MAMMALIA OF

INDIA AND CEYLON.

NATURAL HISTORY

OF THE

MAMMALIA OF INDIA

AND CEYLON.

BY

ROBERT A. STERNDALE,

F.R.G.S., F.Z.S., &c.

GYAN

Published by

Gyan Publishing House
5, Ansari Road
Daryaganj, New Delhi-110002
Phone: 011-47034999, 9811692060
E-mail: books@gyanbooks.com

Distribution Network
gyanbooks.com
India, USA, Canada, UK, Australia, France

ISBN: 978-81-212-8013-6 (PB)
First Published, 1884

2nd Impression 2023

Printed at: Gyan Press, Delhi.

MAMMALIA OF INDIA AND CEYLON
Author: ROBERT A. STERNDALE

MAMMALIA OF

INDIA AND CEYLON.

FELIS TIGRIS.

NATURAL HISTORY

OF THE

MAMMALIA OF INDIA

AND CEYLON.

BY

ROBERT A. STERNDALE,

F.R.G.S., F.Z.S., &c.,

AUTHOR OF "THE DENIZENS OF THE JUNGLE;" "THE AFGHAN KNIFE;"
"SEONEE, OR CAMP LIFE IN THE SATPURA RANGE," ETC.

WITH 170 ILLUSTRATIONS BY THE AUTHOR, T. W WOOD,
AND OTHERS.

CALCUTTA:

THACKER, SPINK, AND CO.

BOMBAY: THACKER AND CO., LIMITED. LONDON: W. THACKER AND CO

1884.

THIS

POPULAR

HISTORY OF OUR INDIAN MAMMALS

IS

Respectfully Dedicated

(BY PERMISSION)

TO ONE WHO TAKES A DEEP INTEREST IN ALL THAT CONCERNS OUR EASTERN EMPIRE,

THE RIGHT HON.

THE EARL OF NORTHBROOK, G.C.S.I.,

LATE GOVERNOR-GENERAL AND VICEROY OF INDIA.

PREFACE.

THIS work is designed to meet an existing want, viz.: a popular manual of Indian Mammalia. At present the only work of the kind is one which treats exclusively of the Peninsula of India, and which consequently omits the more interesting types found in Assam, Burmah, and Ceylon, as well as the countries bordering the British Indian Empire on the North. The geographical limits of the present work have been extended to all territories likely to be reached by the sportsman from India, thus greatly enlarging the field of its usefulness.

The stiff formality of the compiled "Natural Histories" has been discarded, and the Author has endeavoured to present, in interesting conversational and often anecdotal style, the results of experience by himself and his personal friends; at the same time freely availing himself of all the known authorities upon the subject.

CONTENTS.

LIST OF ILLUSTRATIONS.

NATURAL HISTORY

OF THE

MAMMALIA OF BRITISH INDIA AND CEYLON.

INTRODUCTION.

In laying before the public the following history of the Indian Mammalia, I am actuated by the feeling that a popular work on the subject is needed, and would be appreciated by many who do not care to purchase the expensive books that exist, and who also may be more bothered than enlightened by over-much technical phraseology and those learned anatomical dissertations which are necessary to the scientific zoologist.

Another motive in thus venturing is, that the only complete history of Indian Mammalia is Dr. Jerdon's, which is exhaustive within the boundaries he has assigned to India proper; but as he has excluded Assam, Cachar, Tenasserim, Burmah, Arracan, and Ceylon, his book is incomplete as a Natural History of the Mammals of British India. I shall have to acknowledge much to Jerdon in the following pages, and it is to him I owe much encouragement, whilst we were together in the field during the Indian Mutiny, in the pursuit of the study to which he devoted his life; and the general arrangement of this work will be based on his book, his numbers being preserved, in order that those who possess his 'Mammals of India' may readily refer to the noted species.

But I must also plead indebtedness to many other naturalists who have left their records in the 'Journals of the Asiatic Society' and other publications, or who have brought out books of their own, such as Blyth, Elliott, Hodgson, Sherwill, Sykes, Tickell, Hutton, Kellaart, Emerson Tennent, and others; Col. McMaster's 'Notes on Jerdon,' Dr. Anderson's 'Anatomical and Zoological Researches,' Horsfield's 'Catalogue of the Mammalia in the Museum of the East India Company,' 'Dr. Dobson's Monograph of the Asiatic Chiroptera,' the writings of Professors Martin Duncan, Flowers, Kitchen Parker, Boyd Dawkins, Garrod, Mr. E. R. Alston, Sir Victor Brooke and others; the Proceedings and Journals of the Zoological, Linnean, and Asiatic Societies, and the correspondence in *The Asian;* so that after all my own share is minimised to a few remarks here and there, based on personal experience during a long period of jungle life, and on observation of the habits of animals in their wild state, and also in captivity, having made a large collection of living specimens from time to time.

As regards classification, Cuvier's system is the most popular, so I shall adopt it to a certain extent, keeping it as a basis, but engrafting on it such modifications as have met with the approval of modern naturalists. For comparison I give below a synopsis of Cuvier's arrangement. I have placed Cetacea after Carnivora, and Edentata at the end. In this I have followed recent authors as well as Jerdon, whose running numbers I have preserved as far as possible for purposes of reference.

Cuvier divides the Mammals into nine orders, as follows. (*The examples I give are Indian ones, except where stated otherwise*) :—

Order I.—BIMANA. Man.

Order II.—QUADRUMANA. Two families—1st, Apes and Monkeys; 2nd, Lemurs.

Order III.—CARNARIA. Three families—1st, *Cheiroptera*, Bats; 2nd, *Insectivora*, Hedgehogs, Shrews, Moles, Tupaiæ, &c.; 3rd, *Carnivora*: Tribe 1, *Plantigrades*, Bears, Ailurus, Badger, Arctonyx; 2, *Digitigrades*, Martens, Weasels, Otters, Cats, Hyænas, Civets, Musangs, Mongoose, Dogs, Wolves and Foxes.

Order IV.—MARSUPIATA. Implacental Mammals peculiar to America and Australia, such as Opossums, Dasyures, Wombats, and Kangaroos. We have none in India.

Order V.—RODENTIA. Squirrels, Marmots, Jerboas, Mole-Rats, Rats, Mice, Voles, Porcupines, and Hares.

Order VI.—EDENTATA, or toothless Mammals, either partially or totally without teeth. Three families—1st, *Tardigrades*, the Sloths, peculiar to America; 2nd, *Effodientia*, or Burrowers, of which the Indian type is the Manis, but which includes in other parts of the world the Armadillos and Anteaters; 3rd, *Monotremata*, Spiny Anteaters or Echidnas, and the Ornithorynchus.

Order VII.—PACHYDERMATA, or thick-skinned Mammals. Three families—1st, *Proboscidians*, Elephants; 2nd, *Ordinary Pachyderms*, Rhinoceroses, Hogs; 3rd, *Solidungula*, Horses.

Order VIII.—RUMINANTIA, or cud-chewing Mammals. Four families—1st, *Hornless Ruminants*, Camels, Musks; 2nd, *Cervidæ*, true horns shed periodically, Deer; 3rd, *Persistent horns*, Giraffes; 4th, *Hollow-horned Ruminants*, Antelopes, Goats, Sheep and Oxen.

Order IX.—CETACEA. Three families—1st, *Herbivorous Cetacea*, Manatees, Dugongs; 2nd, *Ordinary Cetacea*, Porpoises; 3rd, *Balænidæ*, Whales.

ORDER BIMANA.

SOME people have an extreme repugnance to the idea that man should be treated of in connection with other animals. The development theory is shocking to them, and they would deny that man has anything in common with the brute creation. This is of course mere sentiment; no history of nature would be complete without the noblest work of the Creator. The great gulf that separates the human species from the rest of the animals is the impassable one of intellect. Physically, he should be compared with the other mammals, otherwise we should lose our first standpoint of comparison. There is no degradation in this, nor is it an acceptance of the development theory. To argue that man evolved from the monkey is an ingenious joke which will not bear the test of examination and the Scriptural account, may still be accepted. I firmly believe in man as an original creation just as much as I disbelieve in any development of the Flying Lemur (*Galeopithecus*) from the Bat, or that the habits of an animal would in time materially alter its anatomy, as in the case of the abnormal length of the hind toe and nail of the Jacana. It is not that the habit of running over floating leaves induced the change, but that an all-wise Creator so fashioned it that it might run on those leaves in search of its food. I accept the development theory to the extent of the multiplication of species, or perhaps, more correctly, varieties in genera. We see in the human race how circumstances affect physical appearance. The child of the ploughman or navvy inherits the broad shoulders and thick-set frame of his father; and in India you may see it still more forcibly in the difference between Hindu and Mahomedan races, and those Hindus who have been converted to Mahomedanism. I do not mean isolated converts here and there who intermarry with pure Mahomedan women, but I mean whole communities who have in olden days been forced to accept Islam. In a few generations the face assumes an unmistakable Mahomedan type. It is the difference in living and in thought that effects this change.

It is the same with animals inhabiting mountainous districts as compared with the same living in the plains; constant enforced exercise tells on the former, and induces a more robust and active form.

Whether diet operates in the same degree to effect changes I am inclined to doubt. In man there is no dental or intestinal difference, whether he be as carnivorous as an Esquimaux or as vegetarian as a Hindu; whereas in created carnivorous, insectivorous, and herbivorous animals there is a striking difference, instantly to be recognised even in those of the same family. Therefore, if diet has operated in effecting such changes, why has it not in the human race?

"Who shall decide when doctors disagree?" is a quotation that may aptly be applied to the question of the classification of man; Cuvier, Blumenbach, Fischer, Bory St. Vincent, Prichard, Latham, Morton, Agassiz and others have each a system.

Cuvier recognises only three types—the Caucasian, the Mongolian, and the Negro or Ethiopian, including Blumenbach's fourth and fifth classes, American and Malay in Mongolian. But even Cuvier himself could hardly reconcile the American with the Mongol; he had the high cheek-bone and the scanty beard, it is true, but his eyes and his nose were as Caucasian as could be, and his numerous dialects had no affinity with the type to which he was assigned.

Fischer in his classification divided man into seven races:—

1st.—Homo japeticus, divided into three varieties—*Caucasicus*, *Arabicus* and *Indicus*.

2nd.—H. Neptunianus, consisting of—1st, the Malays peopling the coasts of the islands of the Indian Ocean, Madagascar, &c.; 2nd, New Zealanders and Islanders of the Pacific; and, 3rd, the Papuans.

3rd.—H. Scythicus. Three divisions, viz.: 1st, Calmucks and other Tartars; 2nd, Chinese and Japanese; and, 3rd, Esquimaux.

4th.—H. Americanus, and

5th.—H. Columbicus, belong to the American Continent.

6th.—H. Æthiopicus. The Negro.

7th.—H. Polynesius. The *inland* inhabitants of the Malay Peninsula, of the Islands of the Indian Ocean, of Madagascar, New Guinea, New Holland, &c.

I think this system is the one that most commends itself from its clearness, but there are hardly two writers on ethnology who keep to the same classification.

Agassiz classifies by realms, and has eight divisions.

The Indian races with which we have now to deal are distributed, generally speaking, as follows:—

Caucasian.—(*Homo japeticus*, Bory and Fischer). Northerly, westerly, and in the Valley of the Ganges in particular, but otherwise generally distributed over the most cultivated parts of the Peninsula, comprising the Afghans (Pathans), Sikhs, Brahmins, Rajputs or Kshatryas of the north-west, the Arabs, Parsees, and Mahrattas of the west coast, the Singhalese of the extreme south, the Tamils of the east, and the Bengalis of the north-east.

Mongolians (*H. Scythicus*), inhabiting the chain of mountains to the north, from Little Thibet on the west to Bhotan on the east, and then sweeping downwards southerly to where Tenasserim joins the Malay Peninsula. They comprise the Hill Tribes of the N. Himalayas, the Goorkhas of Nepal, and the Hill Tribes of the north-eastern frontier, viz. Khamtis, Singphos, Mishmis, Abors, Nagas, Jynteas, Khasyas, and

Garos. Those of the northern borders: Bhotias, Lepchas, Limbus, Murmis and Haioos; of the Assam Valley Kachari, Mech and Koch.

The Malays (*H. Neptunianus*) Tipperah and Chittagong tribes, the Burmese and Siamese.

Now comes the most difficult group to classify—the aborigines of the interior, and of the hill ranges of Central India, the Kols, Gonds, Bhils, and others which have certain characteristics of the Mongolian, but with skins almost as dark as the Negro, and the full eye of the Caucasian. The main body of these tribes, which I should feel inclined to classify under Fischer's *H. Polynesius*, have been divided by Indian ethnologists into two large groups—the Kolarians and Dravidians. The former comprise the Juangs, Kharrias, Mundas, Bhumij, Ho or Larka Kols, Santals, Birhors, Korwas, Kurs, Kurkus or Muasis, Bhils, Minas, Kulis. The latter contains the Oraons, Malers, Paharis of Rajamahal, Gonds and Kands.

The Cheroos and Kharwars, Parheyas, Kisans, Bhuikers, Boyars, Nagbansis, Kaurs, Mars, Bhunyiars, Bendkars form another great group apart from the Kolarians and Dravidians, and approximating more to the Indian variety of the Japetic class.

Then there are the extremely low types which one has no hesitation in assigning to the lowest form of the Polynesian group, such as the Andamanese, the jungle tree-men of Chittagong, Tipperah, and the vast forests stretching towards Sambhulpur.

On these I would now more particularly dwell as points of comparison with the rest of the animal kingdom. I have taken but a superficial view of the varieties of the higher types of the human race in India, for the subject, if thoroughly entered into, would require a volume of no ordinary dimensions; and those who wish to pursue the study further should read an able paper by Sir George Campbell in the 'Journal of the Asiatic Society' for June 1866 (vol. xxxv. Part II.), Colonel Dalton's 'Ethnology of Bengal,' the Rev. S. Hislop's 'Memoranda,' and the 'Report of the Central Provinces Ethnological Committee.' There is as yet, however, very little reliable information regarding the wilder forms of humanity inhabiting dense forests, where, enjoying apparently complete immunity from the deadly malaria that proves fatal to all others, they live a life but a few degrees removed from the Quadrumana.

I have in my book on the Seonee District described the little colonies in the heart of the Bison jungles. Clusters of huts imbedded in tangled masses of foliage, surrounded by an atmosphere reeking with the effluvia of decaying vegetation, where, unheedful of the great outer world beyond their sylvan limits, the Gonds pass year after year of uneventful lives.

In some of these hamlets I was looked upon with positive awe, as being the first white man the *Baigas* had seen. But these simple savages rank high in the scale compared with some others, of whom we have as yet but imperfect descriptions.

Some years ago Mr. Piddington communicated to the Asiatic Society an account of some "Monkey-men" he came across on the borders of the Palamow jungle. He was in the habit of employing the aboriginal tribes to work for him, and on one occasion a party of his men found in the jungle a man and woman in a state of starvation, and brought them in. They were both very short in stature, with disproportionately long arms, which in the man were covered with a reddish-brown hair. They looked almost more like baboons than human beings, and their language was unintelligible, except that words here and there resembled those in one of the Kolarian dialects. By signs, and by the help of these words, one of the Dhangars managed to make out that they lived in the depths of the forest, but had to fly from their people on account of a blood feud. Mr. Piddington was anxious to send them down to Calcutta, but before he could do so, they decamped one night, and fled again to their native wilds. Those jungles are, I believe, still in a great measure unexplored; and, if some day they are opened out, it is to be hoped that the "Monkey-men" will be again discovered.*

The lowest type with which we are familiar is the Andamanese, and the wilder sort of these will hardly bear comparison with even the degraded Australian or African Bosjesman, and approximate in debasement to the Fuegians.

The Andamanese are small in stature—the men averaging about five feet, the women less. They are very dark, I may say black, but here the resemblance to the Negro ceases. They have not the thick lips and flat nose, nor the peculiar heel of the Negro. In habit they are in small degree above the brutes, architecture and agriculture being unknown. The only arts they are masters of are limited to the manufacture of weapons, such as spears, bows and arrows, and canoes. They wear no kind of dress, but, when flies and mosquitoes are troublesome, plaster themselves with mud. The women are fond of painting themselves with red ochre, which they lay thickly over their heads, after scraping off the hair with a flint-knife. They swim and dive like ducks, and run up trees like monkeys. Though affectionate to their children, they are ruthless to the stranger, killing every one who happens to be cast away on their inhospitable shores. They have been accused of cannibalism, but this is open to doubt. The bodies of those they have killed have been found dreadfully mutilated, almost pounded to a jelly, but no portion had been removed.†

* There has been lately exhibited in London a child from Borneo which has several points in common with the monkey—hairy face and arms, the hair on the fore-arm being reversed, as in the apes.

† Since the above was written there has been published in the 'Journal of the Anthropological Institute,' vol. xii., a most interesting and exhaustive paper on these people by Mr. E. H. Man, F.R.G.S., giving them credit for much intelligence.

In the above description I speak of the savage Andamanese in his wild state, and not of the specimens to be seen at Port Blair, who have become in an infinitesimal degree civilised—that is to say, to the extent of holding intercourse with foreigners, making some slight additions to their argillaceous dress-suits, and understanding the principles of exchange and barter—though as regards this last a friend informs me that they have no notion of a token currency, but only understand the *argumentum ad hominem* in the shape of comestibles, so that your bargains, to be effectual, must be made within reach of a cookshop or grocery. The same friend tells me he learnt at Port Blair that there were marriage restrictions on which great stress was laid. This may be the case on the South Island; there is much testimony on the other side as regards the more savage Andamanese.

The forest tribes of Chittagong are much higher in the scale than the Andamanese, but they are nevertheless savages of a low type. Captain Lewin says: "The men wear scarcely any clothing, and the petticoat of the women is scanty, reaching only to the knee; they worship the terrene elements, and have vague and undefined ideas of some divine power which overshadows all. They were born and they die for ends to them as incomputable as the path of a cannon-shot fired into the darkness. They are cruel, and attach but little value to life. Reverence or respect are emotions unknown to them, they salute neither their chiefs nor their elders, neither have they any expression conveying thanks." There is, however, much that is interesting in these wild people, and to those who wish to know more I recommend Captain Lewin's account of 'The Hill Tracts of Chittagong.'

ORDER QUADRUMANA.

THE monkeys of the Indian Peninsula are restricted to a few groups, of which the principal one is that of the *Semnopitheci*. These monkeys are distinguished not only by their peculiar black faces, with a ridge of long stiff black hair projecting forwards over the eyebrows, thin slim bodies and long tails, but by the absence of cheek pouches, and the possession of a peculiar sacculated stomach, which, as figured in Cuvier, resembles a bunch of grapes. Jerdon says of this group that, out of five species found on the continent there is only one spread through all the plains of Central and Northern India, and one through the Himalayas, whilst there are three well-marked species in the extreme south of the Peninsula; but then he omits at least four species inhabiting Chittagong, Tenasserim, Arracan, which also belong to the continent of India, though perhaps not to the actual Peninsula. Sir Emerson Tennent, in his 'Natural History of Ceylon,' also mentions and figures three species, of which two are not included in Jerdon's 'Mammals,' though incidentally spoken of. I propose to add the Ceylon Mammalia to the Indian, and therefore shall allude to these further on.

The next group of Indian monkeys is that of the Macaques or Magots, or Monkey Baboons of India, the *Lal Bundar* of the natives. They have simple stomachs and cheek pouches, which last, I dare say, most of us have noticed who have happened to give two plantains in succession to one of them.

Although numerically the *Langurs* or Entellus Monkeys form the most important group of the Quadrumana in India, yet the Gibbons (which are not included by Jerdon) rank highest in the scale, though the species are restricted to but three—*Hylobates hooluck*, *H. lar* and *H. syndactylus.* They are superior in formation (that is taking man as the highest development of the form, to which some people take objection, though to my way of thinking there is not much to choose between the highest type of monkey and the lowest of humanity, if we would but look facts straight in the face), and they are also vastly superior in intellect to either the *Langurs* or the *Macaques*, though inferior perhaps to the Ourangs.

GENUS HYLOBATES—THE GIBBONS,

Which, with the long arms of the Ourangs and the receding forehead of the Chimpanzee, possess the callosities of the true monkeys, but differ from them in having neither tail nor cheek pouches. They are true bipeds on the ground, applying the sole of the foot flatly, not, as Cuvier and others have remarked of the Ourangs, with the outer edge of the sole only, but flat down, as Blyth, who first mentions it, noticed it, with the thumb or big toe widely separated.

No. 1. HYLOBATES HOOLUCK.

The White-fronted Gibbon.

NATIVE NAMES.—*Hooluck, Hookoo.*

HABITAT.—Garo and Khasia Hills, Valley of Assam, and Arracan.

DESCRIPTION.—Males deep black, marked with white across the forehead. Females vary from brownish black to whitish-brown, without, however, the fulvous tint observable in pale specimens of the next species.

"In general they are paler on the crown, back, and outside of limbs, darker in front, and much darker on the cheeks and chin."—*Blyth.*

SIZE.—About two feet.

I think of all the monkey family this Gibbon makes one of the most interesting pets. It is mild and most docile, and capable of great attachment. Even the adult male has been caught, and within the short space of a month so completely tamed that he would follow and come to a call. One I had for a time, some years ago, was a most engaging little creature. Nothing contented him so much as being allowed to sit by my side with his arm linked through mine, and he would resist any attempt I made to go away. He was extremely clean in his habits, which cannot be said of all the monkey tribe. Soon after he came to me I gave him a piece of blanket to sleep on in his box, but the next morning I found he had rolled it up and made a sort of pillow for his head, so a second piece was given him. He was destined for the Queen's Gardens at Delhi, but unfortunately on his way up he got a chill, and contracted a disease akin to consumption. During his illness he was most carefully tended by my brother, who had a little bed made for him, and the doctor came daily to see the little patient, who gratefully accepted his attentions; but, to their disappointment, he died. The only objection to these monkeys as pets is the power they have of howling, or rather whooping, a piercing and somewhat hysterical "Whoop-poo! whoop-poo! whoop-poo!" for several minutes, till fairly exhausted.

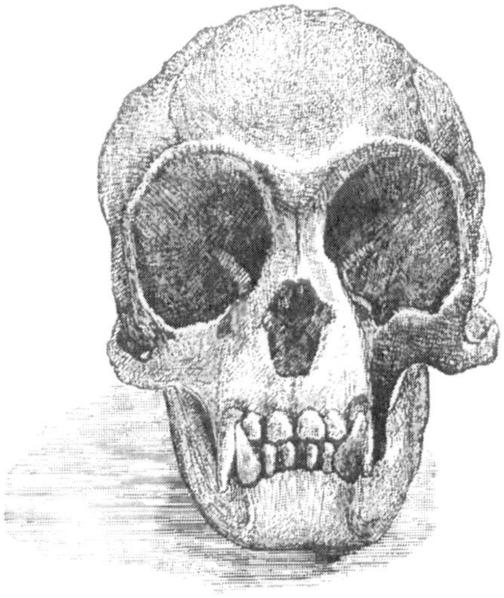

Skull of *Hylobates hooluck*.

They are very fond of swinging by their long arms, and walk something like a tipsy sailor. A friend, resident on the frontiers of Assam, tells me that the full-grown adult pines and dies in confinement. I think it probable that it may miss a certain amount of insect diet, and would recommend those who cannot let their pets run loose in a garden to give them raw eggs and a little minced meat, and a spider or two occasionally.

In its wild state this Gibbon feeds on leaves, insects, eggs and small

HYLOBATES LAR. *HYLOBATES HOOLUCK.*

birds. Dr. Anderson notices the following as favourite leaves: *Moringa pterygosperma* (horse-radish tree), *Spondias mangifera* (amra), *Ficus religiosa* (the pipal), also *Beta vulgaris;* and it is specially partial to the *Ipomœa reptans* (the water convolvulus) and the bright-coloured flowers of the Indian shot (*Canna Indica*). Of insects it prefers spiders and the Orthoptera; eggs and small birds are also eagerly devoured.

No. 2. HYLOBATES LAR.

The White-handed Gibbon.

HABITAT.—Arracan, Lower Pegu, Tenasserim, and the Malayan Peninsula.

DESCRIPTION.—"This species is generally recognisable by its pale yellowish, almost white hands and feet, by the grey, almost white, supercilium, whiskers and beard, and by the deep black of the rest of the pelage."—*Anderson.*

SIZE.—About same as *H. hooluck.*

It is, however, found in every variety of colour, from black to brownish, and variegated with light-coloured patches, and occasionally of a fulvous white. For a long time I supposed it to be synonymous with *H. agilis* of Cuvier, or *H. variegatus* of Temminck, but both Mr. Blyth and Dr. Anderson separate it. Blyth mentions a significant fact in distinguishing the two Indian Gibbons, whatever be their variations of colour, viz.: "*H. hooluck* has constantly a broad white frontal band either continuous or divided in the middle, while *H. lar* has invariably white hands and feet, less brightly so in some, and a white ring encircling the visage, which is seldom incomplete."*

H. lar has sometimes the index and middle fingers connected by a web, as in the case of *H. syndactylus* (a Sumatran species very distinct in other respects). The very closely allied *H. agilis* has also this peculiarity in occasional specimens. This Gibbon was called "*agilis*" by Cuvier from its extreme rapidity in springing from branch to branch. Duvaucel says: "The velocity of its movements is wonderful; it escapes like a bird on the wing. Ascending rapidly to the top of a tree, it then seizes a flexible branch, swings itself two or three times to gain the necessary impetus, and then launches itself forward, repeatedly clearing in succession, without effort and without fatigue, spaces of forty feet."

Sir Stamford Raffles writes that it is believed in Sumatra that it is so jealous that if in captivity preference be given to one over another, the neglected one will die of grief; and he found that one he had sickened

* There is an excellent coloured drawing by Wolf of these two Gibbons in the 'Proceedings of the Zoological Society,' 1870, page 86, from which I have partly adapted the accompanying sketch.

under similar circumstances and did not recover till his rival (a Siamang, *H. syndactylus*) was removed.

No. 3. HYLOBATES SYNDACTYLUS.

The Siamang.

HABITAT.—Tenasserim Province, Sumatra, Malayan Peninsula.

DESCRIPTION.—A more robust and thick-set animal than the two last; deep, woolly, black fur; no white supercilium nor white round the face. The skull is distinguished from the skull of the other Gibbons, according to Dr. Anderson, by the greater forward projection of the supraorbital ridges, and by its much deeper face, and the occipital region more abruptly truncated than in the other species. The index and middle toes of the foot are united to the last phalange.

SIZE.—About three feet.

This Gibbon is included in the Indian group on the authority of Helfer, who stated it to be found in the southern parts of the Tenasserim province. Blyth mentions another distinguishing characteristic—it is not only larger than the other Gibbons, but it possesses an inflatable laryngeal sac. Its arms are immense—five feet across in an adult of three feet high.

The other species of this genus inhabiting adjacent and other countries are *H. pileatus* and *H. leucogenys* in Siam; *H. leuciscus*, Java; *H. Mulleri* and *H. concolor*, Borneo.

GENUS PRESBYTES—CUVIER'S GENUS SEMNOPITHECUS.

These monkeys are characterised by their slender bodies and long limbs and tails. Jerdon says the Germans call them Slim-apes. Other striking peculiarities are the absence of cheek pouches, which, if present, are but rudimentary. Then they differ from the true monkeys (*Cercopithecus*) by the form of the last molar tooth in the lower jaw, which has five tubercles instead of four; and, finally, they are to be distinguished by the peculiar structure of the stomach, which is singularly complicated, almost as much so as in the case of Ruminants, which have four divisions. The stomach of this genus of monkey consists of three divisions: 1st, a simple cardiac pouch with smooth parietes; 2nd, a wide sacculated middle portion; 3rd, a narrow elongated canal, sacculated at first, and of simple structure towards the termination. Cuvier from this supposes it to be more herbivorous than other genera, and considers this conclusion justified by the blunter tubercles of the molars and greater length of intestines and cœcum, all of which point to a vegetable diet. "The head is round, the face but little produced, having a high facial angle."—*Jerdon.*

But the *tout ensemble* of the *Langur* is so peculiar that no one who has once been told of a long, loosed-limbed, slender monkey with a prodigious tail, black face, with overhanging brows of long stiff black hair, projecting like a pent-house, would fail to recognise the animal.

The *Hanuman* monkey is reverenced by the Hindus. Hanuman was the son of Pavana, god of the winds; his strength was enormous, but in attempting to seize the sun he was struck by Indra with a thunderbolt which broke his jaw (*hanu*), whereupon his father shut himself up in a cave, and would not let a breeze cool the earth till the gods had promised his son immortality. Hanuman aided Rama in his attack upon Ceylon, and by his superhuman strength mountains were torn up and cast into the sea, so as to form a bridge of rocks across the Straits of Manar.*

The species of this genus of monkey abound throughout the Peninsula. All Indian sportsmen are familiar with their habits, and have often been assisted by them in tracking a tiger. Their loud whoops and immense bounds from tree to tree when excited, or the flashing of their white teeth as they gibber at their lurking foe, have often told the shikari of the whereabouts of the object of his search. The *Langurs* take enormous leaps, twenty-five feet in width, with thirty to forty in a drop, and never miss a branch. I have watched them often in the Central Indian jungles. Emerson Tennent graphically describes this: "When disturbed their leaps are prodigious, but generally speaking their progress is not made so much by *leaping* as by swinging from branch to branch, using their powerful arms alternately, and, when baffled by distance, flinging themselves obliquely so as to catch the lower boughs of an opposite tree, the momentum acquired by their descent being sufficient to cause a rebound of the branch that carries them upwards again till they can grasp a higher and more distant one, and thus continue their headlong flight."

Jerdon's statement that they can run with great rapidity on all-fours is qualified by McMaster, who easily ran down a large male on horseback on getting him out on a plain.

A correspondent of the *Asian*, quoting from the *Indian Medical Gazette* for 1870, states that experiments with one of this genus (*Presbytes entellus*) showed that strychnine has no effect on *Langurs*—as much as five grains were given within an hour without effect. "From a quarter to half of a grain will kill a dog in from five to ten minutes, and even one twenty-fourth of a grain will have a decided tetanic effect in human beings of delicate temperament."—*Cooley's Cycl.* Two days after *ten* grains of strychnine were dissolved in spirits of wine, and

* The legend, with native picture, is given in Wilkin's 'Hindoo Mythology.'

mixed with rum and water, cold but sweet, which the animal drank with relish, and remained unhurt.

The same experiment was tried with one of another genus (*Inuus rhesus*), who rejected the poisoned fruit at once, and on having strychnine in solution poured down his throat, died.

The *Langur* was then tried with cyanide of potassium, which he rejected at once, but on being forced to take a few grains, was dead in a few seconds.

Although we may not sympathize with those who practise such cruel experiments as these above alluded to, the facts elucidated are worth recording, and tend to prove the peculiar herbivorous nature of this genus, which, in common with other strictly herbivorous animals, instinctively knows what to choose and what to avoid, and can partake, without danger, of some of the most virulent vegetable poisons. It is possible that in the forests they eat the fruit of the *Strychnos nux-vomica*, which is also the favourite food of the pied hornbill (*Hydrocissa coronata*).

No. 4. SEMNOPITHECUS *vel* PRESBYTES ENTELLUS.

The Bengal Langur (*Jerdon's No.* 1).

NATIVE NAMES.—*Langur*, *Hanuman*, Hindi; *Wanur* and *Makur*, Mahratti; *Musya*, Canarese.

HABITAT.—Bengal and Central India.

DESCRIPTION.—Pale dirty or ashy grey; darker on the shoulders and rump; greyish-brown on the tail; paler on the head and lower parts; hands and feet black.

SIZE.—Length of male thirty inches to root of tail; tail forty-three inches.

The *Entellus* monkey is in some parts of India deemed sacred, and is permitted by the Hindus to plunder their grain-shops with impunity; but I think that with increasing hard times the *Hanumans* are not allowed such freedom as they used to have, and in most parts of India I have been in they are considered an unmitigated nuisance, and the people have implored the aid of Europeans to get rid of their tormentors. In the forest the *Langur* lives on grain, fruit, the pods of leguminous trees, and young buds and leaves. Sir Emerson Tennent notices the fondness of an allied species for the flowers of the red hibiscus (*H. rosa sinensis*). The female has usually only one young one, though sometimes twins. The very young babies have not black but light-coloured faces, which darken afterwards. I have always found them most difficult to rear, requiring almost as much attention as a human baby. Their diet and hours of feeding must be as systematically arranged; and if cow's milk be given it must be freely diluted with water—two-thirds to one-third milk when very young, and afterwards decreased to one-half. They are extremely susceptible to cold. In confinement they are quiet and gentle whilst young, but the old males are generally sullen and treacherous. Jerdon says, on the authority of the *Bengal Sporting Magazine* (August 1836), that the males live apart from the females, who have only one or two old males with each colony, and that they have fights at certain seasons, when the vanquished males receive charge of all the young ones of their own sex, with whom they retire to some neighbouring jungle. Blyth notices that in one locality he found only males of all ages, and in another

Presbytes entellus.

chiefly females. I have found these monkeys mostly on the banks of streams in the forests of the Central Provinces; in fact, the presence of them anywhere in arid jungles is a sign that water is somewhere in the vicinity. They are timid creatures, and I have never seen the slightest disposition about them to show fight, whereas I was once most deliberately charged by the old males of a party of *Rhesus* monkeys. I was at the time on field service during the Mutiny, and, seeing several nursing mothers in the party, tried to run them down in the open and secure a baby; but they were too quick for me, and, on being attacked by the old males, I had to pistol the leader.

No. 5. SEMNOPITHECUS *vel* PRESBYTES SCHISTACEUS.*

The Himalayan Langur (*Jerdon's No.* 2).

NATIVE NAMES.—*Langur*, Hindi; *Kamba Suhú*, Lepcha; *Kubup*, Bhotia.

HABITAT.—The whole range of the Himalayas from Nepal to beyond Simla.

DESCRIPTION (after Hodgson).—Dark slaty above; head and lower parts pale yellowish; hands concolorous with body, or only a little darker; tail slightly tufted; hair on the crown of the head short and radiated; on the cheeks long, directed backwards, and covering the ears. Hutton's description is, dark greyish, with pale hands and feet, white head, dark face, white throat and breast, and white tip to the tail.

SIZE.—About thirty inches; tail, thirty-six inches.

Captain Hutton, writing from Mussoorie, says: "On the Simla side I observed them also, leaping and playing about, while the fir-trees, among which they sported, were loaded with snow-wreaths, at an elevation of 11,000 feet."—'Jour. As. Soc. Beng.' xiii. p. 471.

Dr. Anderson remarks on the skull of this species, that it can be easily distinguished from *entellus* by its larger size, the supraorbital ridge being less forwardly projected, and not forming so thick and wide a pent roof, but the most marked difference lies in the much longer facial portion of *schistaceus*; the teeth are also larger; the symphysis or junction of the lower jaw is considerably longer and broader, and the lower jaw itself is generally more massive and deep.

No. 6. SEMNOPITHECUS *vel* PRESBYTES PRIAMUS.

The Madras Langur.

NATIVE NAME.—*Gandangi*, Telugu.

HABITAT.—The Coromandel Coast and Ceylon.

DESCRIPTION.—Ashy grey, with a pale reddish or *chocolat-au-lait* tint overlying the whole back and head; sides of the head, chin, throat, and beneath pale yellowish; hands and feet whitish; face, palms and fingers,

* Mr. J. Cockburn, of the Imperial Museum, has, since I wrote about the preceding species, given me some interesting information regarding the geographical distribution of *Presbytes entellus* and *Hylobates hooluck*. He says: "The latter has never been known to occur on the north bank of the Brahmaputra, though swarming in the forests at the very water's edge on the south bank. The *entellus* monkey is also not found on the north bank of the Ganges, and attempts at its introduction have repeatedly failed." *P. schistaceus* replaces it in the Sub-Himalayan forests.

and soles of feet and toes black; hair long and straight, not wavy; tail of the colour of the darker portion of the back, ending in a whitish tuft.—*Jerdon.*

SIZE.—About the same as *P. entellus.*

Blyth, who is followed by Jerdon, describes this monkey as having a compressed high vertical crest, but Dr. Anderson found that the specimens in the Indian Museum owed these crests to bad stuffing. Kellaart, however, mentions it, and calls the animal "the Crested Monkey." In Sir Emerson Tennent's figure of *P. priamus* a slight crest is noticeable; but Kellaart is very positive on this point, saying: "*P. priamus* is easily distinguished from all other known species of monkeys in Ceylon by its high compressed vertical crest."

Jerdon says this species is not found on the Malabar Coast, but neither he nor McMaster give much information regarding it. Emerson Tennent writes: "At Jaffna, and in other parts of the island where the population is comparatively numerous, these monkeys become so familiarised with the presence of man as to exhibit the utmost daring and indifference. A flock of them will take possession of a palmyra palm, and so effectually can they crouch and conceal themselves among the leaves that, on the slightest alarm, the whole party becomes invisible in an instant. The presence of a dog, however, excites such irrepressible curiosity that, in order to watch his movements, they never fail to betray themselves. They may be frequently seen congregated on the roof of a native hut; and, some years ago, the child of a European clergyman, stationed near Jaffna, having been left on the ground by the nurse, was so teased and bitten by them as to cause its death."

In these particulars this species resembles *P. entellus.*

NO. 7. SEMNOPITHECUS *vel* PRESBYTES JOHNII.

The Malabar Langur (Jerdon's No. 4).

HABITAT.—The Malabar Coast, from N. Lat. 14° or 15° to Cape Comorin.

DESCRIPTION.—Above dusky brown, slightly paling on the sides; crown, occiput, sides of head and beard fulvous, darkest on the crown; limbs and tail dark brown, almost black; beneath yellowish white.—*Jerdon.*

SIZE.—Not quite so large as *P. entellus.*

This monkey was named after a member of the Danish factory at Tranquebar, M. John, who first described it. It abounds in forests, and does not frequent villages, though it will visit gardens and fields, where, however, it shuns observation.

The young are of a sooty brown, or nearly black, without any indication of the light-coloured hood of the adult.

No. 8. SEMNOPITHECUS *vel* PRESBYTES JUBATUS.

The Nilgheri Langur (Jerdon's No. 5).

HABITAT.—The Nilgheri Hills, the Animallies, Pulneys, the Wynaad, and all the higher parts of the range of the Ghâts as low as Travancore.

DESCRIPTION.—Dark glossy black throughout, except head and nape, which are reddish brown; hair very long; in old individuals a greyish patch on the rump.—*Jerdon.*

SIZE.—Length of head and body, 26 inches; tail, 30.

This monkey does not, as a rule, descend lower than 2,500 to 3,000 feet; it is shy and wary. The fur is fine and glossy, and is much prized (Jerdon). Its flesh is excellent food for dogs (McMaster).

Dr. Anderson makes this synonymous with the last.

No. 9. SEMNOPITHECUS *vel* PRESBYTES PILEATUS.

The Capped Langur.

HABITAT.—Assam, Chittagong, Tipperah.

DESCRIPTION.—General colour dark ashy grey, with a slight ferruginous tint; darker near head and on shoulders; underneath and on the inside of the limbs pale yellowish, with a darker shade of orange or golden yellow on the breast and belly. The crown of the head is densely covered with bristly hairs, regularly disposed and somewhat elongated on the vertex so as to resemble a cap, whence the name. Along the forehead is a superciliary crest of long black bristles, directed outwardly; whiskers full and down to the chin: behind the ears is a small tuft of white hairs; the tail is long, one third longer than the body, darker near the end, and tufted; fingers and toes black.

SIZE.—A little smaller than *P. entellus.*

This monkey is found in Northern Assam, Tipperah and southwards to Tenasserim; in Blyth's 'Catalogue of the Mammals of Burmah' it is mentioned as *P. chrysogaster* (*Semnopithecus potenziani* of Bonaparte and Peters). He writes of it: "Females and young have the lower parts white, or but faintly tinted with ferruginous, and the rest of the coat is of a pure grey; the face black, and there is no crest, but the hairs of the crown are so disposed as to appear like a small flat cap laid upon the top of the head. The old males seem always to be of a deep rust-colour on the cheeks, lower parts, and more or less on the outer side of the limbs; while in old females this rust colour is diluted or little more than indicated."

Dr. Anderson says that a young one he had was of a mild disposition, which however is not the character of the adult animal, which is uncertain, and the males when irritated are fierce, and determined in attack. No rule, however, is without its exception, for one adult male, possessed by Blyth, is reported as having been an exceeding gentle animal.

No. 10. SEMNOPITHECUS *vel* PRESBYTES BARBEI.

The Tipperah Langur.

HABITAT.—Tipperah, Tenasserim.

DESCRIPTION.—No vertical crest of hair on the head, nor is the occipital hair directed downwards, as in the next species. Shoulders and outside of arm silvered; tail slightly paler than body, "which is of a blackish fuliginous hue."

More information is required about this monkey, which was named by Blyth after its donor to the Asiatic Society, the Rev. J. Barbe. Blyth considered it as distinct from *P. Phayrei* and *P. obscurus*, which last is from Malacca.

Dr. Anderson noticed it in the valley of the Tapeng in the centre of the Kakhyen Hills, in troops of thirty to fifty, in high forest trees overhanging the mountain streams. Being seldom disturbed, they permitted a near approach.

No. 11. SEMNOPITHECUS *vel* PRESBYTES PHAYREI.

Syn.—SEMNOPITHECUS CRISTATUS.

The Silvery-Leaf Monkey (Blyth).

HABITAT.—Arracan, Malayan Peninsula, Sumatra, Borneo.

DESCRIPTION.—Colour dusky grey-brown above, more or less dark, with black hands and feet; a conspicuous crest on the vertex; under parts white, scarcely extending to the inside of the limbs; sides grey like the back; whiskers dark, very long, concealing the ears in front; lips and eyelids conspicuously white, with white moustachial hairs above and similar hairs below.

SIZE.—Two feet; tail, 2 feet 6 inches.

This monkey was named by Blyth after Captain (now Sir Arthur) Phayre, who first brought it to his notice; but he afterwards reconciled it as being synonymous with *Semnopithecus cristatus*. The colouring, according to different authors, seems to vary considerably, which causes some confusion in description. It differs from an allied species, *S. maurus*, in selecting low marshy situations near the banks of streams. Its favourite food is the fruit of the Nibong palm (*Oncosperma filamentosa*).

No. 12. SEMNOPITHECUS *vel* PRESBYTES OBSCURUS.

The Dusky-Leaf Monkey.

HABITAT.—Mergui and the Malayan Peninsula.

DESCRIPTION.—Adults ashy or brownish black, darker on forehead, sides of face, shoulder, and sides of body; the hair on the nape is lengthened and whitish. The newly-born young are of a golden ferruginous colour, which afterward changes to dusky-ash colour, the terminal half of the tail being last to change; the mouth and eyelids are whitish, but the rest of the face black.

SIZE.—Body, 1 foot 9 inches; tail, 2 feet 8 inches.

This monkey is most common in the Malayan Peninsula, but has been found to extend to Mergui, where Blyth states it was procured by the late Major Berdmore. Dr. Anderson says it is not unfrequently offered for sale in the Singapore market.

No. 13. SEMNOPITHECUS *vel* PRESBYTES CEPHALOPTERUS.

The Ceylon Langur.

NATIVE NAME.—*Kallu Wanderu.*

HABITAT.—The low lands of Ceylon.

DESCRIPTION.—General colour cinereous black; croup and inside of thighs whitish; head rufescent brown; hair on crown short, semi-erect; occipital hairs long, albescent; whiskers white, thick and long, terminating at the chin in a short beard, and laterally angularly pointed; upper lip thinly fringed with white hairs; superciliary hairs black, long, stiff and standing erect; tail albescent and terminating in a beard tuft; face, palms, soles, fingers, toes and callosities black; irides brown.—*Kellaart.*

SIZE.—Length, 20 inches; tail 24 inches.

Sir E. Tennent says of this monkey that it is never found at a higher elevation than 1,300 feet (when it is replaced by the next species).

"It is an active and intelligent creature, little larger than the common bonneted macaque, and far from being so mischievous as others of the monkeys in the island. In captivity it is remarkable for the gravity of its demeanour and for an air of melancholy in its expression and movements, which are completely in character with its snowy beard and venerable aspect. In disposition it is gentle and confiding, sensible in the highest degree of kindness, and eager for endearing attention, uttering a low plaintive cry when its sympathies are excited. It is particularly cleanly in its habits when domesticated, and spends much of its time in trimming its fur and carefully divesting its hair of particles of dust. Those which I kept at my house near Colombo were chiefly fed upon plantains and bananas, but for nothing did they evince a greater partiality than the rose-coloured flowers of the red hibiscus (*H. rosa sinensis*). These they devoured with unequivocal gusto; they likewise relished the leaves of many other trees, and even the bark of a few of the more succulent ones."

No. 14. SEMNOPITHECUS *vel* PRESBYTES URSINUS.

The Great Wanderu.

NATIVE NAME.—*Maha Wanderu.*

HABITAT.—The mountainous district of Ceylon.

DESCRIPTION.—Fur long, almost uniformly greyish black; whiskers full and white; occiput and croup in old specimens paler coloured; hands and feet blackish; tail long, getting lighter towards the lower half. The young and adults under middle age have a rufous tint, corresponding with that of the head of all ages.

SIZE.—Body about 22 inches; tail, 26 inches.

The name Wanderu is a corruption of the Singhalese generic word for monkey, *Ouandura*, or *Wandura*, which bears a striking resemblance to the Hindi *Bandra*, commonly called *Bandar*—*b* and *v* being interchangeable—and is evidently derived from the Sanscrit *Banur*, which in the south again becomes *Wanur*, and further south, in Ceylon, *Wandura*. There has been a certain amount of confusion between this animal and *Inuus silenus*, the lion monkey, which had the name *Wanderu* applied to it by Buffon, and it is so figured in Cuvier. They are both large monkeys, with great beards of light coloured hair, but in no other respect do they resemble. Sir Emerson Tennent says: "It is rarely seen by Europeans, this portion of the country having till very recently been but partially opened; and even now it is difficult to observe its habits, as it seldom approaches the few roads which wind through these deep solitudes. At early morning, ere the day begins to dawn, its loud and peculiar howl, which consists of quick repetition of the sound *how-how!* may be frequently heard in the mountain jungles, and forms one of the characteristic noises of these lofty situations." This was written in 1861; since then much of the mountainous forest land has been cleared for coffee-planting, and the Wanderu either driven into corners or become more familiarised with man. More therefore must be known of its habits by this time, and information regarding it is desirable.

No. 15. SEMNOPITHECUS *vel* PRESBYTES THERSITES.

NATIVE NAME.—*Ellee Wanderu* (Kellaart).

HABITAT.—Ceylon.

DESCRIPTION.—Chiefly distinguished from the others by wanting the head tuft; uniform dusky grey, darker on crown and fore-limbs; slaty brown on wrists and hands; hair on toes whitish; whiskers and beard largely developed and conspicuously white.

Presbytes thersites.

The name was given by Blyth to a single specimen forwarded by Dr. Templeton, and it was for a time doubtful whether it was really a native, till Dr. Kellaart procured a second. Dr. Templeton's specimen was partial to fresh vegetables, plantains, and fruit, but he ate freely boiled rice, beans, and gram. He was fond of being noticed and petted, stretching out his limbs in succession to be scratched, drawing himself up so that his ribs might be reached by the finger, closing his eyes during the operation, and evincing his satisfaction by grimaces irresistibly ludicrous.—*Emerson Tennent.*

Dr. Anderson considers this monkey as identical with *Semnopithecus priamus*, but Kellaart, as I have before stated, is very positive on the point of difference, calling *S. priamus* emphatically the crested monkey, and alleging that *thersites* has no crest, and it is probable he had opportunities of observing the two animals in life; he says he had a young specimen of *priamus*, which distinctly showed the crest, and a young *thersites* of the same age which showed no sign of it.

In Emerson Tennent's 'Natural History of Ceylon,' (1861) page 5, there is a plate of a group in which are included *priamus* and *thersites*; in the original they are wrongly numbered—the former should be 2 and not 3, and the latter 3 and not 2. If these be correct (and Wolf's name should be a voucher for their being so) there is a decided difference. There is no crest in the latter, and the white whiskers terminate abruptly on a level with the eyebrow, and the superciliary ridge of hair is wanting.

No. 16. SEMNOPITHECUS *vel* PRESBYTES ALBINUS (*Kellaart*).

The White Langur.

HABITAT.—Ceylon, in the hills beyond Matelle.

DESCRIPTION.—Fur dense, sinuous, nearly of uniform white colour. with only a slight dash of grey on the head; face and ears black; palm, soles, fingers and toes flesh-coloured; limbs and body the shape of *P. ursinus;* long white hairs prolonged over the toes and claws, giving the appearance of a white spaniel dog to this monkey; irides brown; whiskers white, full, and pointed laterally.—*Kellaart.*

The above description was taken by Dr. Kellaart from a living specimen. He considered it to be a distinct species, and not an Albino, from the black face and ears and brown eyes.

The Kandyans assured him that they were to be seen (rarely however) in small parties of three and four over the hills beyond Matelle, but never in company with the dark kind.

Emerson Tennent also mentions one that was brought to him taken between Ambepasse and Kornegalle, where they were said to be numerous; except in colour it had all the characteristics of *P. cephalopterus.* So striking was its whiteness that it might have been conjectured to be an Albino, but for the circumstance that its eyes and face were black. An old writer of the seventeenth century, Knox, says of the monkeys of Ceylon (where he was captive for some time) that there are some "milk-white in body and face, but of this sort there is not such plenty." —*Tennent's 'Natural History of Ceylon,' page* 8.

NOTE.—Since the above was in type I have found in the List of Animals in the Zoological Society's Gardens, a species entered as *Semnopithecus leucoprymnus*, the Purple-faced Monkey from Ceylon—see P.Z.S.

PAPIONINÆ.

This sub-family comprises the true baboons of Africa and the monkey-like baboons of India. They have the stomach simple, and cheek-pouches are always present. According to Cuvier they possess, like the last family, a fifth tubercle on their last molars. They produce early, but are not completely adult for four or five years; the period of gestation is seven months.

The third sub-family of *Simiadæ* consists of the genera *Cercopithicus*, *Macacus*, and *Cynocephalus*, as generally accepted by modern zoologists, but Jerdon seems to have followed Ogilby in his classification, which merges the long-tailed Macaques into *Cercopithecus*, and substituting *Papio* for the others.

GENUS INUUS.

Cuvier applies this term to the Magots or rudimentary-tailed Macaques. The monkeys of this genus are more compactly built than those of the last. They are also less herbivorous in their diet, eating frogs, lizards, crabs and insects, as well as vegetables and fruit. Their callosities and cheek-pouches are large, and they have a sac which communicates with the larynx under the thyroid cartilage, which fills with air when they cry out.

Some naturalists of the day, however, place all under the generic name Macacus.

Macacus silenus.

No. 17. INUUS *vel* MACACUS SILENUS.

The Lion Monkey (*Jerdon's No.* 6).

NATIVE NAMES.—*Nil bandar*, Bengali; *Shia bandar*, Hindi; *Nella manthi*, Malabari.

HABITAT.—The Western Ghâts of India from North Lat. 14° to the extreme south, but most abundant in Cochin and Travancore (*Jerdon*), also Ceylon (*Cuvier* and *Horsfield*), though not confirmed by Emerson Tennent, who states that the *silenus* is not found in the island except as introduced by Arab horse-dealers occasionally, and that it certainly is not indigenous. Blyth was also assured by Dr. Templeton of Colombo that the only specimens there were imported.

DESCRIPTION.—Black, with a reddish-white hood or beard surrounding the face and neck; tail with a tuft of whitish hair at the tip; a little greyish on the chest.

SIZE.—About 24 inches; tail, 10 inches.

There is a plate of this monkey in Carpenter and Westwood's edition of Cuvier, under the mistaken name of *Wanderoo*.

It is somewhat sulky and savage, and is difficult to get near in a wild state. Jerdon states that he met with it only in dense unfrequented forest, and sometimes at a considerable elevation. It occurs in troops of from twelve to twenty.

No. 18. INUUS *vel* MACACUS RHESUS.

The Bengal Monkey (*Jerdon's No.* 7).

NATIVE NAMES. — *Bandar*, Hindi; *Markot*, Bengali; *Suhu*, Lepcha, *Piyu*, Bhotia.

HABITAT. — India generally from the North to about Lat. 18° or 19°; but not in the South, where it is replaced by *Macacus radiatus*.

DESCRIPTION.—Above brownish ochrey or rufous; limbs and beneath ashy-brown; callosities and adjacent parts red; face of adult males red.

SIZE. — Twenty-two inches; tail 11 inches.

Macacus rhesus.

This monkey is too well-known to need description. It is the common acting monkey of the *bandar-wallas*, the delight of all Anglo-Indian children, who go into raptures over the romance of *Munsur-ram* and *Chameli*, their quarrels, parting, and reconciliation, so admirably acted by these miniature comedians.

NOTE.—For *Macacus rheso-similis*, Sclater, see P.Z.S. 1872, p. 495, pl. xxv., also P.Z.S. 1875, p. 418.

No. 19. INUUS *vel* MACACUS PELOPS. *Syn.*—MACACUS ASSAMENSIS.

The Hill Monkey (Jerdon's No. 8).

HABITAT.—The Himalayan ranges and Assam.

DESCRIPTION.—Brownish grey, somewhat mixed with slaty, and rusty brownish on the shoulders in some; beneath light ashy brown; fur fuller and more wavy than in *rhesus;* canine teeth long; of stout habit; callosities and face less red than in the last species (*Jerdon*). Face flesh-coloured, but interspersed with a few black hairs (*McClelland*).

No. 20. INUUS *vel* MACACUS NEMESTRINUS.

The Pig-tailed Monkey.

HABITAT.—Tenasserim and the Malay Archipelago.

DESCRIPTION.—General colour grizzled brown; the piles annulated

Macacus nemestrinus.

with dusky and fulvous; crown darker, and the middle of the back also darker; the hair lengthened on the fore-quarters; the back stripe extends along the tail, becoming almost black; the tail terminates in a bright ferruginous tuft. This monkey is noted for its docility, and in Bencoolen is trained to be useful as well as amusing. According to Sir Stamford Raffles it is taught to climb the cocoa palms for the fruit for its master, and to select only those that are ripe.

No. 21. INUUS *vel* MACACUS LEONINUS.

The Long-haired Pig-tailed Monkey.

HABITAT.—Arracan.

DESCRIPTION.—A thick-set powerful animal, with a broad, rather flattened head above, and a moderately short, well clad, up-turned tail, about one-third the length of the body and head; the female smaller. —*Anderson.*

Face fleshy brown; whitish round the eyes and on the forehead; eyebrows brownish, a narrow reddish line running out from the external angle of the eye. The upper surface of the head is densely covered with short dark fur, yellowish brown, broadly tipped with black; the hair radiating from the vertex; on and around the ear the hair is pale grey; above the external orbital angle and on the sides of the face the hair is dense and directed backwards, pale greyish, obscurely annulated with dusky brown, and this is prolonged downwards to the middle of the throat. On the shoulders, back of the neck, and upper part of the thighs, the hairs are very long, fully three inches in the first-mentioned localities; the basal halves greyish; and the remainder ringed with eleven bands of dark brown and orange; the tips being dark. The middle and small of the back is almost black, the shorter hair there being wholly dark; and this colour is prolonged on the tail, which is tufted. The hair on the chest is annulated, but paler than on the shoulders, and it is especially dense on the lower part. The lower halves of the limbs are also well clad with annulated fur, like their outsides, but their upper halves internally and the belly are only sparsely covered with long brownish grey plain hairs, not ringed.

The female differs from the male in the absence of the black on the head and back, and in the hair of the under parts being brownish grey, without annulations. The shoulders somewhat brighter than the rest of the fur, which is yellowish olive; greyish olive on outside of limbs; dusky on upper surface of hands and feet; and black on upper surface of tail.

SIZE.—Length of male, head and body 23 inches; tail, without hair, 8 inches; with hair 10 inches.

The above description is taken from Dr. Anderson's account, 'Anat. and Zool. Res.,' where at page 54 will be found a plate of the skull showing the powerful canine teeth. Blyth mentions a fine male with hair on the shoulders four to five inches long.

No. 22. INUUS *vel* MACACUS ARCTOIDES.

The Brown Stump-tailed Monkey.

HABITAT.—Cachar, Kakhyen Hills, east of Bhamo.

DESCRIPTION.—Upper surface of head and along the back dark brown, almost blackish; sides and limbs dark brown; the hair, which is very long, is ringed with light yellowish and dark brown, darker still at the tips; face red; tail short and stumpy, little over an inch long.

This monkey is one over which many naturalists have argued; it is synonymous with *Macacus speciosus*, *M. maurus*, *M. melanotus*, and was thought to be with *M. brunneus* till Dr. Anderson placed the latter in a separate species on account of the non-annulation of its hair. It is essentially a denizen of the hills; it has been obtained in Cachar and in Upper Assam. Dr. Anderson got it in the Kakhyen Hills on the frontier of Yunnan, beyond which, he says, it spreads to the south-east to Cochin-China.

No. 23. INUUS *vel* MACACUS THIBETANUS.

The Thibetan Stump-tailed Monkey.

DESCRIPTION.—Head large and whiskered; form robust; tail stumpy and clad; general colour of the animal brown; whiskers greyish; face nude and flesh-coloured, with a deep crimson flush round the eyes.

SIZE.—Two feet 9 inches; tail about 3 inches.

This large monkey, though not belonging to British India, inhabiting, it is said, "the coldest and least accessible forests of Eastern Thibet," is mentioned here, as the exploration of that country by travellers from India is attracting attention.

GENUS MACACUS.

Tail longer than in *Inuus*, and face not so lengthened; otherwise as in that genus.—*Jerdon.*

No. 24. MACACUS RADIATUS.

The Madras Monkey (Jerdon's No. 9).

NATIVE NAMES.—*Bandar*, Hindi; *Makadu* or *Wanur*, Mahratti; *Kerda mahr* of the Ghâts; *Munga*, Canarese; *Koti*, Telegu; *Vella munthi*, Malabar.

HABITAT.—All over the southern parts of India, as far north as lat. 18°.

DESCRIPTION.—Of a dusky olive brown, paler and whitish underneath, ashy on outer sides of limbs; tail dusky brown above, whitish beneath; hairs on the crown of the head radiated.

SIZE.—Twenty inches; tail 15 inches.

Elliott remarks of this monkey that it inhabits not only the wildest jungles, but the most populous towns, and it is noted for its audacity in stealing fruit and grain from shops. Jerdon says: "It is the monkey most commonly found in menageries, and led about to show various

Macacus radiatus and *Macacus pileatus.*

tricks and feats of agility. It is certainly the most inquisitive and mischievous of its tribe, and its powers of mimicry are surpassed by none." It may be taught to turn a wheel regularly; it smokes tobacco without inconvenience.—*Horsfield.*

No. 25. MACACUS PILEATUS (*vel* SINICUS, *Lin.*).

The Capped Monkey, or *Bonneted Macaque* of *Cuvier.*

NATIVE NAME.—*Rilawa*, Singhalese.

HABITAT.—Ceylon and China.

DESCRIPTION.—Yellowish brown, with a slight shade of green in old specimens; in some the back is light chestnut brown; yellowish brown hairs on the crown of the head, radiating from the centre to the circumference; face flesh-coloured and beardless; ears, palms, soles, fingers, and toes blackish; irides reddish brown; callosities flesh-coloured; tail longish, terminating in short tuft.—*Kellaart.*

SIZE.—Head and body about 20 inches; tail 18 inches.

This is the *Macacus sinicus* of Cuvier, and is very similar to the last species. In Ceylon it takes the place of our rhesus monkey with the conjurors, who, according to Sir Emerson Tennent, "teach it to dance, and in their wanderings carry it from village to village, clad in a grotesque dress, to exhibit its lively performances." It also, like the last, smokes tobacco; and one that belonged to the captain of a tug steamer, in which I once went down from Calcutta to the Sandheads, not only smoked, but chewed tobacco. Kellaart says of it: "This monkey is a lively, spirited animal, but easily tamed; particularly fond of making grimaces, with with which it invariably welcomes its master and friends. It is truly astonishing to see the large quantity of food it will cram down its cheek pouches for future mastication."

No. 26. MACACUS CYNOMOLGUS.

The Crab-eating Macaque.

NATIVE NAME.—*Kra*, Malay.
HABITAT.—Tenasserim, Nicobars, Malay Archipelago.

Macacus cynomolgus.

DESCRIPTION.—"The leading features of this animal are its massive form, its large head closely set on the shoulders, its stout and rather short legs, its slender loins and heavy buttocks, its tail thick at the base" (Anderson). The general colour is similar to that of the Bengal rhesus monkey, but the skin of the chest and belly is bluish, the face livid, with a white area between the eyes and white eyelids. Hands and and feet blackish.

SIZE.—About that of the Bengal rhesus.

According to Captain (now Sir Arthur) Phayre "these monkeys frequent the banks of salt-water creeks and devour shell-fish. In the cheek-pouch of the female were found the claws and body of a crab. There is not much on record concerning the habits of this monkey in its wild state beyond what is stated concerning its partiality for crabs, which can also, I believe, be said of the rhesus in the Bengal Sunderbunds."

No. 27. MACACUS CARBONARIUS.

The Black-faced Crab-eating Monkey.

HABITAT—Burmah.

DESCRIPTION.—In all respects the same as the last, except that its face is blackish, with conspicuously white eyelids.

FAMILY LEMURIDÆ.

The Indian members of this family belong to the sub-family named by Geoffroy *Nycticebinæ.*

GENUS NYCTICEBUS.

No. 28. NYCTICEBUS TARDIGRADUS.

The Slow-paced Lemur (Jerdon's No. 10).

NATIVE NAME.—*Sharmindi billi,* Hindi.

HABITAT.—Eastern Bengal, Assam, Garo Hills, Sylhet, Arracan.—*Horsfield.*

DESCRIPTION.—Dark ashy grey, with a darker band down middle of back, beneath lighter grey; forehead in some dark, with a narrow white stripe between the eyes, disappearing above them; ears and round the eye dark; tail very short.—*Jerdon.*

SIZE.—Length about 14 to 15 inches; tail $\frac{5}{8}$ of an inch.

Nocturnal in its habits; sleeping during the day in holes of trees, and coming out to feed at night. Sir William Jones describes one kept by him for some time; it appeared to have been gentle, though at times petulant when disturbed; susceptible of cold; slept from sunrise to sunset rolled up like a hedgehog. Its food was chiefly plantains, and mangoes when in season. Peaches, mulberries, and guavas, it did not so much care for, but it was most eager after grasshoppers, which it devoured voraciously. It was very particular in the performance of its

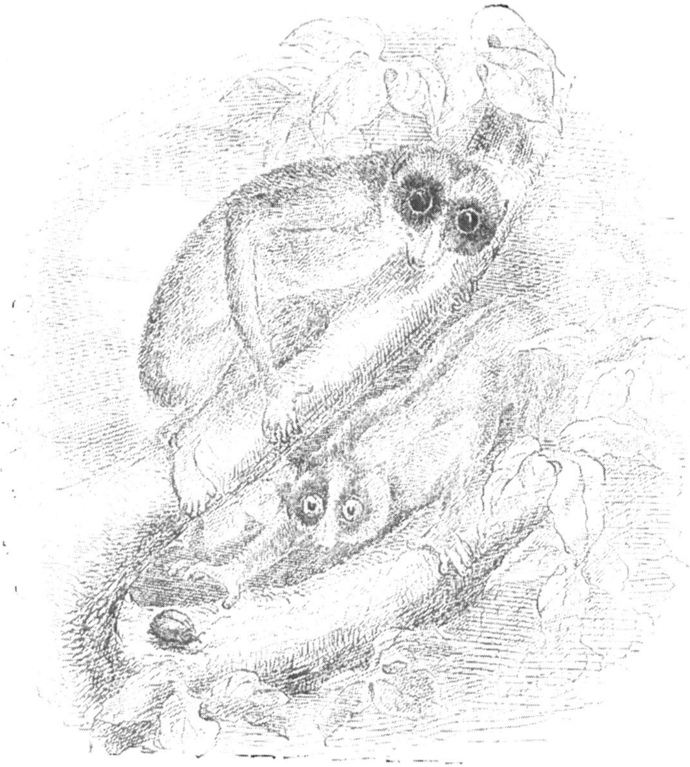

Loris gracilis and *Nycticebus tardigradus.*

toilet, cleaning and licking its fur. Cuvier also notices this last peculiarity, and with regard to its diet says it eats small birds as well as insects. These animals are occasionally to be bought in the Calcutta market. A friend of mine had a pair which were a source of great amusement to his guests after dinner. (See Appendix C, p. 526.)

GENUS LORIS.

Body and limbs slender; no tail; eyes very large, almost contiguous; nose acute.

No. 29. LORIS GRACILIS.

The Slender Lemur (Jerdon's No. 11).

NATIVE NAMES.—*Tevangar*, Tamil; *Dewantsipilli*, Telegu. (*Oona happslava*, Singhalese.—*Kellaart.*)

HABITAT.—Southern India and Ceylon.

DESCRIPTION.—Above greyish rufescent (tawny snuff brown: Kellaart); beneath a paler shade; a white triangular spot on forehead, extending down the nose; fur short, dense, and soft; ears thin, rounded (Jerdon). A hooped claw on inner toes; nails of other toes flat; posterior third of palms and soles hairy (Kellaart).

SIZE.—About 8 inches; arm, 5; leg, 5½.

This, like the last, is also nocturnal in its habits, and from the extreme slowness of its movements is called in Ceylon "the Ceylon sloth." Its diet is varied—fruit, flower, and leaf buds, insects, eggs, and young birds. Sir Emerson Tennent says the Singhalese assert that it has been known to strangle pea-fowl at night and feast on the brain, but this I doubt. Smaller birds it might overcome. Jerdon states that in confinement it will eat boiled rice, plantains, honey or syrup and raw meat. McMaster, at page 6 of his 'Notes on Jerdon,' gives an interesting extract from an old account of 'Dr. John Fryer's Voyage to East India and Bombain,' in which he describes this little animal as "Men of the Woods, or more truly Satyrs;" asleep during the day; but at "Night they Sport and Eat." "They had Heads like an owl. Bodied like a monkey without Tails. Only the first finger of the Right Hand was armed with a claw like a bird, otherwise they had hands and feet which they walk upright on, not pronely, as other Beasts do."

These little creatures double themselves up when they sleep, bending the head down between their legs. Although so sluggish generally, Jerdon says they can move with considerable agility when they choose.

SUB-ORDER PLEUROPTERA.—FAMILY GALÆOPITHECIDÆ.

There is a curious link between the Lemurs and the Bats in the Colugos (*Galæopithecus*): their limbs are connected with a membrane as in the Flying Squirrels, by which they can leap and float for a hundred yards on an inclined plane. They are mild, inoffensive animals, subsisting on fruits and leaves. Cuvier places them after the Bats, but they seem properly to link the Lemurs and the frugivorous Bats. As yet they have not been found in India proper, but are common in the Malayan Peninsula, and have been found in Burmah.

No. 30. GALÆOPITHECUS VOLANS

The Flying Lemur.

NATIVE NAME.—*Myook-hloung-pyan*, Burmese.
HABITAT.—Mergui; the Malayan Peninsula.
DESCRIPTION.—Fur olive brown, mottled with irregular whitish spots

Galæopithecus volans.

and blotches; the pile is short, but exquisitely soft; head and brain very small; tail long and prehensile. The membrane is continued from each side of the neck to the fore feet; thence to the hind feet, again to the tip of the tail. This animal is also nocturnal in its habits, and very sluggish in its motions by day, at which time it usually hangs from a branch suspended by its fore hands, its mottled back assimilating closely with the rugged bark of the tree; it is exclusively herbivorous, possessing a very voluminous stomach, and long convoluted intestines. Wallace says of it, that its brain is very small, and it possesses such tenacity of life that it is very difficult to kill; he adds that it is said to have only one at a birth, and one he shot had a very small blind naked little creature clinging closely to its breast, which was quite bare and much wrinkled. Raffles, however, gives two as the number produced at each birth. Dr. Cantor says that in confinement plantains constitute the favourite food, but deprived of liberty it soon dies. In its wild state it "lives entirely on young fruits and leaves; those of the cocoanut and *Bombax pentandrum* are its favourite food, and it commits great injury to the plantations of these."—*Horsfield's* 'Cat. Mam.' Regarding its powers of flight, Wallace, in his 'Travels in the Malay Archipelago,' says: "I saw one of these animals run up a tree in a rather open space, and then glide obliquely through the air to another tree on which it alighted near its base, and immediately began to ascend. I paced the distance from one tree to the other, and found it to be seventy yards, and the amount of descent not more than thirty-five or forty feet, or less than one in five. This, I think, proves that the animal must have some power of guiding itself through the air, otherwise in so long a distance it would have little chance of alighting exactly upon the trunk."

There is a carefully prepared skeleton of this animal in the Indian Museum in Calcutta.

ORDER CARNARIA.

CHEIROPTERA.

It may seem strange to many that such an insignificant, weird little creature as a bat should rank so high in the animal kingdom as to be but a few removes from man. It has, however, some striking anatomical affinities with the last Order, *Quadrumana*, sufficient to justify its being placed in the next link of the great chain of creation.

"Bats have the arms, fore-arms and fingers excessively elongated, so as to form with the membrane that occupies their intervals, real wings, the surface of which is equally or more extended than in those of birds. Hence they fly high and with great rapidity."—*Cuvier.* They suckle their young at the breast, but some of them have pubic warts resembling mammæ. The muscles of the chest are developed in proportion, and the sternum has a medial ridge something like that of a bird. They are all nocturnal, with small eyes (except in the case of the frugivorous bats), large ears, and in some cases membranous appendages to the nostrils, which may possibly be for the purpose of guiding themselves in the dark, for it is proved by experiment that bats are not dependent on eyesight for guidance, and one naturalist has remarked that, in a certain species of bat which has no facial membrane, this delicacy of perception was absent. I have noticed this in one species, *Cynopterus marginatus*, one of which flew into my room not long ago, and which repeatedly dashed itself against a glass door in its efforts to escape. I had all the other doors closed.

Sternum of *Pteropus*.

Bats are mostly insectivorous; a few are fruit-eaters, such as our common flying-fox. They produce from one to two at a birth, which are carried about by the mother and suckled at the breast, this peculiarity being one of the anatomical details alluded to as claiming for the bats so high a place.

Bats are divided into four sub-families—*Pteropodidæ*, *Vampyridæ*, *Noctilionidæ*, and *Vespertilionidæ*.

MEGACHIROPTERA.

SUB-FAMILY PTEROPODIDÆ.

GENUS PTEROPUS.

These are frugivorous bats of large size, differing, as remarked by Jerdon, so much in their dentition from the insectivorous species that they seem to lead through the flying Lemurs (*Colugos*) directly to the *Quadrumana*. The dentition is more adapted to their diet; they have cutting incisors to each jaw, and grinders with flat crowns, and their intestines are longer than those of the insectivorous bats. They produce but one at birth, and the young ones leave their parents as soon as they can provide for themselves. The tongue is covered with rough papillæ. They have no tail. These bats and some of the following genus, which are also frugivorous, are distinguished from the rest of the bats by a claw on the first or index finger, which is short.

Dental formula: Inc., $\frac{4}{4}$; can., $\frac{1-1}{1-1}$; premolars, $\frac{2-2}{3-3}$; molars, $\frac{3-3}{3-3}$.

No. 31. PTEROPUS EDWARDSII *vel* MEDIUS.

The Common Flying Fox (Jerdon's No. 12).

The Flying Fox at Home.

NATIVE NAMES.—*Badul*, Bengali and Mahratti; *Wurbagul*, Hindi; *Toggul bawali*, Canarese; *Sikurayi*, Telegu.

HABITAT.—All through India, Ceylon, and Burmah.

DESCRIPTION.—Head and nape rufous black; neck and shoulders golden yellow (the hair longer); back dark brown; chin dark; rest of body beneath fulvous or rusty brown; interfemoral membrane brownish black.—*Jerdon.*

SIZE.—Length, 12 to 14 inches; extent of wings, 46 to 52 inches.

These bats roost on trees in vast numbers. I have generally found them to prefer tamarinds of large size. Some idea of the extent of these colonies may be gathered from observations by McMaster, who attempted to calculate the number in a colony. He says: "In five minutes a friend and I counted upwards of six hundred as they passed over head, *en route* to their feeding grounds; supposing their nightly exodus to continue for twenty minutes, this would give upwards of two thousand in one roosting place, exclusive of those who took a different direction."

Head of *Pteropus medius.*

Tickell's account of these colonies is most graphic, though Emerson Tennent has also given a most interesting and correct account of their habits. The former writes:—"From the arrival of the first comer until the sun is high above the horizon, a scene of incessant wrangling and contention is enacted among them, as each endeavours to secure a higher and better place, or to eject a neighbour from too close vicinage. In these struggles the bats hook themselves along the branches, scrambling about hand over hand with some speed, biting each other severely, striking out with the long claw of the thumb, shrieking and cackling without intermission. Each new arrival is compelled to fly several times round the tree, being threatened from all points, and, when he eventually hooks on, he has to go through a series of combats, and be probably ejected two or three times before he makes good his tenure."

For faithful portraying, no one could improve on this description. These bats are exceeding strong on the wing. I was aware that they went long distances in search of food, but I was not aware of the power they had for sustained flight till the year 1869, when, on my way to England on furlough, I discovered a large flying fox winging his way towards our vessel, which was at that time more than two hundred miles from land. Exhausted, it clung on to the fore-yard arm; and a present of a rupee induced a Lascar to go aloft and seize it, which he did after several attempts. The voracity with which it attacked some plantains showed that it had been for some time deprived of food, probably having been blown off shore by high winds. Hanging head-downwards from its cage, it stuffed the fruit into its cheeks, monkey-fashion, and then seemed to chew it at leisure. When I left the steamer at Suez it remained in the captain's possession, and seemed to be tame and reconciled to its imprisonment, tempered by a surfeit of plantains. In flying over water they frequently dip down to touch the surface. Jerdon was in doubt whether they did this to drink or not, but McMaster feels sure that they do this in order to drink, and that the habit is not peculiar to the *Pteropodidæ*, as he has noticed other bats doing the same. Colonel Sykes states that he "can personally testify that their flesh is delicate and without disagreeable flavour;" and another colonel of my acquaintance once regaled his friends on some flying fox cutlets, which were pronounced "not bad." Dr. Day accuses these bats of intemperate habits; drinking the toddy from the earthen pots on the cocoanut trees, and flying home intoxicated. The wild almond is a favourite fruit.

Mr. Rainey, who has been a careful observer of animals for years, states that in Bengal these bats prefer clumps of bamboos for a resting place, and feed much on the fruit of the betel-nut palm when ripe. Another naturalist, Mr. G. Vidal, writes that in Southern India the *P. medius* feeds chiefly on the green drupe or nut of the Alexandrian laurel (*Calophyllum inophyllum*), the kernels of which contain a strong-smelling green oil on which the bats fatten amazingly; and then they in turn yield, when boiled down, an oil which is recommended as an excellent stimulative application for the hair. I noticed in Seonee a curious superstition to the effect that a bone of this bat tied on to the ancle by a cord of black cowhair is a sovereign remedy, according to the natives, for rheumatism in the leg. Tickell states that these bats produce one at a time in March or April, and they continue a fixture on the mother till the end of May or beginning of June.

No. 32. PTEROPUS LESCHENAULTII (CYNONYCTERIS AMPLEXICAUDATA).

The Fulvous Fox-Bat (*Jerdon's No.* 13).

Dobson places this bat in the sub-group *Cynonycteris.* It seems to differ from *Pteropus* only, as far as I can see, in having a small distinct tail, though the above-quoted author considers it closely allied to the next genus.

HABITAT.—The Carnatic, Madras and Trichinopoly; stated also procurable at Calcutta and Pondicherry (*Jerdon*); Ceylon (*Kellaart*).

DESCRIPTION.—Fur short and downy; fulvous ashy, or dull light ashy brown colour, denser and paler beneath; the hairs whitish at the base; membranes dark brown.

SIZE.—Length, 5 to $5\frac{1}{2}$ inches; extent of wing, 18 to 20 inches.

More information is required regarding the habits of this bat.

GENUS CYNOPTERUS.

This genus has four molars less than the last, a shorter muzzle; the cheek-bones or zygomatic arch more projecting; tongue rather longer and more tapering, and slightly extensile.

Dental formula: Inc., $\frac{4}{4}$ or $\frac{4}{2}$; can., $\frac{1-1}{1-1}$; premolars, $\frac{2-2}{3-3}$; molars, $\frac{2-2}{2-2}$.

No. 33. CYNOPTERUS MARGINATUS.

The Small Fox-Bat (*Jerdon's No.* 14).

NATIVE NAME.—*Chamgadili*, Hindi; *Coteekan voulha*, Singhalese.

HABITAT.— India generally, and Ceylon.

Cynopterus marginatus.

DESCRIPTION.—General colour fulvous olivaceous, paler beneath and with an ashy tinge; ears with a narrow margin of white (*Jerdon.*) A reddish smear on neck and shoulders of most specimens; membranes dusky brown. Females paler (*Kellaart*).

SIZE.—Length, $4\frac{1}{2}$ to $5\frac{1}{2}$ inches; extent of wing, 17 to 20 inches.

This bat is found all over India; it is frugivorous exclusively, though some of this sub-order are insectivorous. Blyth says he kept some for several weeks; they would take no notice of the buzz of an insect held to them, but are ravenous eaters of fruit, each devouring its own weight at a meal, voiding its food but little changed whilst slowly munching away; of guava it swallows the juice only. Blyth's prisoners were females, and after a time they attracted a male which hovered about them for some days, roosting near them in a dark staircase; he was also caught, with one of the females who had escaped and joined him. Dr. Dobson writes that in three hours one of these bats devoured twice its own weight. This species usually roosts in trees.

No. 34. MACROGLOSSUS (PTEROPUS) MINIMUS.

The Tenasserim Fox-Bat.

NATVIE NAME.—*Lowo-assu* (dog-bat), Javanese.

HABITAT.—The Himalayas, Burmah, Tenasserim, and the Indian Archipelago.

DESCRIPTION.—Ears half length of head, narrow and rounded at tip; face abruptly narrowed in front of eyes; muzzle long, narrow, cylindrical; lower jaw slightly projecting; eyes large; tongue very long, last third attenuated, covered with brush-like papillæ; interfemoral membrane very narrow, especially at root of tail; fur reddish brown, and very long.

SIZE.—Head and body, $2\frac{3}{10}$ inches.

Like other *Pteropi* this bat feeds on fruit of every description, but particularly attacks the various cultivated varieties of *Eugenia* (Jamoon).

GENUS EONYCTERIS.

Muzzle long and cylindrical; nostrils scarcely projecting; upper lip with a shallow vertical groove in front; *index finger without a claw;* thumb short; part of the terminal phalanx included in the wing membrane; metacarpal bone of the second finger equal to the index finger in length; tail short and distinct; the base contained in the narrow interfemoral membrane; tongue long, as in *Macroglossus.*

Dentition: Inc., $\frac{4}{4}$; can., $\frac{1-1}{1-1}$; premolars, $\frac{2-2}{2-2}$; molars, $\frac{3-3}{3-3}$.

No. 35. EONYCTERIS SPELÆA.

HABITAT.—Burmah.

DESCRIPTION.—Head long; muzzle narrow, cylindrical, abruptly narrowed in front of the eyes; nostrils with an intervening emargination, which also passes down to the lips; tongue very long and pointed; ears conical, with rounded tips; body clothed with very short and thinly-spread fur of a uniform dark brown colour; the fur on the head extends only as far as the inner corners of the eye, leaving the rest of the face naked; tail half an inch. On each side, and a little behind the anal opening, are two small, kidney-shaped subcutaneous glandular bodies.

SIZE.—Head and body, 4 inches; tail, ½ inch.

Found in Farm Caves, Moulmein. The absence of the claw on the index finger is specially to be noted.

MICROCHIROPTERA.

SUB-FAMILY VAMPYRIDÆ.

GENUS MEGADERMA.

Bats with simple or complicated nose-leaves or membranes. The conch of the ear very large, and joined together on the top of the head; tragus large and bifurcated; nasal membranes complicated; no tail; wings remarkably ample. They have four incisors below but none above, the intermaxillaries remaining cartilaginous.

Dental formula: Inc., $\frac{0}{4}$; can., $\frac{1-1}{1-1}$; pre-m., $\frac{2-2}{2-2}$ or $\frac{1-1}{2-2}$; molars, $\frac{3-3}{3-3}$.

NO. 36. MEGADERMA LYRA.

The Large-eared Vampire Bat (Jerdon's No. 15).

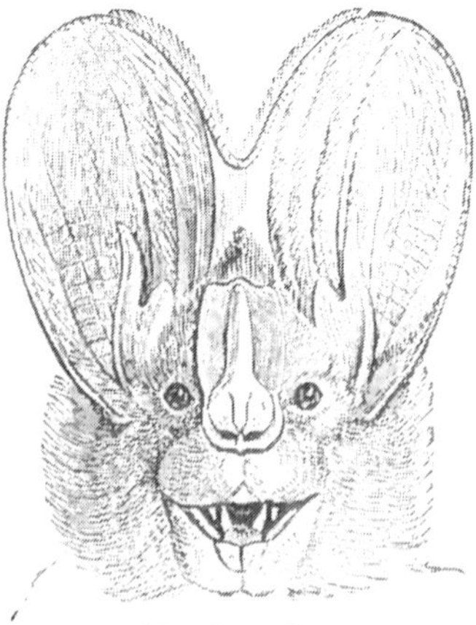

Megaderma lyra.

HABITAT.—India and Ceylon.

DESCRIPTION.—Above ashy blue, slaty or pale mouse colour; albescent or yellowish ashy beneath; nasal appendage large, oblong, free at the tip, reaching to the base of the ears with a fold down the centre; tragus (*oreillon*) cordate, two-lobed, anterior long, narrow and pointed, posterior lobe half the height and rounded; muzzle truncated; under-lip cleft; wing membranes dark brown.

SIZE.—Head and body, 3 or 3½ inches; wing extent, 14 to 19 inches.

Very abundant in old buildings. They are beyond doubt blood-suckers. Blyth noticed one fly into his room one evening with a small *vespertilio*, which it dropped on being chased. The smaller bat was weak from loss of blood, and next morning (the Megaderm having been caught), on both bats being put into the same cage, the little one was again attacked and devoured; it was seized both times behind the ear. McMaster writes that in Rangoon he had a tame canary killed by a bat, and the bird's mate soon afterwards was destroyed in the same way. The case was clearly proved.

Mr. Frith informed Mr. Blyth that these bats were in the habit of resorting to the verandah of his house at Mymensing, and that every morning the ground under them was strewed with the hind quarters of frogs, and the wings of large grasshoppers and crickets. On one occasion the remains of a small fish were observed; but frogs appeared to be their chief diet—never toads; and of a quiet evening these animals could be distinctly heard crunching the heads and smaller bones of their victims.

No. 37. MEGADERMA SPECTRUM.

The Cashmere Vampire (Jerdon's No 16).

HABITAT.—Cashmere.

DESCRIPTION.—Above slaty cinereous, whitish beneath; the vertical nose-leaf of moderate size, oval; inner lobe of tragus ovate (*Jerdon*).

SIZE.—Two and three-quarter inches.

Dobson makes this bat synonymous with the last.

No. 38. MEGADERMA SPASMA.

HABITAT.—Tenasserim, Ceylon.

DESCRIPTION. — Muzzle, ear-conch, and tragus similar to those of *M. lyra;* the posterior portion of the tragus, however, is longer and more attenuated upwards, and more acutely pointed; the nose-leaf is shorter, with convex sides; but the anterior concave disc is considerably larger, and the base of the thickened process is cordate; thumbs and wings as in *M. lyra;* interfemoral membrane deeper; the calcaneum stronger; colour the same.

Megaderma spasma.

SIZE,—Head and body, about 3 inches. This bat is alluded to by Jerdon as *M. Horsfieldii.*

RHINOLOPHINÆ.

Nasal leaf complicated, and crests resting on the forehead, presenting more or less the figure of a horse-shoe; tail long and placed in the interfemoral membrane; ears large, but separate, and not joined at the base, as in the last genus; without a tragus, but often with a lobe at the base of the outer margin; wings large and long; forefinger of a single joint.

GENUS RHINOLOPHUS.

Nose-leaf cordate, or semi-orbicular, bi-lobed in front of the nostrils; a longitudinal crest along the nose and an erect frontal leaf posteriorly more or less lanceolate.—*Jerdon.*

Dental formula: Inc., $\frac{2}{4}$; can., $\frac{1-1}{1-1}$; pre-molars, $\frac{2-2}{2-2}$; molars, $\frac{3-3}{3-3}$.

No. 39. RHINOLOPHUS PERNIGER *vel* LUCTUS.

The Large Leaf-Bat (*Jerdon's No* 17).

Rhinolophus luctus.

HABITAT.—Nepaul, Darjeeling, Khasya Hills.

DESCRIPTION.—Ears very large, much longer than the head; broad, acutely pointed; nasal apparatus very complicated; the lower leaf very large, concealing the upper lip like a door knocker; the upper leaf like a graduated spire; ears transversely striate; a rather large semi-circular lobe at base of ear; fur long, dense, soft, and lax, slightly curled or woolly black with a silvery grizzle, or greyish-black or rich chestnut-brown.—*Jerdon.*

SIZE.—Length, $3\frac{3}{4}$; tail, $1\frac{3}{4}$; wing expanse, 17 inches.

No. 40. RHINOLOPHUS MITRATUS.

The Mitred Leaf-Bat (*Jerdon's No.* 18).

HABITAT.—Chybassa, Central India, Mussoorie (?)

DESCRIPTION—Ears large; anti-helix moderately developed; upper leaf triangular acute; tail extending beyond the tibia; color above light brown; paler beneath.—*Jerdon.*

SIZE.—Head and body, $2\frac{1}{2}$ inches; tail, $1\frac{1}{2}$ inch; wing expanse, 12 to 14 inches.

No. 41. RHINOLOPHUS TRAGATUS *vel* FERRUM-EQUINUM.

The Dark-brown Leaf-Bat (Jerdon's No. 19).

HABITAT.—Nepaul, Mussoorie.

DESCRIPTION.—Upper process like a barbed spear-head; central one

Rhinolophus ferrum-equinum.

small and narrow, a little expanded at the summit; anti tragus less developed than usual; lips simple; colour a uniform deep brown, with tips of the hair paler, and somewhat rusty.—*Jerdon.*

SIZE.—Head and body, $2\frac{5}{8}$ inches; tail, $1\frac{7}{8}$ inch; wing, $15\frac{1}{2}$ inches. The tail of this species seems unusually long. It is found in cavities of rock, and issues forth soon after dusk—sooner, according to Hodgson, than the species of *vespertilio.*

NO. 42. RHINOLOPHUS PEARSONII.

Pearson's Leaf-Bat (*Jerdon's No.* 20).

HABITAT.—Lower Himalayan range, Darjeeling, Mussoorie, &c.

DESCRIPTION.—Colour above dark brown, with a slight shade of chestnut; underneath brown, with a sooty cast; fur very long, dense and soft; ears distinct, with an additional rounded lobe below, measuring anteriorly nearly three-fourths of an inch; point of the facial crest moderately developed; length from the tip of the nose to root of tail three inches; tail half an inch; length of fore-arm two inches; expanse of the wings eleven inches. Although allied to Mr. Hodgson's *R. tragatus*, possesses distinct characters.—*Horsfield.*

SIZE.—As given by Horsfield above.

This bat was first sent from Darjeeling by Mr. J. T. Pearson, and was named after him. It has also, according to Jerdon, been found by Captain Hutton at Mussoorie; it is therefore reasonable to suppose that it inhabits the whole range of the lower Himalayas. One striking difference between it and the last species is the very short tail, and it is easily to be recognised by the great length of the fur.

NO. 43. RHINOLOPHUS AFFINIS.

The Allied Leaf-Bat (*Jerdon's No* 21).

HABITAT.—Ceylon, Burmah, and perhaps the Malabar coast.

DESCRIPTION.—Above bright red ferruginous brown; tips of hair darker, paler beneath; ears pointed and external; edge deeply emarginated; internal edge and basal third of external surface hairy; anti-helix well developed; nasal process apparently very similar to that of *R. mitratus* (*Kellaart*). Upper leaf triangular, emarginate at the tip, reaching above the base of the ears (*Jerdon*).

SIZE.—Head and body about $2\frac{3}{10}$ inches; tail, 1 inch; wing extent, 12 inches.

This bat seems to vary much in colour. Kellaart says some are of a brighter red than others, and a few had a yellower tinge. Another marked variety was of a uniform pale yellow brown.

NO. 44. RHINOLOPHUS ROUXI.

The Rufous Leaf-Bat (*Jerdon's No.* 22).

HABITAT.—India generally.

DESCRIPTION.—Ears large, pointed, externally notched; tragus broad; tips of upper nose-leaf triangular, with its sides well emarginate, reaching above the base of the ears; no upper incisors [as in *Megaderma lyra*];

lower molars only five; canines very large; fur short, crisp; colour above smoky brown in some, reddish brown in others, and golden rufous in some; beneath paler.—*Jerdon.*

SIZE.—Length, $2\frac{3}{8}$ inches; tail, $1\frac{1}{8}$; wing expanse, 13 inches.

Hodgson considers this bat as allied to the two following species. It is the *R. lepidus* of Blyth.

No. 45. RHINOLOPHUS MACROTIS.

The Large-eared Leaf-Bat (*Jerdon's No.* 23).

HABITAT.—Lower Himalayas.

DESCRIPTION.—Ears very large, broad, oval, with pointed recurved tip, and a large obtuse tragus; anterior central crest of nose-leaf produced in front over the top of the flat transverse front edge; hinder leaf lanceolate triangular; above sooty brown or light earthy olive-brown, paler below, some with a rufous or Isabelline tint; no pubic teats.—*Jerdon.*

SIZE.—Head and body, $1\frac{3}{4}$ inch; tail, $\frac{3}{4}$; wing expanse, $9\frac{3}{4}$.

No. 46. RHINOLOPHUS SUB-BADIUS.

The Bay Leaf-Bat (*Jerdon's No.* 24).

HABITAT.—Nepaul.

DESCRIPTION.—Ears not larger than the head, obtusely pointed and ovoid; nasal appendage quadrate, with a transverse bar nearly surmounting it; upper leaf triangular, with slightly emarginate sides; clear brown above, paler below and on head and face.

SIZE.—Head and body, $1\frac{1}{2}$ inch; tail, $1\frac{1}{4}$; wing expanse, $7\frac{1}{2}$.—*Jerdon.*

No. 47. RHINOLOPHUS RAMMANIKA (*Kellaart*).

HABITAT.—Ceylon.

DESCRIPTION.—Above rufescent, beneath ashy brown; face slightly fulvous; round the base of the ears and on the sides of the posterior half of the body bright fulvous; tail enclosed in the interfemoral membrane.

SIZE.—Head and body, $2\frac{1}{2}$ inches; tail, 1; wing expanse, 10 inches.

This is a doubtful species. Dr. Kellaart got one from Amanapoora hill at Kaduganava. He says: "As the specimen reached us in a dried condition, we are unable to say anything more about its nasal processes than that in place of a transverse process above the nostrils it had a small triangular peak over the usual horse-shoe process surrounding the nasal opening. This triangular crest was hairy; superiorly there was no appearance of a sac above it to the best of our recollection.

No. 48. RHINOLOPHUS ANDAMANENSIS.

HABITAT.—Southern Andaman Island.

DESCRIPTION (*apud* Dobson).—Like *R. affinis* generally, but the anterior horizontal horse-shoe shaped membrane is very broad, completely concealing the muzzle when viewed from above, as in *R. Pearsonii*; the posterior terminal leaf is also much longer, produced backwards between the ears, and not concave on the sides as in *R. affinis*. The thumb is also much longer. Fur bright reddish brown above and beneath.

No. 49. RHINOLOPHUS MINOR.

HABITAT.—Burmah, Yunan.

DESCRIPTION.—Light brown above, greyish brown beneath; ears slightly shorter than the head, sub-acutely pointed; anti-tragus large, separated by a deep angular notch; lower lip with three vertical grooves.

SIZE.—Length of head and body from 1 to 1¾ inch.

No. 50. RHINOLOPHUS CŒLOPHYLLUS.

HABITAT.—Burmah.

DESCRIPTION.—Fur brown, with whitish roots, light brownish white below; ears large, with pointed tips projecting outwards; "anti-tragus large, separated by an angular emargination from the outer margin of the ear; horse-shoe large; horizontal margins of central nose-leaf triangular, small; erect portion rather short, with parallel sides and rounded summit, meeting the connected vertical process at the same level" (*Dobson*). For a more detailed description see Dobson's Monograph, page 53. Three vertical grooves on lower lip.

SIZE.—Length of head and body about 2 inches.

No. 51. RHINOLOPHUS GAROENSIS.

HABITAT.—Garo Hills, Assam; Himalayas (Mussoorie).

DESCRIPTION (*apud* Dobson).—Ears acutely pointed, with a large anti-tragus, as in *R. affinis*; anterior vertical process of the sella maintaining the same breadth upwards and rounded off above, considerably exceeded in height by the upper edge of the connecting process, which develops a long acutely pointed projection; terminal portion of the posterior leaf broad with straight sides, forming an almost equilateral triangle.

Wing membrane from the ankles, inter femoral membrane square behind; extreme tip of the tail free.

SIZE.—Length of head and body about 1·5 inch.

This bat is figured (head only) in Dobson's Monograph, page 48.

No. 52. RHINOLOPHUS PETERSII.

HABITAT.—India. Precise locality unknown.

DESCRIPTION.—Ears acutely pointed, with an emargination immediately beneath the tip; anti-tragus large, separated from the outer margin by a deep angular incision; nose-leaf horizontal, horse-shoe-shaped, not so broad as the muzzle; vertical part of the sella almost same breadth upwards, and rounded off above, exceeded considerably in height by the upper margin of the posterior connecting process; lower lip with three vertical grooves; fur dark brown above, greyish brown beneath.

SIZE.—Length of head and body, 2·5 inches; tail, 1 inch.

There are two good woodcuts of the head of this bat in Dobson's Monograph.

No. 53. RHINOLOPHUS TRIFOLIATUS.

HABITAT.—East coast of India.

DESCRIPTION.—Very much like *R. perniger* (*luctus*), but is distinguished by its smaller size and by the more pointed vertical process of the central nose-leaf, which in the other is truncated.

SIZE.—Length of head and body, 2 inches; tail about 1 inch.

GENUS HIPPOSIDEROS (GRAY) VEL *PHYLLORHINA (BONAPARTE)*.

Nasal-leaf broad, depressed, transverse; ears with transverse wrinkles; a circular sac behind the nasal crest, which can be turned inside out; when alarmed the animal blows it out, and then withdraws it at each breath; it contains a waxy matter of green or yellow colour. Blyth thinks that this sac is affected by the amorous season, as in the case of the infra-orbital cavities of various ruminants and analogous glandular follicles in other animals.

This genus is also distinguishable from the last by the form of the ear conch, the small size of the anti-tragus, and, as Dr. Dobson particularly points out, by the presence of *two* joints only in all the toes, as also by the number and character of the teeth, which are as follows:—

Inc., $\frac{2}{4}$; can., $\frac{1-1}{1-1}$; pre-molars, $\frac{2-2}{2-2}$; molars, $\frac{3-3}{3-3}$.

No. 54. HIPPOSIDEROS ARMIGER.

The Large Horse-shoe Bat (*Jerdon's No.* 25).

HABITAT.—Lower Himalaya ranges; Ceylon.

DESCRIPTION.—Nasal-leaf large and square; lips with a triple fold of skin on each side; tragus vaguely developed and wavily emarginate; of a uniform light-brown colour, with maroon tips to the hairs of the upper parts; membranes black.

SIZE.—Head and body, 4½ inches; tail, 2½; wing expanse, 22.

Jerdon makes this out to be the same as Kellaart's *H. lankadiva* and the Malayan *H. nobilis*, but those are synonymous with *Phyllorhina diadema*. Kellaart supposed it to be identical with *H. insignis*, which will be found further on as *Phyllorhina larvata*, all those bats closely resembling each other in a general way. I think this No. 25 of Jerdon is the same as Peter's *Phyllorhina armigera*. Hutton found it at Darjeeling, and writes of it as follows:—

"When captured alive the large ears are kept in a constant state of rapid tremulous motion, and the animal emits a low purring sound, which becomes a sharp scream when alarmed or irritated. When suspended at rest the tail and inter-femoral membrane are turned up, not in front, like the *Rhinolophi*, but behind, over the lower part of the back; neither does it appear to envelope itself in its wings so completely as does *R. luctus*." He then goes on to say he has noticed the tremor of the ears and facial crests in all the *Rhinolophi* when disturbed, and concludes with a graphic description of this species, sallying forth in the evening to prey upon the noisy *Cicadas*; leisurely wheeling with noiseless, cautious flight round some wide-spreading oak, "scanning each branch as he slowly passes by—now rising to a higher circle, and then perchance descending to the lower branches, until at length, detecting the unfortunate minstrel, it darts suddenly into the tree, and snatching the still screaming insect from its perch, bears it away."

Jerdon procured specimens at Darjeeling, and Kellaart says it is found in great abundance at Kandy and its neighbourhood; Kurnegalle Tunnel swarms with them.

No. 55. HIPPOSIDEROS SPEORIS.

The Indian Horse-shoe Bat (*Jerdon's No.* 26).

HABITAT.—India generally and Ceylon.

DESCRIPTION.—Mouse brown or fulvous brown. Occasionally golden fulvous and sometimes dusky black above, paler beneath; membranes dusky brown; interfemoral membrane narrow, enclosing the tail except the last half joint (about 2-10ths of an inch), which is free.

Ear large, erect and pointed, rounded at the base and emarginated on the outer edge; nasal process complicated. "Males have a frontal sac; females none" (*Kellaart*). Pubis naked, with two inguinal warts.

SIZE.—Head and body, 2 inches; tail, $1\frac{2}{10}$; wing expanse, 12.

Inhabits old buildings, wells, &c.

No. 56. HIPPOSIDEROS MURINUS.

The Little Horse-shoe Bat (*Jerdon's No.* 27).

HABITAT.—Southern India, Ceylon, and Burmah.

DESCRIPTION.—Muzzle short; body short and thick; a transverse frontal leaf with a sac behind it; no folds of skin on each side of the horse-shoe as in the last species; ears large, naked and rounded; colour dusky brown or mouse, sometimes light fawn; wing membrane blackish; interfemoral membrane large, and including the tail all but the tip.

SIZE.—Head and body, $1\frac{4}{5}$ inch; tail, $1\frac{1}{5}$ inch; wing expanse, 10.

Jerdon says the mouse-coloured variety is common in the Carnatic, but he has only seen the light fulvous race on the Nilgheries; but Mr. Elliot procured both in the southern Mahratta country. A dark variety of this bat was called *Rhinolophus ater* by Templeton, and *H. atratus* by Kellaart; in other respects it is identical, only a little smaller.

No. 57. HIPPOSIDEROS CINERACEUS.

The Ashy Horse-shoe Bat (*Jerdon's No.* 28).

HABITAT.—Punjab Salt range.

DESCRIPTION.—Similar to the last, but larger, and I should think the argument against *H. atratus* would apply to this as a distinct species.

No. 58. HIPPOSIDEROS LARVATUS. *Syn.*—PHYLLORHINA LARVATA.

HABITAT.—Arracan.

DESCRIPTION.—The fur of the upper part bright fulvous; more or less tinged with maroon on the back, lighter underneath; membranes dusky, but tinged with the prevailing colour of the fur; ears angulated; a minute false molar in front of the carnassial in the upper jaw.

SIZE.—Head and body, $2\frac{3}{4}$ inches; tail, $1\frac{1}{4}$; wing extent, 12.

Kellaart writes of this bat under his *H. aureus*. He describes it as head, neck, and body of a bright golden yellow, with a slight maroon shade on the tips of the hairs on the back. Females paler coloured. Frontal sac only in males; the waxy matter of a yellow colour, and quite transparent.

No. 59. HIPPOSIDEROS VULGARIS. *Syn.*—PHYLLORHINA LARVATA.

The Common Malayan Horse-shoe Bat.

HABITAT.—Arracan and Malayana.

DESCRIPTION.—"It differs from the last in being rather smaller, and of a brown colour above, much paler at the base of the hairs and at their extreme tips, and lighter coloured below; the ears more apiculated, or rather they appear so from being strongly emarginated externally towards the tip."—*Blyth.*

SIZE.—$2\frac{3}{10}$ inches; tail $1\frac{2}{10}$; wing expanse about 12.

No. 60. HIPPOSIDEROS BLYTHII.

HABITAT.—Ceylon, Fort Frederic.

DESCRIPTION.—Above surface colour a rich dark tawny brown; base of hairs much lighter coloured, of a brighter yellow tinge; beneath paler; face partially blackish; ears black; tip of tail excerted; no frontal sac; membranes blackish; nasal processes as in *H. speoris.*

SIZE.—Head and body, $2\frac{2}{10}$ inches; tail, 1; wing expanse, 12.

Dr. Kellaart considered this a new and undescribed species, distinguished from *H. speoris* and *H. vulgaris* (*vel Templetonii*—Kellaart) by the greater length of the fore-arm, which is two inches. This remark however does not apply to *vulgaris*, of which Kellaart himself gives two inches as the length of the radius, and Blyth gives two and a quarter. The absence of the frontal sac would have been a greater proof, but both specimens on which Kellaart made his observations were females; and as colouring is so varied in the bat tribe as to preclude the division of species on this ground, I think we may put this down as a doubtful species on which more information is desirable.

No. 61. PHYLLORHINA DIADEMA.

HABITAT.—India generally; Ceylon and Burmah.

DESCRIPTION.—The fur with three shades—buff, then reddish brown with ashy tips, underneath greyish or pale brown. "The hinder erect nose-leaf," according to Dobson's description, "equals the horse-shoe and slightly exceeds the sella in width, its free margin forming a segment of the circumference of a circle, with a small blunt projection in the centre and three vertical ridges on its concave front surface; sella large, with a prominent ridge in the centre, forming a small projection above and one smaller on each side; sides of the muzzle with prominent vertical leaves, three on each side; no frontal pore."

There is a good figure of the head of this bat in Cuvier's 'Animal Kingdom,' Carpenter's and Westwood's edition, under the name of

Rhinolophus nobilis. It is the same also as Kellaart's *Hipposideros lankadiva.* Captain Hutton, who was a keen observer of the habits of the bats at Mussoorie, says of this one : "Like *R. affinis*, this species may frequently be heard during its flight cracking and crunching the hard wings of beetles, which in the evening hours are usually abundant among the trees ; the teeth are strong, and the *tout ensemble* of its aspect is not unlike that of a bull-dog."—'Proc. Zoo. Soc.,' 1872, page 701.

No. 62. Phyllorhina Masoni.

HABITAT.—Burmah (Moulmein).

DESCRIPTION.—This bat resembles the last closely ; such difference as exists is that the concave surface of the terminal nose-leaf is divided into two cells only by a single central vertical ridge, and from the under surface of the juncture of the mandible a small bony process projects downwards about equal to the lower canine tooth in vertical extent, and covered by the integument.

There is an excellent figure of this bat in Dobson's Monograph, from whence I have also taken the above description.

No. 63. Phyllorhina Nicobarensis.

HABITAT.—Nicobar Island.

DESCRIPTION.—"Ears large, acute ; outer margin slightly concave beneath the tip ; no frontal sac behind the nose-leaf ; upper margin of the transverse terminal leaf simple, forming an arc of a circle, folded back and overhanging the concave front surface, which is divided into *two* cells only by a single central longitudinal ridge ; in front the margin of the horse-shoe is marked by three small points" (*Dobson*). Fur light brown, then greyish, with light brown tips.

SIZE.—Length of head and body, 3 inches.

No. 64. Phyllhorina armigera.

HABITAT.—The entire range of the Himalayas, Khasya Hills, and Ceylon.

DESCRIPTION.—The hinder erect nose-leaf narrow, not so broad as the horse-shoe ; upper edge sinuate, slightly elevated in the centre, and at either extremity ; vertical ridges beneath well developed, prominent, enclosing moderately deep cells ; wart-like granular elevations on each side above the eyes are usually greatly developed, forming large thickened longitudinal elevations extending forward on each side of the posterior erect nose-leaf, and backwards towards the frontal sac (*Dobson*). The colour varies.

SIZE.—Length of head and body from 3 to 4 inches ; tail about 2.

This is the largest of this genus, and one of the most interesting of the species. My space will not admit of extensive quotations from those who have written about it, but there is a fuller description of it in

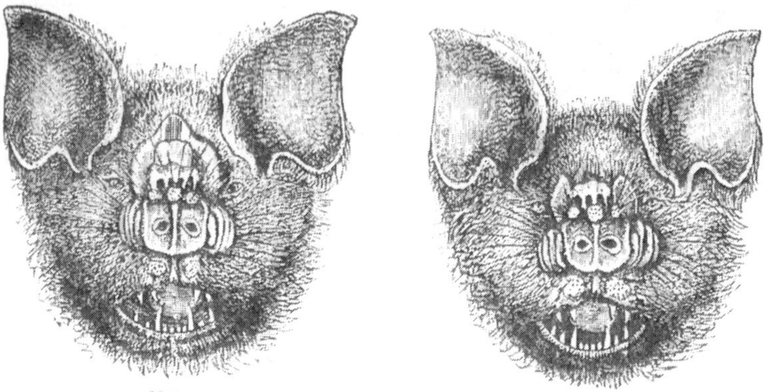

Male. Female.

Phyllorhina armigera.

Dr. Dobson's book, and a very interesting account of its habits by Capt. J. Hutton, in the 'Proceedings of the Zoological Society,' 1872, page 701.

No. 65. PHYLLORHINA LEPTOPHYLLA.

HABITAT.—Khasya Hills.

DESCRIPTION.—Ears large, broad, triangular, with subacute tips; outer margin slightly concave; upper transverse nose-leaf small; upper edge simple, narrower than horse-shoe, thin; three vertical folds in front faintly descernible at base only; horse-shoe with small incision in centre of front free edge; frontal pore small, placed at some distance behind the transverse nose-leaf; fur and integuments dark throughout. —*Dobson.*

SIZE.—Length of head and body, 2 inches; tail, $1\frac{6}{10}$.

No. 66. PHYLLORHINA GALERITA.

HABITAT.—Central India, Deccan.

DESCRIPTION.—"Ear comparatively small, as broad as long; inner margin very convex forward; outer margin slightly concave beneath the tip; nose-leaf as in *P. larvata*, but the transverse terminal leaf is more rectangular; the superior margin less convex, and its concave front surface is marked by three very prominent vertical ridges; frontal pore small, indistinct, not larger than in the females of *P. larvata*."—*Dobson.*

SIZE.—Head and body about 2 inches; tail, 1 inch.

No. 67. PHYLLORHINA BICOLOR.

HABITAT.—India (N. W. Himalaya), Nicobar Islands.

DESCRIPTION.—Fur above reddish chestnut; the base of the hairs pale reddish-white, or base of hair pure white, the tip, dark reddish-brown. Ears as long as the head, broad; the lower half of the inner margin very convex; the summit of the ear conch rounded off broadly as far as a point on the outer side, where a slight but distinct flattening occurs, and indicates the position of the tip. Horse-shoe small, square; the concave front surface divided into four cells by three distinct vertical ridges; no secondary leaflets external to the horse-shoe; frontal sac distinct in males, rudimentary in females (*Dobson*). Blyth includes this bat in his Burmese Catalogue, but does not say much about it.

GENUS CŒLOPS.

Possesses the general characteristics of *Rhinolophus*, but the tail and calcanea wanting entirely; the intercrural membrane acutely emarginate to the depth of a line even with the knees; ears large, broad and rounded; the summit of the facial membranes rising abruptly, obtusely bifid, bent forward; fur long, delicately fine.—*Jerdon.*

Dental formula: Inc., $\frac{1-1}{4}$; can., $\frac{1-1}{1-1}$; pre-molars, $\frac{2-2}{2-2}$; molars, $\frac{3-3}{3-3}$.

No. 68. CŒLOPS FRITHII.

Frith's Tailless Bat (Jerdon's No. 29).

HABITAT.—The Sunderbunds, Bengal.

DESCRIPTION.—Colour dusky or blackish; the fur tipped with ashy brown above, paler and somewhat ashy beneath; membranes fuscous.

SIZE.—Length, $1\frac{7}{8}$ inch; membrane beyond $\frac{3}{4}$ inch; forearm, $1\frac{3}{4}$.

This bat is rare. The above description, given by Jerdon, is based on one specimen sent to Mr. Blyth by Mr. Frith, who obtained it in the Sunderbunds. It also inhabits Java. Dr. Dobson examined a specimen from thence in the Leyden Museum. He says: "Calcanea and tail very short," whereas the above description says entirely wanting. The ears are funnel-shaped, and thickly covered with fine hair. Metacarpal bone of thumb very long; the wing membrane enclosing the thumb up to the base of the claw; wing to the tarsus close to the ankles; feet very slender; toes with strong claws."

GENUS RHINOPOMA.

Ears moderate, but joined above, as in the Megaderms; the nostrils at the end of the muzzle, with a little lamina above, forming a kind of snout; tail slender and joined at the base with the intercrural membrane, but extending far beyond it.

Dental formula: Inc., $\frac{2}{4}$; can., $\frac{1-1}{1-1}$; pre-molars, $\frac{1-1}{2-2}$; molars, $\frac{3-3}{3-3}$.

No. 69. RHINOPOMA HARDWICKII.

Hardwick's Long-tailed Leaf Bat (Jerdon's No. 30).

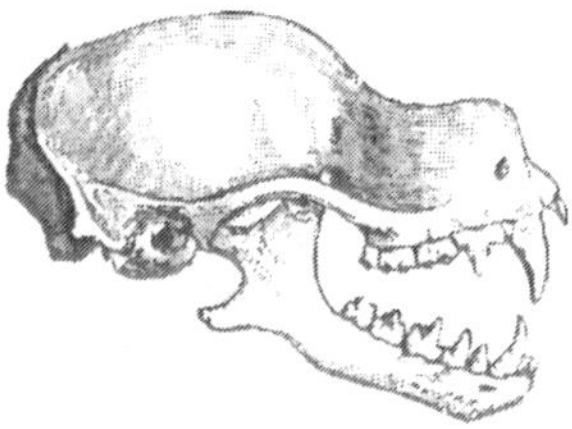

Skull of *Rhinopoma*.

HABITAT.—All over India, Burmah and Malayana.

DESCRIPTION.—Muzzle long, thick, truncated, and surrounded by a small leaf; tragus oblong, bi-acuminate; forehead concave with a channel down the centre; fur soft and very fine, dull brown throughout; face, rump, and part of abdominal region naked.—*Jerdon.*

SIZE.—Head and body, $2\frac{6}{10}$ inches; tail, $2\frac{1}{2}$; expanse, 13.

Frequents old ruins, caves, and clefts in rocks.

SUB-FAMILY NOCTILIONIDÆ.

Bats without facial membranes; with short obtuse and bull-doggish heads; large lips.

GENUS TAPHOZOUS.

Have a small rounded indenture on the forehead; no raised lamina on the nostrils; the head pyramidal; eyes rather large; ears moderate in size and not joined at the base, but widely apart; the tip of the tail free above the membrane, which is much longer.

The males have a transverse cavity under the throat; wings long and narrow, collapsing with a double flexure outwards; fur soft and velvety. (Dobson includes this genus in his Family *Emballonuridæ.*)

Dental formula: Inc., $\frac{1-1}{4}$; can., $\frac{1-1}{1-1}$; pre-molars, $\frac{2-2}{2-2}$; molars, $\frac{3-3}{3-3}$; premaxillaries cartilaginous, supporting only one pair of weak incisors with a gap between them.

No. 70. TAPHOZOUS LONGIMANUS.

The Long-armed Bat (Jerdon's No. 31).

HABITAT.—India generally.

DESCRIPTION.—"Ears oval, with many distinct folds, naked except at the base; tragus securiform; fur thick, close, fuscous-black, or dark fuscous-brown above; beneath paler, except on the throat, the hairs being conspicuously tipped with grey, the upper hairs being all white at their base; face nude, and the membrane dark brownish-black" (*Jerdon*). The gular sac, though represented in the male, is almost absent in the female, being but a rudimentary fold of skin; in this it differs from another common Indian species, *T. saccolaimus*, in which the gular sac is well developed in both sexes, though larger in the male.

SIZE.—Length, 5 inches; expanse, 15 to 16; tail, 1; fore-arm, $2\frac{5}{8}$; tibia, 1 inch.

This bat frequents old buildings, dark cellars, old ruins, &c.; the young are fulvescent, and become darker with age. Blyth states that it has a surprising faculty for creeping about on the vertical board of a cage, hitching its claws into the minute pores of the wood.

No. 71. TAPHOZOUS MELANOPOGON.

The Black-bearded Bat (Jerdon's No. 32).

HABITAT.—Common about Calcutta, East Coast of India, Burmah, and Cochin China.

DESCRIPTION.—"No gular sac, the openings of small pores appearing along a line corresponding to the position of the mouth of the gular sac in other species; in some male specimens the hair behind these pores is very long, forming a dense black beard" (*Dobson*). Ears moderate, oval, with the outer margin extending under the eyes, dilated into a large rounded lobe; the tragus leaf-shaped; the head, muzzle, and chin covered with short hairs.

SIZE.—Length of head and body about $3\frac{1}{2}$; tail, $\frac{2}{3}$; wing expanse, 14 inches.

Horsfield says it occurs in caves in Java inhabited by the esculent swallows (*Collocalia nidifica*), the gelatinous nests of which are used for soup by the Chinese. Dobson remarks that the black beard is not always developed in the males; he conceives it to be owing to certain conditions, probably connected with the amorous seasons. In five males in the Indian Museum the beard is well developed; he found that only two per cent. of the Cochin China specimens in the Paris Museum possessed it.

No. 72. TAPHOZOUS SACCOLAIMUS.

The White-bellied Bat (Jerdon's No. 33).

HABITAT.—Peninsula of India, Burmah, and Ceylon.

DESCRIPTION.—" Muzzle angular, naked, very acute; nostrils small, close; ears distant, shorter than the head, large inner margin recurved, outer margin dilated, reaching to the commissure of the mouth; tragus wide, securiform (i.e. axe-shaped); fur short, smooth, blackish on the head, chestnut brown on the back; beneath, dirty-white or black brown above with white pencillings; pure white below" (*Jerdon*). Dobson says of the fur: " above, white at the base, the terminal three-fourths of the hairs black, with a few irregular small white patches on the back; beneath dark brown." The gular sac is to be found in both sexes, but somewhat larger in the males.

SIZE.—About 5 inches; wing expanse, 17.

No. 73. TAPHOZOUS THEOBALDI.

HABITAT.—Tenasserim.

DESCRIPTION.—The gular sac is absent in both sexes; ears larger than in any others of the sub-genus; the muzzle, from the corners of the eyes downwards, naked.

SIZE.—Head and body about $3\frac{1}{10}$ inches; tail, $1\frac{1}{4}$.

No. 74. TAPHOZOUS KACHHENSIS.

HABITAT.—Kachh, N. W. India.

DESCRIPTION (*apud* Dobson).—" Gular sac absent in both male and female; its usual position indicated in the male by a semi-circular fold of skin and nakedness of the integument in this situation; in other respects similar to *T. nudiventris.* The deposits of fat about the tail very large."

SIZE.—Head and body about 3 inches; tail, $1\frac{1}{4}$.

T. nudiventris, above alluded to, is an inhabitant of Asia Minor, Egypt, and Nubia; similar to the above, only that it has a small gular sac in the male, of which a trace only exists in the female. Its most striking peculiarity is the deposit of fat at the root of the tail, which may possibly be for purposes of absorption during the dormant winter season.

GENUS NYCTINOMUS.

"Ears broad, short, approximate or connate with the outer margin, terminating in an erect lobe beyond the conch; tragus small, concealed" (often very small and quadrate, but never reduced to a mere point, as in *Molossus*—Dobson); "wings narrow, folded as in *Taphozous;* intercrural membrane short, truncate; tail free at the tip; feet short, with strong toes; muzzle thick; lips tumid, lax; upper lip with coarse wrinkles."—*Jerdon.*

Dental formula: Inc., $\frac{2}{6}$ or $\frac{2}{4}$; can., $\frac{1-1}{1-1}$; pre-mol., $\frac{2-2}{2-2}$; mol., $\frac{3-3}{3-3}$.

No. 75. NYCTINOMUS PLICATUS.

The Wrinkle-lipped Bat (*Jerdon's No.* 34).

HABITAT.—India generally.

DESCRIPTION.—Muzzle broad and thick; upper lip overhanging the lower, marked by vertical wrinkles; ears large and quadrilateral; outer margin ending in a decided anti-tragus; tail thick; the lower part of the leg is free from the wing membrane, which however, is connected with the ankle by a strong fibrous band; fur dense, smoky or snuff brown above (or bluish black—*Dobson*); paler beneath.

SIZE.—Head and body about $2\frac{1}{10}$ inches; tail, $1\frac{1}{10}$. Jerdon gives length, $4\frac{1}{4}$ to $4\frac{1}{10}$; expanse, $13\frac{1}{2}$; tail, $1\frac{3}{4}$.

This bat is common about Calcutta, frequenting ruins, dark places and hollow trees. It is allied to *N. tenuis* (*Horsfield*), and it is mentioned as inhabiting hollow trees in such numbers as to attract attention by the hissing noise from within, every available spot in the interior being occupied. A synonym of the genus is *Dysopes.*

No. 76. NYCTINOMUS TRAGATUS.

HABITAT.—India generally.

DESCRIPTION.—This differs from the last in having the wing membrane from the ankles, and in the free portion of the tail being shorter; ears united at the base; tragus broad and rounded above, partially concealed by the large anti-tragus.

SIZE.—About the same as the last.

SUB-FAMILY VESPERTILIONIDÆ.

These bats have simple nostrils, as in the frugivorous ones, with no complications of foliated cutaneous appendages; the muzzle is conical, moderately long, and clad with fur; the ears wide apart; the inner margins springing from the sides, not the top of the head; the tragi are large; eyes usually very small, and the tail, which is long, is wholly included in the membrane.

Dentition (usually): Inc., $\frac{2-2}{6}$; can., $\frac{1-1}{1-1}$; pre-mol., $\frac{3-3}{3-3}$; mol., $\frac{3-3}{3-3}$. The upper incisors are small, and placed in pairs near the canines, leaving a gap in the centre. The lower ones sharp-edged and somewhat notched. At birth there are twenty-two teeth, which are shed, and replaced by others, with sixteen additional ones, the adult bat having thirty-eight teeth.

GENUS PLECOTUS.

Ears very large, united at the base; outer margin of the ear conch terminating opposite the base of the tragus, the inner margin with an abrupt rounded projection directed inwards above the base; tragus very large, tapering upwards, with a lobe at the base of the outer margin.

Dentition: Inc., $\frac{2-2}{6}$; can., $\frac{1-1}{1-1}$; pre-molars, $\frac{2-2}{2-2}$; molars, $\frac{3-3}{3-3}$.

The English species *P. auritus* is very common there, and also in France; its ears are nearly as long as its body, yet, when reposing, they are so folded as to be almost out of sight. The Indian species is only a variety distinguishable by its yet longer ears ("and comparative shortness of the thumbs"—*Dobson*).

Plecotus auritus.

No. 77.

PLECOTUS AURITUS *vel* HOMOCHROUS.

HABITAT. — The Himalayas and the Khasia Hills.

DESCRIPTION. — Head slightly raised above the face-line; ears nearly as long as the fore-arm, joined by a low band across the forehead at the bases of their inner margins; wings from the base of the toes; feet slender; tip of the tail free; fur silky, short, and of a uniform dull brown.

SIZE.—Head and body, 1·7 inch; ears, 1·55 (ears of English type of same size, 1·4 inch); tail, 1·7 inch. Jerdon gives larger results, but I put more reliance on Dobson's figures.

GENUS VESPERUGO.

Bats with very broad and obtuse muzzles; the glandular prominences much developed between the eyes and the nostrils; crown of the head flat; but what distinguishes it from the following genus, *Scotophilus*, is the presence of four incisors in the upper jaw, whereas *Scotophilus* has two only—otherwise the two genera are very similar.

No. 78. VESPERUGO NOCTULA.

HABITAT.—Nepal.

DESCRIPTION.—Head broad and flat; ears oval and broad; the

Vesperugo noctula.

outer margin convex, reflected backwards, and forming a thick lobe terminating close to the angle of the mouth; tragus short and curved inwards; muzzle devoid of hair; fur dark reddish brown.

No. 79. VESPERUGO LEUCOTIS.

HABITAT.—Deserts of Northern India, and Beluchistan.

DESCRIPTION.—"Ears, sides of face, about the eyes, interfemoral membrane, antehumeral membrane, and that portion of the wing membrane along the sides of the body, white, very translucent; remaining portion of wing membrane sepia, traversed by very distinct reticulations; fur on the upper surface black at the base of the hairs for about half their length, remaining portion light yellowish brown; beneath the same, but paler, almost white."—*Dobson.*

No. 80. VESPERUGO MAURUS.

HABITAT.—Khasya Hills.

DESCRIPTION.—Muzzle broad and flat, with large labial development; ears broad, triangular, broadly rounded off above; tragus broad and square; fur long and dense, uniformly sooty brown, with greyish tips; membranes, nose, ears and lips black.

SIZE.—Head and body $1\frac{1}{10}$ inch; tail, 1 inch.

No. 81. VESPERUGO AFFINIS.

HABITAT.—Burmah (Bhamo, Yunan).

DESCRIPTION (*apud* Dobson).—Head flat; upper labial glands so developed as to cause a deep depression between them on the face behind the nostrils; ears broad as long from behind; the outer margin extends from the tip to its termination near the corner of the mouth without emargination or lobe; tragus broad; inner margin straight; outer convex; small triangular lobe at base. Fur chocolate brown above, lighter on head and neck; beneath dark brown with lighter tips on the pubes, and along the thighs dirty white or pale buff.

SIZE.—Head and body, 1·9 inch; tail, 1·65 inch.

There is a good figure of the head of this bat in Dobson's Monograph; it was obtained by Dr. J. Anderson at an elevation of 4500 feet at Bhamo.

No. 82. VESPERUGO PACHYOTIS.

DESCRIPTION.—"This species is readily distinguished by the peculiar thickness of the lower half of the outer side of the ear-conch, which appears as it were excavated out of the thick integument of the neck; tragus short, curved inwards."—*Dobson.*

This bat is more fully described with three illustrations in Dobson's Monograph; he does not mention where it is found, so it may or it may not be an Indian species.

No. 83. VESPERUGO ATRATUS. *Syn.*—NYCTICEJUS ATRATUS.

HABITAT.—Darjeeling.

DESCRIPTION.—Head broad; muzzle obtuse; upper labial glands largely developed; ears large, oval, with rounded tips, which in the natural position of the ears appear acute, owing to the longitudinal folding of the outer side of the conch on the inner, commencing at and almost bisecting the tip (*Dobson*). Fur long, dense and black; Jerdon says rich dark brown; paler beneath.

SIZE.—Head and body, 1·9 inch; tail, 1·8 inch.

No. 84. VESPERUGO TICKELLI.

HABITAT.—Chybassa, Jashpur, and Sirguja.

DESCRIPTION.—Head broad and flat; labial glands developed; ears moderate, rounded above; outer edge straight, emarginate opposite base of tragus, terminating in a small lobe; tragus lunate; tail long; last vertebra free. The face is more clad with fur than in other species of this genus; fur of the body pale, straw brown above, pale buff beneath. For a fuller description and illustration, see Dobson's Monograph.

SIZE.—Head and body, 1·65 inch; tail, 2 inches.

No. 85. VESPERUGO PACHYPUS.

HABITAT.—Darjeeling, Tenasserim, and Andaman Islands.

DESCRIPTION.—Crown of head very flat; ears short, triangular, with broadly rounded tips, tragus short; under surface of the base of the thumb and soles of the feet with broad fleshy pads; wings rather short; fur fine and dense, above reddish brown, paler beneath.

SIZE.—Head and body, 1·75 inch; tail 1 inch.

No. 86. VESPERUGO ANNECTANS.

HABITAT.—Naga Hills and Assam.

DESCRIPTION.—Muzzle sharper; face hairy; ears pointed; tragus long; colour dark brown; illustration in Dobson's Monograph.

SIZE.—about 2 inches; tail, 1·6 inch.

Unites the appearance of a *Vespertilio* to the dentition of *Vesperugo*.

No. 87. VESPERUGO DORMERI.

HABITAT.—Southern India and Bellary Hills.

DESCRIPTION.—Head flat; ears shorter, triangular, with rounded tips; tragus with a small triangular lobe near base of outer margin; fur brown, with ashy tips above, darker brown below, with the terminal third of the hairs white. Dentition approaches the next genus, there being only one pair of unicuspidate upper incisors placed, one by each upper canine.

No. 88. (VESPERUGO) SCOTOPHILUS SEROTINUS. *Syn.*—VESPERUGO SEROTINUS.

The Silky Bat (Jerdon's No. 35).

HABITAT.—Europe, but extending through Asia to the Himalayas, Beluchistan and Kashmir.

DESCRIPTION.—Ears shorter than head, widely separate, ovate, angular, projecting forward, terminating in a convex; lobe ending on a level with the corner of the mouth; tragus twice the length of its breadth, semi-cordate; fur deep bay or chestnut brown; above fulvous, grey beneath; hairs of back long and silky, but the colour of the fur varies considerably.

SIZE.—Head and body, 2½ inches; tail, 2; wing expanse, 13.

This is a rare bat in India, though Captain Hutton has procured it at Mussoorie. In England it is not uncommon even near London; it flies steadily and rather slow, and is found in ruins, roofs of churches, and sometimes old hollow trees.

No. 89. (VESPERUGO) SCOTOPHILUS LEISLERI.

Syn.—VESPERUGO LEISLERI.

The Hairy-armed Bat (Jerdon's No. 36).

Vesperugo leisleri.

HABITAT.—Himalayas.

DESCRIPTION.—Ears short, oval, triangular; tragus short, rounded at tip; membrane attached to base of outer toe; all toes short; membrane over the arms very hairy, some cross-lines of hair on the interfemoral membrane; fur long, deep fuscous brown at base, chestnut at the tip; beneath greyish brown.—*Jerdon.*

SIZE.—Head and body, 2¼ inches; tail, 3¾; expanse, 11½.

SCOTOPHILUS PACHYOMUS.

(Jerdon's No. 37.)

Synonymous with his No. 35; see Dobson's Monograph.

No. 90. (VESPERUGO) SCOTOPHILUS COROMANDELIANUS.

Syn.—VESPERUGO ABRAMUS; VESPERTILIO COROMANDELICUS.

The Coromandel Bat (Jerdon's No. 38).

HABITAT.—India generally, Burmah and Ceylon.

DESCRIPTION.—Ears triangular, rather large; outer margin straight or slightly concave; tragus lunate; feet small; wing membrane attached to the base of the toes; fur short, above dingy brown, the hairs tipped with a lighter tinge, paler beneath.

SIZE.—2½ inches, including tail, which is about 1⅛; wing expanse, 7½.

This is a very common little bat, akin to the English Pipistrelle, and is found everywhere in roofs, hollow bamboos, &c.

No. 91. (VESPERUGO) SCOTOPHILUS LOBATUS.

Syn.—VESPERUGO KUHLII.

The Lobe-eared Bat (Jerdon's No. 39).

HABITAT.—India generally.

DESCRIPTION.—Ears small, triangular; the base of the margin very convex forward; a triangular lobule above the base of the outer margin; tragus short and uniform in width; a short muzzle; wings from the base of the toes; feet small; calcaneum long; tip of tail free; fur blackish yellow above, ashy beneath.

SIZE.—Two and a-half inches, of which the tail is $1\frac{1}{4}$; expanse $7\frac{2}{3}$. Jerdon, quoting Tomes, states that this is the same as *V. Abramus*, but that is the synonym of the last species.

GENUS SCOTOPHILUS.

Muzzle short, bluntly conical, devoid of hair; ears longer than broad; tail shorter than the head and body; wing membrane attached to the base of the toes.

Dentition: Inc., $\frac{1-1}{6}$; can., $\frac{1-1}{1-1}$; premolars, $\frac{1-1}{2-2}$; molars, $\frac{3-3}{3-3}$. Jerdon's formula gives upper incisors 4.

No. 92. SCOTOPHILUS FULIGINOSUS.

The Smoky Bat (Jerdon's No. 40).

HABITAT.—Central Nepal.

DESCRIPTION (*apud* Hodgson).—"Feet very small, included in the wing membrane nearly to the end of the toes; ears acutely pointed, shorter than the head; muzzle groved, nudish; face sharp; rostrum somewhat recurved; wholly sooty brown; a little smaller than *Vesp. formosa.*"

I cannot find this bat mentioned by any other author, and Jerdon says it does not seem to be recognised.

No. 93. SCOTOPHILUS TEMMINCKII.

Syn.—NYCTICEJUS TEMMINCKII (*Jerdon*).

HABITAT.—India generally; Burmah and Ceylon.

DESCRIPTION.—Ears short, rounded and narrow; tragus narrow

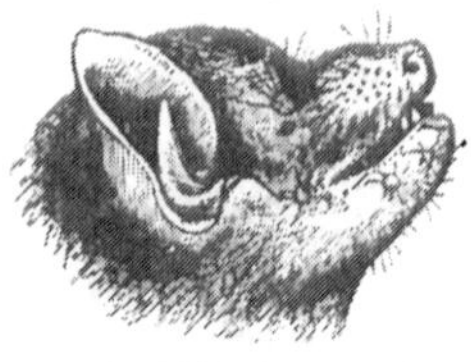

Scotophilus Temminckii.

curved and pointed inwards; muzzle thick, blunt and conical; the fur varies, sometimes dark olive brown, fulvous beneath, and occasionally chestnut, with a paler shade of yellow below.

SIZE.—Four and a-half inches, of which the tail is 1½; expanse, 13.

A very common species, appearing early in the evening. Horsfield says of it that it collects by hundreds in hollow trees, and feeds chiefly on white ants.

No. 94. SCOTOPHILUS HEATHII.

HABITAT.—India and Ceylon (Rajanpore, Punjab).

DESCRIPTION.—Similar to the above, but longer in all its measurements (*Dobson*). Judging from drawings, the head and muzzle of this are more in a line than in the last species, the ears project forward, and are also larger, the tragus especially, and there is a greater width between the ears.

SIZE.—Five inches, of which the tail is 2.

No. 95. SCOTOPHILUS EMARGINATUS.

HABITAT.—India; precise locality unknown.

DESCRIPTION.—Head broad and flat; muzzle obtuse and thick; ears long and large, with rounded tips turning outwards; tragus short; thumb long with a strong claw; wing membrane quite devoid of hair, except on the interfemoral membrane, which is half covered; fur tricolored, first dark chestnut, buff, and then yellowish brown.

SIZE.—Head and body, $2\frac{1}{10}$ inches; tail, 2 inches.

No. 96. SCOTOPHILUS ORNATUS. *Syn.*—NYCTICEJUS ORNATUS.

HABITAT.—India and Burmah.

DESCRIPTION.—Head broad; muzzle short; ears triangular, erect, with rounded tips, and broadly rounded lobe at the base; tragus narrow, semi-lunate, curved towards the front; fur a light Isabelline brown, spotted with white; a white spot on the centre of the forehead, and from the back of the head down the spine for two-thirds of its length a narrow white streak; on each side of the body two white patches; a broad white collar, or rather demi-collar, from one ear spot to the other, passing under the throat. Dr. Dobson says the position of these patches is very constant, but the size varies, being greatest in individuals of a pale rusty red colour, and these he found always to be males.

SIZE.—Head and body, 3 inches; tail, 2 inches; expanse, 15.

No. 97. SCOTOPHILUS PALLIDUS.

HABITAT.—Mian Mir, Lahore.

DESCRIPTION.—Head and muzzle as in *S. Temminckii;* ears slightly shorter than the head; internal basal lobe convex, evenly rounded; tip broadly rounded off; tragus moderately long and rounded at the tip; a prominent triangular lobe at base. Wing membrane from base of toes; lobule at the heel very narrow and long; last rudimentary caudal vertebra free; fur of the body, wings, and interfemoral membrane pale buff thoughout.

SIZE.—Head and body, 2 inches; tail, 1·4 inch.

NOCTULINIA NOCTULA.

(See *ante: Vesperugo noctula—Jerdon's No.* 41.)

NYCTICEJUS HEATHII.

Large Yellow Bat (*Jerdon's No.* 42).

(See *ante: Scotophilus Heathii.*)

NYCTICEJUS LUTEUS.

The Bengal Yellow Bat (*Jerdon's No.* 43).

NYCTICEJUS TEMMINCKII.

The Common Yellow Bat (*Jerdon's No.* 44).

Both the above (Nos. 43 and 44) are, according to Dr. Dobson, synonymous with *Scotophilus Temminckii*, which see.

NYCTICEJUS CASTANEUS.

The Chestnut Bat (*Jerdon's No.* 45).

This is also a variety of *Scotophilus Temminckii.*

NYCTICEJUS ATRATUS.

The Sombre Bat (*Jerdon's No.* 46).

(See *ante: Vesperugo atratus.*)

NYCTICEJUS CANUS.

The Hoary Bat (*Jerdon's No.* 47).

(See *ante: Vesperugo lobatus.*)

NYCTICEJUS ORNATUS.

The Harlequin Bat (Jerdon's No. 48).

(See *ante: Scotophilus ornatus.*)

No. 98. NYCTICEJUS NIVICOLUS.

The Alpine Bat (Jerdon's No. 49).

HABITAT.—Sikim.

DESCRIPTION.—"Head and body above uniform light brown with a slight yellowish shade; underneath, from the throat to the vent, dark grey with a brownish tint, lighter on the sides of the throat. Ears long, attenuated to an obtuse point."—*Jerdon.*

SIZE.—Head and body, 3 inches; tail, 2 inches; expanse, 19 inches.

This bat was described by Hodgson ('Ann. Mag. Nat. Hist.' 1855), but there is some doubt about it, and it has been classed as a *Lasiurus* and also with *Scot. ornatus* and *Vesp. formosa*, but Jerdon thinks it a *distinct* species. I cannot find any mention of it in Dobson's monograph.

GENUS HARPIOCEPHALUS.

This is also the genus *Murina* of Gray. Dr. Dobson explains his acceptance of the former term in the following way: that he first accepted *Murina* on the score of priority in a paper showing that *Harpiocephalus* and *Murina* must be united in a single genus; but finding afterwards that Gray had founded *Murina* on a specimen of what he believed to be *Vesp. suillus* (Temm.), but which was in reality a specimen of a very different species from Darjeeling, belonging to the same section of the genus as *Vespertilio harpia* (Temm.) the type of his genus *Harpiocephalus*, it remained therefore either to discard both names or to retain *Harpiocephalus*, in which course he was supported by Professor Peters, to whom he mentioned the facts.

Horsfield's genus *Lasiurus* is included in this one, though Jerdon considers it distinct from *Murina*.

Muzzle elongated, conical; *nostrils prominent, tubular; produced beyond the upper lip*, opening laterally or sublaterally, emarginate between; crown of the head scarcely raised above the face line; ears thin, generally covered with glandular papillæ; tragus long, attenuated towards the tip, and inclined outwards; thumb very large, with a large, strongly curved claw; wings around interfemoral membrane very hairy. —*Dobson.*

Dentition: Inc., $\frac{2-2}{6}$; can. $\frac{1-1}{1-1}$; premolars, $\frac{2-2}{2-2}$; molars, $\frac{3-3}{3-3}$.

No. 99. HARPIOCEPHALUS HARPIA.

Lasiurus Pearsonii (*Horsfield*) (*Jerdon's No.* 50).

HABITAT.—Darjeeling and Khasia hills.

DESCRIPTION.—"Fur above very soft, silky, and rather long; colour on the head, neck, and shoulders brownish grey, with a ferruginous cast, variegated with whitish hairs; the rest of the body above, with the base of the membrane, the thighs and the interfemoral membrane, have a deep bay or reddish-brown hue, and delicate hairs of the same colour are scattered over the membrane and project from its border; the body underneath is thickly covered with a grey fur, which is paler on the breast and body; the interfemoral membrane marked with regularly parallel transverse lines" (*Horsfield*). Ears ovoid; tragus rather long, nearly straight, acute at the tip (*Jerdon*). Muzzle rather short, obtusely conical; end of nose projecting considerably beyond the lip, consisting of diverging tubular nostrils opening laterally, with a slight emargination between each (*Dobson*).

SIZE.—Head and body, 3 inches; tail, $1\frac{1}{2}$ inch; expanse, 14. Hodgson, who procured it at Darjeeling, writes of it: "Entire legs and caudal membrane clad in fur like the body, which is thick and woolly. Colour bright rusty above; sooty below, the hairs tipped with hoary."

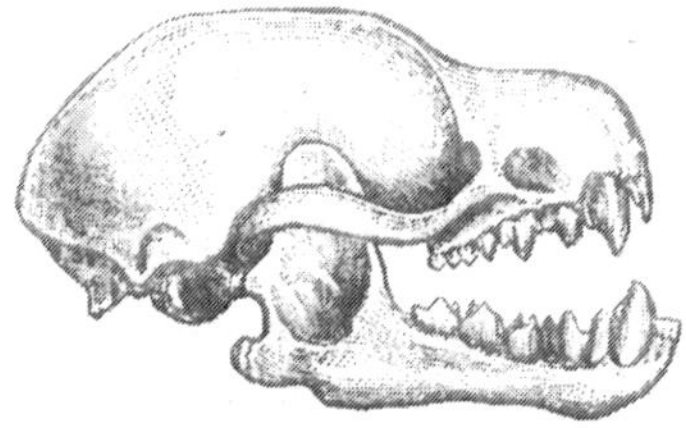

Skull of *Harpiocephalus harpia.*

This bat is, for its size, one of the most powerfully armed with teeth. The skull reminds one of that of a dog or hyæna in miniature; the teeth are very stout, the canines blunt and conical, and the cusps of the molars short and blunt, well coated with enamel; the jaws are correspondingly muscular and adapted to the food of the animal, which consists of hard-shelled beetles, the crushed cases of which have been found in its stomach.

No. 100. HARPIOCEPHALUS (MURINA) SUILLUS.

The Pig-Bat (*Jerdon's No.* 51).

HABITAT.—Darjeeling (*Jerdon*); Malayan archipelago.

DESCRIPTION.—Muzzle narrow, elongated; nostrils very prominent, which, viewed from below, resemble in shape a small hour-glass placed horizontally at the extremity of the muzzle; ears moderate, shorter than the head, rounded at the tips; tragus moderately long, attenuated above and slightly curved outwards; fur light greyish-brown; extremities dark brown; beneath light greyish-brown throughout.—*Dobson.*

SIZE.—Head and body, $1\frac{3}{4}$ to 2 inches; tail, $1\frac{1}{2}$ inch; expanse 9 to 10.

No. 101. HARPIOCEPHALUS AURATUS.

HABITAT.—Thibet.

DESCRIPTION.—Head and muzzle as in *H. suillus*, but the nostrils are differently shaped; each nostril forms a distinct tube directed sub-laterally with a circular aperture marked by a very small notch on the outer and upper margin (*Dobson*). The whole body is thickly clad; the fur on the back is black, with bright golden yellow tips; the back of the fore-arm covered with short golden hair; the hair of the under parts black with silvery tips, whiter on the lower jaw, neck and pubis; the interfemoral membrane is covered with very long hair, which forms a fringe along its free margin extending on the legs and feet, and projecting beyond the toes; underneath short silvery hair.

SIZE.—Head and body 1·4 inch; tail 1·2.

No. 102. HARPIOCEPHALUS GRISEUS.

HABITAT.—Jeripani, N.W. Himalayas.

DESCRIPTION.—Head and muzzle as in *H. suillus;* fur above dark brown, with yellowish-brown extremities; beneath similar, but with the extreme points of the hairs ashy.

SIZE.—Head and body, 1·4 inch; tail 1 inch.

This bat was found near Mussoorie by Captain Hutton, who writes that it occurs, but sparingly, on the outer southern range of hills at 5500 feet. It skims close to the ground, and somewhat leisurely over the surface of the crops and grass; and one which flew into his room kept low down, passing under chairs and tables, instead of soaring towards the ceiling, as bats generally do.

No. 103. HARPIOCEPHALUS LEUCOGASTER.

HABITAT.—N.W. Himalayas, Thibet.

DESCRIPTION.—Head and muzzle as in *H. harpia;* fur long and dense, above brown with grey bases; underneath whitish; sides light brown. It differs from the next species by a small projecting tooth on the inner margin of the ear conch, by the smaller size of the first upper premolar, and by the colour.—*Dobson*.

SIZE.—Head and body, 1·9 inch; tail 1·5.

No. 104. HARPIOCEPHALUS CYCLOTIS.

HABITAT.—Darjeeling, Ceylon.

DESCRIPTION.—Similar to the last, but with round ears; fur bicoloured, the hairs being dark brown at the base, with bright ferruginous tips;

below pale brown; the upper surface of the interfemoral membrane and back of the feet covered with hair, which also extends beyond the toes; the first premolar in the upper jaw nearly equal in size to the second, whereas in the last species it is only about three-fourths.

SIZE.—Head and body, 1·7 inch; tail, 1·5.

GENUS KERIVOULA.

DESCRIPTION.—Muzzle long and narrow; skull very concave between the nasal bones and the vertex, so that the crown appears considerably vaulted; ears funnel-shaped and semi-transparent; tragus very long, narrow and pointed; wings very wide; tail longer than head and body, wholly contained within the interfemoral membrane.

Dentition: Inc., $\frac{2-2}{6}$; can., $\frac{1-1}{1-1}$; premolars, $\frac{3-3}{3-3}$; molars, $\frac{3-3}{3-3}$.

The generic name of this bat is composed of two Singhalese words—*kehel* or *kela*, the plantain, and *voulha*, which is the Singhalese for bat, the specimen on which Gray founded his genus being the following:—

No. 105. KERIVOULA PICTA.

The Painted Bat (*Jerdon's No.* 53).

HABITAT.—India generally, Burmah and Ceylon.

DESCRIPTION—"Fur fine, woolly; above yellowish-red or golden rufous, beneath less brilliant and more yellow; wing membranes inky black, with rich orange stripes along the fingers extending in indentations into the membrane."—*Jerdon.*

Ears moderate, laid forwards; the tips reach midway between the eyes and the middle of the muzzle; tragus very long and straight; thumb short; wings to the base of the toes.

SIZE.—Head and body, 1½ inch; tail, 1·6 inch; expanse about 10 inches.

This beautiful little bat is found all over India, but is not common; it is occasionally caught in plantain gardens, as it resorts to the leaves of that tree for shelter during the night, and may sometimes be discovered in the folds of a leaf. As Jerdon remarks, it looks more like a butterfly or a moth when disturbed during the day time. Dr. Dobson pertinently observes that the colours of this bat appear to be the result of the "protective mimicry" which we see so often in insects, the Mantidea and other genera, the colours being adapted to their abiding places. He alludes to Mr. Swinhoe's account ('P. Z. S.,' 1862, p. 357) of an allied species:—"The body of this bat was of an orange yellow, but the wings were painted with orange yellow and black. It was caught suspended head downwards on a cluster of the round fruit of the longan tree. (*Nephelium* [*Scytalia*] *longanum*) [the *ash phul* of Bengal]. Now this tree is an evergreen, and all the year through some portion of its foliage is undergoing decay, the particular leaves being in such a stage partially orange and black; this bat can therefore at all seasons suspend from its branches and elude its enemies by its resemblance to the leaf of the tree." This bat was named by Pallas *Vespertilio pictus*. Boddaert in 1785 termed it *Vesp. kerivoula*, and Gray afterwards took the second specific name for that of the genus, leaving the first as it is.

KERIVOULA PALLIDA.

(*Jerdon's No.* 54.)

This is synonymous with *Vespertilio formosus*, which see further on, it is the same as the *Kerivoula formosa* of Gray.

No. 106. KERIVOULA PAPILLOSA.

(*Jerdon's No.* 55.)

HABITAT.—Java, but said by Jerdon to have been found in Calcutta and Ceylon.

DESCRIPTION.—Fur fine woolly, long, bicoloured; above light shining brown, paler below; the free edge of the interfemoral membrane margined with small papillæ.

No. 107. KERIVOULA HARDWICKII.

HABITAT.—India (Assam—Shillong, Khasia hills).

DESCRIPTION.—Same size as *K. picta*, but ears larger; fur uniformly dark above and below, with shining greyish-brown extremities.

GENUS VESPERTILIO.

Muzzle long; ears often larger than the head, oval, apart; tragus long, acute; crown of head vaulted; feet moderate; wing membrane from base of toes; tail, wholly included in interfemoral membrane, less than length of head and body.

Dentition: Inc., $\frac{2-2}{6}$; can., $\frac{1-1}{1-1}$; premolars, $\frac{3-3}{3-3}$; molars, $\frac{3-3}{3-3}$.

Vespertilio murinus.

No. 108. MYOTIS (VESPERTILIO) MURINUS.

(*Jerdon's No.* 61.)

HABITAT.—N.W. Himalayas.

DESCRIPTION.—Fur above light reddish or smoke brown beneath darky white, the base of the hairs dark.

SIZE.—Head and body, $2\frac{1}{2}$ inches; tail, 2 inches; expanse, 15 inches.

NOS. 109 & 110. MYOTIS THEOBALDI and MYOTIS PARVIPES.

(*Jerdon's Nos.* 62 & 63.)

Both these appear to be closely allied to the *pipistrelle* of Europe, and are stated to have been found at Mussoorie and in Kashmir.

No. 111. VESPERTILIO LONGIPES.

HABITAT.—Kashmir (caves of Bhima Devi, 6000 feet).

DESCRIPTION.—Wings from the ankles; *feet very large*, about one-fourth the length of the head and body; fur black above, underneath black with whitish tips.

SIZE.—Head and body, 1·75 inch; tail, 1·45 inch.

No. 112. VESPERTILIO MYSTACINUS.

HABITAT.—Himalayas.

DESCRIPTION.—Muzzle narrow; skull vaulted; ears as long as head wings from base of toes; fur dark brown.

No. 113. VESPERTILIO MURICOLA.

HABITAT.—Himalayas, Arracan.

DESCRIPTION.—Similar to the above, but may be distinguished by a small lobe behind the heel, by the deep emargination of the upper third of the outer margin of the ear; by the intensely black colour of the fur and membranes, and by its small size.—*Dobson.*

SIZE.—Head and body, 1·6 inch; tail, 1·55 inch.

No. 114. VESPERTILIO MONTIVAGUS.

HABITAT.—Burmah, Hotha, Yunan.

DESCRIPTION.—Head slightly elevated above the face line; muzzle obtuse; ears narrow, tapering, *with* rounded tips slightly turned outwards; tragus long, narrow, and acutely pointed; feet very small; toes two-thirds the length of the whole foot; tail wholly contained in the membrane; wings from base of toes; fur dark brown above, the tips paler and shining, beneath much darker, almost black, with ashy tips to the hairs; face much covered with hair, which almost conceals the eyes; the tip of the nose alone naked; wing membranes partially covered with fur.

SIZE.—Head and body, 1·8 inch; tail, 1·6 inch.

This bat, of which the above description is taken from Dobson's monograph, was obtained by Dr. J. Anderson during the Yunan Expedition.

No. 115. VESPERTILIO MURINOIDES.

HABITAT.—N.W. Himalayas (Chamba), 3000 feet.

DESCRIPTION.—General form of the ear triangular, with narrow rounded tips; outer margin concave beneath tips; tragus slender and acutely pointed, with a quadrangular lobe at the base of the outer margin; fur dark brown above with light brown tips; dark brown below, almost black with greyish tips.

SIZE.—Head and body, 2·5 inches; tail 2.

No. 116. VESPERTILIO FORMOSUS.

HABITAT.—N.W. Himalayas (Nepal, Darjeeling), Khasia hills.

DESCRIPTION.—Wing membrane broad and variegated with orange and rich dark brown; the portions of the dark-coloured membrane are triangular in form, and occupy the spaces between the second and third and third and fourth fingers; all the remaining portions of the membranes, including interfemoral, are orange, as are also the ears; the orange colour extends in narrow lines along each side of the fingers, and is dispersed over the dark triangular space in dots and streaks.

SIZE.—Head and body, 2 inches; tail, 1·1; expanse 11.

No. 117. VESPERTILIO NEPALENSIS.

HABITAT.—Khatmandu, Nepal.

DESCRIPTION.—Fur of head and back long and dense, bicoloured; base black, tips brown; underneath the hairs are two-thirds black, with the remaining upper third pure white.

SIZE.—Head and body, 1·65 inch; tail, 1·35.

No. 118. VESPERTILIO EMARGINATUS.

VARIETY.—*Desertorum.*

HABITAT.—Beluchistan.

DESCRIPTION.—The upper third of the outer margin of the ears deeply emarginate; colour of fur light brownish; ears and interfemoral membranes pale yellowish white; membranes dusky white.

SIZE.—Head and body, 2 inches; tail 1·6.

Vespertilio formosus.

GENUS MINIOPTERUS (*Bonaparte*).

DESCRIPTION.—Crown of head abruptly and very considerably raised above the face line; ears separate, rhomboidal, the outer margin carried forward to the angle of the mouth; tragus like that in *Vesperugo*; first phalanx of the second or longest finger very short;

feet long and slender; tail as long as head and body, wholly contained in the membrane.

Dentition: Inc., $\frac{2-2}{6}$; can., $\frac{1-1}{1-1}$; premolars, $\frac{2-2}{3-3}$; molars, $\frac{3-3}{3-3}$.

No. 119. MINIOPTERUS SCHREIBERSII.

HABITAT.—Burmah and Ceylon.

DESCRIPTION.—Colour of fur varies, the basal half of the hair always dark greyish black, dark brown or black; the extremities varying from light grey to light reddish-grey, dark reddish-brown and black. For further details see Dobson's monograph.

GENUS BARBASTELLUS.

Synotus barbastellus.

Ears large, connate at the base in front, triangular, emarginate on the outer margin, broad, concealing the back of the head, hairy in the middle; tragus broad at the base, narrow at the tip, and curved outwardly.

Dentition: Inc., $\frac{2-2}{6}$; can., $\frac{1-1}{1-1}$; premolars, $\frac{2-2}{2-2}$; molars, $\frac{3-3}{3-3}$.

No. 120. BARBASTELLUS COMMUNIS.

Jerdon's No. 65.)

HABITAT.—Himalayas, Nepal and Mussoorie.

DESCRIPTION.—Fur above blackish brown; the hairs fulvous at the tips; abdomen greyish brown; hairs fine silky.

SIZE.—Head and body, 2 inches; tail, $1\frac{2}{12}$; expanse; $10\frac{1}{2}$.—*Jerdon.*

This is the same as the English Barbastelle, and it appears in Dobson's monograph as *Synotus Darjeelinensis.*

No. 121. NYCTOPHILUS GEOFFROYI.

(*Jerdon's No.* 66.)

HABITAT.—Mussoorie.

Jerdon here goes back to the nose-leafed bats. I can find no trace of it in Dobson's monograph, which is so exhaustive as far as Asiatic species are concerned.

DESCRIPTION.—Over the eyes, at the hind corner, a tuft of black hair; fur dark brown, above throat and flank brownish-white; below black with white tips. A simple transverse nose-leaf; ears large, ovoid, united at base as in *Plecotus*.

SIZE.—Head and body, $1\frac{3}{4}$ to 2 inches; tail, $1\frac{5}{12}$; expanse, $9\frac{3}{4}$.

We have now concluded our notice of Indian bats but yet much is to be discovered concerning them. Very little is known of the habits of these small nocturnal animals, only a few of the most familiar large ones are such as one can discourse upon in a popular way; the lives and habits of the rest are a blank to us. We see them flit about rapidly in the dusky evening, and capture one here and there, but, after a bare description, in most cases very uninteresting to all save those who are "bat fanciers," what can be said about them? Many of them have been written about for a century, yet how little knowledge has been gained! It has been no small labour to collate all the foregoing species, and to compare them with various works; it would have been a most difficult task but for the assistance I have received from Dr. Dobson's book, which every naturalist should possess if he desires to have a thorough record of all the Indian Chiroptera.

INSECTIVORA.

These are mostly small animals of, with few exceptions, nocturnal habits.

Their chief characteristic lies in their pointed dentition, which enable them to pierce and crush the hard-shelled insects on which they feed. The skull is elongated, the bones of the face and jaw especially, and those of the latter are comparatively weak. Before we come to the teeth we may notice some other peculiarities of this order.

The limbs are short, feet five-toed and plantigrade, with the entire sole placed on the ground in running, and these animals are all possessed of clavicles which in the next order are but rudimentary; in this respect they legitimately follow the Bats. The mammæ are placed under the abdomen, and are more than two. None of them (except *Tupaia*) have a cæcum (this genus has been most exhaustively described in all its osteological details by Dr. J. Anderson: see his 'Anatomical and Zoological Researches'); the snout is usually prolonged and mobile. The dentition is eccentric, and not always easy to determine; some have long incisors in front, followed by other incisors along the sides of their narrow jaws and canines, all shorter than the molars; others have large separated canines, between which are placed small incisors. In Blyth's additions to Cuvier he states that "in this group we are led to identify the canine tooth as simply the first of the false molars, which in some has two fangs, and, as in the Lemurs, to perceive that the second in the lower jaw is in some more analagous in size and character to an ordinary canine than that which follows the incisors. The incisor teeth are never more than six in number, which is the maximum throughout *placental* mammalia (as opposed by *marsupial*), and in several instances one or two pairs are deficient. (It should be remarked that a single tooth with two fangs is often represented by two separate teeth, each with one fang.) The canines, with the succeeding false molars, are extremely variable, but there are ordinarily three tuberculated molars posterior to the representative of the carnivorous or cutting grinder of the true *Carnivora*." All the molar teeth are studded with sharp points or cusps; the deciduous teeth are developed and disappear before birth. This order is divided into four families, viz., *Talpidæ* or Moles, *Soreciddæ* or Shrews, *Erinaceidæ* or Hedgehogs, and the *Tupaiadæ*, Banxrings or Tree-shrews. Of all these well-defined types are to be found in India, but America and Africa possess various genera which we have not, such as the Condylures (*Condylura*, Illiger), the Shrew-moles (*Scalops*, Cuvier), belonging to *Talpidæ*; the Solendons, Desmans, and Chrysochlores to *Soreciddæ*; the Sokinahs, Tenrecs and Gymnures to *Erinaceidæ*; and the Macroscelles or Elephant-mice of the Cape Colony form another group more allied to *Tupaia* than the rest. This last family is the most interesting. Anatomically belonging to this order, they externally resemble the squirrels so closely as to have been frequently mistaken for them. The grovelling Mole and creeping Shrew are as unlike the sprightly Tupaia, as it springs from branch to branch, whisking its long bushy tail, as it is possible to conceive. I intend further on to give an illustration of this little animal. The first we have on record concerning it is in the papers relating to Captain Cook's third voyage, which are now in the British Museum, where the animal is described and figured as *Sciurus dissimilis*; it was obtained at Pulo Condore, an island 100 miles from Saigon, in 1780.

Sir T. Stamford Raffles was the next to describe it, which he did under the generic name *Tupaia—tupai* being a Malayan word applied to various squirrel-like small animals—but he was somewhat forestalled in the publication of his papers by MM. Diard and Duvaucel. Dr. Anderson relates how Sir T. Raffles engaged the services of these two naturalists to assist him in his researches, on the understanding that the whole of the observations and collections were to be the property of the East India Company; but ultimately on this point there arose a disagreement between them, and the paper that was first read before the Asiatic Society of Bengal on the 10th of March, 1820, was drawn up by MM. Diard and Duvaucel, though forwarded by Sir T. Raffles, whose own paper on the subject was not read before the Linnean Society until the 5th of December of that year, nor published till 1821; therefore to the others belongs the credit of first bringing this curious group to notice.

They regarded it in the light of a true Shrew, disguised in the form and habits of a squirrel, and they proposed for it the name *Sorex-Glis*, i.e. Shrew-squirrel (*Glis* properly means a dormouse, but Linnæus used it for his rodential group which he termed *Glires*); this was afterwards changed by Desmarest and Giebel to *Gli Sorex* and *Glisosorex*, which latter stands for one of the generic terms applied to the group. F. Cuvier, objecting to *Tupaia*, proposed *Cladobates* (signifying branch walkers), and Temminck, also objecting to *Tupaia*, suggested *Hylogale* (from Gr. *hyla*, forest, and *gale*, a weasel), so now we have four generic names for this one small group. English naturalists have however accepted *Tupaia*; and, as Dr. Anderson fairly remarks, though it is a pity that some definite rules are not laid down for the guidance of naturalists for the acceptance or rejection of terms, still those who reject *Tupaia* on the ground of its being taken from a savage tongue should be consistent, and refuse all others of similar origin. He is quite right; but how many we should have to reject if we did so—*Siamanga* in Quadrumana, *Kerivoula* in Cheiroptera, *Tupaia* in Insectivora, *Golunda* in Rodentia, *Rusa* in Ruminantia, and others! At the same time these names are wrong; they convey no meaning; and had they a meaning (which only *Kerivoula* or *Kelivoulha*, i.e. plantain-bat, has) it is not expressed in languages common to all western nations, such as the Latin and Greek. *Tupaia* is an unfortunate selection, inasmuch as it does not apply to one type of animal, but reminds me somewhat of the Madras *puchi*, which refers, in a general way, to most creeping insects, known or unknown.

FAMILY TALPIDÆ—THE MOLES.

These animals have a small cylindrical body, very short arm attached to a large shoulder-blade, supported by a stout clavicle or collar-bone. The fore-feet are of great breadth, suppported by the powerful muscles of the arm; the palm of the foot or hand is directed outwards or backwards, the lower edge being trenchant, with scarcely perceptible fingers armed with long, flat nails, strong and sharp, with which to tear up the ground and shovel the earth aside. The hind feet are small and weak in comparison, with slender claws. The head tapers to a point, the long snout being provided with a little bone which assists it in rooting, and the cervical muscles are very strong. The eyes are microscopical.

and almost concealed in the fur. At one time it was a popular delusion that the mole was devoid of the power of sight, but this is not the case. The sense of hearing is extremely acute, and the tympanum is large, although externally there is no aural development. The tail is short, the fur set vertically in the skin, whence it is soft and velvety. The bones of the pubis do not join, and the young when produced are large. The mammæ are six in number. The jaws are weak, the incisors are six above and eight below. The canines (false molars ?) have two roots. There are four false molars above and three below, and three molars with pointed cusps.

Moles live principally on earth-worms, snails, and small insects, though they are also said to devour frogs and small birds. They are more common in Europe than in India, where the few known species are only to be found in hilly parts. I have, I think, procured them on the Satpura range some years ago, but I cannot speak positively to the fact at this lapse of time, as I had not then devoted much attention to the smaller mammalia, and it is possible that my supposed moles were a species of shrew.

They are seldom if ever trapped in India, for the simple reason that they are not considered worth trapping, and the destruction of moles in England has long been carried on in the same spirit of ignorance which led farmers, both there and in France, to destroy small birds wholesale, till they did themselves much injury by the multiplication of noxious insects. Moles, instead of being the farmers' foes, are the farmers' friends. Mr. Buckland in his notes to Gilbert White's 'Natural History of Selborne' (Macmillan's *édition de luxe* of 1876)—says : "After dinner we went round the sweetstuff and toy booths in the streets, and the vicar, my brother-in-law, the Rev. H. Gordon, of Harting, Petersfield, Hants, introduced me to a merchant of gingerbread nuts who was a great authority on moles. He tends cows for a contractor who keeps a great many of the animals to make concentrated milk for the navy. The moles are of great service; eat up the worms that eat the grass, and wherever the moles have been afterwards the grass grows there very luxuriantly. When the moles have eaten all the grubs and the worms in a certain space, they migrate to another, and repeat their gratuitous work. The grass where moles have been is always the best for cows." In another place he says: "M. Carl Vogt relates an instance of a landed proprietor in France who destroyed every mole upon his property. The next season his fields were ravaged with wire-worms, and his crops totally destroyed. He then purchased moles of his neighbours, and preserved them as his best friends."

The poor little despised mole has had its part to play in history. My readers may remember that William the Third's horse is supposed to have put his foot into a mole-pit, and that the king's death was hastened by the unconscious agency of "the little gentleman in black," who was so often toasted afterwards by the Jacobites.

No. 122. TALPA MICRURA.

The Short-tailed Mole (Jerdon's No. 67).

HABITAT.—The Eastern Himalayan range.

NATIVE NAMES.—*Pariam*, Lepcha; *Biyu-kantyen*, Bhotia (*Jerdon*).

DESCRIPTION.—Velvety black, with a greyish sheen in certain lights; snout nude; eyes apparently wanting. Jerdon says there is no perforation of the integument over the eyes, but this I doubt, and think that by examination with a lens an opening would be discovered, as in the case of the Apennine mole, which M. Savi considered to be quite blind. I hope to have an opportunity of testing this shortly. The feet are fleshy white, also the tail, which, as its specific name implies, is very small. "There are three small upper premolars between the quasi-canine tooth and the large scissor-toothed premolar, which is much developed."

SIZE.—Length, $4\frac{3}{4}$ to 5 inches; head alone, $1\frac{3}{4}$; palm with claws, $\frac{7}{8}$ inch; tail, $\frac{3}{16}$ of an inch or less.

Jerdon says: "This mole is not uncommon at Darjeeling, and many of the roads and pathways in the station are intersected by its runs, which often proceed from the base of some mighty oak-tree to that of another. If these runs are broken down or holes made in them they are generally repaired during the night. The moles do not appear to form mole-hills as in Europe." Jerdon's specimens were dead ones picked up, as the Lepchas do not know how to trap them.

No. 123. TALPA MACRURA.

The Long-tailed Mole (Jerdon's No. 68).

HABITAT.—Sikim.

DESCRIPTION.—Deep slaty blue, with a whitish or hoary gloss, iridescent when wet; the tail covered with soft hair.

SIZE.—Head and body, 4 inches; tail, $1\frac{1}{4}$ inch; head alone, $1\frac{1}{8}$ inch; palm, $\frac{3}{4}$ inch.

No. 124. TALPA LEUCURA (*Blyth*).

The White-tailed Mole.

HABITAT.—Sylhet, Burmah (Tenasserim).

DESCRIPTION.—Similar to *micrura*, but with a short tail covered with white hairs, and it has one premolar less.

FAMILY SORECIDÆ.

Small animals, which from their size, shape, and nocturnal habits are frequently confounded with rats and mice, as in the case of the common Indian Shrew, known to most of us as the Musk-rat; they have distinct though small eyes, distinct ears, the conch of which is like that of a mouse. The tail *thick* and tapering, whence the generic name *Pachyura*, applied by De Selys Longchamp, and followed latterly by Blyth; but there is also a sub-family of bats to which the term has been applied. "On each flank there is a band of stiff closely-set bristles, from between which, during the rutting season, exudes an odorous fluid, the product of a peculiar gland" (*Cuvier*); the two middle superior incisors are hooked and dentated at the base, the lower ones slanted and elongated; five small teeth follow the larger incisors on the upper jaw, and two those on the lower. There are three molars with sharp-pointed cusps in each jaw, with a small tuberculous tooth in the upper. The feet are five-toed, separate, not webbed like the moles; the snout is long and pointed and very mobile.

This family has been subdivided in various genera by naturalists, each one having his followers; and it is puzzling to know which to adopt. Simplicity being the great point to aim at in all these matters, I may broadly state that Shrews are divided into land and water shrews (*Sorex* and *Hydrosorex*); the former includes *Crocidura* of Wagner, *Corsira* of Gray, and *Anurosorex* of Milne-Edwards, the latter *Crossopus* and *Chimarrogale*, Gray.

For ages both in the West and East this poor little amimal has been the victim of ignorance. In England, even in the last century, it was looked upon as an evil thing, as Gilbert White says: "It is supposed that a shrew-mouse is of so baneful and deleterious a nature that wherever it creeps over a beast, be it horse, cow, or sheep, the suffering animal is afflicted with cruel anguish, and threatened with loss of the use of the limb," the only remedy in such cases being the application of the twigs of a shrew ash, which was an ash-tree into which a large hole had been bored with an augur, into which a poor little shrew was thrust alive and plugged up (*see* Brand's 'Popular Antiquities' for a description of the ceremonies). It is pleasant to think that such barbarities have now ceased, for though shrew ashes are to be found in various parts of England, I have never heard (in my own county, Derbyshire, at least) of the necessity for their use. In an article I contributed to a magazine some thirteen years ago, I pointed out a coincident superstition prevailing in India. Whilst marching as a Settlement officer in the district of Seonee, I noticed that one of my camels had a sore back and on inquiring into the cause was told by the natives that a musk-rat (our commonest shrew) had run over him. Jerdon also remarks that in Southern India (Malabar) the bite of *S. murinus* is considered venomous, and so it is in Bengal.

GENUS SOREX (*Linn.*).

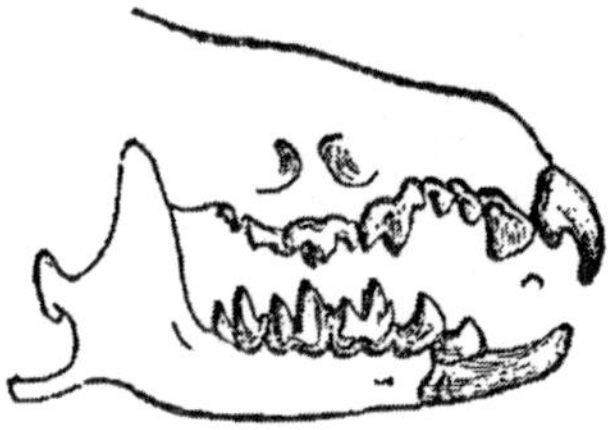

Dentition of Shrew (magnified).

SYNONYM.—*Pachyura*, De S. Long; *Crocidura*, Wagner.

DESCRIPTION.—Upper front teeth large; "inferior incisors entire, or rarely so much as the trace of a serrated upper edge;" between these and the first cutting molar four teeth as follows: large, small, middling, very small; teeth wholly white; tail thick and tapering, with a few scattered hairs, some with glands secreting a pungent musky odour, some without.

NO. 125. SOREX CÆRULESCENS.

The Common Musk Shrew, better known as Musk-rat.

NATIVE NAME.—*Chachhunder*, Hind.; *Sondeli*, Canarese.

HABITAT.—India generally.

DESCRIPTION.—Bluish gray, sometimes slightly mouse-coloured; naked parts flesh-coloured.

SIZE.—Head and body, 6 to 7 inches; tail $3\frac{1}{2}$ to 4 inches.

This little animal is almost too well known, as far as its appearance is concerned, to need much description, though most erroneous ideas prevail about its habits. It is proverbially difficult to uproot an old-established prejudice; and, though amongst my friends I have been fighting its battles for the poor little shrew for years, I doubt whether I have converted many to my opinions. Certainly its appearance and its smell go strongly against it—the latter especially—but even here its powers are greatly exaggerated. I think by this time the old fallacy of musk-rats tainting beer and wine in bottles by simply running over them is exploded. When I came out in 1856 it was a common thing at the mess table, or in one's own house, to reject a bottle of beer or wine, because it was "musk-ratty;" but how seldom is the complaint made now since country-bottled beverages are not used? Jerdon, Kellaart, and every Indian naturalist scouts the idea of this peculiar power to do what no chemist has yet succeeded in, viz., the creation of an essence subtle enough to pass through glass. That musky bottles were frequent formerly is due to impregnated corks and insufficient washing before the bottle was filled. The musk-rat in a quiescent state is not offensive, and its odour is more powerful at certain seasons. I am peculiarly sensitive to smells, and dislike that of musk in particular, yet I have no objection to a musk-rat running about my room quietly if I do not startle him. I never allow one to be killed, and encourage their presence in the house, for I think the temporary inconvenience of a whiff of musk is amply repaid by the destruction of the numerous objectionable insects which lurk in the corners of Indian houses. The notion that they do damage by gnawing is an erroneous one, the mischief done by mice and rats being frequently laid to their charge; they have not the powerful dentition necessary for nibbling through wood and mortar. In my book on 'Camp Life in Seonee,' I say a good word for my little friends, and relate as follows an experiment which I tried many years ago: "We had once been talking at mess about musk-rats; some one declared a bottle of sherry had been tainted, and nobody defended the poor little beast but myself, and I was considerably laughed at. However, one night soon after, as I was dressing before dinner, I heard a musk-rat squeak in my room. Here was a chance. Shutting the door, I laid a clean pocket-handkerchief on the ground next to the wall, knowing the way in which the animal usually skirts round a room; on he came and ran over the handkerchief, and then, seeing me, he turned and went back again. I then headed him once more and quietly turned him; and thus went on till I had made him run over the handkerchief five times. I then took it up, and there was not the least smell. I then went across to the mess house, and, producing the handkerchief, asked several of my brother officers if they could perceive any peculiar smell about it. No, none of them could. 'Well, all I know is,' said I, 'that I have driven a musk-rat five times over that pocket-handkerchief just now.'"

When I was at Nagpore in 1864 I made friends with one of these shrews, and it would come out every evening at my whistle and take grasshoppers out of my fingers. It seemed to be very short-sighted, and did not notice the insect till quite close to my hand, when, with a short swift spring, it would pounce upon its prey.

A correspondent of *The Asian*, writing from Ceylon, gives an account of a musk-rat attacking a large frog, and holding on to it in spite of interference.

McMaster says that these shrews will also eat bread, and adds: "insects, however, form their chief diet, so they thus do us more good than harm. I once disturbed one that evidently had been eating part of a large scorpion."

No. 126. SOREX MURINUS.

The Mouse-coloured Shrew (Jerdon's No. 70).

HABITAT.—India generally, Burmah and Ceylon.

DESCRIPTION. Brownish-grey above, paler beneath; fur coarser and longer than in the last species, and in the young ones the colour is more of a bluish-grey, browner on the back. The ears are larger than those of *S. cærulescens;* tail nearly equal to the body, thick at the base, and sparsely covered with long coarse hairs; feet and tail flesh-coloured in the living animal.

SIZE.—Head and body about 6 inches; tail, 3½ inches.

"This," as Jerdon says, "is the common musk-rat of China, Burmah, and the Malayan countries, extending into Lower Bengal and Southern India, especially the Malabar Coast, where it is said to be the common species, the bite of which is considered venomous by the natives." Kellaart mentions it in Ceylon as the "common *musk shrew* or rat of Europeans;" but he confuses it with the last species. He gives the Singhalese name as "*koone meeyo.*" The musky odour of this species is less powerful, and is almost absent in the young. Blyth states that he was never able to obtain a specimen of it in Lower Bengal, yet the natives here discriminate between the light and dark-coloured shrews, and hold, with the people of Malabar, that the bite of the latter is venomous. Horsfield states that it has been found in Upper India, Nepal, and Assam, and he gives the vernacular name in the last-named country as "*seeka.*"

No. 127. SOREX NEMORIVAGUS.

The Nepal Wood Shrew (Jerdon's No. 71).

HABITAT.—Nepal.

DESCRIPTION.—Differs from the last "by a stouter make, by ears smaller and legs entirely nude, and by a longer and more tetragonal tail; colour sooty black, with a vague reddish smear; the nude parts fleshy grey; snout to rump, $3\frac{5}{8}$ inches; tail, 2 inches, planta, $\frac{11}{16}$ inch. Found only in woods and coppices."—*Hodgson.*

No. 128. SOREX SERPENTARIUS.

The Rufescent Shrew (Jerdon's No. 72).

HABITAT.—Southern India, Burmah and Ceylon.

DESCRIPTION.—Colour dusky greyish, with rufous brown tips to the hairs (*Blyth*). Above dusky slate colour with rufescent tips to the fur; beneath paler, with a faint rufous tinge about the breast (*Jerdon*).

Fur short ashy-brown, with a ferruginous smear on the upper surface; beneath a little paler coloured (*Kellaart*). Teeth and limbs small; tail slender.

SIZE.—Head and body about 4½ inches; tail, 2 inches; skull, 1 2/10 inch.

The smell of this musk shrew is said by Kellaart, who names it *S. Kandianus*, to be quite as powerful as that of *S. cærulescens*. Blyth seems to think that this animal gets more rufescent with age, judging from two examples sent from Mergui. By some oversight, I suppose, he has not included this species in his 'Catalogue of the Mammals of Burmah.'

No. 129. SOREX SATURATIOR.

The Dark Brown Shrew (*Jerdon's No.* 73).

HABITAT.—Darjeeling.

DESCRIPTION.—"Colour uniform deep brown, inclining to blackish, with a very slight rufescent shade; fur short, with an admixture of a few lengthened piles, when adpressed to the body smooth, but reversed somewhat harsh and rough; tail cylindrical, long, gradually tapering; mouth elongated, regularly attenuated, ears moderate, rounded."

SIZE.—Head and body, 5½ inches; tail, 3 inches.

Jerdon seems to think this is the same as *S. Griffithi* or closely allied; I cannot say anything about this, as I have no personal knowledge of the species, but on comparison with the description of *S. Griffithi* (which see further on) I should say they were identical.

No. 130. SOREX TYTLERI.

The Dehra Shrew (*Jerdon's No.* 74).

HABITAT.—Dehra Doon.

DESCRIPTION.—"Light rufescent sandy brown, paler beneath; unusually well clad even on the feet and tail, this last being covered with shortish fur having numerous long hairs intermixed; form very robust; basal portion of tail very thick."

SIZE.—Head and body, 4½ inches; tail, 2¾ inches; hind foot, ⅞ inch.

No. 131. SOREX NIGER.

The Neilgherry Wood Shrew (*Jerdon's No.* 75).

HABITAT.—Ootacamund, Neilgherry hills.

DESCRIPTION.—"Blackish-brown, with a rufescent shade on the upper parts; abdomen greyish; tail equal in length to the entire animal, exclusive of the head, gradually tapering to a point; snout greatly attenuated. Length of head and body, 3½ inches; of the tail, 2½ inches."
—*Horsfield.*

No. 132. SOREX LEUCOPS.

The Long-tailed Shrew (Jerdon's No. 76).

HABITAT.—Nepal.

DESCRIPTION.—Uniform blackish-brown colour; tail very long and slender, exceeding in length the head and body, terminating in a whitish tip of half an inch long.

SIZE.—Head and body, 3 inches; tail, 2½ inches. Jerdon supposes that it is found at great altitudes, from Hodgson having in another place described it (MSS.) under the name *nivicola.*

No. 133. SOREX SOCCATUS.

The Hairy-footed Shrew (Jerdon's No. 77).

HABITAT.—Nepal, Sikim, Mussoorie.

DESCRIPTION.—According to Hodgson, nearly the size of *S. nemorivagus*, "but distinguished by its feet being clad with fur down to the nails, and by its depressed head and tumid bulging cheeks (mystaceal region); ears large and exposed; colour a uniform sordid or brownish-slaty blue, extending to the clad extremities; snout to rump, 3½ inches; tail, 2½ inches; planta, $\frac{13}{16}$ inch. This animal was caught in a wood plentifully watered, but not near the water. It had no musky smell when brought to me dead."

No. 134. SOREX MONTANUS.

The Ceylon Black Shrew.

HABITAT.—Ceylon, mountainous parts.

DESCRIPTION.—" Fur above sooty black without any ferruginous smear, beneath lighter coloured; whiskers long, silvery grey; some parts of legs and feet greyish, clothed with adpressed hairs; claws short, whitish; ears large, round, naked; outer margin lying on a level with the fur of the head and neck, the ears being thus concealed posteriorly; tail tetragonal, tapering, shorter than head and body."—*Kellaart.*

SIZE.—Head and body, 3¾ inches; tail, 2¼ inches; hind feet, ⅓ inch.

No. 135. SOREX FERRUGINEUS.

The Ceylon Rufescent Shrew.

HABITAT.—Ceylon, Dimboola, below Newara Elia.

DESCRIPTION.—" Colour uniform dusky or dusky slate, with the tips of the fur rufescent; fur long; large sebaceous anal glands; smell very powerful."—*Kellaart.*

SIZE.—Head and body, 3¾ inches; tail, 2¼ inches.

No. 136. SOREX GRIFFITHI.

The Large Black Shrew.

HABITAT.—Khasia hills and Arracan.

DESCRIPTION.—"Deep blackish-brown, with a slight rufous reflection in a certain light; fur short, close, soft, and adpressed; tail thick at the base, with a few long very slender straggling hairs along its entire length; ears small and rounded; snout elongated."—*Horsfield.*

SIZE.—Head and body, 5¾ inches; tail, 2½ inches.

Horsfield puts this down as having been found in Afghanistan by Griffiths, but this is an error owing to Griffiths' Afghanistan and Khasia collections having got mixed up.

No. 137. SOREX HETERODON.

HABITAT.—Khasia hills.

DESCRIPTION.—"Very similar to *S. soccatus* in general appearance, but less dark coloured, with shorter fur, and pale instead of blackish feet and tail underneath; the feet too are broader, especially the hind feet, and they have a hairy patch below the heel" (*Blyth*). The skull is narrower, and the upper incisors less strongly hooked.

GENUS FEROCULUS.

Teeth small; upper incisors shorter and less strongly hooked than in restricted *Sorex;* posterior spur large; lower incisors serrated with three coronal points. Feet very large.

No. 138. FEROCULUS MACROPUS.

The Large-footed Shrew.

HABITAT.—Ceylon.

DESCRIPTION.—Fur, long, soft uniform blackish-faint rufescent tinge.

SIZE.—Head and body 4½ inches; tail 2¼.

The following species are of a more diminutive type, and are commonly called "pigmy-shrews;" in other respects they are true shrews.

No. 139. SOREX HODGSONI.

The Nepal Pigmy-Shrew (Jerdon's No. 78).

HABITAT.—Nepal and Sikim.

DESCRIPTION.—Brown, with a slight tinge of chestnut; feet and tail furred; claws white.

SIZE.—Head and body $1\frac{1}{2}$ inch; tail, 1 inch.

Found in coppices and fields; rarely entering houses.

No. 140. SOREX PERROTETI.

The Neilgherry Pigmy-Shrew (*Jerdon's No.* 79).

HABITAT.—Neilgherry hills, probably also other parts of Southern India.

DESCRIPTION.—"Back deep blackish-brown; belly pale; limbs and feet brown; palms and plantæ clad with hairs; ears large, conspicuous."

SIZE.—Head and body, $1\frac{1}{12}$ inch; tail, $\frac{11}{12}$ inch.

No. 141. SOREX MICRONYX.

The Small-clawed Pigmy-Shrew (*Jerdon's No.* 80).

HABITAT.—West Himalayas, Kumaon, Mussoorie.

DESCRIPTION.—Claws very minute, with fine hairs impending them, only to be detected by a lens; fur paler and more chestnut-brown than any other of these minute shrews, and more silvery below.

SIZE.—Head and body, $1\frac{5}{8}$ inch; tail $1\frac{1}{8}$ inch.

No. 142. SOREX MELANODON.

The Black-toothed Pigmy-Shrew (*Jerdon's No.* 81).

HABITAT.—Calcutta.

DESCRIPTION.—Called *melanodon* from the remarkable colouring of its teeth, which are piceous and white-tipped; colour uniform fuscous, scarcely paler beneath.

SIZE.—Head and body, $1\frac{7}{8}$ inch; tail, $1\frac{1}{16}$ inch.

No. 143. SOREX NUDIPES.

The Naked-footed Shrew.

HABITAT.—Tenasserim.

DESCRIPTION.—"Remarkable for its naked feet and very large ears; also for the odoriferous glands on the sides being strongly developed, whereas we can detect them in no other of these minute species" (*Blyth*). Colour brown above, a little grizzled and glistening, more silvery below.

SIZE.—Head and body, $1\frac{3}{4}$ inch; tail, $1\frac{1}{16}$ inch.

No. 144. SOREX ATRATUS.

The Black Pigmy-Shrew.

HABITAT.—Khasia hills.

DESCRIPTION.—"Very dark colour, extending over the feet and tail which is even *blackish underneath*; fur blackish-brown above, a little tinged rufescent, and with dark greyish underneath; the feet and tail conspicuously furred, beside the scattered long hairs upon the latter." —*Blyth.*

This species was determined by Blyth on a single specimen, which was found without its head, impaled by some shrike upon a thorn at Cherrapunji. The same thing occasionally occurs in England, when the common shrew may be found impaled by the rufous-backed shrike (*Lanius collurio*).

SUB-GENUS SORICULUS (Blyth).

The foregoing species being of the *white-toothed* variety (with the exception of *S. melanodon*, which, however, exhibits coloration decidedly the *reverse* of the following type), we now come to the shrews with teeth tipped with a darker colour; the dentition is as in the restricted shrews, with the peculiarity of colour above mentioned. The hind feet of ordinary proportions, unadapted for aquatic habits, and the tail slender and tapering, like that of a mouse, instead of being cylindrical with a stiff brush at the end.

NO. 145. SORICULUS NIGRESCENS.

The Mouse-tailed Shrew (*Jerdon's No.* 82).

HABITAT.—Sikim and Nepal.

DESCRIPTION.—"Above dark-blackish or blackish-brown, slightly tinged rufescent, and with a silvery cast in certain lights; beneath greyish-black" (*Jerdon*). Feet and claws pale; tail slender, straight and naked.

SIZE.—Head and body, $3\frac{1}{4}$ inches; tail, $1\frac{1}{2}$ inch; hind foot, $\frac{5}{8}$ inch.

Jerdon says that Kellaart named an allied species from Ceylon *Corsira newera ellia*, but I have not been able to find it in his 'Prodromus Faunæ Zeylanicæ,' nor elsewhere.

GENUS CROSSOPUS (Wagner).

The hind feet large; the lower surface, as also of the tail, fringed with stiff hairs; tail somewhat compressed towards the tip; habits aquatic.

NO. 146. CROSSOPUS HIMALAICUS.

The Himalayan Water-Shrew (*Jerdon's No.* 83).

NATIVE NAMES.—*Oong lagniyu*, Lepcha; *Choopitsi*, Bhot.

HABITAT.—Darjeeling.

DESCRIPTION.—Fur dark brown above, paler beneath; rusty brown on the lower part of throat and middle of belly, according to Jerdon; slate coloured back with scattered long hairs, which are longer and white-tipped on the sides and rump, according to Blyth's memoir; ears very small, hairy, concealed; tail long, slender, fringed with stiff whitish hair beneath; whiskers long and brown.

SIZE.—Head and body, 5 to 6 inches; tail about $3\frac{1}{2}$ inches; hind foot, $\frac{3}{4}$ to $\frac{11}{12}$ inch.

Jerdon procured this water-shrew at Darjeeling in the Little Rungeet river; it is said to live on small fish, tadpoles, water insects, &c. The movements of the English water-shrew, when swimming, are very agile. It propels itself by alternate strokes of its hind feet, but with an undulating motion, its sides being in a manner extended, and body flattened, showing a narrow white border on each side; then the fur collects a mass of tiny air bubbles which make the submerged portion glow like silver. It prefers clear still water, but at the same time will make its way up running streams and ditches, and occasionally wanders away into fields, and has been found in houses and barns.

Its food is principally aquatic insects, worms, mollusca, and fresh-water crustacea. In Bell's 'British Quadrupeds' its mode of poking about amongst stones in search of fresh-water shrimps (*Gammarus pulex*) is well described. Mr. F. Buckland states that he once dissected a water-shrew and found the intestines to contain a dark fluid pulpy matter, which, on being examined by a microscope, proved to consist entirely of the horny cases and legs of minute water insects. Continental writers declare that it will attack any small animal that comes in its way, giving it quite a ferocious character, and it is said to destroy fish spawn. I can hardly believe in its destroying large fish by eating out their brain and eyes. Brehm, who gives it credit for this, must have been mistaken. I have also read of its attacking a rat in a trap which was dead, and was discovered devouring it, having succeeded in making a small hole through the skin.

In England this animal breeds in May. The young are from five to seven in number, and are brought forth in a small chamber in the bank, which is constructed with several openings, one of which is usually under the level of the water.

Dr. Anderson has very fully described the Himalayan species under the name of *Chimarrogale Himalaica*. He caught a specimen in a mountain stream at Ponsee in the Kakhyen hills, 3500 feet above the sea level, and observed it running over the stones in the bed of the stream and plunging freely into the water hunting for insects.

GENUS NYCTOGALE.

Head and skull as in *Soricidæ*, but with palmated feet and compressed tail, as in *Myogalidæ*. Special characteristic, large pads on the soles of the feet, which form sucking discs.

No. 147. NYCTOGALE ELEGANS.

The Thibet Water-Shrew.

HABITAT.—Moupin in Thibet.

DESCRIPTION.—Fur of two kinds, a soft under down of slaty grey colour through which pass longer hairs, grey at the base with white tips, "causing the animal to vary considerably in appearance according as these hairs are raised or laid flat;" ears quite concealed, and without a conch; tail stout, longer than the body, quadrangular at the base, then triangular, and finally flattened; feet large and palmated, with large pads on the soles, depressed in the middle, forming sucking discs, which are a peculiar characteristic of this animal.

SIZE.—Head and body about 3½ inches; tail about 4 inches. Though this is not properly an Indian animal, I have thought fit to include it as belonging to a border country in which much interest is taken, and which has as yet been imperfectly explored.

GENUS CORSIRA.

Of Gray, *Amphisorex* of Duvernoy; differs in dentition from the last in having the lower quasi-incisors serrated with three or four coronal points, and the anterior point of the upper incisors not prolonged beyond the posterior spur, tipped with ferruginous; the lateral small teeth in the upper jaw are five in number, diminishing in size from the first backwards. Tail cylindrical, not tapering, and furnished with a stiffish brush at the extremity. The common British land-shrew is of this type.

No. 148. CORSIRA ALPINA.

The Alpine Shrew (Jerdon's No. 84).

HABITAT.—Darjeeling.

DESCRIPTION.—Deep blackish brown, very slightly rufescent in certain lights; tail slender, nearly naked, very slightly attenuated, compressed at the tip.

SIZE.—Head and body, 2½ inches; tail 2½ inches.

This is identical with the European Alpine shrew; the *Sorex caudatus* of Horsfield's Catalogue (No. 148), which was a specimen named by Hodgson, is also the same animal.

GENUS ANUROSOREX.

Remarkably for its large head, nude, scaly extremities, and extremely short, nude, scaly tail. "The structure of the ear, limbs and tail has special reference to a burrowing animal—the ear being valvular, so that it may be effectually closed against the entrance of foreign substances, and the feet devoid of hair, but scaly, and the tail reduced to very small dimensions. The eye is also excessively small, and buried deep in the dense silky fur. The hind feet, contrary to what is almost invariably the case in burrowing mammals, are larger than the fore feet." —*Anderson.*

No. 149. ANUROSOREX ASSAMENSIS.

The Assam Burrowing Shrew.

HABITAT.—Assam, Thibet.

DESCRIPTION.—General colour dark slaty, faintly washed with brownish rusty on the long hairs of the rump; fur long and silky, longest over the rump; occasional long brown hairs with pale tips are scattered over the body; long whiskers, yellow claws; naked parts of snout, limbs and tail flesh-coloured.

SIZE.—Head and body nearly 3 inches; tail, $\frac{1}{2}$ inch; forefoot, $\frac{1}{2}$ inch; hind foot, $\frac{3}{4}$ inch.

The skull and dentition of this animal are essentially soricine. The Thibetan species (*A. squamipes*) is described as being over four inches in length, of a greyish colour, with a greenish-brown tinge; feet and nails whitish. It lives in burrows which it digs in the earth. I think it should properly come after the moles, which it resembles in some particulars.

FAMILY ERINACEIDÆ—THE HEDGEHOGS.

The molar teeth broad; the hinder ones nearly square, the tubercles on their upper surface rounded; the other teeth are three incisors on each side, of which the inner one is considerably larger than the rest; behind these, separated by a little gap, come three premolars gradually increasing in size, then one having much the appearance of a true molar, but furnished with a cutting edge; then three molar teeth, two of which are nearly square with strong tubercles. The last molar is small. In the lower jaw the lowermost incisor is very large, and projects almost horizontally forwards, and it is followed by three small teeth now acknowledged to be premolars, with another large premolar, which is of the nature of a carnassial or cutting tooth acting on the one in the upper jaw. Then three molars as above, two large and one small, but with sharp tubercles. The skull has a more carnivorous form; it has "a complete zygomatic arch, and the tympanic bone forms a bundle-like swelling on each side of the back of the skull." Feet pentadactylous or five-toed; legs very short. The tibia and fibula (two bones of the shank) are joined together. The back is clothed with hair intermixed with sharp spines or bristles. Tail short or wanting entirely.

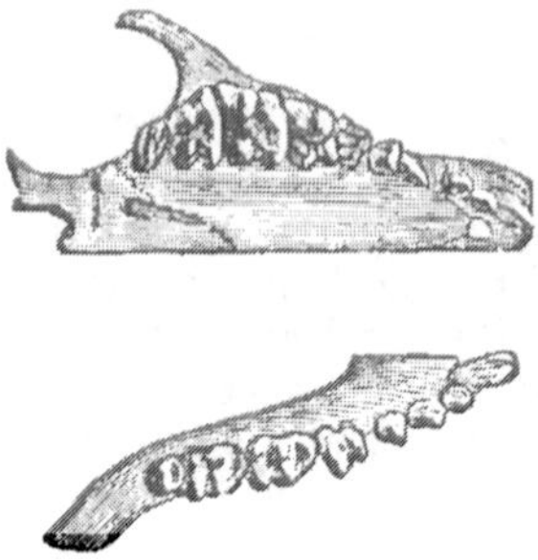

Dentition of Hedgehog.

GENUS ERINACEUS.

The European hedgehog is well known to most of us. Few boys who have lived a country life have been without one at some time or other as a pet. I used to keep mine in a hole at the root of an old apple-tree, which was my special property, and they were occasionally brought into the house at the cook's request to demolish the black-beetles in the kitchen. These they devour with avidity and pursue them with the greatest ardour. They also eat slugs, worms, and snails; worms they seize and eat from end to end, like a Neapolitan boy with a string of maccaroni, slowly masticating, the unconsumed portion being constantly transferred from one side of the mouth to the other, so that both sides of the jaws may come into play. Dr. Dallas quaintly remarks on the process: "This must be an unpleasant operation for the worm, much as its captor may enjoy it." Toads, frogs, mice, and even snakes are eaten by the European hedgehog. It would be interesting to find out whether the Indian hedgehog also attacks snakes; even the viper in Europe is devoured by this animal, who apparently takes little heed of its bite. The European species also eats eggs when it can get them, and I have no doubt does much damage to those birds who make their nests on the ground.

Few dogs will tackle a hedgehog, for the little creature at once rolls itself into a spiny ball, all sharp prickles, by means of the contraction of a set of cutaneous muscles, the most important of which, the *orbicularis panniculi*, form a broad band encircling the body which draws together the edges of the spiny part of the skin. There is a most interesting account of the mechanism of the spines in Mr. F. Buckland's notes to White's 'Natural History of Selborne,' vol. ii., page 76. A jet of water poured on to the part within which the head is concealed will make the creature unroll, and it is said that foxes and some dogs have discovered a way of applying this plan, and also that foxes will roll a hedgehog into a ditch or pond, and thus make him either expose

Hedgehog.

himself to attack or drown. Gipsies eat hedgehogs, and consider them a delicacy—the meat being white and as tender as a chicken (not quite equal to porcupine, I should say); they cook them by rolling them in clay, and baking them till the clay is dry; when the ball is broken open the prickles come off with the crust.

Hedgehogs have had several popular fallacies concerning them. They were supposed to suck cows dry during the night and to be proof against poisons. Mr. Frank Buckland tried prussic acid on one with fatal results, but he says the bite of a viper seemed to have no effect. Pallas, I know, has remarked that hedgehogs will eat hundreds of cantharides beetles with impunity, whereas one or two will cause extreme agony to a cat or dog. The female goes with young about seven weeks, and she has from three to eight in number. The little ones when born have soft spines—which, however, soon harden—are blind, and, with the exception of the rudimentary prickles, quite naked. They are white at birth, but in about a month acquire the colour of the mother.

No. 150. ERINACEUS COLLARIS.

The Collared Hedgehog (Jerdon's No. 85).

HABITAT.—Northern India and Afghanistan. Dallas says from Madras to Candahar; but Jerdon calls it the North Indian hedgehog, and assigns to it the North-west, Punjab, and Sind, giving Southern India to the next species.

DESCRIPTION.—Spines irregularly interwoven, ringed with white and black, with yellowish tips, or simply white and black, or black with a white ring in the middle; ears large; chin white; belly and legs pale brown.

SIZE.—Head and body, 8 to 9 inches; tail, $\frac{7}{12}$ inch.

I have found this species in the Punjab near Lahore. One evening, whilst walking in the dusk, a small animal, which I took to be a rat, ran suddenly between my legs. Now I confess to an antipathy to rats, and, though I would not willingly hurt any animal, I could not resist an impulsive kick, which sent my supposed rat high in the air. I felt a qualm of conscience immediately afterwards, and ran to pick up my victim, and was sorry to find I had perpetrated such an assault on an unoffending little hedgehog, which was however only stunned, and was carried off by me to the Zoological Gardens. Captain Hutton writes of them that they feed on beetles, lizards, and snails; "when touched they have the habit of suddenly jerking up the back with some force so as to prick the fingers or mouth of the assailant, and at the same time emitting a blowing sound, not unlike the noise produced when blowing upon a flame with a pair of bellows." He also says they are very tenacious of life, bearing long abstinence with apparent ease; when alarmed they roll themselves up into a ball like the European species.

Hutton also remarks that *E. collaris*, on hearing a noise, jerks the skin and quills of its neck completely over its head, leaving only the tip of the nose free.

No. 151. ERINACEUS MICROPUS.

The Small-footed Hedgehog (Jerdon's No. 86).

HABITAT.—South India.

DESCRIPTION.—" Ears moderately large; form somewhat elongated;

tail very short, concealed; feet and limbs very small; head and ears nude, sooty-coloured; belly very thinly clad with yellowish hairs; spines ringed dark brown and whitish, or whitish with a broad brown sub-terminal ring, tipped white."—*Jerdon.*

SIZE.—Head and body about 6 inches. Dr. Anderson considers this as identical with *E. collaris.*

No. 152. ERINACEUS PICTUS.

The Painted Hedgehog.

HABITAT.—Central India, Goona, Ulwar, Agra, Kurrachee.

DESCRIPTION.—Similar to the above, but the tips of the spines are more broadly white, and the brown bands below not so dark; the ears are somewhat larger than *micropus*, and the feet narrower and not so long.

No. 153. ERINACEUS GRAYI.

HABITAT.—North-west India.

DESCRIPTION.—The general colour is blackish-brown; the spines are narrowly tipped with black, succeeded by a narrowish yellow band; then a blackish-brown band, the rest of the spine being yellowish; the broad dark-brown band is so strongly developed as to give the animal its dark appearance when viewed from the side; some animals are, however, lighter than others. The feet are large; the fore-feet broad, somewhat truncated, with moderately long toes and powerful claws.

SIZE.—Head and body about 6¾ inches.

No. 154. ERINACEUS BLANFORDI (*Anderson*).

HABITAT.—Sind, where one specimen was obtained by Mr. W. T. Blanford, at Rohri.

DESCRIPTION.—Muzzle rather short, not much pointed; ears moderately large, but broader than long, and rounded at the tips; feet larger and broader than in the next species, with the first toe more largely developed than in the last. The spines meet in a point on the forehead, and there is no bare patch on the vertex. Each spine is broadly tipped with deep black, succeeded by a very broad yellow band, followed by a dusky brown base; fur deep brown; a few white hairs on chin and anterior angle of ear.

SIZE.—Head and body, 5·36 inches.

No. 155. ERINACEUS JERDONI (*Anderson*).

HABITAT.—Sind, Punjab frontier.

DESCRIPTION.—Muzzle moderately long and pointed; ears large

round at tip and broad at base; feet large, especially the fore-feet; claws strong. The spines begin on a line with the anterior margins of the ears; large nude area on the vertex; spines with two white and three black bands, beginning with a black band. When they are laid flat the animal looks black; but on erection the white shows and gives a variegated appearance.

SIZE.—Head and body about 7½ inches.

No. 156. ERINACEUS MEGALOTIS.

The Large-eared Hedgehog.

HABITAT.—Afghanistan.

More information is required about this species. Jerdon seems to think it may be the same as described by Pallas (*E. auritus*), which description I have before me now ('Zoographica Rosso Asiatica,' vol. i. page 138), but I am unable to say from comparison that the two are identical—the ears and the muzzle are longer than in the common hedgehog. This is the species which he noticed devouring blistering beetles with impunity. It has a very delicate fur of long silky white hairs, covering the head, breast and abdomen, "forming also along the sides a beautiful ornamental border" (*Horsfield*, from a specimen brought from Mesopotamia by Commander Jones, I.N.)

The space to which I am obliged to limit myself will not allow of my describing at greater length; but to those of my readers who are interested in the Indian hedgehogs, I recommend the paper by Dr. J. Anderson in the 'Journal of the Asiatic Society of Bengal' for 1878, page 195, with excellently drawn plates of the heads, skulls and feet of the various species. There is one peculiarity which he notices regarding the skull of *E. collaris* (or, as he calls it, *micropus*): the zygomatic arch is not continuous as in the other species, but is broken in the middle, the gap being caused by the absence of the *malar* or cheek-bone. In this respect it resembles, though Dr. Anderson does not notice it, the *Centetidæ* or *Tanrecs* of Madagascar.

Dr. Anderson's classification is very simple and good. He has two groups: the first, containing *E. micropus* and *E. pictus*, is distinguished by the *second upper premolar simple, one-fanged, the feet club-shaped; soles tubercular*. The second group, containing *E. Grayi*, *E. Blanfordi* and *E. Jerdoni*, has *the second upper premolar compound, three-fanged, and the feet well developed and broad.* The first group has also a division or bare area on the vertex; the second has not.

FAMILY HYLOMIDÆ (*Anderson*).

The following little animal has affinities to both *Erinaceidæ* and *Tupaiidæ*, and therefore it may appropriately be placed here. Dr. Anderson on the above ground has placed it in a separate family, otherwise it is generally classed with the *Erinaceidæ*. Its skull has the general form of the skull of *Tupaia*, but in its imperfect orbit, in the rudiment of a post-orbital process, and in the absence of any imperfections of the zygomatic arch and in the position of the lachrymal foramen it resembles the skull of *Erinaceus*. The teeth are 44 in number: Inc., $\frac{3-3}{3-3}$; can., $\frac{1-1}{1-1}$; premolars, $\frac{4-4}{4-4}$; molars, $\frac{3-3}{3-3}$, and partake of the character of both *Tupaia* and *Erinaceus*. The shank-bones being united and the rudimentary tail create an affinity to the latter, whilst its arboreal habits are those of the former.

GENUS HYLOMYS.

Head elongate; ears round; feet arboreal, naked below; tail seminude; pelage not spiny.

NO. 157. HYLOMYS PEGUENSIS.

The Short-tailed Tree-Shrew.

HABITAT.—Burmah, Pegu, Ponsee in the Kakhyen hills.
Appears to be identical with the species from Borneo (*H. suillus*).

FAMILY TUPAIIDÆ.

These interesting little animals were first accurately described about the year 1820, though, as I have before stated, it was noticed in the papers connected with Captain Cook's voyages, but was then supposed to be a squirrel. Sir T. Stamford Raffles writes: "This singular little animal was first observed tame in the house of a gentleman at Penang, and afterwards found wild at Singapore in the woods near Bencoolen, where it lives on the fruit of the kayogadis, &c." Another species, *T. Javanica*, had, however, been discovered in Java fourteen years before, but not published till 1821. They are sprightly little creatures, easily tamed, and, not being purely insectivorous, are not difficult to feed in captivity. Sir T. S. Raffles describes one that roamed freely all over the house, presenting himself regularly at meal-times for milk and fruit. Dr. Sal. Müller describes the other species (*T. Javanica*) as a confiding, simple little animal, always in motion, seeking its food at one time amongst dry leaves and moss on the ground, and again on the stems and branches of trees, poking its nose into every crevice. Its nest, he says, is formed of moss at some height from the ground, supported on clusters of orchideous plants. Dr. Cantor, in his 'Catalogue of the Mammalia of the Malayan Peninsula,' writes as follows: "In a state of nature it lives singly or in pairs, fiercely attacking intruders of its own species. When several are confined together they fight each other, or jointly attack and destroy the weakest. The natural food is mixed insectivorous and frugivorous. In confinement, individuals may be fed exclusively on either, though preference is evinced for insects; and eggs, fish and earth-worms are equally relished. A short, peculiar, tremulous, whistling sound, often heard by calls and answers in the Malayan jungle, marks their pleasurable emotions, as for instance on the appearance of food, while the contrary is expressed by shrill protracted cries. Their disposition is very restless, and their great agility enables them to perform the most extraordinary bounds in all directions, in which exercise they spend the day, till night sends them to sleep in their rudely-constructed lairs in the highest branches of trees. At times they will sit on their haunches, holding their food between their forelegs, and after feeding they smooth the head and face with both fore-paws, and lick the lips and palms. They are also fond of water, both to drink and to bathe in. The female usually produces one young."

The above description reminds one forcibly of the habits of squirrels, so it is no wonder that at one time these little creatures were confounded with the *Sciuridæ*.

GENUS TUPAIA.

The dentition of this genus is as follows: Either four or six incisors in the upper jaw, but always six in the lower; four premolars and three molars in each jaw, upper and lower. The skull has a complete bony orbit, and the zygomatic arch is also complete, but with a small elongated perforation; the muzzle attenuated, except in *T. Ellioti;* ears oval; the stomach possesses a cæcum or blind gut; the eyes are large and prominent, and the tail bushy, like that of a squirrel; the toes are five in number, with strong claws; the shank-bones are not united as in the hedgehogs. The diet is mixed insectivorous and frugivorous.

No. 158. TUPAIA ELLIOTI.

Elliot's Tree-Shrew (Jerdon's No. 87).

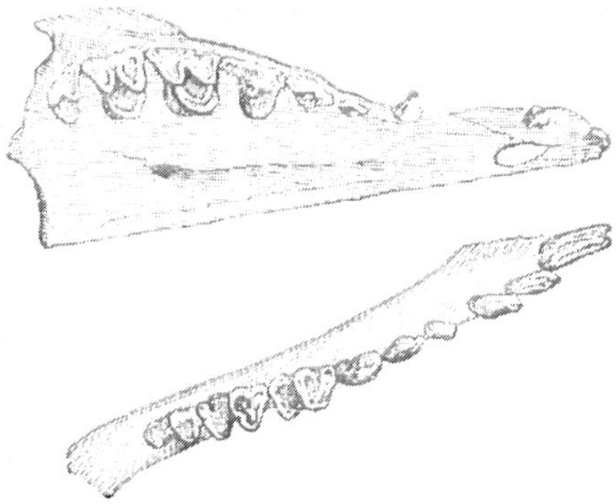

Dentition of *Tupaia.*

HABITAT. — Southern India, Godavery district, Cuttack; the Central Provinces, Bhagulpore range.

DESCRIPTION.—Fur pale rufous brown, darker on the back and paler on the sides; the chin, throat, breast and belly yellowish, also a streak of the same under the tail; the upper surface of the tail is of the same colour as the centre of the back; there is a pale line from the muzzle over the eye, and a similar patch beneath it; the fur of this species is shorter and more harsh, and the head is more blunt than in the Malayan members of the family.

SIZE.—Head and body, 7 to 8 inches; tail, 7 to 9 inches.

No. 159. TUPAIA PEGUANA. *Syn.*—TUPAIA BELANGERI.

The Pegu Tree-Shrew (Jerdon's No. 88).

HABITAT.—Sikim (Darjeeling), Assam and through Arakan to Tenasserim.

DESCRIPTION.—Jerdon says: "General hue a dusky greenish-brown, the hairs being ringed brown and yellow; lower parts the same, but lighter, and with a pale buff line; a stripe from the throat to the vent, broadest between the forearms and then narrowing; ears livid red, with a few short hairs; palms and soles dark livid red." Dr. Anderson remarks that the fur is of two kinds of hairs—one fine and wavy at the extremity, banded with black, yellow and black; the second being strong and somewhat bristly, longer than the other, and banded with a black basal half and then followed by rings of yellow and black, then yellow again with a black tip, the black basal half of the hairs being hidden, the annulation of the free portions produces a rufous olive-grey tint over the body and tail.

SIZE.—Head and body about 7 inches; tail, 6½.

Jerdon says of it that those he procured at Darjeeling frequented the zone from 3000 to 6000 feet; they were said by the natives to kill small birds, mice, &c. The Lepcha name he gives is *Kalli-tang-zhing.* McMaster in his notes writes: "The Burmese Tupaia is a harmless little animal; in the dry season living in trees and in the monsoon freely entering our houses, and in impudent familiarity taking the place held in India by the common palm squirrel. It is, however, probably from its rat-like head and thievish expression, very unpopular. I have found them in rat-traps, however, so possibly they deserve to be so." He adds he cannot endorse the statement regarding their extraordinary agility mentioned by Dr. Cantor and quoted by Jerdon, for he had seen his

Tupaia Peguana.

terriers catch them, which they were never able to do with squirrels; and cats often seize them.

Mason says: "One that made his home in the mango-tree near my house at Tonghoo made himself nearly as familiar as the cat. Sometimes I had to drive him off the bed, and he was very fond of putting his nose into the teacups immediately after breakfast, and acquired a taste both for tea and coffee. He lost his life at last by incontinently walking into a rat-trap."

The Burmese name for it is *Tswai* in Arracan. Jerdon states that it is one of the few novelties that had escaped the notice of Mr. Brian Hodgson, but Dr. Anderson mentions a specimen (unnamed) from Nepal in the British Museum which was obtained by Hodgson.

No. 160. TUPAIA CHINENSIS (*Anderson*).

HABITAT.—Burmah, Kakhyen hills, east of the valley of the Irrawaddy.

DESCRIPTION.—Ferruginous above, yellowish below, the basal two thirds of the hair being blackish, succeeded by a yellow, a black, and then a yellow and black band, which is terminal; there is a faint shoulder streak washed with yellowish; the chest pale orange yellow, which hue extends along the middle of the belly as a narrow line; under surfaces of limbs grizzled as on the back, but paler; upper surface of tail concolorous with the dorsum.

SIZE.—Head and body, 6½ inches; tail, 6·16.

The teeth are larger than those of *T. Ellioti*, but smaller than the Malayan *T. ferruginea*, and the skull is smaller than that of the last species, and the teeth are also smaller. Dr. Anderson says: "When I first observed the animal it was on a grassy clearing close to patches of fruit, and was so comporting itself that in the distance I mistook it for a squirrel. The next time I noticed it was in hedgerows."

The other varieties of *Tupaia* belong to the Malayan Archipelago—*T. ferruginca*, *T. tana*, *T. splendidula*, and *T. Javanica* to Borneo and Java. There is one species which inhabits the Nicobars.

No. 161. TUPAIA NICOBARICA.

HABITAT.—Nicobar Island.

DESCRIPTION.—Front and sides of the face, outside of fore-limbs, throat and chest, golden yellow; inner side of hind limbs rich red brown, which is also the colour of the hind legs and feet; head dark brown, with golden hairs intermixed; back dark maroon, almost black; upper surface of the tail the same; pale oval patch between shoulders, dark band on each side between it and fore-limbs, passing forward over the ears.

SIZE.—Head and body, 7·10; tail, 8 inches.

There is a little animal allied to the genus *Tupaia*, which has hitherto been found only in Borneo and Sumatra, but as Sumatran types have been found in Tenasserim, perhaps some day the *Ptilocercus Lowii* may be discovered there. It has a rather shorter head than the true Banxrings, more like *T. Ellioti*, but its dentition is nearly the same, as also are its habits. Its chief peculiarity lies in its tail, which is long, slender and naked, like that of a rat for two-thirds of its length, the terminal third being adorned with a broad fringe of hair on each side, like the wings of an arrow or the plumes of a feather. There is an excellent coloured picture of it in the 'Proc. Zool. Society,' vol. of Plates.

I had almost concluded my sketch of the Insectivora without alluding to one most interesting genus, which ought properly to have come between the shrews and the hedgehogs, the *Gymnura*, which, though common in the Malay countries, has only recently been found in Burmah—a fact of which I was not aware till I saw it included in a paper on Tenasserim mammals by Mr. W. T. Blanford ('Jour. As. Soc. Beng.,' 1878, page 150.) Before I refer to his notes I may state that this animal is a sort of link between the *Soricidæ* and the *Erinaceidæ*, and De Blainville proposed for it the generic name of *Echinosorex*, but the one generally adopted is *Gymnura*, which was the specific name given to it by its discoverer, Sir Stamford Raffles, who described it as a *Viverra* (*V. gymnura*); however, Horsfield and Vigors and Lesson, the two former in England and the latter in France, saw that it was not a civet, and, taking the naked tail as a peculiarity, they called the genus *Gymnura*, and the specimen *Rafflesii*. There is not much on record regarding the anatomy of the animal, and in what respects it internally resembles the hedgehogs. Outwardly it has the general soricine form, though much larger than the largest shrew. The long tail too is against its resemblance to the hedgehogs, which rests principally on its spiny pelage.

The teeth in some degree resemble *Erinaceus*, the molars and premolars especially, but the number in all is greater, there being forty-four, or eight more. It would be interesting to know whether the zygomatic arch is perfect and the tibia and fibula united, as in the hedgehogs, or wanting and distinct as in the shrews. I have given a slight sketch in outline of the animal.

NO. 162. GYMNURA RAFFLESII.

The Bulau.

HABITAT.—Tenasserim (Sumatra, Borneo); Malacca.

DESCRIPTION.—Long tapering head, with elongated muzzle, short legs, shrew-like body, with a long, round, tapering and scaly rat-like tail, naked, with the exception of a few stiff hairs here and there among the scales. In each jaw on each side three incisors, one canine (those in the upper jaw double-fanged) and seven premolars and molars; feet five-toed, plantigrade, armed with strong claws. Fur of two kinds, fine and soft, with longer and more spiny ones intermixed. The colour varies a good deal, the general tint being greyish-black, with head and neck pale or whitish, and with a broad black patch over the eye. Some have been found almost wholly white, with the black eye-streak and only a portion of the longer hairs black, so that much stress cannot be laid on the colouring; the tail is blackish at the base, whitish and compressed at the tip. Mr. Blanford says: "The small scales covering the tail are indistinctly arranged in rings and sub-imbricate; on the lower surface the scales are convex and distinctly imbricate, the bristles arising from the interstices. Thus the under surface of the tail is very rough, and may probably be of use to the animal in climbing." He also refers to the fact that the claws of his specimen are not retractile, and mentions that in the original description both in Latin and English the retractability of the claws is pointed out as a distinction between *Gymnura* and *Tupaia*. In the description given of the Sumatran animal both by Dallas and Cuvier nothing is mentioned about this feature.

Gymnura Rafflesii.

SIZE.—A Sumatran specimen: head and body, 14 inches; tail, 12 inches. Mr. Blanford's specimen: head and body, 12 inches; tail, 8·5.

Mr. Blanford was informed by Mr. Davison, who obtained it in Burmah, that the *Gymnura* is purely nocturnal in its habits, and lives under the roots of trees. It has a peculiar and most offensive smell, resembling decomposed cooked vegetables. The Bulau has not the power of rolling itself up like the hedgehog, nor have the similar forms of insectivores which resemble the hedgehog in some respects, such as the Tenrecs (*Centetes*), Tendracs (*Ericulus*), and Sokinahs (*Echinops*) of Madagascar.

CARNIVORA.

Speaking generally, the whole range of mammals between the *Quadrumana* and the *Rodentia* are *carnivorous* with few exceptions, yet there is one family which, from its muscular development and dentition, is pre-eminently flesh-eating, as Cuvier aptly remarks, "the sanguinary appetite is combined with the force necessary for its gratification." Their forms are agile and muscular; their circulation and respiration rapid. As Professor Kitchen Parker graphically writes: "This group, which comprises all the great beasts of prey, is one of the most compact as well as the most interesting among the mammalia. So many of the animals contained in it have become 'familiar in our mouths as household words,' bearing as they do an important part in fable, in travel, and even in history; so many of them are of such wonderful beauty, so many of such terrible ferocity, that no one can fail to be interested in them, even apart from the fact likely to influence us more in their favour than any other, that the two home pets, which of all others are the commonest and the most interesting, belong to the group. No one who has had a dog friend, no one who has watched the wonderful instance of maternal love afforded by a cat with her kittens, no one who loves riding across country after a fox, no lady with a taste for handsome furs, no boy who has read of lion and tiger hunts and has longed to emulate the doughty deeds of the hunter, can fail to be interested in an assemblage which furnishes animals at once so useful, so beautiful and so destructive. It must not be supposed from the name of this group that all its members are exclusively flesh-eaters, and indeed it will be hardly necessary to warn the reader against falling into this mistake, as there are few people who have never given a dog a biscuit, or a bear a bun. Still both the dog and several kinds of bears prefer flesh-meat when they can get it, but there are some bears which live almost exclusively on fruit, and are, therefore, in strictness not carnivorous at all. The name must, however, be taken as a sort of general title for a certain set of animals which have certain characteristics in common, and which differ from all other animals in particular ways." I would I had more space at my disposal for further quotations from Professor Parker's 'General Remarks on the Land Carnivora,' his style is so graphic.

The dentition of the Carnivora varies according to the exclusiveness of their fleshy diet, and the nature of that diet.

In taking two typical forms I give below sketches from skulls in my possession of the tiger, and the common Indian black bear; the one has trenchant cutting teeth which work up and down, the edges sliding past each other just like a pair of scissors; the other has flat crowned molars adapted for triturating the roots and herbage on which it feeds. A skull of an old bear which I have has molars of which the crowns are worn almost smooth from attrition. In the most carnivorous forms the tubercular molars are almost rudimentary.

The skull exhibits peculiar features for the attachment of the necessary powerful muscles. The bones of the face are short in comparison with the *cranial* portion of the skull (the reverse of the *Herbivores*); the strongly built zygomatic arch, the roughened ridges and the broad ascending ramus of the lower jaw, all afford place for the attachment of the immense muscular development. Then the hinge of the jaw is peculiar; it allows of no lateral motion, as in the ruminants; the *condyle*, or hinge-bolt of a tiger's jaw (taken from the largest in my collection), measures two inches, and as this fits accurately into its corresponding (glenoid) cavity, there can be no side motion, but a vertical chopping one only. The skeleton of a typical carnivore is the perfection of strength and suppleness. The tissue of the bones is dense and white; the head small and beatifully articulated; the spine flexible yet strong. In those which show the greatest activity, such as the cats, civets and dogs, the spinous processes, especially in the lumbar region, are greatly developed—more so than in the bears. These serve for the attachment of the powerful muscles of the neck and back. The clavicle or collar-bone is wanting, or but rudimentary. The

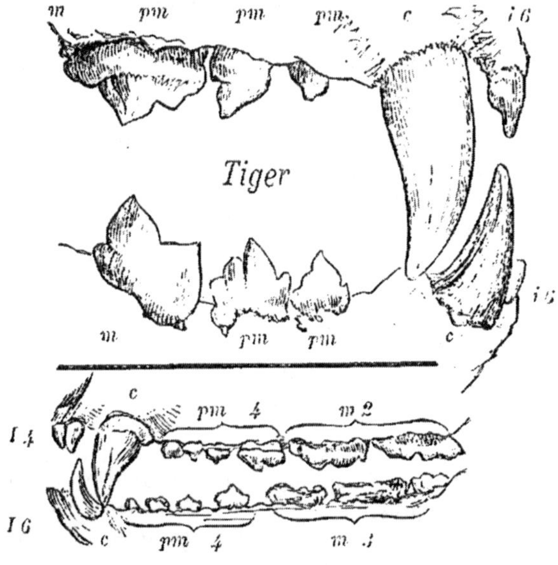

stomach is simple; the intestinal canal short; liver lobed; organs of sight, hearing, and smell much developed.

Now we come to the divisions into which this group has been separated by naturalists. I shall not attempt to describe the various systems, but take the one which appears to me the simplest and best to fit in with Cuvier's general arrangement, which I have followed. Modern zoologists have divided the family into two great groups—the *Fissipedia* (split-feet) or land Carnivora, and the *Pinnipedia* (fin-feet or water Carnivora. Of the land Carnivora some naturalists have made the following three groups on the characteristics of the feet, *viz.*, *Plantigrada*, *Sub-plantigrada* and *Digitigrada*. The dogs and cats, it is well known, walk on their toes—they are the *Digitigrada*; the bears and allied forms on the palms of their hands and soles of their feet, more or less, and thus form the other two divisions, but there is another classification which recommends itself by its simplicity and accuracy. Broadly speaking, there are three types of land carnivores—the cat, the dog, and the bear, which have been scientifically named *Æluroidea* (from the Greek *ailouros*, a cat); *Cynoidea* (from *kuon*, a dog); and *Arctoidea* (from *arctos*, a bear). The distinction is greater between the families of *Digitigrades*, the cat and dog, than between the *Plantigrades* and *Sub-plantigrades*, and therefore I propose to adopt the following arrangement:—

I. ARCTOIDEA	{ *Pantigrades.* { *Sub-plantigrades.*
II. ÆLUROIDEA III. CYNOIDEA	} *Digitigrade.*

I may here remark that the Insectivora are in most cases plantigrade, therefore the term is not an apposite one as applied to the bear and bear-like animals only, but in treating of them under the term *Arctoidea* we may divide them again into *Plantigrades* and *Sub-plantigrades.*

ARCTOIDEA.

PLANTIGRADA.

URSIDÆ.

The bears differ from the dogs and cats widely in form and manner, and diet. The cat has a light springy action, treading on the tips of its toes, a well-knit body glistening in a silky coat, often richly variegated, "a clean cut," rounded face, with beautifully chiselled nostrils and thin lips, and lives exclusively on flesh. The bear shambles along with an awkward gait, placing the entire sole of his foot on the ground; he has rough dingy fur, a snout like a pig's, and is chiefly a vegetarian—and in respect to this last peculiarity his dentition is modified considerably: the incisors are large, tri-cuspidate; the canines somewhat smaller than in the restricted carnivora; these are followed by three small teeth, which usually fall out at an early period, then comes a permanent premolar of considerable size, succeeded by two molars in the upper, and three in the under jaw. The dental formula is therefore: Inc., $\frac{3-3}{3-3}$; can., $\frac{1-1}{1-1}$; premolars, $\frac{4-4}{4-4}$; molars, $\frac{2-2}{3-3}$. In actual numbers this formula agrees with that for the dogs; but the form of the teeth is very different, inasmuch as the large premolars and the molars have flat tuberculated crowns, constituting them true grinders, instead of the

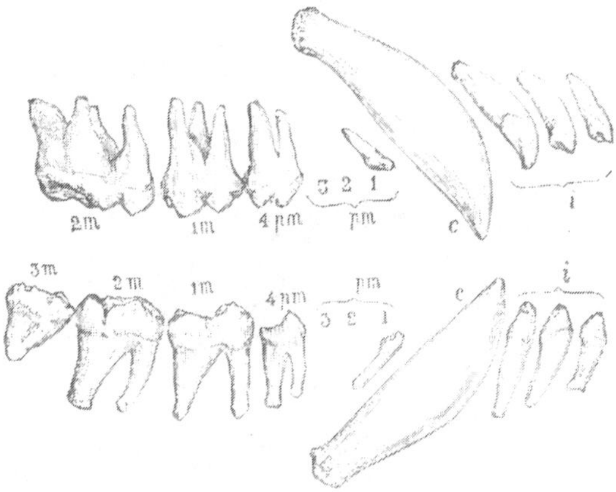

Dentition of Bear.

trenchant shape of the cats, which is also, to a modified extent, possessed by the dogs, of which the last two molars have, instead of cutting edges, a grinding surface with four cusps. The trenchant character is entirely lost in the bear, even in the carnivorous species which exhibit no material difference in the teeth, any more than, as I mentioned at the commencement of this work, do the teeth of the human race, be they as carnivorous as the Esquimaux, or vegetarian as the Hindu.

There is also another peculiarity in the bear's skull as compared with the cat's. In the latter there is a considerable bulging below the aperture of the ear called the *bulla tympani*, or bulb of the drum. This is almost wanting in the bear, and it would be interesting to know whether this much affects its hearing. I myself am of opinion that bears are not acute in this sense, but then my experience has been with the common Indian *Ursus*,

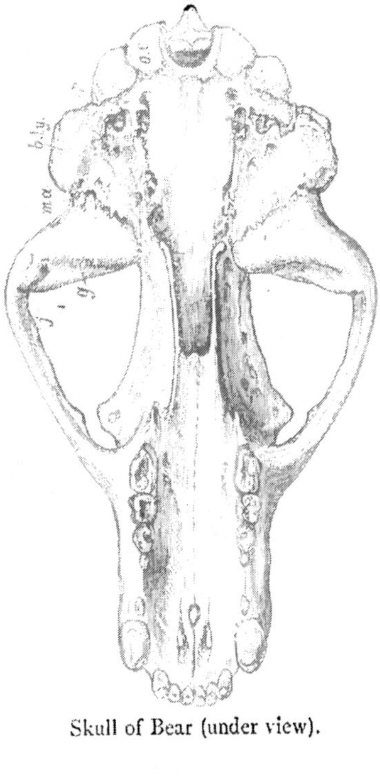

Skull of Bear (under view).

Ursus Isabellinus.

or *Melursus labiatus* only, and the skulls of this species in my possession strongly exhibit this peculiarity.* The cylindrical bones resemble those of man nearer than any other animal, the *femur* especially; and a skinned bear has a most absurd resemblance to a robust human being. The sole of the hind foot leaves a mark not unlike that of a human print.

The Brown Bear of Europe (*Ursus arctos*) is the type of the family, and has been known from the earliest ages—I may say safely prehistoric ages, for its bones have been frequently found in post-pliocene formations along with those of other animals of which some are extinct. An extinct species of bear, *Ursus spelæus*, commonly called the Cave Bear, seems to have been the ancestor of the Brown Bear which still is found in various parts of Europe, and is said to have been found within historic times in Great Britain.

The bear of which we have the oldest record is almost the same as our Indian Brown or Snow Bear. Our bear (*U. Isabellinus*) is but a variety of *U. Syriacus*, which was the one slain by David, and is spoken of in various parts of the Bible. It is the nearest approach we have to the European *U. arctos*.

No. 163. URSUS ISABELLINUS.

The Himalayan Brown Bear (Jerdon's No. 89).

NATIVE NAME.—*Barf-ka-rich* or *Bhalu*, Hind.; *Harput*, Kashmiri; *Drin-mor*, Ladakhi.

DESCRIPTION.—A yellowish-brown colour, varying somewhat according to sex and time of year. Jerdon says: "In winter and spring the fur is long and shaggy, in some inclining to silvery grey, in others to reddish brown; the hair is thinner and darker in summer as the season advances, and in autumn the under fur has mostly disappeared, and a white collar on the chest is then very apparent. The cubs show this collar distinctly. The females are said to be lighter in colour than the males."

Gray does not agree in the theory that *Ursus Syriacus* is the same as this species; in external appearance he says it is the same, but there are differences in the skull; the nose is broader, and the depression in the forehead less. The zygomatic arch is wider and stronger; the lower jaw stronger and higher, and the upper tubercular grinders shorter and thicker than in *Ursus Isabellinus*.

* On referring to Mr. Sanderson's interesting book, 'Thirteen Years among the Wild Beasts of India,' and General Shakespear's 'Wild Sports,' I find that both those authors corroborate my assertion that the sloth bear is deficient in the sense of hearing. Captain Baldwin, however, thinks otherwise; but the evidence seems to be against him in this respect.

URSUS TIBETANUS.

"It is found," Jerdon says, "only on the Himalayas and at great elevations in summer close to the snow. In autumn they descend lower, coming into the forests to feed on various fruits, seeds, acorns, hips of rose-bushes, &c., and often coming close to villages to plunder apples, walnuts, apricots, buckwheat, &c. Their usual food in spring and summer is grass and roots. They also feed on various insects, and are seen turning over stones to look for scorpions (it is said) and insects that harbour in such places. In winter they retreat to caves, remaining in a state of semi-torpidity, issuing forth in March and April. Occasionally they are said to kill sheep or goats, often wantonly, apparently, as they do not feed upon them. They litter in April and May, the female having generally two cubs. This bear does not climb trees well."

The next three species belong to the group of Sun Bears; *Helarctos* of some authors.

No. 164. URSUS (HELARCTOS) TORQUATUS *vel* TIBETANUS.

The Himalayan Black Bear (Jerdon's No. 90).

NATIVE NAME.—*Bhalu*, Hind.; *Thom*, Bhot.; *Sona*, Lepcha.

HABITAT.—The Himalayas, Nepal, Assam, Eastern Siberia, and China.

DESCRIPTION.—Entirely black, with the exception of a broad white V-shaped mark on the chest and a white chin. Neck thick, head flattened; ears large; claws very long and curved; fur short; body and head more slender than the preceding species.

Jerdon remarks that the specific name of this bear is unfortunate, since it is rare in Thibet. However the more appropriate specific name *torquatus* is now more generally adopted. It seems to be common in all the Himalayan ranges, where it is to be found from 5000 to 12,000 feet. Jerdon says it lives chiefly on fruit and roots, apricots, walnuts, apples, currants, &c., and also on various grains, barley, Indian corn, buckwheat, &c., and in winter on acorns, climbing the oak trees and breaking down the branches. They are not afraid of venturing near villages, and destroy not only garden stuff, but—being, like all bears, fond of honey—pull down the hives attached to the cottages of the hill people. "Now and then they will kill sheep, goats, &c., and are said occasionally to eat flesh. This bear has bad eyesight, but great power of smell, and if approached from windward is sure to take alarm. A wounded bear will sometimes show fight, but in general it tries to escape. It is said sometimes to coil itself into the form of a ball, and thus roll down steep hills if frightened or wounded." If cornered it attacks savagely, as all bears will, and the face generally suffers, according to Jerdon; but I have noticed this with the common Indian Sloth Bear, several of the men wounded in my district had their scalps torn. He says: "It has been noticed that if caught in a noose or snare, if they cannot break it by force they never have the intelligence to bite the rope in two, but remain till they die or are killed." In captivity this bear, if taken young, is very quiet, but is not so docile as the Malayan species.*

* Since writing the above, the following letter appeared in *The Asian* of May 11, 1880:—

"THE HIMALAYAN BLACK BEAR.

"SIR,—Mr. Sterndale, in the course of his interesting papers on the Mammalia of British India, remarks of *Ursus Tibetanus,* commonly known as the Himalayan Black Bear, that 'a wounded one will sometimes show fight, but in general it tries to escape.' This description is not, I think, quite correct. As it would lead one to suppose that this bear is not more savage than any other wild animal—the nature of most of the *feræ* being to try to escape when wounded, *unless* they see the hunter who has fired at them, when many will charge at once, and desperately. The Himalayan Black Bear will not only do this *almost invariably*, but often attacks men without any provocation whatever, and is altogether about the most fierce, vicious, dangerous brute to be met with either in the hills or plains of India. They inflict the most horrible wounds, chiefly with their paws, and generally—as Mr. Sterndale states—on the face and head. I have repeatedly met natives in the interior frightfully mutilated by encounters with the Black Bear, and cases in which Europeans have been killed by them are by no means uncommon. These brutes are totally different in their dispositions to the Brown Bear (*Ursus Isabellinus*), which, however desperately wounded, will never charge. I believe there is no case on record of a hunter being charged by a Brown Bear; or even of natives, under any circumstances, being attacked by one; whereas every one of your readers who has ever marched in the Himalayas must have come across many victims of the ferocity of *Ursus Tibetanus*. As I said before, this brute often, unwounded, attacks man without any provocation whatever. Two cases that I know of myself may not be without interest. An officer shooting near my camp was stalking some thar. He was getting close to them, when a Black Bear rushed out at him from behind a large rock on his right and above him. He was so intent on the thar, and the brute's rush was so sudden, that he had barely time to pull from the hip, but he was fortunate enough to kill the animal almost at his feet. I heard this from him on the morning after it happened. On another occasion, I was shooting in Chumba with a friend. One evening he encamped at a village, about which there was, as usual, a little cultivation on terraces, and a good many apricot-trees. Lower down the khud there was dense jungle. The villagers told us that a Black Bear had lately been regularly visiting these trees, and generally came out about dusk, so that if we would go down and wait, we should be pretty sure of a shot. We went, and took up positions behind trees, about 200 yards apart, each of us having a man from the village with us. Intervening jungle prevented us from seeing each other. I had not been at my post more than ten minutes when I was startled by loud shrieks and cries from the direction of my companion. No shot was fired, and the coolie with me said that the bear had killed some one. In less than a minute I had reached the spot where I had left my friend. He, and the man with him, had disappeared; but, guided by the shrieks, which still continued, I made my way into the thick cover in front of his post, and about fifty yards inside it, much to my relief, came upon him, rifle in hand, standing over the dead body of a man, over which two people—the coolie that had been with my friend and an old woman—were weeping, and shrieking loudly, 'Look out!' said he, as I came up, 'the bear has just killed this fellow!' The first thing to be done was to carry him out into the open. I helped to do this, and directly I touched him I felt that he was stone cold, and a further examination showed he must have been dead some hours. That he had

In *The Asian* of January 7th, 1879, page 68, a correspondent ("N. F. T. T.") writes that he obtained a specimen of this bear which was coal black throughout, with the exception of a dark dirty yellow on the lower lip, but of the usual crescentic white mark she had not a trace. This exceptional specimen was shot in Kumaon. Robinson, in his 'Account of Assam,' states that these bears are numerous there, and in some places accidents caused by them are not unfrequent.

All the Sun Bears are distinguished for their eccentric antics, conspicuous among which is the gift of walking about on their hind legs in a singularly human fashion. Those in the London Zoological Gardens invariably attract a crowd. They struggle together in a playful way, standing on their hind legs to wrestle. They fall and roll, and bite and hug most absurdly.

Captain J. H. Baldwin, in his 'Large and Small Game of Bengal,' puts this bear down as not only carnivorous, but a foul feeder. He says: On my first visit to the hills I very soon learnt that this bear was a flesh-eater, so far as regards a sheep, goats, &c., but I could hardly believe that he would make a repast on such abominations (i.e. carrion), though the paharies repeatedly informed me that such was the case. One day, however, I saw a bear busy making a meal off a bullock that had died of disease, and had been thrown into the bed of a stream." In another page Captain Baldwin states that the Himalayan Bear is a good swimmer; he noticed one crossing the River Pindur in the flood, when, as he remarks, "no human being, however strong a swimmer, could have stemmed such a roaring rapid."

---

been killed by a bear was also very evident. He was naked to the waist, and had been cutting grass. His bundle lay by him, and the long curved kind of sickle that the hillmen used to cut grass with was stuck in his girdle, showing that he had not had time to draw it to strike one blow in his defence. The mark of the bear's paw on his left side was quite distinct. This had felled him to the ground, and then the savage brute had given him one bite—no more, but that one had demolished almost the whole of the back of his head, and death must have been instantaneous. The man had apparently cut his load of grass, and was returning with it to the village, when he disturbed the bear, which attacked him at once. The old woman was his mother, and the coolie with J—— some relation. Her son having been away all day, I suppose the old woman had gone to look for him. She found his body, as described, just below J——'s post, and at once set up a lamentation which brought the coolie, J——'s attendant, down to her, and J—— following himself, thought at first that the man had been killed then and there. There was such a row kicked up that no bear came near the apricots that night, and the next day we had to march, as our leave was up. I have heard of many other cases of the Black Bear attacking without any provocation, and from what I know of the brute I quite believe them; and, after all, the animal is not worth shooting. Their skins are always poor and mangy, and generally so *greasy* that they are very difficult to keep until you can make them over to the dresser. The skin of the Snow or Brown Bear, on the other hand, particularly if shot early in the season, is a splendid trophy, and forms a most beautiful and luxurious rug, the fur being extremely soft, and several inches in depth. "SPINDRIFT.

No. 165. URSUS (HELARCTOS) GEDROSIANUS.

Baluchistan Bear.

NATIVE NAME.—*Mamh.*

HABITAT.—Baluchistan.

DESCRIPTION.—Fur ranging from brown to brownish-black, otherwise as in last species.

This is a new species, brought to notice by Mr. W. T. Blanford, and named by him. The skull of the first specimen procured was scarcely distinguishable from that of a female of *Ursus torquatus*, and he was for a time apparently in doubt as to the distinctness of the species, taking the brown skin as merely a variety; but a subsequently received skull of an adult male seems to prove that it is a much smaller animal.

No. 166. URSUS (HELARCTOS) MALAYANUS.

The Bruang or Malayan Sun Bear.

NATIVE NAME.—*Wet-woon*, Arracan.

HABITAT.—Burmah, Malay Peninsula and adjacent islands.

DESCRIPTION.—Smaller than *U. torquatus*, not exceeding four and a half feet in length. Fur black, brownish on the nose; the chest marked with a white crescent, or, in the Bornean variety, an orange-coloured heart-shaped patch; the claws are remarkably long; mouth and lower jaw dirty white; the lower part of the crescent prolonged in a narrow white streak down to the belly, where it is widened out into a large irregular spot. Marsden, in his 'History of Sumatra,' published towards the end of the last century, speaks of this bear under the name of *Bruang* (query: is our *Bruin* derived from this?), and mentions its habit of climbing the cocoa-nut trees to devour the tender part, or cabbage.

It is more tamable and docile than the Himalayan Sun Bear, and is even more eccentric in its ways. The one in the London "Zoo," when given a biscuit, lies down on its back, and passes it about from fore to hind paws, eyeing it affectionately, and making most comical noises as it rolls about. Sir Stamford Raffles writes of one which was in his possession for two years:—"He was brought up in the nursery with the children; and when admitted to my table, as was frequently the case, gave a proof of his taste by refusing to eat any fruit but mangosteens, or to drink any wine but champagne. The only time I ever knew him out of humour was on an occasion when no champagne was forthcoming. He was naturally of a playful and affectionate disposition, and it was never found necessary to chain or chastise him. It was usual for this bear, the cat, the dog, and a small blue mountain bird, or lory, of New Holland, to mess together and eat out of the same dish. His favourite playfellow was the dog, whose teasing and worrying was always borne, and returned with the utmost good humour and playfulness. As he grew up he became a very powerful animal, and in his rambles in the garden he would lay hold of the largest plantains, the stems of which he could scarcely embrace, and tear them up by the roots." The late General A. C. McMaster gives an equally amusing account of his pet of this species which was obtained in Burmah. "Ada," he writes, "is never out of temper, and always ready to play with any one. While she was with me, 'Ada' would not eat meat in any shape; but I was told by one of the

Ursus Malavanus.

ship's officers that another of the same species, 'Ethel' (also presented by me to the Committee of the People's Park of Madras, and by them sent to England), while coming over from Burmah killed and devoured a large fowl put into her cage. I do not doubt the *killing*, for at that time 'Ethel' had not long been caught, and was a little demon in temper, but I suspect that, while attention was taken off, some knowing lascar secured the body of the chicken, and gave her credit for having swallowed it. 'Ada's' greatest delight was in getting up small trees; even when she was a chubby infant I could, by merely striking the bark, or a branch some feet above her head, cause her to scramble up almost any tree. At this time poor 'Ada,' a Burman otter, and a large white poodle were, like many human beings of different tastes or pursuits, very fast friends." In another part he mentions having heard of a bear of this species who delighted in cherry brandy, "and on one occasion, having been indulged with an entire bottle of this insinuating beverage, got so completely intoxicated that it stole a bottle of blacking, and drank off the contents under the impression that they were some more of its favourite liquor. The owner of the bear told me that he saw it suffering from this strange mixture, and evidently with, as may easily be imagined, a terrible headache."

So much for the amusing side of the picture, now for the other.

Although strictly frugivorous, still it has been known to attack and devour man in cases of the greatest want, and it also occasionally devours small animals and birds, in the pursuit of which, according to Dr. Sal Müller, it prefers those that live on a vegetable diet. The Rev. Mr. Mason, in his writings about Burmah, says "they will occasionally attack man when alone;" he instances a bear upsetting two men on a raft, and he goes on to add that "last year a Karen of my acquaintance in Tonghoo was attacked by one, overcome, and left by the bear for dead." In this case there was no attempt to devour, and it may have been, as I have often observed with the Indian Sloth Bear, that such attacks are made by females with young.

Dr. Sal Müller states: "in his native forests this bear displays much zeal and ingenuity in discovering the nests of bees, and in extracting their contents by means of his teeth from the narrow orifices of the branches of the trees in which they are concealed."

The next species constitutes the genus *Melursus* of Meyer or *Prochilus* of Illiger. It is an awkward-shaped beast, from which it probably derives its name of "Sloth Bear," for it is not like the sloth in other respects. It has long shaggy hair, large curved claws (which is certainly another point of resemblance to the sloth), and a very much elongated mobile snout. Another peculiarity is in its dentition; instead of six incisors in the upper jaw it has only four.

Blyth, in his later writings, adopts Illiger's generic name *Prochilus*.

NO. 167. URSUS (MELURSUS) LABIATUS.

The Common Indian Sloth Bear.

NATIVE NAMES.—*Bhalu*, Hind.; *Reench*, Hind.; *Riksha*, Sanscrit; *Aswail*, Mahr.; *Elugu*, Tel.; *Kaddi* or *Karadi*, Can.; *Yerid* or *Asol* of the Gonds; *Banna* of the Coles.

HABITAT.—All over the peninsula of India. Blyth says it is not found in Burmah.

DESCRIPTION.—General shape of the ursine type, but more than usually ungainly and awkward. Hair very long and shaggy, all black, with the exception of a white V-shaped mark on the chest, and dirty whitish muzzle and tips to its feet; snout prolonged and flexible; claws very large.

SIZE.—A large animal of this species will measure from five to six feet in length, and stand nearly three feet high, weighing from fifteen to twenty stones.

Our old friend is so well known that he hardly requires description, and the very thought of him brings back many a ludicrous and exciting scene of one's jungle days. There is frequently an element of comicality

Ursus labiatus.

in most bear-hunts, as well as a considerable spice of danger; for, though some people may pooh-pooh this, I know that a she-bear with cubs is no despicable antagonist. Otherwise the male is more anxious to get away than to provoke an attack.

This bear does not hibernate at all, but is active all the year round. In the hot weather it lies all day in cool caves, emerging only at night. In March and April, when the *mohwa*-tree is in flower, it revels in the luscious petals that fall from the trees, even ascending the branches to shake down the coveted blossoms. The *mohwa* (*Bassia latifolia*) well merits a slight digression from our subject. It is a large-sized umbrageous tree, with oblong leaves from four to eight inches long, and two to four inches broad. The flowers are globular, cream coloured, with a faint greenish tint, waxy in appearance, succulent and extremely sweet, but to my taste extremely nasty, there being a peculiar disagreeable flavour which lingers long in the mouth. However not only do all animals, carnivorous as well as herbivorous, like them, but they are highly appreciated by the natives, who not only eat them raw, but dry them in the sun and thus keep them for future consumption, and also distil an extremely intoxicating spirit from them. The fresh refuse, or *marc*, after the extraction of the spirit is also attractive to animals. Some years ago I sent to Mr. Frank Buckland, for publication in *Land and Water*, an account of a dog which used to frequent a distillery for the purpose of indulging in this refuse, the result of which was his becoming completely intoxicated. This *marc*, after further fermentation, becomes intensely acid, and on one occasion I used it successfully in cleaning and brightening a massive steel and iron gate which I had constructed. I made a large vat, and filling it with this fermented refuse, put the gate in to pickle. The seeds of the *mohwa* yield an oil much prized by the natives, and used occasionally for adulterating *ghee*. The wood is not much used; it is not of sufficient value to compensate for the flower and fruit, consequently the tree is seldom cut down. When an old one falls the trunk and large limbs are sometimes used for sluices in tanks, for the heart wood is generally rotten and hollow, and it stands well under water. If you ask a Gond about the *mohwa* he will tell you it is his father and mother. His fleshly father and mother die and disappear, but the *mohwa* is with him for ever! A good *mohwa* crop is therefore always anxiously looked for, and the possession of trees coveted; in fact a large number of these trees is an important item for consideration in the assessment of land revenues. No wonder then that the villager looks with disfavour on the prowling bear who nightly gathers up the fallen harvest, or who shakes down the long-prayed-for crop from the laden boughs.

The Sloth Bear is also partial to mangos, sugar-cane, and the pods of the *amaltas* or *cassia* (*Cathartocarpus fistula*), and the fruit of the jack-tree (*Artocarpus integrifolia*).

It is extremely fond of honey, and never passes an ant-hill without digging up its contents, especially those of white ants. About twenty years ago my first experience of this was in a neighbour's garden. He had recently built himself a house, and was laying out and sowing his flower-beds with great care. It so happened that one of the beds lay over a large ants' nest, and to his dismay he found one morning a huge pit dug in the centre of it, to the total destruction of all his tender annuals, by a bear that had wandered through the station during the night. Tickell describes the operation thus: "On arriving at an ant-hill the bear scrapes away with the fore-feet till he reaches the large combs at the bottom of the galleries. He then with violent puffs dissipates the dust and crumbled particles of the nest, and sucks out the inhabitants of the comb by such forcible inhalations as to be heard at two hundred yards distant or more. Large larvæ are in this way sucked out from great depths under the soil."

Insects of all sorts seem not to come amiss to this animal, which systematically hunts for them, turning over stones in the operation.

The Sloth Bear has usually two young ones at a birth. They are born blind, and continue so till about the end of the third week. The mother is a most affectionate parent, defending her offspring with the greatest ferocity. A she-bear with cubs is always an awkward customer, and she continues her solicitude for them till they are nearly full grown. The young ones are not difficult to rear if ordinary care be taken. The great mistake that most people make in feeding the young of wild animals is the giving of pure cows' milk. I mentioned this in 'Seonee' in speaking of a bear:—

"The little brute was as savage as his elders, and would do nothing but walk to the end of the string by which he was attached to a tent peg, roll head over heels, and walk in a contrary direction, when a similar somersault would be performed; and he whined and wailed just like a child; one might have mistaken it for the puling of some villager's brat. Milford was going to give it pure cows' milk when Fordham advised him not to do so, but to mix it with one half the quantity of water. 'The great mistake people make,' he said, 'who try to rear wild animals, is to give them what they think is best for them, viz., good fresh cows' milk, and they wonder that the little creatures pine away and die, instead of flourishing on it. Cows' milk is too rich; buffalos' milk is better, but both should be mixed with water. It does not matter what the animal is: tiger-cub, fawn, or baby monkey—all require the same caution.'"

I had considerable experience in the bringing up of young things of all sorts when in the Seonee district, and only after some time learnt the proper proportions of milk and water, and also that regularity in feeding was necessary—two-thirds water to one of milk for the first month; after that half and half.

The Sloth Bear carries her cubs on her back, as do the opossums, and a singular little animal called the koala (*Phascolarctos cinereus*)—and she seems to do this for some time, as Mr. Sanderson writes he shot one which was carrying a cub as large as a sheep-dog.

In that most charming of all sporting books ever written, Campbell's 'Old Forest Ranger,' there is an amusingly-told bit with reference to this habit of cub-carrying which I am sure my readers will forgive me for extracting. Old Dr. Jock M'Phee had been knocked over by a she-bear, and is relating his grievances to Charles:—

"Well, as I was saying, I was sitting at my pass, and thinking o' my old sweethearts, and the like o' that, when a' at ance I heard a terrible stramash among the bushes, and then a wild growl, just at my very lug. Up I jumps wi' the fusee in my hand, and my heart in my mouth, and out came a muckle brute o' a bear, wi' that wee towsie tyke sitting on her back, as conciety as you please, and haudin' the grip like grim death wi' his claws. The auld bear, as soon as she seed me, she up wi' her birse, and shows her muckle white teeth, and grins at me like a perfect cannibal; and the wee deevil he sets up his birse too, and snaps his bit teeth, and tries to grin like the mither o't, with a queer auld farrant look that amaist gart me laugh; although, to tell the blessed truth, Maister Charles, I thought it nae laughing sport. Well, there was naething else for it, so I lets drive at them wi' the grit-shot, thinking to ding them baith at ance. I killed the sma' ane dead enough; but the auld one, she lets a roar that amaist deeved me, and at me she comes like a tiger. I was that frighted, sir, I did na ken what to do; but in despair I just held out the muzzle o' the fusee to fend her off, and I believe that saved my life, for she gripped it atween her teeth, dang me o'er the braid o' my back, and off she set, trailing me through the bushes like a tether-stick; for some way or other I never let go the grip I had o' the stock. I was that stupefied I hae nae recollection what happened after this, till I found mysel' sticking in the middle o' a brier-bush, wi' my breeks rived the way you see, and poor old 'Meg' smashed in bits—de'el be in her skin that did it."

Poor old Jock M'Phee! On the whole he did well to escape with but injury to his garments. I have seen several men mauled by she-bears; one of them was scalped and torn to such an extent that it was a long time before he recovered; and I always marvelled to think he got over it at all.

The British soldier is rather fond of a bear cub as a pet; and Captain Baldwin tells an amusing story of one which followed the men on to the parade ground, and quite disorganised the manœuvres by frightening the colonel's horse. In 1858 I was quartered for a time with a naval brigade; and once, when there was an alarm of the enemy, Jack went to the front with all his pets, including Bruin, which brought up the rear, shuffling along in blissful ignorance of the bubble reputation to be found at the cannon's mouth.

Although as a rule vegetarian, yet this species is not altogether free from the imputation of being a devourer of flesh when it comes in its way. In such cases it possibly has been impelled by hunger, and I doubt whether it ever kills for the sake of eating. I have known even ruminants eat meat, and in their case hunger could not have been urged as an excuse. Mr. Sanderson mentions an instance when a Barking Deer he shot was partially devoured by a bear during the night.

Very few elephants, however steady with tigers, will stand a bear. Whether it is that bears make such a row when wounded, or whether there be anything in the smell, I know not, but I have heard many sportsmen allude to the fact. A favourite elephant I had would stand anything but a bear and a pig. Few horses will approach a bear, and this is one difficulty in spearing them; and for this reason I think bear dancers should be prohibited in towns. Calcutta used to swarm with them at one time. It always makes me angry when I see these men going about with the poor brutes, whose teeth and claws are often drawn, and a cruel ring passed through their sensitive nostrils. I should like to set an old she-bear after the *bhalu-wallas*, with a fair field and no favour.

The bear rising to hug its adversary is a fallacy as far as this species is concerned; it does not squeeze, but uses its claws freely and with great effect.

I think we have now exhausted our Indian bears. Some have spoken of a dwarf bear supposed to inhabit the Lower Himalayas, but as yet it is unknown—possibly it may be the *Ailuropus*. We now come to the Bear-like animals, the next in order, being the Racoons (*Procyon*), Coatis (*Nasua*), Kinkajous (*Cercoleptes*), and the Cacomixle (*Bassaris*) of North and South America, and then our own Panda or Cat-Bear (*Ailurus fulgens*).

This, with the above-mentioned Racoons, &c., forms a small group of curious bear-like animals, mostly of small size. Externally they differ considerably, especially in their long bushy tails, but in all essential particulars they coincide. They are plantigrade, and are without a cæcum or blind gut; the skull, however it may approach to a viverrine or feline shape, has still marked arctoid characteristics. The ear passage is well marked and bony, as in that of the bear, but the bulb of the drum (*bulla tympani*) is much developed, as in the dogs and cats. The molars are more tuberculated than in the bears, resembling the hinder molars of a dog.

AILURIDÆ.

F. Cuvier, who received the first specimen of the type of this family from his son-in-law, M. Duvaucel, was not happy in his selection of a name, which would lead one to suppose that it was affixed to the cats instead of the bears. It certainly in some degree resembles the cat externally, and it has also semi-retractile claws, but in greater measure it belongs to the Arctoidea. There are only two genera as yet known —the Red Cat-Bear, *Ailurus fulgens*, and the Thibetan *Ailuropus melanoleucos*.

GENUS AILUROPUS.

This very rare and most curious animal should properly come between the bears and *Ailurus*, as it seems to form a link between the two. Such also is the idea of a naturalist friend of mine, who, in writing to me about it, expressed it as being a link between *Helarctos Malayanus* and *Ailurus fulgens*. Very little is, however, known of the creature, which inhabits the most inaccessible portions of a little-known country—the province of Moupin in Eastern Thibet. It was procured there by the Abbé David, who, after a prolonged residence in China, lived for nearly a year in Moupin, and he sent specimens of the skull, skin, &c., to M. Alphonse Milne-Edwards, from whose elaborate description in his 'Recherches sur les Mammifères' I have extracted the following notice. The original article is too long to translate *in extenso*, but I have taken the chief points.

NO. 168. AILUROPUS MELANOLEUCOS.

HABITAT.—The hilly parts Moupin, Easter Thibet.

DESCRIPTION.—The *Ailuropus* has a thick-set heavy form. His head is short, rather slender in front, but extremely enlarged in the middle and after part; the nose is small and naked at its extremity; the forehead very large and convex; the eyes are small; the ears short, wide between and rounded at the ends; neck thick and very strong; the body is squat and massive; the tail is so short as to be hardly distinguishable. The feet are short, very large, nearly of the same length, terminated by five toes very large and with rounded ends, the general conformation of which recalls in all respects those of the bears, but of which the lower parts, instead of being completely placed on the sole in walking and entirely naked or devoid of hair, are always in great measure raised, and abundantly clad with fur to almost their full extent.

On the hind feet can be noticed at the base of the toes a transverse range of five little fleshy pads, and towards the anterior extremity of the metatarsal region another naked cushion placed transversely; but between these parts, as well as the posterior two-thirds of the planta, the hair is as abundant and as long almost as on the upper part of the foot. In the fore-limbs the disposition is much the same, though the metacarpal cushion may be larger; and there is another fleshy pad without hair near the claws.

The *Ailuropus* is thus an animal not strictly plantigrade, like the Bears in general, or the same as the Polar Bear, of which the feet, although placed flat on the earth, are not devoid of hair; but, on the contrary, the *Ailuropus* resembles the *Ailurus*, which is semi-plantigrade, yet hairy under its soles.

The colouring of the *Ailuropus* is remarkable: it is white with the exception of the circumferences of the eyes, the ears, the shoulders, and the lower part of the neck which are entirely black. These stand out clearly on a groundwork of slightly yellowishwhite; the spots round the eyes are circular, and give a strange aspect to the animal; those on the shoulders represent a sort of band placed transversely across the withers, widening as they descend downwards to lower limbs. The hinder limbs are also black from the lower part of the thigh down

Ailuropus melanoleucos.

to the toes, but the haunches, as also the greater part of the tail, are as white as the back and belly; the colouring is the same in young and old. The fur is long, thick, and coarse, like that of the bears.

From the general form of the skull it would seem impossible to determine the family to which this animal belongs. In effect the head differs considerably from the *Ursidæ* and the *Mustelidæ*, and presents certain resemblances to that of the hyæna; but there are numerous and important particulars which indicate a special zoological type, and it is only by an inspection of the dental system that the natural affinities of the *Ailuropus* can be determined.

In the upper jaw the incisors are, as usual, in three pairs. They are remarkable for their oblique direction; the centre ones are small and a little widened at the base; the second pair are stronger and dilated towards the cutting edge; the external incisors are also strong and excavated outside to admit the canines of the lower jaw. The canines are stout, but short, with a well-marked blunt ridge down the posterior side, as in the Malayan bears.

The molars are six in number on each side, of which four are premolars, and two true molars. The first premolar, situated behind, a little within the line of the canine, is very small, tuberculiform, and a little compressed laterally. The second is strong and essentially carnassial; it is compressed laterally and obliquely placed. It is furnished with three lobes: the first lobe is short, thick, and obtuse; the second is raised, triangular and with cutting edges; the third of the size of the first, but more compressed—in short, a double-fanged tooth. This molar differs considerably from the corresponding tooth of the bear by its form and relative development, since in that family it is one-fanged, very low and obtuse. On the contrary, it approaches to that of the hyænas and felines. With the panda (*Ailurus fulgens*) the corresponding premolar is equally large, double-fanged and trenchant, but the division in lobes is not so marked.

The third or penultimate molar of the *Ailuropus* is larger and thicker than the preceding, divided in five distinct lobes—three outer ones in a line, and two less projecting ones within.

The last premolar is remarkably large; it is much larger behind than in front, and its crown is divided into six lobes, of which five are very strong; the three external ones are much developed and trenchant, the centre one being the highest and of a triangular shape. Of the internal lobes, the first one is almost as large as the external ones; the second is very small, almost hidden in the groove between the last mentioned; and the third, which is very large, rounded and placed obliquely inwards in front, and outwards behind. Professor Milne-Edwards remarks that he knows not amongst the carnivora a similar example of a tooth so disposed. That of *Ailurus* shows the least difference, that is to say it is nearest in structure, having also six lobes, but more thick-set or depressed.

The true molars are remarkable for their enormous development: the first is almost square, with blunt rounded cusps, four-fanged, and presenting a strange mixture of characteristics, in its outward portion resembling an essentially carnivorous type, and its internal portion that of molars intended to triturate vegetable substances. Amongst bears, and especially the Malayan bears, this character is presented, but in a less striking degree; the panda resembles it more, with certain restrictions, but the most striking analogy is with the genus *Hyænarctos*.

The last molar is peculiar in shape, longer than broad, and is tuberculous, as in the bears, but it differs in this respect from the pandas, in which the last molar is almost a repetition of the preceding one, and its longitudinal diameter is less than its transverse.

In the lower jaw the first premolar, instead of being small and tuberculate, as its corresponding tooth in the upper jaw, is large, double-fanged, trenchant and tri-lobed, resembling, except for size, the two following ones. The second is not inserted obliquely like its correspondent in the upper jaw, its axis is in a line with that of its neighbours; tricuspidate, the middle lobe being the highest. The third premolar is very large, and agrees with its upper one, excepting the lobule on the inner border.

The first true molar is longer than broad, and wider in front; the crown, with five conical tubercles in two groups, separated by a transverse groove; the next molar is thicker and stouter than the preceding one, and the last is smaller, and both much resemble those of the bears, and differ notably from the pandas.

From what M. Milne-Edwards describes, we may briefly epitomise that the pre-molarial dentition of the *Ailuropus* is ailuroid or feline, and that the true molars are arctoid or ursine.

The skull is remarkable for the elongation of the cranium and the elevation of the occipital crest, for the shortness of the muzzle, for the depression of the post-frontal portion, and for the enormous development of the zygomatic arches. In another part M. Milne-Edwards remarks that there is no carnivorous animal of which the zygomatic arches are so developed as in the *Ailuropus*. He states that it inhabits the most inaccessible mountains of Eastern Thibet, and it never descends from its retreats to ravage the fields, as do the Black Bears; therefore it is difficult to obtain. It lives principally on roots, bamboos and other vegetables; but we may reasonably suppose from its conformation that it is carnivorous at times, when opportunity offers, as are some of the bears, and as is the *Ailurus*. I have dwelt at some length on this animal, though not a denizen of India proper; but it will be a prize to any of our border sportsmen who come across it on the confines of Thibet, and therefore I have deemed it worthy of space.

SIZE.—From muzzle to tail, about four feet ten inches; height about twenty-six inches.

GENUS AILURUS.

No. 169. AILURUS FULGENS.

The Red Cat-Bear (*Jerdon's No.* 92).

NATIVE NAMES.—*Wah*, Nepal; *Wah-donka*, Bhot.; *Sunnam* or *Suknam*, Lepch.; *Negalya*, *Ponya* of the Nepalese (*Jerdon*). In the Zoological Gardens in London it is called the *Panda*, but I am unable just now to state the derivation of this name.

HABITAT.—Eastern Himalayas and Eastern Thibet.

Ailurus fulgens.

DESCRIPTION.—"Skull ovate; forehead arched; nose short; brain case ovate, ventricose; the zygomatic arches very large, expanded; crown bent down behind" (*Gray*). The lower jaw is very massive, and the ascending ramus unusually large, extending far above the zygomatic arch, forming almost a right angle with equal arms. Hodgson's description is: "Ursine arm; feline paw; profoundly cross-hinged, yet grinding jaw, and purely triturative and almost ruminant molar of *Ailurus*; tongue smooth; pupil round; feet enveloped in woolly socks with leporine completeness." It walks like the marten; climbs and fights with all the four legs at once, like the *Paradoxuri*, and does not employ its forefeet—like the racoon, coatis, or bears—in eating."

Jerdon's outward description is: "Above deep ochreous-red; head and tail paler and somewhat fulvous, displayed on the tail in rings; face, chin, and ears within white; ears externally, all the lower surface and the entire limbs and tip of tail jet-black; from the eye to the gape a broad vertical line of ochreous-red blending with the dark lower surface; moustache white; muzzle black."

The one at present in the London "Zoo" is thus described: "Rich red-chestnut in colour on the upper surface, jet black as to the lower surface, the limbs also black, the snout and inside of ears white; the tail bushy, reddish-brown in colour and indistinctly ringed."

SIZE.—Head and body 22 inches; tail 16; height about 9; weight about 8 lbs.

Jerdon has epitomised Hodgson's description of the habits of this animal as follows: "The Wah is a vegetivorous climber, breeding and feeding chiefly on the ground, and having its retreat in holes and clefts of rock. It eats fruits, roots, sprouts of bamboo, acorns, &c.; also, it is said, eggs and young birds; also milk and ghee, which it is said to purloin occasionally from the villages. They feed morning and evening, and sleep much in the day. They are excellent climbers, but on the ground move rather awkwardly and slowly. Their senses all appear somewhat blunt, and they are easily captured. In captivity they are placid and inoffensive, docile and silent, and shortly after being taken may be suffered to go abroad. They prefer rice and milk to all other food, refusing animal food, and they are free from all offensive odour. They drink by lapping with the tongue, spit like cats when angered, and now and then utter a short deep grunt like a young bear. The female brings forth two young in spring. They usually sleep on the side, and rolled into a ball, the head concealed by the bushy tail." (For the full account see 'Jour. As. Soc. Beng.' vol. xvi. p. 1113.)

Mr. Bartlett, who has studied the habits of the specimen in the London Gardens, says that in drinking it sucks up the fluids like a bear instead of licking it up like a dog or cat, which disagrees with what Hodgson states above. "When offended it would rush at Mr. Bartlett, and strike at him with both feet, the body being raised like a bear's, and the claws projecting."

General Hardwicke was the first to discover this animal, which he described in a paper read before the Linnæan Society on the 6th of November 1821, but it was not published for some years, and in the meanwhile M. Duvaucel sent one to M. F. Cuvier, who introduced it first to the world. Some years ago I had a beautiful skin of one offered to me for sale at Darjeeling by some Bhotias, but as it was redolent of musk and other abominations quite foreign to its innocent inodorous self, I declined to give the high price wanted for it.

SEMI-PLANTIGRADES.

These form part of the Plantigrada of Cuvier and part of the Digitigrada; they walk on their toes, but at the same time keep the wrist and heel much nearer to the ground than do the true Digitigrades, and sometimes rest on them. Of those Semi-plantigrades with which we now have to deal there are three sections, viz., the *Mustelidæ*, containing the Gluttons, Martens, Weasels, Ferrets, Grisons, &c., the *Melidæ*, *Melididæ* and *Melinidæ* of various authors: i.e. Badgers, Ratels, and Skunks; and the *Lutridæ* or Otters. Some writers bring them all under one great family, *Mustelidæ*, but the above tripartite arrangement is, I think, better for ordinary purposes. To the mind of only moderate scientific attainments, a distinct classification of well-defined groups is always an easier matter than a large family split up into many genera defined by internal anatomical peculiarities.

Of the Semi-plantigrades at large Jerdon remarks: "None of them have more than one true molar above and another below, which, however, vary much in development, and the flesh tooth is most marked in those in which the tuberculate is least developed, and *vice versa*. The great and small intestines differ little in calibre, and many of them (i.e. the family) can diffuse at will a disgusting stench." This last peculiarity is a specialty of the American members of the family, notably the skunk, of the power of which almost incredible stories are told. I remember reading not long ago an account of a train passing over a skunk, and for a time the majority of the passengers suffered from nausea in consequence. Sir John Richardson writes: "I have known a dead skunk thrown over the stockades of a trading port produce instant nausea in several women in a house with closed doors, upwards of a hundred yards distant." The secretion is intensely inflammatory if squirted in the eye.

MELIDIDÆ; OR, BADGER-LIKE ANIMALS.

This group is distinguished by a heavier form, stouter limbs, coarse hair, and slower action; in most the claws are adapted for burrowing. None of them are arboreal, although in olden times marvellous tales were told of the wolverene or glutton as being in the habit of dropping down from branches of trees on the backs of large animals, clinging on to them and draining their life blood as they fled. Some of them are capable of emitting a noisome smell. The teledu of Java (*Mydaus meliceps*) is the worst of the family in this respect, and almost equals the skunk. It is possible that this animal may be found in Tenasserim.

GENUS ARCTONYX.

Dentition much the same as that of the Badger (*Meles*). Incisors, $\frac{6}{6}$; can., $\frac{1-1}{1-1}$; pre-molars, $\frac{3-3}{3-3}$; molars, $\frac{1-1}{1-1}$. The incisors are disposed in a regular curve, vertical in the upper jaw, obliquely inclined in the lower; canines strong, grinders compressed; general form of the badger, but stouter. Feet five-toed, with strong claws adapted for digging, that of the index finger being larger than the other.

No. 170. ARCTONYX COLLARIS.

The Hog-Badger (Jerdon's No. 93).

NATIVE NAMES.—*Balu-suar*, Hind., Sand-pig, or, as Jerdon has it, *Bhalu-soor*, Hind., i.e. Bear-pig; *Khway-too-wet-too*, Arakanese.

HABITAT.—Nepal, Sikim, Assam, Sylhet, Arakan, extending, as Dr. Anderson has observed, to Western Yunnan. The late General A. C.

Arctonyx collaris.

McMaster found it in Shway Gheen on the Sitang river in Pegu. I heard of it in the forests of Seonee in the Central Provinces, but I never came across one.

DESCRIPTION.—"Hair of the body rough, bristly, and straggling; that of the head shorter, and more closely adpressed. Head, throat, and breast yellowish white; on the upper part this colour forms a broad regularly-defined band from the snout to the occiput; ears of the same colour; the nape of the neck, a narrow band across the breast, the anterior portion of the abdomen, the extremities, a band arising from the middle of the upper lip, gradually wider posteriorly, including the eyes and ears, and another somewhat narrower arising from the lower lip, passing the cheek, uniting with the former on the neck, are deep blackish-brown" (*Horsfield*). The tail is short, attenuated towards the end, and covered with rough hairs.

SIZE.—From snout to root of tail, 25 inches; tail, 7 inches; height at the rump, 12 inches.

M. Duvaucel states that "it passes the greatest part of the day in profound somnolence, but becomes active at the approach of night; its gait is heavy, slow, and painful; it readily supports itself erect on its hind feet, and prefers vegetables to flesh."

Jerdon alludes to all this, and adds, "one kept in captivity preferred fruit, p'antains, &c., as food, and refused all kinds of meat. Another would eat meat, fish, and used to burrow and grope under the walls of the bungalow for worms and shells." My idea is *Balu-suar*, or Sand-pig is the correct name, although *Bhalu-suar* or Bear-pig may hit off the appearance of the animal better, but its locality has always been pointed out to me by the Gonds in the sandy beds of rivers in the bamboo forests of Seonee; and Horsfield also has it *Baloo-soor*, Sand-pig.

Bewick, who was the first to figure and describe it, got, as the vulgar phrase hath it, the wrong pig by the lug, as he translates it *Sand-bear*. McMaster also speaks of those he saw as being in deep ravines on the Sitang river.

The stomach of Arctonyx is simple; there is no cæcum, as is the case also with the bears; the liver has five lobes; under the tail it has glands, as in the Badgers, secreting a fatty and odorous substance.

No. 171. ARCTONYX TAXOIDES.

The Assam Badger.

HABITAT.—Assam and Burmah.

DESCRIPTION.—Smaller than the last, with longer and finer fur, narrower muzzle, smaller ears, shorter tail, and more distinct markings. The measurement of the respective skulls show a great difference. The length of a skull of a female of this species given by Dr. Anderson is 4·75 inches against 6·38 of a female of *A. collaris*. The breadth across the zygomatic arch is 2·38 against 3·64 of *A. collaris*. The breadth of the palate between the molars is only 0·81 against 1·07.

GENUS MELES.

SUB-GENUS TAXIDIA.

This sub-genus is that of the American type of Badger, to which Hodgson, who first described the Thibetan *T. leucurus*, supposed his species to belong; but other recent naturalists, among whom are Drs. Gray and Anderson, prefer to class it as *Meles*. Hodgson founded his classification on the dentition of his specimen, but Blyth has thrown some doubt on its correctness, believing that the skull obtained by Hodgson with the skin was that of *Meles albogularis*. Hodgson, however, says: "from the English Badger type of restricted *Meles* our animal may be at once discriminated without referring to skulls by its inferior size, greater length of tail, and partially-clad planta or foot-sole."

NO. 172. MELES (TAXIDIA) LEUCURUS.

The Thibetan White-tailed Badger.

NATIVE NAME.—*Tampha*.

HABITAT.—The plains of Thibet.

DESCRIPTION.—Fur long, flaccid, dark iron-grey and white mixed; hair long, white, with a broad sub-lunate black band and a white tip; under fur abundant, long, white; a streak on each side of the forehead blackish grey, varied; chin, throat, legs and under side of the body black; tail, sides of head, and body whitish."—*Gray*.

The aspect, according to Hodgson, is entirely that of a long-tailed Badger (Gray remarks: "it most resembles the European animal"), with somewhat smaller head, with longer, finer fur than usual; the entire sole of the foot is not naked, but only about two-thirds, and the toe-pads are very much developed, thus raising the powerful long fossorial claws from the ground in walking.

SIZE.—Total length 37 inches, of which the tail, with the hair, is 10 inches, and without the hair 7 inches; the longest hair of the body is 4½ inches.

There is not much known about the *Tampha*. According to what Hodgson was able to gather concerning his habits, "he dwells in the more secluded spots of inhabited districts, makes a comfortable, spacious and well-arranged subterraneous abode, dwells there in peace with his mate, who has an annual brood of two to four young, molests not his neighbour, defends himself if compelled to it with unconquerable resolution, and feeds on roots, nuts, insects and reptiles, but chiefly the two former—on vegetables, not animals—a point of information confirmed by the prevalent triturant character of the teeth." The colouring of this animal is almost identical with the English badger, only that his tail is longer and whiter.

No. 173. MELES ALBOGULARIS.

The White-throated Thibetan Badger.

HABITAT.—Thibet.

DESCRIPTION.—Smaller and much less tufted ears than the last species; a shorter and much less bushy tail; and the fur shorter and coarser, though of finer texture than in the European badger, with much woolly hair at its base. Both the English badger and *M. leucurus* are black throated; this one is white throated. The English animal has a broad band of brownish-black, which begins between the muzzle and the eye, and runs through the eye and ear till it fades off on the neck; the space of white between these two bands on the forehead runs back and contracts behind the ears. In the Thibetan animal it contracts just behind the eyes, and is continued as a faint narrow streak only as far as the ears. In the English one the cheeks are broadly white between the eye-band and the black throat; in the Thibetan there is a little white below the eye, and this is bordered by a narrow black stripe, beneath which is the white throat.

There is another Thibetan badger mentioned by Professor Milne-Edwards in his 'Recherches sur les Mammifères,' a white-throated one, *M. obscurus*, but it appears to be the same as *M. albogularis*.

GENUS MELLIVORA.

Tubercular grinder transverse; flesh-tooth larger, with a small internal lobe, and with a single tubercle; lower flesh-tooth tricuspidate, sharp-edged; head depressed; nose blunt; ears not visible externally; body stout, depressed; legs short, and strong; feet plantigrade, five-toed; front claws elongated and strong; the bald sole of the hind foot occupying the whole under surface, only slightly divided across about one-third of its length from the front; tail very short, with powerfully offensive glands; it has a thick loose skin and a subcutaneous layer of fat, which doubtless protect it from stings of bees, on which this genus is supposed to feed whenever it can.

No. 174. MELLIVORA INDICA.

The Indian Ratel or Honey-Badger (*Jerdon's No.* 94).

NATIVE NAME.—*Biju*, Hind.; *Biyu-khawar*, Telegu; *Tavakaradi*, Tamil; *Bajru-bhal*, at Bhagulpore (Santali?); *Bharsiah*, Nepalese.

HABITAT.—Throughout India.

DESCRIPTION.—The upper half of its body is ashy-grey; the lower half, muzzle, limbs, and tail black; the general appearance is that of a black animal with a grey cloak on its back. The only difference between the Indian and the Cape Ratel is, that the grey cloak of the latter has a conspicuous white border which is wanting in the Indian species; the tail also of the latter is shorter, otherwise they are the same, and were for a long time considered the same.

SIZE.—Head and body, 26 to 32 inches; tail, 5 to 6 inches.

Jerdon says it is chiefly found in hilly districts, and that he has not found it in Lower Bengal nor on the Malabar coast. In Central India it is not uncommon. It has got a reputation for digging into graves, and is called in some parts "the grave-digger;" but I do not believe in its carnivorous propensities to this extent; it lives principally on small fry,

Mellivora Indica.

insects, and small animals, honey and vegetable food. Jerdon says it is destructive to poultry, which is probable, for it will eat small birds. Both it and the Cape species will eagerly look out for bees, but it is not to be supposed, as some books would make out, that bees and honey form the staple diet. Its thick and loose skin, the stiffness of the hair above, and the layer of fat below, effectually preserve it from the effects of the stings. The tail glands contain a very strong and pungent secretion.

Some years ago, before I knew exactly what they were, the Ratels in the London Zoological Gardens used to interest me greatly. They had a low cage, on the ground I think, and their peculiar antics never failed to draw a crowd. They used to run round in an idiotic sort of way, and always at one point gravely turn head over heels and then proceed as before and repeat. In Cassell's 'Natural History' this is alluded to, only the writer says that now they are in fresh quarters, and the flitting seems to have disturbed them. He adds: "We have often watched one of them run round and round the cage in the usual purposeless manner of captive animals, but with this peculiarity: when he reached a particular corner of the den, he quietly, and without effort, turned head over heels, and then went on again. On one occasion, after he had been doing this with great regularity for some rounds he seemed to become abstracted, and passed the usual spot without the somersault; when, however, he had proceeded a few paces he recollected himself, stopped for a moment, returned to the exact place, turned over as usual, and proceeded without further let or hindrance." The African species is said to live largely on bees—I suppose ground bees, such as our English humble bee, for these animals are not arboreal—and it is said to exhibit great skill in tracking the flying insects to their nest. "Sparrman states that it seats itself on a hillock to look for the bees, and shades its eyes with one forepaw against the rays of the setting sun." Here is something for our Indian naturalists to observe. Some other animals are said to do the same; whether the Biju does it or not I cannot say. McMaster says of it: "Two that I saw in confinement appeared very good-tempered, and much more playful than tame bears would have been. They were, I think, fed entirely upon vegetables, rice and milk." This animal is the same as Hodgson's *Ursitaxus inauritus*, the *Bharsiah* which figures as a separate genus in Cuvier. The skull is very like that of the wolverenes in general form.

GENUS GULO—THE GLUTTON OR WOLVERENE.

This animal was placed by Linnæus among the *Ursidæ*, and is classed by some with the *Melididæ*, but its dentition is more that of the Martens, which occupy the next group. The true Glutton (*Gulo luscus*) is not known in India, but we have some so-called Wolverenes (*Helictis*) to which I shall presently allude. Still a few remarks about the typical animal, which is by no means an uninteresting creature, may not be out of place. The Glutton inhabits a wide tract of country in the Northern Hemisphere, the colder regions of Europe, Asia, and America; it is abundant in Siberia and Kamschatka, and is the pest of the trappers in North America. Fabulous stories were told of this animal in olden days, some of which are still propagated at the present time. It was supposed to be of insatiable appetite, and to attack its prey (deer, &c.) by dropping down from the branch of a tree on to the back of its victim, and to eat its way into a vital part, whilst being carried along—a decided fallacy, for neither the Glutton nor our Indian species of *Helictis* are arboreal in their habits. Then it was accused of eating to such a pitch of distention that it had to squeeze itself between two close-growing trees for relief ere it returned again to the repast. There is no doubt, however, that it is to a great extent voracious and extremely cunning; and what it cannot eat it will carry off and hide. The trappers complain bitterly of it, and spare no pains to kill every one they can come across; but it is not easily to be caught, and only a very cunningly-devised bait will succeed.

Were I to relate some of the stories recorded of this animal I might get accused, if not of being a romancer myself, at all events of being a too credulous propagator of other people's romances. It is told of it that it will discover hidden stores, and, digging them up out of the snow, carefully smooth the surface over again; that it will avoid every trap set for itself, and, going round to the back of spring guns, gnaw through the string connected with the trigger before it drags away the bait. It follows up the lines laid down by the trappers, taking the martens out, and devouring them, or hiding what it cannot eat, and by wearying out the patience of the hunters, compel them to strike a new "marten-road."

It is said by Dr. Coues to possess a singular habit of sitting down on its haunches, shading its eyes with a forepaw, and gazing earnestly at the approaching enemy before it takes to flight. I have already alluded to the Cape ratel doing this on the look-out for bees. The Indian form of Wolverene is a slighter and much smaller animal, with a still more weasel-like appearance. The Glutton is comparatively a large beast, the body being about 2½ feet, and the tail 10 inches; the *Helictis* is only half the size, and there is a slight difference in the dentition.

GENUS HELICTIS.

"Head tapering; nose acute, conical; muzzle bald, obliquely truncated; other side hairy, with a central groove; nostrils inferior; ears ovate; body slender; legs short; toes 5·5; front claws elongate, curved; hinder short and acute; sole of foot hairy behind, bald in front, and rhombic for half the length of the foot, with three large oblong pads on the front, and three small ones on the hinder edge; toes elongate; thumb short; fur black, like *Herpestes;* tail moderate, sub-cylindrical; teeth, 38; pre-molars, $\frac{4-4}{4-4}$; grinders, $\frac{5}{6}$."—*Gray.*

There are four species of this genus, and of these two come within the geographical limits of these papers, viz., *Helictis Nipalensis* and *H. moschata;* the third, *H. orientalis*, belongs to Java; and the fourth, *H. subaurantiaca*, to Formosa.

No. 175. HELICTIS NIPALENSIS.

The Nepal Wolverene (Jerdon's No. 95).

NATIVE NAME.—*Oker*, Nepalese; *Kyoung-pyan*, Arakanese.

HABITAT.—Nepal, Arakan, and Pegu.

DESCRIPTION.—Hodgson, who first described this animal in the 'Journal of the Asiatic Society of Beng.' (vol. v. pp. 237–38), says: "Above earthy brown; below, with the edge of the upper lip, the insides of the limbs, and terminal half of the tail, yellow; a white mesial stroke from the nape to the hips, and a white band across the forehead, spreading on the cheeks, and confluent with the pale colour of the animal's lower surface; head and body vermi-formed; digits and nails of the anterior extremities stronger; half way from the os calcis to the fingers hairy; fur of two sorts and abundant, but not lengthened, nor harsh, nor annulated; tail cylindrico-tapered, pointed, half the length of the animal." He goes on to add: "The anterior limbs are decidedly fossorial, and the hinder suited for walking in a sub-plantigrade manner; both wholly unfitted for rapatory or scansorial purposes."

SIZE.—Head and body 16 inches; tail 7½ inches, 9 inches, including hair.

The habits of this animal are nocturnal. Swinhoe mentions this in his account of the Formosan species, and Dr. Anderson relates that he is aware that the Nepal one is similar in its ways, and that it not unfrequently enters Bhotia huts at night; and on one occasion he killed one in a Bhotia hut, thinking it was a large rat, greatly to the chagrin of his host, who informed him that the animal was in the habit of visiting him nightly, and was most useful in destroying cockroaches and other insects.

No. 176. HELICTIS MOSCHATA.

The Chinese Wolverene.

HABITAT.—China, also Burmah (Pegu, Yunnan).

DESCRIPTION.—Similar to the last, but differing in dentition and the formation of certain points in the skull. The teeth are smaller, and the infra-orbital foramen much larger. Both the above species are noted for long skulls and palate, whereas *H. orientalis* has a short skull and palate. The following are the chief characteristics:—

Short head and palate, large teeth, *small* infra-orbital foramen = *H. orientalis.*

Long head and palate, large teeth, *small* infra-orbital foramen = *H. Nipalensis.*

Long head and palate, *small* teeth, *large* infra-orbital foramen = *H. moschata.*

Dr. Anderson obtained a specimen of this species at an elevation of 5000 feet, at Teng-yue-chow in Yunnan.

MUSTELIDÆ—MARTENS AND WEASELS.

In India the members of this family are restricted to the Weasels and Martens, but in other countries are included the Grisons, Zorillas, Skunks, &c. They are small animals of elongated form, with short legs, commonly expressed as vermiform; where the head of a weasel will go his body will follow—at least that was my experience in my boyish days, when I was particularly interested in vermin, and the gamekeeper was my first instructor in natural history. The face is rounded like a cat, but the skull behind the eye is very long and pear-shaped when viewed from above; in proportion to a cat's skull the brain case is a fourth longer. They are most sanguinary in their habits, and their agility is great, so on the whole they are most formidable to many animals, not only smaller, but in many cases four times their own size. The ferocity of the common weasel (*Putorius vulgaris*) ought to be as proverbial as its watchfulness. A case has been known of a kite carrying off one of these animals, but falling dead after a time with the large blood-vessels under the wing cut through by the savage little prisoner, who, on reaching *terra firma*, escaped apparently unhurt. I think in Wolff's admirable 'Illustrations of Natural History' this fact, related by Bell, is made the subject of a picture called "Catching a Tartar."

Most of the animals of this group are eagerly sought for on account of their fur. In Northern India the skin of one species, probably a variety of *Martes abietum*, is sold in the bazaars at Peshawur and Lahore. In 1868 I bought sufficient to line a large overcoat, which proved most comfortable in travelling in the cold weather in the Punjab, as well as in subsequent wanderings on the European continent in winter.

Dr. E. Coues, in his monograph on the North American Mustelidæ, gives the following interesting information regarding the number of skins of various species sold by the Hudson's Bay Company in London during the century 1769–1868:—

Sables, 1,240,511; otters, 674,027; wolverenes, 68,694; minks, 1,507,240; skunks, 218,653; badgers, 275,302; sea otters, 5349. In 1868, which appears to have been a prosperous year, the Company sold: Sables, 106,254; otters, 14,966; wolverenes, 1104; minks, 73,473; skunks, 6298; badgers, 1551; sea otters, 123.*

When one considers the number of those whose skins are damaged

* In the same year were sold by other firms, 22,000 otter skins and 4500 sables. See Appendix *C* for further statistics.

and cast aside, the number that fall victims to larger predatory animals, and the operations of disease, from which no animals, small or great, are free, we may form some idea of the immense multitude of these little creatures.

The ordinary divisions of the restricted Mustelidæ are the Martens (*Martes*), Pole-cats (*Putorius*), and Weasels (*Mustela*), but Gray has further subdivided them chiefly on the characteristics of the feet.

The Martens have four more teeth than the rest, which are distinguished as follows:—

Putorius.—Short ovate head; feet very hairy, especially between the pads; body stout; underside blackish.

Mustela.—Narrow, elongated head; feet very hairy between the pads; slender body; under-side yellow or white.

Vison.—Head elongate, narrow; feet slightly hairy; pads exposed; body rather slender; under-side same colour as upper.

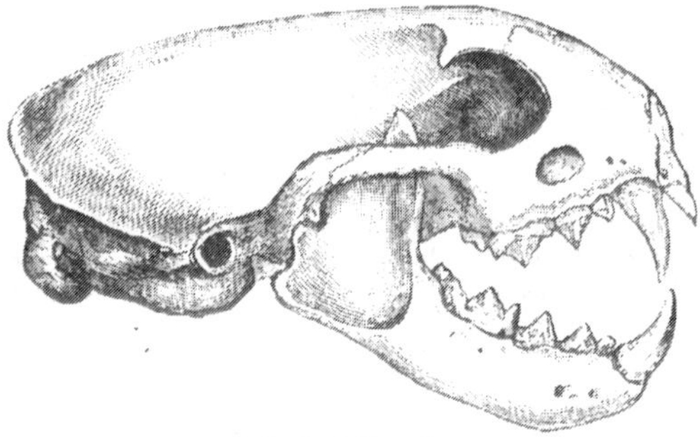

Skull of *Putorius*.

Gymnopus.—Head elongate, narrow; feet rather naked, bald beneath, between, and rather behind the pads; toes largely webbed; soles hairy behind; body slender.

It is doubtful whether these distinctions are of sufficient importance to warrant so much subdivision; and unnecessary multiplication of genera is a thing to be avoided as much as possible.

GENUS MARTES—THE MARTENS.

A more or less arboreal group of larger size, and possibly less sanguinary habits than the weasels, although in this respect I do not think there is much difference. The tail is longer, though not so long as the head and body, and it is bushy; the fur is fine and in general highly prized; the dentition differs from the typical *Mustela* in having four more teeth and an additional false molar on either side in each jaw; and the inner side of the carnassial or flesh tooth has a tubercle which is not present in the weasels; head elongate; feet very hairy; space between the pads hairy, often covering them from sight, except in the case of *Martes flavigula*, of which the soles are nude.

NO. 177. MARTES FLAVIGULA.

The White-cheeked Marten (*Jerdon's No.* 96).

NATIVE NAMES.—*Mal-sampra*, Nepalese; *Tuturala* in Kumaon; *Kusiah* in Sirmoor; *Huniah* or *Aniar*, Bhotia; *Sakku*, Lepcha.

HABITAT.—Nepal, Thibet, Kumaon, Gurhwal, Sirmoor, Assam, Burmah, Ceylon.

DESCRIPTION.—Glossy blackish brown, with the throat and breast yellow; the chin and lower parts white, from which I have preferred to call it after Pennant "the White-cheeked Marten" instead of the "yellow-throated," this characteristic belonging also to some other species. The fur seems to vary a good deal. Jerdon says of it: "The body is at times dirty brownish or chestnut brown, or brown mixed with grey, and the middle of the back is sometimes paler than the rest, or the same tint as the sides of the body. In some the top of the head is pale brown, but it is edged by a dark peripheral line, and in some there are one or more irregular dark spots between the fore-limbs."

Blyth writes of the Burmese specimens that they are "similar to the Himalayan, but differing from the Malayan race—found also in Formosa—by having much longer fur, and a wholly black cap instead of a brown cap with a black periphery." The soles are nude.

SIZE.—Head and body about 20 inches; tail, including fur, 12 inches.

This Indian Marten, according to Jerdon, is also found in Ceylon; it was, however, appparently unknown to Kellaart, nor does Sir Emerson Tennent allude to it. It is to be had in the Neilgherries, the Khasia hills, and the ranges in Arakan, as well as in the valleys of the great Himalayan chain up to 7000 or 8000 feet of elevation. It is found in pairs or in small families of five or six. If hunted it takes to trees at once, being a good climber. According to Captain the Hon. C. Shore, who observed its habits in Kumaon and Gurhwal, "its food is chiefly birds, rats, mice, hares and even young fawns of the kakur or barking-deer." He adds: "The specimen sent to the Zoological Society was brought to me in September 1828, when it was about four months old. It had been caught when not many days old, and was so tame that it was always kept loose about a well, sporting about the windlasses, posts, &c., and playing tricks with the people who came to draw water." This is the one alluded to by Jerdon as having been described by Mr. Bennett in the 'Gardens and Menageries of the Zoological Society.' *Martes Gwatkinsi* of Horsfield's Catalogue (page 99), is evidently, as Jerdon says, the same as *M. flavigula*, although the colouring is different, and is supposed to be the same animal in its summer fur, some specimens being darker than others. It is just one hundred years since this little animal was first described, the earliest record of it being in Pennant's 'History of Quadrupeds' (first edition), published in 1781. It must, however, have been known before that, for Pennant first observed it in Brooks's Menagerie in 1774, and named it the "White-cheeked Weasel," which Boddart afterwards in 1785 introduced into his 'Elenchus Animalium' under the name of *Mustela flavigula (Horsfield)*.

NO. 178. MARTES ABIETUM.

The Pine Marten.

HABITAT.—Ladakh and the Upper Himalayas, Afghanistan (?)

DESCRIPTION.—Brown; throat yellow or yellow spotted (*Gray*). Light yellowish-grey, rather deeper in a line along the back; the hair

Martes abietum.

brown; extremities blackish; chin, throat and breast white (according to Horsfield).

SIZE.—About 18 to 20 inches; tail 12 inches.

Horsfield remarks that the specimens received in the Indian Museum combine the peculiarities of the Pine and Beech Martens respectively, and lead to the conclusion that both are varieties of one species. This idea was prevalent some time ago, and the Beech Marten (*M. foina*) was supposed to be merely a variety of the Pine species, but there are certain differences in the skulls of the two animals. It is stated by the editor of my edition of Cuvier that, on examination of the crania of the two, he found that those of *M. abietum* are constantly smaller, with the zygomatic arch fully twice as strong as in the other. There is also a slight difference in the teeth, the hinder upper tubercular grinder in *M. foina* not being quite so large as in the other.

The Pine Marten has a wide distribution; the finest specimens are found in Sweden; in England it is becoming scarce, but in other parts of Europe and Asia it is common. Professor Parker and his brother write of it: "This animal is essentially arboreal in its habits, inhabiting chiefly thick coniferous woods, whence its name of Pine Marten is derived. In the branches the female makes a nest of leaves or moss, and sometimes spares herself this trouble by ejecting squirrels or wood-peckers, and occupying the vacant dwellings. For its size it is, like all the Mustelidæ, extremely ferocious and strong. It attacks and kills fawns, notwithstanding their superior size; from these down to mice nothing comes amiss to it, and nothing is safe from its attacks." It seems almost incredible that such a small animal should venture on such large game, but the same is reported of *M. flavigula;* and a much smaller creature, the Yellow-bellied Weasel, *M. kathiah*, is reported by Hodgson to attack even goats and sheep.

No. 179. MARTES TOUFŒUS.

NATIVE NAME.—*Toufee.*

HABITAT.—Thibet.

DESCRIPTION (from skins only).—General colour smoky brown, darker along the spine and on the limbs, but without marks, and paler to sordid yellowish hoary on the neck and head; head palest, except the mystaceal region and chin, which are embrowned; moustache moderate and dark brown.

SIZE.—Head and body about 20 to 22 inches.

The above description is taken from Hodgson, who had only received imperfect skins. Jerdon just alludes to it by name, but I cannot find it mentioned by any other author. As much stress cannot be laid on colouring in these animals, I feel inclined to think that it is a variety of *Martes abietum*, probably in its dark summer coat.

GENUS MUSTELA—THE WEASELS.

These are smaller animals of the true vermiform shape; the legs are very short in comparison with the body, and the neck is very thick and very long, and the head is small, so that head, neck, and body are almost equally cylindrical, and the length of the neck gives a far, set-back appearance to the forelegs, so much so that they seem to start from behind the chest instead of in front of it. The teeth are 34 in number, or four less than in the preceding genus; upper tubercular grinder transverse or broader than long; the feet are slightly webbed, covered with hair, and the space between the pads is hairy; the tail is short; fur dark above, white or yellowish beneath.

Mustela.

Some authors contend that the weasel, though commonly referred to the genus *Mustela*, should be *Putorius*, which is an instance of the disagreement which exists among naturalists. I have however followed Gray in his classification, although perhaps Cuvier, who classes the weasels and pole-cats under the genus *Putorius*, has the claim of priority. Ray applied the name of *Mustela* to the restricted weasels, and *Martes* to the martens, but Cuvier gives *Mustela* to the martens, and brings the weasels and pole-cats together under *Putorius*.

No. 180. MUSTELA (VISON: *Gray*) SUB-HEMACHALANA.

The Sub-Hemachal Weasel (*Jerdon's No.* 97).

NATIVE NAMES.—*Zimiong*, Bhotia; *Sang-king*, Lepcha; *Kran* or *Gran*, Kashmiri.

DESCRIPTION.—" Uniform bright brown, darker along the dorsal line; nose, upper lip, and forehead, with two inches of the end of the tail black-brown; mere edge of upper lip and whole of lower jaw hoary; a short longitudinal white stripe occasionally on the front of the neck, and some vague spots of the same laterally, the signs, I suspect, of immaturity; feet frequently darker than the body or dusky brown; whiskers dark; fur close, glossy and soft, of two sorts, or fine hair and soft wool, the latter and the hair basally of dusky hue, but the hair externally bright brown; head, ears, and limbs more closely clad than the body, tail more laxly, tapering to the point."—*Hodgson.*

SIZE.—Head and body about 12 inches; tail, 6 inches.

Jerdon calls this the Himalayan Weasel, but I have preferred to translate Hodgson's name, which, I confess, puzzled me for some time till I found out there was a Hemachal range in Thibet.

No. 181. MUSTELA (GYMNOPUS: *Gray*) KATHIAH.

The Yellow-bellied Weasel (*Jerdon's No.* 98).

NATIVE NAME.—*Kathia-nyal*, Nepalese.

HABITAT.—Nepal, Bhotan.

DESCRIPTION.—Dark brown; upper lip, chin, throat, chest, underside of body and front of thighs, bright yellow; tail dark brown, shorter than the body and head, tapering, and of the same colour to the tip; the soles of the hind feet bald; pads well developed, exposed.

SIZE.—Head and body, 10 inches; tail, 5 inches.

Hodgson states that a horribly offensive yellowish-grey fluid exudes from two subcaudal glands. He says that the Nepalese highly prize this little animal for its services in ridding houses of rats. It is easily tamed, and such is the dread of it common to all murine animals that not one will approach a house wherein it is domiciled. Rats and mice seem to have an instinctive sense of its hostility to them, so much so that when it is introduced into a house they are observed to hurry away in all directions, being apprised, no doubt, of its presence by the peculiar odour it emits. Its ferocity and courage are made subservient to the amusement of the rich, who train it to attack large fowls, geese, and even goats and sheep. It seizes these by the great artery of the neck, and does not quit its hold till the victim sinks exhausted from the loss of blood—a cruel pastime which one could only expect of a barbarous people.

No. 182. MUSTELA (GYMNOPUS: *Gray*) STRIGIDORSA.

The Striped Weasel (Jerdon's No. 99).

HABITAT.—Sikim.

DESCRIPTION.—Dark chestnut-brown, with a narrow streak of long yellow hairs down the back; edge of upper lip, chin, throat, chest, and a narrow stripe down the centre of the belly, yellow, or yellowish-white.

SIZE.—Head and body, 12 inches; tail, 5½ inches without the hair, 6½ inches with it.

This is similar to the last, but is slightly larger, and distinguishable by the dorsal stripe.

No. 183. MUSTELA ERMINEA.

The Ermine or Stoat.

HABITAT.—Europe, America and Asia (the Himalayas, Nepal, Thibet, Afghanistan).

DESCRIPTION.—Brown above; upper lip, chin, and lower surface of body, inside of limbs and feet yellowish-white; tail brown, with a black tip. In winter the whole body changes to a yellowish-white, with the exception of the black tip of the tail.

SIZE.—Head and body, about 10 inches; tail, 4½ inches.

This is about the best known in a general way from its fur being used as part of the insignia of royalty. The fur however only becomes valuable after it has completed its winter change. How this is done was for a long time a subject of speculation and inquiry. It is, however, now proved that it is according to season that the mode of alteration is effected. In spring the new hairs are brown, replacing the white ones of winter; in autumn the existing brown hairs turn white. Mr. Bell, who gave the subject his careful consideration, says that in Ross's first Polar expedition, a Hudson's Bay lemming (*Myodes*) was exposed in its summer coat to a temperature of 30° below zero. Next morning the fur on the cheeks and a patch on each shoulder had become perfectly white; at the end of the week the winter change was complete, with the exception of a dark band across the shoulder and a dorsal stripe.

Hodgson remarks that the Ermine is common in Thibet, where the skins enter largely into the peltry trade with China.

In one year 187,000 skins were imported into England.

No. 184. MUSTELA (VISON: *Gray*) CANIGULA.

The Hoary Red-necked Weasel.

HABITAT.—Nepal hills, Thibet.

DESCRIPTION.—Pale reddish-brown, scarcely paler beneath; face, chin, throat, sides of neck and chest white; tail half as long as body and head, concolorous with the back; feet whitish. Sometimes chest brown and white mottled, according to Gray. Hodgson, who discovered the animal, writes: "Colour throughout cinnamon red without black tip to the tail, but the chaffron and entire head and neck below hoary."

SIZE.—15½ inches; tail without hair 7½ inches, with hair 9½ inches.

No. 185. MUSTELA STOLICZKANA.

HABITAT.—Yarkand.

DESCRIPTION.—Colour pale sandy brown above; hairs light at base, white below; tail concolorous with back; small white spot close to anterior angle of each eye; a sandy spot behind the gape; feet whitish.

SIZE.—Head and body, 12·2; tail, 3 inches, including hair.

No. 186. MUSTELA (VISON) SIBIRICA.

HABITAT.—Himalayas (Thibet?); Afghanistan (Candahar).

DESCRIPTION.—Pale brown; head blackish, varied; spot on each side of nose, on upper and lower lips and front of chin, white; tail end pale brown like back, varies; throat more or less white.

This Weasel, described first by Pallas ('Specil Zool.' xiv. t. 4, f. 1.) was obtained in Candahar by Captain T. Hutton, who describes it in the 'Bengal Asiatic Society's Journal,' vol. xiv. pp. 346 to 352.

No. 187. MUSTELA ALPINA.

The Alpine Weasel.

HABITAT.—Said to be found in Thibet, otherwise an inhabitant of the Altai mountains.

DESCRIPTION.—Pale yellow brown; upper lip, chin, and underneath yellowish-white; head varied with black-tipped hairs; tail cylindrical, unicolour, not so long as head and body.—*Gray.*

No. 188. MUSTELA HODGSONI.

HABITAT.—Himalaya, Afghanistan.

DESCRIPTION.—Fur yellowish-brown, paler beneath; upper part and side of head much darker; face, chin, and throat varied with white; tail long, and bushy towards the end.

No. 189. MUSTELA (VISON) HORSFIELDI.

HABITAT.—Bhotan.

DESCRIPTION.—Uniform dark blackish-brown, very little paler beneath; middle of front of chin and lower lip white; whiskers black; tail slender, blackish at tip, half the length of head and body.

No. 190. MUSTELA (GYMNOPUS) NUDIPES.

Gymnopus leucocephalus of Gray.

HABITAT.—Borneo, Sumatra, Java, but possibly Tenasserim.

DESCRIPTION.—Golden fulvous with white head.

As so many Malayan animals are found on the confines of Burmah, and even extending into Assam, it is probable that this species may be discovered in Tenasserim.

GENUS PUTORIUS—THE POLE-CAT.

This is a larger animal than the weasel, and in form more resembles the marten, except in the shortness of its tail; the body is stouter and the neck shorter than in *Mustela;* the head is short and ovate; the feet generally hairy, and the space between the pads very much so; the under side of the body is blackish; the fur is made up of two kinds, the shorter is woolly and lighter coloured than the longer, which is dark and shining.

The disgusting smell of the common Pole-cat (*Putorius fœtidus*) is well known, and has become proverbial. In my county, as well as in many parts of England, the popular name is "foumart," which is said to be derived from "foul marten." The foumart is the special abhorrence of the game-keeper; it does more damage amongst game and poultry than any of the other *Mustelidæ*, and consequently greater pains are taken to trap and shoot it, in fact, so much so that I wonder that the animal is not now extinct in the British Isles. Professor Parker writes: "It has been known to kill as many as sixteen turkeys in a single night; and indeed it seems to be a point of honour with this bloodthirsty little creature to kill everything it can overpower, and to leave no survivors on its battle-fields." According to Bell, a female Pole-cat, which was tracked to her nest, was found to have laid up in a side hole a store of food consisting of forty frogs and two toads, all bitten through the brain, so that, though capable of living for some time, they were deprived of the power of escape. Now, this is a most wonderful instance of instinct bordering upon reason. Only the Reptilia can exist for any length of time after injury to the brain; to any of the smaller mammalia such a process as that adopted by the Pole-cat, would have resulted in instant death and speedy decomposition.

The Ferret (*Putorius furo*) is a domesticated variety of the Pole-cat, reputed to be of African origin. Certain it is that it cannot stand extreme cold like its wild cousin, and an English winter is fatal to it if not properly looked after. It inter-breeds with the Pole-cat.

Ferrets are not safe pets in houses where there are young children. Cases have been known of their attacking infants in the cradle, and severely lacerating them.

They are chiefly used for killing rats and driving rabbits out of burrows; in the latter case they are muzzled. As pets they are stupid, and show but little attachment. Forbearance as regards making its teeth meet in your fingers is, I think, the utmost you can expect in return for kindness to a ferret, and that is something, considering what a sanguinary little beast it is.

No. 191. PUTORIUS LARVATUS, *vel* TIBETANUS.

Black-faced Thibetan Pole-cat.

HABITAT.—Utsang in Thibet, also Ladakh.

DESCRIPTION.—"Tail one-third of entire length; soles clad; fur long; above and laterally sordid fulvous, deeply shaded on the back with black; below from throat backwards, with the whole limbs and tail, black; head pale, with a dark mask over the face."—*Hodgson.*

SIZE.—Head and body, 14 inches; tail, 6 inches, with hair 7 inches; palma, $1\frac{3}{4}$; planta, $2\frac{3}{8}$.

This animal, according to Gray, is synonymous with the Siberian *Putorius Eversmannii*, although the sudden contraction of the brain case in front, behind the orbit, mentioned of this species, is not perceptible in the illustration given by Hodgson of the skull of this Thibetan specimen. Horsfield, in his catalogue, states that the second specimen obtained by Captain R. Strachey in Ladakh, north of Kumaon, agreed in external character.

In some respects it is similar to the European Pole-cat, but as yet little is known of its habits.

No. 192. PUTORIUS DAVIDIANUS.

HABITAT.—Moupin in Thibet.

DESCRIPTION.—Uniform fulvous brown, yellower under the throat; upper lip and round nostrils to corner of the eye white, darker on nose and forehead.

SIZE.—Head and body about $11\frac{1}{2}$ inches; tail, $6\frac{1}{2}$ inches.

This is one of the specimens collected by the Abbé David, after whom it is named. A fuller description of it will be found in Milne-Edwards's 'Recherches sur les Mammifères,' page 343. There is also a plate of the animal in the volume of illustrations.

No. 193. PUTORIUS ASTUTUS.

HABITAT.—Thibet.

DESCRIPTION.—About the size of Ermine, but with a longer tail. Colour brown, the white of the chest tinted with yellow; tail uniform in colour, darker on head.

SIZE.—Head and body, 10 inches; tail, $4\frac{1}{5}$ inches.

This is also described and figured by Milne-Edwards.

No. 194. PUTORIUS MOUPINENSIS.

HABITAT.—Thibet.

DESCRIPTION.—Reddish-brown, white under the chin, and then again a patch on the chest.

LUTRIDÆ—THE OTTERS.

We now come to the third group of the musteline animals, the most aquatic of all the Fissipedia—the *Lutridæ* or Otters—of which there are two great divisions, the common Otters (*Lutra*) and the Sea-Otters, (*Enhydra*). With the latter, a most interesting animal in all its ways, as well as most valuable on account of its fur, we have nothing to do. I am not aware that it is found in the tropics, but is a denizen of the North Pacific. Of *Lutra* we have several species in two genera. Dr. Gray has divided the Otters into no less than nine genera on three characteristics, the tail, feet, and muzzle, but these have been held open to objection. The classification most to be depended upon is the division of the tribe into long-clawed Otters (*Lutra*), and short or rudimentary-clawed Otters (*Aonyx*). The characteristics of the skulls confirm this arrangement, as the short-clawed Otters are distinguishable from the others by a shorter and more globose cranium and larger molars, and, as Dr. Anderson says, "the inner portion of the last molar being the largest part of the tooth, while in *Lutra* the outer exceeds the inner half; the almost general absence of the first upper pre-molar; and the rudimentary claws, which are associated with much more feebly-developed finger and toe bones, which are much tapered to a point, while in *Lutra* these bones are strong and well developed." Gray has separated a genus, which he called *Pteronura*, on account of a flattened tail arising from a longitudinal ridge on each side, but this flattening of the tail is common to all the genera more or less.

All the Otters, though active on land, are still only thoroughly at home in the water, and they are therefore specially constituted for such a mode of life. They have an elongated flattened form; webbed feet with short claws; compressed and tapering tail; dense fur of two kinds, one of long brown shining hairs; the under fur short and fine, impervious to wet, and well adapted for keeping an equality of temperature; the skull is peculiar, the brain case being very long, and compressed from above downwards; the facial portion forms only about one-fourth of the

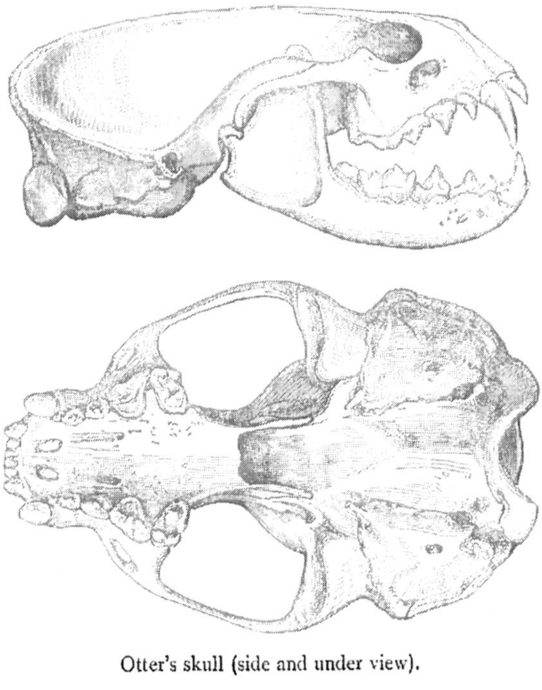

Otter's skull (side and under view).

extreme length; the teeth are strong and sharp; the upper flesh tooth very large.

Dental formula: Inc., $\frac{3-3}{3-3}$; can., $\frac{1-1}{1-1}$; pre-molars, $\frac{4-4}{3-3}$; molars, $\frac{1-1}{2-2}$.

Jerdon states that the otter has a nictitating membrane or additional semi-transparent eyelid, similar to that in the eyes of birds, which he supposes is a defence to them under water; but I have not noticed this myself, and have failed to discover it in the writings of others. I should think that the vision of the animal under water would not require obscuring by a semi-transparent membrane, which none of the marine carnivora possess, though their eyes are somewhat formed for seeing better under water than when exposed to the full light above. Some idea of the rapidity of these animals in the water may be conceived when we think that their food is almost exclusively fish, of which they sometimes kill more than they can eat. They reside in burrows, making the entrance under water, and working upwards, making a small hole for the ventilation of their chamber. The female has about four or five young ones at a time, after a period of gestation of about nine weeks, and the mother very soon drives them forth to shift for themselves in the water.

For a pretty picture of young otters at play in the water, nothing could be better than the following description from Kingsley's 'Water Babies':—

"Suddenly Tom heard the strangest noise up the stream—cooing, grunting, and whining, and squeaking, as if you had put into a bag two stock-doves, nine mice, three guinea-pigs, and a blind puppy, and left them there to settle themselves and make music. He looked up the water, and there he saw a sight as strange as the noise: a great ball rolling over and over down the stream, seeming one moment of soft brown fur; and the next of shining glass, and yet it was not a ball, for sometimes it broke up and streamed away in pieces, and then it joined again; and all the while the noise came out of it louder and louder. Tom asked the dragon-fly what it could be: but of course with his short sight he could not even see it, though it was not ten yards away. So he took the neatest little header into the water, and started off to see for himself; and when he came near, the ball turned out to be four or five beautiful creatures, many times larger than Tom, who were swimming about, and rolling, and diving, and twisting, and wrestling, and cuddling, and kissing, and biting, and scratching, in the most charming fashion that ever was seen. And if you don't believe me you may go to the Zoological Gardens (for I am afraid you won't see it nearer, unless, perhaps, you get up at five in the morning, and go down to Cordery's Moor, and watch by the great withy pollard which hangs over the back-water, where the otters breed sometimes), and then say if otters at play in the water are not the merriest, lithest, gracefullest creatures you ever saw."

Professor Parker, who also notices Kingsley's description,* states that the Canadian otter has a peculiar habit in winter of sliding down ridges of snow, apparently for amusement. It, with its companions, scambles up a high ridge, and then, lying down flat, glides headforemost down the declivity, sometimes for a distance of twenty yards.

* In fact it was his quotation that induced me to buy a copy of that most charming little book, which I recommend every one to read.—R. A. S.

"This sport they continue apparently with the keenest enjoyment, until fatigue or hunger induces them to desist."

The following are the Indian species; *Lutra nair*, *L. simung vel monticola*, *L. Ellioti*, and *L. aurobrunnea* of the long-clawed family, and *Aonyx leptonyx* of the short-clawed.

No. 195. LUTRA NAIR.

The Common Indian Otter (*Jerdon's No.* 100).

NATIVE NAMES.—*Ud* or *Ood*, *Ood-bilao*, *Panikutta*, Hindi; *Nir-nai*, Canarese; *Neeru-kuka*, Telegu; *Jal-manjer*, Mahratti.

HABITAT.—India generally, Burmah and Ceylon.

Lutra nair.

DESCRIPTION.—Hair more or less brown above, sometimes with a chestnut hue, sometimes grizzled, or with a tinge of dun; yellowish-white, or with a fulvescent tinged white below; the throat, upper lip, and sides of head are nearly white; the line of separation of upper and lower parts not very distinctly marked. Some have whitish paws.

SIZE.—Head and body, 29 to 30 inches; tail about 17 inches.

This otter, which is synonymous with *L. Indica*, *L. Chinensis* and Hodgson's *L. Tarayensis*, is well known throughout India, and indeed far beyond Indian limits. They are generally found in secluded spots, in parties of about half a dozen hunting in concert. The young ones are easily tamed, and become greatly attached if kindly treated. I had one for some time. Jerdon tells a curious story of one he had, and which used to follow him in his walks. He says: "As it grew older it took to going about by itself, and one day found its way to the bazaar and seized a large fish from a moplah. When resisted, it showed such fight that the rightful owner was fain to drop it. Afterwards it took regularly to this highway style of living, and I had on several occasions to pay for my pet's dinner rather more than was necessary, so I resolved to get rid of it. I put it in a closed box, and, having kept it without food for some time, I conveyed it myself in a boat some seven or eight miles off, up some of the numerous back-waters on this coast. I then liberated it, and, when it had wandered out of sight in some inundated paddy-fields, I returned by boat by a different route. That same evening, about nine whilst in the town about one and a-half miles from my own house, witnessing some of the ceremonials connected with the Mohurrum festival, the otter entered the temporary shed, walked across the floor, and came and lay down at my feet!" It is to be hoped Dr. Jerdon did not turn him adrift again; such wonderful sagacity and attachment one could only expect in a dog.

McMaster gives the following interesting account of otters hunting on the Chilka Lake: "Late one morning I saw a party, at least six in number, leave an island on the Chilka Lake and swim out, apparently to fish their way to another island, or the mainland, either at least two miles off. I followed them for more than half the distance in a small canoe. They worked most systematically in a semicircle, with intervals of about fifty yards between each, having, I suppose, a large shoal of fish in the centre, for every now and then an otter would disappear, and generally, when it was again seen, it was well inside the semicircle with a fish in its jaws, caught more for pleasure than for profit, as the fish, as far as I could see, were always left behind untouched beyond a single bite. I picked up several of these fish, which, as far as I can recollect, were all mullet." Kingsley notices this. The old otter tells Tom: "We catch them, but we disdain to eat them all; we just bite out their soft throats and suck their sweet juice—oh, so good!" (and she licked her wicked lips)—"and then throw them away, and go and catch another."

General McMaster also quotes from a letter by "W. C. R." in the *Field* about the end of 1868, which gives a very curious incident of a crocodile stealing up to a pack of otters fishing, and got within thirty yards; "but no sooner was the water broken by the hideous head of the reptile, than an otter, which evidently was stationed on the opposite bank as a sentinel, sounded the alarm by a whistling sort of sound. In an instant those in the water rushed to the bank and disappeared among the jungle, no doubt much to the disgust of the *mugger*."

I have not heard any one allude to the offensive glands of the Indian otter, but I remember once dissecting one and incautiously cutting into one of these glands, situated, I think, near the tail. It is now over twenty years ago, so I cannot speak with authority, but I remember the abominable smell, which quite put a stop to my researches at the time.

This otter is trained in some parts of India, in the Jessore district and Sunderbunds of Bengal, to drive fish into nets. In China a species there is driven into the water with a cord round its waist, which is hauled in when the animal has caught a fish.

No. 196. LUTRA MONTICOLA *vel* SIMUNG.

(*Jerdon's No.* 101).

HABITAT.—Nepal, Sumatra, and Borneo.

DESCRIPTION.—" The colour is more rufous umber-brown than *L. nair*, and does not exhibit any tendency to grizzling, and the under surface is only somewhat hoary, well washed with brownish; the chin and edge of the lips are whitish; and the silvery hoary on the sides of the head, on the throat, and on the under surface of the neck and of the chest is marked; the tail above and below is concolorous with the trunk. The length of the skeleton of an adult female, measured from the tip of the premaxillaries to the end of the sacral vertebræ, is 23·25, and the tail measures 17·75 inches" (*Anderson*). Of the Sumatran specimen the first notice was published in 1785 in the first edition of Marsden's 'History of Sumatra.' This otter is larger than the common Indian one, the skull of a female, as given by Dr. Anderson, exceeding in all points that of male of *Lutra nair*.

Jerdon has this as *Lutra vulgaris*, which is the common English otter, but there is a difference in the skull.

No. 197. LUTRA ELLIOTI.

HABITAT.—Southern Mahratta country.

DESCRIPTION.—The colouring is the same as the last, only a little darker; the distribution of the silvery white is the same; the muzzle is however more depressed than in the last species, and it differs from *L. nair* by a broader, more arched head, and shorter muzzle.

Dr. Anderson, who distinguishes it by the feature of its skull from the two preceding species, says: " It may be that this otter has a north-westerly distribution, and that it is the species which occurs in the lake at Mount Abu in Rajputana, and also in Sindh and in the Indus.

No. 198. LUTRA AUROBRUNNEA.

HABITAT.—Nepal.

DESCRIPTION.—Fur of a rich ferruginous brown colour, the upper surface of the head being a deeper brown than the back; the nose is bare; the ears are small and pointed posteriorily. All the strong bristles of the moustache, eyes, cheeks, and chin, are dark brown; claws as in *Lutra* (*Anderson*). Hodgson says it has a more vermiform body than the rest of Indian otters; tail less than two thirds of the body; nails and toes feebly developed (whence it is classed by Gray in the next genus); fur long and rough, rich chestnut-brown above, golden red below and on the extremities.

SIZE.—Head and body, 20 to 22 inches; tail, 12 to 13 inches.

GENUS AONYX—CLAWLESS OTTERS.

Muzzle bald, oblong; skull broad, depressed, shorter and more globose than in *Lutra*; the molars larger than in the last genus; flesh tooth larger, and with a large internal lobe; first upper premolar generally absent; feet oblong, elongate; toes slender and tapering; claws rudimentary.

No. 199. AONYX LEPTONYX.

The Clawless Otter (Jerdon's No. 102).

NATIVE NAMES.—*Chusam*, Bhotia; *Suriam*, Lepcha.

HABITAT.—Throughout the Himalayas, also in Lower Bengal and in Burmah.

DESCRIPTION.—"Above earthy brown or chestnut brown; lips, sides of head, chin, throat, and upper part of breast white, tinged with yellowish-grey. In young individuals the white of the lower parts is less distinct, sometimes very pale brownish."—*Jerdon.*

SIZE.—Head and body, 24 inches; tail, 13.

Mason speaks of this species as common in Burmah, and McMaster mentions his having seen in the Sitang River a colony of white-throated otters smaller than *L. nair*, though larger than *L. aurobrunnea*, but he did not secure specimens.

ÆLUROIDEA.

This section includes the Cat family (*Felidæ*); the Hyænas (*Hyænidæ*); two families unknown in India, viz. the *Cryptoproctidæ* and the *Protelidæ*; and the Civet family (*Viverridæ*).

FELIDÆ—THE CAT FAMILY.

This family contains the typical carnivores. There is in them combined the greatest power of destruction, accompanied by the simplest mechanism for producing it. All complications of dentition and digestion disappear. Here are the few scissor-like teeth with the enormous canines, the latter for holding and piercing the life out of their prey, the former for chopping up the flesh into suitable morsels for swallowing. Then the stomach is a simple sac, undivided into compartments, and the intestine is short, not more than three times the length of the body, instead of being some twenty times longer, as in some herbivores. This family has the smallest number of molars, a class of tooth which would indeed be useless, for the construction of the feline jaw precludes the possibility of grinding, and therefore a flat-crowned tuberculous tooth would be out of place. As I have before described it, the jaw of a tiger is incapable of lateral motion. The condyle of the lower jaw is so broad, and fits so accurately into its socket, the glenoid cavity, that there can be no departure from the up and down scissor-like action. The true Cats have, therefore, only one molar on each side of each jaw; those in the upper jaw being merely rudimentary, and placed almost at

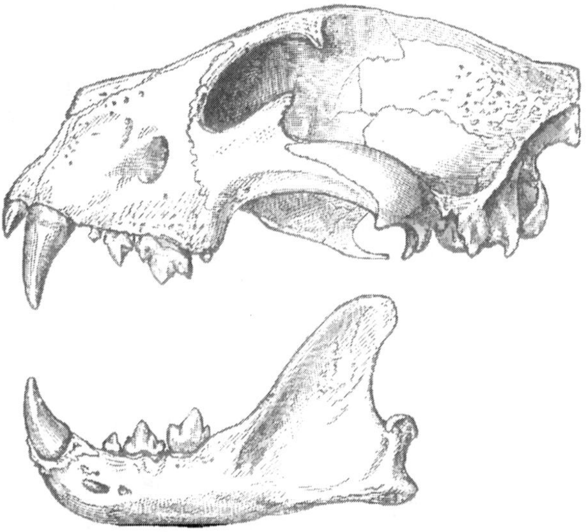

Skull of Tiger (side view).

right angles to the rest of the teeth, and seem apparently of little use; those of the lower jaw are large and trenchant, cutting against the edge of the third upper premolar.

It may interest my readers to know which are premolars and which are molars. This can be decided only by dissection of the jaw of a young animal. True molars only appear as the animal approaches the adult stage. They are never shed, as are all the rest of the teeth, commonly called milk teeth. The deciduous or milk teeth are the incisors, canines, and premolars; they drop out and are replaced, and behind the last premolar comes up the permanent molar.

Another peculiar feature of the Cat family is the power of sheathing their talons. Claws to a cat are of as great importance to him in the securing of his prey as are his teeth. The badger is a digger, Hodge, who carries his mattock on his shoulder; but the feline is the free-lance whose sword must be kept keen in its scabbard, so by a peculiar arrangement of muscles the points of the claws are kept off the ground, while the animal treads noiselessly on soft pads. Otherwise by constant abrasion they would get so blunted as to fail in their penetrating and seizing power. I give here an illustration of the mechanism of the feline claw. In the upper sketch the claw is retracted or sheathed; in the lower it is protruded as in the act of striking.

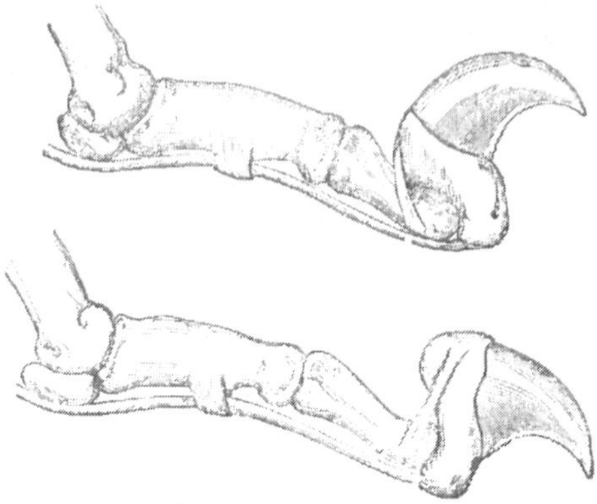

Tendons of Tiger's toe.

The senses of hearing and smell are much developed, and the bulb of the ear (*bulla tympani*) is here found of the largest dimensions. I have once before alluded to this in writing of the bears, in whom this arrangement is deficient. I give here a section of the auditory apparatus. I do not know whether the engraver has effectually rendered my attempt at conveying an idea, based as it is on dissections by Professor Flower; but if he has failed I think the fault lies in the shakiness of my hand in attempting the fine shading after nearly breaking a saw and losing my temper over a very tough old skull which I divided before commencing my illustration. The great cavity is the *bulla tympani* or bulb of the ear; *a m* is the *auditory meatus* or external hole of the ear. On looking into a dry skull the passage seems to be of no great depth, nor can an instrument be passed directly from the outside into the great tympanic cavity, the hindrance being a wall of bone, *s*, the *septum* which divides the *bulla* into two distinct chambers, the reason for which is not very clear, except that one may suppose it to be in some measure for acoustic purposes, as all animals

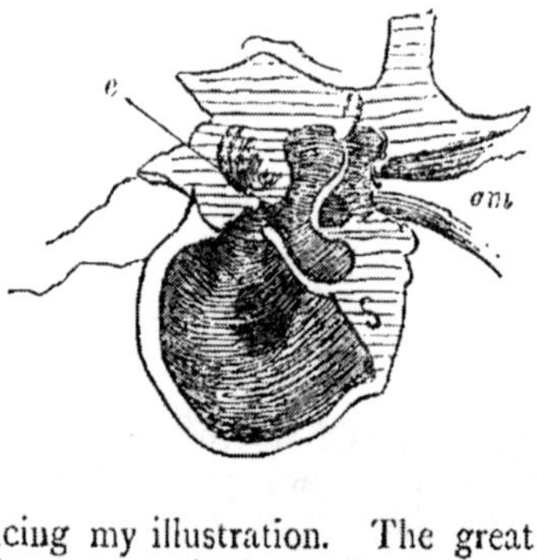

with this development are quick of hearing. The communication between the two chambers lies in a narrow slit over the *septum*, the Eustachian tube, *e*, being on the outside of the *septum* and between it and the tympanum or ear drum, *t*.

The above are the chief characteristics of the family. For the rest we may notice that they have but a rudimentary clavicle imbedded among the muscles; the limbs are comparatively short, but immensely muscular; the body lithe and active; the foot-fall noiseless; the tongue armed with rough papillæ, which enables them to rasp the flesh off bones, and their vision is adapted for both night and day.

None of them are gregarious, as in the case of dogs and wolves. One hears sometimes of a limited number of lions and tigers being seen together, but in most cases they belong to one family, of which the junior members have not been "turned off on their own hook" as yet.

No. 200. FELIS LEO.

The Lion (*Jerdon's No.* 103).

NATIVE NAMES.—*Sher-babbar*, *Singh*, *Unthia-bagh*.

HABITAT.—Guzerat and Central India.

DESCRIPTION.—The lion is almost too well known to need description, and there is little difference between the Asiatic and African animal. It may, however, be generally described as being distinguished from other Cats by its uniform tawny colour, flatter skull, which gives it a more dog-like appearance, the shaggy mane of the male, and by the tufted tail of both sexes.

Felis leo (Indian variety).

SIZE.—From nose to insertion of tail, 6 to $6\frac{1}{2}$ feet; tail, $2\frac{1}{2}$ to 3 feet; height, $3\frac{1}{2}$ feet.

The weight of one measured by Captain Smee, 8 feet $9\frac{1}{2}$ inches, was (excluding the entrails) thirty-five stone. This must be the one alluded to by Jerdon, but he does not state the extraction of the viscera, which would add somewhat to the weight.

Young lions when born are invariably spotted; and Professor Parker states that there were in the Zoological Gardens in 1877 three lions which were born in the menagerie about ten years previously, and which showed "indistinct, though perfectly evident, spots of a slightly darker tawny than the general ground-tint on the belly and flanks." He adds: "This is also the case with the puma, and it looks very much as if all the great Cats were descended from a spotted ancestor." The more dog-like head of the lion is well known to all who have studied the physiognomy of the Cats, and I have not only noticed it in drawing the animal, but have seen it alluded to in the writings of others. It was not, however, till lately that I had an opportunity of comparing the skulls of the lion and tiger in the Calcutta Museum, and I am indebted to Mr. Cockburn of the museum, not only for the trouble he took in getting out the various skulls, but for his assistance in pointing out certain peculiarities known to him, but of which I was at the time ignorant. That the skull of the lion is flatter than, and wants the bold curve of, those of the tiger, leopard and jaguar, is a well-known fact, but what Mr. Cockburn pointed out to me was the difference in the maxillary and nasal sutures of the face. A glance at two skulls placed side by side would show at once what I mean. It would be seen that the nasal bones of the tiger run up higher than those of the lion, the apices of whose nasal and maxillary sutures are on a level. On leaving the museum I compared the tiger skulls in my possession with accurate anatomical drawings which I have of the osteology of the lion, and the result was the same. It is said that there is also a difference in the infra-orbital foramen of the two animals, but this I have failed to detect as yet, though asserted by De Blainville in his magnificent work on osteology ('Ostéographie').

From all that has been written of the African and Indian lions I should say that the tiger was the more formidable of the two, as he is, I believe, superior in size. About twenty-two years ago my attention was drawn to this subject by the perusal of Mr. Blyth's article on the *Felidæ* in the old *India Sporting Review* of 1856–57. If I am not mistaken there was at that time (1861) a fine skeleton of a lion in the museum, as well as those of several tigers, which I measured. I had afterwards opportunities of observing and comparing skeletons of the two animals in various museums in Europe, though not in my own country, for my stay in England on each occasion of furlough was brief, and in almost every instance I found the tiger the larger of the two. The book in which I recorded my observations, and which also contained a number of microscopic drawings of marine infusoria, collected during a five months' voyage, was afterwards lost, so I cannot now refer to my notes.

I believe there was once a case of a fair fight between a well-matched lion and tiger in a menagerie (Edmonds's, I think). The two, by the breaking of a partition, got together, and could not be separated. The duel resulted in the victory of the tiger, who killed his opponent.

The lion seems to be dying out in India, and it is now probably confined only to Guzerat and Cutch. I have not been an attentive reader of sporting magazines of late years, and therefore I cannot call to mind any recent accounts of lion-killing in India, if any such have been recorded. At the commencement of this century lions were to be found in the North-West and in Central India, including the tract of country now termed the Central Provinces. In 1847 or 1848 a lioness was killed by a native shikari in the Dumoh district. Dr. Spry, in his 'Modern India,' states that, when at Saugor in the Central Provinces in 1837, the skin of a full-grown male lion was brought to him, which had been shot by natives in the neighbourhood. He also mentions another lioness shot at Rhylee in the Dumoh district in 1834, of which he saw the skin. Jerdon says that tolerably authentic intelligence was received of the presence of lions near Saugor in 1856; and whilst at Seonee, within the years 1857 to 1864, I frequently heard the native shikaris speak of having seen a tiger *without stripes*, which may have been of the present species. The indistinct spots on the lion's skin (especially of young lions), to which I have before alluded, were noticed in the skin of the lioness shot at Dumoh in 1847. The writer says: "when you place it in the sun and look sideways at it, some very faint spots (the size of a shilling or so) are to be seen along the belly."

Lions pair off at each season, and for the time they are together they show great attachment to each other, but the male has to fight for his spouse, who bestows herself on the victor. They then live together till the young are able to shift for themselves. The lioness goes with young about fifteen or sixteen weeks, and produces from two to six at a litter. But there is great mortality among young lions, especially about the time when they are developing their canine teeth. This has been noticed in menageries, confirming a common Arab assertion. In the London Zoological Gardens, during the last twenty years, there has been much mortality among the lion cubs by a malformation of the palate. It is a curious fact that lions breed more readily in travelling menageries than in stationary ones.

No. 201. FELIS TIGRIS.

The Tiger (*Jerdon's No* 104).

NATIVE NAME.—*Bagh*, *Sher*, Hindi; *Sela-vagh*, *Go-vagh*, Bengali; *Wuhag*, Mahrathi; *Nahar* in Bundelkund and Central India; *Tut* of the hill people of Bhagulpore; *Nongya-chor* in Gorukpore; *Puli* in Telegu and Tamil, also *Pedda-pulli* in Telegu; *Parain-pulli* in Malabar; *Huli* in Caranese; *Tagh* in Tibet; *Suhtong* in Lepcha; *Tukh* in Bhotia.

These names are according to Jerdon. *Bagh* and *Sher* all Indian sportsmen are familiar with. The Gonds of the Central Provinces call it *Pullial*, which has an affinity with the southern dialects.

HABITAT.—The tiger, as far as we are concerned, is known throughout the Indian peninsula and away down the eastern countries to the Malayan archipelago. In Ceylon it is not found, but it extends to the Himalayas, and ranges up to heights of 6000 to 8000 feet. Generally speaking it is confined to Asia, but in that continent it has a wide distribution. It has been found as far north as the island of Saghalien, which is bisected by N. L. 50°. This is its extreme north-eastern limit, the Caspian Sea being its westerly boundary. From parallel 50° downwards it is found in many parts of the highlands of central Asia.

DESCRIPTION.—A large heavy bodied Cat, much developed in the fore-quarters, with short, close hair of a bright rufous ground tint from every shade of pale yellow ochre to burnt sienna, with black stripes arranged irregularly and seldom in two individuals alike, the stripes being also irregular in form, from single streaks to loops and broad bands. In some the brows and cheeks are white, and in all the chin, throat, breast, and belly are pure white. All parts, however, whether white or rufous, are equally pervaded by the black stripes. The males have prolonged hairs extending from the ears round the cheeks, forming a ruff, or whiskers as they are sometimes called, although the true whiskers are the labial bristles. The pupil of the tiger's eye is round, and not vertical, as stated by Jerdon.

SIZE.—Here we come to a much-vexed question, on which there is much divergence of opinion, and the controversy will never be decided until sportsmen have adopted a more correct system of measurement. At present the universal plan is to measure the animal as it lies on the ground, taking the tape from the tip of the nose to the end of the tail. I will undertake that no two men will measure the same tiger with equal results if the body be at all disturbed between the two operations. If care be not taken to raise the head so as to bring the plane of the skull in a line with the vertebræ, the downward deflection will cause increased measurement. Let any one try this on the next opportunity, or on the dead body of a cat. Care should be taken in measuring that the head be raised, so that the top of the skull be as much as possible in a line with the vertebræ. A stake should be then driven in at the nose and another close in at the root of the tail, and the measurement taken between the two stakes, and not round the curves. The tail, which is an unimportant matter, but which in the present system of measurement is a considerable factor, should be measured and noted separately. I am not a believer in tails (or tales), and have always considered that they should be excluded from measurements except as an addition. I spoke of this in 'Seonee' in the following terms: "If all tigers were measured honestly, a twelve-foot animal would never be heard of. All your big fellows are measured from stretched skins, and are as exaggerated as are the accounts of the dangers incurred in killing them—at least in many cases. But even the true method of measuring the unskinned animal is faulty; it is an apparent fact that a tail has very little to do with the worthiness of a creature, otherwise our bull-dogs would have their caudal appendages left in peace. Now every shikari knows that there may be a heavy tiger with a short tail and a light bodied one with a long tail. Yet the measurement of each would be equal, and give no criterion as to the size of the brute. Here's this tiger of yours; I call him a heavy one, twenty-eight inches round the fore-arm, and big in every way, yet his measurement does not sound large (it was 9 feet 10 inches), and had he six inches more tail he would gain immensely by it in reputation. The biggest panther I ever shot had a stump only six inches long; and according to the usual system of measuring he would have read as being a very small creature indeed." Tails do vary. Sir Walter Elliot was a very careful observer, and in his comparison of the two largest males and two largest females, killed between 1829 and 1833, out of 70 to 80 specimens, it will be seen that the largest animal in each sex had the shortest tail:—

—	Adult Male.		Adult Female.	
	ft. in.	ft. in.	ft. in.	ft. in.
Length of head and body	6 2	5 6	5 3½	5 2
Length of tail	3 1½	3 3	2 11	3 2
	9 3½	8 9	8 2½	8 4

Campbell, in his notes to 'The Old Forest-Ranger,' gives the dimensions of a tiger of 9 ft. 5 in. of which the tail was only 2 ft. 10 in. From the other detailed measurements it must have been an enormous tiger. The number of caudal vertebræ in the tiger and lion should be twenty-six. I now regret that I did not carefully examine the osteology of all short-tailed tigers which I have come across, to see whether they had the full complement of vertebræ. The big tiger in the museum is short by the six terminal joints = three inches. This may have occurred during life, as in the case of the above-quoted panther; anyhow the tail should, I think, be thrown out of the calculation. Now as to the measurement of the head and body. I quite acknowledge that there must be a different standard for the sportsman and for the scientific naturalist. For the latter the only reliable data are derived from the bones. Bones cannot err. Except in very few abnormal conditions the whole skeleton is in *accurate* proportion, and it has lately struck me that from a certain measurement of the skull a true estimate might be formed of the length of the skeleton, and approximately the size of the animal over the muscles. I at first thought of taking the length of the skull by a craniometer, and seeing what portion of the total length to the posterior edge of the sacrum it would be, but I soon discarded the idea on account of the variation in the supra-occipital process.

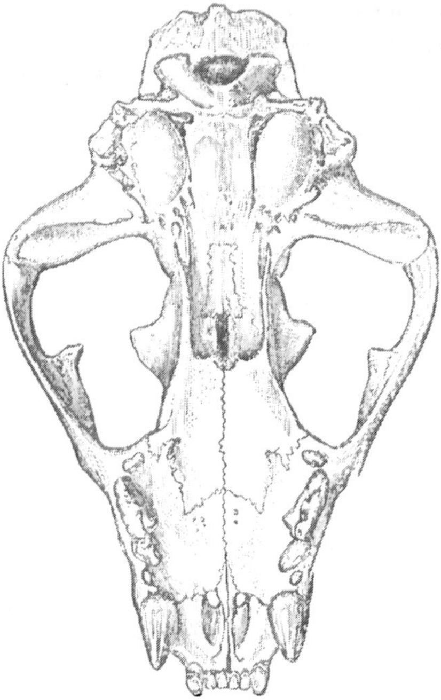

Tiger's skull (under part).

I then took the palatal measurement, from the outer edge of the border in which the incisors are set to the anterior inside edge of the brain-hole, or foramen magnum, and I find that this standard is sufficiently accurate, and is 5·50 of the length taken from the tip of the premaxillaries to the end of the sacrum. Therefore the length of this portion of any tiger's skull multiplied by 5·50 will give the measurement of the head and body of the skeleton.

For the purpose of working out these figures I applied to all my sporting friends for measurements of their largest skulls, with a view to settling the question about tigers exceeding eleven feet. The museum possesses the skeleton of a tiger which was considered one of the largest known, the cranial measurement of whose skull is 14·50 inches, but the Maharajah of Cooch Behar showed me one of his skulls which exceeded it, being 15 inches. Amongst others I wrote to Mr. J. Shillingford of Purneah, and he most kindly not only drew up for me a tabular statement of the dimensions of the finest skulls out of his magnificent collection, but sent down two for my inspection. Now in the long-waged war of opinion regarding the size of tigers I have always kept a reserved attitude, for if I have never myself killed, or have seen killed by others, a tiger exceeding ten feet, I felt that to be no reason for doubting the existence of tigers of eleven feet in length vouched for by men of equal and in some cases greater experience, although at the same time I did not approve of a system of measurement which left so much to conjecture.

There is much to be said on both sides, and, as much yet remains to be investigated, it is to be hoped that the search after the truth will be carried on in a judicial spirit. I have hitherto been ranged on the side of the moderate party; still I was bound to respect the opinion of Sir Joseph Fayrer, who, as not only as a sportsman but as an anatomist, was entitled to attention; and from my long personal acquaintance I should implicitly accept any statement made by him. Dr. Jerdon, whom I knew intimately, was not, I may safely assert, a great tiger shikari, and he based his opinion on evidence and with great caution. Mr. J. Shillingford, from whom I have received the greatest assistance in my recent investigations, and who has furnished me with much valuable information, is on the other hand the strenuous assertor of the existence of the eleven-foot tiger, and with the magnificent skulls before me, which he has sent down from Purneah, I cannot any longer doubt the size of the Bengal tiger, and that the animals to which they belonged were eleven feet, *measured sportsman fashion*—that is round the curves. The larger of the two skulls measures 15·25 inches taken between two squares, placed one at each end; a tape taken from the edge of the premaxillaries over the curve of the head gives 17·37 inches; the width across the zygomatic arches, 10·50.* The palatal measurement, which is the test I proposed for ascertaining the length of the skeleton, is 12·25, which would give 5 feet 7·37 inches; about 3¾ inches larger than the big skeleton in the Museum. This may seem very small for the body of an animal which is supposed to measure eleven feet, but I must remind my readers that the bones of the biggest tiger look very small when denuded of the muscles; and the present difficulty I have to contend with is how to strike the average rate for the allowance to be added to skeleton for muscles, the chief stumbling block being the system which has hitherto included the tail in the measurement. If all tigers had been measured as most other animals (except felines)

* At Mr. Shillingford's request, I made over this skull to the Calcutta Museum.

are—i.e. head and body together, and then the tail separately—I might have had some more reliable data to go upon; but I hope in time to get some from such sportsmen as are interested in the subject. I have shown that the tail is not trustworthy as a proportional part of the total length; but from such calculations as I have been able to make from the very meagre materials on which I have to base them, I should allow one 2·50th part of the total length of skeleton for curves and muscles.

In addition to a careful study of De Blainville's 'Ostéographie,' where the bones are figured in large size to scale, I have made many careful measurements of skulls belonging to myself and friends, and also of the skulls and skeletons in the Calcutta Museum (for most willing and valuable assistance in which I am indebted to Mr. J. Cockburn, who, in order to test my calculations, went twice over the ground); and I have adopted the following formula as a tentative measure. I quite expect to be criticised, but if the crude idea can be improved on by others I shall be glad.

I now give a tabular statement of four out of many calculations made, but I must state that in fixing an arbitrary standard of 36 inches for tail, I have understated the mark, for the tails of most tigers exceed that by an inch or two, though, on the other hand, some are less.

Formula.—Measure from the tip of the premaxillaries or outer insertion of the front teeth (incisors) along the palate to the nearest inner edge of the foramen magnum. Multiply the result by 5·50. This will give the length of the skeleton, excluding the tail. Divide this result by 2·50, and add the quotient to the length for the proportionate amount of muscles and gain in curves. Add 36 inches for tail.

—	Palatal measurement multiplied by 5·50.	Add one 2·50th part of last for curves and muscles.	Total.	Total.	Total in feet and inches.		REMARKS.
					ft.	in.	
Mr. Shillingford's tiger	67·37	26·94	36·00	130·31	10	10	Mr. S——'s tiger's tail was over 3 ft. 2 ins., which would make it 11 ft.
Big tiger in museum .	63·52	25·40	36·00	124·92	10	4¾	Nearly 10 ft. 5 in.
Maharajah of Cooch Behar's tiger	66·00	26·40	36·00	128·40	10	8·4	The Maharajah writes to me that it measured on the ground 9 ft. 11 in. See further on.
A medium-sized one of my own	55·75	23·10	36·00	116·85	9	8¾	

It will be seen that my calculation is considerably out in the Cooch Behar tiger, so I asked the Maharajah to tell me, from the appearance of the skull, whether the animal was young or old. He sent it over to me, and I have no hesitation in saying that it was that of a young tiger, who, in another year, might have put on the extra nine inches; the parietal sutures, which in the old tiger (as in Mr. Shillingford's specimens) are completely obliterated, are in this one almost open. It must be remembered that the bones of the skull do not grow in the same ratio to the others, and that they attain their full size before those of the rest of the body. Therefore it is only in the case of the adult that accurate results can be calculated upon. Probably I have not done wisely in selecting a portion of the skull as a standard—a bone of the body, such as a femur or humerus might be more reliable—but I was driven to it by circumstances. Sportsmen, as a rule, do not keep anything but the skull, and for general purposes it would have been of no use my giving as a test what no one could get hold of except in a museum.

I have always understood that the tiger of the plains grew to a greater size, that is in length, than the tiger of hilly country. I have never shot a tiger in Lower Bengal, therefore I cannot judge of the form of the beast, whether he be more lanky or not. If an eleven-foot Bengal tiger be anything like as robust in proportion as our Central Indian ones, I should say he was an enormous creature, but I believe the Central and Southern tiger to be the heavier one, and this is borne out by an illustration given by Mr. Shillingford in one of his able letters, which have called forth so much hostile criticism. He compares one of his largest with the measurement of a Southern India tiger :—

Locality of Tiger.	Length.	Girth of Chest.	Girth of Head.	Tail.	Round Fore-arm.	Height.	Total of feet and inches.
	ft. in.	ft. in.	ft. in.	ft. in.	ft. in.	ft. in.	ft. in.
Purneah . .	11 0	4 6	2 10	3 4	2 2	3 7	27 5
Southern India.	10 2	6 1	3 5	3 1	2 10	3 .9	29 4

The shorter tiger has an advantage of nearly two feet in all-round measurement.

Sir Joseph Fayrer has also been called in question for his belief in twelve feet tigers, but what he says is reasonable enough. "The tiger should be measured from the nose along the spine to the tip of the tail, as he lies dead on the spot where he fell, before the skin is removed. *One that is ten feet by this measurement is large, and the full-grown male does not often exceed this*, though no doubt larger individuals (males) are occasionally seen, and I have been informed by Indian sportsmen of reliability that they have seen and killed tigers over twelve feet in length." ('Royal Tiger of Bengal,' p. 29).

Sir Joseph Fayrer in a letter to *Nature*, June 27, 1878, brings forward the following evidence of large tigers shot by sportsmen whose names are well known in India.

Lieutenant-Colonel Boileau killed a tiger at Muteara in Oude, in 1861, over 12 feet; the skin when removed measured 13 feet 5 inches.

Sir George Yule has heard once of a 12-foot tiger fairly measured, but 11 feet odd inches is the largest he has killed, *and that twice or thrice.*

Colonel Ramsay (Commissioner) killed in Kumaon a tiger measuring 12 feet.

Sir Joseph Fayrer has seen and killed tigers over 10 feet, and one in Purneah 10 feet 8 inches, in 1869.

Colonel J. Sleeman does not remember having killed a tiger *over* 10 feet 6 inches in the skin.

Colonel J. MacDonald has killed one 10 feet 4 inches.

The Honourable R. Drummond, C.S., killed a tiger 11 feet 9 inches, measured before being skinned.

Colonel Shakespeare killed one 11 feet 8 inches.

However, conceding that all this proves that tigers do reach occasionally to eleven and even twelve feet, it does not take away from the fact that the average length is between nine and ten feet, and anything up to eleven feet is rare, and up to twelve feet still more so.*

VARIETIES OF THE TIGER.—It is universally acknowledged that there is but one species of tiger. There are, however, several marked varieties. The distinction between the Central Asian and the Indian tiger is unmistakable. The coat of the Indian animal is of smooth, short hair; that of the Northern one of a deep furry pelage, of a much richer appearance.

There is an idea which is also to be found stated as a fact in some works on natural history, that the Northern tiger is of a pale colour with few stripes, which arises from Swinhoe having so described some specimens from Northern China; but I have not found this to be confirmed in those skins from Central Asia which I have seen. Shortly before leaving London, in 1878, Mr. Charles Reuss, furrier, in Bond

* Since writing the above I have to thank "Meade Shell" for the measurements of the skull of a tiger 11 ft. 6 in. The palatal measurement is 12 inches, which, according to my formula, would give only 10 ft. 8 in.; but it must be remembered that I have allowed only 3 ft. for the tail, whereas such a tiger would probably have been from 3½ to 4 ft., which would quite bring it up to the length vouched for. The tail of a skeleton of a much smaller tiger in the museum measures 3 ft. 3½ in., which with skin and hair would certainly have been 3½ ft. Until sportsmen begin to measure bodies and tails separately it will, I fear, be a difficult matter to fix on any correct formula.—R. A. S. See Appendix *C*.

Street, showed me a beautiful skin with deep soft hair, abundantly striped on a rich burnt sienna ground, admirably relieved by the pure white of the lower parts. That light-coloured specimens are found is true, but I doubt whether they are more common than the others. Of the varieties in India it is more difficult to speak. Most sportsmen recognise two (some three)—the stout thick-set tiger of hilly country, and the long-bodied lankier one of the grass jungles in the plains. Such a division is in consonance with the ordinary laws of nature, which we also see carried out in the thick-set muscular forms of the human species in mountain tracts.

Some writers, however, go further, and attempt subdivisions more or less doubtful. I knew the late Captain J. Forsyth most intimately for years. We were in the same house for some time. I took an interest in his writings, and helped to illustrate his last work, and I can bear testimony to the general accuracy of his observations and the value of his book on the Highlands of Central India; but in some things he formed erroneous ideas, and his three divisions, based on the habits of the tiger, is, I think, open to objection, as tending to create an idea of at least two distinct varieties.

Native shikaris, he says, recognise two kinds—the *Lodhia Bagh* and the *Oontia Bagh* (which last I may remind my readers is one of the names of the lion). The former is the *game-killing* tiger, retired in his habits, living chiefly among the hills, retreating readily from man. "He is a light-made beast, very active and enduring, and from this, as well as his shyness, generally difficult to bring to bag."

I grant his shyness and comparative harmlessness (I once met one almost face to face)—and the nature of the ground he inhabits increases the difficulty in securing him—but I do not think he physically differs from his brother in the cattle districts. Mr. Sanderson says one of the largest tigers he had killed was a pure game-killer.

"The cattle-lifter again," says Forsyth, "is usually an older and heavier animal (called *Oontia Bagh*, from his faintly striped coat, resembling the colour of a camel), very fleshy and indisposed to severe exertion."

His third division is the man-eater. However, this is merely a classification on the habits of the same animal. I think most Central India sportsmen will agree with me when I say that many a young tiger is a cattle-eater, with a rich coloured hide, although it often happens that an old tiger of the first division, when he finds his powers for game failing by reason of age or increased bulk, transfers himself from the borders of the forest to the vicinity of grazing lands and villages, and he ultimately may come into the third division by becoming a man-eater. So that the *Lodhia* becomes the *Oontia* (for very old tigers become lighter in colour), and may end by being an *Adam-khor*, or man-eater. Tigers roam a great deal at times, and if in their wanderings they come to a suitable locality with convenience of food and water, they abide there, provided there be no occupant with a prior claim and sufficient power to dispute the intrusion. We had ample proof of this at Seonee. Close to the station, that is, within a short ride, were several groups of hills which commanded the pasture lands of the town. Many a tiger has been killed there, the place of the slain one being occupied ere long by another. On the other hand, if a tiger be accommodated with lodgings to his liking, he will stay there for years, roaming a certain radius, but returning to his home; and it is the knowledge of this that so often enables the hunter to compass his destruction. As long therefore as there are human habitations, with their usual adjuncts of herds and flocks, within a dozen miles of the jungle tiger's haunts, so long there will always be the transition from the game-killer to the cattle-lifter and the man-eater. Colour and striping must also be thrown out of the question, for no two individuals of any variety agree, and the characteristics of shade and marking are common to all kinds. The only reliable data therefore are derived from measurements, and from these it may be proved that the grass-jungle tiger of Bengal, though the longer animal, is yet inferior in all round measurement and probably in weight to the tiger of hilly country —see Mr. Shillingford's comparison quoted by me above. Let also any one compare the following measurements of one given by Colonel Walter Campbell with a tiger of equal length shot in the grassy plains of Bengal :—

	ft.	in.
Length from point of nose to end of tail	9	5
Ditto of tail	2	10
Height from heel to shoulder	3	2
Extreme length from shoulder to point of toe	3	11
From elbow to point of toe	2	0
Girth of body just behind the shoulder	5	3
Ditto of forearm	2	7
Ditto of neck	3	0
Circumference of head	3	3

This is a remarkably short-tailed tiger. If the concurrence of evidence establishes the difference beyond doubt, then we may say that there are two varieties in India—the hill tiger, *Felis tigris, var. montanus;* and the other, inhabiting the alluvial plains of great rivers, *Felis tigris, var. fluviatilis.* Dr. Anderson says he has examined skulls and skins of those inhabiting the hill ranges of Yunnan, and can detect no difference from the ordinary Indian species.

The tigress goes with young for about fifteen weeks, and produces from two to five at a birth. I remember once seeing four perfectly formed cubs, which would have been born in a day or two, cut from a tigress shot by my brother-in-law Col. W. B. Thomson in the hills adjoining the station of Seonee. I had got off an elephant, and, running up the glen on hearing the shots, came unpleasantly close to her in her dying throes. When about to bring forth, the tigress avoids the male, and hides her young from him. The native shikaris say that the tiger kills the young ones if he finds them. The mother is a most affectionate parent as a rule, and sometimes exhibits strange fits of jealousy at interference with her young. I heard an instance of this some years ago from my brother, Mr. H. B. Sterndale, who, as one of the Municipal Commissioners of Delhi, took a great interest in the collection of animals in the Queen's Gardens there. Both tiger and leopard cubs had been born in the gardens, and the mother of the latter shewed no uneasiness at her offspring being handled by strangers as they crept through the bars and strayed about; but one day, a tiger cub having done the same, the tigress exhibited great restlessness, and, on the little one's return, in a sudden accession of jealous fury she dashed her paw on it and killed it. I am indebted to Mr. Shillingford for a long list of tigresses with cubs killed during the years 1866 to 1880. Out of 53 cubs (18 mothers) 29 were males and 22 females, the sex of two cubs not being given. This tends to prove that there are an equal number of each sex born—in fact here the advantage is on the side of the males. I have heard it asserted that tigresses are more common, and native shikaris account for it by saying that the male tiger kills the cubs of his own sex; but I have not seen anything to justify this assertion, or the fact of there being a preponderance of females. Mr. Sanderson, however, writes: "Male and female cubs appear to be in about equal proportions. How it is that amongst mature animals tigresses predominate so markedly I am unable to say."

Tigresses have young at all seasons of the year, and they breed apparently only once in three years, which is about the time the cubs remain with their mother.

For the following interesting memorandum I have to thank Mr. Shillingford:—

		Feet.
"Cubs one year old measure	Males	4½ to 5½
	Females	4 to 5
Ditto two years old	Males	5½ to 7
	Females	5 to 6½
Ditto three years old	Males	7 to 8½
	Females	6½ to 7½

"When they reach three years of age they lose their 'milk' canines, which are replaced by the permanent fangs, and at this period the mother leaves them to cater for themselves."

The cubs are interesting pets if taken from the mother very young. I have reared several, but only kept one for any length of time. I have given a full description of Zalim and his ways in 'Seonee.' He was found by my camp followers with another in a nullah, and brought to me. The other cub died, but Zalim lived to grow up into a very fine tiger, and was sent to England. I never allowed him to taste raw flesh. He had a little cooked meat every day, and as much milk as he liked to drink, and he throve well on this diet. When he was too large to be allowed to roam about unconfined I had a stout buffalo-leather collar made for his neck, and he was chained to a stump near the cook-room door. With grown-up people he was perfectly tame, but I noticed he got restless when children approached him, and so made up my mind to part with him before he did any mischief.

I know nothing of the habits of the tiger of the grass plains, but those of the hill tiger are very interesting, the cattle lifter especially, as he is better known to men. Each individual has his special idiosyncrasy. I wrote of this once before as follows: "Strange though it may seem to the English reader that a tiger should have any special character beyond the general one for cruelty and cunning, it is nevertheless a fact that each animal has certain peculiarities of temperament which are well known to the villagers in the neighbourhood. They will tell you that such a one is daring and rash; another is cunning and not to be taken by any artifice; that one is savage and morose; another is mild and harmless. There are few villages in the wilder parts of the Seonee and Mandla districts without an attendant tiger, which undoubtedly does great damage in the way of destroying cattle, but which avoids the human inhabitants of the place. So accustomed do the people get to their unwelcome visitor that we have known the boys of a village turn a tiger out of quarters which were reckoned too close, and pelt him with stones. On one occasion two of the juvenile assailants were killed by the animal they had approached too near. Herdsmen in the same way get callous to the danger of meddling with so dreadful a creature, and frequently rush to the rescue of their cattle when seized. On a certain occasion one out of a herd of cattle was attacked close to our camp, and rescued single-handed by its owner, who laid his heavy iron-bound staff across the tiger's back; and, on our rushing out to see what was the matter, we found the man coolly dressing the wounds of his cow, muttering to himself: 'The robber, the robber! My last cow, and I had five of them!' He did not seem to think he had done anything wonderful, and seemed rather surprised that we should suppose that he was going to let his last heifer go the way of all the others.

"It is fortunate for these dwellers in the backwoods that but a small percentage of tigers are man-eaters, perhaps not five per cent., otherwise village after village would be depopulated; as it is the yearly tale of lives lost is a heavy one."*

* 'Seonee.'

Tigers are also eccentric in their ways, showing differences in disposition under different circumstances. I believe that many a shikari passes at times within a few yards of a tiger without knowing it, the tendency of the animal being to crouch and hide until the strange-looking two-legged beast has passed. The narrowest escape I ever had is an instance. I had hunted a large tiger, well known for the savageness of his disposition, on foot from ravine to ravine on the banks of the Pench, one hot day in June, and, giving him no rest, made sure of getting him about three o'clock in the afternoon. He had been seen to slip into a large nullah, bordered on one side by open country, a small water-course draining into it from the fields; here was one large *beyr* bush, behind which I wished to place myself, but was persuaded by an old shikari of great local reputation to move farther on. Hardly had we done so when our friend bounded from under the bush and disappeared in a thicket, where we lost him. Ten days after this he was killed by a friend and myself, and he sustained his savage reputation by attacking the elephant without provocation—a thing a tiger seldom does. I had hunted this animal several times, and on one occasion saw him swim the Pench river at one of its broadest reaches. It was the only time I had seen a tiger swim, and it was interesting to watch him powerfully breasting the stream with his head well up. Tigers swim readily, as is well known. I believe it is not uncommon to see them take to the water in the Sunderbunds; and a recent case may be remembered when two of them escaped from the King of Oude's Menagerie, and one swam across the Hooghly to the Botanical Gardens.

There has been some controversy about the way in which tigers kill their prey. I am afraid I cannot speak definitely on the subject, although I have on several occasions seen tigers kill oxen and ponies. I do not think they have a uniform way of doing it, so much depends upon circumstances—certain it is that they cannot smash in the head of a buffalo with a stroke, as some writers make out, but yet I have known them make strokes at the head, in a running fight, for instance, between a buffalo and a tiger—in which the former got off—and in the case of human beings. Of two men killed by the same tiger, one had his skull fractured by a blow; the other, who was killed as we were endeavouring to drive the tiger out of the village, was seized by the loins. He died immediately; the man with the fractured skull lingered some hours longer. Another case of a stroke at the head happened once when I had tied out a pony for a tiger that would not look at cows, over which I had sat for several successive nights. A tiger and tigress came out, and the former made a rush at the *tattu*, who met him with such a kick on the nose that he drew back much astonished; the tigress then dashed at the pony, and I, wishing if possible to save the plucky little animal's life, fired two barrels into her, rolling her over just as she struck at his head. But it was too late; the pony dropped at the blow and died—not from concussion, however, but from loss of blood, for the jugular vein had been cut open as though it had been done with a knife. So much for the head stroke, which is, I may say, exceptional. As a general rule I think the tiger bears down his victim by sheer weight, and then, by some means which I should hesitate to define, although I have seen it, the head is wrenched back, so as to dislocate the vertebræ. One evening two cows were killed before me. I was going to say the tiger sprang at one, but correct myself—it is not a spring, but a rush on to the back of the animal; he seldom springs all fours off the ground at once. I have never seen a tiger get off his hind legs except in bounding over a fallen tree, or in and out of a ravine. In this case he rushed on to the cow and bore it to the ground; there was a violent struggle, and in the dusky light I could not tell whether he used his mouth or paws in wrenching back the head, which went with a crack. The thing was done in a minute, when he sprang once more to his feet, and the second cow was hurled to the ground in like manner. As his back was turned to me I fired somewhat hastily, thinking to save the cow, but only wounded the tiger, which I lost. Both the cows, however, had their necks completely broken. I cannot now remember the position of the fang-marks in the throat. On another occasion I came across five out of a herd that had been killed, probably by young tigers; every one had the neck broken.

Mr. Sanderson says that herdsmen have described to him how they have noticed the operation: "Clutching the bullock's fore-quarters with his paws, one being generally over the shoulder, he seizes the throat in his jaws from underneath and turns it upwards and over, sometimes springing to the far side in doing so, to throw the bullock over and give the wrench which dislocates its neck. This is frequently done so quickly that the tiger, if timid, is in retreat again almost before the herdsmen can turn round." This account seems reliable. A tiger may seize by the nape in order to get a temporary purchase, but it would be awkward for him to pull the head back far enough to snap the vertebral column.

Now for a few remarks in conclusion. I have written more on the subject than I intended. That tigers are carrion feeders is well known, but that sometimes they prefer high meat to fresh I had only proof of once. A tiger killed a mare and foal, on which he feasted for three days; on the fourth nothing remaining but a very offensive leg; we tied out a fine young buffalo calf for him within a yard or two of the savoury joint. The tiger came during the night and took away the leg, without touching the calf; and, devouring it, fell asleep, in which condition we, having tracked him up the nullah, found and killed him.

The tiger is not always monarch over all the beasts of the field. He is positively afraid of the wild dog (*Cuon rutilans*), which readily attacks him in packs. Then he often finds his match in the wild boar. I have myself seen an instance of this, in which the tiger was not only ripped to death, but had his chest-bone gnawed and crushed, evidently after life was extinct.

Buffalos in herds hesitate not in attacking a tiger; and I saw one instance of their saving their herdsman from a man-eater. My camp was pitched on the banks of a stream under some tall trees. I had made a *détour* in order to try and kill this man-eater, and had sent on a hill tent the night before. I was met in the morning by the *khalasi* in charge, with a wonderful story of the tiger having rushed at him, but as the man was a romancer I disbelieved him. On the other side of the stream was a gentle slope of turf and bushes, rising gradually to a rocky hill. The slope was dotted with grazing herds, and here and there a group of buffalos. Late in the afternoon I heard some piercing cries from my people of "*Bagh! Bagh!*" The cows stampeded, as they always do. A struggle was going on in the bush, with loud cries of a human voice. The buffalos threw up their heads, and, grunting loudly, charged down on the spot, and then in a body went charging on through the brushwood. Other herdsmen and villagers ran up, and a charpoy was sent for and the man brought into the village. He was badly scratched, but had escaped any serious fang wounds from his having, as he said, seen the tiger coming at him, and stuffed his blanket into his open mouth, whilst he belaboured him with his axe. Anyhow but for his buffalos he would have been a dead man in three minutes more.

THE PARDS OR PANTHERS.

To these are commonly assigned the name of Leopard, which ought properly to be restricted to the hunting leopard (*Felis jubata*), to which we have also misappropriated the Indian name *Chita*, which applies to all spotted cats, *Chita-bagh* being spotted tiger. The same term, derived from the adjective *chhita*, spotted or sprinkled, applies in various forms to the other creatures, such as *Chital*, the spotted deer (*Axis*), *Chita-bora*, a kind of speckled snake, &c. *Leopardus* or lion-panther was, without doubt, the name given by the ancients to the hunting leopard, which was well known to them from its extending into Africa and Arabia. Assuredly the prophet Habakkuk spoke of the hunting chita when he said of the Chaldæans: "That bitter and hasty nation . . . . their horses also are swifter than the leopards," for the pard is not a swift animal, whereas the speed of the other is well known.

The name was given to it by the ancients on the supposition that it was a cross between the lion and the pard, from a fancied resemblance to the former on account of the mane or ruff of hair possessed by the hunting leopard. Apparently this animal must have been more familiar to our remote ancestors than the pard, for the name has been attached for centuries to the larger spotted Cats indiscriminately. I have not time just now to attempt to trace the species of the leopard which formerly graced the arms of the English kings, but I should not be surprised if it were the guepard or chita. The old representations were certainly attenuated enough; and the animal must have been familiar to the crusaders, as we know it was before them to the Romans.

Mr. Blyth, who speculated on the origin of the name, in one of his able articles on the felines of India in the *India Sporting Review* of April 1856, makes no allusion to the above nor to the probable confusion that may have arisen in the middle ages over the spotted Cats. Although the term leopard, as applied to panthers, has the sanction of almost immemorable custom, I do not see why, in writing on the subject, we should perpetuate the misnomer, especially as most naturalists and sportsmen are now inclined to make the proper distinction. I have always avoided the use of the term leopard, except when speaking of the hunting chita, preferring to call the others panthers.

Then again we come on disputed ground. Of panthers how many have we, and how should they be designated? I am not going farther afield than India in this discussion beyond alluding to the fact that the jaguar of Brazil is almost identical with our pard as far as marking goes, but is a stouter, shorter-tailed animal, which justifies his being classed as a species; therefore we must not take superficial colouring as a test, but class the black and common pards together; the former, which some naturalists have endeavoured to made into a separate species (*Felis melas*), being merely a variety of the latter. They present the same characteristics, although Jerdon states that the black is the smaller animal. They have been found in Java to inhabit the same den, according to Professor Reinwardt and M. Kuhl, and they inter-breed, as has been proved by the fact that a female black pard has produced a black and a fulvous cub at the same birth. This is noticed by Mr. Sanderson in his book, and he got the information from the director of the Zoological Society's Menagerie at Amsterdam. "Old Fogy," a constant contributor to the old *India Sporting Review*, a good sportsman and naturalist, with whom Blyth kept up a correspondence, wrote in October 1857 that, "in a litter of four leopard cubs one was quite black; they all died, but both the parents were of the ordinary colour and marking; they were both watched at their cave, and at last shot, one with an arrow through the heart. Near a hill village a black male leopard was often seen and known to consort with an ordinary female. I have observed them myself once, if not twice."

An observant sportsman, "Hawkeye," in one of his letters to the *South of India Observer*, remarks that "on one occasion a gentleman saw an old leopard accompanied by two of her offspring, one red, the other black." He also says he has never known "of two black leopards in company," but black pards have bred in zoological gardens. I am told that cubs have been born in the Calcutta Garden, but they did not live. General MacMaster, in his notes on Jerdon, makes the pertinent remark: "If however black panthers are only accidental, it is odd that no one has yet come on a black specimen of one of the larger cats, *F. leo tigris.*" I see no reason why such should not yet be discovered; he was perhaps not aware that the jaguar of Brazil, which comes next to the tiger, has been found black (*Felis nigra* of Erxleben). A black tiger would be a prize. General MacMaster relates that he once watched a fine black cat basking in the sun, and noticed that in particular lights the animal exhibited most plainly the regular brindled markings of the ordinary gray wild or semi-wild cat. These markings were as black or blacker than the rest of his hair. His mother was a half-wild gray brindle.

I think we have sufficient evidence that the black pard is merely a variety of the common one, but now we come to the pards themselves, and the question as to whether there are two distinct species or two varieties; Blyth, Jerdon and other able naturalists, although fully recognizing the differences, have yet hesitated to separate them, and they still remain in the unsatisfactory relation to each other of varieties. I feel convinced in my own mind that they are sufficiently distinct to warrant their being classed, and specifically named apart. It is not as I said before, that we should go upon peculiarities of marking and colour, although these are sufficiently obvious, but on their osteology and also the question of interbreeding and production. Grant their relative sizes, one so much bigger than the other, and the difference in colour and marking, has it ever been known that out of a litter of several cubs by a female of the larger kind, one of the smaller sort has been produced, or *vice versâ?* This is a question that yet remains for investigation. My old district had both kinds in abundance, and I have had scores of cubs, of both sorts, brought to me—cubs which could be distinguished at a glance as to which kind they belonged to, but I never remember any mixture of the two. As regards the difference in appearance of the adults there can be no question. The one is a higher, longer animal, with smooth shiny hair of a light golden fulvous, the spots being clear and well defined, but, as is remarked by Sir Walter Elliot, the strongest difference of character is in the skulls, those of the larger pard being longer and more pointed, with a ridge running along the occiput, much developed for the attachment of the muscles, whereas the smaller pard has not only a rougher coat, the spots being more blurred, but it is comparatively a more squat built animal, with a rounder skull without the decided occipital ridge. There is a mass of evidence on the point of distinctness—Sir Walter Elliot, Horsfield, Hodgson, Sir Samuel Baker, Johnson (author of 'Field Sports in India'), "Mountaineer," a writer in the *Bengal Sporting Review*, even Blyth and Jerdon, all speak to the difference, and yet no decided separation has been made. There is in fact too much confusion and too many names. For the larger animal *Felis pardus* is appropriate, and the *leopardus* of Temminck, Schreber and others is not. Therefore that remains; but what is the smaller one to be called? I should say *Felis panthera* which, being common to Asia and Africa, was probably the panther of the Romans and Greeks. Jerdon gives as a synonym *F. longicaudata* (Valenciennes), but I find on examination of the skulls of various species that *F. longicaudata* has a complete bony orbit which places it in Gray's genus *Catolynx*, and it is too small for our panther. We might then say that we have the pard, the panther, and the leopard in India, and then we should be strictly correct. Some sportsmen speak of a smaller panther which Kinloch calls the third (second?) sort of panther, but this differs in no respect from the ordinary one, save in size, and it is well known that this species varies very much in this respect. I am not singular in the views I now express. Years ago Colonel Sykes, who was a well known naturalist, said of the pard: "It is a taller, stronger, and slighter built animal than the next species, which I consider the *panther*."

The skull of the pard in some degree resembles that of the jaguar, which again is nearest the tiger, whereas that of the panther appears to have some affinity to the restricted cats. In disposition all the pards and panthers are alike sanguinary, fierce and incapable of attachment. The tiger is tameable, the panther not so. I have had some experience of the young of both, and have seen many others in the possession of friends; and though they may, for a time, when young, be amusing pets, their innate savageness sooner or later breaks out. They are not even to be trusted with their own kind. I have known one to turn on a comrade in a cage, kill and devour him, and some of my readers may possibly remember an instance of this in the Zoological Gardens at Lahore, when, in 1868, a pard one night killed a panther which inhabited the same den, and ate a goodly portion of him before dawn. They all show more ferocity than the tiger when wounded, and a man-eating pard is far more to be dreaded than any other man-eater, as will be seen farther on from the history of one I knew.

No. 202. FELIS PARDUS.

The Pard (Jerdon's No. 105).

NATIVE NAMES.—*Tendua*, *Chita* or *Chita-bagh*, *Adnara;* Hindi, *Honiga;* Canarese, *Asnea;* Mahratti, *Chinna puli;* Telegu, *Burkal;* Gondi, *Bay-heera;* and *Tahr-hay* in the Himalayas.

HABITAT.—Throughout India, Burmah, and Ceylon, and extending to the Malayan Archipelago.

DESCRIPTION.—A clean, long limbed, though compact body; hair close and short; colour pale fulvous yellow, with clearly defined spots in rosettes; the head more tiger-like than the next species; the skull is longer and more pointed, with a much developed occipital ridge.

SIZE.—Head and body from 4½ to 5½ feet; tail from 30 to 38 inches.

This is a powerful animal and very fierce as a rule, though in the case of a noted man-eater I have known it exhibit a curious mixture of ferocity and abject cowardice. It is stated to be of a more retiring disposition than the next species, but this I doubt, for I have frequently come across it in the neighbourhood of villages to which it was probably attracted by cattle. It may not have the fearlessness or impudence of the panther, which will walk through the streets of a town and seize and devour its prey in a garden surrounded by houses, as I once remember, in the case of a pony at Seonee, but it is nevertheless sufficiently bold to hang about the outskirts of villages. Those who have seen this animal once would never afterwards confuse it with what I would call the panther. There is a sleekness about it quite foreign to the other, and a brilliancy of skin with a distinctness of spots which the longer, looser hair does not admit of. But with all these external differences I am aware that there will be objection to classifying it as a separate species, unless the osteological divergences can be satisfactorily determined, and for this purpose it would be necessary to examine a large series of authenticated skulls of the two kinds.

The concurrence of evidence as to the habits of this species is that it is chiefly found in hilly jungles preying on wild animals, wild pigs, and monkeys, but not unfrequently, as I know, haunting the outskirts of villages for the sake of stray ponies and cattle. The largest pard I have ever seen was shot by one of my own shikaris in the act of stalking a pony near a village. I was mahseer-fishing close by at the time, and had sent on the man, a little before dusk, to a village a few miles off, to arrange for beating up a tiger early next day. Jerdon says this is the kind most common in Bengal, but he does not say in what parts of Bengal, and on what authority. I have no doubt it abounds in Sontalia and Assam, and many other hilly parts. At Colgong, Mr. Barnes informed him that many cases of human beings killed by pards were known in the Bhaugulpore district. At Seonee we had one which devastated a tract of country extending to about 18 miles in diameter. He began his work in 1857 by carrying off a follower of the Thakur of Gurwarra, on whom we were keeping a watch during the troublous times of the mutiny. My brother-in-law, Colonel Thomson and I, went after him under the supposition that it was a tiger that had killed the man, and it was not till we found the body at the bottom of a rocky ravine that we discovered it was a pard. During the beat he came out before us, went on, and was turned back by an elephant and came out again a third time before us; but we refrained from firing as we expected a man-eating tiger. I left Seonee for two years to join the Irregular Corps to which I had been posted, and after the end of the campaign, returned again to district work, and found that the most dreaded man-eater in the district was the pard whose life we had spared. There was a curious legend in connection with him, like the superstitious stories of Wehr wolves in Northern Europe. I have dealt fully with it in "Seonee," and Forsyth has also given a version of it in the 'Highlands of Central India,' as he came to the district soon after the animal was destroyed. Some of the aborigines of the Satpura Range are reputed to have the power of changing themselves into animals at will, and back again into the human form. The story runs, that one day one of these men, accompanied by his wife, came to a glade in the jungle where some nilgai were feeding. The woman expressed a wish for some meat, on which the husband gave her a root to hold, and to give him to smell on his return. He changed himself into a pard, killed one of the nilgai, and came bounding back for the root; but the terrified woman lost her nerve, flung away the charm, and rushed from the place. The husband hunted about wildly for the root, but in vain; and then inflamed with rage he pursued her, and tore her to pieces and continued to wreak his vengeance on the human race. Such was the history of the man-eating panther of Kahani, as related in the popular traditions of the country, and certainly everything in the career of this extraordinary animal tended to foster the unearthly reputation he had gained. Ranging over a circle, the radius of which may be put at eighteen miles, no one knew when and where he might be found. He seemed to kill for killing's sake, for often his victims—at times three in a single night—would be found untouched, save for the fatal wound in the throat. The watcher on the high machaun, the sleeper on his cot in the midst of a populous village, were alike his prey. The country was demoralized; the bravest hunters refused to go after him; wild pigs and deer ravaged the fields; none would dare to watch the growing crops. If it had been an ordinary panther who would have cared? Had not each village its Shikari? men who could boast of many an encounter with tiger and bear, and would they shrink from following up a mere animal? Certainly not; but they knew the tradition of Chinta Gond, and they believed it. What could they do?

On the morning of the second day, after leaving Amodagurh, the two sportsmen neared Sulema, a little village not far from Kahani, out of which it was reported the panther had taken no less than forty people within three years. There was not a house that had not mourned the loss of father, or mother, or brother, or sister, or wife or child, from within this little hamlet. Piteous indeed were the tales told as our friends halted to gather news, and the scars of the few who were fortunate enough to have escaped with life after a struggle with the enemy, were looked at with interest; but the most touching of all were the stories artlessly told by a couple of children, one of whom witnessed the death of a sister, and the other of a brother, both carried off in broad daylight, for the fell destroyer went boldly to work, knowing that they were but weak opponents."* I was out several times after this diabolical creature, but without success; as I sat out night after night I could hear the villagers calling from house to house hourly, "*Jágté ho bhiya! jágté ho!*" "Are you awake, brothers? are you awake!" All day long I scoured the country with my elephant, all night long I watched and waited. My camp was guarded by great fires, my servants and followers were made to sleep inside tents, whilst sentries with musket and bayonet were placed at the doors; but all to no purpose. The heated imagination of one sentry saw him glowering at him across the blazing fire. A frantic camp-follower spoilt my breakfast next morning ere I had taken a second mouthful, by declaring he saw him in an adjoining field. Then would come in a tale of a victim five miles off during the night, and then another, and sometimes a third. I have alluded before to his cowardice; in many cases a single man or boy would frighten him from his prey. On one occasion, in my rounds after him, I came upon a poor woman bitterly crying in a field; beside her lay the dead body of her husband. He had been seized by the throat and dragged across the fire made at the entrance of their little wigwam in which they had spent the night, watching their crops. The woman caught hold of her husband's legs, and, exerting her strength against the man-eater's, shrieked aloud. He dropped the body and fled, making no attempt to molest her or her little child of about four years of age. This man was the third he had attacked that night.

He was at last killed, by accident, by a native shikari who, in the dusk, took him for a pig or some such animal, and made a lucky shot; but the tale of his victims had swelled over two hundred during the three years of his reign of terror.

* 'Seonee.'

Felis Panthera

[*From a fine specimen in the Regent's Park Gardens.*]

No. 203. FELIS PANTHERA.

The Panther.

NATIVE NAMES.—*Chita*, *Gorbacha*, Hindi; *Beebeea-bagh*, Mahrathi, *Bibla*, of the Chita-catchers; *Ghur-hay* or *Dheer-hay* of the hill tribes; *Kerkal*, Canarese.

HABITAT.—India generally, Burmah and Ceylon, extending also into the Malayan countries.

DESCRIPTION.—Much smaller than the last, with comparatively shorter legs and rounder head; the fur is less bright; the ground-work often darker in colour, and the rosettes are more indistinct which is caused by the longer hairs intermingling and breaking into the edges of the spots; tail long and furry at the end. According to Temminck the tail is longer than that of the last species, having 28 caudal vertebræ against 22 of the other; if this be found to be the normal state, there will be additional grounds for separating the two.

SIZE.—Head and body, 3 to 3½ feet; tail, 2½ feet; height from 1½ to 2 feet.

This animal is more common than the pard, and it is more impudent in venturing into inhabited places. This is fortunate, for it is seldom a man-eater, although perhaps children may occasionally be carried off. I have before mentioned one which killed and partially devoured a pony in the heart of a populous town, and many are the instances of dogs being carried off out of the verandahs of Europeans' houses. A friend of mine one night being awoke by a piteous howl from a dog, chained to the centre pole of his tent, saw the head and shoulders of one peering in at the door; it retreated but had the audacity to return in a few minutes. Jerdon and other writers have adduced similar instances. It is this bold and reckless disposition which renders it easier to trap and shoot. The tiger is suspicious to a degree, and always apprehensive of a snare, but the panther never seems to trouble his head about the matter, but walks into a trap or resumes his feast on a previously killed carcase, though it may have been moved and handled. There is another thing, too, which shows the different nature of the beast. There is little difficulty in shooting a panther on a dark night. All that is necessary is to suspend, some little distance off, a common earthen *gharra* or water pot, with an oil light inside, the mouth covered lightly with a sod, and a small hole knocked in the side in such a way as to allow a ray of light to fall on the carcase. No tiger would come near such an arrangement, but the panther boldly sets to his dinner without suspicion, probably from his familiarity with the lights in the huts of villages.

I may here digress a little on the subject of night shooting. Every one who has tried it knows the extreme difficulty in seeing the sights of the rifle in a dark night. The common native method is to attach a fluff of cotton wool. On a moonlight night a bit of wax, with powdered mica scattered on it, will sometimes answer. I have seen diamond sights suggested, but all are practically useless. My plan was to carry a small phial of phosphorescent oil, about one grain to a drachm of oil dissolved in a bath of warm water. A small dab of this, applied to the fore and hind sights, will produce two luminous spots which will glow for about 40 or 50 seconds or a minute.

Dr. Sal Müller says of this species that it is occasionally found sleeping stretched across the forked branch of a tree, which is not the case with either the tiger or the pard. According to Sir Stamford Raffles, the *Rimau-dahan* or clouded panther (miscalled tiger) *Felis macrocelis*, has the same habit.

I would remark in conclusion that in the attempt to define clearly the position of these two animals the following points should be investigated by all who are interested in the subject and have the opportunity.

First the characteristics of the skull :—

viz.—Length, and breadth as compared with length of each, with presence or absence of the occipital ridge.

2ndly.—Number of caudal vertebræ in the tails of each.

3rdly.—Whether in a litter, from one female, cubs of each sort have been found.

No. 204. FELIS UNCIA.

The Ounce or Snow Panther (Jerdon's No. 106).

Felis uncia.

NATIVE NAMES.—*Iker*, Tibetan; *Sah*, Bhotia; *Phalé*, Lepcha; *Burrel-hay*, Simla hillmen; *Thurwag* in Kunawur. *The Snow-Leopard* of European sportsmen.

HABITAT.—Throughout the Himalayas, and the highland regions of Central Asia.

DESCRIPTION.—Pale yellowish or whitish isabelline, with small spots on the head and neck, but large blotchy rings and crescents, irregularly dispersed on the shoulders, sides and haunches; from middle of back to root of tail a medium irregular dark band closely bordered by a chain of oblong rings; lower parts dingy white, with some few dark spots about middle of abdomen; limbs with small spots; ears externally black; tail bushy with broad black rings.

SIZE.—Head and body about 4 feet 4 inches; tail, 3 feet: height, about 2 feet.

I have only seen skins of this animal, which is said to frequent rocky ground, and to kill *Barhel*, *Thar*, sheep, goats, and dogs, but not to molest man. This species is distinguishable from all the preceding felines by the shortness and breadth of the face and the sudden elevation of the forehead—*Gray*. Pupil round—*Hodgson*.

No. 205. FELIS DIARDII *vel* MACROCELIS.

The Clouded Panther (*Jerdon's No.* 107).

NATIVE NAMES.—*Tungmar*, Lepcha; *Zik*, Bhotia; *Lamchitta*, of the Khas tribe (*Jerdon*). *Riman dahan* of Sumatra.

HABITAT.—Nepal, Sikim, Assam, Burmah, and down the Malayan Peninsula to Sumatra, Java and Bornea.

DESCRIPTION.—A short-legged long-bodied animal, with a very elongated skull; the upper canines are the longest in comparison of all living felines, and in this respect it comes nearest to the extinct species *Felis smilodon*. The ground-work of the colouring is a pale buff, with large, irregular, cloud-like patches of black. Blyth remarks that the markings are exceedingly beautiful, but most difficult to describe, as they not only vary in different specimens, but also in the two sides of one individual. Jerdon's description is as follows: "Ground colour variable, usually pale greenish brown or dull clay brown, changing to pale tawny on the lower parts, and limbs internally, almost white however in some. In many specimens the fulvous or tawny hue is the prevalent one; a double line of small chain-like stripes from the ears, diverging on the nape to give room to an inner and smaller series; large irregular clouded spots or patches on the back and sides edged very dark and crowded together; loins, sides of belly and belly marked with irregular small patches and spots: some black lines on the cheeks and sides of neck, and a black band across the throat; tail with dark rings, thickly furred, long; limbs bulky, and body heavy and stout; claws very powerful." Hodgson stated that the pupil of the eye is round, but Mr. Bartlett, whose opportunities of observation have been much more frequent, is positive that it is oval.

SIZE.—Head and body, $3\frac{1}{2}$ feet; tail, 3 feet, but Jerdon states it grows to a larger size.

This is one of the most beautiful of all the cat family. It is not, however, one of the most elegant in form and motion, but its colouring is exquisite; it is quite an arboreal feline, and is found only in forests, frequently sleeping or lying in wait across the forked branches of trees, from which habit it acquires its Malayan name, *dahan*, signifying the forked branch of a tree. The young seem to be easily tamed, according to Sir Stamford Raffles, who describes two which he had in confinement. Dr. Jerdon also states the same, he having procured a young one in the

Felis Diardii.

neighbourhood of Darjeeling. In the Zoological Gardens in London there was a very fine specimen about four years ago. Professor Parker says of it: "It was not always to be seen, as it was kept during the day fastened up in one of the sleeping apartments at the back of a cage in the lion-house, and was left out only for about half an hour before the gardens closed. It was well worth stopping to see. As soon as the iron door of its cell was raised, it would come out into the large cage with a peculiar sailor-like slouch, for owing to the shortness of its legs, its gait was quite different to that of an ordinary cat, and altogether less elegant. The expression of the face, too, was neither savage nor majestic nor intelligent, but rather dull and stupid. It was fond of assuming all sorts of queer attitudes. Brehm describes one as lying prone on a thick branch placed in its cage, with all four legs hanging down straight, two on each side of the branch—certainly a remarkable position for an animal to assume of its own free will.

The type of this animal constitutes the genus *Neofelis* of Gray, containing two species, this and the *Neofelis* (*leopardus*) *brachyurus* of Formosa.

No. 206. FELIS VIVERRINA.

The Large Tiger-Cat (*Jerdon's No.* 108).

NATIVE NAMES.—*Mach-bagral*, *Bagh-dasha*, Bengali; *Bunbiral*, *Khupya-bagh*, Hindi; *Handoon-deeva*, Singhalese.

HABITAT.—India generally, Burmah, the Malay countries, and Ceylon. Jerdon says he has not heard of it in Central India nor in the Carnatic, nor farther west of Nepal. I have been, however, informed that a wild cat was killed lately at Jeypore in the act of carrying off an infant of four months old. I know of no cat, save this species, capable of such a proceeding. The child was rescued alive.

DESCRIPTION.—"Of a mouse gray colour, more or less deep and sometimes tinged with tawny, with large dark spots, more or less numerous, oblong on the back and neck and in lines, more or less rounded elsewhere, and broken or coalescing" (but never ocellate: *Blyth*); "cheeks white; a black face stripe; beneath dull white; chest with five or six dark bands; belly spotted," (whence the name *celidogaster* applied by Temminck) "tail with six or seven dark bands and a black tip" (sometimes spots only); "feet unspotted."—*Jerdon.*

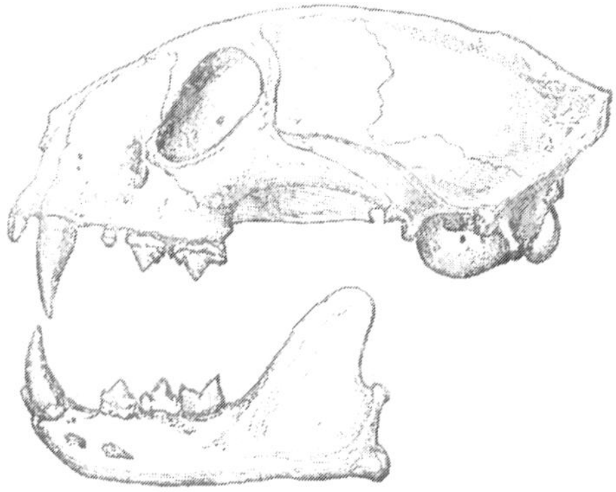

Skull of *Felis viverrina*.

SIZE.—Head and body 30 to 34 inches; tail only 10 to 13; height about 15 or 16; weight according to Hodgson and Jerdon, about 17 lbs.

The frontal and jugal bones in old specimens of this species are united by a bar which forms a complete bony orbit—a peculiarity possessed, as I have before observed, by *F. longicaudata*, but by few other felines. *Felis rubiginosa*, *F. planiceps*, and *F. Ellioti* are also cats of this type, which Gray has separated into the genus *Viverriceps*.

This large cat is not uncommon near Calcutta, and is reputed to live much on fish and fresh-water shells, but also I should say on larger game. According to some authors (Buchanan-Hamilton, for instance), it is fierce and untameable, but Blyth states that he had several big toms, quite tame, and in the Surrey Zoological Gardens there was many years ago a very fine male which he had frequently handled and had even on his lap. He relates, however, in another part, that a newly caught male of this species killed a tame young leopardess of twice its own size, having broken through the partition of a cage, but he did not eat any portion of her. The Prince of Wales took home a very fine specimen of this cat among his collection of living animals.

Mr. Rainey writes of the ferocity of this cat in the following terms: "I can testify to the existence of the above qualities in this animal (*Felis viverrina*, Bennett), which is rather abundant in these parts, generally taking up its quarters in low, swampy jungle, where it often carries off calves, for which the leopard (*F. leopardus*, Linn.), undeservedly gets credit. Lately, a couple of months ago, a pair of them at night broke into a matted house, and went off with a brace of ewes, which had half-a-dozen lambs between them, born only a short time before their mothers met with their bloody end. I have caught this species in traps, and when let loose in an indigo vat with a miscellaneous pack of dogs, they have invariably fought hard, and at times proved too much for their canine adversaries, so that I have had to go to their rescue, and put an end to the fight, by a spear-thrust, or a heavy whack on the back of the head with a stout club. Some years ago one got into my fowl-house at night, and just as I opened the door to enter inside, it made a fierce jump at me from a perch on the opposite side. I had just time to put the barrel of my gun forward, on the muzzle of which it fell, and had its chest blown to atoms, as I pulled the trigger instantly it alighted there."

No. 207. FELIS MARMORATA.

The Marbled Tiger-Cat (*Jerdon's No.* 109).

HABITAT.—The Sikim Himalayas, Assam, Burmah, and the Malayan countries.

DESCRIPTION.—"Size of a domestic cat, but with stouter limbs and a much longer and thicker tail, of uniform thickness throughout and reaching back to the occiput when reflected; the upper canines are not remarkably elongated as in *F. macroceloides* (*macrocelis*); ears rather small and obtusely angulated, with a conspicuous white spot on their hinder surface" (*Blyth*). "Ground colour dingy-fulvous, occasionally yellowish grey; the body with numerous elongate wavy black spots, somewhat clouded or marbled; the head and nape with some narrow blackish lines, coalescing into a dorsal interrupted band; the thighs and part of the sides with black round spots; the tail black, spotted, and with the tip black; belly yellowish white."—*Jerdon.*

SIZE.—Head and body, 18 to 24 inches; tail, 14 to 16.

This beautiful little cat is almost a miniature of the clouded panther, and Blyth confuses the Malayan name of the latter, and applies it to this species, which probably arose from his quoting as a synonym, *F. diardii*, which, however, in the same paper he repudiates, as the description of the

Felis marmorata.

size of *F. diardii* clearly proved a much larger animal. This is the type of Grey's genus *Catolynx*, the other species in India being *F. charltoni.* The genus is peculiar from the resemblance of the nasal bones to those of the lynx, and from the complete or nearly complete bony orbit; the skull differs, however, greatly from the *viverriceps* form, being much more spherical with very short nasal bones. There is an admirable illustration in De Blainville's 'Ostéographie' of it under the name of *F. longicaudata.* Very little is known as yet of the habits of this cat.

No. 208. FELIS BENGALENSIS.

The Leopard-Cat (*Jerdon's No.* 110).

NATIVE NAMES.—*Bun Beral*, Bengali; *Jungli Bilao, Chhita Bilao*, Hindi; *Theet-kyoung* in Arakan; *Lhan-rahn-manjur*, Mahrathi; *Wagati*, Mahratti of the Ghats.

HABITAT.—India generally, in hilly parts; Assam, Burmah, and the Malay countries: also Ceylon.

DESCRIPTION.—About the size of the domestic cat, but with extremely variable colouring and a short, thick, cylindrical tail reaching, when turned back, above half way up the spine. Blyth says of it: "In general the ground hue is pale fulvous, with under parts of the purest white, richly marked with deep black; black lines on the crown and nape; angular spots on the body wholly or partially black, or, *en rosette*, with deeper fulvous within and round; black spots on the limbs and tail; sometimes the body markings unite more or less into longitudinal streaks and rarely a marbled appearance is assumed on the upper parts."

SIZE.—Head and body, 24 to 26 inches; tail 11 to 12.

It is useless to lay down, as in Jerdon, a very accurate description of the markings of this cat, for it varies to such an extent as to have given rise to at least sixteen synonymous names, if not more. You will find the same cat repeated over and over again in Gray's catalogue, and a different name in almost every book of natural history; it figures at large as *Felis Bengalensis*, *undata*, *Javanensis*, *Sumatrana*, *minuta*, *torquata Nipalensis*, *wagati*, *pardochrous*, *undulata*, *Ellioti*, *Horsfieldi*, *inconspicua*, *Chinensis*, *Reevesii*, and *Diardii*. Blyth pertinently remarks: "The varieties of this handsome little cat are endless, and nominal species may be made of it, *ad libitum*, if not rather *ad nauseam*."

This is a very savage animal, and not tameable. Jerdon and Blyth both agree in this from specimens they kept alive. Hutton also writes: "I have a beautiful specimen alive, so savage that I dare not touch her." I should like to possess a young one, having been successful with many so-called savage animals. I had a wild-cat once which was very savage at first, but which ultimately got so tame as to lie in my lap whilst I was at work in office or writing, but she would never allow me to touch or stroke her; she would come and go of her own sweet will, and used to come daily, but she would spit and snarl if I attempted a caress. Blyth says that in confinement it never paces its cage, but constantly remains crouched in a corner, though awake and vigilant; but I have always found that the confinement of a cage operates greatly against the chance of taming any wild animal. Sir Walter Elliot says that the Shikaris attribute to it the same habit as that which used erroneously to be ascribed to the glutton, viz., that of dropping from trees on to its prey and eating its way into the neck. It preys chiefly on small game—poultry, hares, and is said to destroy small deer. McMaster relates he "saw one carry off a fowl nearly as large as itself, shaking it savagely meanwhile, and making a successful retreat in spite of the abuse, uproar, and missiles which the theft caused." Dr. Anderson says it is essentially arboreal, and the natives assert it lives on birds and small mammals, such as *Squirrels* and *Tupaiæ*. According to Hutton it breeds in May, producing three or four young in caves or beneath masses of rock.

No. 209. FELIS JERDONI.

The Lesser Leopard-Cat (Jerdon's No. 111).

HABITAT.—Peninsula of India, probably also Assam and Burmah.

DESCRIPTION.—"Very like *F. Bengalensis;* but smaller, the ground colour of the upper part grey, untinged with fulvous" (*Blyth*). A few small distinct black spots; spots of sides of legs round, long in the centre of the back; tail and feet dark greyish brown, but slightly spotted, if at all; chin, throat, and under parts white, with black spots.

No. 210. FELIS AURATA.

The Bay Cat (Jerdon's No. 112).

HABITAT.—The Nepal and Sikim Himalayas, probably also Assam; and as it occurs in the Malayan islands, it should be found in Burmah. It is likewise an African species, Gold Coast.

DESCRIPTION. — Deep bay red above, paler below; a few indistinct dark spots on the hind legs and sides; throat white; inside of ears black; the head beautifully striped with black, white and orange; the cheeks are yellowish, with two black streaks; a pale black edged line over the eyes; whiskers black, with white tips; claws black. Jerdon says that the lower surface in some is reddish white, with large and small maroon spots.

Felis aurata.

SIZE.—Head and body, 31 inches and over; tail, 19. There is a fine illustration of this cat in Cassell's 'Natural History,' edited by Professor Martin Duncan, vol. ii., page 58.

Very little is known of the habits of this cat. Mr. Hodgson's first specimen "was caught in a tree by some hunters in the midst of an exceedingly dense forest. Though only just taken it bore confinement very tranquilly, and gave evident signs of a tractable disposition, but manifested high courage, for the approach of a huge Bhotea dog to its cage excited in it symptoms of wrath only, none of fear." That it is found in Burmah is extremely probable, as it inhabits the Malay countries, and the Rev. J. Mason speaks of a tiger cat in Tenasserim, "which the Karens call the *Fire Tiger* from the colour of its skin, which is of an uniform red."

No. 211. FELIS RUBIGINOSA.

The Rusty-spotted Cat (*Jerdon's No.* 113).

NATIVE NAME.—*Namali pelli*, Tamil.—*Jerdon.*

HABITAT.—Southern India and Ceylon. Jerdon says he never saw or heard of it in Central India, or on the Malabar Coast, but I got it at Seonee in the Central Provinces.

DESCRIPTION.—Size of a small domestic cat, with a tail half the length of the body; colour greyish with a rufous tinge, or greenish grey tinged with rufous; the under parts white, with large rufous spots; ears small; four well defined dark brown or black lines along the forehead and nape, and three along the back, the latter being interrupted into longish spots; a series of rusty coloured spots on the sides; fur very short; tail uniform in colour, more rufous than the body, sometimes indistinctly spotted; insides of limbs with large brown spots; feet reddish grey above with black soles, whiskers long and white.

SIZE.—Head and body, 16 to 18 inches; tail, 9½.

Jerdon says: "This very pretty little cat frequents grass in the dry beds of tanks, brushwood, and occasionally drains in the open country and near villages, and it is said not to be a denizen of the jungles. I had a kitten brought to me when very young, in 1846, and it became quite tame, and was the delight and admiration of all who saw it. Its activity was quite marvellous, and it was very playful and elegant in its motions. When it was about eight months old I introduced it into a room where there was a small fawn of the gazelle, and the little creature flew at it the moment it saw it, seized it by the nape, and was with difficulty taken off. I lost it shortly after this. It would occasionally find its way to the rafters of bungalows and hunt for squirrels."

Jerdon doubted the existence of this cat in Central India, but, in 1859 or 1860, I had two kittens brought to me by a Gond in the Seonee district, and I kept them for many months. They became perfectly tame, so much so that, although for nine months of the year I was out in camp, they never left the tents, although allowed to roam about unconfined. The grace and agility of their motions was most striking. I have seen one of them balance itself on the back of a chair, and when one of the pair died it was ludicrous to see the attempts of a little gray village cat, which I got to be a companion to the survivor, to emulate the gymnastics of its wild comrade. At night the little cats were put into a basket, and went on with the spare tents to my next halting place; and on my arrival next morning I would find them frisking about the tent roof between the two canvasses, or scrambling up the trees under which we were pitched. Whilst I was at work I usually had one in my lap and the other cuddled behind my back on the chair. One day one of them, which had been exploring the hollows of an old tree close by, rushed into my tent and fell down in convulsions at my feet. I did everything in my power for the poor little creature, but in vain, it died in two or three minutes, having evidently been bitten by a snake. The survivor was inconsolable, refused food, and went mewing all over the place and kept rolling at my feet, rubbing itself against them as though to beg for the restoration of its brother. At last I sent into a village and procured a common kitten, which I put into the basket with the other. There was a great deal of spitting and growling at first, but in time they became great friends, but the villager was no match for the forester. It was amusing to see the wild one dart like a squirrel up the walls of the tent on to the roof; the other would try to follow, scramble up a few feet, and then, hanging by its claws, look round piteously before it dropped to the ground.

No. 212. FELIS TORQUATA.

The Spotted Wild-Cat (Jerdon's No. 114).

NATIVE NAME.—*Lhan-rahn-manjur,* Mahrathi.

HABITAT.—North-Western, Central, and Southern India.

DESCRIPTION.—Ground colour pale greyish fulvous or cat-grey, with numerous round black spots, smaller on the head, nape, and shoulders; longitudinal lines on the occiput; cheek striped; breast spotted, but belly free from spots; on the limbs distinct cross bands; within the arms one or two broad black streaks; tail tapering more or less, and marked with a series of well-defined rings and a black tip; smallish ears, as in the domestic cat, reddish outside with a small dusky tuft at tip; paws black underneath.

SIZE.—Head and body, from 16 to 24 inches; tail, about half the length.

Blyth first obtained this from Hansi, where it was stated to frequent open sandy plains, living on field rats. Jerdon at Hissar and in the Central Provinces. At Hissar he found it among low sand-hills, where it appeared to feed on the jerboa-rat (*Gerbillus indicus*), which is common there. Sykes seems to have confused this species with a domestic variety run wild, as the habits differ from the present species.

No. 213. FELIS MANUL.

The Black-chested Wild-Cat.

HABITAT.—Tibet, Central and Northern Asia.

DESCRIPTION.—Rufescent pale grey; chest and front of neck and part of belly sooty black, "terminating forward near the ears horn-wise or crescent-wise; on the crown of the head several series of black dots are disposed more or less linearly and length-wise. On the cheeks, from eyes to articulation of jaws, are two sub-parallel zig-zag lines of jet black; five to seven straighter lines, less deep in hue, cross the lower back and blend gradually with the caudal rings, which, including the black tip, are about nine in number. These rings of the tail are narrow, with large intervals, diminishing towards its tip, as the interstices of the dorsal bars do towards the base of the tail; the black caudal rings are perfect, save the two basal, which are deficient below, whilst the two apical on the contrary are rather wider below and nearly or quite connected there. Outside the arms and sides are two or three transverse black bars, more or less freckled with the grey hairs of the body; ears outside grey, like the back, but paler, small and much rounded. The young show the marks more clearly" (*Blyth*, abridged from *Hodgson*).

SIZE.—Head and body, 22 to 24 inches: tail, 10 to 11 inches.

This animal which is allied to the European wild-cat, was first discovered by Pallas, who, however, has left little on record concerning its habits beyond that it is found in woody rocky countries preying on the smaller quadrupeds.

No. 214. FELIS SCRIPTA.

HABITAT.—Thibet.*

No. 215. FELIS SHAWIANA.

The Yarkand Spotted Wild-Cat.

NATIVE NAME.—*Molun*, Turki.

HABITAT.—Turkistan, Yarkand.

DESCRIPTION.—"General colour pale greyish fulvous above, the back rather darker than the sides; under parts white; the body marked throughout with rather small black spots which are largest on the abdomen, smaller and closer together on the shoulders and thighs, tending to form cross lines on the latter, and indistinct on the middle of the back; anterior portion of the face and muzzle whitish; cheek stripes of rusty red and black; hairs mixed; ears rather more rufous outside, especially towards the tip, which is blackish brown and pointed; the hairs at the end scarcely lengthened; interior of ears white; there are some faint rufous spots at the side of the neck; breast very faintly rufous, with one narrow brownish band across; inside of limbs mostly white; a black band inside the forearm, and a very black spot behind the tarsus; tail dusky above near the base, with five or six black bars above on the posterior half, none below, the dark bars closer together

* Milne-Edwards describes this animal in his 'Recherches sur les Mammifères,' page 341.

towards the tip; fur soft, moderately long, purplish grey towards the base."

SIZE.—Apparently exceeds that of the common cat, and equals *F. chaus;* the tail about half the length of the body.

I have taken the above description from Mr. W. T. Blanford ('Report on the Second Yarkand Mission: Mammalia') who has first described and named this new species. There is also an excellent plate in the same portion of the report, which unfortunately is published at an almost prohibitive price, and to be obtained at the Government Press. The black spots on the belly have been inadvertently left out; otherwise the plate is excellent, as are all the others, especially the osteological ones.

No. 216. FELIS CHAUS.

The Common Jungle-Cat (Jerdon's No. 115).

NATIVE NAMES.—*Kutas* (according to Jerdon, but I have always found this applied to the *Paradoxurus*), *Jangli-billi, Ban-bilao,* Hindi; *Ban beral,* Bengali; *Birka,* Bhagalpor Hill Tribes; *Maut-bek,* Canarese; *Kada-bek* or *Bella-bek* of Waddars; *Mota lahn manjur,* Mahrathi; *Bhaoga* Mahrathi of the Ghats; *Jinki-pilli,* Telegu; *Cheru-pali,* Malabarese (*Jerdon*); *Khyoung-Tsek-koon* in Arakan.

HABITAT.—Common all over India from 7,000 or 8,000 feet of elevation in the Himalayas, down to Cape Comorin and the Island of Ceylon. It is also found in Assam and Burmah. This species appears to have a wide range, as it has been found also in Persia, on the borders of the Caspian and in Egypt.

DESCRIPTION.—Larger somewhat, and more lanky than the domestic cat. The general appearance of the fur a rusty or grizzly grey; the hairs being pale fulvous brown with dark tips; more rufous on the sides of the abdomen and neck, the lower parts being white; faint transverse stripes, occasionally broken into spots on the sides, but these markings disappear with old age, and are more difficult to trace in the deeper furred specimens from cold countries; the markings are darker on the limbs, and there is a distinct black bar on the forearm near the elbow; inside are two or three dark stripes; the feet are blackish underneath; often a dark bar across the chest, and sometimes faint spots on the belly; rufous stripes on the cheek; a dark stripe ascends from the eye, especially in the young animal, and it has sometimes faint stripes on the nape mingling on the forehead; the ears are slightly tufted, dark externally, white within; the tail, which is short, is more or less ringed from the middle to the tip, which is black. Melanoid specimens have been found.

SIZE.—Head and body, about 26 inches; tail, nine to ten; height at shoulder, 14 to 15 inches.

This rather common cat is, in some degree, related to the lynxes, sufficiently distinct, yet resembling the latter in its tufted ears, short tail, long limbs, and some few peculiarities of the skull.

Jerdon says of it: "It frequents alike jungles and the open country, and is very partial to long grass and reeds, sugar-cane fields, corn fields, &c. It does much damage to game of all kinds—hares, partridges, &c., and quite recently I shot a pea fowl at the edge of a sugar-cane field when one of these cats sprang out, seized the pea fowl, and after a short struggle (for the bird was not dead) carried it off before my astonished eyes, and in spite of my running up, made good his escape with his booty. It must have been stalking these birds, so immediately did its spring follow my shot." Blyth writes: "In India the *chaus* does not shun, but even affects populous neighbourhoods, and is a terrible depredator among the tame ducks and poultry, killing as many as it can get at, but I have not known him to attack geese, of which I long kept a flock out day and night, about a tank where ducks could not be left out at night on account of these animals. A pair of them bred underneath my house, and I frequently observed them, and have been surprised at the most extraordinary humming sound which they sometimes uttered of an evening. Their other cries were distinguishable from those of the domestic cat." This species will, however, interbreed with the domestic cat. According to Hodgson it breeds twice a year in the woods, producing three or four kittens at a birth. It is said to be untameable, but in 1859, at Sasseram, one of the men of my Levy caught a very young kitten, which was evidently of this species. I wrote at the time to a friend about a young mongoose which I had just got, and added, "It is great fun to see my last acquisition and a little jungle cat (*Felis chaus*) playing together. They are just like two children in their manner, romping and rolling over each other, till one gets angry, when there is a quarrel and a fight, which, however, is soon made up, the kitten generally making the first advances towards a reconciliation, and then they go on as merrily as ever. The cat is a very playful, good tempered little thing; the colour is a reddish-yellow with darker red stripes like a tiger, and slightly spotted; the ears and eyes are very large; the orbits of the last bony and prominent. What is it? *Chaus* or *Bengalensis*? * I am not as yet learned in cats when very young. If it be a real jungle cat—which my shikaris declare it to be—it strangely belies the savage nature of its kind, as Thomson says:—

> 'The tiger darting fierce
> Impetuous on the prey his glance has doom'd
> The lively shining leopard speckled o'er
> With many a spot the beauty of the waste
> And scorning all the taming arts of man.'

* Both reputed to be untameable.

"Poets are not always correct. Tigers have often been tamed, though they are not to be depended on."

Now we come to the true Lynxes, which are cats with very short tails, long limbs, tufted ears, the cheeks whiskered almost as long as Dundreary's, and feet the pads of which are overgrown with hair. Some naturalists would separate them from the other cats, but the connection is supplied by the last species which, though possessing certain features of the lynx, yet interbreeds with the true cats. The lynx was well known to the ancients, and was one of the animals used in the arena from its savage disposition, and its sight was considered so piercing as to be able to penetrate even stone walls! There are no true lynxes in India proper; we must look to the colder Trans-Himalayan countries for them. The following is from Thibet:—

No. 217. FELIS ISABELLINA.

The Thibetan Lynx.

HABITAT.—Thibet.

DESCRIPTION.—"Pale isabella-brown, with scarcely a trace of markings, but in some the spots come out even conspicuously in summer *pelage*, especially on the limbs and belly, and the crown and middle of the back are generally more or less infuscated, occasionally very much so; in some the face is almost white, with traces of frontal streaks, and there is always (the same as in the European lynx) a short, narrow, dark streak on each side of the nose towards its tip."—*Blyth.*

This species is similar in some respects to the European animal, but the principal difference lies in the feet, the pads of which in the Thibetan species are prominent and bare, with short, close fur between them, whereas in the European lynx the long fur completely conceals the pads, and the latter is the larger animal. There is a very good photograph of *F. isabellina* in Kinloch's 'Large Game Shooting in Thibet and the North-West,' taken from a carefully stuffed specimen. The author says: "On the 4th of July 1866, I was hunting *Oves Ammon* on the high ground between Hanle and Nyima, when I suddenly came upon a female lynx with two young cubs. I shot the mother, and as the cubs concealed themselves among some rocks, I barricaded them in, and went on with my hunting. On arriving in camp I sent men back to try and catch the cubs; in this they succeeded, and brought them to me. They were about the size of half grown cats, and more spiteful vicious little devils cannot be imagined; they were, however, very handsome, with immense heads and paws. For two or three days they refused all food; but at the end of that time they fed quite ravenously from the hand. They soon became very tame and playful, though always ready to set their backs up if at all teased, or if a dog came near them."

The next species differs from the typical lynx in wanting the ruff of hair round the face, and also in having the pads of the feet bald. The skull is that of a lynx, but the processes of the frontals and intermaxillæ are not quite so much produced, and they do not entirely separate the nasal from the maxillæ. There is a good illustration to be found in De Blainville's 'Ostéographie.'

No. 218. FELIS CARACAL.

The Red Lynx (*Jerdon's No.* 116).

NATIVE NAME.—*Siagosh*, Persian, i.e., black ear.

HABITAT.—Scattered throughout India generally, Assam (Burmah and Ceylon ?), but it has also a much wider range, being found throughout Africa, Syria, and Arabia, and also in Persia.

DESCRIPTION.—Colour sandy fulvous, varying somewhat in individuals; paler beneath, in some almost white; tail the same colour as the body, with a black tip; the lower parts with some obscure spots, more or less distinct on the belly, flanks and insides of limbs; ears black externally, with a long dark ear tuft, white inside; a small blackish spot on the upper lip, and another above the eye, also a line down each side of the nose. In some individuals faint bars and caudal rings are discernible, and the chest is obscurely banded.

SIZE.—Head and body, 26 to 30 inches; tail, 9 or 10; height, 16 to 18 inches.

This handsome lynx is found, though not very common, in most parts of the Indian Peninsula, although Jerdon states that it is unknown in the Himalayas, Bengal, and the eastern countries. In those parts where it abounds it is very destructive to small game, such as gazelles, the smaller deer and hares. It also catches such birds as pea-fowl, florican, cranes, &c., frequently springing at them from the ground as they fly over. They are easily tamed. I had a young one at Seonee, and the natives of some parts are said to train them for sporting purposes in the manner in which the hunting leopard is trained.

Blyth says a brace of siagosh are often pitted against each other by the natives who keep them, a heavy wager pending as to which of the two will disable the greater number out of a flock of tame pigeons feeding, before the mass of them can rise out of reach, and ten or a dozen birds are commonly struck down right and left.

"It is a most sanguinary creature, yet the keepers manage them with facility, and slip the hood over their eyes with extreme dexterity, while they are engaged with their prey. In general they become quite tame to persons they know, and often sufficiently so to bear handling by a stranger. Much as I have seen of them I never heard one utter a sound, except hissing and growling."

With regard to this last assertion of Mr. Blyth's I may say that the caracal differs very much from the European lynx, who, according to Tschudi, betrays his presence by horrible howlings audible at a great distance. Professor Kitchen Parker writes that the specimen now in the Zoological Gardens is a most cantankerous beast.* "If the American

Felis caracal.

lynx, who is unfortunate enough to live in the same cage with him, dares to come betwixt the wind and his nobility, or even if he, in the course of his peregrinations, should, by chance, get sufficiently near his companion to be annoyed with the sight of so vulgar a beast, he immediately arches his back, lays back his ears, uncovers his great canines, and swears in a most fearful manner until the other unlucky animal is quite cowed, and looks as meek as its feline nature will allow it, evidently deprecating the anger of my lord; and although not

* I can bear witness to this, having lately made his acquaintance.

conscious of having done wrong, quite ready to promise faithfully never to do it again."

We now take up the last member of the Cat family; one differing so much in certain respects as to have been classed by some authors as a separate genus, to which Wagner gave the name of *Cynælurus,* or dog-cat, which, however, is not appropriate, as the animal, though having the slender form of the greyhound, and in having the claws of its middle front toes but imperfectly retractile, is, in its anatomy and all osteological features, a true cat. As I have before remarked it is to this animal alone that the name leopard should be applied, the peculiar ruff or shagginess of hair on the neck having given rise to the ancient superstition that this animal was a cross between the lion and the pard, whence its name Leo-Pardus. There are three varieties found in Africa and India—one, the maneless leopard, is confined to Africa, where also is found in the south a woolly variety with light brown spots. The maned leopard is found all over South-West Asia, including India.

NO. 219. FELIS JUBATA.

The Hunting Leopard (Jerdon's No. 117).

NATIVE NAMES.—*Chita,* Hindi; *Yuz* of the Chita-catchers; *Kendua-bagh,* Bengali; *Laggar* in some parts; *Chita Puli,* Telegu; *Chircha* and *Sivungi,* Canarese.

HABITAT.—Central or Southern India, and in the North-West from Kandeish, through Scinde and Rajpootana, to the Punjab. It is also found in all Africa, with Syria and Arabia, and throughout Asia Minor. In India the places where it is most common are Jeypur in Upper India, and Hyderabad in Southern India.

DESCRIPTION.—A tall, slim animal, with body much drawn in at the flanks like a greyhound; purely cat-like head with short round ears; long tail, much compressed at the end; in colour a bright rufous fawn, more or less deep, sometimes what Blyth calls a bright *nankeen,* dotted with numerous small black spots which are single, and not in rosettes, as in the pards; a black streak from the corner of the eye down the face; ears black at base externally, the rest whitish; the tail spotted, but having three or four black rings at the tip: the extreme tip is always white; the hair of the belly is lengthened with a shaggy

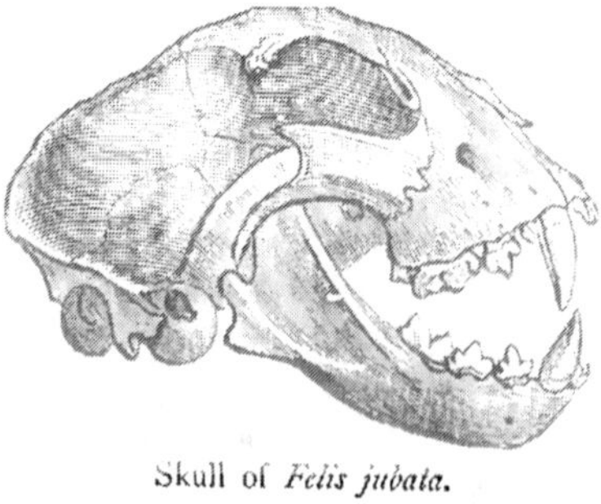

Skull of *Felis jubata.*

fringe-like appearance; the fur generally is coarse; the nozzle is black, whereas in the tiger it is pink, and in a pard dusky pink; the pupils of the eye contract circularly.

SIZE.—Head and body, about $4\frac{1}{2}$ feet; tail, $2\frac{1}{2}$; height, $2\frac{1}{2}$ to $2\frac{3}{4}$ feet.

This animal is one of the most interesting of all the felines, both as regards its appearance, disposition, habits, and the uses to which it can be put. Throughout India it is in much request as a necessary appanage to regal state; and, therefore, a class of men devote themselves to the trapping of this creature which, when trained, finds a ready sale at the courts of Indian nobles. For this purpose the adult animal is always caught, it being considered by the chita-catchers that a young leopard would never turn out well for the purposes of the chase. A similar idea prevails amongst the falconers of Hindustan regarding nestlings, and it is surprising how soon a large adult and apparently savage animal

Felis jubata.

can be reduced to a state of comparative slavery and obedient to the orders of his keepers.

Dr. Jerdon describes one which he brought up from its earliest infancy; his bungalow was next to the one I inhabited for a time at Kampti, and consequently I saw a good deal of Billy, as the leopard was named. At my first interview I found him in the stables amongst the dogs and horses, and, as I sat down on his charpoy, he jumped up alongside of me, and laid down to be scratched, playing and purring and licking my hands with a very rough tongue. He sometimes used to go out with his master, and was gradually getting into the way of running down antelope, when Dr. Jerdon was ordered off on field service.

The mode of hunting with the chita is so well known, and has been so frequently described, that I think I need not attempt a description.

Its habits in a state of nature, and the mode of capture, are more to the purport of this work. It is said by shikarees to feed only once every third day, when, after gorging itself, it retires to its den for the other two. On the morning of the third day he visits some particular tree, which the animals of his species in the neighbourhood are in the habit of frequenting. Such trees are easily to be recognised by the scoring of the bark on which he whets his claws. Here, after having relieved himself in various ways and played about with such of his comrades as may be there, they go off on a hunting expedition.

There is an interesting letter from "Deccanee Bear" in *The Asian* of the 22nd of July, 1880, giving a description of the snaring of some of these animals, and the remarks he makes about their rendezvous at a particular tree, corroborates what has been asserted by other writers. He says: "Arrived at the spot the bullocks were soon relieved of their burden, and then work commenced. The nooses were of the same kind as those used for snaring antelope, made from the dried sinews of the antelope. These were pegged down in all directions, and at all angles, to a distance of 25 to 30 feet from the tree. The carts and bullocks were sent off into a road about a mile away. An ambush was made of bushes and branches some fifty or sixty yards away, and here, when the time came, I and three Vardis ensconced ourselves. I have sat near some dirty fellows in my life, but the stench of those three men baffles description; you could cut it with a knife. I could not smoke, so had to put up with the several smells until I was nearly sick. At last the sun commenced to sink, and the men who were looking round in all directions, suddenly pointed in the direction of the north. Sure enough there were four cheetahs skying away and playing together about 400 yards off; they came closer and closer, when they stopped about 100 yards off, looking about as if they suspected danger. However, they became reassured, and all raced away as hard as they could in the direction of the tree. Two were large and the other two smaller; the larger had the best of the race, and were entangled by all four feet before they knew where they were. The Vardis made a rush. I did the same, but in a second was flat on the ground, having caught my feet in the nooses. One of the men came and released me from my undignified position, and I could then see how the cheetahs were secured. A country blanket was thrown over the heads of the animal, and the two fore or hind legs tied together. The carts had come up by this time; a leather hood was substituted for the blanket—a rather ticklish operation, during which one man was badly bitten in the hand. The cheetahs know how to use their teeth and claws. Having been securely fastened on the carts, and the nooses collected, we started for camp, which we reached about eight in he evening. I was much pleased with what I had seen and learnt, but it took me a long time to get the smell of the Vardis out of my head. The next morning I went to see the cheetahs and found that they had been tied spread-eagle fashion on the carts, and with their hoods firmly tied. They were a pair, and in all probability the parents of the two smaller ones. Women and children are told off to sit all day long close to the animals, and keep up a conversation, so that they should get accustomed to the human voice. The female was snarling a good deal, the male being much quieter; they go through various gradations of education, and I was told they would be ready to be unhooded and worked in about six months' time. The man who had his hand bitten was suffering from considerable inflammation. I had him attended to, and, after rewarding them with 'baksheesh,' I let them proceed on their way rejoicing."

Chita kittens are very pretty little things, quite grey, without any spots whatever, but they can always be recognised by the black stripe down the nose, and on cutting off a little bit of the soft hair I noticed that the spots were quite distinct in the under fur. I have not seen this fact alluded to by others. As a rule the young of all cats, even the large one-coloured species, such as the lion and puma, are spotted, but the hunting leopard is externally an exception, although the spots are there lying hid. I had several of them at Seonee.

HYÆNIDÆ—THE HYÆNAS.

The second family of the Æluroidea contains only one genus, the *Hyæna*, which, though somewhat resembling the dog in outward appearance, connects the cat with the civet. The differences between the *Felidæ* and the *Viverridæ*, setting aside minor details, are in the teeth, and the possession by the latter of a caudal pouch. My readers are now familiar with the simple cutting form of the feline teeth, which are thirty in number. The civets have no less than forty, and the grinders, instead of having cutting scissor-like edges, are cuspidate, or crowned with tubercles. Now the hyæna comes in as an intermediate form. He has four more premolars than the typical cat, and the large grinding teeth are conical, blunt and very powerful, the base of the cone being belted by a strong ridge, and the general structure is one adapted for crushing rather than cutting. Professor Owen relates that an eminent engineer, to whom he showed a hyæna's jaw, remarked that the strong conical tooth, with its basal ridge, was a perfect model of a hammer for breaking stones.

Of course, such a formation would be useless without a commensurate motive power, and we may, therefore, look to the skull for certain signs of the enormous development of muscles, which this animal possesses. In shape it somewhat resembles the cat's skull, though not so short, nor yet so long as that of the civet or dog. The zygomatic arches are greatly developed, also the bony ridges for the attachment of the muscles, especially the sagittal or great longitudinal crest on the top of the head, which is in comparison far larger than that of even the tiger, and to which are attached the enormous muscles of the cheek working the powerful jaws, which are capable of crushing the thigh-bone of a

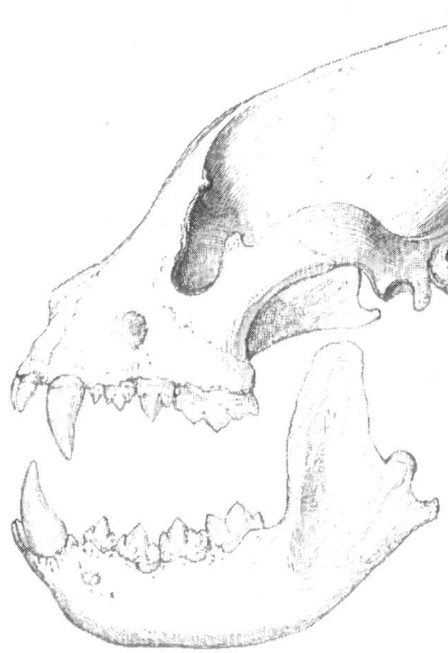

Skull of Hyæna.

bullock. Captain Baldwin, in his book, says he remembers once, when watching over a kill, seeing a hyæna, only some twelve feet below where he sat, snap with a single effort through the rib of a buffalo.

The hyæna also possesses the sub-caudal pouch of the civets, which gave rise amongst the ancients to various conjectures as to the dual character of its sex.

The *bulla tympani* or bulb of the ear is large as in the cats, but it is not divided into two compartments by a bony partition (which in the dogs is reduced to a low wall), but the paroccipital process or bony clamp on the external posterior surface is closely applied to the bulb as in the cats, and not separated by a groove as in the dogs.

The cervical vertebræ sometimes become anchylosed, from whence, in former times, arose the superstition that this animal had but one bone in the neck.

In its internal anatomy, digestive as well as generative, the hyæna is nearer to the cat than the dog, but it possesses the *cæcum*, or blind gut, which is so large in the canidæ, small in the felines, and totally absent in the bears.

The tongue is rough, with a circular collection of retroflected spines. The hind legs are much shorter than the front, and the feet have only four toes with blunt worn claws, not retractile, but like those of the dog.

The hair is coarse and bristly, and usually prolonged into a sort of crest or mane along the neck and shoulders, and to a slighter degree down the back; the tail is bushy.

Dental formula: Inc., $\frac{3-3}{3-3}$; can., $\frac{1-1}{1-1}$; pre-molars, $\frac{4-4}{3-3}$; molars, $\frac{1-1}{1-1}$.

There are only three known species of hyæna, of which one, our common Indian animal, belongs to Asia, and two, *H. crocuta* and *H. brunnea*, to Africa.

No. 220. HYÆNA STRIATA.

The Striped Hyæna (*Jerdon's No.* 118).

NATIVE NAMES.—*Taras*, *Hundar*, *Jhirak* (in Hurriana); *Lakhar-baghar*, *Lokra-bagh*, Hindi; *Naukra-bagh*, Bengali; *Rerha* in Central India; *Kirba* and *Kat-Kirba*, Canarese; *Korna-gandu*, Telegu.

HABITAT.—All over India; but as far as I can gather not in Burmah nor in Ceylon; it is not mentioned in Blyth's and Kellaart's catalogues. It is also found in Northern Africa and throughout Asia Minor and Persia; it is common in Palestine.

DESCRIPTION.—Pale yellowish-grey, with transverse tawny or blackish bands which encircle the body, and extend downwards on to the legs. The neck and back are maned.

SIZE.—Head and body, 3½ feet; tail, about 1½ feet.

This repulsive and cowardly creature is yet a useful beast in its way. Living almost exclusively on carrion, it is an excellent scavenger. Most wild animals are too active for it, but it feeds on the remains left by the larger felines, and such creatures as die of disease, and can, on a pinch, starve for a considerable time. The African spotted hyæna is said to commit great havoc in the sheep-fold. The Indian one is very destructive to dogs, and constantly carries off pariahs from the outskirts of villages. The natives declare that the hyæna tempts the dogs out by its unearthly cries, and then falls upon them. Dr. Jerdon relates a story of a small dog belonging to an officer of the 33rd M. N. I. (the regiment he was with when I first knew him) being carried off by a hyæna whose den was known. Some of the sepoys went after it, entered the cave, killed the hyæna, and recovered the dog alive, and with but little damage done to it.

The hyæna is of a timorous nature, seldom, if ever, showing fight. Two of them nearly ran over me once as I was squatting on a deer run waiting for sambar, which were being beaten out of a hill. I flung my hat in the face of the leading one, on which both turned tail and fled. The Arabs have a proverb, "As cowardly as a hyæna."

The *Cryptoprocta ferox* is not an inhabitant of India, being found only in the interior of Madagascar. The genus contains only one species, a most savage little animal; it is the most perfect link between

Hyæna striata.

the cats and the civets, having retractile claws, one more premolar in each jaw; five toes, and semi-plantigrade feet. It should properly come before the hyænas, to which the next in order is the South African Aard-wolf (*Proteles Lalandii*), which forms the connection between the hyæna and the civet, though more resembling the former. It is placed in a family by itself, which contains but one genus and species. It has the sloping back of the hyæna, the hind legs being lower than the fore, and it might almost, from its shape and colouring, be taken for that animal when young. The skull however is prolonged, and the teeth are civet-like. It is nocturnal and gregarious, several living in the same burrow. Like the hyæna it lives on carrion. It has a fifth toe on the fore feet.

VIVERRIDÆ—THE CIVET FAMILY.

The Civets are confined to the Old World; they are mostly animals with long bodies, sharp muzzle, short legs, long tapering tail and coarse fur; they are semi-plantigrade, walking on their toes, but keeping the wrist and ankle nearer to the ground than do the cats; the claws are only partially retractile; the skull is longer in the snout than that of felines, and, altogether narrower, the zygomatic arches not being so broad, the base of the skull is much the same, and the *bulla tympani* shews little difference; the teeth, however, are decidedly different. There

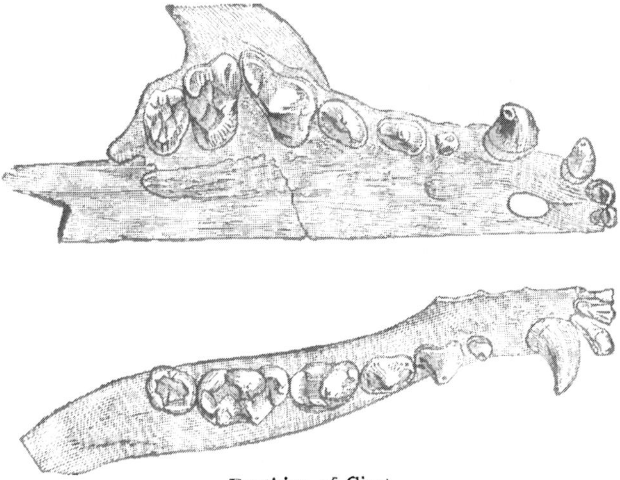

Dentition of Civet.

are four premolars and two molars on each side of each jaw, which, with the normal number of canines and incisors, give forty teeth in all; the canines are moderate in size, and sharp; the premolars conical, and the molars cuspidate, which gives them a grinding surface instead of the trenchant character of the cats; the tongue is rough, the papillæ being directed backwards; the pupils are circular. The most striking characteristics of the family is, however, the sub-caudal pouch, which in most produces an odorous substance, and in the typical civet the perfume of that name.

Dental formula: inc., $\frac{3-3}{3-3}$; can., $\frac{1-1}{1-1}$; premolars, $\frac{4-4}{3-3}$; molars $\frac{2-2}{3-3}$

The family contains the Civet, Genette, Linsang, Suricate, Binturong and Mongoose, though this last is separated by Jerdon, who follows Blyth.

GENUS VIVERRA.

Anal pouch large, and divided into two sacs secreting the *civet* perfume of commerce; pupil vertical and oblong; fur spotted and coarse, lengthened into an erectile mane on the back; diet mixed carnivorous and vegetivorous.

No. 221. VIVERRA ZIBETHA.

The Large Civet Cat (*Jerdon's No* 119).

NATIVE NAMES.—*Katas*, Hindi; *Mach-bhondar*, Bengali, also *Bagdos* and *Pudo-gaula* in some parts; *Bhran* in the Nepal Terai; *Nit-biralu*,

Viverra zibetha.

Nepalese; *Kung*, Bhotia; *Saphiong*, Lepcha, (*Jerdon*); *Khyoung-myen*, Aracanese.

HABITAT.—According to Jerdon this species inhabits Bengal, extending northwards in Nepal and Sikhim, and into Cuttack, Orissa, and Central India on the south, but is replaced in Malabar by the next species; it is also found in Assam and Burmah, but apparently not in Ceylon, where *V. Malaccensis* represents the family.

DESCRIPTION.—Hoary or yellowish grey, generally spotted and striped with black; some specimens are marked with wavy bands, others are almost free from marks; throat white, with a transverse black band, another on each side of the neck; under-parts white; tail with six black rings; limbs dark.

SIZE.—Head and body, 33 to 36 inches; tail 13 to 20.

"This animal frequents brushwood and grass, and the thorny scrub that usually covers the bunds of tanks. It is very carnivorous and destructive to poultry, game, &c., but will also, it is said, eat fish, crabs and insects. It breeds in May and June, and has usually four or five young. Hounds, and indeed all dogs, are greatly excited by the scent of this civet, and will leave any other scent for it. It will readily take to water if hard pressed."—*Jerdon.*

The drug civet is usually collected from the glands of this and other species, which are confined for the purpose in cages in which they can hardly turn round, and it is scraped from the pouch with a spoon. Sometimes the animal rubs off the secretion on the walls and bars of its cage, which are then scraped; but the highest price is given for the pouch cut from the civet when killed. In the London Zoological Gardens the collection of the perfume, which is rubbed off against the walls of the cage, is a valued perquisite of the keeper. Cuvier says of a civet which was kept in captivity in Paris: "Its musky odour was always perceptible, but stronger than usual when the animal was irritated; at such times little lumps of odoriferous matter fell from its pouch. These masses were also produced when the animal was left to itself, but only at intervals of fifteen to twenty days."

No. 222. VIVERRA CIVETTINA.

The Malabar Civet-Cat (*Jerdon's No.* 120).

HABITAT.—Throughout the Malabar coast, abundant in Travancore, and found occasionally in the uplands of Wynaad and Coorg.

DESCRIPTION.—Hair long, coarse, and of a dusky or brownish-grey, and marked with interrupted transverse bands or spots in rows, two obliquely transverse black lines on the neck; the snout, throat, and neck are white; the tail tinged with black. From the shoulders along the back a mane or crest of lengthened hair.

SIZE.—Same as last species.

This species closely resembles the African civet—only that in the latter the mane begins on the occiput. Jerdon supposes that it may be found in Ceylon, but it is not mentioned by Kellaart. It is found chiefly in forests and richly-wooded lowlands, and is stated to be very destructive to poultry. The young may, however, be reared on farinaceous food, with the addition of a little fish and raw meat; when older on flesh alone.

No. 223. VIVERRA MEGASPILA.

NATIVE NAME.—*Khyoung-myen.*

HABITAT.—Burmah, also Malayan peninsula and archipelago (?)

Viverra megaspila.

DESCRIPTION.—The body markings larger, blacker and fewer in number than in last species.

SIZE.—Same as last.

Blyth states that this is nearly allied to the last species, but differs from *V. tangalunga* of Sumatra (with which some consider it synonymous) as the latter is smaller, with a more cat-like tail, and more numerous spots. Gray says that *V. tangalunga* has the tail black above and ringed on the lower side.

The next species is smaller and more vermiform, with acute compressed claws, a shorter tail, and no crest, and of more scansorial habits. It forms the sub-genus *Viverricula* of Hodgson, but it is not desirable to perpetuate the sub-division.

NO. 224. VIVERRA MALACCENSIS.

The Lesser Civet-Cat (Jerdon's No. 121).

NATIVE NAMES.—*Mushak-billi*, *Katas*, *Kasturi*, Hindi; *Gando-gaula*, *Gandha-gokul*, Bengali; *Jowadi-manjur*, Mahrathi; *Punagin-bek*, Canarese; *Punagu-pilli*, Telegu; *Sayer*, *Bug-nyul*, Nepalese; *Wa-young-kyoung-bauk*, Aracanese; *Kyoung-ka-do*, Burmese; *Ooralawa*, Singhalese.

Viverra Malaccensis.

HABITAT.—India generally, with Assam, Burmah, and Ceylon. It extends also to the Malayan countries, Java and China.

DESCRIPTION.—General colour greyish-brown, spotted black; the dorsal spots elongated, and forming longitudinal interrupted streaks or stripes on the back and croup; the sides and limbs have also spots in lines; a long black streak from ear to shoulder, and some transverse lines on the sides of the neck. Abdomen nearly spotless; feet and part of legs dusky-brown; tail long and tapering, marked with eight or nine black rings.

SIZE.—Head and body, 22 to 24 inches; tail, 16 to 17 inches.

According to Jerdon, "it lives in holes in the ground or in banks, occasionally under rocks or in dense thickets, now and then taking shelter in drains and out-houses." Hodgson says: "These animals dwell in forests or detached woods and copses, whence they wander freely into the open country by day (occasionally at least) as well as by night. They are solitary and single wanderers, even the pair seldom being seen together, and they feed promiscuously upon small animals, birds' eggs, snakes, frogs, insects, besides some fruits or roots. In the Terai a low caste of woodmen, called Mushahirs, eat the flesh." Mr. Swinhoe affirms that the Chinese also eat its flesh, and adds: "but a portion that I had cooked was so affected with the civet odour that I could not palate it." The fur is valued in China as a lining for coats, and is bought by those who cannot afford the more expensive skins. Jerdon had one which was perfectly tame; it caught rats and squirrels at times, as also sparrows and other birds. It is kept alive by the natives in India and Ceylon for the sake of the secretion. Kellaart says it is a great destroyer of poultry, and that it will enter a yard in daylight and carry off a fowl or a duck. It is much dreaded by the Chinese for the havoc it commits in the hen-roost.

GENUS PRIONODON.

Between the last genus and this should come the *Genets*, which are not found in India, but chiefly in Africa, and one species is common in the south of Europe, where in some parts it is domesticated for the purpose of catching mice. It has rudimentary pouches only, which do not yield the musky secretion of the civets. The Linsang or *Prionodon* is a very cat-like animal, which was once classed with the Felidæ; the body is long and slender; the limbs very short; fur soft, close and erect, very richly coloured and spotted with black; the grinders are tubercular; claws retractile; soles furred; tail long, cylindrical, and ringed with black; no sub-caudal pouch. The female has two pectoral and two inguinal mammæ. Teeth, 38; molars, $\frac{5-5}{6-6}$.

No. 225. PRIONODON PARDICOLOR.

The Tiger Civet or Linsang (Jerdon's No. 122).

NATIVE NAME.—*Zik-chum*, Bhotia; *Suliyu*, Lepcha.
HABITAT.—Nepal, Sikim.

DESCRIPTION.—"Rich orange buff or fulvous, spotted with black; the neck above with four irregular lines; the body above and on the sides with large, entire elliptic or squarish marks, eight in transverse, and seven in longitudinal series, diminishing in size on the dorsal ridge, which has an interrupted dark line, and extending outside the limbs to the digits; below entirely unspotted; tail with eight or nine nearly perfect and equal rings" (*Jerdon*). "Skull elongate; nose rather short, compressed; brain-case narrow in front, swollen over the ears, and contracted and produced behind; orbits, not defined behind, confluent with the temporal cavity; zygomatic arch slender; palate contracted behind" (*Gray*). Jerdon's description is a very good one, but it must not be taken as an accurate one, spot for spot, for the animal varies somewhat in colour. Take, for instance, a description from Gray: "Pale *whitish grey;* back of neck and shoulders with *three* streaks diverging from the vertebral line; back with two series of large square spots; the shoulders, sides, and legs with round black spots; an elongated spot on the middle of the front part of the back, between the square spots on the sides of the body."

SIZE.—Head and body, 16 inches; tail, 14 inches; height, 6 inches.

Our Indian animal is closely allied to the Malayan species, which was first described as *Felis* and afterwards *Prionodon gracilis*. It is mentioned in the English translation of Cuvier as the delundung, "a rare Javanese animal, of which there is only one species," but another was subsequently found by Mr. Hodgson in Nepal, and now a third has been discovered in Tenasserim. They are beautiful little creatures, with all the agility of cats, climbing and springing from branch to branch in pursuit of small mammals and birds, and I have no doubt it is a great enemy of the *Tupaiæ* and squirrels. It breeds in the hollows of trees. It is capable of being tamed, and according to several authors becomes very gentle and fond of being noticed.

Hodgson says it never utters any kind of sound. He fed his on raw meat.

NO. 226. PRIONODON MACULOSUS.

The Spotted Linsang.

HABITAT.—Tenasserim.

DESCRIPTION.—"Upper part brownish-black, broken up by greyish-white bands, lower parts white; tail brownish-black, with seven white rings; tips whitish; two broad black bands run down each side of the upper part of the neck, between them is a narrow greyish-white band with a faint mesial dark streak somewhat interrupted, and passing into two bands of elongate spots between the shoulders. The two broad dark bands pass into the dark patches on the back; on each side of these bands is a white rather wavy stripe, commencing at the ear, and continued along the neck above the shoulder and down the side to the thighs, becoming more irregular behind; below this again is a dark band somewhat broken up into spots in front, passing over the shoulder and continued as a line of large spots along the side. The back is chiefly brownish-black, crossed by six narrow transverse whitish bands, the first five equidistant, the foremost communicating with the mesial neck band, and the hinder all uniting with the white band on the side, so as to break up the dark colour into large spots. There are small spots on the fore neck, lower portion of the sides, and outside of the limbs, the spots in the neck forming an imperfect gorget. The white rings on the tail are not much more than half the breadth of the dark

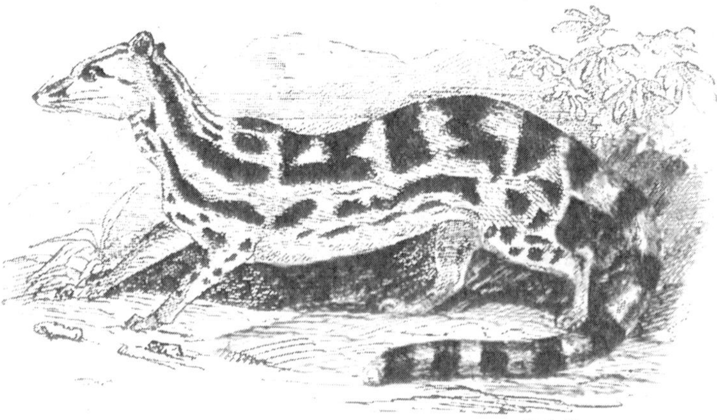

Prionodon maculosus.

rings; the last ring near the tip and the first white ring are narrower than the others; nose dark brown mixed with grey; a dark ring round each orbit, with a streak running back to below the ear, and another passing up to the crown; forehead between and behind the eyes and in front of the ears and cheeks pale grey; ears rounded and clad with blackish hairs outside and near the margin inside, a few long pale hairs on the inner surface of the ear conch; whiskers long, extending to behind the ears, the upper brown, the lower entirely white; soles, except the pads, which are naked, covered with fine hair." The above careful description is by Mr. W. T. Blanford on specimens collected by Mr. Davison in Burmah. Mr. Davison lately showed me a beautiful specimen, which I should describe by a reverse process to Mr. Blanford's, taking the light colour as the ground work, and stating it to be of a yellowish-white or pale buff, with broad black bands and blotches as above described, or in general terms broad black patches over the back, two longitudinal interrupted black bands along the neck and sides, with two lines of elongated spots above and below the lower band, and numerous small spots on the throat, chest and limbs.

SIZE—Head and body, 18¼ inches; tail, 16 inches without the hair, 16¾ with it.

This is a larger animal than *P. pardicolor*, and is distinguished from it by its larger marking. The fur is beautifully soft and close. From the richness of its colouring, the elegance of its shape, and the agility of its movements, it is one of the most beautiful and interesting of our smaller mammals.

No. 227. PRIONODON GRACILIS.

The Malayan Linsang.

HABITAT.—Malacca, Siam, Sumatra, and Tenasserim.

DESCRIPTION.—Fur white, back with broad black cross-bands, sides of neck with a broad black streak continued along the sides of the body, confluent with the bands of the neck; back of neck with five parallel black streaks; tail with seven black and white streaks; a second streak, broken into spots, from the side of the neck to the haunches; legs with small black spots.

Very similar to the last, only somewhat smaller.

Between *Prionodon* and the next comes a genus *Hemigalea*, which contains one species, *H. Hardwickii*, inhabiting the Malay countries. It is a perfect link between *Prionodon* and *Paradoxurus.*

GENUS PARADOXURUS—THE MUSANGS.

Paradoxurus is a misnomer, signifying *queer-tailed*, which originated in an abnormal twist in the tail of the specimen first described and named by M. F. Cuvier. I do not think that it is even occasional, as stated by some naturalists, but is of comparatively rare occurrence; and such deformities are by no means confined to this genus only.

The tail can be rolled up towards the end, and the hair is occasionally worn off, and some have a habit of curling it sideways; but I have never seen one as described by Kellaart when speaking of the genus: "The extreme or more distant half being, when extended, turned over so that the lower side is uppermost, and the animal can roll it up spirally from above downwards, and from the extremity to the base."

In general appearance the musang resembles the civet, and it has in some species a sub-caudal glandular fold which contains a secretion, but without the musky odour of civet.

The dentition is singularly like that of the dog, save that the flesh tooth is proportionally much stouter.

The feet are five-toed, webbed; pads bald; claws semi-retractile; tail very long, with from thirty-six to thirty-eight vertebræ; the pupil of the eye is linear and erect.

NO. 228. PARADOXURUS MUSANGA.

The Common Musang (*Jerdon's No.* 123.)

NATIVE NAMES.—*Khatas*, *Menuri* (in Southern India), *Lakati*; *Jhar-ka-kutta*, Hindi; *Bhonar*, Bengali; *Ud*, Mahrathi; *Kera-bek*, Canarese; *Manupilli*, Telegu; *Marra-pilli*, Malayan (toddy-cat and tree-cat of Europeans); *Sakrala*, *Khoonla*.

HABITAT.—Throughout India, Burmah and Ceylon, extending to the Malay countries.

DESCRIPTION.—It is difficult to lay down any precise rule for the colour of this animal, for it varies much. In general it is a fulvous grey, marked or clouded with black, or with black longitudinal stripes. No two naturalists describe it exactly alike. The limbs are, however, always dark, and there is usually a dark stripe down from the top of head to the centre of the nose. I will quote a few descriptions by various authors: "General colour brownish-black, with some dingy yellowish stripes on each side, more or less distinct, and sometimes not noticeable. A white spot above and below each eye, and the forehead with a whitish band in some; a black line from the top of the head down the centre of the nose is generally observable. In many individuals the ground colour appears to be fulvous, with black pencilling or mixed fulvous and black; the longitudinal stripes then show dark; limbs always dark brown; some appear almost black throughout, and the young are said to be nearly all black" (*Jerdon*). "General colour fulvous grey, washed with black; face darker coloured, with four white spots, one above and one below each eye, the latter more conspicuous; from three to five—more or less interrupted—black lines run from shoulder to root of tail, the central one broader and more distinct than the lateral lines; some indistinct black spots on the sides and upper parts of limbs; tail nearly all black; feet black, soles bald to the heel, flesh-coloured" (*Kellaart*). "Nose brown in the centre, with the brown colour extending under the eyes; the spot under the eye is small and indistinct" (*Gray*). The last remark is reverse of what Kellaart says. The muzzle of the young animal is flesh coloured; they are said to lose their black hairs when kept long in confinement, and become generally lighter coloured.

SIZE.—Head and body about 20 to 25 inches; tail from 19 to 21 inches.

This is a very common animal in India, frequently to be found in the neighbourhood of houses, attracted no doubt by poultry, rats, mice, &c. It abounds in the suburbs of Calcutta, taking up its abode sometimes in out-houses or in secluded parts of the main building. During the years 1865–66 a pair inhabited a wooden staircase in the Lieutenant-Governor's house at Alipore (Belvedere). We used to hear them daily, and once or twice I saw them in the dusk, but failed in all my attempts to trap them. That part of the building has since been altered, so I have no doubt the confiding pair have betaken themselves to other quarters. In a large banyan-tree in my brother's garden at Alipore there is a family at the present time, the junior members of which have lately fallen victims to a greyhound, who is often on the look-out for them. As yet the old ones have had the wisdom to keep out of his way.

They are very easily tamed. I had one for a time at Seonee which had been shot at and wounded, and I was astonished to find how soon it got accustomed to my surgical operations. Whilst under treatment I fed it on eggs. In confinement it is better to accustom it to live partly on vegetable food, rice, and milk, &c., with raw meat occasionally. Its habits are nocturnal. I cannot affirm from my own experience that it is partial to the juice of the palm tree, for *toddy* (or *tari*) is unknown in the Central Provinces, and I have had no specimens alive since I have been in Bengal, but it has the character of being a toddy-drinker in those parts of India where the toddy-palms grow; and Kellaart confirms the report. It is arboreal in its habits, and climbs with great agility.

NO. 229. PARADOXURUS (PAGUMA *of Gray*) GRAYII.

The Hill Musang (Jerdon's No. 124).

HABITAT.—South-east Himalayas and Burmah, from Nepal to Arakan.

DESCRIPTION.—"Colour above light unspotted fulvous brown, showing in certain lights a strong cinereous tinge, owing to the black tips of many of the hairs; beneath lighter and more cinereous; limbs ash-coloured, deeper in intensity towards the feet, which are black; tail of the same colour as the body, the end dark, white-tipped; ears rounded, hairy, black; face black, except the forehead; a longitudinal streak down the middle of the nose, and a short oblique band under each of the eyes, which are gray or whitish."—*Jerdon.*

SIZE.—Head and body, 30 inches; tail, 20 inches. According to Hodgson, this species keeps to the forests and mountains, feeding on small animals and birds, and also vegetable food. "One shot had only seeds, leaves, and unhusked rice in its stomach. A caged animal was fed on boiled rice and fruits, which it preferred to animal food. When set at liberty it would lie waiting in the grass for mynas and sparrows, springing upon them from the cover like a cat, and when sparrows, as it frequently happened, ventured into its cage to steal the boiled rice, it would feign sleep, retire into a corner, and dart on them with unerring aim. It preferred birds, thus taken by itself, to all other food.

"This animal was very cleanly, nor did its body usually emit any unpleasant odour, though when it was irritated it exhaled a most fœtid stench, caused by the discharge of a thin yellow fluid from four pores, two of which are placed on each side of the intestinal aperture."

No. 230. PARADOXURUS BONDAR.

The Terai Musang (Jerdon's No. 125).

NATIVE NAMES.—*Chinghar*, Hindi; *Bondar*, *Baum*, Bengali; *Machabba* and *Malwa* in the Nepal Terai.

HABITAT.—Nepal, North Behar and Terai.

DESCRIPTION.—Clear yellow, tipped with black, the fur coarse and harsh; under fur soft and woolly; legs blackish-brown outside; body without marks, but the bridge of the nose, upper lip, whiskers, broad cheek-band, ears, chin, lower jaw, and the terminal third of the tail blackish-brown; pale yellow round the eyes; snout and feet flesh-grey; nails sharp and curved. The female smaller and paler.

SIZE.—Head and body, about 22 inches; tail, 20 to 22; skull of one $4\frac{1}{6}$ inches, less ventricose than that of *P. Grayii.*

This species is found, like *P. musanga*, in the vicinity of houses; it lives in hollow trees, where it also breeds. Its habits are in great measure those of the common musang, though it is probably more carnivorous; it will, however, eat fruit. Jerdon says: "It sleeps rolled up like a ball, and when angered spits like a cat. It is naturally very ferocious and unruly, but capable of domestication, if taken young. It has a keen sense of smell, but less acute hearing and vision by day than the mungooses."

No. 231. PARADOXURUS TRIVIRGATUS.

The Three-striped Musang.

NATIVE NAME.—*Kyoung-na-ga*, in Arakan.

HABITAT.—Tenasserim and the Malay countries; also Assam.

DESCRIPTION.—Fur blackish-brown, slightly silvered with pale tips; three narrow black streaks down the back; under parts dirty white; head, feet, and tail black or blackish-brown. This animal forms a separate genus of Gray, following Professor Peters' *Arctogale*, on account of the smallness of the teeth and the protraction of the palate.

I had a specimen of this Paradoxurus given to me early in the cold season of 1881 by Dr. W. Forsyth. I brought it home to England with me, and it is now in the Zoological Society's Gardens in Regent's Park. It was very tame when Dr. Forsyth brought it, but it became more so afterwards, and we made a great pet of it.

It used to sleep nearly all day on a bookshelf in my study, and would, if called, lazily look up, yawn, and then come down to be petted, after which it would spring up again into its retreat. At night it was very active, especially in bounding from branch to branch of a tree which I had cut down and placed in the room in which it was locked up every evening. Its wonderful agility on ropes was greatly noticed on board ship. Its favourite food was plantains, and it was also

Paradoxurus trivirgatus.

very fond of milk. At night I used to give it a little meat, but not much; but most kinds of fruit it seemed to like.

Its temper was a little uncertain, and it seemed to dislike natives, who at times got bitten; but it never bit any of my family, although one of my little girls used to catch hold of it by the forepaws and dance it about like a kitten. Its carnivorous nature showed itself one day by its pouncing upon a tame pigeon. The bird was rescued, and is alive still, but it was severely mauled before I could rescue it, having been seized by the neck.

No. 232. PARADOXURUS LEUCOTIS.

The White-eared Musang.

NATIVE NAME.—*Na-zwet-phyoo*, Arakanese.

HABITAT.—Burmah and Assam.

DESCRIPTION.—Fur longish, soft, and silky; upper parts tawny;

reddish-brown on back and sides; thighs, legs, throat, and belly lighter; tail long, deep chestnut brown; nose with a central white line; ears yellowish.

No. 233. PARADOXURUS ZEYLANICUS.

The Golden Musang.

NATIVE NAME.—*Coolla-weddah*, Singhalese.

HABITAT.—Ceylon.

DESCRIPTION.—A golden-brown colour arising from the longer hairs having a bright golden tint; the shorter hairs brown, paler beneath; head and legs dark brown; muzzle and lips blackish; whiskers white or yellowish; ears small, dark brown externally, almost naked internally; tail sub-cylindrical, long; sometimes with a single pale sub-terminal band; tip rounded, paler than the body. According to Kellaart, three inconspicuous brown dorsal streaks diverging and terminating on the crupper, and some very indistinct spots seen only in some lights. Gray says these animals differ in the intensity of the colour of the fur—some are bright golden and others much more brown. The latter is *P. fuscus* of Kellaart.

SIZE.—Head and body, 19 inches; tail, 15 to 16 inches.

Kellaart writes of this species: "The golden paradoxure appears to be a more frugivorous animal than the palm-cat (*Paradoxurus typus**). Their habits are alike nocturnal and arboreal. In all the individuals of the former species examined at Newera-Ellia the stomach contained Cape gooseberries (*Physalis Peruviana*†), which grow there now in great abundance; and only one had the remains of animal matter in the stomach. When young they are tolerably docile, but as they grow up their natural ferocity returns." This seems strange, as they appear to be less carnivorous than the others.

No. 234. PARADOXURUS (PAGUMA) LANIGER.

HABITAT.—Thibet.

This requires further investigation. Gray says: "This species is only known from a skin without any skull, and in a very bad state."

P. strictus, *quadriscriptus* and *prehensilis* are three species alluded to by Gray as requiring further examination, but probably Jerdon is right in considering them as varieties of *P. musanga*.

A specimen with very large canines has been reported from the Andaman Islands (*P. Tytleri ?*) in addition to these. Gray enumerates as an Indian species *P. nigrifrons*, which is likely to be a variety of

* Cuvier's name for *P. musanga*.—R. A. S.

† The *Tipari* of Bengal.—R. A. S.

P. musanga; it was described from a single specimen. The dorsal streaks and spots were absent, but then he says the animal had been in confinement, and, as I have said before, this tends to make the dark parts disappear.

GENUS ARCTICTIS.

This is a very curious animal, which, like the panda and the linsang, at first misled naturalists in assigning it a place. It was formerly classed with the racoons, which it superficially resembles; and, as Jerdon remarks, it may be considered as a sort of link between the plantigrade and digitigrade carnivora. The skeleton however is similar to that of the musangs as regards the great number (thirty-four) of the caudal vertebræ, but the bones of the feet have a more plantigrade character; the skull resembles that of a badger; the head is conical, with a large brain-case and acute turned-up nose; the orbit of the skull is imperfect, only defined by a prominence above; the ears are pencilled or tufted; the tail is very long, muscular and prehensile—although this was doubted by F. Cuvier, but it is now a well-known fact—and in climbing trees it is much assisted by the tail; the teeth are thirty-six in all; canines stout, upper ones long; grinders small and far apart; of the false grinders, the first and second are conical, the third compressed; the flesh-tooth is triangular, and as broad as long; the tubercular grinders are smaller than the flesh-tooth, the first triangular, the hinder cylindrical and smaller still; toes five in each foot, with powerful semi-retractile claws.

No. 235. ARCTICTIS BINTURONG.

The Binturong (Jerdon's No. 126).

HABITAT.—Assam, Nepal, Simla hills, also Tenasserim, Arakan, and the Malayan countries.

DESCRIPTION.—Long body, short legs, long prehensile tail, very thick at the base, and gradually tapering to a point, clad with very long bristling hair; the hair of the body very coarse; general colour, deep black, with a white border to the ears, a few brown hairs on the head and anterior surface of fore-legs. Some of the Malayan specimens are slightly sprinkled with brown, and have the head, face, and throat grizzled. It has a large sub-caudal gland, secreting an oily fluid.

SIZE.—Head and body 28 to 30 inches; tail about the same. Jerdon gives 28 to 33 inches; tail 26 to 27 inches.

According to Jerdon it is nocturnal, arboreal, and omnivorous, eating small animals, birds, insects, fruit and plants; more wild than viverrine animals in general, but easily tamed. Its howl is loud. In an illustration I have of one of these animals, it is drawn with white patches over the eyes. Cantor says the young are marked with eye spots. I have

Arctictis binturong.

added the Simla hills to the list of places it inhabits, as Mr. Hume possesses the skin of one which I have lately examined, and which was procured in this neighbourhood.

HERPESTIDÆ.

THE ICHNEUMON OR MUNGOOSE FAMILY.

A well-defined genus of animals, with long vermiform bodies, clad with long, harsh grizzled hair, long muscular tails, thick at the base, and tapering to a fine point; semi-plantigrade feet with five toes, and partially retractile claws; the eyes are small, but glittering and snake-like; the tongue rough like a cat's. Dr. Gray has divided this family into two groups, *Herpestina* and *Cynictidina*, the former containing thirteen genera, the latter one, which is separated on account of its having four toes only. Of the thirteen genera in Herpestina, we have only to do with *Herpestes*, *Calogale*, *Calictis*, *Urva*, *Tæniogale*, and *Onychogale*, which six are by most naturalists treated under *Herpestes*, and I will continue to do so, as the differences are hardly sufficient to warrant so much subdivision.

GENUS HERPESTES.

Long vermiform body; short legs with five semi-palmated toes with short compressed claws; eyes small, with linear erect pupils; long skull with forty teeth; the orbit complete in many cases, or only slightly imperfect; the hairs are long, rigid, and ringed like the quill of a porcupine, which gives the grizzled appearance peculiar to these animals. The female has only four mammæ. They are very active and sanguinary, chiefly hunting along the ground, but can climb with facility. There are several species found within the limits of British India, and many more in Africa.

No. 236. HERPESTES PALLIDUS *vel* GRISEUS.

The Common Grey Mungoose (*Jerdon's Nos.* 127 *and* 128).

NATIVE NAMES.—*Mungus, Newul, Newra*, *Nyul*, Hindi; *Mungli*, Canarese; *Yentawa*, Telegu; *Koral*, Gondi; *Moogatea*, Singhalese.

HABITAT.—India generally and Ceylon, but apparently not in Burmah.

DESCRIPTION.—Light iron grey with a yellowish tint, some more rufous, the hairs being ringed with brown and grey or yellowish-white; muzzle and feet brown; irides light brown.

SIZE.—Head and body, 16 to 20 inches; tail, 14 to 16½ inches.

Jerdon calls this the Madras mungoose, and separates it from the next species, but they are apparently the same. Dr. Anderson prefers the specific name *pallidus* to either *griseus* or *Malaccensis*, as *griseus* originally included an African species, and the latter name is geographically misleading. Hodgson's name *H. nyula* is objectionable, as *nyul* or *newul* is applied by natives to all mungooses generally. Jerdon's Nos. 127 and 128 differ only in colour and size; according to him the lighter and larger, *griseus*, being the Southern India mungoose, and the browner and smaller, *Malaccensis*, the Bengal and the Northern India one. But at Sasseram in Behar, I some years ago obtained a very large specimen of the lighter species, and have lately seen a skin from the North-west Provinces. This animal is familiar to most English residents in the Mofussil; it is, if unmolested, fearless of man, and will, even in its wild state, enter the verandahs and rooms of houses. In one house I know a pair of old ones would not only boldly lift the bamboo chicks and walk in, but in time were accompanied by a young family. When domesticated they are capable of showing as much attachment as a dog. One that I had constantly with me for three years died of grief during a temporary separation, having refused food from the time I left. I got it whilst on active service during the Indian Mutiny, when it was a wee thing, smaller than a rat. It travelled with me on horseback in an empty holster, or in a pocket, or up my sleeve; and afterwards, when my duties as a settlement officer took me out into camp, "Pips" was my constant companion. He knew perfectly well when I was going to shoot a bird for him. He would stand up on his hind legs when he saw me present the gun, and rush for the bird when it fell; he had, however, no notion of retrieving, but would scamper off with his prey to devour it at leisure. He was a most fearless little fellow, and once attacked a big greyhound, who beat a retreat. In a rage his body would swell to nearly twice its size from the erection of the hair, yet I had him under such perfect subjection that I had only to hold up my finger to him when he was about to attack anything, and he would desist. I heard a great noise one day outside my room and found Master "Pips," attacking a fine male specimen I had of the great bustard, *Eupodotis Edwardsii*, and had just seized it by the throat. I rescued the bird, but it died of its injuries. Through the carelessness of one of my servants he was lost one day in a heavy brushwood jungle some miles from my camp, and I quite gave up all hopes of recovering my pet. Next day, however, in tracking some antelope, we happened to cross the route taken by my servants, when we heard a familiar little yelp, and down from a tree we were under rushed "Pips." He went to England with me after that, and was the delight of all the sailors on board, for his accomplishments were varied; he could sit on a chair with a cap on his head, shoulder arms; ready, present, fire!—turn somersaults, jump, and do various other little tricks.

From watching him I observed many little habits belonging to these animals. He was excessively clean, and after eating would pick his teeth with his claws in a most absurd manner. I do not know whether a mungoose in a wild state will eat carrion, but he would not touch anything tainted, and, though very fond of freshly-cooked game, would turn up his nose at high partridge or grouse. He was very fond of eggs, and, holding them in his fore-paws, would crack a little hole at the small end, out of which he would suck the contents. He was a very good ratter, and also killed many snakes against which I pitted him. His way seemed to be to tease the snake into darting at him, when, with inconceivable rapidity, he would pounce on the reptile's head. He seemed to know instinctively which were the poisonous ones, and acted with corresponding caution. I tried him once with some sea-snakes (*Hydrophis palamoides*), which are poisonous, but he could get no fight out of them, and crunched their heads off one after the other. I do not believe in the mungoose being proof against snake poison, or in the antidote theory. Their extreme agility prevents their being bitten, and the stiff rigid hair, which is excited at such times, and a thick loose skin, are an additional protection. I think it has been proved that if the poison of a snake is injected into the veins of a mungoose it proves fatal. The female produces from three to four young at a time.

The cry of the mungoose is a grating mew, varied occasionally by a little querulous yelp, which seems to be given in an interrogative sort of way when searching for anything. When angry it growls most audibly for such a small beast, and this is generally accompanied by a bristling of the hair, especially of the tail.

No. 237. HERPESTES JERDONI *vel* MONTICOLUS.

The Long-tailed Mungoose (Jerdon's No. 129).

HABITAT.—Indian peninsula, it having been found in the extreme south as well as Kashmir in the north and Singbhoom in the centre.

DESCRIPTION.—Colour like the last, but more yellow in general tone; tail long, tipped with maroon and black, very hairy; feet dark reddish-brown; muzzle slightly tinged with red; under fur pale yellowish, the long hairs being broadly tipped with brown, darkest at the tip, paler at the base, then a white band; then three brown bands separated by white, the base of the hair being broadly white; the skull is distinguishable by the breadth of the frontal region across the post-orbital processes, and between the anterior margins of the orbit. Dr. Anderson considers this as identical with the Kashmir *H. thysanurus*, which has also been found by Mr. Ball in Singbhoom. Dr. Gray says it is very like the African *H. ichneumon*, only paler. Dr. Jerdon had only obtained it from the Eastern Ghâts inland from Nellore, where it inhabits forests among the hills.

SIZE.—Head and body, 20 inches; tail, 19 inches.

No. 238. HERPESTES SMITHII.

The Ruddy Mungoose (Jerdon's No. 130).

NATIVE NAME.—*Deeto,* Singhalese.

HABITAT.—Southern India and Ceylon.

DESCRIPTION.—Reddish ferruginous brown, long hair, well grizzled, more red on the head and outer part of limbs; hairs annulated dark and white, with reddish tips; muzzle long and flesh-coloured; feet black; tip of tail black.

SIZE.—Head and body, 15 inches; tail, 12 to 13 inches.

This is the same as *H. Ellioti* of Blyth, and *H. rubiginosus* of Kellaart, and *Calictis Smithii* of Gray.

No. 239. HERPESTES AUROPUNCTATUS.

The Gold-speckled Mungoose (Jerdon's No. 131).

HABITAT.—The plains near the hills from Afghanistan to Bengal, also Assam and Burmah, and on into the Malayan peninsula.

DESCRIPTION.—General colour olive brown with a golden hue, or finely speckled with golden yellow, due to the fine annulation of the hair; the sides of the body slightly paler, and not so yellow; under parts dirty yellowish-white; limbs the same colour as the body; the under fur is purplish-brown in its lower two-thirds, and pale yellow in its terminal third; the long hair is smooth, fine, short, and adpressed; the tips are dark brown, then yellow, then brown, twice repeated; occasionally a yellow band at the base; in the tail there are generally eight bands, with the terminal dark brown; the skull is remarkable for the narrow and elongated character of its facial portion; the orbit is perfect in the adult. Length of skull about $1\frac{5}{12}$ inches; width at the zygoma, $1\frac{1}{4}$.

SIZE.—Head and body, 12 to 13 inches; tail, 9 to 10 inches.

This and *H. persicus* are the smallest of the genus; it is included in Gray's genus *Calogale*, and he gives the specific name followed by Jerdon, *Nipalensis*, which is geographically misleading. I have therefore followed Dr. Anderson in retaining the more appropriate title. *H. persicus* is closely allied, but the nasal portion of the palate is narrower.

NO. 240. HERPESTES FUSCUS.

The Nilgherry Brown Mungoose (Jerdon's No. 132).

HABITAT.—Madras Presidency, Neilgherries.

DESCRIPTION.—General colour, brown; hair ringed black and yellow, tawny at the base; throat dusky yellowish.—*Jerdon.*

SIZE.—Head and body, 18 inches; tail, with hair, 17 inches.

241. HERPESTES (ONYCHOGALE *of Gray*) MACCARTHIÆ.

HABITAT.—Ceylon.

DESCRIPTION.—Reddish-brown; elongate, flaccid, pale brown, with a broad thick sub-terminal band and a long whitish-brown tip; fur of hands and face shorter; feet blackish brown; hair white-tipped; tail redder; hair elongate, one coloured red; ears rounded, hairy.—*Gray.*

NO. 242. HERPESTES FERRUGINEUS.

HABITAT.—Sind.

DESCRIPTION.—Resembles rufous specimens of *H. pallidus*, but the skull shows differences in the greater breadth of the post-orbital contraction of the frontals, and a shorter, broader muzzle, more particularly with posterior or nasal part of the palate.

The next species, which is included in Gray's genus *Tæniogale*, has the bony orbit always perfect, and the molars are $\frac{6-6}{7-7}$.

No. 243. HERPESTES VITTICOLLIS.

The Stripe-necked Mungoose (Jerdon's No. 133).

NATIVE NAME.—*Loco-moogatea*, Singhalese.

HABITAT.—Southern India, Ceylon, Burmah?

DESCRIPTION.—Grizzled grey, more or less ferruginous, especially on the rump and tail; a dark stripe from the ear to the shoulder; tail rufous black at the tip; skull characteristics: large, with flattened and expanded frontal region, projected narrow muzzle and powerful teeth, larger than other Asiatic *Herpestes*, the last molar being proportionately greater.

SIZE.—Head and body 21 inches; tail 15 inches.

I have put Burmah in the list of places where this mungoose is found, having lately been shown by Mr. Davison the skin of a stripe-necked mungoose obtained by him in Burmah, which seemed to be of this species.

The next has been formed into a separate genus, *Urva;* the teeth are blunter than in *Herpestes.*

No. 244. URVA CANCRIVORA.

The Crab-eating Mungoose (Jerdon's No. 134).

HABITAT.—South-east Himalayas, Assam, and Burmah.

DESCRIPTION.—"General colour fulvous iron-grey, inner fur woolly, outer of long straggling lax hairs, generally ringed with black, white,

Urva cancrivora.

and fulvous; in some the coat has a variegated aspect; in other as uniform tawny tint prevails, and in a few dark rusty brown mixed with grey is the prevalent hue; abdomen brown; limbs blackish-brown; a white stripe on either side of the neck from the ear to the shoulder; tail rufous or brown, with the terminal half rufous" (*Jerdon*). Gray's account is: "black grizzled hairs with a very broad white sub-terminal ring; a white streak on the side of the neck; legs and feet black; tail ashy red at the end."

SIZE.—Head and body, 18 inches; tail, 11 inches.

Somewhat aquatic in its habits, living on frogs and crabs. It has two anal glands, from which it can squirt a fœtid secretion. It is the only mungoose mentioned in Blyth's 'Catalogue of the Mammals of Burmah,' but there are at least two more, and probably some of the Malayan species are yet to be found in Tenasserim.

CYNOIDEA.

This is the next and last section in the order I have adopted, of the land Carnivora, and contains the typical family *Canis*. All the animals that we shall have to deal with might and would be by some authors brought into this one genus, the only others recognised by them being the two African genera, *Megalotis* and *Lycaon*, the long-eared fox and the hyæna-dog, and the *Nyctereutes* or racoon-dog of Northern China and Amoorland. But although all our Indian species might be treated of under the one genus *Canis*, it will be better to keep to the separation adopted by Jerdon, and classify the wolves and jackals under *Canis*, and the foxes under *Vulpes*. As regards the wild dog of India, its dentition might warrant its being placed in a separate genus, but after all the name chosen for it is but merely a difference in sound, the two being the same thing in Latin and Greek.

But although this group contains the smallest number of forms, the varieties of the domestic dog are endless, and no part of the world is without a species of the genus, except certain islands, such as the West Indies, Madagascar, the Polynesian isles, New Zealand and the Malayan archipelago; in these territories there is no indigenous dog. I speak of dogs in its broad sense of *Canis*, including wolves and foxes.

The proper position of the *Cynoidea* should be between the bears and the cats, as in their dentition they approximate to the former, and in their digitigrade character to the latter; but, with a view to make this work concurrent with that of Jerdon's, I have accepted the position assigned by him, though it be a little out of place.

The general form of the skeleton of a dog resembles that of a feline, though the limbs may be to a certain extent longer; they also walk on the tips of their toes, but their claws are not retractile, although the ligament by which the process of retraction in the cat is effected is present in a rudimentary form, but is permanently overpowered by the greater flexor muscles. A dog's paw is therefore by no means such a wonderful piece of mechanism and example of power as that of the cat, but is feeble in comparison, and is never used as a weapon of offence, as in the case of felines, the prey being always seized by the teeth.

The skull partakes of the characteristics of both cat and bear. It departs from the simple cutting dentition of the former by the addition of two tuberculated molars in each upper jaw, or one more than the rudimentary molar in the cat, whilst the lower jaw has two extra molars on each side; the premolars are also in excess, being four in number on each side of the upper and lower jaws, whereas in the feline there are three above and two below.

There is also a difference in the lower carnassial or first molar, which impinges on the upper carnassial or fourth premolar; it has a protuberance behind, termed the heel, which is prominently marked, but it is in the molars in which the greatest deviation from the specially carnivorous dentition occurs. The incisors are somewhat larger than, but the canines and premolars approximate to, those of the felines; the crown of the incisors is cuspidate, and the premolars increase gradually in size, with the exception of the fourth in the upper jaw, the carnassial, which is treble the size of the one next to it.

But it is in the molars that we find the similarity to the semi-herbivorous bears. The last two molars on each side of the upper and lower jaws are true grinders, divided into four cusps, which suits the dog to a mixed diet.

Of course the increased number of teeth (the dog has forty-two against thirty of the cat) necessitates a prolonged muzzle, and therefore the skull has more of the bear than the cat shape. The nasal bones are long, the zygomatic arch smaller, but it has the ear-bulb or *bulla tympani*, so conspicuous in the cat and wanting in the bear, yet the character of the aperture of the ear or *auditory meatus* approaches that of the latter, as the margins of its outer aperture are somewhat prolonged into a short tube or spout, instead of being flush, as in the felines. Then the bony clamp or par-occipital process, which in the cats is fixed against the hinder end of the bulla, is in the dogs separated by a decided groove.

The intestinal peculiarities of this section consist of a very large *cæcum* or blind gut, which is small in the cats and wholly absent in the bears, and in the very long intestines. Some have a sub-caudal gland secreting a pungent whey-like matter.

GENUS CANIS—THE DOG.

Muzzle obtuse; tail short; no caudal gland.

Dental formula: inc., $\frac{6}{6}$; can., $\frac{1-1}{1-1}$; premolar, $\frac{4-4}{4-4}$; molar, $\frac{2-2}{3-3}$.

This genus contains the wolf and the jackal, as well as the dog proper.

The origin of the domestic dog (*Canis familiaris*) is involved in obscurity; it is mentioned in its domestic state and in an infinity of

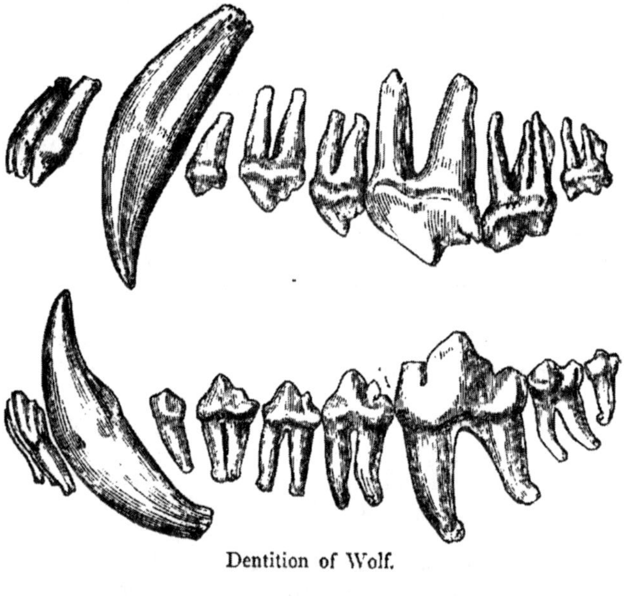

Dentition of Wolf.

varieties in records of remote ages. Job talks of "the dogs of my flock," and in the Assyrian monuments, as far back as 3400 years before Christ, various forms are represented; and in Egypt not only representations of known varieties, easy to be recognised, are found, but numerous mummies have been exhumed, the animal having been held in special veneration. There is a preponderance of opinion strongly in favour of the theory that the domestic dog sprang from the wolf, and much argument has been advanced in support of this idea. The principal objection made to this by those who hold opposite views is the fact that no dog in a wild state barks, but only howls.

Now for the evidence adduced in support of the former assertion, some domesticated species of dog closely resembling the wild wolf.

Sir John Richardson says of the Eskimo dog that it is not only extremely like the North American wolf (*Canis lupus*), both in form, colour, and nearly in size, but that the howl of both animals "is prolonged so exactly in the same key that even the practised ear of an Indian fails at times to discriminate them." He adds of the dog of the Hare Indians, a distinct breed, that it is almost the same as the prairie wolf (*Canis latrans*), the skull of the dog appeared to him a little smaller, otherwise he could detect no difference in form, nor fineness of fur, nor the arrangement of spots of colour.

Professor Kitchen Parker writes: "Another observer remarks that, except in the matter of barking, there is no difference whatever between the black wolf-dog of the Indians of Florida and the wolves of the same country. The dogs also breed readily with the wild animals they so closely resemble. The Indians often cross their dogs with wolves to improve the breed, and in South America the same process is resorted to between the domesticated and the wild dogs." He then goes on to allude to many varieties of dogs closely resembling wolves—the shepherd dog of Hungary, which is so like that a Hungarian has been known to mistake a wolf for one of his own dogs. Some Indian pariahs, and some dogs of Egypt, both now and in the condition of mummies, closely resemble the wolf of their country. The domestic dogs of Nubia and certain mummified forms are closely related to jackals. The Bosjesman's dog is very like the black-backed jackal (*Canis mesomelas*). Domestic dogs which have run wild do in some measure, though not entirely, revert to the wolf type. The dingo of Australia is thought to be derived from some imported variety of dog. The wolf is easily tamed, and even in its wild state has some of the peculiarities of the dog; for instance, a young wolf, when surprised and threatened by the hunter, will crouch and fawn like a spaniel. Mr. Bell tells of a she-wolf in the Regent's Park Zoological Gardens which would bring her cubs to the bars of the cage, that they might be caressed by the visitors; and there is a most interesting account, too long for insertion here, in the third volume of the old *India Sporting Review* (new series) chiefly taken from Major Lloyd's 'Scandinavian Adventures,' of the tameability of wolves, giving an instance of two cubs out of a litter of three becoming as faithfully attached as any dog. The period of gestation (sixty-three days) is the same in both animals, and they will interbreed freely, the progeny being also fertile. There only now remains the question of the bark, which, singularly enough, is peculiar to the domesticated dog only, and may have arisen in imitation of the gruffer tones of the human voice. The domestic dog run wild will in a few generations lose the power of barking. This happened on the island of Juan Fernandez; the dogs left there quite lost their bark in thirty-three years, and it is said that a few caught and removed after that period reacquired it very slowly. We may then, I think, accept Darwin's opinion that "it is highly probable that the domestic dogs of the world have descended from two good species of wolf (*C. lupus* and *C. latrans*), and from two or three other doubtful species of wolves (namely, the European, Indian, and North African forms), from at least one or two South American canine species, and from several races or species of the jackal."

No. 245. CANIS PALLIPES.

The Indian Wolf (*Jerdon's No.* 135).

NATIVE NAMES.—*Bheria*, *Bhera*, North and Central India; *Landagh*, South India; *Nekra*, in some parts; *Bighana*, *Hunder*, or *Hurar*, in Bundelcund; *Tola*, Canarese; *Toralu*, Telegu.

HABITAT.—Throughout the whole of India, though Hodgson says he has not found it in the Himalayas, nor can I find any notice of it in Burmah, and it is likewise absent in Ceylon.

DESCRIPTION.—"Hoary fulvous or dirty reddish-white, some of the hairs tipped with black, which gives it a grizzled appearance; somewhat reddish on the face and limbs, the latter paler than the body; lower parts dingy white; tail thinly bushy, slightly black-tipped; ears rather small" (*Jerdon*). But, as a matter of fact, wolves vary greatly in colour. Every one who has seen much of them will bear testimony to this. Sir Walter Elliot says: "Several adults that I shot differed in their colours and general character." The late Brigadier-General McMaster, in his notes on Jerdon, wrote: "Wolves vary a good deal in colour and length of hair, probably with season and climate. I have seen some of light reddish-grey, and others much darker than any jackal;" and he speaks of another "nearly as red as an Irish setter."

SIZE.—Head and body, about 3 feet; tail, 16 to 18 inches; height at shoulder, 26 inches.

The Indian wolf is somewhat inferior in size to the European one, and is probably less ferocious, or at all events its ferocity is not called out by the severity of the climate, as in the case of *C. lupus*. We never hear of them attacking bodies of men and overwhelming them by numbers. In 1812 twenty-four French soldiers were surrounded by an immense troop of wolves; and though, it is said, the men killed two or three hundred of their assailants, they had to succumb at last to numbers, and were all devoured. This was doubtless an extreme case, but in the severe winters of the north, when these animals band together and roam abroad in search of food, they will attack anything that comes in their way, although a single wolf will hardly ever dare to meddle with a man.

In India one seldom hears of their attacking grown-up men. I remember an instance in which an old woman was a victim; but hundreds of children are carried off annually, especially in Central India and the North-west provinces.

Stories have been related of wolves sparing and suckling young infants so carried off, which, if properly authenticated, will bring the history of Romulus and Remus within the bounds of probability. I have not by me just now the details of the case of the "Boy-Wolf" of Lucknow,

Canis pallipes.

which was, I believe, a case vouched for by credible witnesses. It was that of a boy found in a wolf's lair, who had no power of speech, crawled about on his hands and knees, ate raw flesh, and who showed great wildness in captivity. I think he died soon after being caught. The story of the nursing is not improbable, for well-known instances have been recorded of the *feræ*, when deprived of their young, adopting young animals, even of those on whom they usually prey. Cats have been known to suckle young leverets. The wolf in its wild state is particularly partial to dog as an article of diet, yet in confinement it will attach itself to its domesticated canine companions, and interbreed with them. A writer in the *India Sporting Review*, vol. vi. of 1847, page 252, quoted by McMaster, says he received from Dr. Jameson, Superintendent of the Botanical Gardens at Saharunpore, a hybrid, the produce of a tame female wolf and a pointer dog. This hybrid died when twenty months old, and is said to have been mild and gentle; its howl seems to have had more of the bark in it than the cry of the hybrid jackal, and to have been more dog-like. "It exactly resembled the coarse black pariah to be seen about Loodhiana and Ferozepore," the black colour doubtless coming from the pointer sire. As General McMaster remarks, it would be interesting to know what the colours of the rest of the litter were. Wolves do, I think, get light-coloured with great age. I remember once having one brought into my camp for the usual reward by a couple of small boys, the elder not more than ten or twelve years of age, I should think. The beast was old and emaciated, and very light coloured, and, doubtless impelled by hunger, attacked the children, as they were herding cattle, with a view to dining off them; but the elder boy had a small axe, such as is commonly carried by the Gonds, and, manfully standing his ground, split the wolf's skull with a blow—a feat of which he was justly proud.

Sir Walter Elliot's description of the manner in which wolves hunt has been quoted by Jerdon and others, but, as it is interesting, I reproduce it here:—

"The wolves of the southern Mahratta country generally hunt in packs, and I have seen them in full chase after the goat antelope *Gazella Arabica* (*Bennettii?*). They likewise steal round the herd of *Antilope cervicapra* and conceal themselves on different sides till an opportunity offers of seizing one of them unawares as they approach, while grazing, to one or other of their hidden assailants. On one occasion three wolves were seen to chase a herd of gazelle across a ravine in which two others were lying in wait. They succeeded in seizing a female gazelle, which was taken from them. They have frequently been seen to course, and run down hares and foxes; and it is a common belief of the ryots that in the open plains, where there is no cover or concealment, they scrape a hole in the earth, in which one of the pack lies down and remains hid, while the others drive the herd of antelope over him. Their chief prey, however, is sheep; and the shepherds say that part of the pack attack, and keep the dogs in play, while others carry off their prey, and that, if pursued, they follow the same plan, part turning and checking the dogs, while the rest drag away the carcase, till they evade pursuit. Instances are not uncommon of their attacking man. In 1824 upwards of thirty children were devoured by wolves in one pergunnah alone. Sometimes a large wolf is seen to seek his prey singly; these are called *Won-tola*, and are reckoned particularly fierce."

McMaster corroborates the account of wolves hiding themselves by scratching holes in the ground whilst antelope were quietly walking up to the ambush; and there is a most amusing account given by Major Lloyd, in his 'Scandinavian Adventures,' of the wiles of a tame wolf in her efforts to get young pigs within her reach. He says: "When she saw a pig in the vicinity of her kennel, she evidently, with the purpose of putting him off his guard, would throw herself on her side or back, wag her tail most lovingly, and look innocence personified; and this amicable demeanour would continue until the grunter was beguiled within reach of her tether, when, in the twinkling of an eye, 'Richard was himself again!'" Major Lloyd asserts that but for this *penchant* for his neighbours' pigs he would have trained this wolf as a pointer.

Jerdon states that he has known wolves turn on dogs that were running at their heels, and pursue them smartly till close up to his horse. He adds: "A wolf once joined with my greyhounds in pursuit of a fox, which was luckily killed almost immediately afterwards, or the wolf might have seized one of the dogs instead of the fox. He sat down on his haunches, about sixty yards off, whilst the dogs were worrying the fox, looking on with great apparent interest, and was with difficulty driven away."

NO. 246. CANIS LANIGER (LUPUS CHANCO *of Gray*).

The Thibetan Wolf.

NATIVE NAMES.—*Chanko, Changu.*

HABITAT.—Thibet.

DESCRIPTION.—Yellowish-grey, with long soft hairs (*Kinloch*). Long sharp face, elevated brows, broad head, large pointed ears, thick woolly pelage, and very full brush of medial length; above dull earth-brown; below, with the entire face and limbs, yellowish-white; no marks on limbs; tail concolourous with the body, that is brown above and yellowish below, and no dark tip (*Hodgson*).

SIZE.—Length, 4 feet; tail, 20 inches; height, 30 inches.

Hodgson says this animal is common all over Thibet, and is a terrible depredator among the flocks, or, as Kinloch writes: "apparently preferring the slaughter of tame animals to the harder task of circumventing wild ones." The great Bhotea mastiff is chiefly employed to guard against it. According to Hodgson the chanko has a long, sharp face, with the muzzle or nude space round the nostrils produced considerably beyond the teeth, and furnished with an unusually large lateral process, by which the nostrils are much overshadowed sideways and nearly closed. The eye is small and placed nearer to the ear than to the nose; the brows are considerably elevated by the large size of the frontal sinuses; the ears are large and gradually tapered to a point from their broad bases, and they have the ordinary fissure towards their posteal base; the head is broad; the teeth large and strong; the body long and lank, the limbs elevated and very powerful; the brush extends to half-way between the mid-flexure (*os calcis*) of the hind limbs and their pads, and is as full as that of a fox.

The fur or pelage is remarkable for its extreme woolliness, the hairy piles being few and sparely scattered amongst the woolliness, which is most abundant; the head as far as the ears, the ears, and the limbs are clad in close ordinary hair; the belly is thinly covered with longer hairs; but all the rest of the animal is clothed in a thick sheep-like coat, which is most abundant on the neck above and below. Gray ('P. Z. S.,' 1863, p. 94) says: "The skull is very much like, and has the same teeth as the European wolf (*C. lupus*)," but in this I think he is mistaken, as the upper carnassial in *C. lupus* is much larger than in any of the Asiatic wolves, and in this particular *C. laniger* is affined to *C. pallipes*. There is a black variety of the chanko, as there is of the European wolf, and by some he is considered a distinct species, but is really a melanoid variety, though Kinloch writes: "The black chanko is rather larger than the grey one; he is of a beautiful glossy black, with a small white star on the chest and a few grey hairs about the muzzle." He was fortunate enough to secure two cubs of this variety. "They fed ravenously on raw meat, and before long became pretty tame." After accompanying him for two months he left them at the hill station of Kussowlie, fearing that the heat at Meerut might prove too great for them; at the end of 2½ months they were sent down. "By this time they had immensely increased in size, but, although they had not seen me for so long, they recognised me, and also my greyhound, of which they had previously been very fond. They soon became much attached to me, and would fawn on me like dogs, licking my face and hands; they were always, however, ready to growl and snap at a stranger. I took them to Agra at the time of the great Durbar there, and used to let them loose in camp with my dogs, so tame had they become."

He eventually presented them to the Zoological Gardens in Regent's Park, and their portraits appeared in the *Illustrated London News* of November 21st, 1868. Whether the skins purchased at Kashgar by the Yarkand Mission were of *C. laniger* or *lupus* is doubtful, as no skulls were procured. In some particulars they seem to agree with the chanko in being rather larger (i.e., larger than *pallipes*); the hair long, and the under fur ash-grey and *woolly*, but the black line down the fore-legs is like *C. lupus*. It is not stated whether the tail was dark-tipped or not, the absence of this dark tip, common to most other wolves, is a point noticed by Hodgson in speaking of *C. laniger*. Mr. Blanford describes another skin which was purchased at Kashgar, and which he supposes may belong to a new species, but there was no skull with it—it is that of a smaller canine, midway between a wolf and a jackal, the prevailing tint being black, mixed with pale rufous, and white along the back and upper surface of the tail; pale rufous on the flanks, limbs, anterior portion of the abdomen and under the tail; a distinct black line down the front of each foreleg; upper part of head rufous, mixed with whitish and black, the forehead being greyer, owing to the white tips to the hairs; the tip of the tail is quite black, and the tail itself is short, as in the jackal, but more bushy, the feet larger than the common jackal—a short, bushy tail agrees with *Cuon*, so also does the large foot.

No. 247. CANIS LUPUS.

The European Wolf.

HABITAT.—All over Europe and Northern Asia, in Turkestan and Yarkand (?)

DESCRIPTION.—Fur long and coarse, dark yellowish-grey, sometimes almost black, but there is a good deal of variation in both colour and texture of the hair according to the country, whether cold or warm, from which the animal comes; a dark streak on the forelegs; the carnassial tooth is however the chief point of distinction between this and the Indian and Thibetan species; it is very much larger in the European animal, approximating to, and sometimes exceeding in size, the two molars together, which is not the case with the others. Mr. Blanford, in his report on the Mammalia of Yarkand published by Government in the 'Scientific Results of the Second Yarkand Mission,' quotes from Professor Jeitteles, of Vienna, the opinion that none of the larger domestic dogs could have descended from the European wolf, because of the relative proportions of their teeth, but that all must have been derived from the Indian wolf or from allied forms.

SIZE.—Head and body, 3½ to 4 feet; tail, 20 inches; height, about 30 to 32 inches.

Mr. Blanford supposes, and with some degree of reason, that the flat skins purchased at Kashgar were those of this species; but unfortunately the absence of the skulls must for the present leave this in doubt, as variations in colour and texture of fur are frequent and dependent on climatic conditions.

No. 248. CANIS AUREUS.

The Jackal (Jerdon's No. 136).

NATIVE NAMES.—*Srigala*, Sanscrit; *Geedhur*, Hindi; *Shial*, *Sial*, *Siar* and *Shialu*, Bengali; *Kola*, Mahrathi; *Nari*, Canarese; *Nakka*, Telegu;

Nerka, Gondi; *Shingal* or *Sjekal*, Persia; *Amu*, Bhotia; *Myae-khawae*, Burmese; *Nareeah*, Singhalese.

HABITAT.—Throughout India, Burmah, and Ceylon; it is found over a great part of Asia, Southern Europe, and Northern Africa.

DESCRIPTION.—"Fur dusky yellowish or rufous grey, the hairs being mottled black, grey, and brown, with the under fur brownish yellow; lower parts yellowish-grey; the tail reddish-brown, ending in a darkish tuft; more or less rufous on the muzzle and limbs; tail moderately hairy."—*Jerdon.*

SIZE.—Head and body, 28 to 30 inches; tail, 10 or 11 inches; height, 16 to 18 inches.

The jackal is one of our best-known animals, both as a prowler and scavenger, in which capacity he is useful, and as a disturber of our midnight rest by his diabolical yells, in which peculiarity he is to be looked upon as an unmitigated nuisance.

He is mischievous too occasionally, and will commit havoc amongst poultry and young kids and lambs, but, as a general rule, he is a harmless, timid creature, and when animal food fails he will take readily to vegetables. Indian corn seems to be one of the things chiefly affected by him; the fruit of the wild behr-tree (*Zizyphus jujuba*) is another, as I have personally witnessed. In Ceylon he is said to devour large quantities of ripe coffee-berries, the seeds, which pass through entire, are carefully gathered by the coolies, who get an extra fee for the labour, and are found to be the best for germination, as the animal picks the finest fruit. According to Sykes he devastates the vineyards in the west of India, and is said to be partial to sugar-cane. The jackal is credited with digging corpses out of the shallow graves, and devouring bodies. I once came across the body of a child in the vicinity of a jungle village which had been unearthed by one. At Seonee we had, at one time, a plague of mad jackals, which did much damage. Sir Emerson Tennent writes of a curious horn or excrescence which grows on the head of the jackal occasionally, which is regarded by the Singhalese as a potent charm, by the instrumentality of which every wish can be realised, and stolen property will return of its own accord! This horn, which is called *Nari-comboo*, is said to grow only on the head of the leader of the pack.

The domestic dog is supposed to owe its origin to this species, as well as to the wolf, but all conjecture on this point can be but pure speculation. Certain it is that the pariahs about villages are strikingly like jackals, at least in many cases, and they will freely interbreed.

The writer in the *India Sporting Review* alluded to by me in writing of the wolf, mentions some experiments made in crossing dogs with jackals. "First cross, hybrid between a female jackal and Scotch terrier dog, or half jackal and half dog; second cross, between the hybrid jackal and terrier, or quarter jackal and three-quarters dog; third cross between the quarter jackal and terrier, or seven-eighths dog and one-eighth jackal. Of the five pups comprising the litter, of which the last was one, two were fawn-coloured and very like pariahs, while three had the precise livery of the jackal; noses sharp and pointed; ears large and erect; head and muzzle like the jackal. This cross, he remarks, appears to have gone back a generation, and to have resembled the jackal much more than their mother, whose appearance, with the exception of the very sharp muzzle, although she had so much jackal blood, was that of a sleek, well-fed pariah dog, colour yellow fawn, but her gait and gallop were precisely that of the jackal."—*McMaster.*

GENUS CUON.

Dentition as in restricted *Canis*, but wanting the second grinder behind the flesh-tooth in the lower jaw; the nose is short; skull arched; the forehead broad, convex, and gradually shelving from the nose line; nasals long, produced behind the hinder upper edge of the maxillaries.

NO. 249. CANIS (CUON) RUTILANS.

The Indian Wild Dog (*Jerdon's No.* 137).

NATIVE NAMES.—*Jungli-kutta; Son-kutta; Ban-kutta, Ram-kutta,* Hindi; *Kolsun, Kolusna, Kolsa* and *Kolasra,* Mahrathi; *Reza-kutta, Adavi-kutta,* Telegu; *Shen-nai,* Malabarese; *Eram-naiko,* Gondi; *Sakki-sarai,* at Hyderabad; *Ram-hun* in Kashmir; *Siddaki,* Thibetan, in Ladakh; *Suhu-tum,* Lepcha; *Paoho,* Bhotea; *Bhaosa, Bhoonsa, Buansu* in the Himalayas, generally from Simla to Nepal (*Jerdon*); *Tao-khwae,* Burmese; *Assoo-adjakh, Assoo-kikkee,* Javanese; *Oesoeng-esang,* Sundese; *An-jing Utan,* Malay; *Hazzee,* Thibetan.

HABITAT.—The whole of India and down the Burmese country to the Malayan archipelago, but not in Ceylon, although Jerdon asserts that it is common there. I however cannot find any authority for this, and both Kellaart and Sir Emerson Tennent affirm that there are no wild dogs in Ceylon.

DESCRIPTION.—General colour bright rusty or red, somewhat paler beneath; ears large and erect, round at the tips; large, hairy-soled feet; very bushy, straight tail, reaching half-way from the hough to the sole, with a dark tip. It stands lower in front than behind; and, though somewhat resembling a jackal, has an unmistakable canine physiognomy; the eye is fuller and better placed, and forehead broader, and the muzzle less pointed.

SIZE.—Head and body, 32 to 36 inches; tail, 16 inches; height 17 to 20 inches.

It has been supposed that there were two or three species of wild dog to be found within the limits of British India, but it is now, I think, conclusively settled that the Malayan and Indian species are one, and that those from Darjeeling and other hills, which showed variation, are the same, with slight differences caused by climate. They are certainly not canine in disposition; the wolf and jackal are much more so, for in confinement they are as ill-conditioned brutes as it is possible to conceive. Those in the Regent's Park Gardens are active, snappy' snarly, wild-looking creatures. Hodgson writes of them: "Those I kept in confinement, when their den was approached, rushed into the remotest corner of it; huddled one upon another, with their heads concealed as much as possible. I never dared to lay hands on them, but if poked with a stick they would retreat from it as long as they could, and then crush themselves into a corner, growling low, and sometimes, but rarely, seizing the stick and biting it with vehemence. After ten months' confinement they were as wild and shy as the first hour I got them. Their eyes emitted a strong light in the dark, and their bodies had the peculiar fœtid odour of the fox and jackal in all its rankness." McMaster sent one to the People's Park, at Madras, which he obtained in Burmah, and says of her: "'Evangeline,' as she is named, is certainly though an interesting and rare creature to have in a museum or wild-beast show, the most snarling, ill-mannered, and detestable beast I have ever owned." "Hawkeye," whose most interesting paper on the wild dog appeared in the *South of India Observer*, of January 7th, 1869, alludes to "Evangeline" in the following terms:—"I saw the beast at the People's Park, and a more untameable wretch I never met with; and why so fair a name for such a savage de'il, I know not." It is strange that the most dog-like of the wild canines should refuse domestication when even the savage European wolf has become so attached as to pine during the absence of his master. Jesse, in his 'History of the British Dog,' relates that a lady near Geneva had a tame wolf, which was so attached that when, on one occasion, she left home for a while he refused food and pined. On her return, when he heard her voice, he flew to meet her in an ecstasy of delight; springing up, he placed a paw on each of her shoulders, and the next moment fell backwards and expired. The wild dog, however, refuses all endearments, and keeps his savage nature to the last. I have never heard of their attacking men, but few four-footed beasts, even of large size, escape them. Fortunately they are not as common as jackals, otherwise little game would be left in the country. During my residence in the Seonee district from 1857 to 1864, I only came across them two or three times. Their mode of hunting has been described by various writers—Hodgson, Elliot, Jerdon, and others of less reliability—but one of the best descriptions, which I regret I have not space for *in extenso*, is that to which I have already alluded as written by "Hawkeye," and which may be found in the paper above mentioned, and also in McMaster's notes on Jerdon; but I give a few extracts:—

"Generally speaking, however, the wild dog has not been known to be the aggressor against mankind; and, though not displaying much dread of man, has hitherto refrained from actual attack, for I have never heard of any case proving it otherwise; at the same time it is well known and an established fact that the tiger and leopard are often driven away by these dogs. It is uncertain whether they really attack with intent to kill either the one or the other, but that they have been repeatedly seen following both there is no question. The wild dog in appearance bears much similitude to the English fox; he is however larger, and stands some inches higher, and has no white tip to his tail, which, with his

Cuon rutilans.

muzzle, is perfectly black. The muscular development all over the body is extraordinary. One that I shot, when skinned, was a most perfect specimen of thews and sinews I ever beheld." He describes various hunts by packs of these dogs, in one of which, witnessed by a brother sportsman, the dogs, five in number, in pressing a Sambar stag, spread themselves out like a fan, which he considers a matter of instinct, so that in case of a flank movement the outer dogs would have a chance; in this case however the stag kept straight on, and, the ground being precipitous, he managed to escape. The evidence produced tends to confirm the opinion that the wild dog endeavours to seize the quarry by the flanks and tear out the entrails. According to Hodgson the *buansu*, as it is called in Nepal, runs in a long, lobbing canter, unapt at the double, and considers it inferior in speed to the jackal and fox. It hunts chiefly by day. Six or eight, or more, unite to hunt down their victim, maintaining the chase more by power of smell than by the eye, and usually overcome by force and perseverance, though occasionally mixing stratagem with direct violence. He asserts that in hunting they bark like hounds, but their barking is in such a voice as no language can express. "Hawkeye," however, states that the wild dog does not throw his tongue when in chase; he has heard them make a kind of tremulous whimper.

The stories of their attacking and killing tigers must be received with caution, though it is certain they will harass both tigers and leopards. I wrote some time back, in 'Seonee': "The natives in all parts of India declare that even tigers are attacked by them; and we once heard a very circumstantial account given of a fight, which took place near the station of Seonee, between a tiger and a pack of these dogs, in which the latter were victors. They followed him about cautiously, avoiding too close a contact, and worried him for three successive days—a statement which should be received with caution. We have, however, heard of them annoying a tiger to such an extent as to make him surrender to them the prey which he had killed for himself."

I agree with Jerdon in disbelieving the native superstition that the wild dog sheds a pungent secretion on his tail, and whisks it in the eyes of the animals it attacks, or covers the leaves of the bushes through which the victim graze, and then takes advantage of the temporary blindness thus caused; but it is a curious fact that the idea is prevalent in all parts of India, north and south, and has been accepted by many writers on Indian sports.

The wild dog dwells and breeds in holes and caves in rocks. The breeding season is from January to March, and about six whelps are born at a time. The mammæ are more numerous than in any other canine—from twelve to fourteen. Jerdon notices that Mr. Wilson at Simla discovered a breeding-place in holes under some rocks, where evidently several females were breeding together. At such times they endeavour to hunt their game towards their den, and kill it as near to it as possible.

GENUS VULPES.

The foxes form a distinct group of the Canidæ; their bodies are long, with short legs, the muzzle more lengthened in comparison and much sharper, and the pupil of the eye contracts vertically instead of circularly; the tail is very bushy, with a gland at the base secreting a strong odorous substance. The female has six mammæ. There are two types in India—the desert fox or fox of the plains, *Cynalopex* of Hamilton Smith; and the hill fox, which approximates to the European species. The former has longer ears and longer and more slender limbs.

No. 250. VULPES BENGALENSIS.

The Indian Fox (*Jerdon's No.* 138).

NATIVE NAMES.—*Lomri*, *Lokri*, *Lokria*, Hindi; *Kokri*, Mahrathi; *Khekar* and *Khikir* in Behar; *Khek-sial*, Bengali; *Konk*, *Kemp-nari*, *Chanaak-nari*, Canarese; *Konka-nakka* or *Gunta-nakka*, *Poti-nara*, Telegu.—*Jerdon.*

HABITAT.—Throughout India; probably Ceylon, as Kellaart mentions having heard of a fox there, but I cannot trace it, or any other, in Burmah.

DESCRIPTION.—Reddish-grey; rufous on the legs and muzzle; reddish white beneath; ears long dark brown externally; tail long bushy, with a broad black tip; muzzle very acute; chin and throat whitish."—*Jerdon.*

Here is Colonel Sykes's description of it in Southern India:—

"It is a very pretty animal, but smaller than the European fox; head short; muzzle very sharp; eyes oblique; irides nut-brown; legs very slender; tail trailing on the ground, very bushy; along the back and on the forehead fawn colour, with hair having a white ring to its tip; back, neck, between the eyes, along the sides, and half way down the tail reddish-grey; each hair banded black and reddish-white; all the legs reddish outside, reddish-white inside; chin and throat dirty white; along the belly reddish-white; ears externally dark brown, and with the fur so short as to be scarcely discoverable; edges of eyelids black; muzzle red brown."

The colour however varies a good deal, according to season and locality. It becomes more grey in the cold season. McMaster writes that he once killed one silvery grey, almost white.

SIZE.—Head and body, 20 to 21 inches; tail, 12 to 14 inches; weight, $5\frac{1}{2}$ lbs.

This fox is common, not only in open country, but even in cantonments and suburbs of cities. Hardly a night passes without its familiar little chattering bark in the Dalhousie Square gardens, or on the Maidan, being heard; and few passengers running up and down our railway lines, who are on the look-out for birds and animals as the train whirls along, fail to see in the early morning our little grey friend sneaking home with his brush trailing behind him.

Jerdon says of the manner in which he carries this that he trails it when going slowly or hunting for food; holds it out horizontal when running; and raises it almost erect when making a sudden turn.

It also, like the jackal, will eat fruit, such as melons, ber, &c., and herbs. It breeds in the spring, from February to April, and has four cubs. Jerdon says the cubs are seldom to be seen outside their earth till nearly full grown. It is much coursed with greyhounds, and gives most amusing sport, doubling constantly till it gets near an earth; but it has little or no smell, so its scent does not lie.

Sir Walter Elliot wrote of it in the Madras *Journal of Literature and Science* (vol. x. p. 102): "Its principal food is rats, land-crabs, grasshoppers, beetles, &c. On one occasion a half-devoured mango was found in the stomach. It always burrows in open plains, runs with great speed, doubling like a hare; but instead of stretching out at first like that animal, and trusting to its turns as a last resource, the fox turns more at first; and, if it can fatigue the dogs, it then goes straight away."

It is easily tamed if taken young, and is very playful, but Jerdon, in repeating the assertion that tame foxes sooner or later go mad, says he has known one or two instances where they have done so; but McMaster throws doubt on this, and puts the supposed madness down to excitement at the amorous season. He gives an interesting account of a pair kept by a friend, which lived on amicable terms with his greyhounds. The owner writes: "I sometimes took them on to the parade ground, and slipped a couple of greyhounds after them. They never ran far, as when tired they lay down on their backs, and were at once recognised by the dogs. On one occasion one fox was tired before the other, and after he had made friends with the dogs he joined them in the chase after the other."

No. 251. VULPES LEUCOPUS.

The Desert Fox (Jerdon's No. 139).

HABITAT.—Northern India, and also on the Western Coast about Cutch.

DESCRIPTION—"Light fulvous on the face, middle of back and upper part of tail; cheeks, sides of neck and body, inner side, and most of the fore parts of the limbs, white; shoulder and haunch, and outside of the limbs nearly to the middle joint, mixed black and white; tail darker at the base above, largely tipped with white; lower parts nigrescent; ears black posteriorly; fur soft and fine as in *V. montanus*, altogether dissimilar from that of *V. Bengalensis.* The skull with the muzzle distinctly narrower, and the lower jaw weaker. One I killed at Hissar had the upper parts fulvous, the hair black-tipped; sides paler; whole lower parts from the chin, including the inside of the arm and thigh, blackish; feet white on the inner side anteriorly, with a blackish border on the anterior limbs; legs fulvous externally; all feet white; tail always with a white tip."—*Jerdon.*

SIZE.—Head and body, 20 inches; tail, 14 inches; weight, 5½ lbs.

According to Mountstuart Elphinstone the backs of the foxes in Hurriana are of the same colour as the common fox, but in one part of the desert their legs and belly, up to a certain height, are black, and in another white—the one seems to have been wading up to the belly in ink, and the other in whitewash.

This fox lives chiefly on the jerboa-rat (*Gerbillus Indicus*) common on sandy plains. Jerdon thinks it more speedy than the common Indian fox.

NO. 252. VULPES FERRILATUS.

The Thibetan Grey Fox.

NATIVE NAME.—*Iger*, Thibetan.

HABITAT.—Thibet.

DESCRIPTION.—Pale fulvous, with grizzled white or iron-grey sides; shorter ears than in the Indian fox.

We now come to the true foxes, with shorter legs and moderate ears.

NO. 253. VULPES MONTANUS.

The Hill Fox (*Jerdon's No.* 140).

NATIVE NAMES.—*Loh*, Kashmiri; *Lomri*, Hindi, at Simla; *Wamu*, Nepalese.

HABITAT.—Throughout the Himalayas.

DESCRIPTION.—Pale fulvous, with a dark brownish or deep chestnut streak down the back; sides deeper fulvous; the haunches a steely grey, mixed with yellowish hairs; tail grey and very bushy, largely tipped with white; ears deep black on outside; cheeks and jowl greyish-white; moustaches black; legs chestnut in front, paling off behind.

SIZE.—Head and body, 30 inches; tail, 19 inches; weight, 14 lbs.

Not at all unlike an English fox, only more variegated. The foregoing description is taken chiefly from a very fine specimen shot in the garden of the house in which I stayed at Simla; but it is subject to great variation, and is in its chief beauty in its winter dress. Several specimens which I have seen are all more or less different in colour. I have never seen a handsomer fox; the fur is extremely rich, the longer hairs exceeding two inches, and the inner fur is fine and dense. It is said to breed in April and May, the female usually having three to four cubs.

NO. 254. VULPES PUSILLUS.

The Punjab Fox (*Jerdon's No.* 141).

HABITAT.—Punjab Salt Range.

DESCRIPTION.—Similar to the last, but much smaller, being about the size of the Indian fox. Jerdon suggests that it may be a variety of the last species, dwarfed by a warmer climate, but Blyth and others keep it apart.

No. 255. VULPES FLAVESCENS.

The Persian Fox.

NATIVE NAMES.—*Tulke*, at Yarkand; *Wamu*, Nepalese.

HABITAT.—Eastern Turkestan, Ladakh, Persia, and, according to Gray, Indian Salt Range; Thibet.

DESCRIPTION.—Fulvous, darker on back, very similar to *V. montanus*, only more generally rufous and paler, with longer hair and larger teeth; face, outer side of fore-legs and base of tail pale fulvous; spot on side of face, chin, front of fore-legs, and a round spot on upper part of hind foot blackish; hairs of tail tipped black; ears externally black; tail tipped largely with white. The skull of one mentioned by Mr. Blanford had larger auditory bullæ than either the European fox or *V. montanus*.

No. 256. VULPES GRIFFITHII.

The Afghanistan Fox.

This was at first reckoned by Blyth as synonymous with the last, but was afterwards separated and renamed. It is stated by Hutton to be common about Candahar, where the skins are made into *reemchas* and *poshteens*, the price in 1845 being about six annas a skin.

MARINE CARNIVORA.

WE disposed of the land Carnivora in the last article, and now, before proceeding to the Cetacea, I will give a slight sketch of the marine Carnivora, of which, however, no examples are to be found on the Indian coasts. The Pinnipedia or Pinnigrada are amphibious in their habits, living chiefly in the water, but resorting occasionally to the land. There are some examples of the land Carnivora which do the same—the polar bear and otter, and more especially the sea-otter, *Enhydra lutris*, which is almost exclusively aquatic, but these are all decidedly of the quadrupedal type, whereas in the amphibia we see the approach to the fish form necessary for their mode of life. The skeleton reveals the ordinary characteristics of the quadruped with somewhat distorted limbs. The bones of the forelimbs are very powerful and short, a broad scapula, short humerus and the ulna and radius are stout, parallel to each other, and the latter much broader at the base; often in old animals the two are ankylosed at the joint, which is also the case with the tibia and fibula. The hip-bones are narrow and much compressed, the femur remarkably short, the shank-bones and the bones of the feet very long. In walking on land the feet are, in the case of the *Otaria* or eared seals placed flat on the full sole; the common seals never use their hind limbs on the shore. The dentition is essentially carnivorous, but varies considerably in the different families, and even in the *Phocidæ* themselves. The stomach is simple, but the intestines are considerably longer than in the *Felidæ*, averaging about fifteen times the length of the body; the digestion is rapid. The bones are light and spongy, and the spine particularly flexible, from the amount of cartilage between the bones. They have a large venous cavity in the liver, and the lungs are capacious, the two combining to assist them in keeping under water; the blood is dark and abundant. The brain is large, and in quantity and amount of convolution exceeds that of the land Carnivores. Their hearing is acute, but their sight out of water is defective.

Their external features are an elongated pisciform body, the toes joined by a membrane converting the feet into broad flippers or fins, the two hind ones being so close as to act like the caudal fin of a fish. The head is flattish and elongated, or more or less rounded, but in comparison with the body it is small. Except in the *Otaridæ* there are no perceptible ears, and in them the ear is very small. The fur is of two kinds, one long and coarse, but the other, or under fur, is beautifully soft and close, and is the ordinary sealskin of commerce. The roots of the coarse hair go deeper into the skin than those of the under fur, so the furrier takes advantage of this by thinning the skin down to the coarse roots, cutting them free, and then the hairs are easily removed, leaving the soft fur attached to the skin.

The Pinnigrada are divided into three families—the *Trichechidæ*, or walruses; the *Otaridæ*, or sea-lions or eared seals; and the *Phocidæ*, or ordinary seals.

As none of these animals have been as yet observed in the Indian seas, being chiefly denizens of cold zones, I will not attempt any further description of species, having merely alluded to them *en passant* as forming an important link in the chain of animal creation.

We must now pass on to the next order, a still more aquatic one.

ORDER CETACEA—THE WHALES.

THESE curious creatures have nothing of the fish about them, save the form, and frequently the name. In other respects they are warm-blooded, viviparous mammals, destitute of hinder limbs, and with very short fore-limbs completely enclosed in skin, but having the usual number of bones, though very much shortened, forming a kind of fin.

The fin on the back is horizontal, and not rayed and upright like that of a fish; the tail resembles that of a fish in form, the caudal vertebræ running through the middle of it. The immense muscular power of this tail, with its broad flanges, arises from the flesh of the body, terminating in long cords of tendon, running to the tip. The vertebral column is often ankylosed in the fore-part, but is extremely elastic, owing to the cartilaginous cushion between each bone in the latter half. Thus, whilst the fore-part is rigid, the hinder is flexible in the extreme. The brain is large and much convoluted; the heart is very large, and the blood-vessels extremely full and numerous, with extensive ramifications, which, being filled with oxygenated blood, assist in supporting life whilst submerged. The lungs are also very large. The laryngeal and nasal passages are peculiar. The following description is by Dr. Murie: "In front of the larynx of man we all know that there is an elastic lid, the epiglottis, which folds over and protects the air passage as food is swallowed. The side cartilages constitute the walls of the organ of voice and protect the vocal chords. Now, in the comparatively voiceless wh le, the cartilages, including the epiglottis, form a long rigid cylindrical tube, which is thrust up the passage at the back of the palate in continuity with the blow-hole. It is there held in place by a muscular ring. With the larynx thus retained bolt upright, and the blow-hole being meanwhile compressed or closed, the cetacean is enabled to swallow food under water without the latter entering the lungs." The stomach is peculiar, being composed of several sacs or chambers with narrow passages between; the intestines are long, glandular and, according to Dr. Murie, full of little pouches. There is no gall bladder; the gullet is very narrow in some and wider in others. Some have teeth, others are without. The eyes are small; the ears deficient externally, though the interior small ear-bones of ordinary mammals are in these massive and exceedingly dense, so much so, as Murie observes, as to be frequently preserved fossil when other osseous structures are destroyed.

The cetacea have been divided into the *Denticete*, or Toothed Whales, and the *Mysticete*, or Whalebone Whales. The former contains the river dolphins, the ziphoid whales, the gigantic sperm whale, the sea dolphins, and the narwhal or sea unicorn. The latter contains the baleen whales.

DENTICETE—THE TOOTHED WHALES.

None of the larger species are found on these coasts, or in the Indian Ocean, the two most interesting of which are the gigantic sperm whales (*Physeter macrocephalus*), and the curious narwhal or sea unicorn (*Monodon monoceros*). The latter is an inhabitant of the northern seas only, but the sperm abounds in warmer waters, being frequently found in the sub-tropical oceans. I have occasionally seen them in the South Atlantic, though they are said to have diminished there of late years. It is a wonder that the species does not get scarce in many localities, so great is the chase after them. During the last forty years the Americans alone have taken at the rate of 10,000 barrels of sperm oil per annum, or upwards of four million barrels since 1835. The sperm whale, though of such enormous bulk and courage, yet has enemies besides man. The thrasher and the killer whale both attack it, and sailors assert that the sword-fish and thrasher combine against it, the latter stabbing from below, whilst the former leaps on it with stunning blows. I think by sword-fish (*Xiphias*), which is also a large but not so very sanguinary a fish, they mean the saw-fish (*Pristis*), which is allied to the sharks, and which attacks the largest whales. The sword-fish has however the character of being pugnacious. The old sperms, especially males, will show fight at times, but the younger ones are easily alarmed, and on being molested rush off in various directions, each looking out for himself. The sperm whale is known from the others by the way in which it spouts, the jet being thrown up obliquely forwards, and it blows at regular intervals. Although the old "bulls" show a certain amount of ferocity at times, their savageness is considerably exaggerated by the whalers, who love to spin yarns about them. Having watched the habits of these and the baleen whales with curiosity, I tried to get as much information about them as I could, from the whalers, but, with the exception of the officers of whaling ships, there was much that was unreliable in Jack's notions about the sperm. On one occasion I was just too late to see one killed. The boats, under full sail, were towing the carcase towards the ship. I would have given a good deal to have seen the encounter. The food of the sperm consists greatly of the huge rock squid or cuttle-fish, which they swallow in large lumps. I have heard whalers assert that a wounded sperm in the death agony will vomit immense pieces of squid. In this respect it differs much from the baleen whales, which have a narrow gullet. According to Professor Flower there is no sufficient evidence of the existence of more than one species of sperm whales, but an allied species, *Physeter* (*Euphysetes*) *simus*, is found on the Madras coast, and to this I will allude further on.

FAMILY DELPHINIDÆ—THE DOLPHINS OR PORPOISES.

GENUS PLATANISTA—THE RIVER DOLPHINS.

A globular head with a long, compressed and, towards the end, spoon-shaped rostrum or snout; flippers short, broad and triangular; a long body of moderate girth; no back fin, but a slight elevation which takes its place. There is a decided depression between the head and body on the region of the neck; the eye is remarkably small, so much so as to be

Platanista Gangetica.

hardly perceptible; in an adult of eight feet long the whole eye-ball is no bigger than a pea, and the orifice of the ear is like a pin-hole.

The skull has peculiar features. "The apparently rounded skull behind the snout has broad, thick zygomatic arches, and above and in front of these the cheek-bones (*maxillæ*) each send forwards and inwards a great roughened sheet of bone or crest, which forms a kind of open helmet. In the large hollow between these bony plates, and somewhat behind, are situated the nasal orifices, which are slightly awry" (*Murie*).* Professor Flower's notice of the skull ('Osteology of the Mammalia') is thus worded: "The orbit is extremely small, the temporal fossa large, and the zygomatic processes of the squamosal are greatly developed. From the outer edge of the ascending plates of the maxillæ, which lie over the frontals, great crests of bone, smooth externally, but reticulated and laminated on their inner surface, rise upwards, and, curving inwards, nearly meet in the middle line above the upper part of the face."

* See Appendix B for illustration.

The dentition is also curious, the upper and lower jaws being provided with a number of teeth, pointed and conical in front, and smaller and more flattened behind. They vary in number. In an example quoted by Dr. Murie the total was 117, viz., $\frac{27-28}{30-32}$, but in a specimen examined by Dr. Anderson, who has most exhaustively described these animals, the total number of teeth amounted to 128, i.e. $\frac{33-32}{32-31}$. (See Appendix B, p. 525.)

The cervical vertebræ are movable, and not ankylosed, as in many of the cetacea; the cæcum is small; the blow-hole is a narrow slit, not transverse as in other whales, but longitudinal. I have somewhat gone out of order in Jerdon's numbering in bringing in this genus here instead of letting it follow Delphinus, as he has done. These river Dolphins naturally come after the extinct Phocodontia or seal-toothed whales, and bear considerable resemblance in the dentition to the extinct genus Squalodon.

No. 257. PLATANISTA GANGETICA.

The Gangetic Porpoise (Jerdon's Nos. 144 *and* 145).

NATIVE NAMES.—*Soonse*, *Soosoo*, *Soosa*, Hindi; *Susak*, *Shishuk*, Bengali; *Sisumar*, Sanscrit; *Bulhan* or *Sunsar*, on the Indus; *Hihoo*, *Siho*, Assamese; *Huhh* in Cachar and Sylhet.

HABITAT.—In the larger rivers connected with the Ganges nearly up to the hills; also in the Brahmaputra and in the Indus, but in fresh water; only it does not go out to sea.

DESCRIPTION.—"A long compressed snout with a formidable array of teeth; a vaulted compressed forehead; longitudinal blow-hole; scarcely perceptible eye; distinct neck; broad and abruptly truncated pectoral fins, and small dorsal fin; and the male, a smaller but heavier-built animal than the female, with a shorter snout" (*Anderson*). The colour is from a dark lead to a sooty black; according to Jerdon "when old with some lighter spots here and there; shining pearl-grey when dry."

SIZE.—From six to eight feet.

This animal, though not often captured, at all events in the vicinity of Calcutta, is familiar to most people who have travelled on the larger Indian rivers. It is common enough in the Hooghly. I have frequently observed it in the river abreast of the Fort whilst we were slowly driving down the Course.

I am largely indebted to Dr. Anderson for information concerning it, for he has not only most carefully watched the habits of this curious animal, but has most exhaustively described its anatomy in his 'Anatomical and Zoological Researches.' It is found in the Hooghly, chiefly in the cold weather, migrating during the hot and rainy season; at least so it was supposed, and Dr. Cantor conjectured that at such times it visited the sea, but this has been proved to be not the case. The *soosoo* never leaves fresh water; and it is in the river during the rains, for fishermen catch it in their nets, but it is hardly ever seen at that time. It rises so as to expose the blow-hole only, and the rush of the swollen waters prevents the peculiar sound of respiration being heard. But in the cold weather, when the river is calm, the ear is attracted at once by the hissing puff of expiration, and the animal may be seen to bound almost out of the water. Dr. Anderson had one alive in captivity for ten days, and carefully watched its respirations. "The blow-hole opened whenever it reached the surface of the water. The characteristic expiratory sound was produced, and so rapid was the inspiration that the blow-hole seemed to close immediately after the expiratory act." He states that "the respirations were tolerably frequent, occurring at intervals of about one-half or three-quarters of a minute, and the whole act did not take more than a few seconds for its fulfilment." But it is probable that in a free state and in perfect health the animal remains longer under water. It has certainly been longer on several occasions when I have watched for the reappearance of one in the river. The food of the Gangetic dolphin consists chiefly of fish and crustacea; occasionally grains of rice and remains of insects are found in the stomach, but these are doubtless, as Dr. Anderson conjectures, in the fish swallowed by the dolphin. The period of gestation is said to be eight to nine months, and usually only one at a time is born, between April and July. The young are sometimes caught with their mothers, and are said to cling by holding on by the mouth to the base of the parent's pectoral fins. "The flesh and blubber are occasionally eaten by many of the low caste Hindus of India, such as the Gurhwals, the Domes of Jessore and Dacca districts, the Harrees, Bourees, Bunos, Bunpurs, Tekas, Tollahas, the Domes of Burdwan and Bhagulpore, who compare it to venison; also by the Teewars and Machooas of Patna, the Mussahars of Shahabad, the Gourhs and Teers of Tirhoot, and the Mullahs of Sarun. In the North-west Provinces about Allahabad, the Chumars, Passees, Kooras, Khewuts or Mullahs, have rather a high estimate of the flesh, which they assert resembles turtle. The Koonths of Benares, Phunkeahs, Natehmurrahs, and Buahoas of Moradabad, and also such gipsy tribes as the Sainsees, Kunjars and Hubbossahs, in the neighbourhood of Meerut, do not despise it. In the Punjab we find the Choorahs, Dhapels, Sainsees, Budcus, and Burars eating the flesh; and in Sind the Kehuls. The Moras, a tribe of Mahomedan boatmen who lead a wandering life on the streams in the Punjab and in Sind, subsist on the dolphin when by good chance they catch one; this is also the case with the Cacharies and the Nagas of Assam. The Sansee women on the Indus eat the flesh under the idea that it makes them prolific. All along the Ganges, Bramahputra, and Indus, the oil is universally considered as of great value as an embrocation in rheumatism and for giving much strength when rubbed on the back and loins. But many other animal oils, such as those of various species of turtle, the crocodile, and the pelican, have a similar reputation. It is said to be of a very penetrating nature, and, owing to this property, it is highly prized for preserving leather, such as harness, &c. The illuminating powers of this oil are said to be very high." (Anderson's 'Anatomical and Zoological Researches.')

Jerdon gives, on the authority of Blyth, another species, *Platanista Indi*, or the Indus porpoise, but Dr. Anderson has conclusively proved that this is identical with the Gangetic dolphin. The dentition of the *soosoo* is most curious. The perfect tooth in the young animal is sharp and pointed, but as the creature advances in age the fangs get broader, and the point wears down, till in old age the crown is so worn as to leave but a bony lump in its place.

GENUS ORCELLA—THE ROUND-HEADED RIVER DOLPHINS.

The generic characteristics of these dolphins are, according to Dr. Anderson, as follows: "Head globular; dorsal fin low, situated behind the middle of the body; pectoral fins oval, about one-sixth the length of the animal; teeth conical, large, and fewer in the lower than in the upper jaw, thirteen to seventeen teeth in the upper and twelve to fourteen teeth in the lower jaw; skull beaked; beak broad at the base, anteriorly pointed; premaxillary not much laterally dilated, bearing one tooth; vertebræ sixty-two to sixty-three; first two cervical vertebræ ankylosed; lumbar transverse process moderately long; vertebræ ribs twelve to thirteen, with one or two free ribs; pelvic bones opposite thirty-fifth and thirty-sixth vertebræ."

These are the dolphins which were procured by Mr. Blyth in the Hooghly, and were supposed by him to be the young of the ca'ing whale (*Globicephalus*), which idea has also been adopted by Jerdon; but it has been since proved that the skeletons prepared from these supposed young whales are those of adults fully matured, and not of young animals, which have certain resemblances to *Globicephalus* as well as to the killer whales, *Orca*, from which the generic name has been derived, but yet was undoubtedly distinct. The killer whales have a very high dorsal fin in the middle of the back, with very large pectoral flippers as broad as long; in *Orcella* the back fin is low and behind the middle of the body, and the pectoral fin is only half as broad as long. In the ca'ing whale the back fin is more towards the shoulders, and the flippers are long and narrow; the genus *Orcella* in fact seems to be intermediate between the dolphin and the ca'ing whale, combining the head of *Globicephalus* with the body of *Delphinus*. Dr. Anderson, however, points out further differences than the external ones I have above alluded to. *Orca*, he says, is distinguished by a "more powerfully built skeleton, with considerably fewer vertebræ, there being only a maximum of fifty-three in it to a maximum of sixty-three in *Orcella*." In *Orca* generally four or five cervical vertebræ are ankylosed as in the cachelots, but in the two species of *Orcella* only the atlas and axis are joined. "In the killers and ca'ing whales the ribs are transferred to the transverse processes at the seventh dorsal, whilst in *Orcella* the transference does not take place until the eighth." The skull resembles that of *Orca* in the breadth of the upper jaw being produced by the maxillaries, whereas in *Globicephalus* this effect is caused by the premaxillaries. The teeth resemble the killer's.

As I have said so much about the killer whale, I may digress a little to explain what it is, though it is not a denizen of the Indian seas. It is to the Cetacea what the shark is to fishes—a voracious tyrant with a capacious mouth, armed with formidable teeth. It hesitates not to attack the largest sperm and Greenland whales, and the smaller whales, porpoises and seals will spring out of water and strand themselves on shore in terror at its approach. It ranges from twenty to thirty feet in length, and is of so gluttonous a character that in one recorded case a killer had been found choked in the attempt to swallow a *fifteenth* seal, the other fourteen, with thirteen porpoises, being found in its stomach!

According to Scammon three or four of them do not hesitate to grapple with the largest baleen whale; and, as described by Dr. Murie, "the latter often, paralysed through fear, lie helpless and at their mercy. The killers, like a pack of hounds, cluster about the animal's head, breach over it, seize it by the lips, and haul the bleeding monster under water; and, should the victim open its mouth, they eat its tongue." In one instance he relates that a Californian grey whale and the young one were assaulted; the *Orcas* killed the latter, and sprang on the mother, tearing away large pieces of flesh, which they greedily devoured.

"These brutes have been known to attack a white-painted herring boat, mistaking it for a beluga; and it is stated that occasionally they will boldly lay siege to whales killed by the whalers, almost dragging them perforce under water. Near some of the Pacific sealing grounds they continually swim about, and swoop off the unwary young; even the large male sea-lions hastily retreat ashore and give these monsters a wide berth. The walrus also, with his powerful tusks, cannot keep the killers at bay, especially if young morses are in the herd. The cubs on such occasions will mount upon the mother's back for refuge, clinging for dear life, but the *Orca*, diving, comes suddenly up with a spiteful thud, and the cub, losing its balance, falls into the water, when in an instant it is seized by the remorseless whales." The speed of the killer whale is immense, as may be supposed when it can overtake the swift dolphins, which it catches and swallows alive. It has also been seen chasing salmon up the mouths of rivers.

The genus *Orcella* seems to come in between the sea and river dolphins, although *Orcellà fluminalis* of Dr. Anderson is a purely fluviatile animal, which apparently never goes out to sea.

No. 258. ORCELLA BREVIROSTRIS.

The Short-nosed Round-headed River Dolphin.

HABITAT.—The estuaries of the Ganges and Brahmaputra rivers.

DESCRIPTION.—" The head is convex from the blow-hole to the upper lip, but its sides immediately below the angle of the mouth are somewhat anteriorly convergent, but rounded; the gape posteriorly has a long upward curve; the eye, which is well developed, is near the angle at the gape, and in the adult is placed about one inch above it, with a slightly downward slope; the ear is nearly on the same level as the angle of the mouth, but is extremely small, crescentic, and not measuring more than 0·12 inch in diameter. The posterior margin of the blow-hole is immediately behind the anterior angle of the eye; the blow-hole is crescentic and unsymmetrical, being more to the left than to the right side; there are two slight eminences about one inch behind the blow-hole; the construction of the neck occurs below the ear and slightly behind it" (Anderson's 'Anatomical and Zoological Researches,' p. 370). The other characteristics are triangular flippers half as broad as long. The back fin rises behind the centre of the back; it is comparatively small, falcate, curved over the top to a blunt point, and concave behind. The line of the back is sharp from this fin down to the tail. The ventral line is the same for some inches behind the anus. The colour is dark slaty-blue above, almost black, a little paler below, without any streaks or marks, such as in *O. fluminalis* and Risso's grampus.

SIZE.—From snout to caudal notch, about 7 feet.

I cannot find much on record concerning the habits of this dolphin, and my own acquaintance with it is too limited for me to afford much original information.

No. 259. ORCELLA FLUMINALIS (*Anderson*).

The Fresh-water Round-headed Dolphin.

HABITAT.—The Irrawaddy river; Burmah.

DESCRIPTION.—This differs from the last in a " rather smaller, lower, and more falcate dorsal fin, its more pointed and less anteriorly bulging head, and rather shorter and broader pectoral fins" (*Anderson*). The colour is a pale bluish above, and white underneath, with numerous streaks, as in Risso's grampus.

SIZE.—From 7 to 7½ feet from snout to fork of tail.

Dr. Anderson, who has fully described this species, says that he has "never observed it in tidal waters, so that it is even more strictly fluviatile than the Gangetic dolphin. From a little below Prome to as far up as Bhamo, which is about 550 miles, as the crow flies, from the sea, these animals abound. It is asserted by the Shans of Upper Burmah that these dolphins are not to be found beyond a point thirty miles above Bhamo, where the course of the river is interrupted by rocks, and which they style *Labine* or Dolphin Point, from the circumstance that, according to them, it is the residence of certain *Nâts*, who there impose so heavy a toll on dolphins as to deter them from proceeding upwards."

This dolphin is somewhat like its marine cousins, being fond of gambolling round the river steamers. Solitary ones are seldom met with, usually two or three being together. When they rise to breathe the blow-hole is first seen; then, after respiration, the head goes down, and the back as far as the dorsal fin is seen, but rarely the tail flippers. They rise to breathe every 70 to 150 seconds, and the respiratory act is so rapid that it requires a very expert marksman to take aim and fire before the animal disappears.

Dr. Anderson says: "I have observed some of them disporting themselves in a way that has never yet been recorded of *Cetacea*, as far as I am aware. They swam with a rolling motion near the surface, with their heads half out of the water, and every now and then nearly fully exposed, when they ejected great volumes of water out of their mouths—generally straight before them, but sometimes nearly vertically. The sight of this curious habit at once recalled to me an incident in my voyage up the river, when I had been quite baffled to explain an exactly similar appearance seen at a distance, so that this remarkable habit would appear to be not uncommonly manifested. On one occasion I noticed an individual standing upright in the water, so much so that one-half of its pectoral fins was exposed, producing the appearance against the background as if the animal was supported on its flippers. It suddenly disappeared, and again, a little in advance of its former position, it bobbed up in the same attitude, and this it frequently repeated. The Shan boatmen who were with me seemed to connect these curious movements with the season—spring—in which the dolphins breed."

A similar thing has been noticed in the case of marine dolphins off the coast of Ceylon by Mr. E. W. H. Holdsworth, whose observations confirm the opinion of the Shan boatmen. (See 'P. Z. S.' 1872, p. 586.)

"The food of the Irrawady dolphin is apparently exclusively fish. The fishermen believe that the dolphin purposely draws fish to their nets, and each fishing village has its particular guardian dolphin, which receives a name common to all the fellows of his school, and it is this supposition that makes it so difficult to obtain specimens of this cetacean. Colonel Sladen has told me that suits are not unfrequently brought into the native courts to recover a share in the capture of fish in which a plaintiff's dolphin has been held to have filled the nets of a rival fisherman" (*Anderson*). This reminds me that in the surveying voyage of the *Herald*, as related by Mr. H. Lee, the natives of Moreton Bay entreated the seamen not to shoot their tame porpoises, which helped them in their fishing.

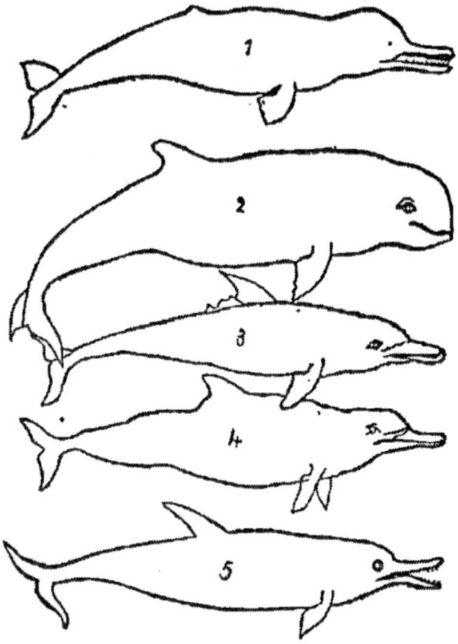

1. Gangetic Dolphin—*Platanista Gangetica.*
2. Round-headed River Dolphin — *Orcella brevirostris.*
3. Gadamu Dolphin—*Delphinus Gadamu.*
4. Freckled Dolphin—*Delphinus lentiginosus.*
5. Black Dolphin—*Delphinus pomegra.*

GENUS DELPHINUS—THE MARINE DOLPHINS.

These are characterised by a convex forehead, with a protruding muzzle which forms a sort of beak; they have teeth in both jaws, numerous and conical, broad and high cranium, nasal passages vertical, no cæcum. They are gregarious in habit, carnivorous and extremely swift, but they must not be confounded with the dolphin of sailors, which is a true fish (*Coryphæna hipparis*) of great velocity and brilliant colours, which change like rainbow tints when the fish is dying. I have several times in vain tried to catch the fleeting shades with both oil and water-colours, but without success; for within a few minutes they change from the most vivid of greens and blues to a pale silvery grey. The true dolphin, of which we are treating, is the dolphin of the ancients, represented in all the old pictures and sculptures. They have a medium dorsal fin, and the pectoral flippers are about two-thirds longer than the breadth.

No. 260. DELPHINUS PERNIGER.

The Black Dolphin (*Jerdon's No.* 142).

HABITAT.—Bay of Bengal.

DESCRIPTION.—"Twenty-six teeth on each side above and below, obtuse, slightly curved inwards; of a uniform shining black above, beneath blackish."—*Jerdon.*

SIZE.—Total length, 5 feet 4 inches.

This species was taken in the Bay of Bengal and sent to the Asiatic Society's Museum by Sir Walter Elliot, but it does not appear to be mentioned by Professor Owen in his notice of the Indian Cetacea collected by Sir Walter Elliot.

No. 261. DELPHINUS PLUMBEUS.

The Lead-coloured Dolphin (*Jerdon's No.* 143).

HABITAT.—Malabar coast.

DESCRIPTION.—Thirty-six teeth in each side in the upper jaw and thirty-two in the lower jaw; of a uniform leaden colour, with the lower jaw white.

SIZE.—About 8 feet.

Whether this be the same as or a different species to the next I am unable to say, as the description is meagre, and the number of teeth vary so much in the same species that no definite rule can be laid down on them.

The following are the species named by Professor Owen and collected by Sir Walter Elliot.

No. 262. DELPHINUS GADAMU.

NATIVE NAME.—*Gadamu.*

HABITAT.—Madras coast.

DESCRIPTION.—Body fusiform, gaining its greatest diameter at the fore-part of the dorsal fin, decreasing forward to the head by straight converging lines, and with a gentle convex curve to the eyes and blow-hole; the forehead descends with a bold convex curve; the sides of the head converge from the eyes to the base of the snout, which is divided from the forehead by a transverse groove extending almost horizontally to the angles of the mouth, and it equals in length the distance from the base to the eyes, which is five inches and a-half; the lower jaw projects a little beyond the upper; the blow-hole is crescentic, in a line with the eyes, exactly in the middle of the head, with the horns of the crescent pointing towards the snout; the pectoral and dorsal fins are falcate and about equal in size; the colour is a dark plumbeous grey, almost black upon the fins, especially at their fore-part; the body below being of a pinkish ashy-grey, with a few small irregular patches of light plumbeous grey.

The dentition varies from $\frac{24-24}{24-24} = 96$, to $\frac{23-23}{27-28} = 101$, and $\frac{27-27}{27-27} = 108$.

SIZE.—About seven feet from snout to fork of tail; girth about 3 feet 9 inches.

No. 263. DELPHINUS LENTIGINOSUS.

The Freckled Dolphin.

NATIVE NAME.—*Bolla Gadimi*, Telegu.

HABITAT.—Madras coast.

DESCRIPTION.—Body fusiform, as in the last, but with smaller pectoral and dorsal but larger caudal fin; the back is straighter and not so much rounded on the shoulders, and the colour is bluish-cinerous or slaty, freckled with small irregular spots of brown or plumbeous, and longitudinal streaks of the same flecked with white; the under parts a shade lighter than rest of the body. The snout is six inches in length.

Dentition: $\frac{32-32}{32-33} = 129$.

SIZE.—Seven to eight feet; girth four feet.

No. 264. DELPHINUS MACULIVENTER.

Spot-bellied Dolphin.

NATIVE NAME.—*Suvva.*

HABITAT.—Madras coast.

DESCRIPTION.—Forehead more convex than even *D. gadamu*, and head proportionately larger and body deeper. A deep shining plumbeous black on the upper part, becoming paler near the belly, which from the underpart of the jaw to the perineum is ashy-grey, with irregular spots and blotches.

Dentition: $\frac{27-27}{30-30} = 114$.

SIZE.—About seven feet.

No. 265. DELPHINUS FUSIFORMIS.

The Spindle-shaped Dolphin.

HABITAT.—Madras coast.

DESCRIPTION.—More slender in proportion to its length; a less elevated and less convex forehead than the last species; a proportionally thicker, broader, and more obtusely terminated snout; a deeper mandible or under jaw, especially posteriorly, and smaller dorsal and pectoral fins, especially the latter. The greatest girth is in middle or fore-part of the dorsal fin, from which the body tapers to both ends, presenting the true spindle form. Colour plumbeous, lighter below, darkest on the fins and snout.

Dentition: $\frac{22-22}{21-21} = 86$ teeth.

Size.—About six feet.

No. 266. DELPHINUS POMEEGRA.

The Black or Pomeegra Dolphin.

NATIVE NAME.—*Pomeegra.*

HABITAT.—Madras coast.

DESCRIPTION.—More slender than any of the foregoing species; longish snout, with 173 teeth, viz. $\frac{41-41}{45-46}$. It is well to note the irregularity here, not only an odd number, but the lower jaw has the greater number, whereas it is generally the other way. Colour almost black, lighter beneath. Professor Owen's description is not so full as in other cases, but from the illustration it seems that the flukes of the caudal fin are longer, and the posterior edge of the dorsal straighter than in the others.

No. 267. DELPHINUS LONGIROSTRIS.

The Long-snouted Dolphin.

HABITAT.—Indian Ocean; coast of Ceylon.

DESCRIPTION.—Similar to the last, but with a longer and more slender snout.

No. 268. DELPHINUS VELOX.

This is also given by Dr. Kellaart as a species found on the coast of Ceylon.

Sir Walter Elliot mentions another species of dolphin, of which he had lost the drawing, about thirty-two inches long, of a uniform black colour, small mouth, and no dorsal fin, called by the Tamil fishermen *Molagan.*

GENUS PHOCÆNA—THE PORPOISES.

No beak or rostrum; snout short and convex; numerous teeth in both jaws. Kellaart testifies to the existence of a true porpoise on the coasts of Ceylon—which he identifies with *Phocæna communis*—of a blackish colour above and whitish beneath.

GENUS GLOBICEPHALUS—THE CA'ING OR PILOT WHALE.

Head globular in front; teeth few in number; the dorsal fin is high, situated nearer to the head than to the tail; the flippers very long and narrow; the fingers possessing an unusually large number of bones.

No. 269. GLOBICEPHALUS INDICUS.

The Indian Ca'ing Whale (Jerdon's No. 146).

HABITAT.—Bay of Bengal.

DESCRIPTION.—Body cylindrical, tapering to the tail; dorsal fin high, falcate, and placed about the middle of the body proper, excluding the tail portion; the forehead with a prominent boss over the snout, which is short; pectoral fins long and narrow; colour uniform leaden black, paler beneath.

SIZE.—Fourteen feet, flippers 2 feet; dorsal fin, 2¼ feet long, 11 inches high; tail flukes, 3 feet broad.

Blyth's specimens were procured in the Salt Lakes near Calcutta. It was for the young of this that he mistook *Orcella brevirostris*.

PHYSETERIDÆ—THE CACHELOTS OR SPERM WHALES.

GENUS EUPHYSETES.

No. 270. PHYSETER *or* EUPHYSETES SIMUS.

The Snub-nosed Cachelot.

NATIVE NAME.—*Wonga*, Telugu.

HABITAT.—Bay of Bengal.

DESCRIPTION.—The general form of this animal resembles the porpoise, but the position of the mouth at once distinguishes it. It is small and situated, like that of the shark, considerably under the blunt rostrum, so much so as to lead one to conjecture whether or not it turns on its back in seizing its prey, as do the sharks. The blow hole is crescentic, but eccentrically placed to the left of the middle line of the head, and the horns of the crescent are turned diagonally backwards —that is to say, the lower limb points to the back whilst the upper one touches the middle line and points across; the eye is small; the pectoral fins are triangular, about one foot in length and four and a-half inches broad in the male, and four inches in the female; the dorsal fin is sub-falcate, standing about a foot high, and is nine to ten inches broad at the base; the male being the broader; the colour is a shining black above, paler and pinkish below.

Dentition: $\frac{1-1}{9-9} = 20$.

SIZE.—Six to seven feet.

The peculiarity of this cetacean is the preponderance of the cranial over the rostral part, more so, as Professor Owen remarks, than in any other species. The asymmetry of the bones too is remarkable, although this is characteristic of all the catodon whales, especially as regards the bones of the anterior narial passages, the left of which is very much larger than the right. This is also the case in the large sperm whale, but in *Euphysetes* the disproportion is still greater. In a notice on a New Zealand species (*E. Pottsii*), by Dr. Julius Haast, he gives the difference as fifteen times the size of the right aperture; the mouth is also peculiar from its position and small size, being very much overshot by the snout. It may, as Dr. Haast supposes, be a ground feeder, existing on the smaller hydroid zoophytes, otherwise it must, I think, turn on its side in seizing its prey.

MYSTICETE—WHALEBONE OR BALEEN WHALES.

GENUS BALÆNA—THE RIGHT WHALES.

They are distinguished from the last group by their enormous heads, with more symmetrical skulls, the facial portion of which is greatly in excess of the cranial. The bones of the lower jaw are not united at the symphysis, but are held together by strong fibrous bands; the two rami are very much rounded and arched outwards; there are no teeth. The maxillary and premaxillary bones are much produced, forming a rostrum tapering, narrow, compressed and much arched in the right whales. From this depends the mass of whalebone, which grows from a fleshy substance "similar," as is aptly described by Dr. Murie, "to the roots of our finger-nails. It grows continuously from the roots like the latter, and in many respects corresponds, save that the free end is always fringed. Baleen, therefore, though varying from a few inches to a number of feet long, in fact approximates to a series of, so to say, mouth nail-plates, which laminæ have a somewhat transverse position to the cavity of the mouth, and thus their inner split edges and lower free ends cause the mouth to appear as a great hairy archway, shallower in front and deeper behind" (Cassell's Natural History).

The object of this vast amount of whalebone is to strain from the huge gulps of water the mollusca, &c., on which this animal feeds. The tongue of these whales is very large, filling up the space between the lower jaws. The gullet is small in comparison. The nasal aperture differs from the *Denticete* in being symmetrical, that is, having the double aperture, and in being directed forwards as in most mammals, instead of upwards and backwards as in the dolphins. The whale produces generally one at a birth, which it suckles for some length of time. The mammæ are pudendal. The right whales have no fin on the back; those that have form a separate genus, *Balænoptera*, i.e. fin-whales.

They are the most valuable of the cetacea, except perhaps the cachelot or sperm whale, as producing the greatest amount of oil and whalebone. Of the various species the most sought after is the Greenland or right whale (*Balæna mysticetus*), which ordinarily attains a length of fifty to sixty feet. An average whale between forty and fifty feet in

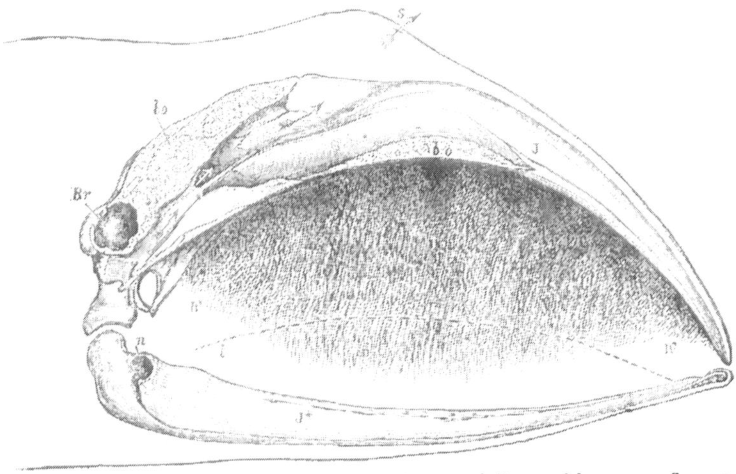

Br, brain cavity; J J*, upper and lower jawbones; the arrows indicate narial passages; S, spout-hole; W, whalebone; *t*, tongue in dotted line; *n*, nerve aperture in lower jaw; *bo*, bone sawed through.

Skull of Baleen Whale.

length will yield from sixty to eighty barrels of oil and a thousand pounds of baleen.

Formerly all whaling vessels were sailers, but now powerful steamships are used, and the harpoon often gives way to the harpoon gun. A whale, when struck, will sometimes run out a mile of line before it comes up again, which is generally in about half an hour. The whalers judge as best they can, from the position of the line, in which direction he will rise, and get as near as possible so as to use the lance or drive in another harpoon. When killed, the animal is towed to the vessel and fastened on the port side, belly uppermost, and head towards the stern; it is then stripped of its blubber, the body being canted by tackles till all parts are cleared. The baleen is then cut out, and the carcase abandoned to the sharks, killer whales, and sea birds.

The baleen whales are not found in the intertropical seas. Of the known species there are the Greenland whale (*B. mysticetus*), the Biscay whale (*B. Biscayensis*), the Japan whale (*B. Japonica*), the Cape whale (*B. australis*), and the South Pacific whale (*B. antipodarum*).

GENUS BALÆNOPTERA—FINBACK WHALES OR RORQUALS.

Are distinguished by their longer and narrower bodies, smaller heads, being one-fourth instead of one-third the length of the body, smaller mouths, shorter baleen, plaited throats, and smaller flippers; they have a dorsal fin behind the middle of the back, and the root of the tail is compressed laterally. They also present certain osteological differences from the right whales; the latter have the whole of the seven cervical vertebræ anchylosed, that is to say generally, for sometimes the seventh is free. In the finbacks the cervical vertebræ are, as a rule, all distinct and free, although occasionally anchylosis may take place between two or more of them. The sternum of the *Balæna* consists of a broad, flattened, heart-shaped or oval presternum. "In the fin whales (*Balænoptera*) it is transversely oval or trilobate, with a projecting backward xiphoid process" (*Professor Flower*). The ulna and radius in the rorquals are also comparatively longer than in the baleen whales. In the skull the supraorbital processes of the frontals are broader in the rorquals than in others, and the olfactory fossa is less elongated.

They are more muscular and active animals than the right whales, and have a less amount of blubber and much shorter whalebone, consequently are not so much sought after by whalers, as the risk in attacking them is not compensated for by the commercial results. Many of them grow to enormous size, far exceeding any of the baleen whales. The common rorqual, razorback, or pike-whale of the English coasts (*B. musculus*) attains a length of seventy feet; it is black above and pure white below. The sulphur-bottom whale (*B. sulfureus*) is known by its yellowish belly, and with Sibbald's whale (*B. Sibbaldii*) grows to a length of one hundred feet, to which size our Indian species also approaches.

No. 271. BALÆNOPTERA INDICA.

The Indian Rorqual (*Jerdon's No.* 147).

HABITAT.—The Indian Ocean.

DESCRIPTION.—External characteristics those of the genus, but from Mr. Blyth's observations the lower jaw of this species is more slender in proportion to its size than that of any other rorqual or even right whale.

SIZE.—Up to 90 and possibly 100 feet.

There is a most interesting article on the great rorqual of the Indian Ocean by Mr. Blyth in the 'Journal of the Asiatic Society' for 1859, p. 481. He notices that the existence of great whales was known to and recorded by the ancients. Nearchus, the commander of Alexander's fleet, which sailed from the Indus to the Persian Gulf in B.C. 327, mentions having met with them, and that on the coast of Mekran the people constructed houses of the bones of stranded whales. In modern times an occasional one gets on shore, as was the case with one at Chittagong in 1842, another on the Arakan coast in 1851. In 1858 one of 90 feet was stranded at Quilon on the west coast, as reported by the Rev. H. Baker of Aleppi, who also mentions that one, said to be 100 feet long, was cast ashore some years previously. He writes to Mr. Blyth: "Whales are very common on the coast. American ships, and occasionally a Swedish one, call at Cochin for stores during their cruises for them; but no English whalers ever come here that I have heard of."

Rorqual.

I wonder at any whaling vessel coming out of their way after this species, for I have always heard from whalers that the finback is not worth hunting. It is possible that in cruising after sperms they may go a little out of their way to take a finback or two. However, to return to Blyth's remarks. Of the whale stranded on the Arakan coast a few bones were sent to the Society's Museum in Calcutta; they consisted of the two rami of the lower jaw, measuring 20 feet 10 inches, a right rib, the left radius, and five vertebræ, which are now to be seen at the Indian Museum. He writes as follows on them: "The proportional length of the radius indicates the animal to have been a Balænoptera or rorqual, while the remarkable slenderness of the lower jaw suffices to prove it a distinct species from any hitherto-described rorqual."

The finback does not confine itself entirely, or even chiefly, as stated by Blyth, to a diet of *Cephalapoda*, but is a fish-eater to boot, doing great damage to shoals of such fish as cod, herrings, &c., as many as six to eight hundred fish having been found in the stomach of one.

They are not particularly shy, and will sometimes follow a vessel closely for days. I read not very long ago an account in one of the Indian newspapers of a steamer running over one of these animals, and nearly cutting it in two; the agony of the poor brute as he struggled in the water, vainly trying to sound, was graphically described. A similar adventure occurred some years ago to the B.I.S.N. Company's steamer *Euphrates*, on a voyage from Kurrachee to Bombay, when about sixty miles from the latter place. The captain writes: "It appears that the animal had for about half an hour amused itself by crossing and recrossing the bow, and then at last suddenly turned and came straight for the vessel, striking us about ten feet from the stem. It struck with such force as to send a considerable quantity of spray on deck. The only other instance that has occurred here lately was in the case of the S.S. *Dalhousie*, when about twelve miles from Kurrachee; it was in September of last year, and the Bombay papers had a full account of it at the time." I am indebted to my friend Mr. M. C. Turner for this and some other interesting letters on this subject. Captain A. Stiffe, of the late Indian Navy, writes regarding the drowning of a whale by entanglement with a submarine cable, off the coast of Mekran: "The telegraph cable was broken, and a dead whale hove up to the surface, with three turns of cable round the neck of his tail, by which he was drowned. I had the three turns in my office at Kurrachee, and there they are now I dare say. I don't remember any more details. There are always shoals of whales about that part, and it is supposed a 'bight' of the cable lying off the ground got wound up like a rope round a screw." I myself was in a sailing vessel going about five or six knots, when a whale played about for a time, and then rose and spouted just under the bow, covering the forecastle with spray. The captain, who was standing by me, quite expected a shock, and exclaimed—"Look out! hold on!"

SIRENIA—THE MANATEES.

This group contains the *phytophagous* or *herbivorous* cetacea. Their teeth have flat crowns, and they live on aquatic vegetation, though, according to Cuvier, they sometimes leave the water for pasture on shore, but this has not been authenticated, and is probably a mistake. The other characteristics of the group are pectoral mammæ and hairy moustaches. The anterior narial aperture in the skull opens upwards, but the orifices of the nostrils are placed at the end of the muzzle. The stomach is complex, being divided into four sacs, and they have a large cæcum. The flippers are broad, and the animal uses them with some dexterity in supporting its young in the act of suckling. As at such times they frequently raise the upper part of the body out of water, they have given rise to the ancient fables regarding mermaids and sirens. There is something human-like, although repulsive, in the aspect of these creatures, especially in the erect attitude just alluded to. No wonder the ancient mariners, with their restricted knowledge and inclination to the marvellous, should have created the fabulous mermaid, half-fish and half-woman, and have peopled the rocks and seas of Ceylon with seductive sirens with imaginary flowing tresses and sweet ensnaring voices. As regards the latter it may be that the strange phenomena related by Sir Emerson Tennent, of musical sounds ascending from the bottom of the sea, and ascribed by him to certain shell-fish, gave rise to the mermaid's song. Sir Emerson's account has in itself a touch of the romantic and marvellous. He says: "On coming to the point mentioned I distinctly heard the sounds in question. They came up from the water like the gentle thrills of a musical chord, or the faint vibrations of a wineglass when its rim is rubbed by a moistened finger. It was not one sustained note, but a multitude of tiny sounds, each clear and distinct in itself, the sweetest treble mingling with the lowest bass. On applying the ear to the wood-work of the boat the vibration was greatly increased in volume." Similar sounds have been heard elsewhere in the Indian seas, and doubtless the ancients connected this mysterious music of the ocean with the animals round which they had thrown such a halo of romance. But to return to the prose of the subject. The Sirenia consists of the Manatees (*Manatus*), the Dugongs (*Halicore*), and the Stellerines (*Rhytina*); the latter is almost extinct; it used to be found in numbers in Behring Straits, but was exterminated by sailors and others, who found it very good eating. The Manatee inhabits the African and American coasts, along the west coast of the former continent, and in the bays, inlets, and rivers of tropical America, but the one with which we have to do is the dugong or halicore, of which the distribution is rather widespread, from the Red Sea and East African coasts to the west coast of Australia. The latter country possesses an organised dugong fishery, which bids fair to exterminate this harmless animal. They are prized for the excellent quality of the oil they yield, which is clear and free from objectionable smell.

GENUS HALICORE—THE DUGONG.

Have grinders of two cones laterally united. The premaxillary region is elongated and bent downwards, overlapping the very deep lower jaw, which is similarly bent down. They have ordinarily two incisors in the upper jaw, none in the lower. No canines, and molars $\frac{3-3}{3-3}$, total fourteen teeth. The incisor tusks in the bent-down upper jaw are longer in the male, and sometimes project beyond the thick fleshy lips, but in the female they are small. The head is round, the lips thick and bristled with moustaches, the body is elongated, and the tail terminated by a crescent-shaped flapper.

NO. 272. HALICORE DUGONG. (*Jerdon's No.* 240.)

The Dugong.

NATIVE NAME.—*Mooda Oora*, Singhalese.

HABITAT.—Indian Ocean off Ceylon.

DESCRIPTION.—Body pisciform, terminated by a horizontal fin with

Halicore dugong.

two lobes; colour slaty brown above, sometimes bluish black, whitish below.

SIZE.—From 5 to 7 feet long usually, but said to reach 10.

Dr. Kellaart says that at an early age this animal has as many as 32 teeth, viz. inc. $\frac{4}{8}$, and molars $\frac{5-5}{5-5}$, but when adult there are only 14, as mentioned above. The molars, according to Dr. Murie, succeed each other, the fore ones dropping out, and others from behind taking their places. It feeds on fucus and other seaweeds, and the flesh is considered good eating, and not unlike veal or, some say, pork. They are lethargic in disposition, and in those countries where they have been unmolested they are so fearless of man as to allow themselves to be handled—a confidence somewhat betrayed by the natives, who on such occasions manage to abstract the fattest calves, which are considered a delicacy.

ORDER RODENTIA.

THE GNAWERS.

THIS order, GLIRES of Linnæus and his followers, is composed of animals, chiefly of small size, which differ from all others by the peculiarity of their teeth. No one, even though he be most ignorant of comparative anatomy, could mistake the rat or rabbit-like skull of a rodent for that of any other creature. The peculiar pincer-like form of the jaws, with their curved chisel-shaped teeth in front, mark the order at a glance. There is no complexity in their dentition. There are the cutters or incisors, and the grinders; and of the cutters there are never more than two in each jaw, that is to say efficient and visible teeth, for there are in some species rudimentary incisors, especially in the young, but these either disappear or take no part in work. Between the grinders and incisors are toothless gaps. The formation and growth of the teeth are peculiar; and it is strange that the gigantic elephant should be the nearest approach to these small creatures in this respect. The teeth—in most cases the grinders, but always the incisors—grow continuously from a persistent pulp, and therefore loss from attrition is kept constantly supplied by growth from behind. The incisors are planted in a socket which is the segment of a circle. These segments are not equal in both jaws. The lower one is a small segment of a large circle, the upper one is the reverse, being a larger segment of a smaller circle. The angle at which they meet is always the same. Some curious malformations are occasionally found which illustrate the growth of these teeth. Should by any chance, accident or design, one of these incisors get diverted from its proper angle and not meet with the friction which is necessary to keep it in its normal condition, it goes on growing and growing, following its natural curve till it forms a ring, or by penetrating the mouth interferes with the animal's feeding. A case is recorded by Blyth of a rat which had an eye destroyed by a tooth growing into it. Here again occurs a similarity to the elephant, whose tusks grow in the same maner, and if abnormally deflected will occasion, as in the case of one lately described to me, serious hindrance to the movement of the trunk. The incisors of rodents are composed of dentine coated in front with a layer of hard enamel, the other surfaces being without this protection, except in the case of some, amongst which are the hares and rabbits, which have a thin coating as well all over. These forms are those with rudimentary incisors, and constitute the links connecting the other mammalia with the Gnawers.

The molars are much alike in structure, and can hardly be divided, as they are by some naturalists, into molars and premolars. They take the three hindmost as molars, regarding the others as premolars. Sometimes these grinders have roots, but are more commonly open at the end and grow from a permanent pulp. They are composed of tubular and convoluted portions of enamel filed up with dentine, and their worn surfaces show a variety of patterns, as in the case of the Proboscidea. These enamelled eminences are always transverse, and according to Cuvier those genera in which these eminences are simple lines, and the crown is very flat, are more exclusively frugivorous; others, in which the teeth are divided into blunt tubercles, are omnivorous; whilst some few, which have no points, more readily attack other animals, and approximate somewhat to the Carnivora.

The head is small in proportion to the body, the skull being long and flat above; the nasal bones are elongated; the premaxillaries very large on account of the size of the incisor teeth, and the maxillaries are, therefore, pushed back; the zygomatic arch is well developed in most, but is in general weak; the orbit of the eye is never closed behind; the tympanic bulla is very large; the jaw is articulated in a singular manner; instead of the lateral and semi-rotary action of the Herbivora, or the vertical cutting one of the flesh-eating mammals, the rodent has a longitudinal motion given by the arrangement of the lower jaw, the condyle of which is not transverse, but parallel with the median line of the skull, and the glenoid fossa, or cavity into which it fits, and which is situated on the under side of the posterior root of the zygoma, is so open in front as to allow of a backwards and forwards sliding action. The vertebral column is remarkable for the great transverse processes directed downwards, forwards, and widening at the ends. In the hare these processes are largely developed; the metapophyses or larger projections on each side of the central spinous process are very long, projecting upwards and forwards; the anapophyses or smaller projection in rear of the above are small; and the hypapophyses or downward processes are remarkably long, single and compressed;

according to Professor Flower these latter are not found in the Rodentia generally. The tail varies greatly, being in some very small indeed, whilst in others it exceeds the length of the body; the sternum or breast-bone is narrow and long, and collar-bones are to be found in most of the genera; the pelvis is long and narrow. In most cases the hind limbs are longer and more powerful than the fore-limbs; in some, as in the jerboas (*Dipus*) and the Cape jumping hare (*Pedetes caffer*), attaining as disproportionate a length as in the kangaroos, their mode of progression being the same; the tibia and fibula are anchylosed; the fore-limbs in the majority of this order are short, and are used as hands in holding the food to the mouth, the radius and ulna being distinct, and capable of rotatory motion. The feet have usually five toes, but in some the hind feet have only four, and even three. In point of intelligence, the rodents do not come up to other mammals, being as a rule timid and stupid; the brain is small and remarkably free from convolution. The cerebellum is distinctly separated from and not overlapped by the hemispheres of the cerebrum; the organs of smell, sight and hearing are usually well developed; the stomach is simple or in two sacs; the intestinal canal and cæcum long. The latter is wanting in one family.

Rodents have been divided in various ways by different authors. Jerdon separates his into four groups, viz. "*Sciuridæ*, squirrels; *Muridæ*, rats; *Hystricidæ*, porcupines; and *Leporidæ*, hares; which indeed are considered by some to embrace the whole of the order; to which has recently been added the *Saccomyidæ*, or pouched rats, whilst many systematists make separate families of the dormice, *Myoxidæ;* jerboas, *Dipodidæ;* voles, *Arvidolidæ;* mole-rats, *Aspalacidæ* and *Bathyergidæ*; all included in the MURIDÆ; and the *Caviadæ*, *Octodontidæ*, and *Hydrochæridæ*, belonging to the HYSTRICIDÆ" ('Mammals of India,' p. 164).

However, the system that most commends itself is that of Mr. E. R. Alston, proposed in the 'Proceedings' of the Zoological Society, and founded on the original scheme of Professor Gervais, by which the order is subdivided into two on the character of the incisor teeth. Those which have never more than two incisors, coated only in front with enamel are termed SIMPLICIDENTATA, or *Simple-toothed Rodents.* The other sub-order, the genera of which have rudimentary incisors, as in the case of hares, rabbits, &c., and in which the enamel is spread more or less over all the surface, is termed DUPLICIDENTATA or *Double-toothed Rodents*, and this is the system I propose to follow.

SUB-ORDER SIMPLICIDENTATA.

SIMPLE-TOOTHED RODENTS.

These, as I before observed, are those of the order which never have more than two incisors in the upper jaw, and the enamel on these is restricted to the front of the tooth. They have also a well-developed bony palate, which in the Duplicidentata is imperfect, forming in fact but a narrow bridge from one jaw to the other. In the latter also the fibula, which is anchylosed to the end of the tibia, articulates with the calcaneum or heel-bone, which is not the case with the simple-toothed rodents.

We now come to the subdivisions of the Simplicidentata. The order GLIRES has always been a puzzling one to naturalists, from the immense variety of forms, with their intricate affinities, and there is not much help to be gained from extinct forms, for such as have been found are mostly referable to existing families. The classification which I have adopted is, as I said before, that elaborated by Mr. E. R. Alston, F.G.S., F.Z.S., and reported in the 'Proceedings' of the Zoological Society for 1876. I said that he had founded it on Professor Gervais' scheme, but I see that the groundwork of the system was laid down in 1839 by Mr. G. R. Waterhouse, then curator of the Zoological Society, and it was afterwards, in 1848, taken up by Professor Gervais, and subsequently added to by Professor Brandt in 1855, and Lilljeborg in 1866. About ten years later Mr. Alston, working on the data supplied by the above, and also by Milne-Edwards, Gray, Günther, Leidy, Coues, and Dr. Peters, produced a complete system of classification, which seems to be all that is to be desired.

We have already divided the rodents into two sub-orders, to which, however, Mr. Alston adds a third, viz., *Hebetidentati*, or Blunt-toothed Rodents, which contains only the *Mesotherium*, a fossil form. We have now to subdivide the two. The Double-toothed Rodents are easily disposed of in two families—*Leporidæ* and *Lagomyidæ*. The Simple-toothed Rodents are more numerous, and consist of about eighteen families arranged under three sections, which are *Sciuromorpha*, or Squirrel-like Rodents, *Myomorpha* or Rat-like Rodents, and *Hystricomorpha*, or Porcupine-like Rodents. It would perhaps render it clear to the reader were I to tabulate the differences chiefly noticeable in these three sections:—

SECTION I.—SCIUROMORPHA, OR SQUIRREL-LIKE RODENTS.

Molar dentition $\frac{4-4}{4-4}$ or $\frac{5-5}{4-4}$. In the latter case the foremost upper molar is small; the fibula is distinct, and never united, except in some cases where it is attached to the extremity of the tibia; the zygomatic arch is formed chiefly by the malar, which is not supported beneath by a continuation of the zygomatic process of the maxillary; collar-bones perfect; upper lip cleft; the muffle small and naked; tail cylindrical and hairy (except in *Castoridæ*). Five families.

SECTION II.—MYOMORPHA, OR RAT-LIKE RODENTS.

Molar dentition from $\frac{3-3}{3-3}$ to $\frac{6-6}{6-6}$, the former being the usual number; the tibia and fibula are united for at least a third of their length. The zygomatic arch is slender, and the malar process rarely extends so far forward as in the preceding section, and is generally supported below by a continuation of the maxillary zygomatic process; collar bones are perfect (except in *Lophiomyidæ*); upper lip and muffle as in the last; tail cylindrical, sometimes hairy, but commonly covered with scales arranged in rings. Seven families.

SECTION III.—HYSTRICOMORPHA, OR PORCUPINE-LIKE RODENTS.

With one exception (*Ctenodactylus*) have four molars in each upper and lower jaw; the tibia and fibula are distinct in young and old; the zygomatic arch is stout, and the malar does not advance far forward, nor is it supported by the maxillary zygomatic process; collar-bones perfect in some; the upper lip is rarely cleft; the muffle clad with fine hair; tail hairy, sub-naked or scaly.

SECTION I.—SCIUROMORPHA.

Contains the following families, those that are not Indian being in *italics*:—

(1) *Anomaluridæ*; (2) Sciuridæ; (3) *Ischyromyidæ*, a fossil genus; (4) *Haplodontidæ*; (5) *Castoridæ*.

The Anomalures are African animals resembling our flying squirrels, to which they were at first thought to belong, but were separated and named by Mr. Waterhouse, the chief peculiarity being the tail, which is long and well covered with hair, though not bushy as in the squirrels, and which has, at its basal portion, a double series of projecting horny scales, which probably help it in climbing trees. There are several other peculiarities, which I need not dwell on here, which have justified its separation from the true squirrels. The flying membrane, which is quite as large as that of the flying squirrels, extends from the elbow to the heel instead of from the wrist, and it is held out by a strong cartilaginous spur starting from the elbow.

Of the Sciuridæ we have many examples in India, which will be noticed further on.

The *Ischyromyidæ* is founded on a single North American fossil genus (*Ischyromys typus*), which is nearly allied to the Sciuridæ, but also shows some affinity to the beavers.

The *Haplodontidæ* is also an American family, founded on one genus, but an existing and not a fossil animal. The *Haplodon rufus* is a small burrowing rodent, valued by the Indians both for its flesh and its skin, of which from twenty to thirty are sewn together to form a robe; the teeth are rootless, simple, and prismatic, the surface of each being surrounded by a mere border of enamel.

The *Castoridæ* is the beaver family, which is also unknown in India. Unlike as this animal is externally to the squirrels, its anatomy warrants its position in the Sciuromorpha, otherwise one would feel inclined to include it in the next section.

We see that of the five families, of which this section is composed, only the second has its representatives in India.

SCIURIDÆ—THE SQUIRRELS.

This family contains the true squirrels, including the flying ones, and the marmots. The distinctive characteristics of the former are as follows: The gnawing teeth are smooth, compressed. The grinding teeth are $\frac{5-5}{4-4}$ or $\frac{4-4}{4-4}$; in the former case the first upper premolar is small, and sometimes deciduous; they are tubercular, at least in youth, and rooted. Skull with distinct post-orbital processes; infra-orbital opening small, usually placed in front of the maxillary zygomatic process; palate broad and flat; twelve or thirteen pairs of ribs; tail cylindrical and bushy; feet either pentadactylous or with a tubercle in place of a thumb on the fore-feet. Mostly quite arboreal.

GENUS SCIURUS.

Pre-molars, $\frac{2-2}{1-1}$; molars, $\frac{3-3}{3-3}$; gnawing teeth smooth, orange-coloured, or brown; no cheek pouches; mammæ three or four pairs; first upper pre-molar soon lost in many cases; limbs free; form agile; tail long and very bushy.

Jerdon states that "there are three well marked groups in India distinguished by size, coloration and habits," by which he means the large forest squirrels, the medium size grizzled ones, and the little striped squirrels, to which however I must add one more form, which is found out of the geographical limits assigned to his work—the

Rhinosciurus, or long-snouted squirrel, an animal singularly like a Tupaia. The squirrels, as a whole, form a natural and well-defined group, with a remarkable uniformity of dentition and skull, but of infinite variation in colour. In fact, it is most puzzling and misleading to find so great a diversity of pelage as is exhibited by a single species. I was shown by a friend a few months ago a fine range of colours in skins of a single species from Burmah—*S. caniceps*. I cannot attempt to describe them from memory, but the diversity was so marked that I believe they would have been taken by unscientific observers for so many different species. Now in domesticated animals there is great variation in colouring, but not in the majority of wild species. What the causes are that operate in the painting of the skin of an animal no one can say, any more than one can say how particular spots are arranged on the petal of a flower or the wing of a butterfly. That specific liveries have been designed by an all-wise Creator for purposes of recognition I have no doubt, as well as for purposes of deception and protection—in the former case to keep certain breeds pure, and in the latter to protect animals from attack by enabling them better to hide themselves, as we see in the case of those birds and quadrupeds which inhabit exposed cold countries turning white in winter, and in the mottled skin of the Galeopithicus, which is hardly discernible from the rough bark of the tree to which it clings. I have hardly ever noticed such varied hues in any wild animals, although the *Viverridæ* are somewhat erratic in colouring, as in the Indian squirrels, and it is doubtful whether several recorded species are not so nearly allied as to be in fact properly but one and the same. There is much in common in at least five species of Burmese squirrels, and it is open to question whether *S. caniceps* and *S. Blanfordii* are not the same. Dr. Anderson writes: "I have examined a very extensive series of squirrels belonging to the various forms above described, viz., *S. pygerythrus*, *S. caniceps*, *S. Phayrei* and *S. Blanfordii*, and of others which appears to indicate at least, if not to prove, that all of them are in some way related to each other." In another place he says: "The skull of an adult male, *S. caniceps*, which had the bright red golden colour of the back well developed, presents so strong a resemblance to the skull of *S. Blanfordii*, that it is

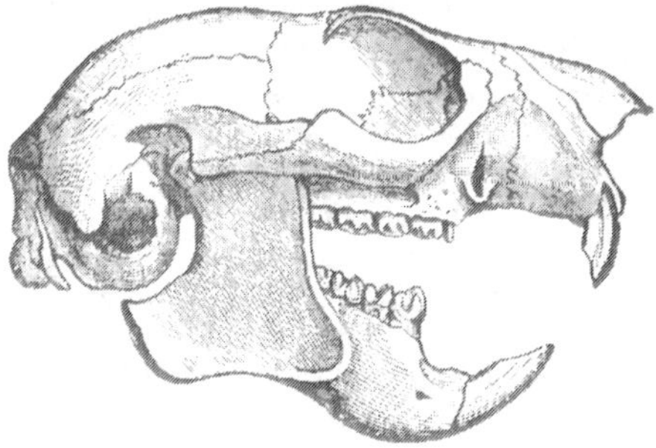

Skull of *Pteromys* (Flying Squirrel).

extremely difficult to seize on any point wherein they differ." After comparison of the above with skulls of *S. griseimanus* and *S. Phayrei*, he adds: "such facts taken in conjunction with those mentioned under *S. Blanfordii*, suggest that there is a very intimate connection between all of these forms, if they do not ultimately prove to be identical" ('Anat. and Zool. Researches,' pp. 229, 231).

Blyth also, speaking of the larger squirrels, says: "It is difficult to conceive of the whole series as other than permanent varieties of one species; and the same remark applies to the races of *Pteromys*, and at least to some of those of *Sciuropterus*, as also to various named *Sciuri*" ('Cat. Mam.,' p. 98).

The large forest squirrels come first on our list. They inhabit lofty tree jungle, making their nests on the tops of the tallest trees. They are most active in their habits, and are strictly arboreal, being awkward on the ground. When kept as pets they become very tame, though some are crotchety tempered, and bite severely.

No. 273. SCIURUS INDICUS.

(*Sciurus Malabaricus and S. Elphinstonei in Jerdon, Nos.* 148 *and* 150.)

The Bombay Squirrel of Pennant.

NATIVE NAMES.—*Jangli-gilheri*, Hindi; *Shekra*, Mahrathi; *Kesaunalu*, Canarese of the Halapyks.

HABITAT.—The dense forests of the Western Ghâts, but extending easterly as far as Midnapore and Cuttack.

DESCRIPTION.—Upper surface of body dark maroon red, lower part of back and rump and upper portions of limbs and the whole of the tail black, the latter ending in a broad brownish-yellow tip; the outside of the hind-legs and half-way down the outside of the fore-legs a uniform rich maroon red; the under parts from chin to vent, inside of limbs, lower part of fore-legs, the inter-aural region and the cheeks bright orange yellow; forehead and nose reddish-brown, with white hairs interspersed; ears small and tufted; a narrow maroon line from the anterior angle of the ear extends downwards to the side of the neck, with a yellow line behind it; whiskers and bristles black.

Dr. Anderson also remarks on the skull of this species that it is considerably smaller than that of *S. maximus*, and has a narrower and less concave inter-orbital space; the nasals are also broader posteriorly, and less dilated anteriorly, the upper dental line being also shorter.

SIZE.—Head and body, 20 inches; tail, 15¼ inches.

Jerdon's description of this animal is taken *verbatim* from Sykes, who named it after the Honourable Mountstuart Elphinstone, under the impression that it was a new species, but it is apparently the same as *S. Indicus* of Erxleben and *S. Malabaricus* of Schinz.

No. 274. SCIURUS MAXIMUS.

The Central Indian Red Squirrel (*Jerdon's No.* 149).

NATIVE NAMES.— *Kat-berral,* Bengali; *Karat,* Hindi; *Rasu* and *Ratuphar* at Monghyr, according to Hamilton; *Kondeng* of the Coles; *Per-warsti,* Gondi; *Bet-udata,* Telegu; *Shekra,* Mahrathi.

Sciurus maximus.

HABITAT.—Malabar coast, Central India, and, according to Dr. F. B. Hamilton, the hills about Monghyr, whence doubtless the Calcutta market is supplied. Hodgson records it from the Himalayan Terai.

DESCRIPTION.—"The upper surface and the sides of the neck, the shoulders, and the outside of the fore-limbs, the lumbar and sacral regions, the outside of the thighs and the tail are black, the black of the hind-quarters being prolonged forwards along the mesial line towards the black of the shoulders; a large dark maroon spot on the vertex, separated from the maroon of the nape by yellowish inter-aural area, which extends downwards and forwards to the cheeks; a maroon-coloured line passes downward from the front of the ear, with a yellow area behind it. The sides of the face and muzzle are pale yellowish, the latter being flesh-coloured; the other portions of the trunk and the lower half of the tibial portion of the hind limbs are maroon. The tail is either black or maroon black, sometimes tipped with yellowish brown. The whole of the under-parts and inside of the limbs and the hands and feet are rich yellowish; the ears strongly maroon and tufted" (*Dr. Anderson*). Jerdon's description of this animal is very meagre and doubtful.

SIZE.—About the same as the last.

This squirrel was tolerably common in the forests of Seonee, and we had one or two in confinement. One belonging to my brother-in-law was so tame as to allow of any amount of bullying by his children, who used to pull it about as though it were a puppy or kitten, but I have known others to bite severely and resent any freedom.

NO. 275. SCIURUS MACROURUS.

The Long-tailed Forest Squirrel (*Jerdon's No.* 152).

NATIVE NAMES.—*Rookecah* or *Dandoleyna*, Singhalese.

HABITAT.—Ceylon, Southern India, i.e. Malabar, Travancore, Mysore, Neilgherries.

DESCRIPTION.—"Fur of the upper parts coarse and slightly waved; above, the colour varies from maroon-black to rufous brown; hairs sometimes grizzled and tipped white or pale yellow, particularly on the croup, sides, and upper parts of limbs; crown of the head darker in most specimens than other parts; cheeks, under-parts, and lower two-thirds of limbs of a fulvous white; occiput of a deeper fulvous, sometimes yellow or ferruginous brown; an indistinct dark spot on the cheek, which is sometimes absent; two-thirds or more of the basal portion of the tail black or brown; the rest grizzled grey or fulvous. In some the hairs of the whole tail are tipped white, and in others grizzled white throughout. In the young there is very little of brown or black; the whole tail is more or less formed of grey hairs, and the terminal third is nearly white. Grey is also the prevailing colour on the posterior half of the body; toes in all black or blackish brown; ears hairy, only slightly tufted in adults."—*Kellaart.*

SIZE.—Head and body, 13½ inches; tail, 11 inches.

This squirrel also varies greatly in colouring, and has led several naturalists astray. Kellaart, in his 'Prodromus Faunæ Zeylanicæ,' says he has seen them in a transition state from dark brown to grizzled grey.

No. 276. SCIURUS GIGANTEUS.

The Black Hill Squirrel (*Sciurus macrouroides in Jerdon, No.* 151).

NATIVE NAMES.—*Shingsham*, Bhotia; *Le-hyuk*, Lepcha; *Jelarang*, Javanese; *Chingkrawah-etam*, Malay; *Leng-thet*, in Arakan; *Sheu*, in Tenasserim.

HABITAT.—North-west Himalayas to Assam, the Garo hills, Sylhet, and Cachar, spreading from Northern Assam across to Yunnan, and through Arakan and Tenasserim on to the Malayan peninsula and Borneo.

DESCRIPTION.—"This species has well-tufted ears; the upper surface is either wholly black or reddish-brown, without any trace of white; the tail is generally jet black, also the outside of the fore and hind limbs, and the upper surface of the feet; an elongated black spot is almost invariably found below the eye from beyond the moustache, and the eye is encircled with black. There are generally two black spots on the under surface of the chin; the under parts and the inside of the limbs vary from pale yellowish-white to a rich rufous orange; the basal portion of the hairs of the under-parts is dark brown or black, and the ventral area has frequently a dull hue where the yellow tips are sparse; the coats of these squirrels are generally sleek, glossy and deep black, and while in this condition the under surface is most brilliant, especially at its line of junction with the black, along the sides of the body and limbs, tending to form a kind of bright band.

"In some the upper parts have a brownish hue, but this is not characteristic of any particular locality, as two individuals, one from Nepal and the other from Borneo, are equally brown. While the fur is of this colour it is long and coarse, and the under-parts are less brilliant. These phases are probably seasonal, and connected with the breeding period."—*Anderson.*

SIZE.—Head and body, about 15 inches; tail, about 16 inches.

The next group consists of squirrels of medium size with grizzled fur, as Jerdon remarks of the two species he mentions; but with the rich fields of Burmah and Assam we can swell our list to over a dozen. It is doubtful whether one or two of the named species are not varieties of one and the same, so nearly are they allied, but this remains to be proved.

No. 277. SCIURUS LOKRIAH.

The Orange-bellied Grey Squirrel (*Jerdon's No.* 153).

NATIVE NAMES.—*Lokriah*, Nepalese; *Zhamo*, Bhotia, *Killi*, or *Kallitingdong*, Lepcha (*Jerdon*).

HABITAT.—Nepal, Sikim, Assam (Khasia Hills), and Burmah (Arakan).

DESCRIPTION.—A deep ferruginous olive-brown, the hairs tipped with orange, soft and silky; the under-parts from chin to vent and the outside of the thighs a rich orange; the tail is shorter than that of the next species, concolorous with the body above, but the banding of the hair is coarser, the apical black band being very broad, tipped with orange or white, generally the latter, the general hue being blackish washed with orange or white. In some the general hue is orange brown with obscure annuli; the arrangement of the hair is distichous or in two rows.

SIZE.—Head and body, about 8 inches; tail, 6½ to 8 inches, including hair.

There is some confusion between this and the next species, *S. lokroides*, and the distinctive characteristics quoted by Jerdon and others, founded on colouring alone, are not to be depended upon, for colouring varies, but there is considerable difference in the skulls of the two, *S. lokriah* having a smaller skull, with distinct peculiarities. The inter-orbital portion of the skull is narrower anteriorly and posteriorly, and the muzzle is narrow at the base, and of nearly equal breadth throughout. The nasals are long and narrow, and reach further back than in *S. lokroides*. These points, which are brought forward by Dr. Anderson, are sufficient to indicate that they are quite distinct species. As regards colouring *S. lokriah* has normally red thighs, but even this is absent at times. Dr. Anderson says: "It is much more richly coloured than *S. lokroides*, with no rufous even on the thighs, and with generally a tuft of pure white hair behind the ear, by which it can be recognised, as it occurs in twenty instances out of twenty-five, and even when absent the hairs in that locality have a paler colour. As this whitish tuft lies backwards, it is only seen when the ear is carefully examined."

No. 278. SCIURUS LOKROIDES.

The Hoary-bellied Grey Squirrel (*Jerdon's No.* 154).

HABITAT.—In the lower ranges of the South-eastern Himalayas, Nepal, Sikim, Assam, Tipperah and Arakan.

DESCRIPTION.—This is a most difficult species to describe. Dr. Anderson writes: "I have before me sixty-two examples of various squirrels which have been referred to *S. lokroides*, *S. Assamensis* and *S. Blythii* by Hodgson, M'Clelland and Tytler, also the types of *S. similis* (Gray), which were forwarded to the British Museum as *S. lokroides* by Hodgson. After a careful consideration of these materials, they appear to me to be referable to one species. Hodgson, who first described it, referred to it all those Himalayan squirrels slightly larger than *S. lokriah*, and which had the ventral surface either pale whitish or slightly washed with rufous, the sides also being sometimes suffused with this tinge especially on the anterior half of the thigh, which in many is bright orange red; but this colour is variable, and many squirrels have this portion of the body white, of which *S. Blythii* is an example; and others similar to it are before me from Bhutan and Assam which do not differ from *S. lokroides* except in the presence of this white area, which is evidently only a variation on the red area, and probably a seasonal change, as many show merely a faint rufous tinge in the inguinal region, that colour being entirely absent on the outside of the thigh.

It is, however, worthy of note that those squirrels which have a rufous tinge in the inguinal region rarely, if ever, have the outside of the thigh bright red, and that the squirrels distinguished by white on their thighs are from Bhutan, Assam, and the Garo hills. But I do not see that these latter differ in any other respect from the squirrels sent by Hodgson as specimens of *S. lokroides*, with and without red thighs. Moreover, one of Hodgson's specimens of *S. lokroides* shows a tendency in the thigh to become white" ('Anat. and Zool. Researches,' pp. 247, 248).

The difficulty in laying down precise rules for colouring is here evident, but in general I may say that the upper parts are rufescent olive brown, the hair being grizzled or banded black and yellow, commencing with greyish-black at the base, then yellow, black, yellow with a dark brown or black tip; the lower parts are rufous hoary or grey, tinged with rufous, or the latter shade may be restricted to the groin or inguinal parts. The fur is coarser and more broadly ringed than in *S. lokriah*, and the ventral surface is never tinged with orange, as in that species: the tail is concolorous with the back; the hair more coarsely annulated; there is no white tuft behind the ears, as in the last species.

SIZE.—About the same as the last, or Dr. Anderson says: "In the form referable to *S. Blythii*, a white spot occurs on the inguinal region of the thigh in the position in which the rufous of the so-called red-legged squirrels is developed. The groin in some of these squirrels shows also a decided rufous tinge, while the remainder of the belly is sullied grey white. If these forms were without the white thigh-spot, they would exactly conform to the type of *S. Assamensis*. A squirrel in the British Museum, labelled *S. Tytleri* (Verreau, 'Indes Orientales'), agrees with *S. Blythii*" ('A. and Z. Res.', p. 249).

Blyth has seen a squirrel of this species renewing its coat, and assuming a variegated appearance during its transition to the breeding dress.

A jet-black squirrel of the same proportion occurs in Sylhet and Cachar, which Dr. Anderson is inclined to think belongs also to this species.

We may, therefore, regard the following as being the same as *S. lokroides*, viz., *S. Assamensis*, *S. Blythii*, *S. similis*, and the black one, which has apparently not been named.

Jerdon states that these squirrels are mostly seen in the autumn when the chestnuts, of which they are very fond, ripen.

No. 279. SCIURUS PYGERYTHRUS.

HABITAT.—Burmah (Lower Pegu, and common in the neighbourhood of Rangoon).

DESCRIPTION.—Upper parts dark olive grey; basal third of the tail concolorous with the back, its latter two-thirds ringed olive-yellow and black; the tip black; feet olive grey, sometimes washed with yellowish; under surface and inside of limbs orange yellow, which extends also along the middle of the under part of the tail. Paler varieties occur. The skull of this species is smaller than those of *S. caniceps*, *S. Phayrei* and *S. Blanfordii.*

No. 280. SCIURUS CANICEPS.

The Golden-backed Squirrel.

HABITAT.—Burmah (Upper Tenasserim and Tavoy).

DESCRIPTION.—General colour grey or fulvous above; limbs outside grizzled grey; feet yellowish-grey; in some cases the nape, shoulders, and upper parts of back are vivid light ferruginous or golden fulvous, sometimes extending downwards on to the base of the tail. Some have only a trace of this colouring, others none at all. There is infinite variety of colouring in this species, as I observed in my remarks on the genus, and it is closely allied to the next three, if they do not ultimately prove to be the same.

"Out of a large series of specimens referable to *S. caniceps*, the males illustrate three phases of colouring, associated with a difference in the character of the fur. The first is a grey, the second a yellowish, and the third a phase in which the back becomes brilliant yellowish-red."—*Anderson.*

No. 281. SCIURUS PHAYREI.

The Laterally-banded or Phayre's Squirrel.

HABITAT.—Burmah. Common in Martaban; has also been obtained at Tounghu.

DESCRIPTION.—Upper parts dark olive grey; lower parts rich orange red; the same colour being more or less continued along the under surface of the tail; the orange colour extends over the inside of the limbs, the front of the thigh and on the feet; the fore-limbs are dusky outside, with pale rufous yellow feet. Its chief distinguishing mark is a brown well-defined dark band on the flanks between the colour of the upper and lower parts.

No. 282. SCIURUS BLANFORDII.

Blanford's Squirrel.

HABITAT.—Upper Burmah.

DESCRIPTION.—Pale grey above, finely punctulated with black and grey; tail concolorous, with a black tip; under parts pale orange yellow; hands and feet yellow. Dr. Anderson shot a female at Pudeepyo, in the beginning of January, which had a distinct tendency to the formation of a dusky lateral stripe, as in the last species; the under-parts also were much more rich orange than in the type of this species. In the grey phase of *S. caniceps* that species is so like *S. Blanfordii* in the colouring of the upper parts and feet that it is almost impossible to distinguish them, but, according to Dr. Anderson, "on examining the under parts it is found that in these phases of *S. caniceps* they are grey, whereas in *S. Blanfordii* they are a beautiful rich orange, and the feet are yellow."

Before proceeding to the next species, which is a better marked one, I will quote one more passage from Dr. Anderson's careful comparison of the four preceding squirrels. "*S. Phayrei* corresponds in the colour of the upper fur to the yellow phase of *S. caniceps*, and the tail is the same as in it, having a black tip, which is the character also that that appendage has in *S. pygerythrus*. In some examples of *S. Phayrei* the dusky or blackish is not confined to the lateral line, but extends over the outside of the fore-limbs, the feet being always yellow in squirrels presenting these characters. Some specimens of *S. pygerythrus* show a distinct tendency to have yellow feet, and further research will probably prove *S. Phayrei* to be only a variety of *S. pygerythrus*. When Blyth first encountered this form, he simply regarded it as a variety of *S. pygerythrus*, and I believe his first opinion will be ultimately found to be more in accordance with the real interpretation of the facts than the conclusion he afterwards adopted. In the Paris Museum there is an example of *S. Blanfordii* from Upper Burmah which distinctly shows a dark lateral streak, so that, taking into consideration the other examples to which I have already referred, there seems to be a presumption that it and *S. Phayrei* are one and the same species, and that they are probably identical with *S. pygerythrus;* moreover, my impression is that a more extensive series will establish their identity with *S. caniceps.* This view of the question is also supported by a small series of these squirrels in the Leyden Museum from Tounghu in Upper Burmah, presented by the Marquis of Tweeddale. From the characters manifested by these squirrels, and the circumstances that they were all shot in one locality, they are of great interest. One is an adult, and in its upper parts it exactly resembles *S. Blanfordii,* also in its yellow feet and black tip to its tail, but, like *S. Phayrei,* it has a broad blackish-brown lateral stripe. The others are smaller, and resemble the foregoing specimens in all their characters, except that they have no dark lateral streak, and that the feet of two are concolorous with the upper parts, while in the remaining squirrel the feet appear to be changing to yellow, as in the adult. The two former of these, therefore, conform to the type of *S. pygerythrus,* but the fur of the upper parts is greyer and not so richly coloured as in it, but the annulation of the fur has the same character in both. The remaining specimen in its features is distinctly referable to *S. Blanfordii* ('Anat. and Zool. Researches,' p. 232).

No. 283. SCIURUS ATRODORSALIS.

The Black-backed Squirrel.

HABITAT.—Burmah and the Malayan countries. Common in Martaban.

DESCRIPTION.—There are two phases of colouring, in which both old and young of this species are found: with the black on the back, and again without it. In the latter case the upper parts and feet are a yellowish-rufous. The upper surface of the head, as far back as to include the ears, orange red; under parts and inside of limbs more or less chestnut; under surface of neck orange yellow, with a centre line of the same on the chest; tail variable—in the young it has seven alternate orange and black bands, the orange being terminal; but the adults have sometimes only five bands, the apical one so broad as to make a rich orange tail with yellowish-white tipped hair. In those with black backs the colour of the upper fur is less fulvous, and the chestnut of the lower parts is darker; in some the tail has broad orange tipped hairs, whilst in others it is, with the exception of the base, wholly black, and not annulated. These differences in colouring are not sexual, nor due to age. The skull of *S. atrodorsalis* resembles that of *S. caniceps,* but is broader, with a somewhat shorter muzzle, has smaller teeth, and would appear to be, from comparisons made by Dr. Anderson, smaller.

No. 284. SCIURUS ERYTHRÆUS.

The Assam Red-bellied Squirrel.

HABITAT.—Assam, Garo hills, Munipur.

DESCRIPTION.—The upper parts glistening deep reddish-black, minutely grizzled with light fulvous or yellowish-brown, each hair having two annulations; under parts and inside of limbs dark reddish maroon; feet black; tail concolorous with the back from the basal third, then gradually less grizzled; the terminal half black; whiskers black. Pallas describes the black of the tail as passing upwards in a mesial line.

SIZE.—Head and body, about 9 to 10 inches; tail with hair, from 11 to 12 inches.

No. 285. SCIURUS GORDONI.

Gordon's Squirrel.

HABITAT.—Upper Burmah.

DESCRIPTION.—Dr. Anderson, who first named this species, describes it as follows: "*S. Gordoni* has the upper surface and a narrow line from between the fore-limbs along the middle of the body grizzled olive-brown or greyish, with a variable rufous tint; the annulations are not so fine as in *S. erythræus*. The chin and sides of the throat are paler grizzled than on the back and the lower part of the throat; the chest, belly, and inside of the limbs are either pale yellow or rich orange-yellow, or passing into pale chestnut in the Assam variety, in which the belly is rarely lineated. The ears are feebly pencilled; the tail has the same proportion as in *S. erythræus* and *S. castaneoventris* * but it is more persistently and uniformly concolorous with the body than in these species, and is finely ringed with black and yellow, the rings being most distinct on the latter fourth; the tip is generally washed with orange yellow" ('Anat. and Zool. Res.').

SIZE.—Head and body, 9 inches; tail, 7 inches.

No. 286. SCIURUS HIPPURUS.

The Chestnut-bellied Assam Squirrel.

HABITAT.—Assam; also in the Malayan peninsula.

DESCRIPTION.—Upper parts of the body, with base of tail yellowish-rufous, punctulated with yellow and black; the lower parts deep ruddy ferruginous or chestnut; feet, tail (which is bushy) and whiskers black.

Dr. Anderson, however, mentions several varieties. He writes: "The specimen in the British Museum referred by Dr. Gray to *S. rufogaster*, var. *Borneoensis* differs from Malayan specimens in having portions

* A Chinese species: Western China, Formosa and Hainau.—R. A. S.

of the upper parts unannulated and of a deep rich chestnut, which embraces the upper surface of the base of the tail, and is concolorous with the chestnut of the under parts. This, however, is evidently not a persistent form, because I have seen a specimen from the same island in which the red portion of the upper parts is grizzled and much of the same tint as Malayan individuals, except in the mesial line of the neck and back, where the colour is rich red-brown extending along the dorsum of the tail for about three inches.

Müller and Schlegel mention a variety that I have not seen, and of which they state that the red colour of the under parts extends to the heel, the forefoot and the toes, while the colour of the upper parts passes into a uniform lustrous black. They also remark, however, that the back not unfrequently assumes a pale yellowish brown tint" ('Anat. and Zool. Res.' p. 242).

Horsfield remarks:—"This species is nearly allied to the *S. erythræus* of Pallas, but it varies in the depth of the colours both above and underneath."

"In the skull the orbit is rather large, and the muzzle is so contracted at its base that the extremity is but little narrower."—*Anderson.*

No. 287. SCIURUS SLADENI.

Sladen's Squirrel.

HABITAT.—Upper Burmah.

DESCRIPTION.—After Dr. Anderson ('Proc. Zool. Soc.' 1871, p. 139) who first obtained and named this species: "grizzled, rufous olive above, the annulations fine, and the fur of moderate length; the forehead, face, chin, throat, belly, inside of limbs, front of thighs, lower half of forelimbs, and the hind-feet rich chestnut red; tail rather bushy, as long as the body without the neck and head, concolorous with the upper surface of the body, but slightly more rufous, with a bright chestnut red tip."

SIZE.—Head and body, 10¼ inches; tail, including rufous tip, 8 inches.

This handsome squirrel is figured in the volume of plates belonging to Dr. Anderson's work on the Zoology of the Yunnan Expedition. Speaking of the skull he says: "The skull of *S. Sladeni* has a rather short muzzle, with considerable breadth across its base superiorly, and it is a shorter and broader skull than the skulls of squirrels referred to *S. Blanfordii.* Compared with the skull of the red-headed specimen of *S. erythræus* from Bhutan, there is a decided resemblance between the two, the chief distinction being the less breadth of the base of the muzzle of the latter, but the teeth of this specimen show it to be young, while the teeth of *S. Sladeni* are much worn by use."—'A. and Z. Res.' p. 243.

No. 288. SCIURUS FERRUGINEUS.

The Rusty-coloured Squirrel.

HABITAT.—From Assam to Burmah and Siam, and the adjacent islands of Pulo Condor and Sichang.

DESCRIPTION.—Colouring most diverse, no less than ten named species being referable to this one, viz., *S. Finlaysoni*, *S. ferrugineus*, *S. Keraudrenii*, *S. splendidus*, *S. cinnamomeus*, *S. Siamensis*, *S. splendens*, *S. Germani*, *S. Bocourtii*, *S. leucogaster;* some are rich red, one jet black, and another is white, but apparently most of the varieties come from Siam; the Assam and Burmah specimens being reddish, of which the following description is by Blyth, according to Horsfield's Catalogue, where it is entered as *S. Keraudrenii:* "Entirely of a deep rufo-ferruginous colour, rather darker above than below; the fur of the upper parts somewhat glistening; toes of all the feet blackish, as in the three preceding, and the extreme tip of the tail yellowish-white."

The following group consists of the striped squirrels, a smaller and more terrestrial species, allied to the ground squirrels (*Tamias*).

No. 289. SCIURUS PALMARUM.

The Common Indian Ground Squirrel (*Jerdon's No.* 155).

NATIVE NAMES.—*Gilehri*, Hindi; *Beral*, *Lakki*, Bengali; *Kharri*, Mahrathi; *Alalu*, Canarese; *Vodata*, Telegu; *Urta* of Waddurs (*Jerdon*).

HABITAT.—India generally, except in some parts of Malabar and North-eastern Bengal.

DESCRIPTION.—The upper parts are dusky greenish-grey, with five yellowish-white dorsal lines, the two outer ones being faint and indistinct; under parts whitish; the hairs of the tail are annulated with red and black; ears round. But the colouring varies; some are much darker than others; one I have is a deep ferruginous brown between the dorsal stripes.

SIZE.—Head and body, 6½ to 7 inches; tail, 5½ to 6 inches.

This beautiful little animal is well known to almost all who have lived in India, and it is one of the most engaging and cheerful of all the frequenters of our Mofussil bungalows, although I have heard the poor little creature abused by some in unmeasured terms, as a nuisance on account of its piercing voice. I confess to liking even its shrill chatter; but then I am not easily put out by noise, and am rather like the deaf old King of Oude, who sits and reads in his cockatoo house, and looks up smilingly, as half a dozen of them give vent to extra diabolical shrieks, and pleasantly remarks: "Ah: the birds are singing a little this morning!" I am not quite so bad as that; but as I now sit writing, I have a hill myna on one side of me imitating an ungreased cart-wheel and the agonies of an asthmatic *derzie*, and on the other side a small female of the rose-headed parrakeet, which has a most piercing selection of whistles and small talk, to say nothing of two small bipeds of five and seven, who cap all the rest for noise, till I sometimes wish I had the aural afflictions of the old king. I can, however, quite imagine the irritation the sharp chirrup-chirrup of this little squirrel would cause to an invalid, for there is something particularly ear-piercing about it; but their prettiness and familiarity make up in great measure for their noisiness. They are certainly a nuisance in a garden, and I rather doubt whether they are of any use, as McMaster says, "in destroying many insects, especially white ants, beetles, both in their perfect and larval state," &c. He adds: "They are said to destroy the eggs of small birds, but I have never observed this myself." I should also doubt this, were it not that the European squirrel is accused of the same thing. General McMaster, I think, got his idea from a quaint old book, which he quotes at times, Dr. John Fryer's 'Voyage to East India and Bombain,' who, writing on the nests of the weaver bird (*Ploceus baya*), says: "It ties it by so slender a Thread to the Bough of the Tree, that the Squirrel dare not venture his body, though his Mouth water at the eggs and Prey within." McMaster himself writes: "This familiar little pest is accused, but I believe unjustly, of robbing nests; were he guilty of this, it would in the breeding season cause much excitement among the small birds, in whose society he lives on terms of the most perfect friendship." There is much truth in this. Wood and others, however, state that the European squirrel has been detected in the act of carrying off a small bird out of a nest, and that it will devour eggs, insects, &c.

Jerdon relates the Indian legend that, when Hanuman was crossing the Ganges, it was bridged over by all the animals; one small gap remained, which was filled by this squirrel, and as Hanuman passed over he put his hand on the squirrel's back, on which the marks of his five fingers have since remained. It is not unlike the chipmunk of America (*Tamias striatus*), but these true ground squirrels have cheeks pouches and live in burrows. Our so-called palm squirrel (though it does not affect palms any more than other trees) builds a ragged sort of nest of any fibrous matter, without much attempt at concealment; and I have known it carry off bits of lace and strips of muslin and skeins of wool from a lady's work-box for its house-building purposes. The skins of this species nicely cured make very pretty slippers. They are very easily tamed, and often fall victims to their temerity, in venturing unknown into their owner's pockets, boxes, boots, &c. One I have now is very fond of a mess of parched rice and milk. It sleeps rolled up in a ball, not on its side, but with its head bent down between its legs.

No. 290. SCIURUS TRISTRIATUS.

The Three-striped Ground-Squirrel (Jerdon's No. 156).

NATIVE NAMES.—As in the last. *Leyna* in Singhalese.

HABITAT.—Ceylon and Southern India; on the Neilgherries. Has been found in Midnapur, and it is stated to range northward to the Himalayas.

DESCRIPTION.—Somewhat larger and darker than the last species, manifesting considerable variation in the colour of the dark lines of the back. In some the lines are rufous; in others dark brown or blackish throughout, or black only from the shoulder to the lumbar region. The general tints are rusty red on the head, greyish on the shoulders, blackish in the middle of the back, rusty on the haunches. Three well-defined yellow dorsal lines, not extending the whole length of the back; the tail rusty beneath, darker than *S. palmarum* on the sides.

SIZE.—Head and body, 7½ inches; tail, 7½ inches.

This squirrel is more shy than the last, and keeps to the woods, although occasionally it will approach houses. Dr. Jerdon says a pair frequented his house at Tellicherry, but they were less familiar than *S. palmarum*, and endeavoured to shun observation. Kellaart gives a careful description of it, but does not say anything about its habits, at which I wonder, for it is common there, and takes the place of our little Indian friend, though probably its more retiring disposition has prevented so much notice being taken of it. Were it in the habit of frequenting houses in the manner of its Indian cousin, I am sure Sir Emerson Tennent would have devoted a page to it, whereas he does not mention it at all. It had also escaped McMaster's notice, careful observer though he was. Waterhouse, in his description ('Proc. Zool. Soc.' 1839, p. 118), describes some differences in the skull of this and *S. palmarum*, but Dr. Anderson finds no difference whatever.

No. 291. SCIURUS LAYARDI.

Layard's Striped Ground-Squirrel (Jerdon's No. 157).

HABITAT.—Ceylon; in the highlands and the mountains of Travancore in Southern India.

DESCRIPTION.—Dark dingy olive, inclining more to ashy than fulvous, except on the head and flanks. Lower parts ferruginous, paler on the breast; middle of back very dark, with a narrow bright fulvous streak in the middle, reaching from between the shoulders to near the tail, and an obscure shorter stripe on either side, barely reaching to the croup; tail ferruginous along the centre, the hairs margined with black, with white tips; a narrower black band near the base of each hair; tip of tail black, forming a pencil tuft three inches long. In some specimens the centre dorsal streak is bright orange, the two intervening bands being jet black. In those in which the streaks are pale, the intervening bands differ only from the surrounding fur in being darker, but are grizzled like it. There is a narrow rufous area round the eye; the whiskers are black; the under-parts and inside of limbs are bright reddish-chestnut, and this colour extends along the under-part of the tail. Jerdon calls this squirrel *the Travancore striped squirrel*, but I see no reason to retain this name, as it is not peculiar to Travancore, but was first found in Ceylon by Mr. E. Layard, after whom Blyth named it.

No. 292. SCIURUS SUBLINEATUS.

The Dusky-striped Ground-Squirrel (*Jerdon's No.* 158).

HABITAT.—The mountains of Ceylon and Southern India.

DESCRIPTION.—Smaller than the palm squirrel; fur soft, dense, grizzled olive brown; base of hairs dusky black; three pale and four dark lines on the back and croup, the lineation being obscure, and reaching only from the shoulder to the sacral region. Under-parts variable, but always dusky, never bright, from grey to dusky brown washed with rufous; tail concolorous with the upper part of the body and obscurely annulated.

SIZE.—Head and body, 5 to 6 inches; tail, 4½ to 6 inches.

Kellaart calls this *the Newara Elia ground-squirrel*, and Jerdon *the Neilgherry striped squirrel*, but, as it is not peculiar to either one or the other place, I think it better to adopt another popular name. It is common about Newara Elia and Dimboola, but it does not seem to descend lower than 3000 feet. In Southern India it is found in the Neilgherries, Wynaad and Coorg, but only at considerable elevations.

No. 293. SCIURUS MCCLELLANDI.

McClelland's Ground-Squirrel (*Jerdon's No.* 159).

NATIVE NAME.—*Kalli-gangdin*, Lepcha.

HABITAT.—"This species has a wide distribution, ranging from Nepal and Thibet to the east of China and Formosa, and through Assam and Cachar south-eastward to Tenasserim and Siam."—*Anderson*.

DESCRIPTION.—General hue olive brown, each hair having a blackish tip, a sub-apical yellow band, and a slaty black base. A pale yellowish band on the side of the nose, passing underneath the eye and ear along the side of the neck, and continued along the side of the back to the base of the tail; its upper margin has a dusky line; a narrow black line from between the shoulders over the vertebræ to the root of the tail;

tail grizzled dark above, fulvous beneath; whiskers black; limbs concolorous with the body: ears small, black edged, fulvous white within, and with white pencil tufts.

SIZE.—Head and body, 5 inches; tail, 4 inches.

Dr. Anderson obtained this species at Ponsee in Burmah, at an elevation of 3500 feet, and Dr. Jerdon, at Darjeeling, at from 4000 to 6000 feet. This species is synonymous with Blyth's *S. Barbei.*

NO. 294. SCIURUS BERDMOREI.

Berdmore's Ground-Squirrel.

HABITAT.—Tenasserim and Martaban.

DESCRIPTION.—General colour brownish, with a distinct rufous tinge on the middle of the back. It is punctulated with yellowish on the head, sides of face and body and outside of limbs, and with rich rufous on the middle of the back. An obscure narrow black line along the middle of the back from between the shoulders, but only extending half way down the trunk. On the sides of the back a yellow line from shoulder to articulation of femur; this is margined below with a broad black band, and above by an obscure dusky line. There is a broad pale yellow linear area below the former of these two dark bands, the portion of the side below it being concolorous with the thighs and fore-limbs. The rufous area of the back is confined between the two uppermost yellow lines; ears are large; all under-parts white, slightly washed here and there with yellowish; the tail moderately bushy, all the hairs annulated with four alternative orange and black bands, the terminal black band being occasionally tipped with white, and being as broad as the three remaining bands, so that the tail has a decidedly black tint washed with whitish, the orange bands, however, appearing through the black.

SIZE.—Head and body, about $7\frac{3}{4}$ inches; tail without hair, 5 inches.

NO. 295. SCIURUS QUINQUESTRIATUS.

The Stripe-bellied Squirrel.

HABITAT.—Kakhyen hills, on the Burmo-Chinese frontier.

DESCRIPTION.—"Above grizzled olive, brownish-grey, with a distinct rufous tint, deepest on the dorsal surface; annulation fine, as in the grizzled squirrels generally; chin and throat obscurely grizzled greyish, washed with reddish; a rufous grizzled blackish-brown band from the chest along the middle line of the belly to the vent; external of this, on either side, a broad pure white well-defined band from the side to the chest along the belly and prolonged along the inguinal region to the vent; a broad black band from the hollow of the axilla along the side of the belly, expanding on the inside of the thighs, where it is faintly washed with greyish; inside of the fore-limbs blackish, washed with greyish; toes black, with rufous annulations. Tail nearly as long as the body and head, concolorous with body, but the black and rufous annulations much broader and more marked, assuming the form of indistinct rufous and black rings on the posterior third; tip of tail jet black, narrowly terminated with greyish."—*Dr. J. Anderson* in 'Proc. Zool. Soc.' 1871, p. 142.

SIZE.—Head and body, about 9½ inches; tail, 7¼ inches.

This curious squirrel was first discovered and named by Dr. Anderson, who states that it was common at Ponsee on the Kakhyen range of hills east of Bhamo, at an elevation of from 2000 to 3000 feet, and as yet it has only been found on those hills. There is a coloured plate of it in the 'Proceedings of the Zoological Society' for 1871.

The next animal forms a curious link in resemblance between the Tupaiidæ and the squirrels. I mentioned some time back that the first Tupaia was taken for a squirrel; and certainly, to look at this long-snouted squirrel, one might easily be misled into supposing it to be a Tupaia, till an examination of its dentition proved it to be a rodent. It is supposed to be a Malayan species, but I was shown not long ago a specimen in Mr. Hume's collection which I understood Mr. Davison to say he had procured in Burmah. It has been classed by Dr. Gray in a separate genus, *Rhinosciurus*.

NO. 296. SCIURUS (RHINOSCIURUS) TUPAOIDES.

The Long-nosed Squirrel.

HABITAT.—The Malayan peninsula and Borneo, and I believe the Tenasserim provinces.

DESCRIPTION.—This animal differs from all other squirrels by the extreme length of its pointed muzzle, with which is associated a long and narrow skull. The coloration varies from light to dark, and almost blackish-brown; the tail is shorter than the body, moderately bushy, narrow at the base, but expanding towards the tip; the hairs are broadly banded with four alternate pale and dark brown bands, the last being the darkest and broadest, with a pale tip; the under-parts are white in some, rich orange yellow in others.

SIZE.—Head and body, 7½ inches; tail reaches to the eye.

The Flying Squirrels next engage our attention. In several groups of animals of strictly arboreal habits, nature has gone beyond the ordinary limits of agility afforded by muscular limbs alone, and has supplemented those limbs with elastic membranes which act like a parachute when the animal takes a leap into space, and gives it a gradual and easy descent. Amongst the lemurs the *Galeopithecus*, the *Pteromys* in the squirrels, and the *Anomalurus* in another family of rodents, are all thus provided with the apparatus necessary to enable them to float awhile in the air, for flying is scarcely the proper term for the letting-down easy principle of the mechanism in question.

The flying squirrels, with which we have now to deal, are in general details the same as ordinary squirrels, but the skin of the flanks is extended between the fore and hind limbs, which, when spread out, stretches it into a wide parachute, increased in front by means of a bony spur which projects from the wrist. These animals have been subdivided into the large round-tailed flying squirrels, *Pteromys*, and the small flat-tailed flying squirrels, *Sciuropterus*. The distinction was primarily made by F. Cuvier on the character of the teeth, as he considered *Sciuropterus* to have a less complex system of folds in the enamel of the molars, more like the ordinary squirrels than *Pteromys;* but modern research has proved that this is not a good ground for distinction. Dr. Anderson has lately examined the dentition in eleven species of *Pteromys* and *Sciuropterus*, and he says: "According to my observations the form of the enamel folds in youth are essentially similar, consisting of a series of tubercular folds which are marked with wavy lines in some, and are smooth in others, but in all there is a marked conformity to a common type. The seemingly more complex character of the folds appears to depend on the extent to which the tubercular ridges are worn by use." He also questions the propriety of the separation according to the distichous arrangement of the hairs of the tail. After a careful examination of the organ in nearly all the members of the series, he writes: "I have failed to detect that it is essentially distinctive of them—that is, that the distichous arrangement of the hairs is always associated with a diminutive species; but at the same time there can be no doubt that it is more prevalent among such." He then goes on to show that the tail is bushy in seventeen species, partially distichous in one, and wholly so in ten, and concludes by saying: "I am therefore disposed to regard the flying squirrels generally as constituting a well-defined generic group, the parallel of the genus *Sciurus*, which consists of an extensive series of specific forms distinguished by a remarkable uniformity of structure, both in their skulls and skeletons, and in the formations of their soft parts." There is a laudable tendency nowadays amongst mammalogists to reduce as far as possible the number of genera and species, and, acting on this principle, I will follow Dr. Anderson, and treat all the Indian flying squirrels under *Pteromys*.

GENUS PTEROMYS.

General anatomy that of the squirrel, except that the skin of the flanks is extended between the limbs in such a manner as to form a parachute when the fore and hind legs are stretched out in the act of springing from tree to tree.

No. 297. PTEROMYS ORAL.

Pteromys petaurista in Jerdon, No. 160.

The Brown Flying Squirrel.

NATIVE NAMES.—*Oral* of the Coles; *Pakya*, Maharathi; *Parachatea*, Malabarese; *Egala dandoleyna*, Singhalese.

HABITAT.—India, wherever there are large forests; Ceylon.

DESCRIPTION.—Upper parts dusky maroon black grizzled with white;

Pteromys oral.

this effect being due to the ends of the hairs being white, tipped with a small black point.

The muzzle and around the eyes, and the feet are black; the limbs and side membrane a lighter rufous maroon; the male has an irregular rufous patch on the sides of the neck, according to Elliot, which in the female is a pale fawn colour; the tail is rather longer than the body, and very bushy; its terminal two-thirds or three-fourths are black or blackish—sometimes (rarely) a little white at the extreme tip; the under-parts are dingy brownish-grey or nearly white. The female has six mammæ—two pectoral and four ventral.

SIZE.—Head and body, 20 inches; tail, 21 inches; breadth of expanse, 21 to 24.

This species is nocturnal in its habits as noticed by Mr. Baker ('Journ. As. Soc. Beng.' 1859, vol. xxviii. p. 287), Jerdon and others.

Mr. Baker says it makes a noise at night in the depths of the jungle which is alarming to strangers. On the other hand Tickell, who was one of the first to bring it to notice, says its voice is seldom heard, and it is a weak, low, soft monotone quickly repeated, so low that in the same room you require to listen attentively to distinguish it. "It is to the Coles a sound ominous of domestic affliction. When angry the oral seldom bites, but scratches with its fore-claws, grunting at the same time like a guinea-pig." "When taken young it becomes a most engaging pet. It can be reared on goat's or cow's milk,* and in about three weeks will begin to nibble fruit of any kind. During the day it sleeps much, either sitting with its back bent into a circle, and its head thrust down to its belly, or lying on its back with the legs and parachute extended—a position it is fond of in sultry weather. During the night time it is incessantly on the move."

Jerdon says of it: "It frequents the loftiest trees in the thickest parts of the forest, and is quite nocturnal in its habits, usually making its appearance when quite dusk. The natives discover its whereabouts by noting the droppings beneath the trees it frequents. It is said to keep in holes of trees during the day, and breeds in the same places. In the Wynaad many are killed, and a few captured alive by the Coorumbars, a jungle race of aborigines, who are usually employed to fell the forest trees in clearing for coffee; and I have had several sent to me alive, caught in this way, but could not keep them for any time. It lives chiefly on fruits of various kinds; also on bark, shoots, &c., and, Tickell says, occasionally on beetles and the larvæ of insects."

Jerdon says he had several times witnessed the flight of this species from tree to tree, and on one occasion he noted a flight of over sixty yards.

"Of course it was very close to the ground when it neared the tree, and the last few feet of its flight were slightly upwards, which I have also noticed at other times." I think Wallace has observed the same of the *Galeopithecus*. How this upward motion is accomplished more careful investigation will show; in all probability the depression or elevation of the tail may cause a deviation from a fixed course. According to Elliot it is very gentle, timid, and may be tamed, but from its delicacy is difficult to preserve. The fur is soft, beautiful and much valued. Jerdon gives the localities in which he has found it to be most

* I advise half water in the case of cow's milk, or one quarter water with buffalo milk.—R. A. S.

common: Malabar, Travancore (the Marquis of Tweeddale, according to Dr. Anderson, got a specimen from this locality of a much lighter colour than usual), the Bustar forests in Central India, Vindhian mountains near Mhow, the Northern Circars, and the Midnapore jungles.

No. 298. PTEROMYS CINERACEUS.

The Ashy Flying Squirrel.

NATIVE NAME.—*Shau-byau* in Arakan.

HABITAT.—Assam, Burmah, viz. Arakan, Pegu and Tenasserim provinces.

DESCRIPTION.—Very like the last, but with a greyish fur, and almost white tail, with a black tip.

The fur generally is a mixture of pale grey and brownish, the hairs of the head and back having a whitish subterminal band; the tail consists almost entirely of the greyish hairs; the parachute is reddish brown; the under-parts white. Blyth, however, mentions a specimen from Tenasserim which is unusually rufous, with the tail concolorous with the upper parts.

SIZE.—Same as the last.

It is open to question whether this is not identical with *Pteromys oral*, merely a local variety. Blyth so termed it; and from what Dr. Anderson has written on the subject, I gather that he, too, inclines to the same opinion, as he says: "The dimensions are the same as those of *P. oral*, Tickell, of which it will probably prove to be a local race."

No. 299. PTEROMYS YUNNANENSIS.

The Yunnan Flying Squirrel.

HABITAT.—Kananzan mountains; Burmo-Chinese frontier.

DESCRIPTION.—Dr. Anderson, who discovered and named this species, describes it as follows: "The general colour is a rich dark maroon chestnut on all the upper parts, the head and back in some being finely speckled with white, which is most marked in the young, but is always most profuse on the posterior half of the back, which in some individuals has almost a hoary tinge, from the extent to which the annulation of the hairs is carried.

"In the adult, the upper surface of the parachute is of the same colour as the back, and the hairs are not annulated, except along its margin; but in younger specimens they are partially so on the upper surface, as are also the hairs on the first three or six inches of the tail, which are concolorous with the back, but broadly tipped with black, while the remaining portion of the tail is rich glossy black; the sides of the face, below the eye and ear, are yellowish-grey, mixed with chestnut, and the chin is dusky; the paws are rich black, also the margins of the limbs; the under surface is clad with a yellowish-white, rather woolly fur, which in some tends to a chestnut tint in the middle line, and to a darker tint of the same colour at the margin of the parachute.

"The basal portion of the fur of the upper parts is a dark greyish-brown, the hairs at their base being wavy; then follows a palish chestnut band, succeeded by a dark maroon chestnut, which either may or may not have a pure white sub-apical band, the tips of the hairs being glossy deep maroon chestnut, in some verging on black.

"The ears are large and rounded, and very sparsely covered with black hairs externally, with chestnut-coloured hairs on the anterior, and black on the posterior half of the dorsal surface.

"The hairs on the outer side of the tarsus form a rather long and dense brush; the tail is moderately bushy."—'Anat. and Zool. Res.,' p. 282.

SIZE.—Dr. Anderson only got skins of this beautiful squirrel, so accurate dimensions cannot be given, but the largest skin measured from muzzle to root of tail 24 inches, the tail being the same.

No. 300. PTEROMYS MELANOPTERUS.

The Black-flanked Flying Squirrel.

HABITAT.—Thibet.

DESCRIPTION.—The back and top of the head are greyish-yellowish, the hairs being leaden grey at the base, passing into yellow, the sub-terminal part being brown, with a minute dark point; the upper surface of the parachute is almost wholly black, with a greyish-white border; under surface yellow; the belly greyish-ashy; feet black; limbs and tail concolorous with the body, the latter very bushy.

SIZE.—Head and body, about 19½ inches; tail, 17½ inches.

I have included this species, although it does not belong to India proper; still it would be well if travellers and sportsmen exploring our Thibetan frontiers would keep a look-out for this animal. At present all we know of it is from Professor Milne-Edwards's description of animals collected by the Abbé David, to whom we are also indebted for the next species.

No. 301. PTEROMYS ALBORUFUS.

The Red and White Flying Squirrel.

HABITAT.—Thibet; district of Moupin.

DESCRIPTION.—I have but a bare note of this species taken long ago from Milne-Edwards's work on the Mammals of Thibet, so I will quote

Dr. Anderson's description from the types he examined: "The head, the sides of the neck, the throat and upper part of the chest, variegated with white, through which the rich maroon of the ground colour is partially seen, and it forms a ring around the eye; the hinder part of the back is yellow, and the tail, immediately beyond its base, is also yellowish for a short way, fading into the deep maroon of its latter two-thirds. It has no black tip. The feet are concolorous with the body; the under parts are pale rich orange yellow; the ears are large and moderately pointed."—'Anat. and Zool. Res.,' p. 284.

SIZE.—Head and body, about 23 inches; tail, 16 inches.

No. 302. PTEROMYS MAGNIFICUS.

The Red-bellied Flying Squirrel (Jerdon's No. 162).

NATIVE NAME.—*Biyom*, Lepcha.

HABITAT.—South-eastern Himalayas, Nepal, Sikim, Bhotan; also in the hill ranges of Assam.

DESCRIPTION.—Upper parts dark chestnut or a rich lustrous dark maroon chestnut, with a golden yellow mesial line in some; the hairs are black tipped, the dark portions of the back being finely but obscurely punctulated with dark orange; the shoulders and thighs are golden yellow, and the under-parts are orange fawn or orange red; so is also the margin of the parachute; the ears are large, semi-nude, sparsely clad with pale red hair externally, and bright red posteriorly, the base of the upper surface being clad with long hair; the sides of the face below the eyes are yellowish; there is a black zone round the eyes; the chin and the feet are blackish; the tail is orange red, tipped more or less broadly with black.

SIZE.—Head and body, about 16 inches; tail, 22 inches.

The young of this species have not the dorsal line, the head and neck are concolorous with the body, as is also the tail at its base; the under parts are pale yellowish-red. According to Dr. Anderson the skulls of *Pteromys magnificus* and *P. oral* differ in the shorter muzzle and the more elevated character of the inter-orbital depression of the latter. This animal is occasionally found at Darjeeling, and according to Jerdon it used to be more common there before the station was so denuded of its fine trees. It frequents the zone from 6000 to 9000 feet, and feeds on acorns, chestnuts and other hard fruit; also on young leaves and shoots. There is a coloured plate of this species in the 'Journal of the Asiatic Society of Bengal,' vol. xiii. part i. p. 67.

No. 303. PTEROMYS ALBIVENTER.

Pteromys inornatus of Jerdon, No. 161.

The White-bellied Flying Squirrel.

NATIVE NAME.—*Rusigugar*, i.e., flying rat, Kashmiri.

HABITAT.—From Nepal, along the North-western Himalayas to Kashmir.

DESCRIPTION.—Upper parts grizzled reddish-brown or dark grey with a rufous tinge, or a reddish-bay, darker on the upper surface of the parachute, and outside of limbs; head, neck, and breast greyish-rufous; cheeks grey; chin, throat and lower part of breast white, faintly tinged with rufous in the belly; under part of parachute rufous, tinged white, with a greyish posterior margin. Occasionally a dark brown band over the nose and round the eyes; the whiskers and feet blackish.

SIZE.—Head and body, 14 inches; tail, 16 inches.

This is a common squirrel at Simla. One was killed close to the house in which I was staying in 1880 at the Chota Simla end of the station by a native servant, who threw a stick at it, and knocked it off a bough, and I heard of two living ones being hawked about for sale about the same time—which, to my regret, I failed to secure, some one having bought them. They are common also in Kashmir, where they live in holes made in the bark of dead fir-trees. They are said to hybernate during the season there. A melanoid variety of this species is mentioned by Dr. Anderson as being in the Leyden Museum. It was obtained by Dr. Jerdon in Kashmir, and presented to the Museum by the late Marquis of Tweeddale.

No. 304. PTEROMYS CANICEPS.

Sciuropterus caniceps of Jerdon, No. 163.

The Grey-headed Flying Squirrel.

NATIVE NAME.—*Biyom-chimbo*, Lepcha.

HABITAT.—Sikim and Nepal.

DESCRIPTION.—At first sight this seems to be a grey-headed form of the last species, but with larger ears; the head is iron grey; round the eyes and a patch above and below orange fulvous or chestnut; the base of the ears the same. Regarding this Dr. Anderson, on comparing it with the last, writes: "On a more critical examination of *P. caniceps* it appears to me, judging from Hodgson's types of the species, that it has larger ears, and if this should prove to be a persistent character, then the grey head and the chestnut speck above and below the eye, and the bright chestnut tuft behind the ears, assume a specific importance which they would not otherwise have." But he adds that his observations are merely from preserved specimens, and that the question of the magnitude of the ears is one yet to be settled by further investigation of the living animal. Jerdon's description is "entire head iron-grey; orbits and base of ears deep orange fulvous; whole body above, with parachute and tail, a mixture of blackish and golden yellow; limbs deep orange ochreous; margin of parachute albescent; beneath the neck whitish; rest of the lower parts pale orange-red; tip of tail black; ears nearly nude; tail sub-distichous." The fur is softer, denser, and longer than in the last two species.

SIZE.—Head and body, about 14 inches; tail, 15 to 16 inches.

No. 305. PTEROMYS PEARSONII.

Sciuropterus villosus of Jerdon, No. 166.

The Hairy-footed Flying Squirrel.

HABITAT.—Sikim and Upper Assam.

DESCRIPTION.—Upper part of head and back rich glossy reddish-brown, grizzled with black; the parachute blackish-brown, sparsely washed with faint reddish brown.

"Fur very fine, soft, and rather long, but adpressed, and the hidden portion is almost black, narrowly tipped with the reddish-brown, the sides of the hair being blackish-brown. On the parachute only a few hairs have the reddish band, and these are most numerous towards the margin; the tail is rather bushy and but slightly distichous, and the hidden portion of its fur is pale fawn at the base, passing into pale chestnut brown, washed with dusky brown on the sides and upper surface; the margins of the eyelids are dark brown, and the sides of the face are pale rufous; the ears are moderately large and rounded, rather dark brown towards the tips, and pencilled at the base, anteriorly and posteriorly, with long delicate hairs. There are no true cheek bristles, but the moustachial hairs are very long; the under surface is pale ferruginous, palest on the mesial line, and most rufescent on the outer half of the membrane, the margin of which inferiorly is pale yellowish; the hairs on the membrane have dark slaty—almost black—bases, the ferruginous being confined to the tips; the fur of the under-parts is very soft and dense; the feet are well clad, more especially so those of the hind limbs."—*Anderson.*

SIZE.—Head and body, 8 inches; tail, 8 inches.

Jerdon says it is found at elevations of 3000 to nearly 6000 feet.

No. 306. PTEROMYS FUSCOCAPILLUS.

Sciuropterus of Jerdon, No. 167.

The Small Travancore Flying Squirrel.

HABITAT.—Southern India and Ceylon.

DESCRIPTION.—Upper parts rufous chestnut according to Kellaart, who named it *Sciuropterus Layardii;* rufescent fulvous or dark brownish isabelline hue, as Jerdon describes it; the fur dusky blackish colour for three-fourths of its length; the tips coarser and coloured rufous chestnut (*Kellaart*); hairs fuscous with a fulvous tip (*Jerdon*); two-thirds of the base dusky ashy, the remainder reddish-brown with a black tip (*Anderson*); the ears are moderate in size, posteriorly ovate with a long pencil of blackish hairs at the base of the posterior margin and at the external surface of the upper angle; cheek bristles well developed; the cheeks white, washed with yellowish, as also before the ears; the margin round the eyes blackish; the parachute is dark brown above washed with pale brown, and the edge is pale yellow; lower parts yellowish-white; the tail is very bushy, and not distichous in the adult, though partially so in the young; it is sometimes yellowish-brown, sometimes dusky brown, especially in the latter half, the under surface being pale brown at the base, passing into blackish-brown. Kellaart says of the Ceylon specimens: "Tail flat and broad, of a lighter chestnut above, washed with black, and under surface of a deep black, except at tip," but apparently he had only one specimen to go upon, and therefore we cannot accept his observations as conclusive.

SIZE.—Head and body, $7\frac{3}{4}$ inches; tail, $6\frac{3}{4}$ inches with hair.

NO. 307. PTEROMYS FIMBRIATUS.

Sciuropterus of Jerdon, No. 164.

The Grey Flying Squirrel.

HABITAT.—North-west Himalayas.

DESCRIPTION.—Fur long, soft greyish, with sometimes a tinge of brown; the hairs are grey at the base, then brown with a black tip; face white; orbits dark brown; chin and under-parts white; the tail is broad, bushy, and rather tapering, more or less fulvous washed with black, black towards the tip; the feet are broad, and according to Dr. Gray the outer edges of the hind feet have a broad fringe of hair, whence probably its specific name; but Dr. Anderson is of opinion that this character is unreliable.

SIZE.—Head and body, 12 inches; tail, 11 inches.

Blyth's *S. Barbei* was probably the same as this; he had only drawings and assertions to go upon. The species is extremely doubtful.

NO. 308. PTEROMYS ALBONIGER.

Sciuropterus of Jerdon, No. 165.

The Black and White Flying Squirrel.

NATIVE NAMES.—*Khim*, Lepcha; *Piam-piyu*, Bhotia.

HABITAT.—Nepal, Sikim, Bhotan, Assam, Sylhet, Burmah, Western Yunnan and Cambodia.

DESCRIPTION.—Dr. Anderson says the name applied to the species is not appropriate, as many individuals have the upper parts more or less yellowish, but it is dark above, blackish, faintly washed with hoary or rufous; white beneath with a slight yellow tinge; the ears and feet flesh-coloured.

Jerdon says the young are pure black and white; the teeth are bright orange red.

SIZE.—Head and body, 11 inches; tail, $8\frac{1}{4}$ to 9 inches.

Jerdon procured it near Darjeeling; it frequents elevations from 3000 to 5000 feet.

No. 309. PTEROMYS SPADICEUS.

The Red Flying Squirrel.

NATIVE NAME.—*Kywet-shoo-byan*, Arakanese.

HABITAT.—Arakan.

DESCRIPTION.—Upper parts bright ferruginous bay; under parts woolly and dull white; the membrane, limbs, and tail dusky; the terminal third of the tail pale rufous.

SIZE.—Head and body, 5 inches; tail, $4\frac{1}{2}$ inches.

ARCTOMYDINÆ—THE MARMOTS.

Stout-bodied, short-tailed animals, with a rudimentary thumb with a flat nail. They are gregarious and terrestrial, living in burrows, where they store provisions against inclement seasons. Some of the genera have cheek pouches, but the true marmots, such as our Indian species, have not. They differ somewhat in dentition from the squirrels in having the first upper molar somewhat larger, and the other molars also differ in having transverse tubercles on the crown. The first upper tooth is smaller than the rest; the ears are short and round, as is also the tail; the hind-feet have five toes, the fore-feet a tubercle in the place of the thumb.

GENUS ARCTOMYS.

Stout body, short tail, large head and eyes, no cheek pouches, mammæ ten to twelve.

Dental formula: Inc., $\frac{1-1}{1-1}$; pre-molars, $\frac{1-1}{1-1}$; molars, $\frac{4-4}{3-3}$.

No. 310. ARCTOMYS BOBAC.

Thibet Marmot of Jerdon, No. 168.

The Bobac, or Poland Marmot.

NATIVE NAMES.—*Brin*, Kashmiri; *Kadia-piu*, Thibetan; *Chibi*, Bhotia; *Lho*, or *Potsammiong*, Lepcha.

HABITAT.—The Himalayan range from Kashmir to Sikim, in Thibet, Ladakh, Yarkand, also throughout Central Asia and Eastern Europe from the south of Poland and Gallicia over the whole of Southern Russia and Siberia, to the Amoor and Kamtchatka.

DESCRIPTION.—Above sub-rufescent cat-grey, washed with blackish brown on the back and sides and front of face, rufescent yellow beneath; the hind limbs more rufous; fur close, adpressed, rather harsh; tail with a black tip.

The hairs are tinged with three bands of dusky rufescent yellow and blackish-brown, the latter being most intense on the face, forehead, head and back (*see* 'P. Z. S.' 1871, p. 560). In the plate given in the report by Mr. Blanford on the mammalia collected during the second Yarkand Mission the back is somewhat barred with dark brown, as is also the tail. The sexes are alike, and of nearly equal size.

SIZE.—Head and body, about 24 inches; tail, 5 to 6 inches. This animal is seldom found at a lower elevation than 12,000 feet, and from that to 16,000 feet according to Jerdon, but Dr. Stoliczka noticed it in Ladak at a height of 17,800 feet.

"It burrows in the ground, living in small societies, and feeding on roots and vegetables. It lifts its food to its mouth with its fore-feet. It is easily tamed. One was brought alive to Calcutta some years ago, and did not appear, says Mr. Blyth, to be distressed by the heat of that place. It was quite tame and fearless, and used to make a loud chattering cachinnation. It was fond of collecting grass, &c., and carrying it to its den. Travellers and sportsmen often meet with this marmot, and speak of its sitting up in groups, and suddenly disappearing into its burrows. The cured skins form an important item of commerce, and are brought to Nepal, and in great numbers to China" (*Jerdon*). Mr. Blanford, in alluding to the conditions under which marmots are liable to produce permanent varieties, says: "each colony or group being isolated, and frequently at a distance of many miles from the next colony, the two in all probability rarely, if ever, breed with each other." Therefore several which are recorded as distinct species may in time be proved to be merely varieties of one. Mr. Blanford keeps to the specific name *Himalayanus* of Hodgson in his report.

No. 311. ARCTOMYS CAUDATUS.

The Red Marmot.

NATIVE NAME.—*Drun*, Kashmiri.

HABITAT.—The North-western Himalayan range. It is found in Kashmir, the Wurdan Pass, Ladakh, the valley of the Dras river.

DESCRIPTION.—General colour rufous-ochreous, darkest above, "the tips of the hairs are washed with black, which is most intense on the back from the occiput to the lumbar region; pale yellow on the shoulders, which have few, if any, black-tipped hairs, and also along the sides, which are nearly free from them; chin, throat, belly, fore-legs and inside of front of lower limbs deep rusty red; the outside of thighs pale rufous yellow, with a few black-tipped hairs; greyish hairs around the lips; cheeks washed with blackish; a large deep black spot on the upper surface of the nose; the rest of the front of the face rufous yellow; tail black, washed more or less with yellowish-grey, the last four inches black; the fur coarse and nearly $2\frac{1}{2}$ inches in length, loose and not adpressed; the black tips are not very long, and the yellow shows through them as a rule, but there are patches where they wholly obscure it; the base of the hair generally is rather rufous dark brown, and is succeeded by a broad rufous yellow band followed by the apical black one. Palm, including nails, $2\frac{4}{12}$ inches; sole, including nails, $3\frac{10}{12}$ inches; the heel is more sparsely clad with hairs along its margin than is the tarsus of *A. bobac*" (*Dr. J. Anderson*, 'P. Z. S.' 1871, pp. 561, 562). Mr. Blanford, who writes of this as *Arctomys caudatus* of Jacquemont, being of opinion that Hodgson's *A. Hemachalanus* is a smaller and differently-coloured species, and doubting whether *A. caudatus* inhabits the Eastern Himalayas, says: "*Arctomys caudatus* is one of the largest species of marmot, being nearly two feet long exclusive of the tail, which measures with the hairs at the end half as much more. The general colour is yellowish-tawny, more or less washed with black on the back, and with all the under-parts and limbs rusty red. In some specimens (males?) the back is much blacker than in others, the hairs being dusky or black throughout, whilst other specimens have only the tips of the hairs black." I am inclined to think that Mr. Blanford is right, for Jerdon thus describes *A. 'Hemachalanus:* "General colour dark grey, with a full rufous tinge, which is rusty, and almost ochreous red on the sides of the head, ears, and limbs, especially in summer; the bridge of the nose and the last inch of the tail dusky brown; head and body above strongly mixed with black, which he equals or exceeds the pale one on these parts; claws long; pelage softer and fuller than in the last."

SIZE.—Jerdon says of the *drun:* "Head and body, about 13 inches."

Now the size given in the 'P. Z. S.' above quoted is, "length, 22 inches from tip of nose to vent; tail, 10½ inches, exclusively of the hair, nearly half the length of the body and head." This agrees better with Mr. Blanford's account.

No. 312. ARCTOMYS HEMACHALANUS.

The Eastern Red Marmot (*Jerdon's No.* 169).

NATIVE NAMES.—*Sammiong*, Lepcha; *Chipi*, Bhotia.

HABITAT.—The Eastern Himalayas, Sikim, Nepal.

DESCRIPTION.—As given above by Dr. Jerdon.

SIZE.—Head and body, 13 inches; tail, 5½ inches. Hodgson kept some of this species in his garden for some time. They were somnolent by day, active by night, and did not hybernate in Nepal. They were fed on grain and fruit, and would chatter a good deal over their meals, but in general were silent. They slept rolled up into a ball, were tame and gentle usually, but sometimes bit and scratched like rabbits, uttering a similar cry.

No. 313. ARCTOMYS AUREUS.

The Golden Marmot.

HABITAT.—Yarkand, Kaskasee pass, 13,000 feet, on the road from Kashgar to Sarikol and the Pamir.

DESCRIPTION—after Blanford, who described and named this species ('Jour. As. Soc. Beng.' 1875): "General colour tawny to rich brownish-yellow, the dorsal portion conspicuously tinged with black from all the hairs having black tips, but these are far more conspicuous in some specimens (males?) than in others; face grey to blackish, with a rufous tinge covered with black and whitish hairs mixed, about half an inch long on the forehead. The black hairs on the face are more prevalent in those specimens (perhaps males) which have the blackest backs; the middle of the forehead is in some cases more fulvous. On the end of the nose is a blackish-brown patch, and there is a narrow band of black hairs with a few white mixed round the lips; the sides of the nose are paler; whiskers black. Hairs of the back, 1¼ to 1½ inches long, much mixed with woolly fibres, dark slaty at the extreme base for about a quarter inch, then pale straw colour, becoming deeper golden yellow towards the extremity, the end black. In the blackest specimens the black tips are wanting on the posterior portion of the back. Tail yellow, the same colour as the rump, except the tip, which is black, from a length varying from an inch to about 2½ inches (in three specimens out of four it does not exceed an inch); hairs of the tail about two inches long, brown at the base. Lower parts rather browner, and sometimes with a rufous wash; the hairs shorter and thinner, chocolate brown at the base without the short woolly under fur, which is very thick on the back. Feet above yellowish-tawny, like the sides" ('Scientific Results of the Second Yarkand Mission': Mammalia).

SIZE.—Head and body, 16 to 18 inches; tail, 5 to 6 inches. Though this agrees in size with *A. Hemachalanus* it differs considerably in colour, and, according to Mr. Blanford, also in the skull. There is a beautifully drawn and coloured plate of this marmot in the work from which I have just quoted; also of *A. Himalayanus* and *A. caudatus*.

NO. 314. ARCTOMYS DICHROUS.

HABITAT.—Afghanistan; mountainous country north of Cabul.

DESCRIPTION.—Less yellow than the last, without any black on the back, and having the upper parts pale dull tawny, and the lower rufous brown. The tail concolorous with the belly, tinged here and there with rich rufous brown, the tip paling to nearly yellowish-brown.

SIZE.—Head and body, 17 inches; tail, 6½ inches.—*Anderson*, 'Ann. and Mag. Nat. Hist.,' vol. xvi. 1875.

NO. 315. ARCTOMYS ROBUSTUS.

Is a Thibetan species, described by Prof. Milne-Edwards, 'Recherches sur les Mammifères,' p. 309. I have not the work by me just now.

SECTION II.—MYOMORPHA—RAT-LIKE RODENTS.

The second section of the order GLIRES, containing the following families—those that are not Indian being in italics:—

Myoxidiæ, *Lophiomyidæ*, Muridæ, Spalacidæ, *Geomyidæ*, *Theridomyidæ* (fossil), Dipodidæ.

The molar dentition is from $\frac{3-3}{3-3}$ to $\frac{6-6}{6-6}$, the former being the usual number; the tibia and fibula are united for at least a third of their length; the zygomatic arch is slender, and the malar process rarely extends so far forwards as in the preceding section, and is generally supported below by a continuation of the maxillary zygomatic process; the collar-bones are perfect (except in *Lophiomyidæ*). Upper lip cleft; the muffle small and naked; tail cylindrical, sometimes hairy, but commonly covered with scales arranged in rings.

In all the Indian mammalogy this section is probably the most difficult to write about. Our knowledge of the smaller rodents is extremely imperfect, and is just engaging increased attention. In the meanwhile I feel that, while I make use of such material as is now available, before long much will have to be revised and corrected after the exhaustive inquiries now being made by Dr. Anderson are published.

The Indian families with which we have to deal are but three—the *Muridæ*, *Spalacidæ*, and the *Dipodidæ*. The *Arvicolidæ* of Jerdon's work is merely a sub-family of *Muridæ*. Of these the *Muridæ* take the first place, as containing the greater number of genera. It is estimated that the total number of species known of this family throughout the world exceed 330, of which probably not more than one-fourth or fifth are to be found in India and adjacent countries.

FAMILY MURIDÆ.

CHARACTER.—"Lower incisors compressed; no premolars; molars rooted or rootless, tuberculate or with angular enamel folds; frontals contracted; infra-orbital opening in typical forms high, perpendicular, wide above and narrowed below, with the lower root of the maxillary zygomatic process more or less flattened into a perpendicular plate; very rarely the opening is either large and oval, or small and sub-triangular. Malar short and slender, generally reduced to a splint between the maxillary and squamosal processes; external characters very variable; pollex rudimentary, but often with a small nail; tail generally sub-naked and scaly, rarely densely haired."—*Alston*, 'P. Z. S.' 1876.

This family is divided into about ten sub-families, of which the Indian ones are as follows: *Platacanthyominæ; Gerbillinæ; Phlæomyinæ; Murinæ; Arvicolinæ; Cricetinæ.*

The other four are *Sminthinæ*, *Hydromyinæ*, *Dendromyinæ*, and *Siphneinæ*, none of which are found within our limits.

GENUS PLATACANTHOMYS.

CHARACTER.—Molars $\frac{3}{3}$, divided into transverse laminæ; infra-orbital opening as in typical *Muridæ;* incisive foramina and auditory bullæ small; form *myoxine* (or dormouse-like); fur mixed with flat spines; tail densely hairy. The general resemblance of this animal to the dormouse (*Myoxus*) is striking, to which its hairy tail and its habits conduce, but on closer examination its small eyes, thin ears, short thumb of the fore-foot bring it into the murine family. The genus was first noted and named by Blyth, who seemed inclined to class it as a dormouse, but this has not been upheld for the reasons given above, and also that *Platacanthomys* has the normal *murine* number of molars, viz.: $\frac{3-3}{3-3}$, whereas *Myoxus* has an additional premolar above and below. These points were first brought to notice by Prof. Peters of Berlin (*see* 'P. Z. S.' 1865, p. 397. There is a coloured plate of the animal in the same volume, but it is not so well executed as most of the illustrations in the Society's works.

No. 316. PLATACANTHOMYS LASIURUS.

The Long-tailed Spiny Mouse (*Jerdon's No.* 198).

HABITAT.—Southern India.

DESCRIPTION.—Light rufescent brown; the under fur paler, more rufous on the forehead and crown; whiskers black; under parts dull white; the hairs on the tail, which are arranged distichously, are darker than those of the body, infuscated except at the tip of the tail, where they are whitish; the muzzle is acute; ears moderate and naked; the fur above is mixed densely with sharp flat spines; the under coat is delicate and fine; the few spines on the lower parts are smaller and finer; the thumb is without a nail.

SIZE.—Head and body, 6 inches; tail, 3½, or five inches including the hair; planta, 1 inch.

This species was discovered by the Rev. Mr. Baker in the Western Ghâts of Malabar, and in Cochin and Travancore, at an elevation of about 3000 feet. He writes of it: "It lives in clefts in the rocks and hollow trees, and is said to hoard ears of grain and roots, seldom comes into the native huts, and in that particular neighbourhood the hillmen told me they are very numerous. I know they are to be found in the rocky mountains of Travancore, but I have never met with them on the plains." In another place he adds: "I have been spending the last three weeks in the Ghâts, and, amongst other things, had a great hunt for the new spiny dormice. They are most abundant, I find, in the elevated vales and ravines, living only in the magnificent old trees there, in which they hollow out little cavities, filling them with leaves and moss. The hill people call them the 'pepper-rat,' from their destroying large quantities of ripe pepper (*Piper nigrum*). Angely and jackfruit (*Artocarpus ovalifolia* and *integrifolia*) are much subject to their ravages. Large numbers of the *shunda* palm (*Caryota*) are found in these hills, and toddy is collected from them. These dormice eat through the covering of the pot as suspended, and enjoy themselves. Two were brought to me in the pots half drowned. I procured in one morning sixteen specimens. The method employed in obtaining them was to tie long bamboos (with thin little branches left on them to climb by) to the trees; and, when the hole was reached, the man cut the entrance large enough to admit his hand, and took out the nest with the animals rolled up in it, put the whole into a bag made of bark, and brought it down. They actually reached the bottom sometimes without being disturbed. It was very wet, cold weather, and they may have been somewhat torpid; but I started a large brown rat at the foot of one of these trees, which ran up the stem into a hole, and four dormice were out in a minute from it, apparently in terror of their large friend. There were no traces of hoarding in any of the holes, but the soft bark of the trees was a good deal gnawed in places. I had two of these dormice alive for some time, but, as they bit and gnawed at everything intended to keep them in durance, I was obliged to kill both. I noticed that when their tails were elevated, the hairs were perfectly erect like a bottle-brush" ('Proc. As. Soc. Beng.' 1859, p. 290).

SUB-FAMILY GERBILLINÆ.

Incisors narrow; molars divided into transverse laminæ; pterygoid fossæ short; auditory bullæ usually large; hind limbs very long; tail long and hairy.

GENUS GERBILLUS.

Form murine, with the exception of the elongated hind-limbs; muzzle pointed; ears moderate and oval; eyes very large and bright; occipital region broad; auditory bullæ large; upper incisors grooved; first molar with three laminæ, the second with two, and third with one only; hinder tarsus and toes much elongated; the fore-limbs small; tail long and hairy, with a tuft at the end.

NO. 317. GERBILLUS INDICUS.

The Indian Jerboa-Rat, or Kangaroo-Rat (Jerdon's No. 170).

NATIVE NAMES.—*Hirna-mus*, Hindi; *Jhenku-indur*, Sanscrit and Bengali; *Yeri-yelka* of the Waddurs; *Tel-yelka* of the Yanadees; *Billa-ilei*, Canarese.

HABITAT.—All over India and in Ceylon, but apparently not in Burmah.

DESCRIPTION.—Light fulvous brown above or fawn colour, paling on the sides; under-parts white; the hairs of the back are ashy at the base.

with fulvous tips, a few thin black hairs intermixed chiefly on the side and cheeks.

The eyebrow is whitish; whiskers long and black and a few grey; the nose is elongated; the upper jaw projecting nearly half an inch beyond the lower; tail, which is longer than the body, is blackish above and below, pale laterally, and terminates with a black tufted tip; the ears are large and nearly naked; the eye is particularly large and lustrous, which, with its graceful bounds, have given it its Indian name of "antelope-rat" (*Hirna-mus*).

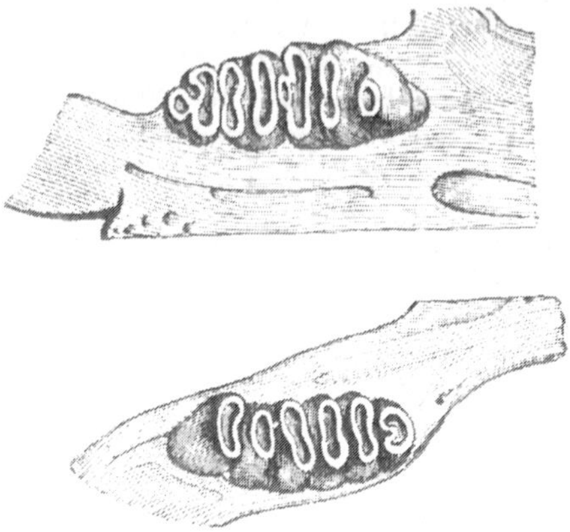

Dentition of *Gerbillus* (magnified).

SIZE.—Head and body, about 7 inches; tail, $8\frac{1}{2}$ inches; fore-foot, $\frac{5}{10}$ inch; hind-foot, 2 inches. Weight, $6\frac{3}{4}$ ounces.

This graceful little creature frequents bare plains and sandy country in general, where it forms extensive burrows. Hardwicke writes of it: "These animals are very numerous about cultivated lands, and particularly destructive to wheat and barley crops, of which they lay up considerable hoards in spacious burrows. A tribe of low-caste Hindus, called Kunjers, go in quest of them at proper seasons to plunder their hoards, and often within the space of twenty yards square find as much corn in the ear as could be crammed in a bushel." Sir Walter Elliot's account of their burrows is most interesting. He says: "The entrances, which are numerous, are small, from which the passage descends with a rapid slope for two or three feet, then runs along horizontally, and sends off branches in different directions. These galleries generally terminate in chambers from half a foot to a foot in width, containing a bed of dried grass. Sometimes one chamber communicates with another furnished in like manner, whilst others appear to be deserted, and the entrances closed with clay. The centre chamber in one burrow was very large, which the Wuddurs attributed to its being the common apartment, and said that the females occupied the smaller ones with their young. They do not hoard their food, but issue from their burrows every evening, and run and hop about, sitting on their hind legs to look round, making astonishing leaps, and on the slightest alarm flying into their holes." This account differs from that of Hardwicke as regards the hoarding of food, and from what I can learn is the more correct.

The food of this animal is grain, grass, and roots, but Kellaart mentions certain carnivorous propensities, for one night several of them nearly devoured an albino rat which had been put into the same cage with them. McMaster says of its agility: "I have seen them when released from a trap baffle and elude dogs in the most extraordinary manner by wonderful jumps made over the backs, and apparently into the very teeth of their pursuers."

Buchanan-Hamilton's assertion that "these animals live in holes which they dig in the abrupt banks of rivers and ponds" is misleading. They may do so occasionally, but in general they choose sandy plains. The female is prolific, bringing forth from eight to twelve young ones, and Dr. Jerdon states that it is said to have occasionally as many as sixteen to twenty. With regard to Kellaart's accusation of its being carnivorous at times, I may say I have noticed such tendencies amongst several other rodents which are supposed to be purely vegetarians. I have also known ruminants take to flesh-eating when opportunity offered.

No. 318. GERBILLUS HURRIANÆ.

The Desert Jerboa-Rat (Jerdon's No. 171).

HABITAT.—The sandy deserts west of the Jumna and Hurriana; also in Afghanistan according to Horsfield's Catalogue, and probably in Rajpootana, Sindh, and the Punjab.

DESCRIPTION.—Pale rufous or sandy above, with fine dusky lines, the hairs being blackish at the base, the rest fawn coloured, with a blackish tip very minute; sides paler, with fewer dusky lines; under-parts white, tinged more or less with fulvous or fawn on the belly; limbs pale fawn; orbits pale; whiskers whitish, a few of the upper ones dark; tail yellowish-rufous or fawn colour throughout, with a line of dusky brown hairs on the upper surface of the terminal half, gradually increasing in length to the tips.

SIZE.—Smaller than the last species. Head and body, 5 inches; tail, 4½.

Jerdon says of this rat that it is "exceedingly numerous in the sandy downs and sand-hills of Hurriana, both in jungles and in bare plains, especially in the former, and a colony may be seen at the foot of every large shrub almost. I found that it had been feeding on the kernel of the nut of the common *Salvadora oleifolia*, gnawing through the hard nut and extracting the whole of the kernel. Unlike the last species, this rat, during the cold weather at all events, is very generally seen outside its holes at all hours, scuttling in on the near approach of any one, but soon cautiously popping its head out of its hole and again issuing forth. In the localities it frequents it is far more abundant than I have ever seen *G. Indicus* in the most favourable spots" ('Mammals of India,' p. 186).

No. 319. GERBILLUS CRYPTORHINUS.

The Lobe-nosed Jerboa-Rat.

HABITAT.—Yarkand.

DESCRIPTION—after Mr. Blanford, who first described and named the species: "Colour above sandy rufescent, some specimens rather more rufous than others; below white, the two colours sharply divided on the sides; cheeks pale; supercilia whitish; feet white; tail above rather more rufous than the back, paler and occasionally whitish below, becoming dark brown or blackish above near the end, and with the slight tuft of longer hairs at the end of the same dark colour; fur soft and glossy, about half an inch long in the middle of the back, all the basal portion being at least three-quarters of the length, dark ashy; the terminal portion pale yellow brown to pale rufous, with numerous longer hairs with black tips mixed; on the under surface the hairs are white throughout; on the tail the hair is rather short, coarse, and close together; there are a very few longer black tips mixed, but scarcely enough to produce an effect in the general colour.

"The ears are oval and of moderate length, densely clad with brown hairs on the anterior portion of the outer surface, and with a fringe of longer hairs on the anterior margin; the posterior portion of the external surface is nearly naked, except near the margin, and the anterior portion of the inner surface is completely destitute of hair, but the inner surface is more hairy near the hinder margin. The whiskers are very numerous, the longest slightly exceeding the head; the uppermost behind being black, all the rest white; all are mixed at the base with long hairs, which cover the side of the nose; soles of the fore-feet with scattered white hairs, but nearly naked; those of the hind-feet densely covered with hair everywhere except at the extreme tips of the toes and at the heel.

"Mammæ, eight—four pectoral and four inguinal, as usual in the genus.

"The most remarkable character of these species is the presence at the end of the snout of a semi-circular lobe, which forms a flap completely covering the openings of the nostrils. This lobe can, of course, only be well seen in the specimens preserved in spirit. In the dried skin its presence can sometimes be detected, but not always. In the only spirit specimen, an adult female, the flap measures about 0·3 inch in breadth, and is barely an eighth of an inch long.

"It is hairy both outside and inside, the hairs being very short and rather scattered inside; the surface below the nostrils covered by the flap is also hairy. The use of this lobe is evidently to keep out sand and dust from the air passages" (W. T. Blanford's 'Mammalia of the Second Yarkand Mission,' p. 56).

SIZE.—Head and body, about $5\frac{1}{2}$ inches; tail, 5 inches; length of fore-foot, 0·5 inch; hind-foot, 1·4 inch.

The peculiarity of the lobe, which was first detected by Mr. Oscar Fraser in removing a skull from a spirit specimen, distinguishes this species from the other Asiatic forms. There is also a peculiarity in the skull noticed by Mr. Blanford, which is that the lachrymal process, instead of being anchylosed to the adjoining bones, as in others of the genus, is free, and this species is therefore distinguished from the one most resembling it, *G. unguiculatus* from Chinese Mongolia, in which the lachrymal process is united to the frontal.

NO. 320. GERBILLUS ERYTHRURUS.

The Red-tailed Jerboa-Rat.

HABITAT.—Afghanistan and Persia.

DESCRIPTION.—Rufous brown above, with a few long black hairs, more numerous on the rump and thighs; under fur slaty; under-parts white, gradually blending with the colour of the sides; ears much larger than in the last species, hairy outside and near the margin inside; soles of hind feet and toes thickly covered with hair, except on the hinder half of the tarsus; tail very rufous—brown with a black tip, black hairs are scattered along the upper surface, and form a black band towards the end above, finally covering the whole tip.

SIZE.—Head and body, about 6 inches; tail, equal.

Mr. Blanford, to whose 'Eastern Persia' I am chiefly indebted for the above description, writes: "From *G. Hurrianæ*, which Jerdon thought might probably be the same, the present form is distinguished by its much larger ears and by the hind feet, and especially the toes, being more thickly covered with hair beneath; the fur too is longer and the colour browner on the back; the tail is more rufous, and the tip blacker; the skull is larger and broader; the nasal portion more elongate and less concave above, and the hind upper molar has a distinct talon, or rudimentary second transverse ridge, in young specimens, traces of which may be detected in the form of the worn tooth."

Its habits are similar to those of the last species.

NO. 321. GERBILLUS NANUS.

The Dwarf Jerboa-Rat.

HABITAT.—Baluchistan.

DESCRIPTION.—The fur is soft and long, rufous brown or fawn colour above, white below, the colours being less sharply distinguished than in *G. Indicus;* the hairs of the upper parts have no black tips, and the basal two-thirds are slaty grey. There is a broad white supercilium in front, joining the white area of the sides of the face, so that the brown of the nose is reduced to a rather narrow band; ears almost naked, a few short whitish hairs near the edge only; whiskers nearly all white; a few of the upper hairs brown near the base; feet white above, naked beneath, tail light brown above, whitish beneath; towards the end a band of darker brown hairs runs along the upper portion, those at the end lengthened; but there is a less marked tuft than usual, and there are no black hairs at the end (Blanford's 'Eastern Persia,' vol. ii. p. 72, *with plate*).

SIZE.—Head and body, 2·6 inches; tail, exclusive of hair, 4·5 inches; hair, 0·55 inches.

This curious little animal was first found and named by Mr. W. T. Blanford, who obtained two specimens, with others of *G. Hurrianæ*, in a large area of ground that was flooded. He at first supposed them to be the young of *G. Indicus*, but found on subsequent examination that they were full grown.

SUB-FAMILY PHLŒMYINÆ.

Incisors broad; molars divided into transverse laminæ; infra-orbital opening typical; claws large.

GENUS NESOKIA.

Muzzle blunt; ears moderate; claws long; fur rather harsh; tail short, scaly, sparsely haired; palate narrow; incisive foramina short; auditory bullæ rather small; incisors broad; first molars with three laminæ, the rest with only two.—*Alston.*

There has been some confusion regarding the species of this genus. Jerdon, in his 'Mammals of India,' gives only two, including *Arvicola Indica* and *Mus kok* of Gray, *Mus providens* of Elliot, and *Mus pyctoris* of Hodgson, under *Nesokia Indica*, and classifying *Nesokia Huttoni* with *N. Hardwickii;* but Dr. Anderson, after a most careful examination of specimens from all parts of India, has proved the distinctness of *Mus providens vel kok* from the species called by Jerdon *Nesokia Indica*, which, being a synonym of *N. Hardwickii*, he has now renamed *Mus* (*Nesokia*) *Blythianus* (*see* 'Jour. As. Soc. Beng.' 1878, vol. xlvii. pt. ii.), and Mr. Blanford had clearly demonstrated that *N. Huttoni* is a distinct species from *N. Hardwickii* ('Zool. of Persia,' vol. ii. p. 59).

No. 322. NESOKIA HARDWICKII.

Hardwick's Field-Rat (*Jerdon's No.* 173).

HABITAT.—North-western India.

DESCRIPTION.—General colour sandy brown on the upper parts, paler on the sides, dusky grey, with a tinge of yellowish-rufous on the under-parts; muzzle, feet, and tail flesh-coloured; ears of the same, but rather darker; head short and bluff; muzzle broad and deep; eye moderately large; ears moderate, rounded, clad with minute hairs; fur soft and moderately long, of three kinds, viz. short under-fur, ordinary hairs, and mixed with them, especially on the back and rump, numerous long black hairs which project a good way beyond the fur.

SIZE.—Head and body, nearly 8 inches; tail, about $4\frac{1}{2}$ inches.

It is probable that this species is identical with *Mus Griffithi*, though the dimensions given by Horsfield ('Cat. Mam. Mus. E. I. Comp.') and the description do not quite agree. He gives the size of head and body at $6\frac{1}{2}$ inches; tail, 3 inches, and says that the teeth are nearly white.

No. 323. NESOKIA HUTTONI.

Hutton's Field-Rat.

HABITAT.—Northern India, Afghanistan and Persia.

DESCRIPTION.—Colour above from ferruginous brown to sandy brown, lower parts isabelline, but frequently appear dark in consequence of the fur being thin or worn; the basal portion dark slaty grey both above and below the animal; hairs on the back soft and of moderate length, a very few black hairs being scattered amongst the brown ones; tail naked, and ears almost naked, the latter having only a few extremely short hairs, thinly scattered, and the feet are covered above very sparsely with short whitish hairs (*see* Blanford's 'Persia,' vol. ii., for description and plate). Nose and feet flesh-coloured; ears and tail darker and brownish; mammæ eight, as usual in the genus.

According to Dr. A. Barclay (quoted by Dr. Anderson) the holes of this rat do not run deep, but ramify horizontally just below the surface of the ground. It throws out a mound of earth at the exit of the hole.

No. 324. NESOKIA SCULLYI.

Scully's Field-Rat.

NATIVE NAME.—*Mughi*, Turki.

HABITAT.—Kashgaria at Sanju, south-east of Yarkand.

DESCRIPTION.—Light rufescent brown above, dirty white beneath; fur fine and silky, blackish-grey at the base, and for two-thirds, the last third of the longer hairs being fawn colour; face earthy brown;

whiskers black, tipped with white; ears very short, semi-nude; feet and claws flesh-coloured; tail naked, with a few scattered fine short hairs.

SIZE.—Head and body, 6·6 inches; tail, 5·2 inches.

No. 325. NESOKIA PROVIDENS.

The Southern India Field-Rat (Jerdon's No. 172).

NATIVE NAMES.—*Kok*, Canarese; *Golatta-koku*, Telegu of the Yanadees; *Yea-kwet* (?) Burmese.

HABITAT.—Southern India and Ceylon, probably Burmah, as one species is mentioned there by Blyth.

DESCRIPTION.—Head short and truncated, with a deep muzzle; ears nearly round, semi-nude, sparsely covered with minute hairs; eyes moderately large, half-way between snout and ear; feet largish; claws short and stout; tail nearly equalling length of head and body, semi-nude, ringed, and with short brown bristly hairs round the margin of the annuli; whiskers full and long; colour of the fur—which is harsh and long, as in the rest of the genus, and of the usual three kinds—is a brown, mixed with a tinge of fawn; the under-parts are whitish, with a yellowish tinge; the nose, ears, and feet are dark flesh-coloured or brownish, and the feet are covered with short brown hair. The incisors are orange yellow; the claws yellowish.

Sir Walter Elliot states that a variety found in red soil is much redder in colour than that inhabiting the black land. The skull is considerably smaller, according to Dr. Anderson, than that of the Bengal *Nesokia*, *N. Blythiana*, of the same age, from which it is also distinguished by its more outwardly arched malar process of the maxillary; by its considerably smaller teeth and long but less open anterior palatine foramina. The brain case is also relatively shorter and more globular than that of *Nesokia Blythiana*.

SIZE.—Head and body, about 7 inches; tail, 6½ inches.

The habits of this rat are similar to those of the Bengal species, to which I will allude further on, and it has the same way of taking to water when pursued.

Jerdon says that this rat is most destructive to tea-trees, biting the roots just below the surface, more, he believes, because they happen to come in the way of their burrows than to feed on them.

Sir Walter Elliot writes: "In its habits it is solitary, fierce, living secluded in spacious burrows, in which it stores up large quantities of grain during the harvest, and when that is consumed lives upon the *huryale* grass and other roots. The female produces from eight to ten at a birth, which she sends out of her burrow as soon as they are able to provide for themselves. When irritated it utters a low grunting cry, like the bandicoot. The race of people known by the name of

Wuddurs, or tank-diggers, capture this animal in great numbers as an article of food, and during the harvest they plunder their earths of the grain stored up for their winter consumption, which in favourable localities they find in such quantities as to subsist almost entirely upon it during that season of the year. A single burrow will sometimes yield as much as half a seer (1 lb.) of grain, containing even whole ears of jowaree (*Holchus sorghum*)." Sir Walter Elliot goes on to give a most interesting account of the construction of the burrows of this animal.

No. 326. NESOKIA BLYTHIANA.

The Bengal Field-Rat.

NATIVE NAME.—*Yenkrai*, Bengalee.

HABITAT.—From Ghazipur in the North-west to Eastern Bengal and Cachar. Very common about Calcutta.

DESCRIPTION.—Fur coarse as in the genus, profusely intermixed with long piles, more numerous on the lumbar and sacral regions, which project a long way beyond the ordinary pelage. The general colour a dark brown with yellowish hairs intermingled, which give a somewhat rufous tinge, paler beneath. Nose, ears, and feet flesh-coloured; tail naked, ringed, and sparsely covered with short bristly hairs at the margin of the rings; feet moderately large; claws short and stout; eyes moderately large, placed a little nearer to the ear than to the snout; ears rounded, semi-nude, covered with a fine down; whiskers black; incisor teeth rich orange, but generally white towards their tips.

The female has eight pairs of mammæ.

SIZE.—Head and body, 8¼ inches; tail, 6½ inches.

I have already alluded to the distinguishing features of the skull of this species, as compared with *Nesokia providens*. From the skull of *N. Hardwickii* it differs in its considerably narrower incisors and smaller and more irregularly laminated molars, and by its long and open anterior palatine foramina. It has also a more arched skull (*Anderson*).

This animal, which is included in Jerdon's *Nesokia Indica*, is very generally distributed over Lower Bengal. In the neighbourhood of Calcutta, Alipore for instance, it is abundant, and is a great nuisance in gardens. It burrows in tortuous directions, only a few inches below the ground, there being no definite plan, some being more complicated than others—the principal passage leading to a chamber containing a nest of leaves and grass. I have been told by natives that large quantities of grain are stored by these rats. When I first heard of its aquatic powers, I was led to believe that it was a species of vole, and was particularly desirous to get one, not being aware of any true water-rat in India. However, the reports of the natives have been confirmed by what Sir Walter Elliot states regarding the habits of *N. providens*, and by Dr. Anderson, who made several experiments with these rats in captivity. He says: "To test this aquatic power, I had two rats placed in a large wire birdcage, and the cage partially submerged; if the rats, when in those circumstances, were much annoyed, they immediately dived to the bottom of the cage, where they could be observed running about under water. I also had them removed from the cage, and let loose in the large sheet of water in the Zoological Gardens, between the two iron bridges. When let loose at the bank, and an attempt was made to catch them, they immediately dived; and the stronger of the two did not appear at the surface for some time, when it was observed at a considerable distance from the bank making for the opposite side."

In confinement these rats are not engaging pets; they show a considerable amount of surliness and ferocity. I have noticed that on approaching the bars of the cage, one would grind its teeth, put back its ears, and fly at you with a grunt.

No. 327. NESOKIA BARCLAYIANA.

Barclay's Field-Rat.

HABITAT.—Northern India, the North-west and some parts of Bengal (Purneah) and Assam.

DESCRIPTION.—General colour brownish; under surface silvery grey; feet and muzzle flesh-colour; tail nearly black; claws horny white; a white band from the nose through the eye; muzzle short and bluff; forehead slightly arched; tail exceeding the length of the trunk, but not equal to head and body, ringed, and sparsely clad; fur coarse; piles moderately long.

SIZE.—Head and body, about $8\frac{3}{4}$ inches; tail, $7\frac{1}{4}$ inches.

This rat was first discovered by Dr. Arthur Barclay at Goona in Central India, and apparently it appears to be identical with specimens collected at Srinagar in Kashmir, in the Purneah district, and in Cachar.

The next two have usually been classed as true *Mus*, and the latter is to be found in Jerdon; but, from the breadth of the incisors and the lamination of the molars, which are less sinuous and relatively larger than in *Mus*, and from other characteristics of the skull, they are nearer allied to *Nesokia* than to the true rats.

No. 328. MUS (NESOKIA) ELLIOTANUS.

Elliot's Field-Rat.

HABITAT.—Bengal, Assam, Khasia hills.

DESCRIPTION.—This rat is thus described by Dr. Anderson. It is the nearest approach in size to the bandicoot: "Head short and deep;

muzzle deep and broad: eye half-way between ear and nose, moderately large; ears not large, rounded, sparsely covered with short hairs; feet large and well developed, with strong claws, and sparsely clad; tail sparsely covered with short bristles on the margins of the annuli, and nearly equalling the length of the body and head. Pelage coarse, with moderately large piles, most numerous on the back; vibrisæ moderately long.

General colour, above brown, with intermixed yellowish or pale brown hairs producing much the same colour as in *M.* (*N.*) *Blythianus*; paler on the sides, and passing into greyish on the under-parts; nose and feet flesh-coloured; ears dark brown; tail blackish ('J. A. S. B.' 1878, vol. xlvii. pt. ii. p. 231).

No. 329. Mus (Nesokia) giganteus.

The Bandicoot (*Jerdon's No.* 174).

NATIVE NAMES.—*Indur*, Sanscrit; *Ghunse*, Hindi; *Ikria*, Bengali; *Heggin*, Canarese; *Pandi-koku*, i.e. pig-rat, Telegu; *Oora-meyoo*, Singhalese.

HABITAT.—Throughout India; also in Ceylon.

DESCRIPTION.—Fur coarse, consisting of the three kinds, of which the coarser piles are very long, and almost hide the general pelage on the lumbar and dorsal regions. These piles are almost absent on the head, neck, and sides; general colour earthy brown, with yellowish hairs intermixed; the piles blackish-brown; under-parts dusky brown, mixed with grey; limbs brownish; nose, inside of ear and feet flesh-coloured; tail black, ringed, and sparsely haired. The female has twelve mammæ.

SIZE.—Head and body, from 12 to 15 inches; tail, from 11 to 13. Weight, about 3 lbs.

This is a well known rat, but it is not common in Calcutta, although supposed to be so. People frequently mistake very large specimens of the common brown house-rat (*Mus decumanus*) for this animal, which, Blyth remarks, is rare here. Jerdon states that it is common in the fort of Madras, where he killed many, some of large size. When assailed it grunts like a pig, hence its Telegu name *Pandi-koku*, from which the word bandicoot is derived. McMaster states that the bandicoot, though so formidable in appearance, does not show so good a fight as an ordinary English rat, being a sluggish and cowardly animal; and though, from its size and weight, it takes a good deal of worrying, it seldom does much in self defence, and any moderately good dog can kill it with ease. It is however a most destructive animal, doing much damage to granaries, gardens, and even poultry-yards. In some parts of the country, as for instance Fort St. George in Madras, Government used to pay a reward of one anna for every bandicoot killed within the walls.

SUB-FAMILY CRICETINÆ.

CHARACTER.—Molars tuberculate; infra-orbital opening sub-typical, not much narrowed below, and the perpendicular plate little developed; large internal cheek pouches.—*Alston.*

GENUS CRICETUS—THE HAMSTERS.

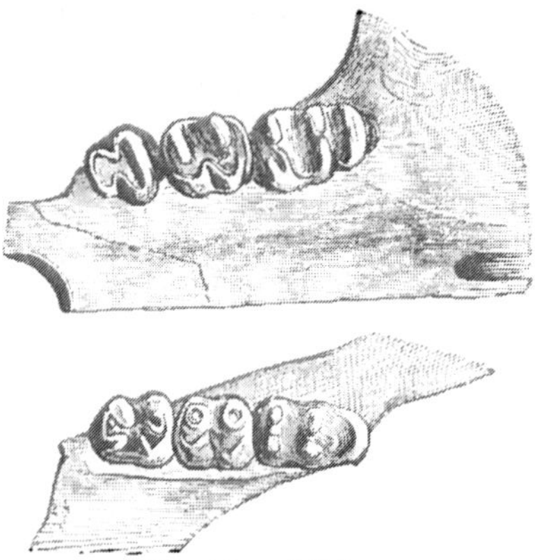

Dentition of *Cricetus.*

Form thick-set, with short limbs and tail, the latter sparsely haired, not scaly. "Skull with marked but rounded supra-orbital ridges continued into temporal ridges; coronoid process high and falcate" (*Alston*). The incisors are plain; the molars tuberculated when young, but in the old animal the tubercles are worn down and exhibit laminæ. They are very nearly related to the true rats, but differ conspicuously in the possession of large cheek pouches—like those of the pouched monkeys, into which they stuff the grain they carry to their burrows. The hind-limbs have five toes, the fore-feet four only, the thumb being represented by a wart. The European hamster is a very destructive little animal, from its numbers and the quantity of grain it stores away in its burrows. They have two sets of burrows for summer and winter, the latter being the deepest and most complicated. They pass the winter in a torpid state, but make up for it by their activity in the summer months. The young are produced twice in the year and in

Cricetus.

number varying from six to eighteen, and they develop very rapidly. Their eyes open in about a week, and when a fortnight old the parents drive them off to shift for themselves. The European hamster is a most savage little creature, and has been known to attack even a red-hot bar, and hold on in spite of the pain.

The two following are dwarf species—*Cricetulus* of some authors:—*

No. 330. CRICETUS PHÆUS.

The Persian Hamster.

HABITAT.—Yarkand, Gilgit, Persia.

DESCRIPTION.—Cinereous above, white below; the colour varies from pure ashey grey to grey with an isabelline tinge.—*Blanford.*

SIZE.—Head and body, about 4 inches; tail, 1¼ inches.

No. 331. CRICETUS FULVUS.

The Sandy Hamster.

HABITAT.—Yarkand, Gilgit.

DESCRIPTION.—Colour above light sandy brown to sandy grey; no band down the back; lower parts, feet, and tail white; fur very soft, fully half an inch long in the middle of the back in some specimens, Rather larger than the last species. (*See* Blanford's 'Second Yarkand Mission,' p. 45.)

SIZE.—Head and body about 4½ inches; tail about 1½ inches.

SUB-FAMILY MURINÆ.

CHARACTER.—Molars tuberculate, at least in youth; infra-orbital opening typical; pterygoid fossæ lengthened; auditory bullæ moderate; cheek pouches absent or very small; tail scaly, more or less naked, cosmopolitan (*Alston*). Three molars in each jaw, the first of which is the largest and the hinder one the least. I think that, with the exception of the islands of the Pacific Ocean, some of the members of this family are known in every quarter of the globe.

GENUS MUS.

"Muzzle pointed; eyes prominent; ears rather large, sub-naked; fur soft (rarely mixed with spines); pollex rudimentary; claws short; tail moderate or long, scaly, with scattered hairs; no cheek pouches;

* Dallas mentions (Cassell's 'Nat. Hist.') a species from Kumaon, *Cricetus songarus.*

skull elongate, narrow; temporal ridges nearly parallel; palate compressed; incisive foramina long; auditory bullæ moderately large; coronoid process high, falcate; incisors rarely grooved; molars with transverse ridges, each composed in youth of three tubercles" (*Alston*).

No. 332. MUS RATTUS.

The Black Rat (*Jerdon's No.* 175).

NATIVE NAMES.—*Kala-mus*, *Kala-chuha*, Hindi; *Kala-meeyo*; Singhalese.

HABITAT.—Chiefly Europe, but is said to be of south Asian origin; it is stated to occur in towns near the sea-coast in India, and Kellaart obtained it in Trincomalee only.

DESCRIPTION.—Greyish-black above, dark ashy beneath, or, as Kellaart describes it, "above blackish-brown, along the dorsal line nearly black; sides paler, some of the hairs with pale fulvous tips; beneath and inside of limbs fur very short, of a uniform sooty ash colour, separated from the colour above by a distinct line of demarcation; ears large, rounded, slightly fulvous externally" ('Prodromus Faunæ Zeylanicæ,' p. 58).

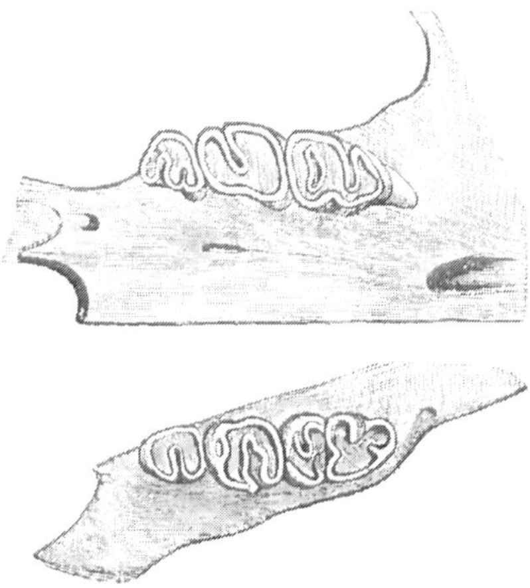

Dentition of Black Rat.

SIZE.—Head and body about $6\frac{1}{2}$ to $7\frac{1}{2}$ inches; tail, $7\frac{1}{2}$ to 8 inches.

Jerdon says of this rat that the muzzle is sharper than that of the brown rat; the ears are more oval; it is lighter in its make, and has much longer hair.

Whether this rat be, as Jerdon seems to suspect, imported into India in ships or not, it is generally supposed to have had its origin in southern Asia, and is almost identical with the Egyptian rat (*M. Alexandrinus*). It was the common rat of England, and indeed of northern Europe, whence it was expelled by its formidable rival, the brown rat, before which it has gradually receded, and it is seldom found now in England.

No. 333. MUS DECUMANUS.

The Brown Rat (Jerdon's No. 176).

NATIVE NAMES.—*Ghur-ka-chuha*, Hindi; *Demsa-indur*, Bengali; *Manei-ilei*, Canarese; *Gaval-meeyo*, Singhalese.

HABITAT.—Throughout India, Ceylon, and in some parts of Burmah.

DESCRIPTION.—Fur greyish-brown, mixed with tawny above, with longer piles of a dark colour, almost black; ears round; tail generally longer than head and body, scaly, with short bristles at the margins of the rings.

SIZE.—Head and body, from 8 to 10 inches; tail, from 6 to 11 inches.

The brown rat of India is identical with that of Europe, most naturalists being now agreed that it originally came from the East. It was supposed by Pallas that the brown rat crossed over into Russia about the year 1727. When frightened by an earthquake, numbers swam over the Volga from countries bordering on the Caspian Sea. It seems to have driven out the black rat before it wherever it made its appearance. In England it was introduced by shipping about the middle of the last century, and has since then increased to such an extent as to swarm over the whole country, and render the old English black rat a comparatively rare animal. From its ferocity and fecundity the brown rat is a veritable pest; if it cannot beat a retreat from an enemy it will show most determined fight, and in large numbers will attack and kill even men. A story is related by Robert Stephenson, the great engineer, that in a coal-pit in which many horses were employed, the rats, allured by the grain, had gathered in large numbers. On the pit being closed for a short time, and the horses being brought up, the first man who descended on the re-opening of the work was killed, and devoured by the starving rats. Similar stories have been told of men in the sewers of Paris. In the horse slaughterhouses at Montfaucon in Paris, the rats swarm in such incredible numbers that the carcases of horses killed during the day would be picked clean to the bone during the night; sometimes upwards of thirty horses would be so devoured. This shows the carnivorous tendencies of these abominable pests. I confess to a general love for all animals, but I draw the line at rats. There is something repulsive about one of these creatures, and a wicked look about his large protruding eye, like a black glistening bead, and his ways are not pleasant; instead of keeping, as he ought, to sweet grain and pleasant roots, he grubs about for all the carrion and animal matter he can get.

I find there is no bait so enticing to the brown rat as a piece of chicken or meat of any kind. I have heard stories of their attacking children, and even grown-up people when asleep, but I cannot vouch for the truth of this beyond what once happened to myself. I was then inhabiting a house which swarmed with these creatures, and one night I awoke with a sharp pain in my right arm. Jumping up, I disturbed a rat, who sprang off the bed, and was chased and killed by me. I found he had given me a nip just below the elbow. I once had a most amusing rat-hunt in the house I now occupy. I had then just taken it over on the part of the Government, in 1868. The whole building is floored with polished marble, which, being new, was like looking-glass. I found an enormous rat, which I took for a bandicoot, in one of the bath-rooms, and, shutting him in for a while, I closed the doors of a very large room adjoining, which was quite empty, and then turned my friend in with a small black-and-tan terrier. The scrimmage that ensued was most laughable, as both rat and dog kept slipping and sliding all over the place. At last the former was pinned in a corner, where he made a most determined stand, and left several marks before he died. They seldom now come so high as the third story, but we had two or three last year which dug a hole through a brick wall into my study, and they were surreptitiously disposed of unknown to my eldest little girl, whose passionate love for every living creature made her take even the rats under her protection, and one of them would come out every morning in the verandah to be fed by her with crumbs and grain. This one was spared for a while, but I was not sorry to find one day that it had fallen into a tub of water in a bath-room and was drowned.

The brown rat breeds several times in the year, and has from ten to fourteen at a time, and it is to be hoped that there is considerable mortality amongst the infants. I have never kept rats as pets, but have noticed amongst mice a tendency on the part of the mother to devour her offspring. I have no doubt that this also is the case with the brown rat, and aids in keeping down its numbers. It is stated that they will attack, kill, and eat each other. The Rev. J. G. Wood remarks in his Natural History: "From some strange cause the male rats far outnumber the females, the proportion being about eight of the former to three or four of the latter. This disproportion of the sexes may possibly be caused by the cannibalistic habits of the rat, the flesh of the female being more tender than that of the opposite sex. Whatever may be the cause, it is clear that the wider increase of these creatures is greatly checked by the comparative paucity of females." During the late siege of Paris by the Germans, amongst the various articles of food which necessity brought into use, rats held a high place as a delicacy. It is a difficult matter to stop the burrowing of rats; the best plan is to fill the holes with Portland cement mixed with bits of bottle glass broken in small pieces. It is said that quicklime will temporarily prevent rats from entering a hole, as the lime burns their feet. A friend of mine lately told me of some wonderful Japanese bird-lime which he uses. It is spread on a board, and will retain any rat that puts even one foot on it. An albino variety is common, and is sold for pets. Rats are partial to certain scents, and some are consequently used by trappers. In Cooley's 'Cyclopædia' the following receipts are given :—

1. Powdered cantharides steeped in French brandy. It is said that rats are so fond of this that if a little be rubbed on the hands they may be handled with impunity.

2. Powdered assafœtida 8 grains, oil of rhodium 2 drams, oil of aniseed 1 dram, oil of lavender ½ dram. Mix by agitation.

3. Oil of aniseed ½ ounce, tincture assafœtida ¼ ounce.

4. Oil of aniseed ¼ ounce, nitrous acid 2 to 3 drops, musk (triturated with a little sugar) 1 grain.

These scents are not only rubbed on traps, but a few drops are mixed with the various rat poisons, of which perhaps the most efficacious is phosphorous paste:

No. 334. MUS ANDAMANENSIS.

The Andaman Rat.

HABITAT.—The Andaman and Nicobar islands.

DESCRIPTION.—A little darker on the back than *Mus decumanus*, paler on the sides, and dull white below. "The long piles are at once distinguished by their flattened spinous character, which is also slightly the case in *M. rattus*, though much less conspicuously than in the present species. It would appear to be a burrower in the ground" (*Blyth*). Ears round as in the brown rat.

SIZE.—Head and body, about 8 inches; tail the same.

No. 335. MUS ROBUSTULUS.

The Burmese Common Rat.

HABITAT.—British Burmah.

DESCRIPTION.—Dark-brown above, under-parts whitish, stoutly formed, with tail not quite so long as head and body; feet conspicuously white.

SIZE.—Head and body, about 6 inches; tail, a little shorter.

Mr. Mason remarks of this rat that they are only second to the white ants for the mischief they perpetrate. "They burrow in the gardens, and destroy the sweet potatoes; they make their nests in the roofs by day, and visit our houses and larders by night. They will eat into teak drawers, boxes, and book-cases, and can go up and down anything but glass. In the province of Tonghoo they sometimes appear in immense numbers before harvest, and devour the paddy like locusts. In both 1857 and 1858 the Karens on the mountains west of the city lost all their crops from this pest." They seem to migrate in swarms, and cross rivers by swimming. Mr. Cross captured one out of a pair he observed swimming the Tenasserim river at a place where it is more than a quarter of a mile wide. *M. Berdmorei* is the same as this species.

The following three are Burmese rats collected by Dr. Anderson during the Yunnan Expedition, and are new species named by him :—

No. 336. MUS SLADENI.

Sladen's Rat.

HABITAT.—Kakhyen hills; Ponsee at 3500 feet.

DESCRIPTION.—Head rather elongated; snout somewhat elongate; muzzle rather deep; ears large and rounded, sparsely clad with short hairs; feet well developed, hinder ones rather strong; claws moderately long and sharp; the feet pads markedly developed, indicating an arboreal habit of life; tail slightly exceeding length of head and body, coarsely ringed, there being three rings to each one-tenth of an inch; the hairs sparse and brown; general colour of upper surface reddish-brown, more rufous than brownish, palest on the head, many hairs with broad yellow tips; cheeks greyish-rufous; chin, throat, and chest whitish, also the remaining under-parts, but with a tinge of yellowish; ears and tail pale brownish. (Abridged from Anderson's 'Anat. and Zool. Res.' p. 305.)

SIZE.—Head and body of one, about 6·30 inches; tail, 7·20 inches.

Dr. Anderson says this species is closely allied to Hodgson's *Mus nitidus*, but its skull is less elongated, with a shorter facial portion, with very much shorter nasals, and with a more abruptly defined frontal contraction than either in *M. nitidus* or *M. rufescens* so called. He adds that this appears to be both a tree and a house rat.

No. 337. MUS RUBRICOSA.

The Small Red Rat of the Kakhyen Hills.

HABITAT.—Kakhyen hills and the Burmo-Chinese frontier at Ponsee, and in the houses of the Shan Chinese at Hotha.

DESCRIPTION.—"Snout moderately pointed and long; ears small, and somewhat pointed; hind foot long and narrow; claws moderately long, compressed and sharply pointed; upper surface dark rusty brown, darkest on the middle and back, and palest on the muzzle, head and shoulder; on the sides and lower part of shoulder the reddish brown tends to pass into greyish; feet greyish; the sides of the snout greyish; all the under-parts silvery grey tending to white, without any trace of rufous, or but with a very faint yellowish blush; the tail, dull brown, is somewhat shorter than the body and head, and it is coarsely ringed, 2½ rings to one-tenth of an inch, the hair being short, sparse, and dark brown" ('Anat. and Zool. Res.' p. 306).

SIZE.—Head and body, 5·70 inches; tail, 5·15 inches.

No. 338. MUS YUNNANENSIS.

The Common House Rat of Yunnan.

HABITAT.—Yunnan, at Ponsee; Hotha and Teng-yue-chow.

DESCRIPTION.—"Muzzle rather short and broad; ear large and rounded, its height considerably exceeding the distance between the inner canthus and the front of the muzzle, sparsely clad with short hairs; feet well developed; hind foot moderately long; pads prominent; claws compressed, strong, curved, and sharp; tail coarsely ringed, three rings to one-tenth of an inch; upper surface dark rich brown, with intermixed pale hairs, with broad brown tips, the sides of the face below the moustachial area, chin, throat, and all the under-parts yellowish washed with rufous; the ears and tail dusky brown; feet pale yellowish, and more or less brownish above; the tail varies in length, but is generally longer than the body and head, although it may occasionally fall short of that length" ('Anat. and Zool. Res.' pp. 306, 307).

SIZE.—Head and body, 5·70 inches; tail, 5·65 inches. An adult female had a much longer tail.

No. 339. MUS INFRALINEATUS.

The Striped-bellied Rat (Jerdon's No. 178).

HABITAT.—Madras; Bustar forests.

DESCRIPTION.—"Above, the fur fulvous, with the shorter hairs lead coloured; throat, breast, and belly pure white, with a central pale fulvous brown streak; tail slightly hairy."—*Jerdon.*

SIZE.—Head and body, 5½ inches; tail, not quite 5 inches; another about 5 inches; tail, 4¼ inches.

Jerdon calls this a field rat in his popular name for it, but I think that the term should be restricted to the *Nesokia* or true field and earth-burrowing rats. He is of opinion that Gray's *Mus fulvescens* from Nepal is the same, the description tallying to some extent, concluding with: "in one specimen a central yellow streak," i.e. on the belly.

No. 340. MUS BRUNNEUS.

The Tree Rat (Jerdon's No. 179).

HABITAT.—India and Ceylon. The common house rat of Nepal.

DESCRIPTION.—Above rusty brown; below rusty, more or less

albescent; extremities pale, almost flesh-coloured; ears rather long; head rather elongated; tail equal to and sometimes exceeding head and body.

SIZE.—Head and body, from 8½ to 9½ inches; tail, from 9 to 9½ inches.

Jerdon states that this rat, which Dr. Gray considered identical with *M. decumanus* (*see* 'Ann. and Mag. Nat. Hist.' vol. xv. 1845, p. 267), "is to be found throughout India, not habitually living in holes, but coming into houses at night; and, as Blyth remarks, often found resting during the day on the *jhil-mil* or venetian blinds. It makes a nest in mango-trees or in thick bushes and hedges. Hodgson calls it the common house rat of Nepal, and Kellaart also calls it the small house rat of Trincomalee." It is probable that this is the rat which used to trouble me much on the outskirts of the station of Nagpore. It used to come in at night, evidently from outside, for the house was not one in which even a mouse could have got shelter, with masonry roof, and floors paved with stone flags. Kellaart evidently considered it as distinct from *M. decumanus*, which he stated to be rare in houses in the town of Trincomalee, though abundant in the dockyard.

NO. 341. MUS RUFESCENS.

The Rufescent Tree Rat (*Jerdon's No.* 180).

NATIVE NAMES.—*Gachua-indur*, Bengali; *Ghas-meeyo*, Singhalese.

HABITAT.—India generally; Ceylon.

DESCRIPTION.—Fur above pale yellowish-brown; under fur lead coloured, mixed with longer piles of stiff, broad, plumbeous black tipped hairs; head long; muzzle narrow; whiskers long and black; ears large, subovate, slightly clad with fine hairs; eyes large; incisor teeth yellow; feet brownish above, but the sides and toes are whitish; tail longer than head and body.

SIZE.—Head and body, from 5½ to 7½ inches; tail from 6½ to 8½ inches.

This is *M. flavescens* of Elliot, and is so noticed in Kellaart's 'Prodromus.' He calls it "the white-bellied tree-rat of Ceylon," and he states that it lives on trees or in the ceiling of houses in preference to the lower parts. Sir Walter Elliot observed it chiefly in stables and out-houses at Dharwar. According to Buchanan-Hamilton it makes its nests in cocoanut-trees and bamboos, bringing forth five or six young in August and September. "They eat grains, which they collect in their nests, also young cocoanuts. They enter houses at night, but do not live there." Kellaart's *M. tetragonurus* is a variety of this, if not identical.

No. 342. MUS NIVEIVENTER.

The White-bellied House Rat (*Jerdon's No.* 181).

HABITAT.—The lower Himalayan ranges.

DESCRIPTION.—"Above blackish-brown, shaded with rufous; below entirely pure white, tail and all."—*Blyth.*

SIZE.—Head and body, $5\frac{1}{4}$ to 7 inches; tail, 6 to $7\frac{1}{2}$ inches. Hodgson stated this to be a house rat in Nepal, but not very common. Jerdon found it common at Darjeeling. Specimens have been received from Mussoorie.

No. 343. MUS NITIDUS.

The Shining Brown Rat (*Jerdon's No.* 182).

HABITAT.—Nepal; Darjeeling.

DESCRIPTION.—Dusky brown above, dusky hoary below. According to Hodgson it is "distinguished for its smooth coat or pelage, wherein the long hairy piles are almost wanting. It is a house rat, like *M. niveiventer*, but much rarer, and frequents the mountains rather than the valleys." The long hairs are $\frac{11}{16}$ inch in length, horny at the base, with black tip, the short fur ashy, with rufous tips.

SIZE.—Head and body, $6\frac{1}{2}$ inches; tail $7\frac{1}{4}$ inches.

Blyth writes of this species ('J. A. S. B.' vol. xxxii. 1863, p. 343): "We have several specimens of what I take to be this rat from Darjeeling. They are especially distinguished by the fineness and softness of the fur. One specimen only, of eight from Darjeeling, which I refer to this species, has the lower parts pure white, abruptly defined."

There is a smaller rat, only four inches in length, which agrees exactly with the above, which Hodgson named *M. horietes.* It is not mentioned in Blyth's Catalogue, but it has not been overlooked by Blyth, as Jerdon's remarks would lead one to suppose, for in the 'Memoir on the Rats and Mice in India,' by the former, in the 'J. A. S. B.' vol. xxxii. for 1863, it is entered with a quotation from Hodgson.

No. 344. MUS CAUDATIOR.

The Chestnut Rat (*Jerdon's No.* 183).

HABITAT.—The lower Eastern Himalayas, i.e., Nepal, Darjeeling, &c.; also in Burmah, Lower Pegu, and Martaban.

DESCRIPTION.—Above a fine bright cinnamon colour, with inconspicuous black tips; the under-parts white, which is abruptly divided from the cinnamon hue above" (*Blyth*). Sometimes yellowish-white (*Jerdon*). Muzzle sharp; ears and tail long.

SIZE.—Head and body, about six inches; tail, $7\frac{3}{4}$ inches.

According to Blyth the Nepal specimens are darker than those from Burmah, which he says "differs only from the Nepalese animal of Mr. Hodgson by having the upper parts entirely of a bright cinnamon colour."

No. 345. MUS CONCOLOR.

The Common Thatch Rat of Pegu.

HABITAT.—Upper and Lower Burmah, Malayan peninsula.

DESCRIPTION.—I have been unable to trace any accurate description of this rat, which Blyth says "conducts from the long-tailed arboreal rats to the ordinary house mice." In his 'Catalogue of the Mammals of Burmah,' published in the 'Jour. Asiatic Soc. Beng.' for 1875, he remarks that "it requires to be critically examined in the fresh state." In the 'J. A. S. B.,' vol. xxviii. p. 295, he describes a young one as dark greyish mouse colour; but this is not reliable, as the young rats and mice change colour as they attain full growth.*

No. 346. MUS PALMARUM.

The Nicobar Tree Rat.

HABITAT.—Nicobar Islands.

No. 347. MUS CEYLONUS.

HABITAT.—Ceylon.

DESCRIPTION.—Fur soft, lead colour; hair of upper parts tipped with dark fawn and black; ears large, naked; whiskers long, black; tail longer than the head and body, scaly.

SIZE.—Head and body, $4\frac{3}{4}$ inches; tail, 6 inches.

"This small rat is found in out-houses in the cinnamon gardens at Colombo. I have no reason to think it to be the young of the former species (*M. decumanus*); the teeth were well developed; the darker colour and long tail will easily distinguish the species from other Colombo rats" (*Kellaart*). The character of the molar teeth is all that can be depended on in the foregoing description, and this may require further investigation. The young of rats and mice are always darker than the adults, and the tail is longer in proportion.

* Since writing the above, Dr. Anderson has kindly allowed me to examine the specimens of *Mus concolor* in the museum, and in the adult state they are considerably more rufescent. In one specimen, allowing for the effects of the spirit, the fur was a bright rufescent brown; but, whatever be the tint of the prevailing colour, it pervades the whole body, being but slightly paler on the under-parts. Size, about 4 inches; tail, about $4\frac{1}{2}$ inches.—R. A. S.

The following are doubtful species :—

NO. 348. MUS PLURIMAMMIS.

Jerdon's No. 177.

This, which Blyth considered a good species, is, I am informed, referable with *M. Taraiyensis* and *M. Morungensis* to Gray's *Nesokia Bengalensis.* The type and drawing of it are in the British Museum.

NO. 349. MUS ÆQUICAUDALIS

of Hodgson, described in Horsfield's Catalogue as pure dark brown above, with a very slight cast of rufescent in a certain aspect; underneath from the chin to the vent, with interior of thighs, yellowish-white; ears nearly an inch long; head proportionately long ('Ann. and Mag. Nat. Hist.' new series, iii. p. 203). This, with Blyth's *M. nemoralis*, seems identical with *M. brunneus.*

Mus arboreus of Horsfield's Catalogue is *Mus rufescens.* It remains to be seen whether there is sufficient difference between *M. rufescens* and *M. niveiventer* to warrant the separation of the latter as a distinct species.

The following species lead on to the mice—beginning with the long-tailed arboreal species, *Vandeleuria* of Gray, which connect the arboreal rats with the house mice.

The characteristics of *Vandeleuria* are: upper incisors triangular, grooved in front; ears hairy; fur soft, with long bristles interspersed; long tail, sparsely haired; hind feet very long, slender; soles bald beneath; toes ·45 long, slender, compressed, the pads much more strongly developed than in ground mice; the inner and outer toes with a small flattened nail.

NO. 350. MUS OLERACEUS.

The Long-tailed Tree Mouse (*Jerdon's No.* 184).

NATIVE NAMES.—*Marad-ilei*, Canarese; *Meina-yelka*, Telegu of the Yanadees (*Jerdon*).

HABITAT.—Throughout India from north to south, but has not been reported from Ceylon. In Burmah Dr. Anderson found it in the valley of the Nampoung, a frontier stream dividing Burmah from China.

DESCRIPTION.—Upper surface rich rufous or chestnut red, paling to brown on the ears and muzzle before the eyes; under-parts white, with a yellowish tinge; feet pale brown, shading off into white on the toes; under surface of feet yellowish; tail brownish or dusky with grey hairs;

it tapers to a point, finely ringed; sparsely haired between the rings, the hairs more numerous and longer towards the tips. The length of the head, according to Dr. Anderson, whose description ('Anat. and Zool. Res.' p. 313) is more complete than Jerdon's, is about one-third the length of the body; the muzzle is moderately long and slightly contracted behind the moustachial area; eyes large; ears ovate, sparsely clad.

SIZE.—Head and body, from 2½ to 3 inches; tail one-half longer than the combined length of body and head.

Jerdon says of this pretty little mouse that "it is most abundant in the south of India, where it frequents trees, and very commonly palm-trees, on which it is said to make its nest generally. It, however, occasionally places its nest in the thatch of houses, on beams, &c. It is very active, and from its habits difficult to procure" ('Mammals of India,' p. 202). According to Sykes it constructs its nest of oleraceous herbs in the fields, and Hodgson states it to tenant woods and coppices in Nepal.

No. 351. MUS NILAGIRICUS.

The Neilgherry Tree Mouse (*Jerdon's No.* 185).

HABITAT.—Ootacamund.

DESCRIPTION.—"Above deep but bright chestnut brown, beneath bright fawn yellow, with a distinct line of demarcation between the two colours; head rather elongated; cars long, oval; tail somewhat hairy." —*Jerdon.*

SIZE.—Head and body, 3½ inches; tail, 5 inches.

This tree mouse was discovered and named by Dr. Jerdon. He says: "The first I observed was brought into the house by a cat. I afterwards, on two or three occasions, found the nest, a mass of leaves and grass, on shrubs and low trees, from four to five feet from the ground, and on one occasion it was occupied by at least eight or ten apparently full-grown mice."

No. 352. MUS BADIUS.

The Bay Tree Mouse.

HABITAT.—The valley of the Sittang, Burmah.

DESCRIPTION.—"Similar to *M. oleraceus*, but with the eye fully twice as large, and black whiskers; colour of the upper parts a more rufous chestnut or cinnamon hue, of the lower parts white, almost pure."—*Blyth.*

SIZE.—Head and body, 3 inches; tail, 4⅜ inches.

No. 353. MUS GLIROIDES.

The Cherrapoonjee Tree Mouse.

HABITAT.—Khasia hills.

DESCRIPTION.—Fur exceedingly dense and fine, of a light brown, tinged with fawn; the basal two-thirds of the piles are dusky ash coloured; the lower parts are white, very faintly tinged with fawn; the white purest about the lips and chin; whiskers long; feet large and sparsely clad with white hairs; a distinct brown mark on each hind foot reaching almost to the division of the toes; ears smallish, ovoid, naked.

SIZE.—Head and body, 2 inches; tail (?) mutilated.

Blyth says this animal has much of the aspect of the European dormouse (*Myoxus avellanarius*), but nothing is said about its dentition, which would at once settle the question whether the young specimen with its imperfect tail were a true *Mus* or a species of *Myoxus*.*

No. 354. MUS PEGUENSIS.

The Pegu Tree Mouse.

HABITAT.—The Sittang valley, Burmah.

DESCRIPTION.—Fulvescent olive brown on the upper parts, yellowish-white below; whiskers remarkably long; the tail very long and conspicuously haired towards the tip; more so, Blyth remarks, than any other mouse, especially when held up to the light.

SIZE.—Head and body, $3\frac{1}{8}$th inches; tail, $3\frac{7}{8}$; in one specimen, $4\frac{1}{2}$ inches.

We now come to the terrestrial or house mice

No. 355. MUS URBANUS.

The Common Indian Mouse (Jerdon's No. 186).

NATIVE NAMES.—*Lengtia-indur*, Bengali; *Mesuri*, *Musi*, *Chuhi*, Hindi.

HABITAT.—Throughout India and Ceylon.

DESCRIPTION.—Somewhat resembling the English mouse, but with very much longer, coarser tail, larger eyes, and smaller ears; dusky reddish-brown above, somewhat paler below; the feet paler still, whitish in some; the tail nude, thick at base, longer by an inch than the head and body, and of a dark brown colour. The young are more dusky.

SIZE.—Head and body, about 2 to 3 inches; tail, 3 to 4 inches.

I have kept these mice in confinement for considerable periods, and have had many opportunities of studying their habits of late. During many years' residence in the Currency Office, I never once found a mouse in my private quarters on the third story, although I frequently

* See Appendix A for description and dentition of *Myoxus*.

observed them in the vaults and strong rooms on the ground floor. During my absence at Simla in 1880 my quarters were unoccupied, as the Public Works Department were giving the building a thorough repair. It was then, I suppose, a few of the mice from the ground floor were driven upstairs, and, being unmolested by us, as we liked to see the little things playing about, they increased to a most uncomfortable extent within eight months. I failed to discover their breeding places, though I suspect they made much use of a large doll's-house for the purpose, for on taking out the front staircase, under which the bells of the establishment were hung, I found a nest of torn paper, and I caught two young ones in one of the rooms. Some of them came out every night whilst we were at dinner, and paid a visit to a rose-headed parraquet (*Palæornis rosa*), mounting up on Polly's perch, and sitting down to supper in the tin receptacles for food at each end. She generally treated them with silent contempt, or gave a snappish little peck if they were too familiar; sometimes, when they were too sky-larky, she retreated to her ring above, where she swung and looked down at them from a coign of vantage. Their agility in running up and down the wires of a cage is marvellous. They have also an extraordinary faculty for running up a perpendicular board, and the height from which they can jump is astounding. One day, in my study, I chased one of these mice on to the top of a book-case. Standing on some steps, I was about to put my hand over him, when he jumped on to the marble floor and ran off. I measured the height, and have since measured it again, 8 feet 9½ inches.

I consider this species the most muscular of all mice of the same size. I have had at the same time in confinement an English mouse (albino), a Bengal field mouse, and house mice from Simla of another species, and none of them could show equal activity. I use, for the purpose of taming mice, a glass fish-globe, out of which none of the other mice could get, but I have repeatedly seen specimens of *M. urbanus* jump clear out of the opening at the top. They would look up, gather their hind quarters together, and then go in for a high leap. They are much more voracious than the Simla or other mice. The allowance of food given would be devoured in less than half the time taken by the others, and they are more given to gnawing. What sort of mothers they are in freedom I know not, but one which produced four young ones in one of my cages devoured her offspring before they were a week old. I have two before me just now as I write, and they have had a quarrel about the highest place on a little grated window. The larger one got the advantage, so the other seized hold of her tail, and gave it a good nip.

Now we come to some doubtful species, doubtful in the sense that they should not be separated, but considered as one to be named afterwards, according to priority of discovery. Dr. Anderson is at present investigating the matter, and we must await his decision, but from such external observations as I have been able to make, it appears probable that the following will prove identical :—

Mus homourus; Mus Darjeelingensis; Mus Tytleri; Mus Bactrianus; Mus cervicolor (?)—*Jerdon's Nos.* 187, 189, 190, 191, *and* 192. These are all hill mice, except the last, and found under the same conditions.

No. 356. MUS HOMOURUS.

HABITAT.—Lower Himalayan range.

DESCRIPTION.—Dark rufescent above, rufescent white below; hands and feet fleshy white; tail equal to length of head and body; "fur more gerbille-like in character than in *M. musculus*" (or *urbanus*), stated to be the common house mouse of the Himalayan hill stations from the Punjab to Darjeeling. Stated by Hodgson to have eight teats only in the female, other mice having ten. Possibly his description was founded on young specimens. I myself was of opinion for some time that I had got two species of hill mice, a larger and a smaller, the latter being so much darker in colour, but I kept them till the young ones attained full size in six months, at which time they were not distinguishable from the old ones. Hodgson may have overlooked the pectoral mammæ when he noted the number.

SIZE.—Head and body, 3½ inches; tail, 3½ inches.

No. 357. MUS DARJEELINGENSIS.

DESCRIPTION.—Dusky brown, with a slight chestnut reflection; underparts pale yellowish-white.

SIZE.—Head and body, 3 inches; tail, 2½ inches.

No. 358. MUS TYTLERI.

HABITAT.—Dehra Doon.

DESCRIPTION.—Fur long and full, pale, sandy mouse-coloured above, isabelline below; pale on the well-clad limbs, and also on the tail laterally and underneath.

SIZE.—Head and body, 2¾ inches; tail, 2¾ inches.

No. 359. MUS BACTRIANUS.

HABITAT.—Punjab, Kashmir, Candahar, Baluchistan, and Southern Persia.

DESCRIPTION.—Upper parts brown above, with a sandy tinge, more on the head; the longer hairs with a dusky tip; the basal two-thirds deep ash; under-parts and feet white; tail clad thinly with fine whitish hair; the fur in general long, dense, and silky.

SIZE.—Head and body, from 2½ to 3½ inches; taïl, about the same.

This is the mouse, I think, that I caught in the house at Simla in 1880. Of eight specimens I got—seven in a cupboard in the dining-room and one in a bath-room—I sent two in spirits to the Indian Museum and brought down to Calcutta three alive, which I kept for about seven months, when they died. I have since then seen living specimens of *M. bactrianus* from Kohat, with which they appear to be identical. They also resemble—I speak under correction—*M. cervicolor*, which is a field mouse found in Bengal. I made the following notes regarding them: Fur very fine, close and silky, rufescent brown, more rufous on the head, isabelline below; feet flesh-coloured, hinder ones large, much larger than those of the English mouse; the hind-quarters are also more powerful; has a very pretty way of sitting up, with the body bent forwards, and its hands clasped in an attitude of supplication. The young mice seem darker both above and below, and are much more shy than the old ones, of which one soon after being caught took bits of cake from my fingers through the bars of its cage. More delicate looking than *Mus urbanus*, with a much shorter and finer tail; less offensive in smell.

Dr. Anderson got, not long ago, two of these mice in a box from Kohat. They bore the journey uncommonly well, and were in lively condition when I saw them at the Museum. Whilst we were talking about them, we noticed an act of intelligence for which I should not have given them credit had I not seen it with my own eyes. They were in a box with a glass front; in the upper left-hand corner was a small sleeping chamber, led up to by a sloping piece of wood. The entrance of this chamber was barred by wires bent into the form of a lady's hair-pin, and passed through holes in the roof of the box.

The mice had been driven out, and the sleeping-chamber barred, for they were having their portraits taken. Whilst we were talking we found, to our surprise, that one mouse was inside the chamber, although the bars were down. There seemed hardly space for it to squeeze through; however, it was driven out, and we went on with our conversation, but found, on looking at the cage again, that our little friend was once more inside, so he was driven out again, and we kept an eye on him. To our great surprise and amusement we saw him trot up his sloping board, put his little head on one side, and seize one of the wires, which worked very loosely in its socket, give it a hitch up, when he adroitly caught it lower down, hitched it up again and again till he got it high enough to allow him to slip in underneath, and then he was quite happy once more. He had only been in the box two days, so he was not long in finding out the weak point. I begin to believe now in rats dipping their tails into oil-bottles, and other wonderful stories of murine sagacity that one reads of. Mice are supposed to live from two-and-a-half to three years. I had the English albino above mentioned for three.

No. 360. MUS CRASSIPES.

The Large-footed Mouse (*Jerdon's No.* 188).

HABITAT.—Mussoorie and, according to Jerdon, the Neilgherries.

DESCRIPTION.—This is stated to be like *M. homourus*, but the difference is well marked in a very much longer tail and much larger feet.

SIZE.—Head and body, 2¾ inches; tail, ¾ inch; hind foot, ¾ inch.

No. 361. MUS SUBLIMIS.

HABITAT.—Ladakh, 13,000 feet.

DESCRIPTION.—Brown above; whitish below; the colours gradually blending; fur soft and long; all except the tips dark slaty grey, the terminal portions of the shorter hairs being light brown, and of the longer hairs dark brown; upper whiskers black; lower white; ears oval; feet thinly clad with short light brown hairs; tail with short bristly hairs, dusky brown above, whitish below; tail longer than head and body.

SIZE.—Head and body, 2·6 inches; tail, 3·05; length of hind foot, 0·83 inch.

Mr. Blanford, who named the above species, which was procured in the expedition to Yarkand, is doubtful whether it may not be referable to the last species.

No. 362. MUS PACHYCERCUS.

HABITAT.—Yarkand.

DESCRIPTION.—Sandy brown above; under-parts white; fur soft and very like *M. bactrianus*; ears large, rounded, hairy; feet clad above with white hair; soles naked; tail thick, shorter than head and body, and thinly clad with white bristles throughout; skin dark above, pale below; incisors deep yellow.

SIZE.—Head and body, 2·35 inches; tail, 1·9 to 2 inches.

Mr. Blanford says this is a house mouse. It is figured in Blanford's 'Mammalia of the Second Yarkand Mission.'

No. 363. MUS ERYTHRONOTUS.

HABITAT.—Yarkand, Persia.

DESCRIPTION.—Rufous, washed with blackish above, white below, abruptly separated; hairs on the back are slaty at the base, then blackish and bright ferruginous at the tips, the extreme points being black, except on the sides, where the black tip is wanting; upper whiskers black, lower white; ears large, rounded, naked; feet white above, dusky and naked below; tail equal to head and body, nearly naked. Mammæ six.

SIZE.—Head and body, 4 inches; tail, 4·2 inches.

This mouse is figured and carefully described in Blanford's 'Eastern Persia,' vol. ii. p. 35.

NO. 364. MUS CERVICOLOR.

The Fawn-coloured Field Mouse.

HABITAT.—Bengal, Nepal, Southern India.

DESCRIPTION.—"Distinguished by its short tail. Above dull fawn, below sordid white; lining of ears and extremities pale" (*Blyth*). "Ears large, hairy" (*Jerdon*). Of the specimens I have seen the fur is soft and of a light sandy brown above and white below, very like *M. bactrianus.*

SIZE.—Head and body, $3\frac{1}{2}$ inches; tail, $2\frac{7}{8}$ inches.

NO. 365. MUS TERRICOLOR.

The Earth-coloured Field Mouse.

HABITAT.—India generally, I think. It has been found in the valley of the Ganges, in Bengal, in the Santal district west of Midnapore, and Southern India.

DESCRIPTION.—The colour varies according to the soil, but in general fawn brown, more or less rufescent—those from the valley of the Ganges being darker than those from the ferruginous soil of other parts. The under-parts are white, abruptly separated from the brown; fur short and soft.

SIZE.—Head and body, $2\frac{1}{2}$ inches; tail, $2\frac{1}{3}$ inches.

NO. 366. MUS PEGUENSIS.

The Pegu Field Mouse.

HABITAT.—The valley of the Sitang River, Burmah.

DESCRIPTION.—"Fur very full and dense, pale fulvescent olive brown on the upper parts, slightly yellowish-white below; whiskers remarkably long" (*Blyth*). Tail longer than head and body, and well clad with hairs, especially towards the tip.

SIZE.—Head and body, $3\frac{1}{8}$ inches; tail, nearly 4 inches.

NO. 367. MUS NITIDULUS.

The Shiny Little House Mouse of Pegu.

HABITAT.—The Sitang valley in Burmah.

DESCRIPTION.—The description given of this mouse by Blyth is extremely vague. He says: "A house mouse apparently, with tail equal to head and body, and uniformly furnished with minute setæ to the end; ears large and ample; colour nearly that of *M. decumanus*, with the under-parts subdued white, tolerably well defined."

He remarks further on that the front teeth are conspicuously larger than those of *M. musculus* and *M. urbanus*.

SIZE.—Head and body, $3\frac{1}{4}$ inches; tail, the same.

No. 368. MUS BEAVENI.

Beaven's Mouse.

HABITAT.—Maubhum, and, according to Blyth's Catalogue, Burmah, valley of the Salween.

DESCRIPTION.—"Above rusty brown, medially black; lips and the whole under side pale ochraceous; feet white, all the hair being slate coloured at the base; tail above brown, below with white hairs; upper whiskers black, lower white. Rather smaller and more delicately built than our common harvest mouse."—*Prof. Peters*, 'P. Z. S.' 1866, p. 559.

No. 369. MUS CUNICULARIS.

The Little Rabbit-Mouse.

HABITAT.—Cherrapunji, Assam.

DESCRIPTION.—"A small field (?) mouse, remarkable for its ample ears and tail shorter than head and body; colour of a wild rabbit above, below white; and the feet with brownish hairs above, but with white hairs upon the toes; tail conspicuously ringed; the setæ minute and inconspicuous."—*Blyth.*

SIZE.—Head and body, $2\frac{1}{2}$ inches; tail, $2\frac{1}{8}$ inches; ears posteriorly half an inch.

No. 370. MUS ERYTHROTIS.

The Cherrapunji Red-eared Mouse.

HABITAT.—Cherrapoonji, Assam.

DESCRIPTION.—A small mouse with very deep soft fur, very long and silky, of a rich dark brown colour, grizzled and brightly tinged with rufous or rufo-ferruginous towards the tail, and upon the ears conspicuously. In such spirit specimens as I have seen the colour was darker than in life, but the soft silkiness of the fur could be seen to advantage as it floated in the clear liquid; the lower parts are whitish, tinged with fawn; feet with brown hairs above; ears small and hirsute, and the tail is also hairy.

SIZE.—Head and body, $2\frac{1}{4}$ inches; tail, $2\frac{3}{8}$ inches.

No. 371. MUS FULVIDIVENTRIS.

HABITAT.—Ceylon, Trincomalee.

DESCRIPTION.—This is a small mouse very like *Mus cervicolor*, or perhaps *M. terricolor*, which it more nearly approaches in size. Kellaart in his ' Prodromus,' calls it *cervicolor*, but Blyth afterwards separated it under the name given above, though after all I think he was doubtful whether it ought to have been so distinguished. The fur is long, soft, and glossy, fulvous fawn brown above, paler below; feet dingy grey.

SIZE.—Head and body, $2\frac{9}{10}$ inches; tail, $2\frac{5}{10}$ inches.

No. 372. MUS KAKHYENENSIS.

The Kakhyen Mouse.

HABITAT.—Burmo-Chinese frontier, Ponsee.

DESCRIPTION.—Differs from *Mus urbanus* by its shorter tail, longer hind feet, and larger ears; muzzle moderately deep, and short; ears large and rounded; fur long, dense, and soft, reddish-brown on the upper parts, with a dark speckled appearance due to the stronger hairs having broad brown tips; sides of the head dusky greyish; chin to vent and under-parts greyish-white, with a silvery sheen; feet dusky pale brown; ears and upper surface of tail dark brown, under surface of tail pale brown.—*Anderson.*

SIZE.—Head and body, 2·90 inches; tail, 3·36 inches.

This mouse was discovered and named by Dr. Anderson, who procured one example at Ponsee, where it occurs, he says, on the old rice and Indian corn clearings. The next species is also a new one discovered and named by him.

No. 373. MUS VICULORUM.

The Kakhyen House Mouse.

HABITAT.—The Burmo-Chinese frontier, Ponsee.

DESCRIPTION.—Muzzle rather sharply pointed, moderately long and not deep; ears moderately large, rounded; its height a little in excess of the distance between the inner canthus and the front of the muzzle; hind-feet not long; tail a little longer than the body and head, finely ringed, five rings to one-tenth of an inch; fur soft, short, dense, dull dark brown on the upper parts, tending to blackish on the back, paling to brownish on the sides, and passing into pale dusky brownish on the under parts with a silvery sheen; feet brownish; toes with shining greyish-yellow hairs; ears and tail brown. (*See* Anderson's 'Anat. and Zool. Res.,' p. 308.)

SIZE.—Head and body, $2\frac{3}{10}$ inches; tail, 3·14 inches.

This species, according to Dr. Anderson, frequents the villages and houses of the Kakhyens. He obtained it at Ponsee.

We now come to an interesting little group of mice, of which the hairs are mixed with flat spines, which form the genus *Leggada* of Gray, a term taken from the Wuddur name for the next species.

GENUS LEGGADA.

CHARACTERISTICS.—Molars high, with somewhat convex crowns; the cross ridges of the upper grinders deeply three-lobed; the front one with an additional lunate lobe at the base of its front edge; fur fine, mixed with numerous spines somewhat flattened.

NO. 374. LEGGADA PLATYTHRIX.

The Brown Spiny Mouse (Jerdon's No. 194).

NATIVE NAMES.—*Leggade* and *Kal-yelka*, of Wuddurs; *Gijeli-gadu*, Telegu, of Yanadees; *Kal-ilei*, Canarese.

HABITAT.—Southern India.

DESCRIPTION.—Sandy brown or light brown fawn above, white underneath, with a band of pale fawn separating the two colours.

The fur mixed with flat transparent spines, smaller beneath; head long; muzzle pointed; ears rather large, oblong, rounded, about half an inch in length.

SIZE.—Head and body, $3\frac{1}{2}$ inches; tail, $2\frac{1}{2}$ inches.

The following description has been given by Sir Walter Elliot and reproduced in Jerdon's 'Mammals': "The Leggade lives entirely in the red gravelly soil in a burrow of moderate depth, generally on the side of a bank. When the animal is inside the entrance is closed with small pebbles, a quantity of which is collected outside, by which its retreat may always be known. The burrow leads to a chamber in which is collected a bed of small pebbles on which it sits, the thick close hair of the belly protecting it from the cold and asperity of such a seat. Its food appears to be vegetable. In its habits it is monogamous and nocturnal.

"In one earth which I opened, and which did not seem to have been originally constructed by the animal, I found two pairs, one of which were adults, the other young ones about three-parts grown. The mouth of the earth was very large, and completely blocked up with small stones; the passage gradually widening into a large cavity, from the roof of which some other passages appeared to proceed, but there was only one communication with the surface, viz. the entrance. The old pair were seated on a bed of pebbles, near which, on a higher level, was another collection of stones probably intended for a drier retreat; the young ones were in one of the passages, likewise furnished with a heap of small stones."

Dr. Jerdon adds he has often opened the burrows of this mouse, and can confirm the above account. He also states that the Yanadees of Nellore declare that one variety uses small sticks instead of stones to sit upon, and they give it a distinct appellation, but he could not detect any difference in the specimens they brought him.

NO. 375. LEGGADA SPINULOSA.

The Dusky Spiny Mouse (*Jerdon's No.* 195).

HABITAT.—Punjab, and also Southern India.

DESCRIPTION.—" Nearly affined to *M. platythrix* (Sykes), but of a dark dusky colour above, with fulvous tips to the softer fur; below and all the feet dull whitish; upper rodential tusks orange, the lower white; whiskers long and fine, the posterior and longer of them black for the basal half or more, the rest white."—*Blyth*, 'J. A. S. B.' 1863.

SIZE.—Head and body, 3¾ inches; tail, 3 inches.

NO. 376. LEGGADA JERDONI.

The Himalayan Spiny Mouse (*Jerdon's No.* 196).

HABITAT.—Himalayan range, up to 12,000 feet.

DESCRIPTION.—" Bright dark ferruginous above, pure white below; some fine long black tips intermingled among the spines of the back; limbs marked with blackish externally; the feet white."—*Blyth's* 'Mem., J. A. S. B.' vol. xxxii.

SIZE.—Head and body, 4 inches; tail, 3½ inches.

Dr. Jerdon first found this mouse at Darjeeling, but afterwards in the valley of the Sutlej in Kunawur, at an elevation of nearly 12,000 feet, living under large stones.

NO. 377. LEGGADA LEPIDA.

The Small Spiny Mouse (*Jerdon's No.* 197).

NATIVE NAMES.—*Chitta-burkani*, *Chit-yelka*, *Chitta-ganda*, Telegu of Wuddurs; *Chitta-yelka* of Yanadees.—*Jerdon.*

HABITAT.—Southern India.

DESCRIPTION.—Similar to *L. platythrix*, but smaller and more weakly spinous; above pale sandy brown, pure white below, the two colours clearly separated. " The spines are small, fine, transparent, and of a dusky tinge, tipped with fawn; head very long; muzzle pointed; ears large, ovate, naked; tail naked, limbs rather long, fine."—*Jerdon.*

SIZE.—Head and body, 2½ to 3 inches; tail, 2¾ inches.

DESCRIPTION.—Jerdon says of this mouse that he has found it in gravelly soil in gardens and woods in most parts of Southern India, making a small burrow, which generally has a little heap of stones placed at a short distance from the hole. It is preyed on now and then by the common Indian roller or jay, and it is very generally used as a bait to catch that bird with bird-lime.

GENUS GOLUNDA.

The following rats are separated by Gray as a distinct genus, which from the Canarese name of the type he has called *Golunda*, the characteristics of which are: "the grinders, when perfect, low, with a broad, flat crown; the cross ridges of the crown of the upper grinders divided into three distinct slightly raised tubercles; upper incisors grooved; rest like *Mus*."

No. 378. GOLUNDA ELLIOTI.

The Bush Rat or Coffee Rat (*Jerdon's No.* 199).

NATIVE NAMES.—*Gulandi*, Canarese; *Gulat-yelka* of Wuddurs; *Sora-panji-gadur*, Telegu of Yanadees; *Cofee-wattee-meeyo*, Singhalese (this name seems to me a corruption of "coffee rat").

DESCRIPTION.—Fur thick and stiff, fulvous brown, mixed with black, some olive brown mixed with fulvous, tawny grey beneath; hairs of upper parts flattened, ashy grey, tipped yellow, with some thinner and longer ones, also tipped yellow, with sub-terminal black band; under fur soft and of a light lead colour; face and cheeks rough; ears moderate, sub-ovate, hairy; tail round, tapering, scaly and hairy, dark brown above, yellowish below; cutting teeth yellow.

SIZE.—Head and body, 4½ inches; tail, 4 inches.

Dr. Kellaart says these are the rats most destructive to coffee-trees, whole plantations being sometimes deprived of buds and blossoms by them.

There is an illustration of one in Sir Emerson Tennent's 'Natural History of Ceylon' in the act of cutting off the slender branches which would not bear its weight in order to feed on the buds and blossoms when fallen to the ground. "The twigs thus destroyed are detached by as clean a cut as if severed with a knife." Sir Walter Elliot writes of it: "The *gulandi* lives entirely in the jungle, choosing its habitation in a thick bush, among the thorny branches of which, or on the ground, it constructs a nest of elastic stalks and fibres of dry grass thickly interwoven. The nest is of a round or oblong shape, from six to nine inches in diameter, within which is a chamber about three or four inches in diameter, in which it rolls itself up. Round and through the bush are sometimes observed small beaten pathways along which the little animal seems habitually to pass. Its motion is somewhat slow, and it does not appear to have the same power of leaping or springing by which the rats in general avoid danger. Its food seems to be vegetable, the only contents of the stomach being the roots of the haryalee grass. Its habits are solitary (except when the female is bringing up her young) and diurnal, feeding in the mornings and evenings." Dr. Jerdon says: "The Yanadees of Nellore catch this rat, surrounding the bush and seizing it as it issues forth, which its comparatively slow actions enable them to do easily. According to Sir Emerson Tennent the Malabar coolies are so fond of their flesh that they evince a preference for those districts in which the coffee-plantions are subject to their incursions, where they fry the rats in cocoanut-oil or convert them into curry." Both he and Dr. Kellaart mention the migratory habits of this animal on the occurrence of a scarcity of food. Kellaart says that in one day on such visits more than a thousand have been killed on one estate alone.

No. 379. GOLUNDA MELTADA.

The Soft-furred Bush Rat (*Jerdon's No.* 200).

NATIVE NAMES.—*Mettade*, of Wuddurs; *Metta-yelka*, Telegu of Yanadees; *Kera ilei*, Canarese.

HABITAT.—Southern India and Ceylon.

DESCRIPTION.—Fur very soft; above deep yellowish, olive brown or reddish-brown, with a mixture of fawn; under fur lead colour; chin and under parts whitish; head short; muzzle sharp; ears long and hairy; tail shorter than body, scaly, but scales covered with short black adpressed hairs; feet pale.

SIZE.—Head and body, 3½ to 5½ inches; tail, 2¼ to 4¼ inches.

The specific name of this rat is an absurd corruption, such as is not unfrequent in Dr. Gray's names, of the native *mettade*, which means soft. According to that accurate observer Sir Walter Elliot, "the *mettade* lives entirely in cultivated fields in pairs or small societies of five or six;* making a very slight and rude hole in the root of a bush, or merely harbouring among the heap of stones thrown together in the fields, in the deserted burrow of the *kok*,† or contenting itself with the deep cracks and fissures formed in the black soil during the hot months. Great numbers perish annually when these collapse and fill up at the commencement of the rains. The monsoon of 1826 having been deficient in the usual fall of rain at the commencement of the season, the *mettades* bred in such numbers as to become a perfect plague. They ate up the seed as soon as sown, and continued their ravages when the grain approached to maturity, climbing up the stalks of jowaree and cutting off the ear to devour the grain with greater facility. I

* In this case probably parents and young.

† *Nesokia providens.*

saw many whole fields completely devastated, so much so as to prevent the farmers from paying their rents. The ryots employed the Wuddurs to destroy them, who killed them by thousands, receiving a measure of grain for so many dozens, without perceptibly diminishing their numbers. Their flesh is eaten by the Tank-diggers. The female produces six to eight at a birth."—'*Madras Journ. Lit. Sc.*' x. 1839.

Kellaart's *Golunda Newera* is, I fancy, the same, although the measurement he gives is less. Head and body, 3¼ inches; tail, 2½. The description tallies, although Kellaart goes upon difference in size and the omission of Gray to state that *G. meltada* had the upper incisors groved. He says that "this rat is found in pairs in the black soil of Newara Elia, and is a great destroyer of peas and potatoes." So its habits agree.

GENUS HAPALOMYS.

This was formed by Blyth on a specimen from Burmah of a murine animal "with a long and delicately fine pelage and exceedingly long tail, the terminal fourth of which is remarkably flattened and furnished with hair more developed than in perhaps any other truly murine form; limbs short, with the toes remarkably corrugated underneath; the balls of the inguinal phalanges greatly developed, protruding beyond the minute claws of the fore-feet, and equally with the more developed claws of the hind-feet; head short; the ears small and inconspicuous; the skull approaches in form that of *Mus Indicus*,* but the rodential tusks are broader and flatter to the front. Molars as in the *Muridæ* generally, but much worn in the specimen under examination; they are considerably less directed outward than usual, and the bony palate has therefore the appearance of being narrow; the superorbital ridges project much outward in form of a thin bony plate, and there is a considerable process at the base of the zygoma anteriorly and posteriorly to the anti-orbital foramen; zygomata broad, and compressed about the middle."

No. 380. HAPALOMYS LONGICAUDATUS.

HABITAT.—Shway Gheen, in the valley of the Sitang river in Burmah, or its adjacent hills.

DESCRIPTION.—"Fur long and soft, measuring about five-eights of an inch on the upper parts, slaty for the basal two-thirds, then glistening brown with black tips, and a few long hairs of very fine texture interspersed; lower parts dull white; whiskers black, long and fine, and there is a tuft of fine blackish-hair anterior to the ears."—*Blyth.*

SIZE.—Head and body of a male, 5¾ inches; tail 7¼ inches. Of

* *Nesokia Blythiana.*

another specimen, female: $5\frac{1}{4}$ inches; tail, $7\frac{1}{2}$ inches; sole, $1\frac{1}{8}$ inch; ears posteriorly, $1\frac{1}{4}$ inch.

Specimens of adult male and female with a young one were forwarded to the Asiatic Society's Museum by Major Berdmore.

We have now come to the end of the purely murine group as far as they exist within the limits assigned to these investigations. I ought perhaps to give some short notices of the following specimens discovered in Thibet by the Abbé David, and described by Professor Milne-Edwards in his 'Recherches sur les Mammifères.'

No. 381. MUS OUANG-THOMÆ.

The Kiangsi Rat.

HABITAT.—Kiangsi in Thibet.

DESCRIPTION.—A tawny grey above, mixed with long hairs, tipped with brown, greyish below; between the fore-paws a crescent of pure white, which is a distinguishing mark of the species.

SIZE.—A little less than *Mus rattus*, which is about seven inches long; tail an inch longer.

This rat Professor Milne-Edwards describes from a single specimen; it is apparently rare, and was named after the Abbé David's Chinese servant.—'Recherches sur les Mammifères,' p. 290.

No. 382. MUS FLAVIPECTUS.

The Yellow-breasted Rat.

HABITAT.—Moupin; Thibet.

DESCRIPTION.—Reddish-brown; chin greyish; throat and chest tawny, mixed with grey; belly and inside of limbs yellowish-grey; ears large, nearly naked; incisors deep yellow; tail brown, covered with short hairs.

SIZE.—About $7\frac{3}{4}$ inches; tail, $6\frac{1}{4}$ inches.—'Mammifères,' p. 289.

No. 383. MUS GRISEIPECTUS.

The Grey-breasted Rat.

HABITAT.—Moupin; Thibet.

DESCRIPTION.—Brown above; the under-parts of a clear grey.

SIZE.—About the same as the last, but with a somewhat shorter tail.—'Mammifères,' p. 290.

No. 384. Mus Confucianus.

Habitat.—Moupin; Thibet.

Description.—Fawn brown above, pure white below; lower part of cheek white; on the back the fur is interspersed with longer hairs of a blackish tint; feet pale.

Size.—Head and body, about 4 inches.—'Mammifères,' p. 286.

No. 385. Mus Chevrieri.

Habitat.—Moupin; Thibet.

Description.—General colour tawny brown, grizzled with dark brown; lower parts of a clear grey, almost white; ears short; feet small; tail covered with short hair.

Size.—About $4\frac{3}{4}$ inches; tail about $3\frac{1}{2}$ inches.—'Mammifères,' p. 288.

No. 386. Mus pygmæus.

The Pigmy Mouse.

Habitat.—Moupin; Thibet.

Description.—Distinguished by its very short ears and the square form of its head; deep brown above; greyish-yellow beneath; tail shorter than in the common mouse.

Size.—About $2\frac{3}{4}$ inches; tail, about 2 inches.—'Mammifères,' p. 291.

ARVICOLINÆ.

In this sub-family the molars are generally semi-rooted or rootless. The *Arvicolinæ* or Voles consist of the American Musquash (*Fiber zibethicus*), a very beaver-like water rat of large size; the Lemmings (*Myodes*), of which there are several species which are celebrated for their vast migrations; and the true Vole (*Arvicola*), which is the only genus found in India, and then only in the colder climate of the Himalayas. There are several species in Europe, of which three are found in England. According to Professor Dallas, the true Voles number about fifty species, arranged by various writers under a considerable number of sub-genera. In India we have only eight known species, and two more from the adjacent country of Thibet.

The European forms of *Arvicolæ* have been divided by Blasius into four sub-genera of two divisions—the first division having rooted molars in the adult animal—containing one sub-genus only, *Hypudæus* of Illiger;

the second division consists of three sub-genera with rootless molars, viz. *Paludicola*, *Agricola*, and *Arvicola*, which last has again been subdivided into long-eared and short-eared Voles—*Arvicola* and *Microtus* — distinguished by the former having eight and the latter four mammæ, and respectively six and four tubercles on the plantæ, the ears of the latter being almost hidden by the fur.

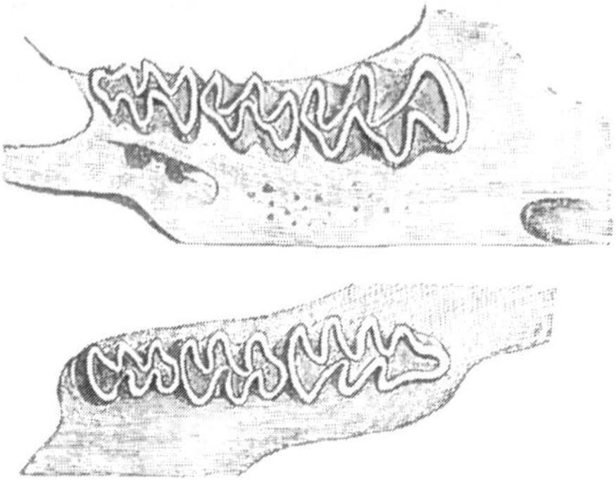

Dentition of *Arvicola*.

None of the forms with which we have now to deal belong to the first division, for, as far as the matter has been investigated, the Indian Voles have rootless molars, but the character of the teeth in some differs from the European forms, and therefore Mr. Blanford has proposed a new section, *Alticola*, for their reception. I have not space here, nor would it accord with the popular character of this work, to go minutely into all the variation of dentition which distinguish the different species. To those who wish to continue to the minutest details the study of the Indian Voles, I recommend a most careful and elaborate paper on them by Mr. W. T. Blanford, F.R.S., in the Journal of the Asiatic Society of Bengal, vol. L., pt. ii.; but without entering into the microscopic particulars of each species, I may here give a general idea of the formation of the teeth of the *Arvicolæ* differing as it does so much from others of the myomorphic or mouse-like group of rodents. In these the general contour of the molar teeth is roundish oblong, the margins being wavy or indented, according to the convolutions of the enamel, but in the Voles there is a sharp angularity about these indentations; the marginal lines, instead of being in well-rounded curves, are sharply zigzag, forming acute angles. If you were to draw two close parallel zigzag lines it would give you some idea of the contour of these teeth. The molars are in fact composed of alternating triangular prisms, with the outer folds of enamel forming deep and acute angles. The other characteristics of this family are: skull, with brain case rhomboidal, frontals much contracted; infra-orbital opening typical; limbs moderate; tail moderate, or short and hairy.

GENUS ARVICOLA.

Muzzle blunt; fore-feet small, with short claws; soles naked; tail longer than the hind-foot, clad with short hairs; incisors plain, smooth in front. The fore-feet in some species have but a small wart in place of a thumb; in others there is a small thumb with a minute claw. The hind-feet have five toes.

No. 387. ARVICOLA STOLICZKANUS.

The Yarkand Vole.

HABITAT.—Yarkand.

DESCRIPTION.—" Bright ferruginous brown above, pure white beneath; fur soft, rather woolly, 0·5 to 0·6 inch long on the middle of the back, the basal portion throughout both head and body being dark leaden grey; this is the case on the back for about three-quarters of the length of the hairs; the remaining quarter is rufous white, tipped with darker rufous, whilst numerous rather longer hairs are dark rufous-brown at the ends; rather a sharp line divides the rufous of the back from the white belly; upper part of the head the same colour as the back; upper whiskers dark brown, lower, including the longest, white; ears small, rounded, hairy, completely concealed by the fur, with rather short bright rufous hair near the margin inside; and covered outside with longer and paler hair; feet small, the thumb of the fore-foot quite rudimentary and clawless; remaining claws long, compressed, sharply pointed, but much concealed by the long white hairs which cover the upper part of the foot, soles naked; tarsus hairy below, a few hairs between the pads of the toes; tail short, apparently about a quarter the length of the body and head together, covered with stiff fulvescent white hair, which extends about half an inch beyond the end."—*W. T. Blanford*, 'Sc. Res. of Second Yarkand Mission,' p. 43.

SIZE.—Head and body, about 4 inches; tail, with hair, 1½.

No. 388. ARVICOLA STRACHEYI.

The Kumaon Vole.

HABITAT.—Kumaon.

DESCRIPTION.—Light brown above, with a greyish tint and dusky forehead; under-parts, feet, and tail white; ears small, not longer than the fur, and thickly clad with hair; feet of moderate size; thumb as in the last; tail short and covered with white hairs.

SIZE.—Head and body, about 3·7 inches; tail; 0·7.

This vole was procured first by Capt. (now Lieut.-Gen.) R. Strachey at Kumaon.

No. 389. ARVICOLA WYNNEI.

The Murree Vole.

NATIVE NAME.—*Kannees.*

HABITAT.—Northern Himalayas; Murree.

DESCRIPTION.—Dark brown above, with a slight greyish tinge; head rufescent, and under-parts pale brown; tail dark brown; ears short and rounded, hidden by the fur; fore-feet rather large; thumb small, with a short claw; incisors orange.

SIZE.—Head and body, about $4\frac{3}{4}$ inches; tail $1\frac{1}{4}$ inch.

No. 390. ARVICOLA ROYLEI.

The Cashmere Vole (Jerdon's No. 202).

HABITAT.—Kashmir; Kunawur near Chini at 12,000 feet.

DESCRIPTION.—Yellowish-brown, with a rufous tint on the back, paler below; tail brown above, whitish underneath; feet concolorous with the under-part; ears small, hairy and nearly hidden by the fur; incisors yellow in front.

SIZE.—Head and body, $3\frac{3}{4}$ inches; tail, $1\frac{2}{12}$ inch.

Jerdon states he got this vole at Kunawur, near Chini, again on the south side of the Barendo pass, and also in the Pir Punjal.

No. 391. ARVICOLA BLANFORDI.

The Gilgit Vole.

HABITAT.—Kashmir territory; Gilgit, at an elevation of 9000 to 10,000 feet.

DESCRIPTION.—Light greyish-brown above, slightly tinged with rufous; greyish-white underneath; fur soft, the basal three-fourths being slaty grey, the rest fawn colour, in some instances with black tips, the hairs of the under-parts being white tipped; ears moderately large, well above the fur, hairy; very long whiskers, chiefly white, a few brown; feet whitish, moderate size; tail cylindrical, not tapering, and well clad with hair, which project about a fifth of an inch beyond the end of the vertebræ.

SIZE.—Head and body, about $4\frac{1}{2}$ inches; tail, 2 inches.

This vole was described by Dr. J. Scully in the 'Annals and Magazine of Natural History,' for November, 1880, vol. vi., and he named it after Mr. W. T. Blanford. It is said to be common on the mountains around Gilgit.

The next two species come under the section *Paludicola.*

No. 392. ARVICOLA BLYTHII.

HABITAT.—Western Thibet, Leh and Ladakh.

DESCRIPTION.—General colour above yellowish-brown, below pale isabelline; fur soft; basal two-thirds of the upper hairs, and one-half of the lower hairs, dark slaty; the upper hairs are tipped, some isabelline and some, which are coarser and longer, dark brown; ears round, small, equal, with the fur thinly clad with pale brown hairs inside, and more thickly so with longer hairs outside; upper whiskers dark brown, lower whitish; feet pale isabelline; soles naked; tail cylindrical, distinctly ringed, covered with short light brown hair like the under-parts in colour.

SIZE.—Head and body, about 3 to 4 inches; tail, 1 to $1\frac{1}{4}$ inch.

Mr. Blanford has written fully regarding this species, which was the type of Blyth's genus *Phaiomys*, in the 'Scientific Results of the Second Yarkand Mission,' page 39, in which he contends, after going through a mass of literature on the subject, that there are no grounds for constituting it the type of a new species; and, if this be conceded, then the specific name given by Blyth, viz. *leucurus*, being forestalled, it is necessary to rename it, which he has done in honour of that well-known naturalist.

No. 393. ARVICOLA MANDARINUS.

The Afghan Vole.

HABITAT.—Afghanistan; Chinese Mongolia.

DESCRIPTION.—Light greyish rufescent brown above, white beneath; ears short, hidden by the fur and hairy; feet whitish; tail rufescent brown.

SIZE.—About 4 inches; tail about 1 inch.

This vole, which is described and figured by Milne-Edwards, is supposed to have been found in Afghanistan from a specimen in Griffith's collection. *A. mandarinus* comes from Chinese Mongolia, and it is figured in the 'Recherches sur les Mammifères.'

The next species was made a separate genus, *Neodon*, by Hodgson, which has been adopted by Jerdon; but there are no good grounds for continuing this separation. Mr. Blanford is certainly of this opinion, and in his remarks on it (*see* his 'Sc. Results Second Yarkand Mission,' pp. 41–42) he writes: "The genus *Neodon*, appears to be founded on characters of only specific importance, and the type *N. Sikimensis* is, I think, a true *Arvicola*.

No. 394. ARVICOLA SIKIMENSIS.

The Sikim Vole (Jerdon's No. 203).

NATIVE NAMES.—*Phalchua*, Nepalese, apparently Hindi; *Cheekyu*, Kiranti; *Singphuei*, Thibetan.

HABITAT.—Nepal; Sikim; Thibet.

DESCRIPTION.—Fur soft and silky. "Deep brownish-black above with a slight rusty shade, minutely and copiously grizzled with hairs of a deep ferruginous tint" (*Horsfield*). Or a deep golden brown from yellow hairs being intermixed; bluish-grey beneath, with a slight fulvous tint; fur leaden grey for the basal three-fourths, the terminal fourth being brownish or tawny with some tipped black; the hairs of the under-parts are dipped with dirty white; ears project beyond the fur moderately, and are hairy; feet very slender; tail thinly clad with short brown hair. The female has six mammæ.

SIZE.—Head and body, about 4¾ inches; tail, 1½ inch. Horsfield gives 5 inches for head and body.

According to Jerdon this vole has only been procured in Sikim near Darjeeling, at heights varying from 7000 to 15,000 feet; but I believe the area it inhabits to be much larger. Hodgson found his specimens at Darjeeling, and on one occasion got a nest in a hollow tree in the forest; it was saucer-shaped, of soft grass without any lining, and contained a male, female, and two young. The latter were "2⅓ inches long, hairy above, nude below, and blind; the ears also closed." Jerdon writes: "Mr. Atkinson found it under fallen trees and stones on the top of Tonglo, near Darjeeling, 10,000 feet, whence also I had a specimen brought me."

The next species is one described and figured by Professor Milne-Edwards, and from Thibet he has two illustrations of it—one of an entire blackish-brown, the other darker above, but with the black belly.

No. 395. ARVICOLA MELANOGASTER.

HABITAT.—Moupin in Tibet.

DESCRIPTION.—"It is characterised by the colour of the lower parts, which are a blackish-grey. The upper parts are sometimes as black as a mole, sometimes grizzled with brown" ('Mammifères,' p. 284). The brown specimen with the dark belly is evidently a rarity.

FAMILY SPALACIDÆ.

The members of this family are characterised by very large incisors; some have premolars, as in *Bathyergus* and two other genera, but not in the *Spalacinæ,* of which our bamboo-rat (*Rhizomys*) is the representative in India. "The grinding teeth are rooted, not tuberculate, but with re-entering enamel folds; infra-orbital opening moderate or small, with no perpendicular plate; occipital plane high, often sloped boldly forward; palate narrow; form cylindrical; eye and ear-conch very small, sometimes rudimentary; limbs short and stout; claws large; tail short or absent" (*Alston*, 'P. Z. S.' 1876, p. 86). There are two subfamilies —*Spalacinæ* and *Bathyerginæ*.

GENUS RHIZOMYS—THE BAMBOO-RAT.

"Form robust; eyes very small; ears very short, naked; pollex rudimentary; tail rather short, partially haired; skull broad; occipital plane only slightly sloped forward; infra-orbital opening small, subtriangular; upper incisors arched forward; no premolar; upper molars with one deep internal and two or more external enamel-folds; the lower molars reversed."—*Alston.*

No. 396. RHIZOMYS BADIUS.

The Chestnut Bamboo-Rat (*Jerdon's No.* 201).

NATIVE NAME.—Known to the Chingpaws or Kakhyens as the *Yewcron.—Anderson.*

HABITAT.—The Sikim and Nepal Terai; Burmah; Arakan; Kakhyen Hills.

DESCRIPTION.—Fine fur, of a grey or slaty grey for two-thirds of the basal portion, the remaining upper third being from a deep to a bright chestnut. "Most intense on the head, and dullest on the rump" (*Anderson*). "Below dark ashy grey" (*Jerdon*). "The fur of the under-parts in these Eastern examples of the species" (referring to those from the Kakhyen hills) "is paler and more reddish than chestnut, whereas in some Nepal animals it inclines even to slaty grey, washed with reddish. The area immediately around the muzzle and the chin is pale brownish, with a tinge of greyish, and the teeth are brilliant reddish, the nose, ears, feet, and tail being pale flesh-coloured" (*Anderson*, 'Anat. and Zool. Res.' p. 329).

Rhizomys badius.

SIZE.—Head and body, 7 inches; tail, about 2½ inches.

Jerdon says of this species that "it eats the roots of bamboos and other trees, constructing burrows under the roots. It is said to be very bold, and easily taken." "In Burmah it constructs its burrows amongst a rank and tall jungle grass, on the roots of which it is said to live" (*Anderson*). Blyth, who writes of the Burmese form, says: "it is barely separable from *R. badius*, from which it seems to differ only in its much brighter colouring."

No. 397. RHIZOMYS ERYTHROGENYS.

The Red-cheeked Bamboo-Rat.

HABITAT.—Burmah; the Salween hill tracts; Tenasserim.

DESCRIPTION.—Upper parts dark iron grey; almost black on the top of the head; the upper lip, chin and upper part of the throat are white, also the chest and belly, which are however more or less tinged with grey and reddish; the lower portion of the throat is dark grey; the sides of the head and cheeks are bright golden red; the feet are sparsely clad and leaden coloured, except the toes of the hind feet, which are fleshy white; tail rather thick at the base, quite naked, not scaly, and of a leaden hue; claws rather broad, and moderately strong.

SIZE (of the living female).—Head and body, 14¾ inches; tail, 5·35 inches.

Dr. Anderson, from whose work I have taken the above description, and who was the first to describe and name this animal, says that a female was recently received in the Zoological Gardens from Mr. A. H. Hildebrand.

No. 398. RHIZOMYS PRUINOSUS.

The Hoary Bamboo-Rat.

HABITAT.—Assam; very common about Cherrapoonjee; Burmah; Kakhyen hills east of Bhamo.

DESCRIPTION.—Brown above, grizzled with white; the base of the fur being slaty grey, tipped with brown, and intermixed with longer hairs, terminating in white bands; underneath much the same, only the white-tipped hairs are shorter and less numerous; whiskers dark brown; the head is generally more grey; ears, nose, feet and tail of a dusky flesh tint; tail one-third of the body.

SIZE.—Head and body, about 11 to 13 inches; tail, 3 to 4 inches.

No. 399. RHIZOMYS MINOR.

The Small Bamboo-Rat.

NATIVE NAME.—*Khai*, Arracanese.

HABITAT.—Burmah, Upper Martaban, and at Yanageen on the Irrawaddy.—*Blyth.*

DESCRIPTION.—"Dark sooty brown above, slightly tinged with deep umber, which is most distinct on the sides of the head and neck, and in reflected light; the under parts are like the upper, only the brown tint is almost absent; the whiskers are black, and tail very sparsely haired" (*Anderson*). "Dusky brown colour, with white muzzle and around the eye, and pale naked feet" (*Blyth*).

SIZE.—Head and body, $6\frac{1}{2}$ inches; tail, $1\frac{3}{4}$ inch.

Blyth says he obtained a living specimen in Upper Martaban, and recognised it as the same as what had been obtained in Siam. The Rev. Mr. Mason writes of it: "This animal, which burrows under old bamboo roots, resembles a marmot more than a rat; yet it has much of the rat in its habits. I one night caught a specimen gnawing a cocoa-nut, while camping out in the jungles."

I may here mention a curious little animal, which is apparently a link between the MURIDÆ and the SPALACIDÆ, *Myospalax fuscocapillus*, named and described by Blyth ('J. A. S. B.' xv. p. 141), found at Quetta, where it is called the "Quetta mole." A full account of it by Mr. W. T. Blanford is to be found in the 'Journal Asiatic Society of Bengal,' (vol. L. pt. ii.).

FAMILY DIPODIDÆ.

This family contains a form of rodent similar to, yet more pronounced than, the jerboa rats, of which I have already treated. It includes the true Jerboas (*Dipus*), the American Jumping Mice (*Zapus*), the *Alactaga*, and the Cape Jumping Hare (*Pedetes caffer*). The characteristics of the family are as follows:—

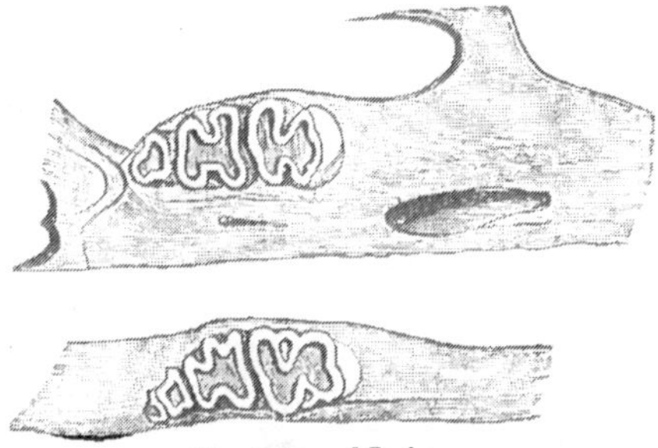

Dentition of Jerboa.

"Incisors compressed; premolars present or absent; grinding teeth rooted or rootless, not tuberculate, with more or fewer transverse enamel folds; skull with the brain-case short and broad; infra-orbital opening rounded, very large (often as large as the orbit); zygomatic arch slender, curved downwards; the malar ascending in front to the lachrymal in a flattened perpendicular plate; facial surface of maxillaries minutely perforated; mastoid portion of

DIPUS.

auditory bullæ usually greatly developed; metatarsal bones elongated, often fused into a cannon bone; form gracile; front portion of body and fore-limbs very small; hind limbs long and strong, with from three to five digits; tail long, hairy. Three sub-families" (*Alston* On the Order GLIRES, 'P. Z. S.' 1876). The three sub-families are *Zapodidæ*,* *Dipodinæ* and *Pedetinæ*, but we have only to deal with the second.

GENUS DIPUS—THE JERBOAS.

Hind feet with three digits; tail cylindrical and tufted; incisors grooved; premolars absent, or, if found, then in the upper jaw and rudimentary; skull with very broad occipital region; greatly developed auditory bullæ; the cervical vertebræ are more or less anchylosed, and the metatarsals are united. They are not found in the plains of India, though one species inhabits Yarkand, and two more are found in Eastern Persia.

NO. 400. DIPUS LAGOPUS.

The Yarkand Jerboa.

HABITAT.—Koshtak, south of Yarkand; Yarkand; and Yangihissar. —*Blanford.*

DESCRIPTION.—"Colour above light sandy brown, slightly washed with dusky, below pure white; a white band across the outside of the thigh; tail pale brown above, whitish below, with a tuft of longer hair, altogether about 2½ inches long; at the end the terminal portion pure white, the proximal portion black or dark-brown on the upper part and sides, but brown or white beneath the tail. The fur is very soft and rather long, 0·6 to 0·8 inch in the middle of the back; on the upper parts it is ashy grey at the base and for the greater parts of its length, pale sandy brown near the end; the extreme tip dusky brown; on the lower parts it is white throughout; ears about half the length of the head, oval, naked inside, thinly clothed with short brown hair outside; face sandy; the hairs grey at the base; sides of head whitish; whiskers as usual very long, exceeding three inches; the uppermost brown; the longest white, except at the base; the lower entirely white; the long hairs beneath the hind feet all white, as are the feet throughout."—*Blanford*, 'Sc. Res. of Sec. Yarkand Mission,' pp. 58, 59.

* Formerly *Jaculinæ*.

GENUS ALACTAGA.

"Hind feet with *five* digits, of which the first and fifth do not reach the ground; tail cylindrical, tufted; skull with the occipital region less broad, and the auditory bullæ smaller; infra-orbital opening with no separate canal for the nerve; incisors plain. One very small premolar present above only."—*Alston.*

NO. 401. ALACTAGA INDICA.

NATIVE NAME.—*Khanee*, Afghan.

HABITAT.—Afghanistan; Eastern Persia.

DESCRIPTION.—Fawn colour above; the hair with black tips and ashy grey at the base; under-parts white; upper parts of thigh white; a black spot behind and inside the thigh just below the white; remainder of the outside and lower part of the inside of the thighs brown; a white line running down the front, and extending over the upper portion of the tarsi and feet; proximal portion of tarsus brown at the sides. (*See* 'Blanford's Eastern Persia,' vol. ii. p. 77.) The tail is brown with a white tip; ears thinly clad with brown hairs; head brown above, whitish around the eyes; whiskers black.

SIZE.—Head and body, 3½ inches; tail, 7 inches.

This animal is unfortunately named, as it is not Indian at all; equally unfortunate, as Mr. Blanford has shown, is Blyth's name *Bactrianus*, for it does not inhabit that tract, so the original title stands. Hutton, in his 'Rough Notes on the Zoology of Candahar' ('J. A. S. B.' xv. p. 137), writes of it as follows: "This beautiful little animal is abundant over all the stony plains throughout the country, burrowing deeply, and when unearthed bounding away with most surprising agility after the manner of the kangaroo-rat. It is easily tamed, and lives happily enough in confinement if furnished with plenty of room to leap about. It sleeps all day, and so soundly that it may be taken from its cage and examined without awaking it; or at most it will half open one eye in a drowsy manner for an instant, and immediately close it again in sleep. It retires to its burrows about the end of October, and remains dormant till the following April, when it throws off its lethargy and again comes forth." There is a good engraving of this animal in Cassel's new Natural History.

We have now closed our account of the Myomorpha or Mouse-like Rodents, and will proceed to the next Section, HYSTRICOMORPHA, or Porcupine-like Rodents.

SECTION III.—HYSTRICOMORPHA.

PORCUPINE-LIKE RODENTS.

This section contains six families, viz. :—

Octodontidæ ..	.. =	3 sub-families, 18 genera.
Hystricidæ ..	.. =	2 sub-families, 5 genera.
Chinchillidæ ..	.. =	5 genera, of which two are fossil.
Dasyproctidæ ..	.. =	2 genera.
Dionymidæ ..	.. =	1 genus.
Caviidæ ..	.. =	3 genera.

Of these we have to deal with but one, the second family, *Hystricidæ*, the rest belonging to Africa in part, but the majority to the American continent, chiefly South America.

I give the general characteristics of the section as laid down by Mr. Alston :—

"One premolar above and below (except in *Ctenodactylus*); grinding teeth rooted or rootless, not tuberculate; frontals with no distinct post-orbital processes (except in *Chætomys*); infra-orbital opening large, subtriangular, or oval; zygomatic arch proportionately stout; molar not advancing far forward, (except in *Ctenodactylinæ* and *Chinchillidæ*) and not supported below by a continuation of the maxillary zygomatic process; incisive foramina small; foramina in the base of skull proportionally large; an inter-pterygoid fissure; mandible with its angular portion springing from the *outer side* of the bony covering of the lower incisor, triangular, usually pointed behind; coronoid process small, and condyle low; clavicles perfect or imperfect; fibula persistent as a distinct bone throughout life; upper lip rarely cleft; muffle clad with fine hairs; nostrils pointed above, sigmoid or linear; ears usually emarginate behind; tail hairy, sub-naked, or scaly."—'P. Z. S.,' 1876, p. 90.

As I have said before, we have only to do with the *Hystricidæ* or Porcupines, but many of the others are familiar by name. Of the *Octodontidæ* the best known is the coypu of the Andes, one of the largest of the rodents, and the ground-rat or ground-pig of western and southern Africa. The chinchilla, which is the typical form of the third family, is known to all, especially ladies, from its delicate soft fur. The agouti of South America is the representative of the *Dasyproctidæ*. The family *Dinomyidæ* consists of one animal only, *Dinomys Branickii*; the only known example of which was obtained in Peru on the Montana de Vitoc. It was found walking about in a yard at daybreak, and showed so little fear of man that it suffered itself to be killed by the stroke of a sword. It is a pity no one was sensible enough to try and take it alive. As yet nothing is known of its habits. Of the last family, *Caviidæ*, the cavy and the capybara are well known to travellers in South America, and the common guinea pig is familiar to us all.

FAMILY HYSTRICIDÆ—THE PORCUPINES.

In this family the hairs of the body are more or less converted into spines or quills; the form of the skull is peculiar, being ovate, often greatly inflated with air cavities in the bones; the facial portion is broad and short; the malar portion of the zygomatic arch has no inferior angular process as in the *Octodontidæ;* the occipital plane or hinder-surface is perpendicular, with a median ridge; the incisor teeth are large and powerful; the molars with external and internal folds, four in each jaw. The form is robust; limbs sub-equal; fore-feet with four toes, and a small wart-like thumb; hind-feet with four and five toes; tail long in some, short in others. There are two sub-families,—*Sphingurinæ* and *Hystricinæ.* With the genera of the first we have nothing to do. They include the prehensile-tailed porcupines of South America, *Sphingurus prehensilis*, *S. villosus*, and *S. Mexicanus*, all arboreal forms, and the Canada porcupine (*Erythizon dorsatus*) which is covered with woolly hairs and spines intermixed. The true porcupines, sub-family *Hystricinæ*, consist of two genera, both of which are represented in India—*Atherura* and *Hystrix*.

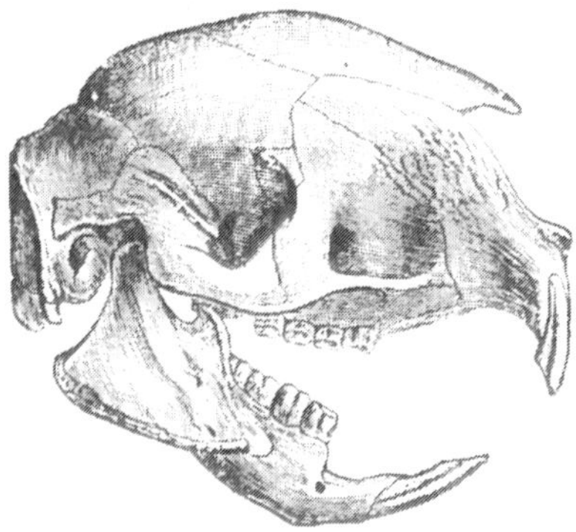

Skull of Porcupine.

SUB-FAMILY HYSTRICINÆ—THE TRUE PORCUPINES.

Grinding teeth semi-rooted; skull rather more elongate; infra-orbital foramen of great size; clavicles imperfect, attached to the sternum, and not to the scapula; upper lip furrowed; tail not prehensile; soles of feet smooth. The female has six mammæ. In these points they differ from the American arboreal porcupines (*Sphingurus*), the skull of which is very short, the tail prehensile, the soles of the feet tuberculated, and the female has only four mammæ.

The two genera, *Atherura* and *Hystrix*, which compose this subfamily, are distinguished by long tail and flattened spines (*Atherura*), and short tail and round spines (*Hystrix*).

GENUS ATHERURA—THE LONG-TAILED PORCUPINE.

Nasal part of skull moderate; upper molars with one internal and three or four external folds, the latter soon separated as enamel loops; the lower teeth similar but reversed; the spines are flattened and channelled; the tail long and scaly, with a tuft of bristles at the end.

No. 402. ATHERURA FASCICULATA.

The Brush-tailed Porcupine.

HABITAT.—Assam, Khasia hills, Tipperah hills, Burmah, Siam, and the Malayan peninsula.

DESCRIPTION.—"The general tint of the animal is yellowish-brown, freckled with dusky brown, especially on the back; the spines, taken separately, are brown white at the root, and become gradually darker to the point; the points of the spines on the back are very dark, being of a blackish-brown colour. The long and stout bristles, which are mixed with the spines on the back, are similarly coloured" (*Waterhouse*, 'Mammalia,' vol. ii. p. 472). The spines are flat on the under-surface and concave on the upper, sharply pointed and broadest near the root. Mixed with the spines on the back are long bristles, very stout, projecting some three inches beyond the spines, which are only about an inch in length; below these is a scanty undergrowth of pale coloured hairs; the tail is somewhat less than half the length of the head and body, scaly, and at the end furnished with a large tuft of flattened bristles from three to four inches long, of a dirty white colour, with sometimes dusky tips; the ears are semi-ovate; whiskers long and stout, and of a brown colour; muzzle hairy; feet short, five toes, but the thumb very small, with a short rounded nail.

SIZE.—Head and body, 18 inches; tail, exclusive of tuft, 7½ inches.

Specimens of this animal were sent home to the Zoological Gardens, from Cherrapoonjee in the Khasia hills, by Dr. Jerdon. This species is almost the same as the African form (*A. Africana*). They are about the same in size and form and in general appearance. This last is found in such plenty, according to Bennett, in the Island of Fernando Po as to afford a staple article of food to the inhabitants. Blyth was of opinion that the Indian animal is much paler and more freckled than the African.

GENUS HYSTRIX—THE PORCUPINE.

"Spines cylindrical; tail short, covered with spines and slender-stalked open quills; nasal cavity usually very large; air sinuses of frontals greatly developed; teeth as in *Atherura*. The hind-feet with five toes; claws very stout."

The hinder part of the body is covered by a great number of sharp spines, ringed black and white, mostly tipped with white; the spines are hollow or filled with a spongy tissue, but extremely tough and resistant, with points as sharp as a needle. The animal is able to erect these by a contraction of the skin, but the old idea that they could be projected or shot out at an assailant is erroneous. They easily drop out, which may have given an idea of discharge. The porcupine attacks by backing up against an opponent or thrusting at him by a sidelong motion. I kept one some years ago, and had ample opportunity of studying his mode of defence. When a dog or any other foe comes to close quarters, the porcupine wheels round and rapidly charges back. They also have a side-way jerk which is effective.

No. 403. HYSTRIX LEUCURA.

The White-tailed Indian Porcupine (Jerdon's No. 204).

NATIVE NAMES.—*Kanta-sahi, Sayi, Sayal, Sarsel,* Hindi; *Sajru,* Bengali; *Chotia-dumsee,* Nepali; *Saori,* Gujrati; *Salendra* and *Sayal,* Mahrathi; *Yed,* Canarese; *Ho-igu,* Gondi; *Phyoo,* Burmese; *Heetava,* Singhalese.

HABITAT.—All over India (except perhaps Lower Bengal), Burmah and Ceylon.

DESCRIPTION.—Blackish-brown; muzzle clad with short, stiff, bristly hairs; whiskers long and black, and a few white spines on the face; spines on the throat short, grooved, some with white setaceous points forming a half-collar; crest of head and neck formed of long black bristles, with here and there one with a long white tip; the spines of the sides are short, flattish, grooved or striated, mostly with white points; the large quills of the back are either entirely black or ringed at the base and middle with white, a few with white tips; the longer and thinner quills on the back and sides have long white terminations; many of these again, particularly the longest, have a basal and one or two central white rings; the short quills on the mesial line of the lumbar region are nearly all white, and the longer striated quills of this region are mostly white; quills of the tail white or yellowish, a few black ones at the root; pedunculated quills are long, broad, and much flattened in old animals.

SIZE.—Head and body, 32 inches; tail, 8 inches.

The description given in his 'Prodromus Faunæ Zeylanicæ' by

Dr. Kellaart, who was a most careful observer, has been of great assistance to me in the above, as it was also, I fancy, to Jerdon, and his subsequent remarks are worthy of consideration. "The identification of species from single characters," he observes, "is at all times difficult and unsatisfactory in the genus *Hystrix*, particularly so as regard the conformation of the skull." And again: "The number of molars varies also in different specimens. In two adults obtained at Trincomalee there were only three molars on each side of the jaw, four being the dental formula of the genus *Hystrix*."

Hystrix leucura.

I think such aberrations ought to warn us from trying to make too many genera out of these animals. Dr. Gray, whose particular forte—or shall I say weakness?—was minute subdivision, classed (in 1847) the Indian porcupines in three sub-families, *Hystrix*, *Acanthion*, and *Atherura*; and *Acanthion* he some years after (1866, *see* 'P. Z. S.' p. 308) divided again into three groups, *Œdocephalus*, *Acanthochœrus* and *Acanthion*. The difference in the skull of *Hystrix* and *Acanthion* lies in the intermaxillaries and the grinders, as follows:—

Hystrix—Inter-max. broad, truncated, wide behind as before; *grinders* oblong, longer than broad, one fold on the inner, and three or four on the outer side.

Acanthion—Inter-max. triangular, tapering behind; *grinders* sub-cylindrical, not longer than broad, one fold on the inner, two or three on the outer side.

According to Waterhouse the European porcupine (*Hystrix cristata* of Linnæus) is the *Acanthion Cuvieri* of Gray; and Gray, who afterwards modified his views of 1847 in 1866, wrote of it: "I am not aware of any external characters by which this species can be distinguished from the *Hystrix cristata*, though the skull is so different." Gray in another place writes that: "Though the skulls of *H. leucurus* preserve a very distinct character, yet they vary so much amongst themselves as to show that skulls afford no better character for the distinction of species than any other single character, such as colour, but can only be depended on when taken in connection with the rest of the organisation." In these circumstances I think it will be better not to attempt any further sub-division of the Indian porcupines in the present work beyond the two already given, viz. *Hystrix* and *Atherura.* There is a great similarity between the Indian *H. leucura* and the European *H. cristata.* According to Waterhouse the quills in the lumbar region, which are white in the Indian, are dusky in the European, which last has long white points to the bristles of the crest, whereas in the Indian one some only of the points are white, and the rest quite brown.

The Indian porcupine lives in burrows, in banks, hill sides, on the bunds of tanks, and in the sides of rivers and nullahs. It is nocturnal in its habits, and in the vicinity of cultivation does much damage to such garden stuff as consists of tubers or roots. In the jungle its food consists chiefly of roots, especially of some kinds of wild yam (*Dioscorea*). I have found porcupines in the densest bamboo jungles of the central provinces, where their food was doubtless young bamboo shoots and various kind of roots.

The porcupine all the world over is known to be good eating, and is in many countries esteemed a delicacy. The flesh is white and tender, and is much prized by most people in those places where it abounds. Brigadier-General McMaster, in his 'Notes on Jerdon,' in speaking of the only instance where he found a porcupine on the move after day-light, says: "Just at dawn a porcupine appeared, and, as I suppose his house was somewhere between us, trotted and fed, grunting hog-like, about the little valley at our feet until long after the sun was well up, and until I, despairing of other game, and bearing in mind his delicious flesh (for that of a porcupine is the most delicate I know of), shot him. Well may the flesh be tender and of delicate flavour, for, as many gardeners know to their cost, porcupines are most scrupulously dainty and epicurean as to their diet. A pine-apple is left by them until the very night before it is fit to be cut. Peas, potatoes, onions, &c., are not touched until the owner has made up his mind that they were just ready for the table." The Gonds in Seonee were always on the look-out for a porcupine. I described in my book on that district the digging out of one.

"The entrance of the animal's abode was a hole in a bank at which the dogs were yelping and scratching; but the bipeds had gone more scientifically to work by countermining from above, sinking shafts downwards at various points, till at last they reached his inner chamber, when he scuttled out, and, charging backwards at the dogs with all his spines erected, he soon sent them flying, howling most piteously; but a Gondee axe hurled at his head soon put an end to his career, for a porcupine's skull is particularly tender."

The female produces from two to four young, which are born with their eyes open. Their bodies are covered with short soft spines, which, however, speedily harden. It is said that the young do not remain long with their mother, but I cannot speak to this from personal experience. I have had young ones, but not those born in captivity.

No. 404. HYSTRIX BENGALENSIS.

The Bengal Porcupine (*Jerdon's No.* 205).

NATIVE NAME.—*Sajaru* or *Sajru*, Bengali.

DESCRIPTION.—"Smaller than the last; crest small and thin; the bristles blackish; body spines much flattened and strongly grooved, terminating in a slight seta or bristle; slender flexible quills much fewer than in *leucura*, white, with a narrow black band about the centre; the thick quills basally white, the rest black, mostly with a white tip; a distinct white demi-collar; spines of lumbar region white, as are those of tail and rattle; muzzle less hirsute than in *leucura*."

SIZE.—Head and body, 28 inches; tail, 8 inches.

There is occasionally a variety to be found of this species with orange-coloured quills, or rather the orange hue is assumed at times. Jerdon mentions the fact that Sclater describes his *H. Malabarica* as having certain orange-coloured quills in place of white, and also that Blyth considered the two species identical. He also states that Mr. Day procured specimens of the orange porcupine from the Ghâts of Cochin and Travancore, and that they were considered more delicate eating by the native sportsmen, who aver that they can distinguish the two kinds by the smell from their burrows; but he was not apparently aware at the time that a specimen of *H. Malabarica* with orange quills in the Zoological Gardens in London moulted, and the red quills were replaced by the ordinary black and white ones of the common Indian kind. Dr. Sclater afterwards (*see* 'P. Z. S.' 1871, p. 234) came to the conclusion that *H. Malabarica* was synonymous with *H. leucura*.

No. 405. HYSTRIX (ACANTHION) LONGICAUDA.

The Crestless Porcupine (*Jerdon's No.* 206).

NATIVE NAMES. — *Anchotia-sahi* or *Anchotia-dumsi* in Nepal; *Sathung*, Lepcha; *O'—e* of the Limbus (*Hodgson*). (N.B.—The *ch* must not be pronounced as *k*, but as *ch* in church.) *Anchotia* means crestless, the crested porcupine being called *Chotia-dumsi*.

HABITAT.—Nepal and Sikim, and on through Burmah to the Malayan peninsula, where it was first discovered.

DESCRIPTION.—Distinguished from the other species "by its inferior size, total absence of crest on its head, neck, and shoulders, by its longer tail, by the white collar of the neck being evanescent, and lastly by the inferior size and smaller quantity of the spines or quills."—*Hodgson.*

It is covered with black spinous bristles from two to three inches long, shortest on the head and limbs. The large quills of the back and croup are from seven to twelve inches long, mostly with one central black ring.

SIZE.—Head and body, 24 inches; tail, 4, or with the quills, $5\frac{1}{2}$ inches.

This is Hodgson's *H. alophus*, which is, I think, a more appropriate name than the one given, for its tail is not so very long in proportion. Hodgson says of it: "They breed in spring, and usually produce two young about the time the crops ripen. They are monogamous, the pair dwelling together in burrows of their own formation. Their flesh is delicious, like pork, but much more delicate flavoured, and they are easily tamed so as to breed in confinement. All tribes and classes, even high-caste Hindoos, eat them, and it is deemed lucky to keep one or two alive in stables, where they are encouraged to breed. Royal stables are seldom without at least one of them."

This animal was described by Gray as *Acanthion Hodgsonii*, the *lesser Indian porcupine*. Waterhouse, in writing of *Hystrix* (*Acanthion*) *Javanica*, says: "The habits of the animal, as recorded by Müller, do not differ from those of *H. Hodgsonii*"; and Blyth, as mentioned by Jerdon, was of opinion that the two species were one and the same. The *Acanthochærus Grotei*, described and figured by Dr. Gray in 1866 ('P. Z. S.' p. 306), is the same as this species. It is to be found at Darjeeling amongst the tea plantations, between 4000 and 5000 feet elevation.

No. 406. HYSTRIX YUNNANENSIS.

HABITAT.—Burmah, in the Kakhyen hills, at elevations of from 2000 to 4500 feet.

DESCRIPTION—after Dr. Anderson, who first discovered and named this species: "Dark brown on the head, neck, shoulders, and sides passing into a deep black on the extremities, a very narrow white line passing backwards from behind the angle of the mouth to the shoulder; under surface brownish; the spiny hairs of the anterior part of the trunk flattened, grooved or ungrooved. The crest begins behind the occiput and terminates before the shoulders; the hairs are long, slender and backwardly curved, the generality of them being about 4½ inches long, while the longer hairs measure about six inches.

"They are all paler than the surrounding hairs, and the individual hairs are either broadly tipped with yellowish-white, or they have a broad sub-apical band of that colour. The short, broad, spiny hairs, lying a short way in front of the quills, are yellow at their bases, the remaining portion being deep brown, whereas those more quill-like spiny hairs, immediately before the quills, have both ends yellow tipped.

"The quills are wholly yellow, with the exception of a dark brown, almost black band of variable breadth and position. It is very broad in the shorter quills, and is nearer the free end of the quill than its base, whereas in the long slender quills it is reduced to a narrow mesial band. The stout strong quills rarely exceed six inches in length, whilst the slender quills are one foot long. Posteriorly above the tail and at its sides many of the short quills are pure white. The modified quills on the tail, with dilated barb-like free ends are not numerous, and are also white. There are three kinds of rattle quills, the most numerous measure 0·65 inch in the length of the dilated hollow part, having a maximum breadth of 0·21 inch, whilst there are a few short cups 0·38 inch in length, with a breadth of 0·17 inch, and besides these a very few more elongated and narrow cylinders occur."—'Anat. and Zool. Res.,' p. 332.

SUB-ORDER DUPLICIDENTATA—DOUBLE-TOOTHED RODENTS.

These rodents are distinguished by the presence of two small additional incisors behind the upper large ones. At birth there are four such rudimentary incisors, but the outer two are shed, and disappear at a very early age; the remaining two are immediately behind the large middle pair, and their use is doubtful; but, as Dallas remarks, "their presence is however of interest, as indicating the direction in which an alliance with other forms of mammalia more abundantly supplied with teeth is to be sought."

Another distinctive characteristic of this sub-order is the formation of the bony palate, which is narrowed to a mere bridge between the alveolar borders, or portions of the upper jaw in which the grinding teeth are inserted.

The following synopsis of the sub-order is given by Mr. Alston :—

Incisors $\frac{4}{2}$; at birth $\frac{6}{2}$; the outer upper incisor soon lost; the next pair very small, placed directly behind the large middle pair; their enamel continuous round the tooth, but much thinner behind; skull with the optic foramina confluent, with no true alisphenoid canal; incisive foramina usually confluent; bony palate reduced to a bridge between the alveolar borders; fibula anchylosed to tibia below, and articulating with the calcaneum; testes permanently external; no vescicular glands. Two families."—'P. Z. S.' 1876, p. 97.

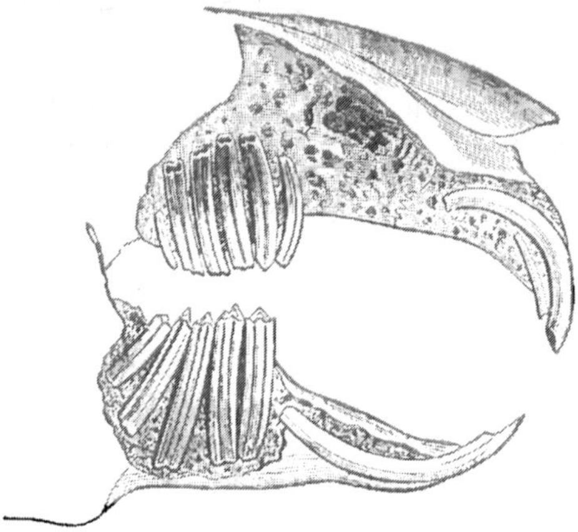

Dentition of Hare.

There are only two families each of one existing genus—LEPORIDÆ, genus *Lepus*, the Hare; and LAGOMYIDÆ, genus *Lagomys*, the Pika, or Mouse-Hare, as Jerdon calls it. There are three fossil genera in the first family, viz. *Palæolagus*, a fossil hare found in the Miocene of Dacota and Colorado, *Panolax* from the Pliocene marls of Santa Fe, and *Praotherium* from Pennsylvanian bone-caves. A fossil Lagomys, genus *Titanomys*, is found in the Post-Pliocene deposits in various parts of Europe, chiefly in the south.

FAMILY LEPORIDÆ—THE HARES.

"Three premolars above and two below; molars rootless, with transverse enamel folds dividing them into lobes; skull compressed; frontals with large wing-shaped post-orbital processes; facial portion of maxillaries minutely reticulated; basisphenoid with a median perforation, and separated by a fissure from the vomer; coronoid process represented by a thin ridge of bone; clavicles imperfect; ears and hind-limbs elongated, tail short, bushy, recurved."—*Alston.*

Hares are found all over the world except in Australasia. The Rabbit is much more localised; in India we have none, unless the Hispid Hare, the black rabbit of Dacca sportsmen, is a true rabbit; it is said to burrow, but whether it is gregarious I know not. Another point would also decide the question, viz. are the young born with eyes open or shut? The hare pairs at about a year old, and has several broods a year of from two to five; the young are born covered with hair and their eyes open, whereas young rabbits are born blind and naked. The hare lives in the open, and its lair or "form" is merely a slight depression in some secluded spot. It has been noticed that the hare always returns to its form, no matter to what distance it may have wandered or have been driven.

No. 407. Lepus ruficaudatus.

The Common Indian Red-tailed Hare (*Jerdon's No.* 207).

Native Names.—*Khargosh*, *Kharra*, Hindi; *Sasru*, Bengali; *Mullol*, Gondi.

Habitat.—India generally.

Description.—"General hue rufescent, mixed with blackish on the back and head; ears brownish anteriorly, white at the base, and the tip brown; neck, breast, flanks and limbs more or less dark sandy rufescent, unmottled; nape pale sandy rufescent; tail rufous above, white beneath; upper lip small; eye-mark, chin, throat, and lower parts pure white." —*Jerdon.*

Size.—Head and body, 20 inches; tail, with hair, 4 inches; ear externally about 5 inches; maximum weight, about 5 lbs.

The Indian hare is generally found in open bush country, often on the banks of rivers, at least as far as my experience goes in the Central Provinces. Jerdon says, and McMaster corroborates his statement, that this species, as well as the next, take readily to earth when pursued, and seem to be well acquainted with all the fox-holes in their neighbourhood, and McMaster adds that they seem to be well aware which holes have foxes or not, and never go into a tenanted one.

The Indian hare is by no means so good for the table as the European one, being dry and tasteless, and hardly worth cooking.

No. 408. Lepus nigricollis.

The Black-naped Hare (*Jerdon's No.* 208).

Native Names.—*Khargosh*, Hindi; *Malla*, Canarese; *Sassa*, Mahrathi; *Musal*, Tamil; *Kundali*, Telegu; *Haba*, Singhalese.

Habitat.—Southern India and Ceylon; stated to be found also in Sind and the Punjab.

Description.—"Upper part rufescent yellow, mottled with black; single hairs annulated yellow and black; chin, abdomen, and inside of hind-limbs downy white; a black velvety spot on the occiput and upper part of neck extending to near the shoulders; the spot under the neck is in some specimens of a bright yellow colour; ears long, greyish-brown, internally with white fringes, at the apical part dusky, posteriorly black at the base; feet yellowish; tail above grizzled with black and yellow, beneath white."—*Kellaart.*

SIZE.—Head and body, 19 inches; tail, 2¼ inches; ears, 4¾ inches.

A friend of Brigadier-General McMaster's, writing to him, says: "The black-naped hare of the Neilgherries, which appears to be the same as that of the plains, only larger from the effect of climate, often, when chased by dogs, runs into holes and hollow trees. I have found some of the Neilgherry hares to be nearly, if not quite, equal to the English hares in flavour. I think a great deal depends upon keeping and cooking.

NO. 409. LEPUS PEGUENSIS.

The Pegu Hare.

NATIVE NAME.—*Yung*, Arakanese.

HABITAT.—Pegu, Burmah.

DESCRIPTION.—Very like *L. ruficaudatus*, but with the tail *black* above; the colour of the upper parts is separated more distinctly from the pure white of the under parts.

SIZE.—Head and body, about 20 inches.

NO. 410. LEPUS HYPSIBIUS.

The Mountain Hare.

HABITAT.—Northern Ladakh.

DESCRIPTION.—Colour rufous brown, more or less mixed with black on the back, dusky ashy on the rump; lower parts white with a slight rufescent tinge, fur long, woolly, rather curly, and thick; head brown, whitish round the eyes; whiskers partly black, partly white; outside surface of ears brown in front, whitish behind, the brown hairs having short black tips; the extreme tip of ears black; tail white; throughout limbs chiefly white, a brownish band running down the anterior portion of the fore-legs.

SIZE.—Of skin about 24 inches. (*See* Blanford's 'Second Yarkand Mission,' p. 60; also plate iii.)

NO. 411. LEPUS PALLIPES.

The Pale-footed Hare.

NATIVE NAMES.—*Togh*, *Toshkhen*, Yarkandi, i.e. Mountain Hare.

HABITAT.—Yarkand; Thibet.

DESCRIPTION.—"Fur long, dense and soft, of a pale ochre colour, but on the back of the animal pencilled with black; haunches greyish;

under-parts white, chest of a delicate yellow rufous tint; the front of the fore-legs and the fore-feet nearly of the same hue; tarsus almost white, but somewhat suffused with rufous in front; tail white, excepting along the middle portion of the upper surface, where it is grey."—Waterhouse's Mammalia,' vol. ii. p. 62.

SIZE.—Head and body, about 18 inches; tail, with hair about 5 inches.

This hare was first described by Hodgson ('J. A. S. B.,' vol. xi.), who also gave a plate; but there is a full description with an excellent plate in Blanford's 'Scientific Results of the Second Yarkand Mission.'

No. 412. LEPUS TIBETANUS.

The Thibet Hare.

HABITAT.—Little Thibet; Ladakh.

DESCRIPTION.—Ears longer than the head, margined with yellow white internally, externally, with the apex, edged with black and with a narrow edging of black extending about half-way down the hinder margin. The general colour seems to vary, as is the case with most of the mountain hares. According to Waterhouse it is "palish-ashy grey; the back mottled with dusky and yellowish-white; the back of neck pale rufous brown." Two specimens, described by Blanford, are "general colour rufous brown (very dark brownish tawny)," and another, "above dusky brown, with an ashy tinge on the rump." Waterhouse's specimens may have been in the winter dress; the under-parts are white; legs longish and white; tail white, with the upper surface sooty or grey-black. The excellent plate in the Yarkand Report is nearer to Waterhouse's verbal portraiture, being of a mottled ashy grey.

SIZE.—Head and body, about 18 inches; tail, with hair, 4½ inches.

No. 413. LEPUS YARKANDENSIS.

The Yarkand Hare.

NATIVE NAME.—*Toshkhan*, Yarkandi.

HABITAT.—The plains of Yarkand and Kashghar.

DESCRIPTION.—General colour sandy, more or less mixed with dusky; pale isabelline on the sides; no grey on rump; tail dark brown above; ears without black tip; lower parts white; fur soft and long; fore-legs very pale, brown in front; hind-legs still paler, brown outside.

SIZE.—Head and body, about 17 inches; tail, 4 inches.

Mr. Blanford remarks that "one striking peculiarity of this very pale coloured hare is the absence of any black patches, and of all grey coloration throughout." The specimens were all shot in winter too. (*See* Blanford's 'Scientific Results, Second Yarkand Mission,' p. 65, and plate iv., fig. 1.)

No. 414. LEPUS PAMIRENSIS.

The Pamir Hare.

HABITAT.—Lake Sirikal, Pamir.

DESCRIPTION.—Pale sandy brown; almost isabelline on back and sides; rump greyish-white; tail black above; face and anterior portion of the ears concolorous with back; terminal portion of ears black outside at the edge; breast light rufous; lower parts white; fur fine, close and soft; fore-legs in front, and hind-legs outside, with a light brownish tinge.

SIZE.—Head and body, about 17 inches; tail, 4 inches.

The hare is described and named by Mr. W. T. Blanford, and from his full description I have abridged the above short notice. It is also well figured in the 'Yarkand Report,' plate v., fig. 1.

No. 415. LEPUS STOLICZKANUS.

Stoliczka's Hare.

HABITAT.—Kashghar, Altum Artush district, north-east of Kashghar.

DESCRIPTION.—"General colour light sandy brown, much mixed with black on the back; the rump very little paler; tail rather long, black above; face and anterior portion of ears the same colour as the back; terminal portion of ears black outside; nape and breast light rufous; lower parts white. The skull differs much from that of *L. Yarkandensis* and *L. Pamirensis*, the nasals being much more abruptly truncated behind than in either, and the parietal region or sinciput flatter" (Blanford's 'Scientific Results, Second Yarkand Mission,' p. 69, and plate v. fig. 2, skull plate, Va. fig. 2).

SIZE.—Head and body, about 17 inches; tail, with hair, 5 inches.

This hare was obtained by Dr. Stoliczka, and was first described and named by Mr. W. T. Blanford ('J. A. S. B.' vol. xiv. 1875, part ii. p. 110).

No. 416. LEPUS CRASPEDOTIS.

The Large-eared Hare.

HABITAT.—Baluchistan, Pishin.

DESCRIPTION.—Colour brown above, white below; the fur of the back is very pale French grey at the base, then black, and the tip is pale brown, almost isabelline; the black rings are wanting on the nape, hind neck and breast, which, like the fore-legs and hinder part of the tarsi, are pale rufous brown; ears externally mouse brown, blackish-brown on the posterior portion near the tip, the anterior edges white, with rather longer hairs, except near the tip, where the hair is short and black; the posterior margins inside pale isabelline, the pale edge becoming broader near the tip; tail black above, white on the sides and below; whiskers black near the base, white except in the shorter ones throughout the greater part of their length; a pale line from the nose, including the eye, continued back nearly to the ear (Blanford's 'Eastern Persia,' vol. ii. p. 81, with plate).

SIZE.—Head and body, 15 inches; tail, with hair, 4·5 inches; ear, 6 inches; breadth of ear laid flat, 3·25 inches.

This is a new species, described and named by Mr. W. T. Blanford.

No. 417. LEPUS HISPIDUS.

The Hispid Hare.

HABITAT.—The Terai and low forests at the base of the Himalayas.

DESCRIPTION.—"General colour dark or iron grey, with an embrowned ruddy tinge, and the limbs shaded outside, like the body, with black, instead of being unmixed rufous" (*Hodgson*). The inner fur is soft, downy, and of an ash colour, the outer longer, hispid, harsh and bristly. Some of the hairs ringed black and brown, others are pure black and long, the latter more numerous; ears short and broad.

SIZE.—Head and body, 19½ inches; tail, with hair, 2⅛ inches; ears, 2¾ inches.

This animal seems to be a link between the hares and the rabbits. Like the latter, it burrows, and has more equal limbs; but, according to Hodgson, it is not gregarious, but lives in pairs. It would greatly help in the identification of its position if some one would procure the young or a gravid female, and see whether the young are born blind and naked as in the rabbits, or open-eyed and clad with fur as in the hares. Jerdon says it is common at Dacca, and is reported to be found also in the Rajmehal hills, and that its flesh is stated to be white, like that of the rabbit.

FAMILY LAGOMYIDÆ—THE PIKAS, OR MOUSE-HARES.

One or two premolars above and below; grinding teeth as in *Leporidæ*; skull depressed; the frontals are contracted, without the wing-like processes of the hares; a single perforation in the facial surface of the maxillaries; a curious prolongation of the posterior angle of the malar into a process extending almost to the ear tube, or auditory meatus; the basisphenoid is not perforated and separated from the vomer as in *Lepus*; the coronoid process is in the form of a tubercle; the clavicles are complete; ears short; limbs nearly equal; no tail.

GENUS LAGOMYS.

Animals of small size and robust form; short-eared and tailless; two premolars above and below.

No. 418. LAGOMYS ROYLEI.

Royle's Pika (Jerdon's No. 210).

NATIVE NAME.—*Rang-runt*, or *Rang-duni*, in Kunawur.—*Jerdon*.
HABITAT.—The Himalayan range, from Kashmir to Sikim.
DESCRIPTION.—Rabbit grey or brown, with a yellowish-grey tinge, more or less rufous on the head, neck, shoulder and sides of body; a hairy brown muzzle, with pale under-lip; long whiskers, some white, the posterior ones dark; under-parts white; fur soft and fine. The upper lip is lobed as in the hare; ears elliptical, with rounded tops.
SIZE.—From 6 to 8 inches.
The first specimen was sent to England by Dr. Royle, in whose honour Mr. Ogilby named it. It was obtained not far from Simla. It lives in rocky ground or amongst loose stones in burrows, and is the tailless rat described by Turner in his 'Journey to Thibet,' which had perforated the banks of a lake by its holes.

No. 419. LAGOMYS CURZONIÆ.

Curzon's Pika.

HABITAT.—The higher ranges of the Himalayas, from 14,000 to 19,000 feet. It has been found northerly in Ladakh, and easterly in Sikim.
DESCRIPTION.—Pale buff above, tinged with rufous, the sides being more rufescent; head, as far back as the ears, decidedly rufescent; ears large and oval; sides of head and nose dirty fulvous white; under-parts white, with a faint yellow tinge; limbs and soles of feet white; whiskers, some black, some white; fur long, fine and silky.
SIZE.—About 7 inches to 8 inches.

No. 420. LAGOMYS LADACENSIS.

The Ladak Pika.

NATIVE NAMES.—*Zabra*, *Karin*, or *Phisckarin*, Ladakhi.
HABITAT.—High plateaux of Ladakh.
DESCRIPTION.—"General hue of the upper body pale buff, fulvous,

with a very slight rufous tint, and tipped with dark brown; below whitish with translucent dusky blue.—*Stoliczka*, quoted by Blanford.

SIZE.—From 7 inches to 9 inches.

It is as yet doubtful whether this is not identical with the last. Mr. Blanford has separated it, and Dr. Günther, agreeing with him, named this species *L. Ladacensis;* but the skull characteristics of *L. Curzoniæ* have not as yet been compared with this, and the separation has been made on external characters only.

No. 421. LAGOMYS AURITUS.

The Large-eared Pika.

HABITAT.—Lukong, on the Pankong lake.

DESCRIPTION.—General colour above smoky or wood brown; the head, shoulders and rump rather paler and more rufous; lower parts whitish, with the dark basal portion of the hair showing through; fur very soft, moderately long; ears large, round, clothed rather thinly inside near the margin with whitish-brown hairs, and outside with much longer hairs of the same colour; whiskers fine and long, the upper dark brown, the lower white; feet whitish. (*See* Blanford's 'Sc. Res. Second Yarkand Mission,' p. 75, plate vi. fig. 2.)

SIZE.—About 8 inches.

No. 422. LAGOMYS MACROTIS.

This seems to be a doubtful species; it may probably prove to be the same as the last, the skulls being similar. Mr. Blanford remarks: "I am strongly disposed to suspect, indeed, that *L. auritus* is the summer *L. macrotis*, the winter garb of the same species; but there are one or two differences which require explanation. The feet appear larger in *L. macrotis*, and the pads of the toes are black, whilst in *L. auritus* they are pale coloured. In the former the long hair of the forehead is lead black at the base, in the latter, pale grey; the feet and lower parts generally are white in *L. macrotis*, buffy white in *L. auritus*, but this may be seasonable."

No. 423. LAGOMYS GRISEUS.

The Grey Pika.

HABITAT.—Yarkand, Kuenlun range, south of Sunju pass.

DESCRIPTION.—General colour dull grey (almost Chinchilla colour), with a slight rufescent tinge on the face and back; lower parts white;

fur very soft, about 0·9 inch long in the middle of the back; glossy leaden black at the base and for about two-thirds of its length, very pale ashy grey towards the end; the extreme tips of many hairs dark brown, and on the back the tips of all the hairs are brownish; the sides are almost pure light ashy; rump still paler; feet white; hair on the face long, light brown on the forehead, greyer on the nose, pure grey on the sides of the head. A few of the upper whiskers black, the rest white; ears large round with rather thin white hairs inside, very short hairs close to the margin, white outside, black inside, outer surface covered with whitish hairs, which become long near the base of the ear. (*See* Blanford's 'Scientific Results, Second Yarkand Mission,' p. 77, and plate vii. fig. 1.)

SIZE.—About 7 inches.

No. 424. LAGOMYS RUFESCENS.

The Red Pika.

HABITAT.—Afghanistan, Persia.

DESCRIPTION.—Pale sandy red, darker on the top of the head, the shoulders and fore part of back; two large patches behind the ears; the feet and the under-parts are pale buff yellow; ears moderately large, subovate and well clad, rusty yellow, paler on the under part; whiskers very long, brown, a few brownish white; toe-pads blackish.

SIZE.—About 8 inches.

This species has been found in the rocky hills of Cabul. *Lagomys Hodgsonii*, from Lahoul, Ladakh and Kulu, is considered to be the same as the above, and *L. Nipalensis*, described by Waterhouse, as synonymous with *L. Roylei.*

Under the systems of older naturalists the thick-skinned animals were lumped together under the order UNGULATA, or *hoofed animals*, subdivided by Cuvier into *Pachydermata*, or thick-skinned non-ruminants, and *Ruminantia*, or ruminating animals; but neither the elephant nor the coney can be called hoofed animals, and in other respects they so entirely differ from the rest that recent systematists have separated them into three distinct orders—*Proboscidea*, *Hyracoidea* and *Ungulata*, which classification I here adopt.

ORDER PROBOSCIDEA.

It seems a strange jump from the order which contains the smallest mammal, the little harvest mouse, to that which contains the gigantic elephant—a step from the ridiculous to the sublime; yet there are points of affinity between the little mouse and the giant tusker to which I will allude further on, and which bring together these two unequal links in the great chain of nature. The order Proboscidea, or animals whose noses are prolonged into a flexible trunk, consists of one genus containing two living species only—the Indian and African Elephants. To this in the fossil world are added two more genera—the *Mastodon* and *Dinotherium*.

The elephant is one of the oldest known of animals. Frequent mention is made in the Scriptures and ancient writings of the use of ivory. In the First Book of Kings and the Second of Chronicles, it is mentioned how Solomon's ships brought every three years from Tarshish gold and silver and ivory (or elephants' teeth) apes and peacocks. In the Apocrypha the animal itself, and its use in war, is mentioned; in the old Sanscrit writings it frequently appears. Aristotle and Pliny were firm believers in the superstition which prevailed, even to more recent times, that it had no joints.

> "The elephant hath joints, but none for courtesy;
> His legs are for necessity, not flexure"—

says Shakespeare. Even down to the last century did this notion prevail, so little did people know of this animal. The supposition that he slept leaning against a tree is to be traced in Thomson's 'Seasons'—

> "Or where the Ganges rolls his sacred waves
> Leans the huge elephant."

Again, Montgomery says—

> "Beneath the palm which he was wont to make
> His prop in slumber."

At a very early period elephants were used in war, not only by the Indian but the African nations. In the first Punic war (B.C. 264–241) they were used considerably by the Carthaginians, and in the second Punic war Hannibal carried thirty-seven of them across the Alps. In the wars of the Moghuls they were used extensively. The domestication of the African elephant has now entirely ceased; there is however no reason why this noble animal should not be made as useful as its Indian brother; it is a bigger animal, and as tractable, judging from the specimens in menageries. It was trained in the time of the Romans for performances in the arena, and swelled the pomp of military triumphs, when, as Macaulay, I think, in his 'Lays of Ancient Rome,' says, the people wondered at—

> "The monstrous beast that had
> A serpent for a hand."

It seems a cruel shame, when one comes to think of it, that thousands of these noble animals should perish annually by all sorts of ignoble means—pitfalls, hamstringing, poisoned arrows, and a few here and there shot with more or less daring by adventurous sportsmen, only for the sake of their magnificent tusks.

Few people think, as they leisurely cut open the pages of a new book or play with their ivory-handled dessert-knives after dinner, of the life that has once been the lot of that inanimate substance, so beautiful in its texture, so prized from time immemorial; still less do they think, for the majority do not know, of the enormous loss of life entailed in purveying this luxury for the market. An elephant is a long-lived beast; it is difficult to say what is the extent of its individual existence; at fifty years it is in its prime, and its reproduction is in ratio slower than animals of shorter life, yet what countless herds must there be in Central Africa when we consider that the annual requirements of Sheffield alone are reported to be upwards of 46,000 tusks, which represent 23,000 elephants a year for the commerce of one single city! The African elephant must be decreasing, even as it has been extirpated in the north of that continent, where it abounded in the time of the Carthaginians, and the time may come when ivory shall be counted as one of the precious things of the past. Even now the price is going up, and is nearly double what it was a year ago. Now enhanced price means either greater demand or deficient supply, and it is probably to this last we must look for an answer to the question. True it is that if we want ivory animals must be killed to get it, for the notion that some people have gained from obsolete works on natural history, to the effect that elephants shed their tusks, is an erroneous one. It is generally supposed that elephants do not shed their tusks at all, not even milk-teeth, but that they grow *ab initio*, as do the incisors of rodents, from a persistent pulp, and continue growing through life. Mr. G. P. Sanderson, the author of 'Thirteen Years among the Wild Beasts,' whom I have to thank for much and valuable information about the habits of these animals, assured me, when I spoke to him about the popular idea of there being milk-tusks, that he had watched elephants from their birth, and had never known them to shed their tusks, nor had his mahouts ever found a shed tusk; but Mr. Tegetmeier has pointed out that there are skulls in the museum of the Royal College of Surgeons, showing both the milk and permanent tusks, the latter pushing forward the former, which are absorbed to a great extent, and leave nothing but a little blackened stump, the size of one's finger. This was brought to my notice by a correspondent of *The Asian*, "Smooth-bore," and I have lately had the pleasure of meeting Mr. Tegetmeier, and speaking to him on the subject. There is apparently no limit to the growth of tusks, so that under favourable circumstances they might attain enormous dimensions, owing to the age of the animal, and absence of the attrition which keeps the incisors of rodents down. As in the case of rodents, malformations of whose incisors I have alluded to some time back, the tusks of elephants assume various freaks. I have heard of their overlapping and crossing the trunk in a manner to impede the free use of that organ. The tusks of fossil elephants are in many cases gigantic. There is a head in the Indian Museum, of which the tusks *outside the socket* measure 9¾ feet, and are of very curious formation. The two run parallel some distance, and then diverge, which would lead one to suppose that the animal inhabited open country, for such a formation would be extremely uncomfortable in thick forest. That tusks of such magnitude are not found nowadays is probably due to the fact that the elephant has more enemies, the most formidable of all being man, which prevent his reaching the great age of those of the fossil periods. It may be said, by those who disbelieve in the extermination of this animal, that, as elephants have provided ivory for several thousand years, they will go on doing so; but I would remind them that in olden days ivory was an article in limited demand, being used chiefly by kings and great nobles; it is only of late years that it has increased more than a hundred-fold. Our forefathers used buck-horn handled knives, and they were without the thousand-and-one little articles of luxury which are now made of ivory; even the requirements of the ancient world drove the elephant away from the coasts, where Solomon, and later still the Romans, got their ivory; and now the girdle round the remaining herds in Central Africa is being narrowed day by day. Mr. Sanderson is of opinion that it is not decreasing in India under the present restrictions, but there is no doubt the reckless slaughter of them in Ceylon has greatly diminished their numbers. Sir Emerson Tennent states that the Government reward was claimed for 3,500 destroyed in part of the northern provinces alone in three years prior to 1848, and between 1851 and 1856, 2000 were killed in the southern provinces.

GENUS ELEPHAS—THE ELEPHANT.

In the writings of older naturalists this animal, so singular in its construction, will be found grouped with the horse, rhinoceros, hippopotamus, tapir, coney, and pig, under the name of pachydermata, the seventh order of Cuvier, but these are now more appropriately divided, as I have said before, into three different orders—Proboscidea, the elephants;

Hyracoidea, the conies; and the rest come under Ungulata. Apparently singular as is the elephant in its anatomy, it bears traces of affinity to both Rodentia and Ungulata. The composition of its massive tusks or incisors, and also of its grinders, resembles that of the Rodents. The tusks grow from a persistent pulp, which forms new ivory coated with enamel, but the grinders are composed of a number of transverse perpendicular plates, or vertical laminæ of dentine, enveloped with enamel, cemented together by layers of a substance called *cortical.* The enamel, by its superior hardness, is less liable to attrition, and, standing above the rest, causes an uneven grinding surface. Each of these plates is joined at the base of the tooth, and on the grinding surface the pattern formed by them distinguishes at once the Indian from the African elephant. In the former, the transverse ridges are in narrow, undulating loops, but in the African they form decided lozenges. These teeth, when worn out, are succeeded by others pushing forward from behind, and not forced up vertically, as in the case of ordinary deciduous teeth, so that it occasionally happens that the elephant has sometimes one and sometimes two grinders on each side, according to age. In the wild state sand and grit, entangled in the roots of plants, help in the work of attrition, and, according to Professor W. Boyd Dawkins, the tame animal, getting cleaner food, and not having such wear and tear of teeth, gets a deformity by the piling over of the plates of which the grinder is composed. An instance of this has come under my notice. An elephant belonging to my brother-in-law, Colonel W. B. Thomson, then Deputy Commissioner

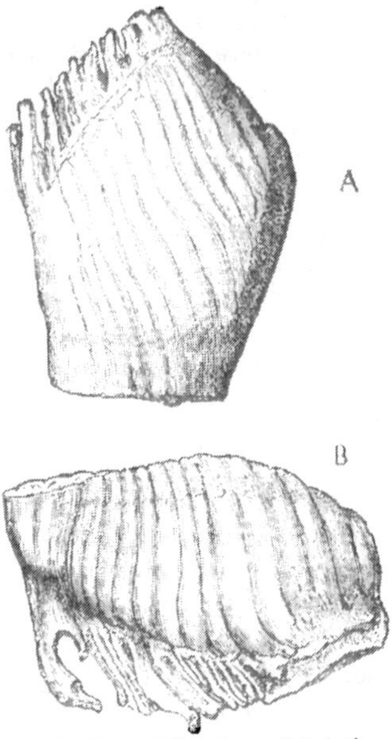

Side view of Grinders of Asiatic Elephant.

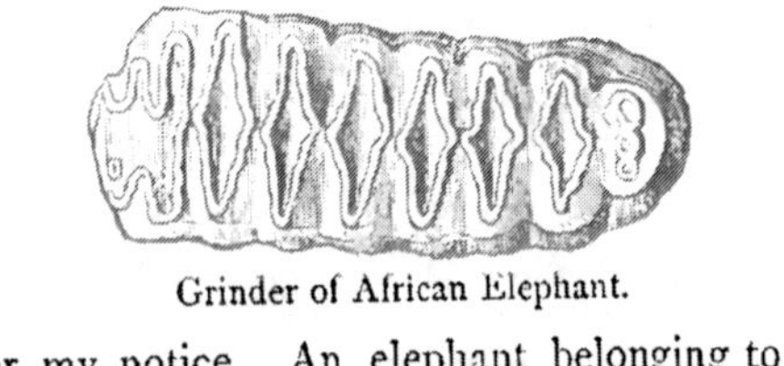
Grinder of Asiatic Elephant.

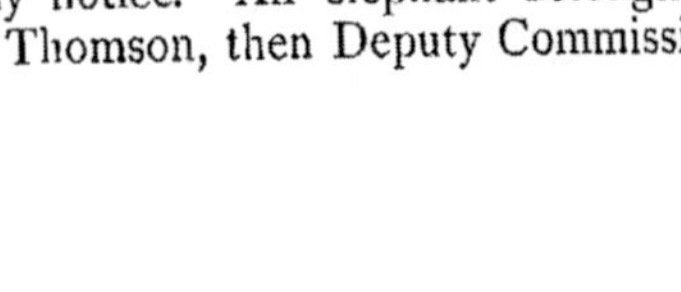
Grinder of African Elephant.

of Seonee, suffered from an aggravated type of this malformation. He was relieved by an ingenious mahout, who managed to saw off the projecting portion of the tooth, which now forms a paper-weight. In my account of Seonee I have given a detailed description of the mode in which the operation was effected.

The skull of the elephant possesses many striking features quite different from any other animal. The brain in bulk does not greatly exceed that of a man, therefore the rest of the enormous head is formed of cellular bone, affording a large space for the attachment of the

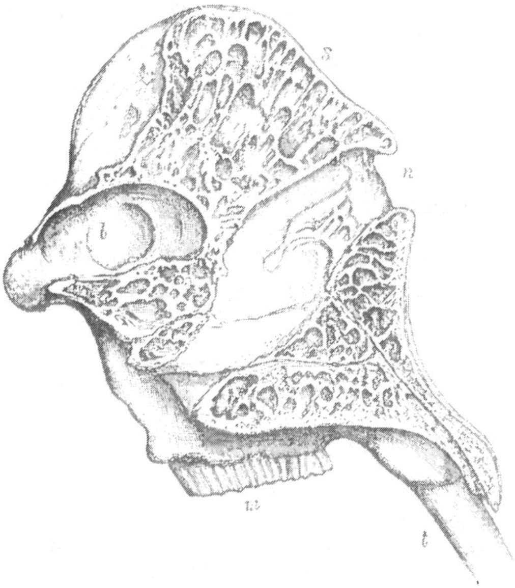

Section of Elephant's Skull.

b, Brain; *s*, Skull; *n*, Narial passage; *m*, Molar; *t*, Tusk.

powerful muscles of the trunk, and at the same time combining lightness with strength. This cellular bone grows with the animal, and is in great measure absent at birth. In the young elephant the brain nearly fills the head, and the brain-case increases but little in size during growth, but the cellular portion progresses rapidly with the growth of the animal, and is piled up over the frontals for a considerable height, giving the appearance of a bold forehead, the brain remaining in a small space at the base of the skull, close to its articulation with the neck. According to Professor Flower, the cranial cavity is elongated and depressed, more so in the African than the Indian elephant. The tentorial plane is nearly vertical, so that the cerebellar fossa is altogether behind the cerebral fossa, or, in plainer terms, the division between the big brain (cerebrum) and the little one (cerebellum) is vertical, the two brains lying on a level plane fore and aft instead of overlapping. The brain itself is highly convoluted. The nasal aperture, or olfactory fossa, is very large, and is placed a little below the brain-case. Few people who are intimate with but the external form of the elephant would suppose that the bump just above the root of the trunk, at which the hunter takes aim for the "front shot," is really the seat of the organ of smell, the channels of which run down the trunk to the orifice at the end. The maxillo-turbinals, or twisted bony laminæ within the nasal aperture, which are to be found in most mammals, are but rudimentary in the elephant—the elongated proboscis, according to Professor Flower, probably supplying their place in warming the inspired air. The premaxillary and maxillary bones are largely developed, and contain the socket of the enormous tusks. The narial aperture is thus pushed up, and is short, with an upward direction, as in the Cetacea and Sirenia, with whom the Proboscidea have certain affinities.

There are no lower incisors (except in a fossil species), and only two of the molar teeth are to be seen on each side of the jaw at a time, which are pushed out and replaced by others which grow from behind. During the life-time of the animal, twenty-four of these teeth are produced, six in each side of the upper and lower jaws.

The elephant has seven cervical vertebræ, the atlas much resembling the human form; of the thoracic and lumbar vertebræ the number is 23, of which 19 or 20 bear ribs; the caudal vertebræ are 31, of a simple character, without chevron bones.

The pelvis is peculiar in some points, such as the form of the ileum and the arrangement of its surfaces, resembling the human pelvis.

The limbs in the skeleton of the elephant are disposed in a manner differing from most other mammalia. The humerus is remarkable for the great development of the supinator ridge. "The ulna and radius are quite distinct and permanently crossed; the upper end of the latter is small, while the ulna not only contributes the principal part of the articular surface for the humerus, but has its lower end actually larger than that of the radius—a condition almost unique among mammals" (*Prof. Flower*).

On looking at the skeleton of the elephant, one of the first things that strikes the student of comparative anatomy is the perpendicular column of the limbs; in all other animals the bones composing these supports are set at certain angles, by which a direct shock in the action of galloping and leaping is avoided. Take the skeleton of a horse, and you will observe that the scapula and humerus are set almost at right angles to each other. It is so in most other animals, but in the elephant, which requires great solidity and columnar strength, it not being given to bounding about, and having enormous bulk to be supported, the scapula, humerus, ulna and radius are all almost in a perpendicular line. Owing to this rigid formation, the elephant cannot spring. No greater hoax was ever perpetrated on the public than that in one of our illustrated papers, which gave a picture of an elephant hurdle-race. Mr. Sanderson, in his most interesting book, says: "He is physically incapable of making the smallest spring, either in vertical height or horizontal distance. Thus a trench seven feet wide is impassable to an elephant, though the step of a large one in full stride is about six and a half feet."

The hind-limbs are also peculiarly formed, and bear some resemblance

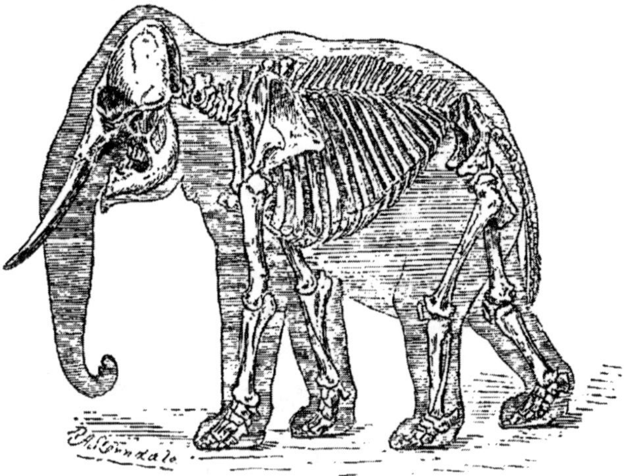

Skeleton of Elephant.

to the arrangement of the human bones, and in these the same perpendicular disposition is to be observed; the pelvis is set nearly vertically to the vertebral column, and the femur and tibia are in an almost direct line. The fibula, or small bone of the leg, which is subject to great variation amongst animals (it being merely rudimentary in the horse, for instance), is distinct in the elephant, and is considerably enlarged at the lower end. The tarsal bones are short, and the digits have the usual number of phalanges, the ungual or nail-bearing ones being small and rounded.

I have thus briefly summarised the osteology of the elephant, as I think the salient points on which I have touched would interest the general reader; but, in now proceeding to the internal anatomy, I shall restrict myself still more, referring only to certain matters affecting externally visible peculiarities. The trunk of the elephant differs somewhat from other nasal prolongations, such as the snouts of certain insectivora, which are simply development of the nasal cartilages. The nasal cartilages in the Proboscidea serve merely as valves to the entrance of the bony nares, the trunk itself being only a pipe or duct leading to them, composed of powerful muscular and membranous tissue, and consisting of two tubes, separated by a septum. The muscles in front (*levatores proboscidis*), starting from the frontal bone, run along a semicircular line, arching upwards above the nasal bones and between the orbits. They are met at the sides by the lateral longitudinal muscles, which blend, and their fibres run the whole length of the proboscis down to the extremity. The depressing muscles (*depressores proboscidis*), or posterior longitudinals, arise from the anterior surface and lower border of the premaxillaries, and form "two layers of oblique fasciculi along the posterior surface of the proboscis; the fibres of the superficial set are directed downwards and outwards from the middle line. They do not reach the extremity of the trunk, but disappear by curving over the sides a little above the end of the organ. The fibres of the deeper set take the reverse direction, and are attached to a distinct tendinous raphe along the posterior median line" ('Anat. Ind. Elep.,' Miall and Greenwood). These muscles form the outer sheath of other muscles, which radiate from the nasal canals outwards, and which consist of numerous distinct fasciculi. Then there are a set of transverse muscles in two parts—one narrow, forming the septum or partition between the

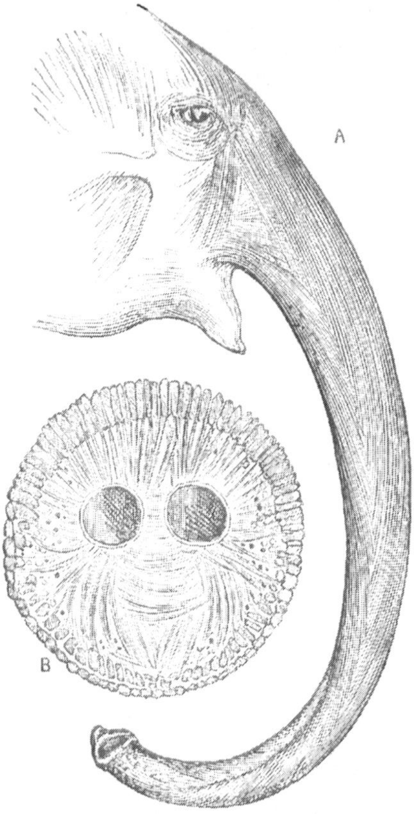

A. Muscles of Elephant's Trunk.
B. Cross-section of ditto.

nasal passages, and the other broader between the narrow part and the posterior longitudinal muscles.

When we consider the bulk of these well-knit muscles we can no longer wonder at the power of which this organ is capable, although, according to Mr. Sanderson, its capabilities are much exaggerated; and he explodes various popular delusions concerning it. He doubts the possibility of the animal picking up a needle, the common old story which I also disbelieve, having often seen the difficulty with which a coin is picked up, or rather scraped up; but he quite scouts the idea of an elephant being able to lift a heavy weight with his trunk, giving an instance recorded of one of these creatures lifting with his trunk the axle of a field-piece as the wheel was about to pass over a fallen gunner, which he declares to be a physical impossibility. Certainly the story has many elements of improbability about it, and his comments on it are caustic and amusing: *par exemple*, when he asks: "How did the elephant know that a wheel going over the man would not be agreeable to him?" That is the weak point in the story—but, however intelligent the animal might be, Mr. Sanderson says it is physically impossible.

Another thing that strikes every one is the noiseless tread of this huge beast. To describe the mechanism of the foot of the elephant concisely and simply I am going to give a few extracts from the observations of Professor W. Boyd Dawkins and Messrs. Oakley, Miall, and Greenwood: "It stands on the ends of its five toes, each of which is terminated by comparatively small hoofs, and the heel-bone is a little distance from the ground. Beneath comes the wonderful cushion composed, of membranes, fat, nerves, and blood-vessels, besides muscles, which constitutes the sole of the foot" (*W. B. D. and H. O.*). "Of the foot as a whole—and this remark apples to both fore and hind extremities—the separate mobility of the parts is greater than would be suspected from an external inspection, and much greater than in most Ungulates. The palmar and plantar soles, though thick and tough, are not rigid boxes like hoofs, but may be made to bend even by human fingers. The large development of muscles acting upon the carpus and tarsus, and the separate existence of flexors and extensors of individual digits, is further proof that the elephant's foot is far from being a solid unalterable mass. There are, as has been pointed out, tendinous or ligamentous attachments which restrain the independent action of some of these muscles, but anatomical examinations would lead us to suppose that the living animal could at all events accurately direct any part of the circumference of the foot by itself to the ground. The metacarpal and metatarsal bones form a considerable angle with the surface of the sole, while the digits, when supporting the weight of the body, are nearly horizontal" (*M. and G.*). This formation would naturally give

2 C

elasticity to the foot, and, with the soft cushion spoken of by Professor Dawkins, would account for the noiselessness of the elephant's tread. On one occasion a friend and myself marched our elephant up to a sleeping tiger without disturbing the latter's slumbers.

It is a curious fact that twice round an elephant's foot is his height; it may be an inch one way or the other, but still sufficiently near to take as an estimate.

Now we come to a third peculiarity in this interesting animal, and that is the power of withdrawing water or a similar fluid from apparently the stomach by the insertion of its trunk into the mouth, which it sprinkles over its body when heated. The operation and the *modus operandi* are familiar to all who have made much use of elephants, but the internal economy by which the water is supplied is as yet a mystery to be solved, although various anatomists have given the subject serious attention. It is generally supposed that the receptacle for the liquid is the stomach, from the quantity that is ejected. An elephant distressed by a long march in the heat of the sun withdraws several quarts of water, but that it is water, and not a secretion produced by salivatory glands, is not I think sufficiently evident. In talking over the matter with Mr. Sanderson, he informed me that an elephant that has drunk a short time before taking an arduous march has a more plentiful supply of liquid at his disposal. Therefore we might conclude that it is water which is regurgitated, and in such quantity as to preclude the idea of its being stored anywhere but in the stomach; but the question is, how it is so stored there without assimulating with the food in the process of digestion. Sir Emerson Tennent, in his popular and well-known, but in some respects incorrect, account of the elephant, has adopted the theory that the cardiac end of the stomach is the receptacle for the water; and he figures a section of it showing a number of transverse circular folds; and he accepts the conclusion arrived at by Camper and Sir Everard Home that this portion can be shut off as a water chamber by the action of the fold nearest to the œsophagus; but these folds are too shallow to serve as water-cells, and it has not been demonstrated that the broadest fold near the œsophagus can be contracted to such an extent as to form a complete diaphragm bisecting the stomach. Messrs. Miall and Greenwood say: "The stomach is smooth, externally elongate, and nearly straight. The cardiac end is much prolonged and tapering. A number of transverse, nearly circular, folds project inwards from the cardiac wall; they almost disappear when the stomach is greatly distended, and are at all times too shallow to serve as water-cells, though they have been figured and described as such."

That the stomach is the reservoir is, I think, open to doubt; but there is no other possible receptacle as yet discovered, though I shall allude to a supposed one presently, which would hold a moderate supply of water, and further research in this direction is desirable. Most of the dissections hitherto made have been of young and immature specimens. Dr. Watson's investigations have thrown some light on the way in which the water is withdrawn, which differs from Dr. Harrison's conclusions, which are quoted by Sir Emerson Tennent. Dr. Watson says regarding this power of withdrawal: "It is evident that were the throat of this animal similar to that of other mammals, this could not be accomplished, as the insertion of a body, such as the trunk, so far into the pharynx as to enable the constrictor muscles of that organ to grasp it, would at once give rise to a paroxysm of coughing; or, were the trunk merely inserted into the mouth, it would be requisite that this cavity be kept constantly filled with water, at the same time that the lips closely encircled the inserted trunk. The formation of the mouth of the elephant, however, is such as to prevent the trunk ever being grasped by the lips so as effectually to stop the entrance of air into the cavity, and thus at once, if I may so express it, the pump action of the trunk is completely paralysed. We find, therefore, that it is to some modification of the throat that we must look for an explanation of the function in question." He then goes on to explain minutely the anatomical details of the apparatus of the throat, which I will endeavour to sketch as simply, though clearly, as I can. The superior aperture of the pharynx is extremely narrow, so much so as to admit, with difficulty, the passage of a closed fist; but immediately behind this the pharynx dilates into a large pouch capable of containing a certain quantity of fluid—according to Dr. Watson a considerable quantity; but this is open to question. Professor Miall states that in the young specimen examined by him and Mr. Greenwood, a pint was the capacity of the pouch. However, according to Dr. Watson, it is capable of distention to a certain extent. The pouch is prolonged forward beneath the root of the tongue, which forms the anterior boundary, whilst the posterior wall is completed by depression of the soft palate; when the latter is elevated the pouch communicates freely with the œsophagus. I omit Dr. Watson's minute description of the anatomy of this part in detail, which the reader who cares to study the matter more deeply can find in his 'Contributions to the Anatomy of the Indian Elephant,' 'Journal of Anatomy and Physiology,' 1871–74, but proceed to quote some of his deductions from the observations made: "An elephant can," he says, "as the quotations sufficiently prove, withdraw water from his stomach in two ways—first, it may be regurgitated directly into the nasal passages by the action of the diaphragm and abdominal muscles, the soft palate being at the same time depressed, so as to prevent the passage of water into the mouth. Having in this manner filled the large nasal passages communicating with the trunk, the water contained in them is then forced through the trunk by means of a powerful expiration; or, in the second place, the water may be withdrawn from the cavity of the mouth by means of the trunk inserted into it."

The second deduction is, I think, the more probable one. Before an elephant spirts water over his body, he invariably puts his trunk into his mouth for the liquid, whatever it may be. Messrs. Miall and Greenwood are also against the former supposition, viz. that the fluid is regurgitated into the nasal passages. They say: "We are disposed to question the normal passage of water along this highly-sensitive tract. Examination of the parts discovers no valve or other provision for preventing water, flowing from behind forward, from gaining free entrance into the olfactory recesses." Mr. Sanderson, in discussing the habits of elephants with me, informed me that, from his observations, he was sure that an elephant, in drawing up water, did not fill more than fifteen to eighteen inches of his trunk at a time, which confirms the opinion of the two last-mentioned authors. Now we go on with Dr. Watson's second deduction:—

"It is manifestly impossible that the water can be contained within the cavity of the mouth itself, as I have already shown that the lips in the elephant are so formed as effectually to prevent this. The water regurgitated is, however, by means of the elevation of the soft palate, forced into the pharyngeal pouch. The superior aperture of this pouch being much narrower than the diameter of the pouch itself, and being completely surrounded by the muscular fibres of the stylo-glossus on each side, and the root of the tongue in front, which is prolonged backwards so as to form a free sharp margin, we have thus, as it were, a narrow aperture surrounded by a sphincter muscle, into which the trunk being inserted, and grasped above its dilated extremity by the sphincter arrangement just referred to, air is thus effectually excluded; and, the nasal passages being then exhausted by the act of inspiration, water is lodged within these passages, to be used as the animal thinks fit, either by throwing it over his body, or again returning it into his mouth."

This is doubtless a correct conclusion. The question still remaining open is, What is the fluid—water or a secretion? If water, where is it stowed in sufficient quantity? The testimony of several eminent anatomists appears to be against stomach complications such as before suggested. Dr. Anderson has told me that he had the opportunity of examining the stomachs of two very large elephants, which were perfectly simple, of enormous size; and he was astonished at the extent of mucous surface. If water were drawn from such a stomach, it would be more or less tainted with half-digested food, besides which, when drunk, it would be rapidly absorbed by the mucous surfaces. I think therefore that we may assume that these yield back a very fluid secretion, which is regurgitated, as before suggested, into the pharyngeal pouch, to be withdrawn as required. Sir Emerson Tennent figures, on the authority of Dr. Harrison, a portion of the trachea and œsophagus, connected by a muscle which he supposes "might raise the cardiac orifice of the stomach, and so aid this organ to regurgitate a portion of its contents into the œsophagus," but neither Dr. Watson nor Messrs. Miall and Greenwood have found any trace of this muscle.

Before proceeding to a detailed account of the Indian elephant, I will cursorily sketch the difference between it and its African brother.

The African elephant is of larger size as a rule, with enormously developed ears, which quite overlap his withers. The forehead recedes, and the trunk is more coarsely ringed; the tusks are larger, some almost reaching the size of those mentioned above in the fossil head at the museum. An old friend of mine, well known to all the civilised—and a great portion of the uncivilised—world, Sir Samuel Baker, had, and may still have, in his possession a tusk measuring ten feet nine inches. This of course includes the portion within the socket, whereas my measurement of the fossil is from the socket to tip.

The lamination of the molar teeth also is very distinct in the two species, as I have before stated—the African being in acute lozenges, the Indian in wavy undulations.

Another point of divergence is, that the African elephant has only three nails on the hind feet, whereas the Asiatic has four.

No. 425. ELEPHAS INDICUS.

The Indian or Asiatic Elephant (*Jerdon's No.* 211).

NATIVE NAMES.—*Hasti* or *Gaja*, Sanscrit; *Gaj*, Bengali; *Hati*, Hindi; *Ani* in Southern India, i.e. in Tamil, Telegu, Canarese, and Malabari; *Feel*, Persian; *Allia*, Singhalese; *Gadjah*, Malayan; *Shañh*, Burmese.

HABITAT.—India, in most of the large forests at the foot of the Himalayas from Dehra Doon down to the Bhotan Terai; in the Garo hills, Assam; in some parts of Central and Southern India; in Ceylon and in Burmah, from thence extending further to Siam, Sumatra and Borneo.

DESCRIPTION.—Head oblong, with concave forehead; small ears as compared with the African animal; small eyes, lighter colour, and four instead of three nails on the hind foot; the laminations of the molar teeth in wavy undulations instead of sharp lozenges, as in the African, the tusks also being much smaller in the female, instead of almost equal in both sexes.

SIZE.—The maximum height appears to be about 11 feet, in fact the only authentic measurement we have at present is 10 feet 7 inches.

"The huge elephant, wisest of brutes,"

has had a good deal of the romance about it taken away by modern observers. The staid appearance of the animal, with the intellectual aspect contributed by the enormous cranial development, combined with its undoubted docility and aptitude for comprehending signs, have led to exaggerated ideas of its intelligence, which probably does not exceed that of the horse, and is far inferior to that of the dog. But from time immemorial it has been surrounded by a halo of romance and exaggeration. Mr. Sanderson says, however, that the natives of India never speak of it as an intelligent animal, "and it does not figure in their ancient literature for its wisdom, as do the fox, the crow, and the monkey;" but he overlooks the fact that the Hindu god of wisdom, *Gunesh*, is always depicted with the body of a man, but the head of an elephant. However this is apparently an oversight, for both in his book and lecture he alludes to *Gunesh*. The rest of his remarks are so good, and show so much practical knowledge, that I shall take the liberty of quoting *in extenso* from a lecture delivered by him at Simla last year, a printed copy of which he kindly sent me, and also from his interesting book, 'Thirteen Years amongst the Wild Beasts.'

He says: "One of the strongest features in the domesticated elephant's character is its obedience. It may also be readily taught, as it has a large share of the ordinary cultivable intelligence common in a greater or less degree to all animals. But its reasoning faculties are undoubtedly far below those of the dog, and possibly of other animals; and in matters beyond the range of its daily experience it evinces no special discernment. Whilst quick at comprehending anything sought to be taught to it, the elephant is decidedly wanting in originality."

I think one as often sees instances of decided stupidity on the part of elephants as of sagacity, but I think the amount of intelligence varies in individuals. I have known cases where elephants have tried to get their mahouts off their backs—two cases in my own district—in the one the elephant tried shaking and then lying down, both of which proved ineffectual; in the other it tried tearing off the rafters of a hut and throwing them over its back, and finally rubbing against low branches of trees, which proved successful. The second elephant, I think, showed the greatest amount of original thought; but there is no doubt the sagacity of the animal has been greatly overrated. I quote again from Mr. Sanderson, whose remarks are greatly to the point:—

"What an improbable story is that of the elephant and the tailor, wherein the animal, on being pricked with a needle instead of being fed with sweetmeats as usual, is represented as having deliberately gone to a pond, filled its trunk with dirty water, and returned and squirted it over the tailor and his work! This story accredits the elephant with appreciating the fact that throwing dirty water over his work would be the peculiar manner in which to annoy a tailor. How has he acquired the knowledge of the incongruity of the two things, dirty water and clean linen? He delights in water himself, and would therefore be unlikely to imagine it objectionable to another. If the elephant were possessed of the amount of discernment with which he is commonly credited, is it reasonable to suppose that he would continue to labour for man instead of turning into the nearest jungle? The elephant displays less intelligence in its natural state than most wild animals. Whole herds are driven into ill-concealed inclosures which no other forest creatures could be got to enter; and single ones are caught by being bound to trees by men under cover of a couple of tame elephants, the wild one being ignorant of what is going on until he finds himself secured. Escaped elephants are re-taken without trouble; even experience does not bring them wisdom. Though possessed of a proboscis which is capable of guarding it against such dangers, the wild elephant readily falls into pits dug in its path, whilst its fellows flee in terror, making no effort to assist the fallen one, as they might easily do by kicking in the earth around the pit. It commonly happens that a young elephant falls into a pit, in which case the mother will remain until the hunters come, without doing anything to assist her offspring—not even feeding it by throwing in a few branches.

"When a half-trained elephant of recent capture happens to get loose, and the approach of its keeper on foot might cause it to move off, or perhaps even to run away altogether, the mahout calls to his elephant from a distance to kneel, and he then approaches and mounts it. The instinct of obedience is herein shown to be stronger than the animal's intelligence. When a herd of wild elephants is secured within a stockade, or *kheddah*, the mahouts ride trained elephants amongst the wild ones without fear, though any one of the wild ones might, by a movement of its trunk, dislodge the man. This they never do."

On the other hand we do hear of wonderful cases of reasoning on the part of these creatures. I have never seen anything very extraordinary myself; but I had one elephant which almost invariably attempted to get loose at night, and often succeeded, if we were encamped in the vicinity of sugar-cane cultivation—nothing else tempted her; and many a rupee have I had to pay for the damage done. This elephant knew me perfectly after an absence of eighteen months, trumpeted when she saw me, and purred as I came up and stroked her trunk. I then gave her the old sign, and in a moment she lifted me by the trunk on to her head. I never mounted her any other way, and, as I used to slip off by a side rope, the constant kneeling down and getting up was avoided.

Sir Emerson Tennent says: "When free in its native woods the elephant evinces rather simplicity than sagacity, and its intelligence seldom exhibits itself in cunning;" yet in the next page he goes on to relate a story told to him of a wild elephant when captured falling down, and feigning to be dead so successfully that all the fastenings were taken off; "while this was being done he and a gentleman by whom he was accompanied leaned against the body to rest. They had scarcely taken their departure and proceeded a few yards when, to their astonishment, the elephant arose with the utmost alacrity, and fled towards the jungles screaming at the top of its voice, its cries being audible long after it had disappeared in the shades of the forest." If this be correct it shows a considerable amount of cunning.

Both Mr. Sanderson and Sir Emerson Tennent agree on the subject of the rarity of the remains of dead elephants. I have never been in real elephant country; the tracks of such as I have come across have been merely single wanderers from the Bilaspore herds, or probably elephants escaped from captivity. Forsyth once came upon the bones of a small herd of five that had been driven over a precipice from the summit of a hill, on which there was a Hindoo shrine, by the drums and music of a religious procession.

The following taken from Mr. Sanderson's lecture is interesting as regards the constitution of the herds: "Herds of elephants usually consist of from thirty to fifty individuals, but much larger numbers, even upwards of a hundred, are by no means uncommon. A herd is always led by a female, never by a male. In localities where fodder is scarce a large herd usually divides into parties of from ten to twenty. These remain at some little distance from each other, but all take part in any common movement, such as a march into another tract of forest. These separate parties are family groups, consisting of old elephants with their children and grandchildren. It thus happens that, though the gregarious instincts of elephants prompt them to form large gatherings, if circumstances necessitate it a herd breaks up under several leaders. Cases frequently occur when they are being hunted; each party will then take measures for its individual safety. It cannot be said that a large herd has any *supreme* leader. Tuskers never interest themselves in the movement of their herds; they wander much alone, either to visit cultivation, where the females, encumbered with young ones, hesitate to follow, or from a love of solitude. Single elephants found wandering in the forests are usually young males—animals debarred from much intimate association with the herds by stronger rivals; but they usually keep within a few miles of their companions. These wandering tuskers are only biding their time until they are able to meet all comers in a herd. The necessity for the females regulating the movements of a herd is evident, as they must accommodate the length and time of their marches, and the localities in which they rest and feed at different hours, to the requirements of their young ones."

It is a curious fact that most of the male elephants in Ceylon are what are called *mucknas* in India, that is, tuskless males—not one in a hundred, according to Sir Emerson Tennent, being found with tusks; nearly all, however, are provided with tushes. These, he says, he has observed them "to use in loosening earth, stripping off bark, and snapping asunder small branches and climbing plants, and hence tushes are seldom seen without a groove worn into them near their extremities." Sir Samuel Baker says that the African elephant uses his tusks in ploughing up ground in search of edible roots, and that whole acres may be seen thus ploughed, but I have never seen any use to which the Indian elephant puts his tusks in feeding. I have often watched mine peeling the bark off succulent branches, and the trunk and foot were alone used. Mr. Sanderson, in his 'Thirteen Years,' remarks: "Tusks are not used to assist the elephant in procuring food;" but he says they are formidable weapons of offence in the tusker, the biggest of whom lords it over his inferiors.

The elephant usually brings forth, after a period of gestation of from eighteen to twenty-two months, a single calf, though twins are occasionally born. Mr. Sanderson says: "Elephant calves usually stand exactly thirty-six inches at the shoulder when born, and weigh about 200 lbs. They live entirely upon milk for five or six months, when they begin to eat tender grass. Their chief support, however, is still milk for some months. I have known three cases of elephants having two calves at a birth. It cannot be said that the female elephant evinces any special attachment to her offspring, whilst the belief that all the females of a herd show affection for each other's calves is certainly erroneous. During the catching of elephants many cases occur in which young ones, after losing their mothers by death or separation, are refused assistance by the other females, and are buffeted about as outcasts. I have only known one instance of a very gentle, motherly elephant in captivity, allowing a motherless calf to suck along with her own young one. When a calf is born the mother and the herd usually remain in that place for two days. The calf is then capable of marching. Even at this tender age calves are no encumbrance to the herd's movement; the youngest climb hills and cross rivers, assisted by their dams. In swimming, very young calves are supported by their mothers' trunks, and are held in front of them. When they are a few months old they scramble on to their mother's shoulders, and hold on with their fore-legs, or they swim alone. Though a few calves are born at other seasons, the largest number make their appearance about September, October, and November."

Until I read the above I, from my limited experience, had come to the conclusion that elephant mothers are very fussy and jealous of other females. (See Appendix C, p. 527.)

I have only once seen an elephant born in captivity, and that was in 1859, when I was in charge of the Sasseram Levy on the Grand Trunk road. Not far from the lines of my men was an elephant camp; they were mostly Burmese animals, and many of them died; but one little fellow made his appearance one fine morning, and was an object of great interest to us all. On one occasion, some years after, I went out after a tiger on a female elephant which had a very young calf. I repented it after a while, for I lost my tiger and my temper, and very nearly my life. Those who have read 'Seonee,' may remember the ludicrous scene in which I made the doctor figure as the hero. An elephant is full grown at twenty-five, though not in his prime till some years after. Forty years is what mahouts, I think, consider age, but the best elephants live up to one hundred years or even more.*

A propos of my remarks, in the introductory portion of this paper on Proboscidea, regarding the probable gradual extinction of the African elephant, the following reassuring paragraphs from the lecture I have so extensively quoted will prove interesting and satisfactory. Mr. Sanderson has previously alluded to the common belief, strengthened by actual facts in Ceylon, that the elephant was gradually being exterminated in India; but this is not the case, especially since the laws for their protection have come into force: "The elephant-catching records of the past fifty years attest the fact that there is no diminution in the numbers now obtainable in Bengal, whilst in Southern India elephants have become so numerous of late years that they are annually appearing where they had never been heard of before."

He then instances the Billigarungun hills, an isolated range of three hundred square miles on the borders of Mysore, where wild elephants first made their appearance about eighty years ago, the country having relapsed from cultivation into a wilderness owing to the decimation of the inhabitants by three successive visitations of small-pox. He adds: "The strict preservation of wild elephants seems only advantageous or desirable in conjunction with corresponding measures for keeping their numbers within bounds by capture. It is to be presumed that elephants are preserved with a view to their utilisation. With its jungles filled with elephants, the anomalous state of things by which Government, when obliged to go into the market, finds them barely procurable, and then only at prices double those of twenty, and quadruple those of forty years ago, will I trust be considered worthy of inquiry. Whilst it is necessary to maintain stringent restrictions on the wasteful and cruel native modes of hunting, it will I believe be found advantageous to

* See note in Appendix C on this subject.

allow lessees every facility for hunting under conditions that shall insure humane management of their captives. I believe that the price of elephants might be reduced one-half in a year or two by such measures. The most ordinary elephant cannot be bought at present for less than Rs. 2,000. Unless something be done, it is certain that the rifle will have to be called into requisition to protect the ryots of tracts bordering upon elephant jungles. To give an idea of the numbers of wild elephants in some parts of India, I may say that during the past three years 503 elephants have been captured by the Dacca kheddah establishment, in a tract of country forty miles long by twenty broad, in the Garo hills, whilst not less than one thousand more were met with during the hunting operations. Of course these elephants do not confine themselves to that tract alone, but wander into other parts of the hills. There are immense tracts of country in India similarly well stocked with wild elephants.

"I am sure it will be regarded as a matter for hearty congratulation by all who are interested in so fine and harmless an animal as is the elephant that there is no danger of its becoming extinct in India. Though small portions of its haunts have been cleared for tea or coffee cultivation, the present forest area of this country will probably never be practically reduced, for reasons connected with the timber supply and climate of the country; and as long as its haunts remain the elephant must flourish under due regulations for its protection."

Elephants are caught in various ways. The pitfall is now prohibited, so also is the Assam plan of inclosing a herd in a salt lick. Noosing and driving into a *kheddah* or inclosure are now the only legitimate means of capture. The process is too long for description here, but I may conclude this article, which owes so much to Mr. Sanderson's careful observations, with the following interesting account of the mode in which the newly-caught elephant is taught to obey:—

"New elephants are trained as follows: they are first tied between two trees, and are rubbed down by a number of men with long bamboos, to an accompaniment of the most extravagant eulogies of the animal, sung and shouted at it at the top of their voices. The animal of course lashes out furiously at first; but in a few days it ceases to act on the offensive, or, as the native say, 'shurum lugta hai'—'it becomes ashamed of itself,' and it then stands with its trunk curled, shrinking from the men. Ropes are now tied round its body, and it is mounted at its picket for several days. It is then taken out for exercise, secured between two tame elephants. The ropes still remain round its body to enable the mahout to hold on should the elephant try to shake him off. A man precedes it with a spear to teach it to halt when ordered to do so; whilst, as the tame elephants wheel to the right or left, the mahout presses its neck with his knees, and taps it on the head with a small stick, to train it to turn in the required direction. To teach an elephant to kneel it is taken into water about five feet deep when the sun is hot, and, upon being pricked on the back with a pointed stick it soon lies down, partly to avoid the pain, partly from inclination for a bath. By taking it into shallower water daily, it is soon taught to kneel even on land.

"Elephants are taught to pick up anything from the ground by a rope, with a piece of wood attached, being dangled over their foreheads, near to the ground. The wood strikes against their trunk and fore-feet, and to avoid the discomfort the elephant soon takes it in its trunk, and carries it. It eventually learns to do this without a rope being attached to the object."

Sir Emerson Tennent's account of the practice in Ceylon is similar.

As regards the size of elephants few people agree. The controversy is as strong on this point as on the maximum size of tigers. I quite believe few elephants attain to or exceed ten feet, still there are one or two recorded instances, the most trustworthy of which is Mr. Sanderson's measurement of the Sirmoor Rajah's elephant, which is 10 ft. 7½ in. at the shoulder—a truly enormous animal. I have heard of a tusker at Hyderabad that is over eleven feet, but we must hold this open to doubt till an accurate measurement, for which I have applied, is received. Elephants should be measured like a horse, with a standard and cross bar, and not by means of a piece of string over the rounded muscles of the shoulder. Kellaart, usually a most accurate observer, mentions in his 'Prodromus Faunæ Zeylanicæ' his having measured a Ceylon elephant nearly twelve feet high, but does not say how it was done. Sir Joseph Fayrer has a photograph of an enormous elephant belonging to the late Sir Jung Bahadur, a perfect mountain of flesh.

WE in India have nothing to do with the next order, HYRACOIDEA or Conies, which are small animals, somewhat resembling short-eared rabbits, but which from their dentition and skeleton are allied to the rhinoceros and tapir. The Syrian coney is frequently mentioned in the Old Testament, and was one of the animals prohibited for food to the Jews, "because he cheweth the cud and divideth not the hoof." The chewing of the cud was a mistake, for the coney does not do so, but it has a way of moving its jaws which might lead to the idea that it ruminates. In other parts of Scripture the habits of the animal are more accurately depicted—"The rocks are a refuge for the conies;" and again: "The conies are but a feeble folk, yet make they their houses in the rocks." Solomon says in the Proverbs: "There be four things which are little upon the earth, but they are exceeding wise." These are the ants, for they prepare their meat in summer, as we see here in India the stores laid up by the large black ant (*Atta providens*); the conies for the reason above given; the locusts, which have no king, yet go forth by bands; and the spider, which maketh her home in kings' palaces.

ORDER UNGULATA.

THESE are animals which possess hoofs; and are divided into two sub-orders—those that have an odd number of toes on the hind-foot, such as the horse, tapir, and rhinoceros, being termed the PERISSODACTYLA; and the others, with an even number of toes, such as the pig, sheep, ox, deer, &c., the ARTIODACTYLA; both words being taken from the Greek *perissos* and *artios*, uneven or overmuch, and even; and *daktulos*, a finger or toe. We begin with the uneven-toed group.

SUB-ORDER PERISSODACTYLA.

This consists of three living and two extinct families—the living ones being horses, tapirs, and rhinoceroses, and the extinct the *Paleotheridæ* and the *Macrauchenidæ*. I quote from Professor Boyd Dawkins and Mr. H. W. Oakley the following brief yet clear description of the characteristics of this sub-order:—

"In all the animals belonging to the group the number of dorso-lumbar vertebræ is not fewer than twenty-two; the third or middle digit of each foot is symmetrical; the femur or thigh-bone has a third trochanter, or knob of bone, on the outer side; and the two facets on the front of the astragalus or ankle-bone are very unequal. When the head is provided with horns they are skin deep only, without a core of bone, and they are always placed in the middle line of the skull, as in the rhinoceros.

"In the *Perissodactyla* the number of toes is reduced to a minimum. Supposing, for example, we compare the foot of a horse with one of our own hands, we shall see that those parts which correspond with the thumb and little finger are altogether absent, while that which corresponds with the middle finger is largely developed, and with its hoof, the equivalent to our nail, constitutes the whole foot. The small splint bones, however, resting behind the principal bone of the foot represent those portions (metacarpals) of the second and third digits which extend from the wrist to the fingers properly so-called, and are to be viewed as traces of a foot composed of three toes in an ancestral form of the horse, which we shall discuss presently. In the tapir the hind foot is composed of three well-developed toes, corresponding to the first three toes in man, and in the rhinoceros both feet are provided with three toes, formed of the same three digits. In the extinct *Paleotherium* also the foot is constituted very much as in the rhinoceros."

FAMILY EQUIDÆ—THE HORSE.

This family consists of the true horses and the asses, which latter also include the zebra and quagga. Apart from the decided external differences between the horse and ass, they have one marked divergence, viz. that the horse has corns or callosities on the inner side of both fore and hind limbs, whilst the asses have them only on the fore limbs; but this is a very trifling difference, and how closely the two animals are allied is proved by the facility with which they interbreed. It is, therefore, proper to include them both in one genus, although Dr. Gray has made a separation, calling the latter *Asinus*, and Hamilton Smith proposed *Hippotigris* as a generic name for the zebras.

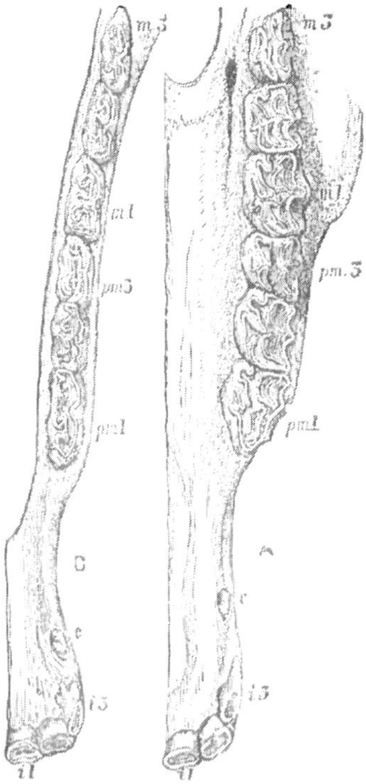

Dentition of Horse.

We have no wild horse in India; in fact there are no truly wild horses in the world as far as we know. The tarpan or wild horse of Tartary, and the mustang of South America, though *de facto* wild horses, are supposed to be descended from domesticated forms. In Australia too horses sometimes grow wild from being left long in the bush. These are known as *brumbies*, and are generally shot by the stock farmer, as they are of deteriorated quality, and by enticing away his mares spoil his more carefully selected breeds. According to Mr. Anthony Trollope they are marvels of ugliness.

The Indian species of this genus are properly asses; there are two kinds, although it has been asserted by many—and some of them good naturalists, such as Blyth—that the *Kiang* of Thibet and the *Ghor-khur* of Sind and Baluchistan are the same animal.

GENUS EQUUS.

Incisors, $\frac{6}{6}$; canines, $\frac{1-1}{1-1}$; molars, $\frac{6-6}{6-6}$; these last are complex, with square crowns marked by wavy folds of enamel. The incisors are grooved, and are composed of folds of enamel and cement, aptly described by Professor Boyd Dawkins and Mr. Oakley as being folded in from the top, after the manner of the finger of a glove the top of which has been pulled in. The marks left by the attrition of the surface give an approximate idea of the age of the animal. The stomach is simple—the intestinal canal very long and cæcum enormous.

NO. 426. EQUUS ONAGER.

The Wild Ass of Kutch (Jerdon's No. 214).

NATIVE NAMES.—*Ghor-khur*, Hindi; *Ghour*, or *Kherdecht*, Persian; *Koulan* of the Kirghiz.

HABITAT.—Sind, Baluchistan, Persia.

DESCRIPTION.—Pale sandy colour above, with a slight rufescent tinge; muzzle, breast, lower parts and inside of limbs white; a dark chocolate brown dorsal stripe from mane to tail, with a cross on the shoulder, sometimes a double one; and the legs are also occasionally barred. The mane and tail-tuft are dark brown or black; a narrow dark band over the hoof; ears longish, white inside, concolorous with the body outside, the tip and outer border blackish; head heavy; neck short; croup higher than the withers.

SIZE.—Height about 11 to 12 hands.

The following account I extract from Jerdon's 'Mammals of India,' p. 238, which epitomises much of what has been written on the subject:—

"The *ghor-khur* is found sparingly in Cutch, Guzerat, Jeysulmeer and Bikaneer, not being found further south, it is said, than Deesa, or east of 75° east longitude. It also occurs in Sind, and more abundantly west of the Indus river, in Baluchistan, extending into Persia and Turkestan, as far north as north latitude 48°. It appears that the Bikaneer herd consists at most of about 150 individuals, which frequent an oasis a little elevated above the surrounding desert, and commanding an extensive view around. A writer in the *Indian Sporting Review*, writing of this species as it occurs in the Pât, a desert country between Asnee and the hills west of the Indus, above Mithunkote, says: 'They are to be found wandering pretty well throughout the year; but in the early summer, when the grass and the water in the pools have dried up from the hot winds (which are here terrific), the greater number, if not all, of the *ghor-khurs* migrate to the hills for grass and water. The foaling season is in June, July, and August, when the

Equus onager.

Beluchis ride down and catch numbers of foals, finding a ready sale in the cantonments for them, as they are taken down on speculation to Hindustan. They also shoot great numbers of full-grown ones for food, the ground in places in the desert being very favourable for stalking.' In Bikaneer too, according to information given by Major Tytler to Mr. Blyth: 'Once only in the year, when the foals are young, a party of five or six native hunters, mounted on hardy Sindh mares, chase down as many foals as they succeed in tiring, which lie down when utterly fatigued, and suffer themselves to be bound and carried off. In general they refuse sustenance at first, and about one-third only of those taken are reared; but these command high prices, and find a ready sale with the native princes. The profits are shared by the party, who do not attempt a second chase in the same year, lest they should scare the herd from the district, as these men regard the sale of a few ghor-khurs annually as a regular source of subsistence.'

"This wild ass is very shy and difficult to approach, and has great speed. A full-grown one has, however, been run down fairly and speared more than once."

I remember we had a pair of these asses in the Zoological Gardens at Lahore in 1868; they were to a certain extent tame, but very skittish, and would whinny and kick on being approached. I never heard of their being mounted.

It is closely allied to, if not identical with, the wild ass of Assyria (*Equus hemippus*). The Hon. Charles Murray, who presented one of the pair in the London Zoological Gardens in 1862, wrote the following account of it to Dr. Sclater: "The ghour or kherdecht of the Persians is doubtless the onager of the ancients. Your specimen was caught when a foal on the range of mountains which stretch from Kermanshah on the west in a south-easterly direction to Shiraz; these are inhabited by several wild and half-independent tribes, the most powerful of which are the Buchtzari. The ghour is a remarkably fleet animal, and moreover so shy and enduring that he can rarely be overtaken by the best mounted horsemen in Persia. For this reason they chase them now, as they did in the time of Xenophon, by placing relays of horsemen at intervals of eight or ten miles. These relays take up the chase successively and tire down the ghour. The flesh of the ghour is esteemed a great delicacy, not being held unclean by the Moslem, as it was in the Mosaic code. I do not know whether this species is ever known to bray like the ordinary domestic ass. Your animal, whilst under my care, used to emit short squeaks and sometimes snorts not unlike those of a deer, but she was so young at the time that her voice may not have acquired its mature intonation."

No. 427. EQUUS HEMIONUS.

The Kiang or Wild Ass of Thibet.

NATIVE NAMES.—*Kiang* or *Dizightai*, Thibetan.

HABITAT.—Thibet and Central Asia; Ladakh.

DESCRIPTION.—Darker in hue than the *ghor-khur*, especially on the flanks, contrasting abruptly with the white of the under-parts. It has the dark line along the back, but not the cross band on the shoulder; ears shorter.

SIZE.—About 12 to 14 hands in height.

From its larger size, shorter ears, and its shrill bray, which has been mistaken for a neigh, this animal has at times been taken for a horse, and described as such. The kiang, of which there is a living specimen in the London Zoological Gardens, inhabits the high plateaux of Thibet, ranging up to fifteen and sixteen thousand feet above the sea level. It is very swift and wary.

The late Brigadier-General McMaster, in his 'Notes on Jerdon,' page 248, says: "An excellent sportsman and very close observer, who, being a cavalry officer, should be able to give a sound opinion on the matter, assured me that the voice of the wild horse of the snowy Himalayas is 'an unmistakeable *neigh, not a bray*,' and that he certainly looked on them as horses. He had seen several of these animals, and killed one." Captain (now General) R. Strachey wrote of it: "My impression as to the voice of the *kyang* is that it is a shrieking bray and not a neigh;" and again: "the *kyang*, so far as external aspect is concerned, is obviously an ass and not an horse." Of this there is but little doubt. Moorcroft, in his travels, vol. i. p. 312, states: "In the eastern parts of Ladakh is a nondescript wild variety of horse which I may call *Equus kiang*. It is perhaps more of an ass than a horse, but its ears are shorter, and it is certainly not the gur-khor or wild ass of Sind." Further on, at page 442, he adds: "We saw many herds of the kyang, and I made numerous attempts to bring one down, but with invariably bad success. Some were wounded, but not sufficiently to check their speed, and they quickly bounded up the rocks, where it was impossible to follow. They would afford excellent sport to four or five men well mounted, but a single individual has no chance. The kyang allows his pursuer to approach no nearer than five or six hundred yards; he then trots off, turns, looks and waits till you are almost within distance, when he is off again. If fired at he is frightened, and scampers off altogether. The Chanthan people sometimes catch them by snares—sometimes shoot them. From all I have seen of the animal I should pronounce him to be neither a horse nor an ass. His shape is as much like that of the one as the other, but his cry is more like braying than neighing. The prevailing colour is a light reddish-chestnut, but the nose, the under-part of the jaw and neck, the belly and the legs are white, the mane is dun and erect, the ears are moderately long, the tail bare and reaching a little below the hock. The height is about fourteen hands. The form, from the fore to the hind leg and feet to a level with the back is more square than that of an ass. His back is less straight, and there is a dip behind the withers and a rounding of the crupper which is more like the shape of the horse; his neck also is more erect and arched than that of the ass. He is perhaps more allied to the quagga, but without stripes, except a reported one along each side of the back to the tail. These were seen distinctly in a foal, but were not distinguished in the adults."

FAMILY TAPIRIDÆ—THE TAPIRS.

These are somewhat hog-like animals, with elongated snouts, possessing four toes on their fore-feet, and three on the hinder ones. They live in dense forests, are nocturnal in habit, and live exclusively on a

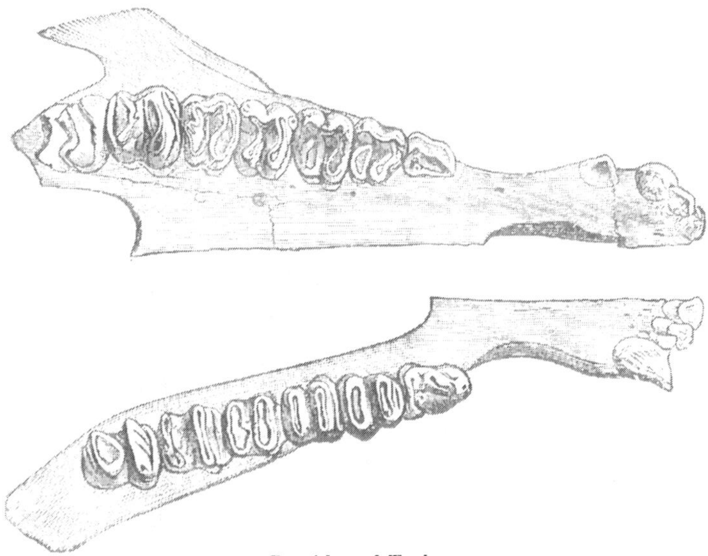

Dentition of Tapir.

vegetable diet. The Indian tapir has a more powerful and extensile trunk than the American, and its skull shows in consequence a greater space for the attachment of the muscles. The dentition is as follows:— Inc., $\frac{3-3}{3-3}$; can., $\frac{1-1}{1-1}$; premolars, $\frac{4-4}{4-4}$; molars, $\frac{3-3}{3-3}$. The outer incisors somewhat resemble canines, whilst the others are very small. The canines themselves are not large.

The tapir is not found in India proper, but the Malayan species is occasionally to be come across in Burmah, having been killed in Tenasserim.

No. 428. TAPIRUS MALAYANUS.

The Malay Tapir.

NATIVE NAMES.—*Ta-ra-shu*, Burmese; *Kuda-ayer*, Malayan; *Saladang* of the Limuns in Sumatra; *Gindol* of the Mannas in Sumatra; *Babi-alu* in Bencoolen; *Tennu* in Malacca.

HABITAT.—Tenasserim provinces, as high as the fifteenth degree north latitude; Lower Siam; the Malayan peninsula; Sumatra and Borneo.

DESCRIPTION.—General colour glossy black, but with the back, rump,

Tapirus Malayanus.

and sides of the belly white. The young are beautifully variegated, being striped and spotted with yellow fawn on the upper parts of the body, and with white below.

Mr. Mason writes: "Though seen so rarely, the tapir is by no means uncommon in the interior of the Tavoy and Mergui provinces. I have frequently come upon its recent footmarks, but it avoids the inhabited parts of the country. It has never been heard of north of the valley of the Tavoy river."

The tapir is naturally all the world over a very shy, retiring animal, but it is capable of being tamed when taken young, and of showing great attachment.

FAMILY RHINOCEROTIDÆ.

"The skeleton of the rhinoceros viewed generally has a resemblance to that of the little hyrax, the tapir, and the horse. The skull is very much elevated at the base, being somewhat of a pyramidal form, and the nasal bones curve upwards and downwards, and are of such a size and thickness, in order to support one or more immense horns, that they are quite unparalleled for their development in any other existing quadruped. The nasal bones, together with the premaxillary and maxillary bones, form the general contour for the external apertures of the nostrils. This is peculiar, and found in no other animal with the exception of the tapir."—*Prof. W. Boyd Dawkins and Mr. Oakley.*

The external appearance of this animal is familiar to most—a large ungainly creature, with a long head, a massive horn on its nose, sometimes two horns; a round unwieldly body covered with an immensely thick hide arranged in heavy folds; short tail and short legs, with three toes covered with broad nails or hoofs.

The stomach is simple; the intestines about eight times the length of the body, and the cæcum is large and sacculated. The horn is a mere agglutinated mass of hair or fibre superimposed on the skin, and has no bony core. The females have two inguinal mammæ.

The dentition is peculiar; "the grinders are implanted by distinct roots, and in the upper jaw their crowns are traversed by two deep folds of enamel which constitute open valleys. In the lower jaw they are composed of two crescent-shaped lobes, also open. The covering of cement is thin, and never fills up the valleys, as in the case of the more complex dental system in the horse. The normal number of grinders is seven in each jaw, while the incisors, as we have already remarked, vary not only in form but also are sometimes absent, and canines are not developed in any of the living or fossil members of the family."—*Boyd Dawkins and Oakley.*

The Rhinocerotidæ are divided into two groups—the Asiatic and the African; and the former consist of two genera—RHINOCEROS and CERATORHINUS, the former with one and the latter with two horns.

It is a moot point whether the rhinoceros is or is not the unicorn of Scripture, though it is by no means clear that the animal in question was a one-horned creature, but according to some might have been the great wild ox or urus of Macedonia. An Indian single-horned rhinoceros was sent from India to the king of Portugal in 1513, and from it various most distorted pictures were disseminated throughout Europe. It was represented as covered with a wondrous suit of armour beautifully decorated, and with a second horn on its shoulders!

The first one brought alive to England was in 1685. Parsons

describes and figures one brought to Europe in 1739, and another in 1741 ('Philosophical Transactions,' xlii.).

The Asiatic rhinoceroses differ from the African in having the skin divided into shields by well-marked folds, long upper cutting teeth, the African having none, and by the produced conical nasal bones of the skull instead of broad and rounded ones. There are one or two other minor yet well-marked differences which we need not mention here.

GENUS RHINOCEROS.

"The skin divided into shields by well-marked folds, lumbar and neck-folds well developed; horn single, anterior; part of occipital bone

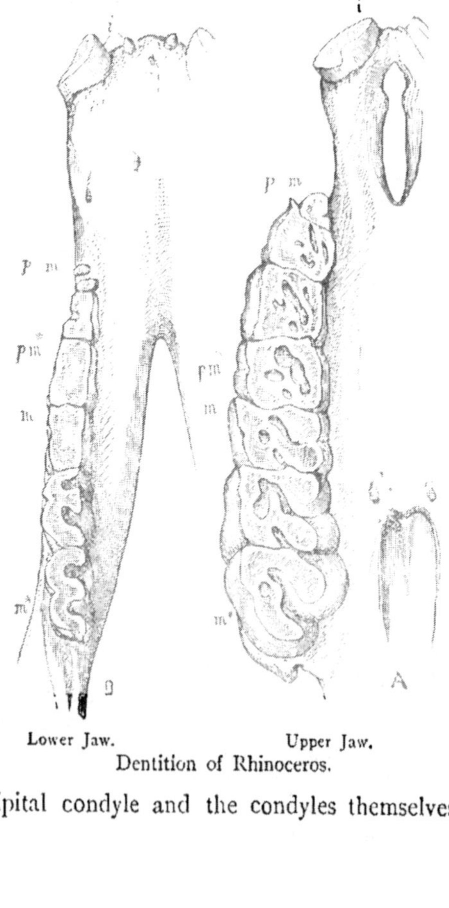

Lower Jaw. Upper Jaw.

Dentition of Rhinoceros.

near the occipital condyle and the condyles themselves prominent." —*Gray*.

There are two species in India, viz. *Rhinoceros Indicus* and *R. Sondaicus*, the latter being the Javan species.

For the following description of the former I have to thank Mr. J. Cockburn, who, with most unselfish kindness, kept back the article he was about to publish, and gave it to me to incorporate in this work. The following remarks on dentition are also his :*—

"The normal dentition of *R. Indicus* is: Inc., $\frac{1-1}{2-2}$; premolars, $\frac{4-4}{4-4}$; molars, $\frac{3-3}{3-3}$; but the dentition varies to a great extent; for example, in a specimen of *R. Sondaicus* it stood: Inc., $\frac{1-1}{2-2}$; molars, $\frac{6-7}{6-6}$. The first premolar in both *Indicus* and *Sondaicus* is a deciduous tooth, which is not usually replaced, and gradually drops out with age, but it may be retained till extreme old age. In the majority of cases it is either lost or worn down before the last molar is in wear. The incisors also vary greatly in the adult animal; they are $\frac{1-1}{2-2}$, the outer pair below being the formidable dagger-shaped tushes, with which they inflict the terrible gashes they can produce. The median pair lower are usually lost or absorbed by advancing age, having no functions, and the incisive tusks themselves are subject to very rapid wear, being often worn down before the animal has reached middle age. Occasionally *R. Indicus* has six incisors in the lower jaw (the normal number in other mammalia), and four in the upper, but this is very exceptional."—*J. Cockburn*, MS.

No. 429. RHINOCEROS INDICUS.

(*Jerdon's No.* 212).

NATIVE NAMES.—*Genda, Gonda, Ganda,* or *Genra*, Hindi; *Gor*, Assamese.

HABITAT.—Himalayan Terai, from Central Nepal to the extreme eastern corner of the valley of Assam.

"About three centuries ago this animal existed on the banks of the Indus. The Indian rhinoceros inhabits by preference heavy grass jungle, rarely entering forest. In this respect it differs from its ally *Sondaicus*, which is a forest-loving species, and even frequents mountainous countries. It is still numerous in the mighty grass jungles which extend along the foot of the Eastern Himalayas from their slopes to the banks of the Brahmaputra. It is yearly becoming more scarce

* There are some interesting notes on the dentition of the rhinoceros, especially in abnormal conditions, by Mr. Lydekker in the 'J. A. S. B.' for 1880, vol. xlix., part ii.

in the Nepal Terai, but is found there from Rohilkund to the Bhootan Doars."

DESCRIPTION.—The accompanying outline sketch, taken from *Nature* for April 1874, will give a better idea of the animal than a mere verbal description :—

"For convenience of description I will divide the body into five segments—the head, the cervical, the scapular, the abdominal, and the gluteal. At the junction of the head with the neck is a large deep collar or ruff or fold of skin, which gives a very peculiar appearance to the animal. Behind this is a second similar but smaller ruff, which does not hang so low down from the throat as the first. On the dorsal surface it transversely crosses the nape. It is then continued down angularly to about the centre of the anterior edge of the scapular shield, where it forms an obtuse angle with its posterior but major half. It is at the point where it forms this angle that it gives off what I call the cervical fold, which forms the boundary of the top front edge of the scapular shield, but is lost at a point in the shoulder nearly over the centre of the fore limb.

Rhinoceros Indicus.

"The scapular shield is a thick cuirass-like plate of skin, studded with round projections about the size of a shilling, and bearing much resemblance to the heads of bolts by which the shield was riveted to the body, and hence called 'boiler-bolt tubercules.' This shield is often removed from the carcase of a slain rhinoceros as a trophy, 'and it is in its centre, but slightly low, that the fatal spot lies which will take him in the heart' (*Pollock*).

"Between the scapular and the gluteal shields lies the abdominal segment. It calls for no particular description, except that the tubercles here are very much flatter and smaller than on either segments three and four. They are here about the size of a four-anna piece, and they seem to be crowded along the centre line of the body, while the dorsal surface is nearly free from them, and smooth.

"We next come to the gluteal segment. It is in this portion that the boiler-bolt tubercles attain their greatest development, some of them being perhaps three-tenths of an inch high.

"The gluteal segment is laterally crossed by three ridges of skin. The first, which is the only one indicated in the drawing, goes right across the buttock. In some animals there is an indication of a second below this, and about fourteen inches lower down a third, which only goes about a quarter of the way across. The tail is almost concealed in a deep groove, in which lie the perineum, &c. Both the front and hind limbs from the point at which they project from the body are finely covered with reticulated skin, forming pentagonal and hexagonal scales, very much as in *R. Sondaicus*, only much finer and less prominent.

"The Indian rhinoceros has the same habit as the African species of depositing its droppings in one spot till they form huge mounds, which

Rhinoceros Indicus.

the animal levels with its horns. It is probable that this rhinoceros was found throughout the plains of the N.W. Provinces in unreclaimed spots as late as the fifth or sixth century. According to the observation of Dr. Andrew Smith in South Africa these huge pachyderms do not absolutely require for their support the dense tropical vegetation we should think necessary to supply food to such huge beasts. This gentleman saw over fifty of them in one day in an open country covered with short grass and thorn-bushes about four feet high. From the affinities of the fauna of the N.W. Provinces, which are strongly African, it is probable that the plains of the N.W. Provinces were rather covered with scrubby open jungles and grass than with tropical primeval forests.

"Here and there belts of Dhak (*Butea frondosa*) were found, and in favoured spots doubtless other tree jungle, but it is improbable that primeval forest has existed since the depression of the Indo-Gangetic plain."—*J. Cockburn*, M.S.

The rhinoceros is supposed to be a very long-lived animal. Dr. Gray ('P. Z. S.' 1867, p. 1011) states on the authority of Mr. Blyth that a pair lived in the Barrackpore Park for forty-five years. They were exactly alike in size and general appearance; they never bred. There is no difference in the horns or form of the skull in the two sexes (*Blyth*, 'J. A. S. B.' vol. xxxi. p. 155).

No. 430. RHINOCEROS SONDAICUS.

The Javan Rhinoceros (*Jerdon's No.* 213).

NATIVE NAMES.—The same as last in Hindi; *Khyen-hsen*, Burmese; *Warak*, Javanese; *Badak*, Malayan.

HABITAT.—"The Bengal Sunderbunds, Tipperah, the swamps at the base of the Garo, Khasia, and Naga Hills" (*Pollock*). "Munipurf, extending into the western provinces of China, southward into Burmah, the Malayan peninsula, Sumatra, Java, and Borneo" (*J. Cockburn*, MS.).

Rhinoceros Sondaicus.

DESCRIPTION.—"Folds somewhat on the same plan as in *Indicus*, one marked distinction being that the lateral shoulder fold is continued upward over the back of the neck to form an independent saddle-shaped shield on the nape. The whole body covered with pentagonal or hexagonal warty insulæ. Females hornless" (*J. Cockburn*, MS.). Males with one horn.

SIZE.—Mr. Cockburn gives the following measurements of a female, which he states is the largest recorded specimen: "Length of body (head and body?), 12 feet 3 inches; tail, 2 feet $4\frac{1}{2}$ inches; height, 5 feet 6 inches." Dr. Jerdon gives: "Length 7 to 8 feet; height, $3\frac{1}{2}$ to $3\frac{3}{4}$ feet;" and he calls the animal "the lesser Indian rhinoceros," whereas Mr. Cockburn's measurement gives an animal somewhat longer, though not so high as the largest recorded specimen of *Indicus*. Blyth again writes ('Mammals of Burmah,' *see* 'J. A. S. B.' vol. xliv. part ii. 1875, p. 50):

"It is about a third smaller than *R. Indicus*, from which it is readily distinguished by having the tubercles of the hide uniformly of the same small size, and also by having a fold or plait of the skin crossing the nape in addition to that behind the shoulder-blades."

This rhinoceros seems to be found at all elevations, like the Sumatran one which was found by General Fytche at an altitude of 4000 feet; it is much more of a forester than the last. Blyth and Jerdon suppose it to be the same as the species hunted by the Moghul Emperor Baber on the banks of the Indus.

GENUS CERATORHINUS.

"The skin divided into shields by deep folds; the lumbar fold rudimentary, short, only occupying the middle of the space between the groin and the back; horns two, the front longer, curved backward, the hinder small; conical skull; forehead narrow, flat; the upper part of the nose on each side of the horns narrow, rounded, sub-cylindrical; the occipital region erect, the part near the condyles rather concave; the occipital condyle short, broad, oblong, placed obliquely inferior, scarcely prominent; lachrymal bone very large, irregular shaped."—*Dr. Gray*, 'P. Z. S.' 1867, p. 1021.

NO. 431. RHINOCEROS *vel* CERATORHINUS (CROSSI?) LASIOTIS.

The Ear-fringed Rhinoceros.

HABITAT.—Arakan, Tenasserim provinces; one was caught near Chittagong in 1868.

DESCRIPTION.—A thinner hide than with the preceding, and not tuberculated; the folds also are fewer in number; there is one great groove behind the shoulder-blades, and a less conspicuous one on the flank, and some slight folds about the neck and top of the limbs; the horns are two in number, the posterior one being the centre of the nose behind the anterior one, and almost over the anterior corner of the eye; the body (of a young specimen) is covered with long, fine, reddish hair, and the posterior margins of the ears have very long fringes of the same; the tail is short and hairy.

A young specimen of this animal (of which there is an excellent coloured plate in 'P. Z. S.' 1872, p. 494) was captured in 1868 in Chittagong. She had got into a quicksand, and had exhausted herself by floundering about. The natives contrived to attach two ropes to her neck, and, hauling her out, managed to make her fast to a tree. Next morning they found her so refreshed and vigorous that they were afraid to do anything more to her, and so sent messengers to the magistrate of Chittagong to report the capture. The same evening Captain Hood and Mr. Wickes started with eight elephants to secure the prize, and after a march of sixteen hours to the south of Chittagong, they came up to the animal. The elephants at first sight bolted, but were brought back by considerable exertion, and the rhinoceros was made fast to one by a rope. The poor creature roared with fright, and a second

Rhinoceros lasiotis.
(*R. Indicus* and *R. Sondaicus* in the distance.)

stampede ensued, in which luckily the rope slipped off the leg of the rhinoceros to which it was attached. Ultimately she was secured between two elephants and marched into Chittagong, where she soon got very tame. Eventually she was sent to England, and was purchased by the Zoological Society for £1250—a very handsome price, owing doubtless to the rarity of the specimen.

No. 432. RHINOCEROS *vel* CERATORHINUS SUMATRENSIS.

The Sumatran Rhinoceros.

NATIVE NAMES.—*Kyen-shan*, Burmese; *Bodok*, Malayan.

HABITAT.—Tenasserim provinces; Burmah, extending into Siam; the Malayan peninsula and Sumatra.

DESCRIPTION.—A smaller animal than the preceding, with a hard, black, rough, bristly skin; a deep fold behind the shoulder; ears set closer than in the last species, and filled with black hair internally; the muzzle in front of the first horn is broader; the horns are two in number, and attain a good size, curving, but slightly, backward; the tail is conspicuously longer than in *R. lasiotis*, and is tapering and not tufted. There is a well drawn and coloured plate of this species in the 'Proceedings of the Zoological Society' for 1872, p. 794, as also several engravings showing the heads of the two animals in juxtaposition.

SIZE.—About 3 feet 8 inches in height at the shoulder.

At first it was considered that *R. lasiotis* was of this species, and as such it was described and sent to England; but on the subsequent arrival of a genuine *R. Sumatrensis* from Malacca it was apparent that *R. lasiotis* was quite distinct. The latter is of larger size, lighter colour, with wide-set ears and a tufted tail. The former is smaller, darker, with narrow-set ears and a long tapering semi-nude tail.* The Society paid Mr. Jamrach £600 in 1872 for the female specimen from Malacca, which settled the question of separate species. A young *R. Sümatrensis* was born in the Victoria Docks in London on December 7th, 1872, on board the steamship *Orchis*. There is a coloured sketch of the little one in the 'P. Z. S.' for 1873, and an interesting account of it and the mother by Mr. Bartlett, the Superintendent of the Society's Gardens. From the circumstances of the capture of the mother it appears that the period of gestation of the rhinoceros is about the same as that of the hippopotamus, viz. seven months.

Although the number of species of living rhinoceros is but few, there are a great many fossil species which show that the animal was more plentiful and in greater variety in prehistoric times.

Remains of the woolly rhinoceros (*R. trichorhinus*) have been found, like those of the mammoth, imbedded in ice; it was about eleven and a-half feet in length, and its body was covered with woolly hair. A specimen found in 1771 or 1772 was entire, and clothed with skin, but so far decomposed as to prevent more than the head and feet being preserved; remains of other fossil species are found throughout Europe, including Great Britain, and also in India. In 'A Sketch of the History of the Fossil Vertebrata of India' by Mr. R. Lydekker, published in the 'Journal of the Asiatic Society of Bengal,' vol. xlix., 1880, will be found the names of eight species of fossil rhinoceros, inclusive of *R. Indicus*, which is found in *recent alluvia*—it is found with two others in the Pleistocene formation, and five others are from the Pleiomiocene.

SUB-ORDER ARTIODACTYLA.

We now come to the second division, and a very large one, of the UNGULATA, which in itself is again subdivided into non-ruminants and ruminants. The former comprises the pigs of the Old and the peccaries of the New World and the hippopotami; the latter contains the camels, llamas, deerlets, oxen, antelope, and deer. In the *Artiodactyla* the toes are even on all feet, being normally four (perfect and rudimentary) with the exception of the camel, giraffe and a few antelope, in which two only are present. To understand the subject thoroughly one must

* There is a very interesting letter in *The Asian* for July 20, 1880, p. 109, from Mr. J. Cockburn, about *R. Sumatrensis*, of which he considers *R. lasiotis* merely a variety. He says it has been shot in Cachar.—R. A. S.

compare the fore-foot of a deer or pig with our own hand; what we call the knee of the former is merely our wrist. The bones which run through the palm of the hand to the knuckles are the metacarpals; they are five in number, corresponding with the thumb and four fingers. In the *Artiodactyla*—or, I should say, in the *Ungulata* generally—the thumb is entirely wanting; in the *Artiodactyla* the fore and little fingers are shorter, rudimentary, or entirely wanting, and the two centre metacarpals, the middle and ring fingers are prolonged into what we call the leg below the knee in these animals, which consist of separate or fused bones terminated by the usual three joints of the finger, on the last of which is placed the hoof.

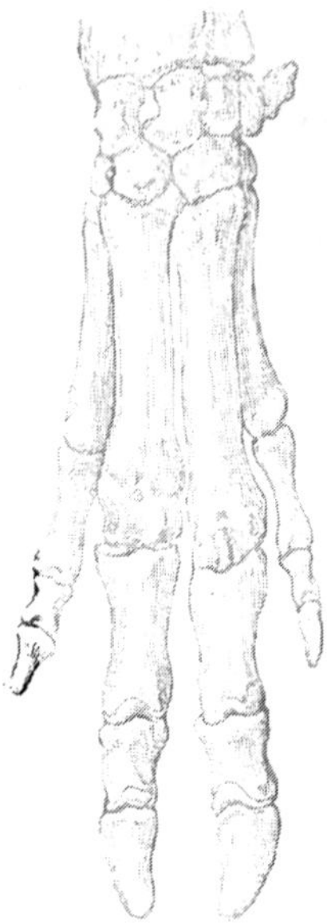

Bones of a Pig's foot.
(See also p. 528.)

The two halves are always symmetrical, and from this we may affirm that it is the thumb and not the little finger which is absent, for we know that, counting from the knuckles, our fingers have three joints, whereas the thumb has only two; so in the digits of the *Artiodactyla* are three joints at the end of each metacarpal. In the pig the metacarpals of the fore and little fingers are produced from the carpus or wrist, or, as is popularly termed in the case of these animals, the knee. They are more attenuated in the chevrotains or deerlets, of which our Indian mouse-deer is an example; in the *Cervidæ* they are more rudimentary, detached from the carpus, and are suspended free and low down, forming the little hoof-points behind; and a little above the proper hoofs in these the two large metacarpals are more or less joined or fused into one bone, and they are still more so in the camel, in which the fore and little finger bones are entirely absent. In the giraffe and prong-horn antelope they are also wanting. The hind feet are similarly constructed.*

Of the non-ruminantia we have only the Suidæ—the peccaries belonging to America, and the hippopotami to Africa.

FAMILY SUIDÆ—THE HOGS.

These have incisors in both jaws, which vary in number, the lower ones slanting forward. Their canines are very large and directed outwards and upwards in a curve, grinding against each other to a sharp edge and fine point. Their metacarpal bones are four in number, and are all distinct, in which respect they differ from the peccaries, in which

* See notes in Appendix C.

the central metacarpals and metatarsals are fused into a solid bone. The hogs have a prolonged snout, flexible at the end, with a firm cartilaginous tip, with which they are enabled to plough up the ground

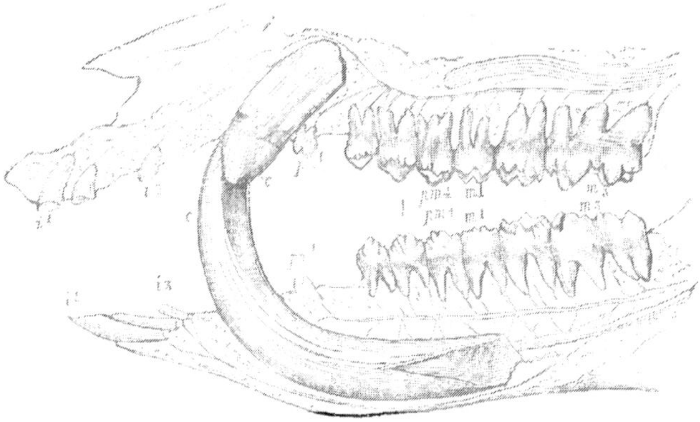

Dentition of Wild Boar.

in search of roots. They have also a very keen sense of smell. The normal dentition of the true hogs is as follows:—

Inc., $\frac{6}{6}$; can., $\frac{1-1}{1-1}$; premolars, $\frac{4-4}{4-4}$; molars, $\frac{3-3}{3-3}$ = 44.

The hogs, unlike other pachyderms, are noted for their fecundity.

GENUS SUS.

Incisors, $\frac{4}{6}$ or $\frac{6}{6}$; the lower ones slanted; the canines large and curved outwards and upwards; molars tuberculate; four toes on each foot—that is, two major and two minor, each hoofed.

No. 433. SUS SCROFA.

The European Wild Boar.

NATIVE NAMES.—*Guraz* or *Kuk*, Persian.

HABITAT.—Persia and the Thian Shan mountains near Kashgar.

DESCRIPTION.—Body dusky or greyish-brown, with a tendency to black, with black spots; large mouth with long projecting tusks; the hairs of the body coarse, mixed with a downy wool; bristles on the neck and shoulders. The young are marked with longitudinal stripes of reddish colour.

The wild boar of Europe apparently extends to the limits sometimes reached by Indian sportsmen. It is found in Persia, and specimens were brought back from Kashgar by the Yarkand Mission in 1873–74. The only divergence which these specimens showed from the European boar was the darker colour of the feet and legs, which were nearly black.

No. 434. SUS INDICUS.

The Indian Boar (*Jerdon's No.* 215).

NATIVE NAMES.—*Soor* or *Süar*, *Bura-janwar*, or *Bad-janwar*, *Barha*, Hindi; *Dukar*, Mahratti; *Paddi*, Gondi; *Pandi*, Telegu; *Handi*, *Mikka*, *Jewadi*, Canarese; *Kis* of the Bhaugulpore hill-tribes; *Tan-wet*, Burmese; *Walura*, Singhalese.

Sus Indicus.

HABITAT.—Throughout India, from a considerable elevation (12,000 feet according to Jerdon) down to the sea level. It is also common in Burmah and in Ceylon.

DESCRIPTION.—The head of the Indian wild boar differs considerably from the German one. Sir Walter Elliot says: "The head of the former is larger and more pointed, and the plane of the forehead straight, while it is concave in the European, the ears of the former are small and pointed; in the latter larger and not so erect. The Indian is altogether a more active-looking animal, the German has a stronger, heavier appearance."

Jerdon, who has in some measure adopted these remarks, adds that the tail is more tufted, and the malar beard is well marked.

The colour of the full-grown animal is brownish-black, sparsely clad with black hair; the ears are scantily covered with black hairs externally, but more abundantly inside. A crest of stiff black bristles extends from the occiput over the neck and shoulders and down the back; the bristles of the throat and breast are reversed, growing forwards instead of backwards, the tips being sometimes white; the limbs, which are well covered with bristly hair outside, are nearly naked within, and the tail is short, slightly hairy, and with a flat tip fringed with lateral bristles set like the barbs of a feather. The young are more hairy, and are striped with brown and fulvous yellow.

SIZE.—Head and body, about 5 feet; tail, 1 foot; height, from 30 to 36 inches.

This species is so well known to residents in India, not only from personal experience but from the numerous accounts of its chase—one of the most exciting of Indian field sports—that it would be almost superfluous to add anything more to the already redundant porcine literature, so I will confine myself to the habits of the animal in the jungles. It is gregarious, living in herds, usually called *sounders*, the derivation of which has often puzzled me as well as others; but McMaster says it is to be found in Bailey's English Dictionary, of which the fifteenth edition was published in 1753 as (among hunters) *a herd or company of swine*. An old boar is generally the chief, but occasionally he gets driven from the herd, and wanders solitary and morose, and is in such a case an awkward customer to tackle. An old boar of this kind is generally a match for a tiger; in fact few tigers, unless young and inexperienced, would attack one. I have known two instances of tigers being killed by boars; one happened a few miles from the station of Seonee, to which place we had the animal carried. (See Appendix C.) On another occasion, whilst on tour in the district, a deputation from a distant village came into my camp to beg of me to visit them, and shoot a large boar which had taken possession of a small rocky hill, and from it made his nightly forays into their rice fields, and was given to attacking those who approached him. I went and got the boar out and shot him, but lost a tiger, which also sneaked out and broke through a line of beaters; these two were the sole occupants of this small isolated knoll, and lived evidently on terms of mutual respect. The boar was the largest I had ever seen or killed, but, as the sun was getting fierce, and I had far to ride to camp, I regret I left him to the villagers without taking any measurements. It is allowable to shoot hogs in some hilly parts of India where riding is out of the question, otherwise the shooting of a boar in riding country is deservedly looked upon as the crime of vulpecide would be in Leicestershire—a thing not to be spoken of. The boar possesses a singular amount of courage; he is probably the most courageous of all animals, much more so than the tiger, but unless irritated he is not prone to attack at first sight, except in a few cases of solitary individuals, like the one above mentioned. I was once rather ludicrously and very uncomfortably held at bay by a boar who covered the retreat of his family. One evening, after dismissing my *amlah*, I took up a shot gun, and, ordering the elephant to follow, strolled across some fields to a low scrub-covered hill where I thought I might pick up a few partridges or a peafowl before dusk. On entering the bush which skirted the base of the hill I was suddenly brought up by a savage grunt, and there in front of me stood an old boar with his bristles up, whilst the rest of his family scampered off into the thicket. I remembered Shakespeare's (the poet's—not the gallant shikari general's) opinion :—

> "To fly the boar before the boar pursues
> Were to incense the boar to follow us,"

and therefore stood my ground, undergoing the stern scrutiny of my bristly friend, who cocked his head on one side and eyed me in a doubtful sort of way, whilst he made up his mind whether to go for me or not, whilst I on my part cogitated on the probable effect at close quarters of two barrels of No. 6 shot. However, he backed a bit, and then sidled to the rear for a few paces, when he brought up with another grunt, but, finding I had not moved, he finally turned round and dashed after his spouse and little ones. (See also Appendix C, p. 528.)

Colonel (now General) Shakespear winds up a thrilling account of a fight with one with the following paragraph, which will give a good idea of the endurance of these creatures :—

"There he was with a broken spear in his withers, the shaft sticking up a foot and a-half from the blade, knocking over a horseman and wounding his horse; receiving two bullets—ten to the pound each—the first in his neck and throat, a very deadly part in all animals; the second breaking his jaw, and fired within a few feet of the muzzle; making good his charge, cutting down his enemy like grass, wounding him, knocking over a second man armed with a spear, defying the dogs, and then, when in the act of charging again, shot to the brain and dying without a groan."

Although I had not intended giving any shikar stories, I cannot resist quoting one from General McMaster's 'Notes on Jerdon.' He writes :—

"In further proof of the savage courage of a boar I may mention the following instance which is recorded in the 'Hunt Annals' of the 25th December, 1869. A large *unwounded* boar had succeeded in getting into some thick bushes. On being bullied by a terrier he charged the nearest hunter, and ripped the horse very badly. Two other sportsmen who were not riding then tried to tempt the boar to charge, one by firing No. 10 or quail shot into the bush, the other by riding a camel into it.

The last was successful, for, charging straight at the camel's legs (receiving some shot in his face on his way) he completely routed the whole arrangement, knocked over and ripped the camel, which broke its leg in falling, and then made away across the fields; he was followed and twice speared, but he was as cunning as courageous, and managed to give his pursuers the slip in some long grass and thick bushes. This boar's savage charge at the camel was within a few yards of all of us, for every one was trying to entice him to come forth; after his headlong rush out of the bush he reared so upright in his attempt to reach his clumsy disturber, which was quite frantic from deadly fear, that he succeeded in ripping it in what in a horse would be termed the stifle joint. The poor brute rolled over in its agony, smashed one of its legs in the fall, and was of course shot. Luckily the rider, one of the best known among the Nagpore Hunt, was not hurt."

I believe a wild pig will charge at anything when enraged. I had an elephant who, though perfectly staunch with tigers, would bolt from a wild boar. The period of gestation is four months, and it produces twice a year; it is supposed to live to the age of twenty years, and, as its fecundity is proverbial, we might reasonably suppose that these animals would be continually on the increase, but they have many enemies, whilst young, amongst the felines, and the sows frequently fall a prey to tigers and panthers. Occasionally I have come across in the jungles a heap of branches and grass, and at first could not make out what it was, but the Gonds soon informed me that these heaps were the nests or lairs of the wild pigs, and they invariably turned them over to look for squeakers. These are funny little things, of a tortoiseshell colour, being striped reddish yellow and dark brown. There is an old writer on Indian field sports, Williamson, who makes some correct observations on the habits ot the wild hog, although much in his book (now, I fancy, out of print) is open to question. He writes: "The wild hog delights in cultivated situations, but he will not remain where water is not at hand, in which he may, unobserved, quench his thirst and wallow at his ease; nor will he resort for a second season to a spot which does not afford ample cover, whether of heavy grass or of underwood jungle, within a certain distance, for him to fly to in case of molestation, and especially to serve as a retreat during the hot season, as otherwise he would find no shelter. The sugar-cane is his great delight. both as being his favourite food and as affording a high, impervious, and unfrequented situation. These hogs commit great devastation, especially the breeding sows, which not only devour, but cut the canes for litter, and throw them up into little huts, which they do with much art, leaving a small entrance which they stop up at pleasure. Sows never quit their young pigs without completely shutting them up. This is, indeed, requisite only for a few days, as the young brood may be seen following the mother at a round pace when not more than a week or ten days old." The fields of *urhur* or *ruhur dâl* (*Cajanus Indicus*) also afford good shelter to pigs. They feed chiefly at night, and in Central India numbers are shot by native shikaries in moonlight nights over water and favourite crops or in particular runs. Many castes of Hindus, who would turn with abhorrence from the village pig, will not scruple to eat the flesh of the wild boar. On the whole it is probably a cleaner feeder, but it will not hesitate to devour carrion if it should come across a dead animal in its wanderings.

No. 435. SUS ANDAMANENSIS.

The Andaman Island Pig.

HABITAT.—Andaman islands; Nicobars (?)

DESCRIPTION.—Much smaller than the last. "The concavity of the cheeks in front of the orbit deeply concave." Tail short, a mere tubercle in fact; the body well clad with somewhat shaggy black hair, probably allied to *Sus Papuensis.*

Dr. Gray was of opinion (*see* his article on the *Suidæ*, 'P. Z. S.' 1868) that the skull of this species is more allied to the *Babirussa* than any others of the pigs, the front of the canines being rather more produced than in other species, but not nearly so much so as in *Babirussa.*

No. 436. SUS MOUPINENSIS.

HABITAT.—Thibet.

A description of this, which I have not by me at present, will be found in Professor Milne Edwards's 'Recherches sur les Mammifères,' p. 377.

GENUS PORCULA.

Head conical, moderate; ears small, erect, hairy; cheeks without any tubercles; tail very short, rudimentary; cutting teeth $\frac{6}{6}$, the two upper front largest, the lateral lower small; intermaxillary moderate, not produced; canines small, scarcely elevated above the other teeth, the upper one rather spread out, but not reflexed; premolars, $\frac{4-4}{4-4}$ (*Gray*); molars, $\frac{3-3}{3-3}$; the fourth toe on all the feet small and unequal. Jerdon observes: "This genus, it will be remarked, makes an approach to the American peccaries in the non-excerted canines, the short tail, and the small fourth toe." Hodgson's dental formula shows one premolar less, viz. teeth: $\frac{6}{6}, \frac{1-1}{1-1}, \frac{6-6}{6-6}$.

No. 437. PORCULA SALVANIA.

The Pigmy Hog of the Saul Forests (*Jerdon's No.* 216).

NATIVE NAMES.—*Sano-banel*, Nepalese; *Chota-suar*, Hindi.

HABITAT.—The Saul forests of the Sikim and Nepal Terai.

DESCRIPTION.—According to Mr. Hodgson "the pigmy hog is about the size of a large hare, and extremely resembles both in form and size a young pig of the ordinary wild kind of about a month old, except in its dark and unstriped pelage. The likeness of the limbs and members to those of the common hog is so close that every purpose of general description of the pigmy hog is served by pointing to that

Porcula Salvania.

resemblance, desiring only that heed should be taken by the observer of the shorter jaws, and eye consequently placed midway between the snout and ear; of the much shorter tail, nude, straight, and not extending so far as the bristles of the rump, and lastly of the smallness of the inner hind toe. The ears also are quite nude, and the abdominal surface of the neck, as well as the insides of the limbs and the belly, are nearly so, but the upper and lateral external parts are covered thickly with bristles, even longer and more abundant than those of the wild or tame hog—save upon the ridge of the neck, where the common hog has more or less of, and generally a conspicuous mane, but the pigmy hog little or none"—"the colour of the animal is a black brown, shaded vaguely with dirty amber or rusty red."

SIZE.—Head and body, from 18 to 20 inches; height, 8 to 10 inches; weight, 7 to 10 lbs.

This little animal, according to Hodgson's account of it (a most interesting one, which will be found in the 'Journal of the Asiatic Society of Bengal,' vol. xvi. May 1847), seems to have the disposition of the peccary as well as the resemblance; it goes, he says, in herds, and the males fearlessly attack intruders, "charging and cutting the naked legs of their human or other attackers with a speed that baffles the eyesight, and a spirit which their straight sharp laniaries renders really perplexing, if not dangerous."

RUMINANTIA—THE RUMINANTS

These differ materially from the foregoing section of the Artiodactyla by the construction of their digestive organs. Instead of the food being masticated and passed at once into the stomach, each mouthful is but slightly bruised and passed into the paunch, whence at leisure it is regurgitated into the mouth to be chewed. For such an operation the machinery is of course more complicated than in other animals, and I must therefore attempt to describe briefly and as clearly as I can the construction of the ruminating stomach. Taking the ox as a typical specimen, we find four well-defined chambers varying in size. The first of these is the rumen or paunch, in which the unmasticated food is stored; it is a large sac partly bent on itself, and narrowing towards its junction with the œsophagus or gullet, and the entrance into the second chamber. It is lined with a mucous membrane, which is covered with a pile or villous surface, and this membrane is what is sold in butchers' shops as tripe. From this bag (the paunch) in the act of rumination a certain portion of the food is ejected into the second chamber, which is termed the reticulum (i.e. a little net) from the peculiar arrangement of its inner or mucous surface, which is lined with a network of shallow hexagonal cells. The functions of this receptacle are probably the forming of the food into a bolus, and by a spasmodic contraction the forcing of it back through the gullet into the mouth for mastication. Here it is well chewed, and, being thoroughly mixed with saliva passes back; on being swallowed in a soft pulpy state it passes the groove or valve communicating with the chamber from which it issued, and goes straight into the psalterium or manyplies, as the third chamber is called. This is globular, but most of its interior is filled up with folds like the leaves of a book, more or less unequal. It is not quite clear what the peculiar functions of this chamber are, but the semi-liquid food, passing through it, goes into the proper stomach (abomasum or reed) and is here acted upon by the gastric juice. Professor Garrod thus describes the probable order of events in the act of rumination: "The paunch contracts, and in so doing forces some of the food into the honeycomb bag, where it is formed into a bolus by the movement of its walls, and then forced into the gullet, from which by a reverse action it reaches the mouth, where it is chewed and mixed with the saliva until it becomes quite pulpy, whereupon it is again swallowed. But now, because it is soft and semi-fluid, it does not devaricate the walls of the groove communicating with the manyplies, and so, continuing on along its tubular interior, it finds its way direct into the third stomach, most of it filtering between the membrous laminæ on its way to the fourth stomach, where it becomes acted on by the gastric juice. After the remasticated food has reached the manyplies, the groove in the reticulum is pushed open by a fresh bolus, and so the process is repeated until the food consumed has all passed on towards the abomasum or true digestive stomach."

The ruminants are peculiar also in their dentition; in the so-called true ruminants there are no incisors or cutting teeth in the upper jaw, but the teeth of the lower jaw are opposed to a hard callous pad; the herbage is cropped by being nipped between these teeth and the pad, and detached by an upward motion; in some few, such as the musk deer, Chinese water deer and the rib-faced deer or muntjac the upper canines exist, and are largely developed.

The camels and llamas possess two cutting teeth in the upper jaw, and in this respect they differ from the true ruminants, as also in some internal features.

The grinding teeth are six on each side of the jaw, and are composed of alternate convolutions of enamel, dentine and cement, which wear unequally by the lateral motion of grinding, and so form the necessary inequality of surface.

The centre metacarpal bones in the Ruminantia are fused into one common bone, except in the deerlets, which also have the two outer fore and little finger metacarpals distinct, whereas they are but rudimentary in the rest of the true ruminants, and totally absent in the camels.

The following is the classification at present adopted: SUB-ORDER *Ruminantia*, containing two sections, viz. True Ruminants and the Camels (*Tylopoda*). SECTION *True Ruminants*, containing two divisions, viz. Horned Ruminants and Hornless Ruminants, such as the chevrotains or deerlets (*Tragulidæ*). DIVISION Horned Ruminants, containing two groups, viz. Hollow-horned Ruminants (*Bovidæ*), and Solid-horned Ruminants (*Cervidæ*). The deerlets possess no psalterium or third stomach, except in a rudimentary form, and their feet approximate to those of the pigs, and they are destitute of horns. The hollow-horned ruminants are these which bear a persistent sheath of horn on a bony core; the others bear solid antlers which are periodically shed, and grow afresh.

FAMILY BOVIDÆ—HOLLOW-HORNED RUMINANTS.

In these there is an elongated process of bone on the frontals, termed the "horn cores," which are covered with a horny sheath which is never shed, but continues to grow till full adult life, and probably whilst life lasts, the growth being from the base. In some of these the females are horned, but the majority are hornless. These have all the typical organs of rumination and digestion, and they consist of the goats, sheep, antelope, oxen, and buffalos.

SUB FAMILY CAPRINÆ—GOATS AND SHEEP.

These are noted for having, as a general rule, horns in both sexes, though of varying quality; they are usually compressed, triangular, rugose, with transverse ridges, and curving backwards or spirally; no canines. Feet pits in some; sub-orbital gland small or absent.

GENUS OVIS—THE SHEEP.

Horns in both sexes; in the male very large, angular, deeply wrinkled, turned downwards in a bold circle, with the point curved outwards; the nasal bones are arched; small feet pits; two mammæ.

No. 438. OVIS POLII.

Marco Polo's Sheep.

NATIVE NAMES.—*Rass* or *Roosh* on the Pamir; *Kuch-kar* (male), *Mesh* (female), in Wakhan.

HABITAT.—Thian Shan mountains, north of Kashgar, and Yarkand, at elevations exceeding 9000 feet.

DESCRIPTION.—During winter light greyish-brown on the sides of the body, with a dark line down the middle of the back, white below. In summer the grey changes to dark brown. The horns describe a circle of about one and a quarter when viewed from the side, and point directly outwards. One of the finest specimens I have seen, which was exhibited at a meeting of the Asiatic Society in December

1879, and is now in the Indian Museum, measures over sixty-seven inches from base to tip along the curve, with a circumference at base of sixteen inches and a width from tip to tip in a straight line of fifty-three inches; one in the British Museum measures sixty-three inches, but is wider in its spread, being fifty-four inches across at the tips. Major Biddulph, who presented the head to our museum, remarked

Ovis Polii.

that the strength of the neck muscles must be enormous to allow of so great a weight being easily carried, and it was doubtless owing to this weight that the *Ovis Polii* and other great sheep that he had observed had a very erect carriage, which has also been noticed by others of the *Ovis Ammon.*

I have never seen this animal in the flesh, and can only therefore give what I gather from others about it, which is not much, as it is not very well known.

SIZE.—Stands nearly four feet at the shoulder.

In the article on Asiatic sheep by Sir Victor Brooke and Mr. B. Brooke in the 'Proceedings of the Zoological Society' in 1875, there is an excellent series of engravings of horns of these animals, amongst which are two of *Ovis Polii.* The description of the animal itself appears to be faulty, for it is stated that around the neck is a pure white mane, whereas Mr. Blanford wrote to the Society a few months later to the effect that he had examined a series of skins brought from Kashgar, and found that none possess a trace of a mane along the neck, as represented in a plate of the animal, there being some long hair behind the horns and a little between the shoulders, but none on the back of the neck. The animal has a very short tail also—so short it

Horns of *Ovis Polii.*

can hardly be seen in life. According to M. Severtzoff there is a dark line above the spinal column from the shoulders to the loins; a white anal disc surrounds the tail; this disc above is bordered by a rather dark line, but below it extends largely over the hinder parts of the thighs, shading gradually into the brown colour of the legs. The light greyish-brown of the sides shades off into white towards the belly.

He gives the following particulars concerning its habits: "It is not a regular inhabitant of the mountains, but of high situated hilly plains, where *Festuca*, *Artemisia*, and even *Salsolæ* form its principal food. It only takes to the mountains for purposes of concealment, avoiding even then the more rocky localities. It keeps to the same localities summer and winter. Its speed is very great, but the difficulty in overtaking wounded specimens may be partly attributed to the distressing effect of the rarefied air upon the horses, which has apparently no effect whatever on the sheep. The weight of an old specimen killed and gralloched by

M. Severtzoff was too much for a strong mountain camel, the animal requiring four hours to do four versts (2·6 miles), and being obliged to lie down several times during the journey. He reckons the entire weight of a male *Ovis Polii* to be not less than 16 or 17 poods (576 to 612lbs.); the head and horns alone weigh over two poods (72 lbs.)." *

I have before me a beautiful photograph by Mr. Oscar Malitte, of Dehra Doon, of a very large skull of this sheep, with the measurements given. The photograph is an excellent one of a magnificent head, and I should say if the measurements have been correctly made, that the horns are the longest, though not the thickest, on record.

The dimensions given are as follows:—

	Inches.
Round the curve	73
From tip to tip	48
Girth at base	14

The next largest head to this is the very fine one in the Indian Museum, presented by Major Biddulph:—

	Inches.
Round the curve	67
From tip to tip	53
Girth at base	16

There is another in the British Museum:—

	Inches.
Round the curve	63
From tip to tip	54
Girth at base	16

From the above measurements it will be seen that the horns in the photograph before me are of greater length, but not so massive as the other two. They are also more compressed in their curvature than the others, and so the tip to tip measurement is less. The skull appears to be that of a very old animal; the horns are quite joined at the base, and from the incrustation on the bones I should say it had been picked up, and was not a shikar trophy. Anyhow it is a valuable specimen.†

No. 439. OVIS HODGSONI.

The Argali or Ovis Ammon of Thibet.

NATIVE NAMES.—*Hyan*, *Nuan*, *Nyan*, *Niar*, *Nyaud* or *Gnow*.

HABITAT.—The Thibetan Himalayas at 15,000 feet and upwards.

DESCRIPTION.—The following description was given by a correspondent of the *Civil and Military Gazette* in the issue of the 21st October,

* It must be remembered that at such great elevations a camel is unable to bear a very heavy load.

† See notes to *Ovis Polii* in Appendix C, p. 528.

OVIS HODGSONI.

1880: "The male dark earthy brown above, lighter below; rump lighter coloured; tail one inch; white ruff of long hairs on throat and chin; hair of body short, brittle, and close-set. The female darker coloured than the male, and may often be distinguished, when too far to see the horns, by the dark hue of the neck." Both male and female are horned; the horns of the former are very large, some are reported as being as much as four feet long, and 22 inches in circumference at the base. Dr. Jerdon quotes Colonel Markham in giving 24 inches as the circumference of one pair. They are deeply rugose, triangular, and compressed, deeper than broad at the base, forming a bold sweep of about four-fifths of a circle, the points turning outwards, and ending obtusely. The horns of the female are mentioned by various writers as being from 18 to 22 inches, slightly curved; but the correspondent of the *Civil and Military Gazette* above quoted gives 24 inches as his experience.

SIZE.—From 10 to 12 hands, sometimes an inch over.

A very interesting account of this animal, with a good photograph of the head, is given in Kinloch's 'Large Game-shooting in Thibet and the North-west.' He says: "In winter the *Ovis Ammon* inhabits the lower and more sheltered valleys, where the snow does not lie in any great quantity. As summer advances, the males separate from the females, and betake themselves to higher and more secluded places. They appear to be particular in their choice of a locality, repairing year after year to the same places, where they may always be found, and entirely neglecting other hills which apparently possess equal advantages as regards pasturage and water. Without a knowledge of their haunts a sportsman might wander for days and never meet with old rams, although perhaps never very far from them. I have myself experienced this, having hunted for days over likely ground without seeing even the track of a ram, and afterwards, under the guidance of an intelligent Tartar, found plenty of them on exactly similar ground a mile or two from where I had been. The flesh of the *Ovis Ammon*, like that of all the Thibetan ruminants, is excellent; it is always tender, even on the day it is killed, and of very good flavour, possibly caused by the aromatic herbs which constitute so large a portion of the scanty vegetation of those arid regions.

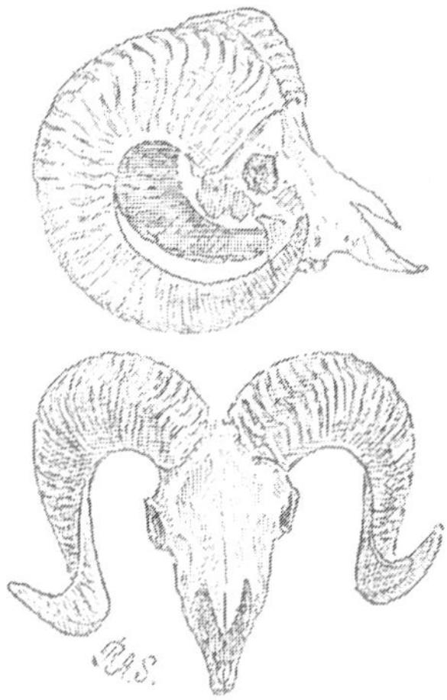

Ovis Hodgsoni.

"No animal is more wary than the *Ovis Ammon*, and this, combined with the open nature of the ground which it usually inhabits, renders it perhaps the most difficult of all beasts to approach. It is however, of course, sometimes found on ground where it can be stalked, but even then it is most difficult to obtain a quiet shot, as the instant one's head is raised one of the herd is nearly sure to give the alarm, and one only gets a running shot.

"*Ovis Ammon* shooting requires a great deal of patience. In the first place, unless the sportsman has very good information regarding the ground, he may wander for days before he discovers the haunts of the old rams; and, secondly, he may find them on ground where it is hopeless to approach them. In the latter case all that can be done is to wait, watch them until they move to better ground, and if they will not do this the same day, they must be left till the next. Sooner or later they will move to ground where they can be stalked, and then, if proper care is exercised, they are not much more difficult to get near than other animals; but the greatest precautions must be taken to prevent being seen before one fires. Some men may think this sort of shooting too troublesome, and resort to driving, but this is very uncertain work, and frightens the animals away, when, by the exercise of patience, a quiet shot might be obtained."

A writer in *The Asian*, whose 'Sportsman's Guide to Kashmir and Ladakh' contains most valuable information, writes thus in the issue of August 30, 1881, of the keen sense of smell possessed by this animal, and I take the liberty of quoting a paragraph :—

"The *Ovis Ammon* is possessed of the sense of smell to a remarkable degree, and, as every one who has stalked in Ladakh is aware, the wind is treacherous. If the stalker feels a puff of wind on his back when within 700 or 800 yards of the game, he well knows that it is 'all up.' On the tops of the mountains and in the vicinity of glaciers these puffs of wind are of frequent occurrence ; often they will only last for a few seconds, but that is sufficiently long to ruin the chance of getting a shot at the *Ovis*. Except for this one fact, we cannot admit that the nyan is harder to approach than any other hill sheep."

No. 440. OVIS KARELINI.

Karelin's Wild Sheep.

NATIVE NAMES.—*Ar* or *Ghuljar* (male), *Arka* (female), Khirghiz; *Külja*, Turki of Kashgar.

HABITAT.—Mountains north-west of Kashgar, and thence northwards beyond the Thian Shan mountains on to the Semiretchinsk Altai.

DESCRIPTION (by Sir Victor Brooke and Mr. Brooke, translated and abstracted from Severtzoff, *see* 'P. Z. S.' 1875, p. 512).—"The horns are moderately thick, with rather rounded edges; frontal surface very prominent, orbital surface rather flat, narrowing only in the last third of its length. The horns are three times as long as the skull. The basal and terminal axis of the horns rise parallel with each other; the median axis parallel with the axis of the skull. The neck is covered by a white mane, shaded with greyish-brown. The light brown of the back and sides is separated from the yellowish-white of the belly by a wide dark line. The light brown of the upper parts gets gradually lighter towards the tail, where it becomes greyish-white, but does not form a sharply marked anal disc. On the back there is a sharply marked dark line running from the shoulders to the loins. I did not find any soft hair under the long winter hair in October."

SIZE.—Height at the shoulder, 3 feet 6 inches; length of the horns, from 44 to 45 inches.

The following is a description by Dr. Stoliczka of this animal, which

Horns of *Ovis Karelini.*

he took to be *Ovis Polii*, and described it as such in the 'P. Z. S.' for 1874, page 425. In the same volume is a plate which, however, is shewn by Mr. Blanford ('Sc. Res. Second Yarkand Mission,' p. 83) to be inaccurate:—

"*Male in winter dress.*—General colour above hoary brown, distinctly rufescent or fawn on the upper hind neck and above the shoulders, darker on the loins, with a dark line extending along the ridge of tail to the tip. Head above and at the sides a greyish-brown, darkest on the hind head, where the central hairs are from four to five inches long, while between the shoulders somewhat elongated hairs indicate a short mane. Middle of upper neck hoary white, generally tinged with fawn; sides of body and the upper part of the limbs shading from brown to white, the hair becoming more and more tipped with the latter colour. Face, all the lower parts, limbs, tail, and all the hinder parts, extending well above towards the loins, pure white.

"The hairs on the lower neck are very much lengthened, being from five to six inches long. Ears hoary brown externally, almost white internally. Pits in front of the eye distinct, of moderate size and depth, and the hair round them generally somewhat darker brown than the rest of sides of the head. The nose is slightly arched and the muzzle sloping. The hair is strong, wiry, and very thickly set, and at the base intermixed with scanty, very fine fleece; the average length of the hairs on the back is 2 to 2½ inches. The iris is brown. The horns are subtriangular, touching each other at the base, curving gradually with a long sweep backwards and outwards; and, after completing a full circle, the compressed points again curve backwards and outwards; their surface is more or less closely transversely ridged.

"The colour of full-grown females does not differ essentially from that of the males, except that the former have much less white on the middle of the upper neck. The snout is sometimes brown, sometimes almost entirely white, the dark eye-pits becoming then particularly conspicuous. The dark ridge along the tail is also scarcely traceable. In size, both sexes of *Ovis Polii* appear to be very nearly equal, but the head of the female is less massive, and the horns, as in allied species, are comparatively small: the length of horn of one of the largest females obtained is 14 inches along the periphery, the distance at the tips being 15 inches, and at the base a little more than one inch. The horns themselves are much compressed; the upper anterior ridge is wanting on them; they curve gradually backwards and outwards towards the tip, though they do not nearly complete even a semicircle. In young males, the horns at first resemble in direction and slight curvature those of the female, but they are always thicker at the base and distinctly triangular.

"The length of the biggest horn of male along the periphery of curve was 56 inches, and the greatest circumference of a horn of a male specimen at the base 18½ inches.

"Mr. Blyth, the original describer of *Ovis Polii*, from its horns, was justified in expecting, from their enormous size, a correspondingly large-bodied animal; but in reality such does not appear to exist. Although the distance between the tips of the horns seems to be generally about equal to the length of the body, and although the horns are very much larger, but not thicker or equally massive, with those of the *Ovis Ammon* of the Himalayas, the body of the latter seems to be comparatively higher. Still it is possible that the *Ovis Polii* of the Pamir may stand higher than the specimens described, which were obtained from the Tian Shan range.

"Large flocks of *Ovis Polii* were observed on the undulating high plateau to the south of the Chadow-Kul, where grass vegetation is abundant. At the time the officers of the Mission visited this ground, i.e. in the beginning of January, it was the rutting season. The characters of the ground upon the Pamir and upon the part of the Tian Shan inhabited by these wild sheep are exactly similar."

The following remarks on the habits of this species are from Sir Victor Brooke's abstract of Servertzoft's description : "*Ovis Karelini*, like other sheep, does not live exclusively amongst the rocks, as is the case with the different species of *Capra*. It is not satisfied, like the latter, with small tufts of grass growing in the clefts of the rocks, but requires more extensive feeding grounds ; it is, therefore, more easily driven from certain districts than is the case with *Capra*. In the neighbourhood of Kopal, for instance, the goats are abundant in the central parts of the steppes of Kara, whilst the sheep have been partially driven from these places, only visiting them in autumn.

"On the southern ranges of the Semiretchinsk Altai, in the vicinity of the river Ili, wherever good meadows and rocky places are found, *Ovis Karelini* occurs at elevations of from 2000 to 3000 feet ; at the sources of the rivers Lepsa, Sarkan, Kora, Karatala, and Koksa it goes as high as 10,000, and even to 12,000 feet in the neighbourhood of the Upper Narin. In winter it is found at much lower elevations."

In a paper by Captain H. Trotter, R.E., read before the Royal Geographical Society on the 13th of May, 1878, on the geographical results of the mission to Kashgar under Sir Douglas Forsyth ('Journal R. G. S.' vol. xlviii., 1878, p. 193), I find the following account refering to this sheep, there mentioned under the name of *Ovis Polii* : "For twenty-five miles above Chakmák the road continues gently ascending along the course of the frozen stream, passing through volcanic rocks to Turgat Bela, a little short of which the nature of the country alters, and the precipitous hills are replaced by gently undulating grassy slopes, abounding with the *Ovis Polii*.*

"These extensive grassy slopes, somewhat resembling the English downs, are a very curious feature of the country, and not only attract the Kirghiz as grazing grounds for their cattle, but are equally sought after by the large herds of guljar, in one of which Dr. Stoliczka counted no less than eighty-five."

The Chakmák and Turgat Bela spoken of are on the southern slopes of the Thian Shan mountains, which form the boundary between Russia and Eastern Turkestan, separating the provinces of Semiretchinsk and Kashghar. The Turgat pass, about 12,760 feet, lies between the Kashgharian fort of Chakmák and the Russian fort Naryn or Narin. Captain Trotter mentions in a foot-note that these sheep, as well as ibex, abound in these hills in such large quantities that they form the principal food of the garrisons of the outposts. At Chakmák they saw a large shed piled up to the roof with the frozen carcases of these

* *Ovis Heinsi* and *Ovis nigromontana* are doubtful species allied to the foregoing, and are not found within the limits assigned to this work.

animals. (A most valuable map of the country is published in the 'Journal' with this paper.)

The chief difference between this species and *Ovis Polii* consists in the much greater length and divergence of horns of the latter and the longer hair on the neck.

No. 441. Ovis Brookei.

Brooke's Wild Sheep.

HABITAT.—Ladakh, or probably the Kuenluen range north of Ladakh.

DESCRIPTION.—This species is founded on a single specimen, which, in the opinion of Mr. Blyth, Mr. Edwin Ward, F.Z.S., Sir Victor Brooke and others, differed materially from all other wild sheep, but, as they had only a head to go upon, further investigation in this direction is

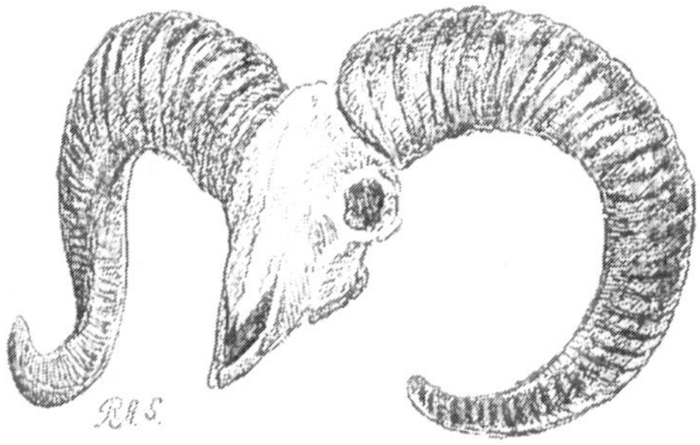

Ovis Brookei.

necessary. It is not even certain where the animal was shot, but it is believed to have been obtained in the vicinity of Leh in Ladakh. It is apparently allied to the *O. Ammon* of Thibet, which Sir Victor and Mr. B. Brooke term in their paper *O. Hodgsonii*, but it differs in its much smaller size, in its deeply sulcated horns, the angles of which are very much rounded, and the terminal curve but slightly developed. It differs also from *O. Vignei* and *O. Karelini*. The orbits project less, with greater width between them, the length of the molar teeth also exceeds the others. There are two wood-cuts of the skull and horns in the 'P. Z. S.' 1874, page 143, illustrating Mr. Edwin Ward's paper on the subject.

The following are the dimensions of the specimen :—

	Inches.
Length of skull	11
Smallest breadth between orbits	$4\frac{5}{8}$
Length of horns, round curve	$33\frac{1}{2}$
Circumference of horns	$13\frac{3}{8}$

No. 442. OVIS VIGNEI.

Vigne's Wild Sheep.

NATIVE NAMES.—*Sha* or *Shapoo.*

HABITAT.—Little Thibet; Ladakh, from 12,000 to 14,000 feet.

DESCRIPTION.—General colour brownish-grey, beneath paler; belly white; a short beard of stiffish brown hair; the horns of the male are sub-triangular, rather compressed laterally and rounded posteriorly, deeply sulcated, curving outward and backward from the skull; points divergent. The female is beardless, with small horns. The male horns run from 25 to 35 inches, but larger have been recorded.

This sheep was for some time, and is still by some, confounded with the oorial (*Ovis cycloceros*), but there are distinct differences, as will be seen further on, when I sum up the evidence. It inhabits the elevated ranges of Ladakh, and is found in Baltistan, where it is called the *oorin.*

No. 443. OVIS CYCLOCEROS.

The Punjab Wild Sheep (Jerdon's No. 236).

NATIVE NAMES.—*Oorial* or *Ooria*, in the Punjab; *Koch* or *Kuch*, in the Suleiman range.

HABITAT.—The Salt range of the Punjab; on the Suleiman range; the Hazarah hills; and the vicinity of Peshawar.

DESCRIPTION.—General colour rufous brown; face livid, side of mouth and chin white; a long thick black beard mixed with white hairs from throat to breast, reaching to the knees; legs below knees and feet white; belly white, a blotch on the flanks; outside of legs and a lateral line blackish. The horns of the male are sub-triangular, much compressed laterally and posteriorly; in fact one may say concave at the sides, that is, from the base of the horn to about one half; transversely sulcated; curving outwards, and returning inward towards the face; points convergent. The female is more uniform pale brown, with whitish belly; no beard, and short straight horns.

SIZE.—About 5 feet in length, and 3 feet high; horns from 25 to 30 inches round the curve.* The marked distinctions between the two species may be thus briefly summed up:—

Ovis Vignei.	*Ovis cycloceros.*
Horn rather compressed laterally.	Much compressed laterally.
Rounded posteriorly.	Much compressed posteriorly.
Curving outward and backward.	Curving outward and inward.
Points divergent.	Points convergent.
General colour, brownish-grey.	General colour, rufous brown, with blotch on flanks and lateral line blackish.
Beard short, of stiffish brown hairs.	Beard profuse, reaching to knees, black intermixed with white hairs.

* See also Appendix C, p. 529.

Mr. Sclater, with reference to the two in his paper on the Punjab Sheep living in the Zoological Society's Garden in 1860 ('P. Z. S.' 1860, page 126), says: "On comparing the skull (of *O. cycloceros*) with that of the shapoo we observe a general resemblance. But it may be noted that the sub-orbital pits in the present species are smaller, deeper, and more rounded; the nasal bones are considerably shorter and more pointed, and the series of molar teeth (formed in each skull of three

Ovis cycloceros.

premolars and three molars) measures only 2·85 instead of 3·20 inches in total length."

There is a fine coloured plate of this animal in that magnificent folio work—Wolf's 'Zoological Sketches,' showing the male, female, and lambs; and in that valuable book of Kinloch's, 'Large Game-shooting in Thibet and the North-west' is a very clear photograph of the oorial's head, from which I give the above sketch. He gives the following account of its habits: "The oorial is found among low stony hills and ravines, which are generally more or less covered with thin jungle, consisting principally of thorny bushes. During the heat of the day the oorial conceal themselves a good deal, retiring to the most secluded places, but often coming down to feed in the evening on the crops surrounding the villages. Where not much disturbed, they will stay all day in the neighbourhood of their feeding grounds, and allow sheep and cattle to feed amongst them without concern; but where they have been much fired at they usually go a long distance before settling themselves for the day. They are generally found on capital ground for stalking, the chief drawback being the stony nature of the hills, which renders it difficult to walk silently. When fired at, oorial usually go leisurely away, stopping to gaze every now and then, so that several shots may often be fired at one herd."

Dr. Leith Adams says regarding it, that it "frequents bleak and barren mountains, composed of low ranges intersected by ravines and dry river courses, where vegetation is scanty at all seasons, and goats and sheep are seldom driven to pasture. It is found in small herds, and, being fond of salt, is generally most abundant in the neighbourhood of salt mines. Shy and watchful, it is difficult to approach, and possesses in an eminent degree the senses of sight and smell. It is seldom seen in the day-time, being secreted among rocks, whence it issues at dusk to feed in the fields and valleys, returning to its retreat at daybreak.

"When suddenly alarmed the males gives a loud shrill whistle, like the ibex. This is an invariable signal for the departure of the herd, which keeps moving all the rest of the day until dusk. Their bleat is like that of the tame species; and the males fight in the same way, but the form of the body and infra-orbital pits simulate the deer, hence it is often called the 'deer-sheep.' It equals the deer in speed and activity. The female gestates seven months. The rutting season is in September."

According to Captain Hutton the flesh is good and well-flavoured, "while the horns are placed as trophies of success and proofs of skill upon tombs and temples."

This sheep has bred in the Gardens of the Zoological Society in London. (*See* notes to *Oorial* in Appendix C.)

No. 444. OVIS BLANFORDII.

Blanford's Wild Sheep.

HABITAT.—Central hills of Khelat.

DESCRIPTION.—The horns of this species are longer and more slender than those of *Ovis Vignei*, *O. cycloceros*, or *O. Gmelini*. Mr. Hume says ('J. A. S. B.' 1877, p. 327): "In all these three species, as far as I can make out, each horn lies in one plane, whereas in the present species the horn twists out in a capital-S fashion. There is, in fact, much the same difference between the horns of the present species and of *O. cycloceros*, that there is between those of *O. Kareleni* and *O. Hodgsoni*.

The lower part of the forehead at the nasal suture, and the whole of the frontals, are more raised and convex than in either *O. cycloceros* or *O. Vignei.*

The frontal ridge between the bases of the horns is less developed in *O. Blanfordii*, and in this latter the posterior convex margin of the bony palate is differently shaped, being more pointed, and not nearly semi-circular as in *O. cycloceros.*"

The dimensions of the skull are given in detail by Mr. Hume in the paper above quoted, out of which I extract those of the horns :—

	Inches.
Length along curve	35·75
Circumference at base	9·0
Width from tip to tip	16·5
Greatest breadth of horn at base	2·25
Greatest depth of ditto	3·25

The horns of a specimen of *O. cycloceros* of about the same age were 29·5 in length and 10 inches in circumference at base, so that the greater length and slenderness of the horns of *Ovis Blanfordii* are apparent. Mr. Hume writes to me that there is a living specimen of this sheep at present in the London Zoological Gardens.

NO. 445. OVIS NAHURA *vel* BURHEL.

The Blue Wild Sheep (Jerdon's No. 237).

NATIVE NAMES.—*Burhel*, *Buroot*, in the Himalayas; *Napu*, *Na*, or *Sna*, Thibet and Ladakh; *Nervati*, in Nepal. *Wa'* or *War* on the Sutlej.

HABITAT.—This animal has a wide range; it is found from Sikim, and, as Jerdon says, probably Bhotan, right away through Thibet, as Père David found it in Moupin, and it extends up to the Kuenluen mountains north of Ladakh, and in Ladakh itself, and it has been obtained by Prejevalski on the Altyn-Tagh, therefore the limits assigned by Jerdon must be considerably extended.

DESCRIPTION.—General colour a dull slaty blue, slightly tinged with fawn; the belly, edge of buttocks, and tail, white; throat, chest, front of fore-arm and cannon bone, a line along the flank dividing the darker tint from the belly; the edge of the hind limbs and the tip of the tail deep black; horns moderately smooth, with few wrinkles, rounded, nearly touching at the base, directed upwards, backwards and outwards, the points being turned forwards and inwards. The female is smaller, the black marks smaller and of less extent; small, straight, slightly recurved horns; nose straighter. The young are darker and browner.

SIZE.—Length of head and body, 4½ to 5 feet; height, 30 to 36 inches; tail, 7 inches; horns, 2 to 2½ feet round the curve; circumference at base, 12 to 13 inches.

An excellent coloured plate is to be found in Blanford's 'Scientific Results of the Second Yarkand Mission' and a life-like photograph of the head in Kinloch's 'Large Game-shooting.' According to the latter author the burrel prefers bare rocky hills, and when inhabiting those which are clothed with forest, rarely or never descends to the limits of the trees. "The favourite resorts of burrel are those hills which have slopes well covered with grass in the immediate vicinity of steep precipices, to which they can at once betake themselves in case of alarm. Females and young ones frequently wander to more rounded and accessible hills, but I have never met with old males very far from some rocky stronghold. The males and females do not appear to

Ovis nahura.

separate entirely during the summer, as I have found mixed flocks at all seasons, though, as a rule, the old males form themselves into small herds and live apart. In my opinion the flesh of the burrel surpasses in flavour the best mutton, and has moreover the advantage of being generally tender soon after the animal is killed."

According to Jerdon the burrel is fattest in September and October. In the 'Indian Sporting Review' a writer, "Mountaineer," states that in winter, when they get snowed in, they actually browse the hair off each other, and come out miserably thin.

The name *Ovis nahura* is not a felicitous one, as it was given under a mistake by Hodgson, the nahoor being quite another animal. I think

Blyth's name of *Ovis burhel* should be adopted to the exclusion of the other, which, however, is in general use.

There is a very interesting paper on this animal by Mr. R. Lydekker in the 'Journal of the Asiatic Society of Bengal,' vol. xlix., 1880, in which he points out its affinity to the goats from the absence of eye-pits and their larminal depression in the lachrymal bone—from the similarity of the basi-occipital and in the structure and colour of its horns. On the other hand it agrees with *Ovis* in the form of its lower jaw, in the absence of beard and any odour, and in the possession of interdigital pores in all feet.

GENUS CAPRA—THE GOATS.

Horns in both sexes curving backwards, angular and flattened, or in some cases twisted spirally. The nose is arched, and the chin of both sexes is more or less bearded; there are no eye-pits or inguinal pits, and feet-pits only in the fore-feet in most, and none in some. Mr. Blyth some years ago pointed out that a hind-quarter of goat with the foot attached can always be told from the same piece of mutton by the absence of the feet-pits in the goat. The males especially emit a strong odour. In other respects there is little difference between goats and sheep, and by interbreeding they produce a fertile offspring. Our domestic goat is supposed to have descended from the ibex, but certainly some of our Indian varieties may claim descent from the markhor. I noticed in 1880 at Simla herds of goats with horns quite of the markhor type, and one old fellow in a herd of about one hundred, which was being driven through the station to some rajah's place in the vicinity, had a remarkably fine head, with the broad flat twist of the markhor horn. I tried in vain to get a similar one; several heads were brought to me from the bazaar, but they were poor in comparison. Goats are more prolific than sheep. The power of gestation commences at the early age of seven months; the period is five months, and the female produces sometimes twice a year, and from two to occasionally four at a birth. The goat is a hardy animal, subsisting on the coarsest herbage, but its flesh and milk can be immensely improved by a selected diet. Some of the small domestic goats of Bengal are wonderful milkers. I have kept them for years in Calcutta for the use of my children, and once took two of them with me to Marseilles by the 'Messageries' Steamers. I prefer them to the larger goats of the North-west. My children have been singularly free from ailments during their infancy, and I attribute the immunity chiefly to the use of goats' milk drawn fresh as required. Of the wild goats, to which I must now confine my attention, there are two groups, viz. the true goats and the antelope goats. Of the former there is a sub-genus—*Hemitragus*—which have no feet-pits, but have a muffle and occasionally four mammæ, which form a connecting link with the *Cervidæ*. In all other respects *Hemitragus* is distinctly caprine.

No. 446. CAPRA MEGACEROS.

The Markhor (*Jerdon's No.* 234).

NATIVE NAMES.—*Mar-khor* (i.e. snake-eater), in Afghanistan, Kashmir, &c.; *Rá-che*, or *Ra-pho-che*, Ladakhi.

HABITAT.—The mountain districts of Afghanistan, and the highest parts of the Thibetan Himalayas. On the Pir Panjal, in Kashmir, the Hazarah hills, the hills north of the Jhelum, the Wurdwan hills west of the Beas river, on the Suleiman range, and in Ladakh.

DESCRIPTION.—General colour a dirty light-blue gray, with a darker beard; in summer with a reddish tinge; the neck and breast clad with long dark hair, reaching to the knees; hair long and shaggy; fore-legs brown. The females are redder, with shorter hair, short black beard, but no mane, and with small horns slightly twisted.

The horns of an old male are a magnificent trophy. Kinloch records having seen a pair, of which the unbroken horn measured sixty-three inches, and its fellow, which had got damaged, had fifty-seven inches left. Forty to fifty inches is, however, a fair average. According to Kinloch the very long horns are not so thick and massive as those of average length. Jerdon says the longest horns have three complete spiral twists.

The horns of certain varieties differ so much that I may say species have been settled with less to go upon. Kinloch notes four varieties. I have hitherto reckoned only two, but he gives—

No. 1.—Pir Panjal markhor; heavy, flat horns, twisted like a corkscrew.

No. 2.—Trans-Indus markhor; perfectly straight horns, with a spiral flange or ridge running up them.

No. 3.—Hazarah markhor; a slight corkscrew, as well as a twist.

No. 4.—Astor and Baltistan markhor; large, flat horns, branching out very widely, and then going up nearly straight with only a half turn.

Of the two kinds I have seen, the one has the broad flat horn twisted like a corkscrew; the other a perfectly straight core, with the worm of a screw turned round it. Nothing could be more dissimilar than these horns, yet, in other respects the animal being the same, it has not been considered necessary to separate the two as distinct species.*

* Colonel Kinloch writes on my remarks as above, and gives the following interesting information: "I cannot consider the spiral-horned and the straight-

SIZE.—Height, about 46 inches.

There is a life-like photograph of No. 1 variety in Kinloch's 'Large Game of Thibet,' and of No. 3 a very fine coloured plate in Wolf's folio of 'Zoological Sketches.'

Capra megaceros. No. 1 variety.

The markhor frequents steep and rocky ground above the forests in summer, but descending in the winter. I cannot do better than quote

---

horned markhor to be one species, any more than the Himalayan and Sindh ibex. The animals differ much in size, habits, and coat, as well as in the shape of their horns. Mr. Sterndale considers that the markhor is probably the origin of some of our breeds of domestic goats, and states that he has seen tame goats with horns

Kinloch, who gives the following graphic little description: "The markhor inhabits the most precipitous and difficult ground, where nearly perpendicular faces of rock alternate with steep grassy slopes and

Capra megaceros. No. 2 variety.

patches of forest. It is very shy and secluded in its habits, remaining concealed in the densest thickets during the day-time, and only coming

quite of the markhor type. Has he ever observed that (as far as my experience goes) the horns of domestic goats invariably twist the *reverse way* to those of markhor? I have observed that the horns of not only markhor, but also antelope, always twist one way; those of domestic goats the other."

out to feed in the mornings and evenings. No animal's pursuit leads the sportsman over such dangerous ground as that of the markhor. Living so much in the forest, it must be followed over steep inclines of short grass, which the melting snow has left with all the blades flattened downwards; and amid pine-trees, whose needle-like spines strew the ground and render it more slippery and treacherous than ice. If one falls on such ground, one instantly begins to slide down the incline with rapidly increasing velocity, and, unless some friendly bush or stone arrests one's progress, the chances are that one is carried over some precipice, and either killed or severely injured. Many hair-breadth escapes occur, and the only wonder is that fatal accidents so seldom happen.

"Early in the season the males and females may be found together on the open grassy patches and clear slopes among the forest, but during the summer the females generally betake themselves to the highest rocky ridges above the forest, while the males conceal themselves still more constantly in the jungle, very rarely showing themselves. They are always very wary, and require great care in stalking them."

No. 447. CAPRA SIBIRICA.

The Himalayan Ibex (Jerdon's No. 235).

NATIVE NAMES.—*Sakin*, *Iskin*, or *Skeen* of the Himalayas; *Buz*, in the upper part of the Sutlej; *Kale*, Kashmiri; *Tangrol*, in Kulu; *Skin*, the male, *L'Dâmuo* the female, in Ladakh.

HABITAT.—Throughout the Himalayas from Kashmir to Nepal. The localities given by Kinloch are Kunawar, Kulu, Lahoul, Spiti, Kashmir, Baltistan, and various parts of Thibet; also Ladakh according to Horsfield.

DESCRIPTION.—General colour light brownish, with a dark stripe down the back in summer, dirty yellowish-white in winter; the beard, which is about six to eight inches long, is black; the horns, which are like those of the European ibex, are long and scimitar-shaped, curving over the neck, flattened at the sides, and strongly ridged in front; from forty to fifty inches in length. A pair is recorded in the 'Proceedings of the Zoological Society' for 1840 of fifty-one inches in length. The females have thin slightly curved horns about a foot long.

Under the hair, which is about two inches long, is a soft down, and is highly prized for the fine soft cloth called *tusi*.

SIZE.—Height at shoulder, about 44 inches.

According to Colonel Markham the ibex "frequents the highest ground near the snows where food is to be obtained. The sexes live apart generally, often in flocks of one hundred and more. In October the males descend and mix with the females, which have generally twins in June and July. It is an extremely wary and timid animal, and can make its way in an almost miraculous manner over the most

Capra Sibirica.

inaccessible-looking ground. No animal can exceed the ibex in endurance and agility."

Kinloch writes as follows concerning it :—

"The ibex inhabits the most precipitous ground in the highest parts of the ranges where it is found, keeping above the forest (when there is any), unless driven down by severe weather. In the day-time it generally betakes itself to the most inaccessible crags, where it may sleep and rest in undisturbed security, merely coming down to the grassy feeding grounds in the mornings and evenings. Occasionally, in very remote and secluded places, the ibex will stay all day on their feeding grounds, but this is not common. In summer, as the snows melt, the old males retire to the highest and most unfrequented mountains, and it is then generally useless to hunt for them, as they have such a vast range, and can find food in places perfectly inaccessible to man. The females and young ones may be met with all the year round, and often at no very great elevation.

"Although an excessively wary animal, the ibex is usually found on such broken ground that, if due care be taken, it is not very difficult to obtain a shot. The grand rule, as in all other hill stalking, is to keep well above the herd, whose vigilance is chiefly directed beneath them. In places where they have been much disturbed, one or two of the herd usually keep a sharp look-out while the rest are feeding, and on the slightest suspicion of danger the sentries utter a loud whistle, which is a signal for a general rush to the nearest rocks. Should the sportsman succeed in obtaining a shot before he is observed by the ibex, he may often have time to fire several shots before they are out of range, as they appear to be completely stupefied and confused by the sudden noise, the cause of which they are unable to account for if they neither see nor smell their enemy."

Jerdon states that Major Strutt killed in the Balti valley an ibex of a rich hair-brown colour, with a yellowish-white saddle in the middle of its back, and a dark mesial line; the head, neck and limbs being of a dark sepia brown, with a darker line on the front of the legs; others were seen in the same locality by Major Strutt of a still darker colour. These seem to be peculiar to Balti; the horns are the same as the others. Kinloch remarks that a nearly black male ibex has been shot to the north of Iskardo.

NO. 448. CAPRA ÆGAGRUS.

The Wild Goat of Asia Minor.

NATIVE NAMES.—*Pasang* (male), *Boz* (female), generally *Boz-Pasang*, Persian (*Blanford*); *Kayeck* in Asia Minor (*Danford*).

HABITAT.—Throughout Asia Minor from the Taurus mountains; through Persia into Sindh and Baluchistan; and in Afghanistan. M. Pierre de Tchihatchef, late a distinguished member of the Russian Diplomatic Service, and well known as an author and a man of science, whose acquaintance I had the pleasure of making some time ago in

Florence, found these goats most abundant on the Aladagh, Boulgerdagh and Hussandagh ranges of the Taurus. He made a very good collection of horns and skulls there, which are now in the Imperial Museum, St. Petersburg. Captain Hutton found it in Afghanistan.

DESCRIPTION.—Hair short and brown, becoming lighter in summer; a dark, almost black line down the back; the males have a black beard; the young and females are lighter, with fainter markings; the horns are of the usual ibex type, but there is a striking difference between those of this species and all the others. As a rule the ibex horn is triangular in section, that is, the front part of the horn is square, with transverse knobs at short intervals all the way up, for about three-fourths of the length, whereas the horn of *C. ægagrus* is more scimitar-like, flattish on the inner side and rounded on the outer, with an edge in front; the sides are wavily corrugated, and on the outer edge are knobs at considerable distances apart. It is believed that an estimate of the age of the animal can be made by these protuberances—after the third year a fresh knob is made in each succeeding one. Mr. Danford says: "The yearly growths seem to be greatest from the third to the sixth year, the subsequent additions being successively smaller." The horns sometimes curve inwards and sometimes outwards at the tips. Mr. Danford figures a pair, the tips of which, turning inwards, cross each other. The female horns are shorter and less characteristic. The size of the male horns run to probably a maximum of 50 inches. There is a pair in the British Museum 48½ inches on the curve. Mr. Danford's best specimen was 47½, the chord of which was 22½, basal circumference 9¾, weight 10¼ lbs. Captain Hutton's living specimen had horns 40½ inches in length.

SIZE.—According to Herr Kotschy "it attains not unfrequently a length of 6½ feet." Mr. Danford measured one 5 feet 5½ inches from nose to tip of tail, 2 feet 9½ inches at shoulder. (See also p. 529)

I have not had an opportunity of measuring a very well-stuffed specimen in the Indian Museum, but I should say that the Sind variety was much smaller. Standing, as it does, beside a specimen of *Capra Sibirica*, it looks not much bigger than some of the Jumnapari goats. (See Appendix C, p. 529.)

The *ægagrus* is commonly supposed to be the parent stock from which the domestic goat descended, and certainly the European and many Asiatic forms show a similarity of construction in the horn, but the common goat descended from more than one wild stock, for, as I have before stated, there are goats in India, which show unmistakable signs of descent from the markhor, *Capra megaceros*. In the article on *Capra ægagrus* in the 'P. Z. S.' for 1875, p. 458, by Mr. C. G. Danford, F.Z.S., written after a recent visit to Asia Minor, it is stated that the late Captain Hutton found it common in Afghanistan, in the Suleiman and Pishin hills, and in the Hazarah and western ranges. I confess I had thought the ibex of these parts to be identical with *C. Sibirica*. Mr. Danford, describing where he met with it, says:—

"The picturesque town of Adalia is situated at the head of the gulf of the same name, and is the principal place in the once populous district of Pamphylia. It is surrounded on its landward side by a wide brushwood-covered plain, bounded on the north and north-east by the Gok and other mountains of the Taurus, and on the west by the Suleiman, a lofty spur of the same range, in which latter the present specimens were collected.

"These mountains, the principal summit of which, the Akdagh (white mountain), attains a height of 10,000 feet (*Hoskyn*), rise abruptly from the plain and sea, and are of very imposing and rugged forms. The pure grey tints of the marble and marble-limestone, of which they are principally composed, show beautifully between the snowy summits, and the bright green of the pines and darker shades of the undergrowth of oak, myrtle and bay, which clothe their lower slopes.

"The wild goat is here found either solitary or in small parties and herds, which number sometimes as many as 100; the largest which I saw contained 28. It is called by the natives *kayeek*, which word, though applied in other parts of the country to the stag, and sometimes even the roe, is here only used to designate the *ægagrus*, the fallow deer of this district being properly known as *jamoorcha*. The old males of the *ægagrus* inhabit during summer the higher mountains, being often met with on the snow, while the females and young frequent the lower and easier ridges; in winter, however, they all seem to live pretty much together among the rocks, scattered pines, and bushy ground, generally preferring elevations of from 2000 to 5000 feet. Herr Kotschy says they never descend below 4000 feet in Cilicia; but his observations were made in summer.

"Like all the ibex tribe, the *ægagrus* is extremely shy and wary at ordinary times, though, as in the case with many other animals, they may be easily approached during the rutting season. I was told that they were often brought within shot at that time by the hunter secreting himself, and rolling a few small stones down the rocks. When suddenly disturbed they utter a short angry snort, and make off at a canter rather than a gallop. Though their agility among the rocks is marvellous, they do not, according to Mr. Hutton ('Calcutta Journ.' vii. p. 524), possess sufficient speed to enable them to escape from the dogs which are employed to hunt them in the low lands of Afghanistan. It is interesting to see how, when danger is dreaded, the party is always led by the oldest male, who advances with great caution, and carefully surveys the suspected ground before the others are allowed to follow; their food consists principally of mountain grasses, shoots of different small species of oak and cedar, and various berries. The young are dropped in May, and are one or two (Kotschy says sometimes three) in number. The horns appear very early, as shown in a kid of the year procured in the beginning of January."

It appears to be very much troubled with ticks, and an *œstrus* or bot which deposits its larvæ in the frontal sinuses and cavities of the horns.

SUB-GENUS HEMITRAGUS.

Some naturalists do not separate this from *Capra*, but the majority do on the following characteristics, viz. that they possess a small muffle, and one of the two species has four mammæ. The horns are trigonal, laterally compressed and knotted on the upper edge.

No. 449. CAPRA *vel* HEMITRAGUS JEMLAICUS.

The Tahr (*Jerdon's No* 232).

NATIVE NAMES.—*Tehr*, *Jehr*, near Simla; *Jharal*, in Nepal; *Kras* and *Jagla*, in Kashmir; *Kart*, in Kulu; *Jhula* the male, and *Thar* or *Tharni* the female, in Kunawur; *Esbu* and *Esbi*, male and female, on the Sutlej above Chini (*Jerdon*).

HABITAT.—Throughout the entire range of the Himalayas, at high elevations between the forest and snow limits. According to Dr. Leith Adams it is very common on the Pir Panjal, and more so near Kishtwar.

DESCRIPTION.—The male is of various shades of brown, varying in tint from dark to yellowish, the front part and mane being ashy with a bluish tinge, the upper part of the limbs rusty brown, the fronts of legs and belly being darker. There is no beard, the face being smooth and dark ashy, but on the fore-quarters and neck the hair lengthens into a magnificent mane, which sometimes reaches to the knees. There is a dark mesial line; the tail is short and nude underneath; the horns are triangular, the sharp edge being to the front; they are about ten or eleven inches in circumference at the base where they touch, then, sweeping like a demi-crescent backwards, they taper to a fine point in a length of about 12 to 14 inches. The male has at times a very strong odour. The female is smaller, and of a reddish-brown or fulvous drab above, with a dark streak down the back, whitish below; the horns are also much smaller.

SIZE.—Length of head and body, about 4½ feet. Height, 36 to 40 inches.

Col. Kinloch, whose two volumes are most valuable, both as

regards interesting details and perfect illustrations, speaks thus of this species:—

"The tahr is a fine-looking beast, although his horns are small, and he cannot compare with his majestic relatives, the ibex and the markhor. The male tahr is about the same size as the ibex, but rather more heavily made. The general colour is a reddish-brown, deepening into a much darker tint on the hind-quarters, but individuals vary a good deal, and I have shot one which was of a yellowish-white. The face is covered with smooth short hair, and is nearly black; the hair of the body is long and coarse, attaining its greatest length on the neck, chest and shoulders, where it forms a fine flowing mane reaching below the animal's knees. The horns are curious, being triangular, with the sharp edge to the front; they are very thick at the base, and taper rapidly to a fine point, curving right back on to the neck. The largest horns attain a length of about 14 inches, and are 10 or 11 inches in circumference at the base.

Hemitragus Jemlaicus.

"The female tahr is very much smaller than the male; the hair is short, and the horns diminutive. The colour is a lightish red, with a dark stripe down the back.

"The tahr is like the markhor, a forest-loving animal, and, although it sometimes resorts to the rocky summits of the hills, it generally prefers the steep slopes, which are more or less clothed with trees. Female tahr may be frequently found on open ground, but old males hide a great deal in the thickest jungle, lying during the heat of the day under the shade of trees or overhanging rocks. Nearly perpendicular hills with dangerous precipices, where the forest consists of oak and ringall cane, are the favourite haunts of the old tahr, who climb with ease over ground where one would hardly imagine that any animal could find a footing. Tahr ground indeed is about the worst walking I know, almost rivalling markhor ground; the only advantage being that, bad as it is, there are generally some bushes or grass to hold on to.

Owing to the ground it inhabits being so covered with jungle, the pursuit of the tahr is attended with a great deal of labour and uncertainty. Forcing one's way for hours through tangled bushes is very fatiguing, and, as it is impossible to do so without noise, chances are often lost which would be easy enough if the ground was more open. Frequently, although the tracks show that old tahr must be near, and in spite of the utmost care and caution, the first intimation one has of the presence of the game is a rush through the bushes, a clatter of falling stones, and perhaps a glimpse of the shaggy hind-quarters of the last of the herd as he vanishes over some precipice where it is perfectly impossible to follow him.

"Early in the spring, when grass and leaves are scarce, and again in the rutting season, are the best times for tahr shooting, as the old males then come out on open slopes.

"The tahr is very tenacious of life, and, even when mortally wounded, he will frequently make his escape into utterly impracticable ground. In autumn the tahr becomes immensely fat and heavy, and his flesh is then in high favour with the natives, the rank flavour suiting their not very delicate palates. An Englishman would rather not be within one hundred yards to leeward of him, the perfume being equal to treble-distilled 'bouquet de bouc.' Ibex is bad enough, but tahr is 'a caution.' The flesh of the female is, however, excellent."

Colonel Markham says: "Seen at a distance it looks like a great wild hog, but when near it is a noble beast." According to Hodgson, it has interbred with a female spotted deer, and the offspring, which more resembled the mother, grew up a fine animal. There is a beautifully clear photograph in Kinloch's 'Large Game of Thibet,' and a large coloured plate in Wolf's 'Zoological Sketches.'

NO. 450. CAPRA *vel* HEMITRAGUS HYLOCRIUS.

The Neilgherry Wild Goat, or Ibex of Madras Sportsmen (Jerdon's No. 233).

NATIVE NAMES.—*Warra-adu* or *Warri-atu*, Tamil.

HABITAT.—The Western Ghâts, southerly towards Cape Comorin.

DESCRIPTION.—According to Jerdon, "the adult male, dark sepia brown, with a pale reddish-brown saddle, more or less marked, and paler brown on the sides and beneath; legs somewhat grizzled with white, dark brown in front, and paler posteriorly; the head is dark, grizzled with yellowish-brown, and the eye is surrounded by a pale fawn-coloured spot; horns short, much curved, nearly in contact at the base, gradually diverging, strongly keeled internally, round externally, with numerous close rings not so prominent as in the last species. There is a large callous spot on the knees surrounded by a fringe of hair, and the male has a short stiff mane on the neck and withers. The hair is short, thick, and coarse."

Colonel Douglas Hamilton, writing to the late Brigadier-General McMaster, says: "I think Jerdon's description is good, but I should call the saddles of the old males grizzled with white, and not pale reddish-brown. A real old 'saddle-back' has a white saddle and amost jet-black points. He makes a mistake about the length of the tail, 6 or 7 inches; it is not more than 3 inches."

SIZE.—Height at shoulder, 41 to 42 inches. Jerdon gives 32 to 34, but he appears to have under-estimated the animal, unless it be a misprint for 42 and 44; although he questions Colonel W. Campbell's measurements of length and height, the former of which does seem excessive (6 feet 5 inches, including tail, probably taken from a skin), but the latter, 42 inches, is corroborated by Colonel Hamilton and several others.

The size of the horns is given by Jerdon as occasionally 15 inches, rarely more than 12. Colonel Douglas Hamilton says, 9 inches in circumference and 15 to 15½ or 15¾ in length is the average of a large horn. General McMaster writes, referring to the latter opinion: "Both he and I know of one 16 inches in length, shot by a well-known South Indian sportsman of the Madras Civil Service, and in February 1869 at Ootacamund, he and I measured the horn of a magnificent buck ibex, shot within 15 or 20 miles of that place. The exact measurements of this mighty horn were 17 inches in length, and 9¾ in circumference at the base."

Jerdon states that this goat chiefly frequents the northern and western slopes of the Neilgherries, where the hills run down in a succession of steep stony slopes or rocky ridges to the high table-land of Mysore and the Wynaad, both of which districts are themselves hilly. It is occasionally seen on the summit of the northern and western faces, but more generally some distance down, at an elevation of 4000 to 6000 feet, and, if carefully looked for, the herd may be seen feeding on an open grassy glade at the foot of some precipice. "I have," he adds, "seen above twenty individuals in a flock occasionally, but more generally not more than six or seven. With the large herds there is almost always one very large old male conspicuous by his nearly black colour."

Colonel D. Hamilton says he has seen 120 pass out of one valley, which he thinks were probably the aggregate of several herds, but he has counted sixty and sixty-five in a herd, and thirty-five in another, without a single adult buck amongst them. In the *South of India Observer* for the 3rd and 17th of September, 1868, will be found most interesting descriptions of ibex-shooting by "Hawkeye" whose letters are largely quoted by McMaster; but I can only find space for one extract here, interesting to both sportsman and naturalist:—

"It is a pleasant sight to watch a herd of ibex, when undisturbed, the kids frisking here and there on pinnacles or ledges of rocks and beetling cliffs, where there seems scarcely safe foothold for anything much larger than the grasshopper or a fly; the old mother looking calmly on or grazing steadily while the day is young, cropping the soft moss or tender herbs and sweet short grass springing from the crevices of the craggy precipices in rich abundance. Then, again, to see the caution observed in taking up their resting or abiding places for the day, where they may be warmed by the sun, listening to the roar of many waters, and figuratively, we may say, chewing the cud of contentment, and giving themselves up to the full enjoyment of their nomadic life and its romantic haunts. Usually before reposing one of the herd, generally an old doe, may be observed intently gazing below, apparently scanning every spot in the range of her vision, sometimes for half an hour or more before she is satisfied that 'all is well;' strange to say, seldom or ever looking up to the rocks above. Then, being satisfied on the one side, she observes the same process on the other, eventually calmly lying down, contented with the precautions she has taken that all is safe. Her post as sentinel is generally a prominent one, on the edge and corner perhaps of some ledge, to be well sheltered from the wind and warmed by the sun, along which the rest of the herd dispose themselves as inclined, fully trusting in the watchful guardian, whose manœuvres I have been describing. Should the sentinel be joined by another, or her kid come and lie down by her, they invariably place themselves back to back, or in such a manner that they can keep a look-out on either side. A solitary male goes through all this by himself, and wonderfully careful he is, but when with the herd he reposes in security, leaving it to the females to take precautions for their mutual safety. I have stated that these animals seldom look above them, except when any cause of alarm leads them to do so. I recollect an instance which I will relate, partly to show the advantage of a good colour for a stalker's dress, and to illustrate what I have mentioned above. I had disturbed a buck ibex accidentally one morning, and, after watching him a long distance with the glass, observed him to take up a position and commence the vigilant process previously mentioned. By this I knew he was preparing to lie down. He was a long time about it, but eventually he was satisfied, and took up his post on a prominent rock, from which, as lying with his back to the mountain, he held a clear view in front and on both sides. I approached from above, the wind all right, and the ibex reposing comfortably in fancied security. I had to pass a large rock to clear an intervening impediment, and gain a full view of the buck, as I could at first only see his horns. I had taken the precaution to remove my shoes, the grass being very dry and noisy. The crunching of the dry grass as I moved attracted the notice of the ibex, and suddenly he looked back and up towards me. He was not more than eighty or ninety yards below. I leaned against the rock, my shikar dress blending with the dark grey of the stone and burnt-up grass so completely as to deceive even my lynx-eyed prey. Long, long he looked, till my very knees trembled with anxiety. At last he turned his head, but I knew better than to move, being sure he would have another look. He did so and it proved to be his last, for, when he again turned his head away, I quietly subsided, and in another moment the buck died on his rocky bed."

There is an illustration by Wolf of the animal in Colonel Walter Campbell's 'My Indian Journal.'

The female has only two mammæ, and usually produces two young at a time.

THE GOAT ANTELOPES, OR CAPRICORNS.

These animals form the link between the goats and the antelopes; their general characteristics are short, conical horns, ringed at the base, upright and curving backwards, and of nearly equal size in both sexes. The body is heavier than is usual amongst antelopes; the feet are large, and have false hoofs.

GENUS NEMORHŒDUS.

" Horns in both sexes round, black and ringed; a small muffle; eye-pits wanting or small; large feet-pits in all feet; no inguinal pits nor calcic tufts; tails short, hairy; four mammæ" (*Jerdon*).

No. 451. NEMORHŒDUS BUBALINA.

The Serow, or Forest Goat (*Jerdon's No.* 230).

NATIVE NAMES.—*Serow*, or *Serowa*, Pahari; *Eimu*, on the Sutlej; *Ramu*, *Halj*, *Salabhir*, Kashmiri; *Nga*, Leesaws of the Sanda valley; *Paypa*, of the Shans; *Shanli*, Chinese of the Burmo-Chinese frontier.

HABITAT.—The whole of the wooded ranges of the Himalayas from Kashmir down past Sikim on to the ranges dividing China from Burmah.

DESCRIPTION.—I have before me several descriptions of this animal, of which I have little personal knowledge. The best of all is that of Colonel Kinloch, which has been, to some extent, quoted by Professor Garrod in Cassell's Natural History. I give it *in extenso*:—

"The serow is an ungainly-looking animal, combining the characteristics of the cow, the donkey, the pig, and the goat! It is a large and powerful beast, considerably larger than a tahr, and longer in the leg. The body is covered with very coarse hair, which assumes the form of a bristly mane on the neck and shoulders, and gives the beast a ferocious appearance, which does not belie its disposition. The colour is a dull black on the back, bright red on the sides, and white underneath, the legs also being dirty white. The ears are very large, the muzzle is coarse, and two singular circular orifices are situated two or three inches below the eyes. The horns are stout at the base, are ringed nearly to the tips, and curve back close to the neck, growing to the length of from nine to fourteen inches; they are very sharp-pointed, and the serow is said to be able to make good use of them.

"The sexes vary very little, less than in any ruminating animal with which I am acquainted; both are furnished with horns of nearly the same size, those of an old male being rather thicker than those of the female.

"The serow has an awkward gait; but in spite of this it can go over the worst ground; and it has, perhaps, no superior in going down steep hills.

Nemorhœdus bubalina.

"It is a solitary animal, and is nowhere numerous; two or three may be found on one hill, four or five on another, and so on. It delights in the steepest and most rocky hill-sides, and its favourite resting-places are in caves, under the shelter of overhanging rocks, or at the foot of shady trees. It constantly repairs to the same spots, as testified to by the large heaps of its droppings which are to be found in the localities above alluded to. Although very shy and difficult to find, the serow is a fierce and dangerous brute when wounded and brought to bay. I have even heard of an unwounded male charging when his mate had been shot.

"It is said that the serow will sometimes beat off a pack of wild dogs, and I believe that serow and dogs have been found lying dead together. It is therefore advisable to be cautious when approaching a wounded one.

"When disturbed, the serow utters a most singular sound, something between a snort and a screaming whistle, and I have heard them screaming loudly when they had apparently not been alarmed."

Colonel Markham says of it that it is something in appearance between a jackass and a *thar*, with long stout legs, and a strong neck. Jerdon's description is not clear; it is: "above black, more or less grizzled and mixed on the flanks with deep clay colour; a black dorsal stripe; fore-arms and thighs anteriorly reddish brown; the rest of the limbs hoary; beneath whitish." The deep clay colour is indefinite, as there are many sorts of clay, and people's ideas may differ as to the shade by the particular clay to which they are most accustomed. Dr. Anderson found it in the Western provinces of Yunnan; and General McMaster, in his 'Notes' (page 143), says that when he was quartered at Shuaygheen, on the Sitang river, in Burmah, a female of this species was brought alive to Major Berdmore by some Burmans, who had caught it in the river, by which it had probably been washed down from the Karanee mountains. He adds that even in its exhausted and dying state it was exceedingly savage, butting at every one who approached it.

SIZE.—Height, about 3 feet, or an inch or two over; length, about 5 to 5½ feet; weight, about 200 lbs.; horns, about a foot long as an average, varying from 9 to 14 inches.

The female usually produces one kid in the autumn, about September or October, and the period of gestation is about seven months.

NO. 452. NEMORHŒDUS RUBIDA *vel* SUMATRENSIS.

The Arakanese Capricorn.

NATIVE NAME.—*Tan-Kseik*, Arakanese.

HABITAT.—Arakan, through Pegu to (according to Blyth) the extremity of the Malayan peninsula, and occurs in Siam and Formosa, and also in Sumatra. Has been shot near Shillong in Assam.

DESCRIPTION.—Blyth is of opinion ('Cat. Mam. British Burmah,' 'J. A. S. B.' 1875) that his *N. rubida* is identical with *Sumatrensis* and *Swinhoei*, and he could detect no difference in their skulls and skins. I therefore take the following description of *Capricornis Swinhoei* from the 'P. Z. S.' 1862, page 263, where it is also figured, plate xxxv.:—

"The fur harsh and crisp, brown, with a narrow streak down the back of the neck; a spot on the knee and the front of the fore-legs below the knee black; the hind-legs are bay; the sides of the chin pale yellowish; the under-side of the neck yellow bay, this colour being separated from the darker colour of the upper part of the neck by a ridge of longer, more rigid hairs; the ears are long, brown, paler internally; the horns are short and conical; the skull has a deep and wide concavity in front of the orbits, and a keeled ridge on the cheek."

Blyth says: "This species varies much in colour from red to black, and the black sometimes with a white nape, or the hairs of the nape may be white at the base only." Lieut. Bevan described one ('P. Z. S.' 1866) shot on the Zwagaben mountain, near Moulmein, as being of a mingled black and ferruginous colour.

No. 453. NEMORHŒDUS EDWARDSII.

The Thibetan Capricorn.

HABITAT.—Thibet.

DESCRIPTION.—This differs from the Indian *N. bubalina* by the uniform blackish brown of the upper parts tending to ferruginous on the thighs, and the red colour in place of the grey on the lower parts of the legs.

It was discovered by the Abbé David, who named it after the well-known Professor A. Milne-Edwards.

No. 454. NEMORHŒDUS GORAL.

The Small Himalayan Capricorn (*Jerdon's No.* 231).

NATIVE NAMES.—*Goral*, Pahari; *Pijur*, Kashmiri (*Jerdon*); *Rein* or *Rom*, Kashmiri (*Kinloch*); *Sah* or *Sarr*, in the Sutlej valley; *Suh-ging*, Lepcha; *Ra-giyu*, Bhotia.

HABITAT.—The whole range of the Himalayas from Bhotan to Kashmir.

DESCRIPTION.—Dull brownish-grey above, with a dark mesial line, paler below; a large white spot under the throat; chest and front of fore-legs dark brown; female paler. The general appearance is that of a high, or arched-backed goat. The females and young are lighter coloured; the horns spring from the crest of the frontals and incline backward, and are slightly curved and very sharp pointed, ringed at the base, and smooth for the apical half or third; some have more rings than others. Jerdon says from twenty to twenty-five rings, but a specimen from Bhutan, which I have before me as I write (a female, I think) has but ten annuli, or little more than one-third ringed.

The following description is from Kinloch's 'Large Game of Thibet':—

"Gooral are not gregarious, like the true goats, all of which frequently assemble in large flocks, but are usually scattered about the hills, three or four being occasionally found close together, but more commonly they feed alone or in pairs. They are to be found in all sorts of ground, from bare crags to thick undulating forests, but their favourite resorts are steep rocky hills, thinly sprinkled with forest, especially where it consists of the Kolin pine. In bright weather they conceal themselves in shady places during the day-time, and only come out to feed on the open slopes in the morning and evening; but when the weather is cloudy they sometimes feed nearly all day.

"From living so near human habitations, and constantly seeing shepherds and wood-cutters, gooral are not alarmed by seeing men at a distance, and where the ground is much broken they are not difficult to stalk. Where they are at all plentiful they afford very good sport, and

Nemorhœdus goral.

their pursuit is a capital school for the young sportsman. Gooral-shooting is in fact like miniature ibex-shooting. The ground they inhabit is frequently difficult walking; the animals are quite sufficiently wary to test the generalship of the stalker; and as they do not present a very large mark, good shooting is required.

"The best way to hunt them is (having discovered a good hill) to be on the ground by daylight and work along the face of the hill, keeping as high up as possible. Every slope should be carefully examined, and on reaching the edge of each ravine it should be thoroughly reconnoitred. Being good climbers, the gooral may be found in all sorts of places—on narrow ledges, on the face of steep precipices, on gentle slopes of young grass, and among scattered bushes or forest trees, As little noise as possible should be made; talking should never be allowed, for nothing frightens game so much. Frequently after firing a shot or two on a hill-side, other animals may be found quietly feeding a little further on, whereas if there has been any shouting or talking the beasts will have been driven away. Shooting over a hill does not appear to have the effect of frightening gooral away; when disturbed they seldom go far, and may be found again on their old ground in the course of a day or two. On detecting the presence of danger, the gooral generally stands still, and utters several sharp hisses before moving away."

SIZE.—Height, 28 to 30 inches; length, about 4 feet; horns, from 6 to 9 inches.

I must here include one of the most curious animals in India, a creature resembling at first sight the African gnu. About a couple of years ago, a friend of mine, who hails from the "land o' cakes,' called to ask me about a strange animal he had noticed in the Museum. "They call it a 'takin,'" said he; "and if I did not think they were above jokes in such a dry-bone establishment, I should say in the language of my native country, that it is a 'tak' in,' for it does not look natural at all." I turned up Hodgson's account of the creature for him, to prove that it was not a hoax. It was first brought to notice by the above naturalist about thirty years ago, and he gave it the name *Budorcas,* from the two Greek words signifying ox and gazelle.

His account of it appears in the 'Journal of the Asiatic Society,' vol. xix., 1850. It is again mentioned in the 'P. Z. S.' for 1853, with a plate (No. xxxvi.), and a further account of it, with several plates, will be found in Professor Milne-Edwards's 'Recherches sur les Mammifères' (pp. 367 to 377).

As my time has been very much occupied lately, I have not been able to go through all that has been written on this singular antelope, but I have been fortunate enough to find a willing helper in Mr. J. Cockburn, who, always ready to assist in the study to which he has devoted himself, has given me the following notes, which I have given in the following notice, as they stand under the heading DESCRIPTION.

GENUS BUDORCAS.

A heavily-built, somewhat cow-shaped animal, with curiously bent horns, which spring upwards, but soon bend laterally outward and then upwards and backwards with angular curves; a front view resembles a trident with the centre prong removed. The chevron is highly arched, and the false hoofs are very large.

No. 455. BUDORCAS TAXICOLOR.

The Takin.

NATIVE NAMES.—*Takin* or *Takhon*, pronounced nasally.
HABITAT.—The Mishmi hills, Assam, Thibet.
DESCRIPTION.—"The takin is a large, heavily-built ruminant, about

Budorcas taxicolor.

3 feet 6 inches high at the shoulder and 6 feet in total length. The external peculiarities of the animal are: first, peculiar angularly curved horns in both sexes; second, the enormously arched chevron; third, the very great development of the spurious hoofs, which are obtusely conical, and about $1\frac{1}{2}$ inches in length in a small specimen.

"The colour of the adult in one stage is fulvous throughout, some of the hairs being dark tipped. Legs, tail, muzzle and dorsal stripe black.

"Old bulls appear to become of an uniform brownish-black at times, but the colour doubtless depends on the season, as each hair has the basal two-thirds yellow, and its apical third black, and the young its hair brown with a dark tint. The takin, pronounced takhon (nasally), is found just outside British limits in the Mishmi and Akha hills, north of Assam. It extends into the mountainous parts of Chinese Thibet, whence it has lately been procured by the adventurous Abbé David, and has been described by the great French naturalist A. Milne-Edwards, in his work 'Recherches sur les Mammifères,' with some osteological details which were hitherto wanting, but no more than the limb bones appear to have been obtained.

"The horns of the takin have been considered to bear some likeness to those of the gnu (*Catoblepas*), but I fail to trace a resemblance. Hodgson's description of the horns is as follows :—

"'The horns of the takin are inserted on the highest part of the forehead. The horns are nearly in contact at their bases. Their direction is first vertically upwards, then horizontally outwards, or to the sides, and then almost as horizontally backwards. The length of each horn is about 20 inches along the curves, but their thickness is great. The tail is about three inches long.'

"This remarkable animal was originally described by Brian Hodgson in 1850, from specimens procured by Major Jenkins from the Mishmis, north-east of Sadya. Skulls and skins are fairly common among the residents of Debroogurh, and two perfect skins of adults were lately presented by Colonel Graham to the Indian Museum.

"It is to be regretted that the skeleton of the animal remains unknown to science; from information collected by myself from the Mishmis, it was apparent that they might easily be procured.

"The animal would appear to range from about 8000 feet to the Alpine region, which is stated to be its habitat.

"While at Sadya a Mishmi chief pointed me out various spurs of the Himalayas, tantalisingly close, where he stated that he had hunted the animal.

"Hodgson's paper on the takin was published in the 'Jour. As. Soc.' vol. xix., pp. 65, 75, with three plates, a drawing of the animal, and two views of the skull.

"The next figure was by Wolf, in the 'Proc. of the Zool. Soc.' for 1853, pt. xxxvi., and is perhaps the worst he has ever done. Neither of these drawings are correct; and it is to be hoped that Professor Milne-Edwards has more materials for his picture than flat skins and limb bones.

"Professor Milne-Edwards was inclined to consider his specimens a distinct variety from the Mishmi animal, and calls it *Budorcas taxicola* (*sic*) var. *Tibetana*.

"The difference the professor points out, namely the fulvous colour and the thinner undeveloped horns, exist in various specimens of the Mishmi takin, and there can be no question but that the animals are identical.

"The slaty colour of Wolf's drawing is probably due to an incorrect conception of Hodgson's term grey, which he defines as a yellowish-grey.

"The takin is essentially a serow (*Nemorhædus*), with affinities to the bovines through the musk ox (*Ovibos moschata*), and other relationship to the sheep, goat and antelope. The development of the spurious hoofs would indicate that it frequents very steep ground."—*J. C.*

GENUS GAZELLA—THE GAZELLES.

These are small animals of slender frame; bovine muzzle; of sandy colour above and white underneath; small annulated horns, curved gracefully backwards, and in some species so elegantly formed as to take the shape of a lyre on looking at them full in front. The females of some have smaller, smoother horns, but others are hornless. The skull has an anteorbital vacuity, with a small anteorbital fossa. The auditory bullæ are large; "eye-pits small; groin-pits distinct; large feet-pits in all feet; knees tufted" (*Jerdon*). The face has a white band running from the outer side of the base of each horn down to the muzzle, the space between forming a dark triangular patch bordered with a deeper tint. Sir Victor Brooke classifies the twenty or so known species as follows:—

I.—BACK UNSTRIPED.

Dentition:—Inc. $\frac{0}{3}$; can. $\frac{0}{1}$; prem. $\frac{3}{3}$; molars, $\frac{3}{3}$.

A.—*The white colour of the rump not encroaching on the fawn of the haunches.*

a. BOTH SEXES WITH HORNS.

Horns lyrate or semi-lyrate: *Gazella dorcas; G. Isabella; G. rufifrons; G. lævipes; G. melanura.*

Horns non-lyrate: *Gazella Cuvieri; G. leptoceros; G. Spekii; G. Arabica; G. Bennetti; G. fuscifrons.*

b. FEMALES HORNLESS.

Gazella subgutterosa; G. gutterosa; G. picticaudata.

B.—*White of rump projecting forwards in an angle into the fawn colour of the haunches.*

Gazella dama; G. mohr; G. Sœmmerringii; G. Granti.

II.—BACK WITH A WHITE MEDIAN STRIPE.

One premolar less in the lower jaw: *Gazella euchore.*

Of the above species the following come under the scope of this work: *Gazella Bennetti; G. fuscifrons; G. subgutterosa; G. picticaudata.*

No. 456. GAZELLA BENNETTI.

The Indian Gazelle (Jerdon's No. 229).

NATIVE NAMES.—*Chikara*, Hindi; *Kal-punch*, Hindi; *Kal-sipi*, Mahratti; *Hirni*, in the Punjab; *Tiska*, also *Budari* and *Mudari*, Canarese; *Barudu-jinka*, Telegu; *Porsya* (male) and *Chari* (female), of Baoris.

HABITAT.—Mr. W. Blanford defines the limits of this species as follows ('P. Z. S.,' 1873, p. 315)—the italics are mine: "It is found throughout the Punjab, North-west Provinces, Rajputana, Sind (unless in part replaced by the next species), Kachh, Kathiawar, Guzerat, and the whole Bombay Presidency, *with the exception of the Western Ghâts and the low land on Konkan, along the western coast, south of the neighbourhood of Daman.* It is also met with in the Narbada and Tapti valleys, Bandelkand, the Son valley, and Rewah, in the Nagpur and Chanda country, Berar, the Hyderabad territories, and other parts of Southern India, *with the complete exception of the Malabar coast and the adjacent hills.*" He adds that from the evidence of Colonel McMaster and Colonel Douglas Hamilton, both good authorities, it is not known to occur much south of the Krishna river, nor is it found in the Ganges valley east of

Gazella Bennetti (male and female).

Benares, in Eastern Behar, the Santal Pergunnahs, Chotia Nagpur, Birbhum, &c., Chhatisgurh, the Mahanadi valley, Orissa, Bastar, and the east coast, generally north of the river Krishna. He says it is met with in the Narbada valley, but I have also found it common on the plateaux of the Satpura range.

DESCRIPTION.—"Fawn brown above, darker where it joins the white of the sides and buttocks; chin, breast, lower parts and buttocks behind white; tail, knee-tufts and fetlocks behind black; a dark brown spot on the nose, and a dark line from the eyes to the mouth, bordered by a light one above" (*Jerdon*).

SIZE.—Length, 3½ feet; height, 26 inches at shoulder, 28 inches at croup.

The horns run from 10 to 14 inches in the male, but, in fact, few exceed a foot. The longest of six pairs in my collection measure 12 inches, and the head is looked upon as a fine one. I agree with Jerdon that there must be some mistake about 18-inch horns recorded from the Punjab.

This pretty little creature, miscalled "ravine-deer," is familiar to most shikaris. How it got called a *deer* it is difficult to say, except on the principle of "rats and mice, and such small deer." The Madras term of "goat-antelope" is more appropriate. I remember once, when out on field service with the late Dr. Jerdon during the Indian Mutiny, a few *chikara* crossed our line of march. A young and somewhat bumptious ensign, who knew not of the fame of the doctor as a naturalist, called out: "There are some deer, there are some deer." "Those are not deer," quietly remarked Jerdon. "Oh, I say," exclaimed the boy, thinking he had got a rise out of the doctor; "Jerdon says those are not deer!" "No more they are, young man—no more they are; much more of the goat—much more of the goat."

This gazelle frequents broken ground, with sandy nullahs bordered by scrub jungle, and is most common in dry climates. It is unknown, I believe, in Bengal and, according to Jerdon, on the Malabar coast, but is, I think, found almost everywhere else in India. It abounds in the Central provinces, and I have found it in parts of the Punjab, and it is common throughout the North-west. It is a wary, restless little beast, and requires good shooting, for it does not afford much of a mark. When disturbed they keep constantly shifting, not going far, but hovering about in a most tantalising way. Natives it cares little for, unless it be a shikari with a gun, of which it seems to have intuitive perception; but the ordinary cultivator, with his load of wood and grass, may approach within easy shot; therefore it is not a bad plan, when there is no available cover, to get one of these men to walk alongside of you, whilst, with a horse-cloth or blanket over you, you make yourself look as like your guide as you can. A horse or bullock is also a great help. I had a little bullock which formed part of some loot at Banda—a very handsome little bull, easy to ride and steady under fire—and I found him most useful in stalking black buck and gazelle.

When alarmed, the *chikara* stamps its foot and gives a sharp little hiss. It is generally found in small herds of four or five, but often singly. Jerdon, however, says that in the extreme North-west he had seen twenty or more together, and this is corroborated by Kinloch.

They are sometimes hunted by hawks and dogs combined, the *churrug* (*Falco sacer*) being the hawk ususally employed, as mentioned both by Kinloch and Hodgson, writing of opposite ends of the great Himalayan chain. The hawk stoops at the head of its quarry and confuses it, whilst the dogs, who would otherwise have no chance, run up and seize it.

The poor little gazelle has also many other enemies — jackals and wolves being amongst the number. Captain Baldwin, in his interesting book, writes: "Like other antelopes, the little ravine-deer has many enemies besides man. One day, when out with my rifle, I noticed an old female gazelle stamping her feet, and every now and then making that hiss which is the alarm note of the animal. It was not I that was the cause of her terror, for I had passed close to her only a few minutes before, and she seemed to understand by my manner that I meant no harm; no, there was something else. I turned back, and, on looking down a ravine close by, saw a crafty wolf attempting a stalk on the mother and young one. Another day, at Agra, a pair of jackals joined in the chase of a wounded buck." Brigadier-General McMaster also relates how he and two friends, whilst coursing, watched for a long time four jackals trying to force one of a small herd of young bucks to separate from the rest. "The gazelles stood in a circle, and maintained their ground well by keeping their heads very gallantly outwards to their foes, until at length, seeing us, both sides made off. We laid the greyhounds into and killed one of the jackals."

No. 457. GAZELLA FUSCIFRONS.

The Baluchistan Gazelle.

HABITAT.—The deserts of Jalk between Seistan and Baluchistan.

DESCRIPTION.—"Central facial band strongly marked, grizzled black; light facial streak grey, fairly definite, as is also the blackish dark facial streak; cheeks and anterior of neck grey; back of the neck, back, sides, haunches and legs sandy; lateral streaks wanting; belly and rump whitish; knee-brushes long, black; ears very long; horns (of female only known) strongly annulated, bending forwards and very slightly inwards at the tips" (*Sir V. Brooke*, 'P. Z. S.,' 1873, p. 545).

SIZE.—Total length, from tip of nose to end of tail, 4 feet; height at shoulder, 1 foot 11 inches.

This curious species was first brought to notice by Mr. Blanford. It is distinguished, he says, from the Indian *G. Bennetti*—first by colour, and secondly by the greater length and more strongly marked annulation of the horns of the female. "The face in the Indian gazelle," he says, "is nearly uniform rufescent fawn colour; the parts that are black and blackish in *G. fuscifrons* being only a little darker than the rest in *G. Bennetti;* the back also in the latter is more rufescent and less yellow, and the hairs are less dense."

The following two species belong to section *B*, of which the females are hornless.

NO. 458. GAZELLA SUBGUTTEROSA.

The Persian Gazelle.

NATIVE NAMES.—*Kik*, *Sai-kik*, and *Jairan*, Turki of Yarkand and Kashgar (*Blanford*).

HABITAT.—The high lands of Persia; to the north-west it is found

Gazella subgutterosa.

as far as Tabriz; it is probably, according to Blanford, the gazelle of Meshed and Herat; on the east it extends to the frontier of India, and is found in Afghanistan and northern Baluchistan; a variety also exists in Yarkand.

DESCRIPTION.—"Hair in winter rough and coarse, in summer much softer and smoother. During both seasons the dirty white of the face and cheeks is only relieved by the dark facial streak, which is short and narrow, but defined by a sprinkling of rufous hairs; the lateral and pygal bands are very faintly indicated, the dark bands being more rufous, the light band rather paler than the grey fawn colour of the upper parts of the body; breast and belly white; tail and ears moderate in length, the former blackish-rufous. Horns absent in the female; in the male long, annulated and lyrate, the points projecting inwards" (*Sir V. Brooke*). According to Blanford, who seemed doubtful whether it should not be raised to the rank of a species, the Yarkand variety differs from the typical *G. subgutterosa* in the very much darker markings on the face, and in the much smaller degree to which the horns diverge; he adds, however, that as there is some variation in face-markings amongst Persian specimens, it is perhaps better to consider the Yarkand race as only a variety. He gives a very good coloured plate of the animal. ('Sc. Results, Second Yarkand Mission—Mammalia.')

NO. 459. GAZELLA PICTICAUDATA.

Thibetan Gazelle.

NATIVE NAME.—*Goa*, Thibetan.

HABITAT.—Ladakh. Abundant, according to Kinloch, on the plateau to the south-east of the Tsomoriri lake, on the hills east of Hanlé, and in the Indus valley from Demchok, the frontier village of Ladakh, as far down as Nyima. He had also seen it on the Nakpogoding pass to the north of the Tsomoriri, and picked up a horn on the banks of the Sutlej beyond the Niti pass.

DESCRIPTION.—Hair in winter long and softish; facial and lateral markings wanting; breast, belly and anal disk which surrounds the tail dirty white; the rest of the body grizzled fawn-colour, becoming more rusty towards the anal disk, a rusty line sometimes running through the disk to the short tail, the tip of which is rusty brown; the hairs about the corners of the mouth elongated. In the summer the coat is short and of a slaty-grey colour. Ears very short; horns long, annulated — diverge as they rise, bending forwards and backwards, again forwards, and a little inwards at the tips. Skull: anteorbital fossa *very* shallow, nasals converging to a point, and rather elongated (*Sir Victor Brooke*, 'P. Z. S.,' 1873, p. 547).

SIZE.—Height, about 18 inches.

There is a lovely little photograph of this gazelle in Kinloch's 'Large Game of Thibet,' wonderfully life-like; the head seems to stand out from the page. He describes it under Hodgson's generic name, *Procapra*, but there is no reason for separating it from *Gazella.* He says: "The goa avoid rocky and steep ground, preferring the undulating plains and gently sloping valleys. Early in the season they are to be found in small herds, frequently close to the snow; as this melts they appear to disperse themselves over the higher ground, being often found singly or in twos and threes."

GENUS PANTHOLOPS

Between the gazelles and antelopes proper comes the *chiru* (*Pantholops Hodgsonii*), though strictly speaking it is, with the saiga antelope (*Saiga Tartarica*), though in a somewhat less degree, connected by cranial affinities with the sheep. The saiga is notable for its highly-arched nose and inflated nostrils, which are so much lengthened as to necessitate the animal's walking backwards when it feeds. The *chiru* is not quite so developed in this respect. The skull of the saiga is unique among ruminants, and those who wish to become acquainted with its most minute osteological details should refer to an article on this animal by Dr. James Murie in the 'P. Z. S.,' 1870, p. 457. I can only here give a very brief summary of the chief characteristics. Looked at in profile, the nasal bones we find to be remarkably short, the face being hollowed out, as it were, between the upper nasal cartilage and the very long and narrow maxillary and pre-maxillary bones; great vertical depth from the top of the nasal to the bottom of the maxillary bones; a very prominent bovine orbit, above and a little behind which the short tapering horns of a gazelle type are placed. The lower nasal cartilage is prolonged on to the fibrous cord of the nares, and the profile view of the animal in life is that of a grotesquely Roman-nosed antelope with swollen nostrils. Its nearest relative in India is the *chiru*, which has certain points of resemblance. The nose is but slightly arched, but the nostrils are more swollen than in antelopes as a rule. This is not sufficiently rendered in an otherwise admirable coloured plate in Blanford's 'Scientific Results of the Second Yarkand Mission,' but it is more apparent in the photograph of the head

Saiga Antelope.

in Kinloch's 'Large Game of Thibet.' Another approach to the saiga is in the position of the horns, which, though of the same class, are much longer and more attenuated, but the position over the eye and the osseous development of the orbit are the same. The nasal bones are also shorter in proportion to other antelopes. The super-orbital foramina just under the horns, which are marked in most antelope and deer, are very minute in *Pantholops*. Dr. Murie notices the inflation of the post-maxilla in the saiga, and states that a similar extension is to be found in the *chiru*.

No. 460. PANTHOLOPS HODGSONII.

The Chiru.

NATIVE NAMES.—*Chiru* in Nepal; *Isos* in Thibet (*Strachey*); also *Isors* or *Choos* (*Kinloch*).

HABITAT.—The open plains of Thibet from Lhassa to Ladakh.

DESCRIPTION.—The following description was written in 1830, apparently by Mr. Brian Hodgson himself, and was published in 'Gleanings in Science' (vol. ii., p. 348), probably the first scientific magazine in India. As I have seen no better account of this curious antelope I give it as it stands. Mr. Hodgson had the advantage of drawing from life, he having had a living specimen as a pet:—

"Antelope with very long, compressed, tapering, sub-erect (? sub-lyrated) horns, having a slight concave arctuation forwards, and blunt annulations (prominently ridged on the frontal surface), except near the tips; a double coat throughout, greyish blue internally, but superficially fawn-coloured above, and white below, a black forehead, and stripes down the legs; and a tumour or tuft above either nostril.

"The ears and tail are moderate and devoid of any peculiarity; so likewise are the sub-orbital sinuses.* The horns are exceedingly long, measuring in some individuals nearly 2½ feet. They are placed very forward on the head, and may popularly be said to be erect and straight, though a reference to the specific character will show that they are not strictly one or the other.

"The general surface of the horns is smooth and polished, but its uniformity is broken by a series of from fifteen to twenty rings extending from the base to within six inches of the tip of each horn. Upon the lateral and dorsal surfaces of the horns these rings are little elevated, and present a wavy rather than a ridgy appearance; but on the frontal surface the rings exhibit a succession of heavy, large ridges, with furrows between; the annulation is nowhere acutely edged. The horns have a very considerable lateral compression towards the base, where their extent fore and aft is nearly double of that from side to side; upwards

* These are wanting.—R. A. S.

from the base the lateral compression becomes gradually less, and towards their tips the horns are nearly rounded. Compared with their length the thickness of the horns is as nothing—in other words they are slender, but not therefore by any means weak. The tips are acute rather than otherwise; the divergence at the points is from one-third to one-half of the length. At the base a finger can hardly be passed between the horns. Throughout five-sixths of their length from the base the horns describe an uniform slightly inward curve, and on the top angle of the curve they turn inwards again more suddenly, but still slightly, the points of the horns being thus directed inwards; the lateral view of the horns shows a considerable concave arctuation forwards, but chiefly derived from the upper part of the horns."

Pantholops Hodgsonii.

There is an excellent coloured plate of this animal in Blanford's 'Mammalia of the Second Yarkand Mission.' The only fault I see lies in the muzzle, especially of the male, which the artist has made as fine as that of a gazelle. The photograph in Kinloch's 'Large Game of Thibet' shows the puffiness of the nostrils much better; the latter author says of it:—

"The Thibetan antelope is a thoroughly game-looking animal; in size it considerably exceeds the common black buck or antelope of India, and is not so elegantly made. Its colour is a reddish fawn, verging on white in very old individuals. A dark stripe runs down the shoulders and flanks, and the legs are also dark brown. The face alone is nearly black, especially in old bucks. The hair is long and brittle, and extraordinarily thick-set, forming a beautiful velvety cushion, which must most effectually protect the animal from the intense cold of the elevated regions which it inhabits. A peculiarity about this antelope is the existence of two orifices in the groin, which communicate with long tubes running up into the body. The Tartars say that the antelope inflates these with air, and is thereby enabled to run with greater swiftness! The muzzle of the Thibetan antelope is quite different from that of most of the deer and antelope tribe, being thick and puffed looking, with a small rudimentary beard; the eyes are set high up in the head; the sub-orbital sinus is wanting; the horns are singularly handsome, jet black, and of the closest grain, averaging about twenty-three or twenty-four inches in length. They are beautifully adapted for knife handles. The females have short black horns, and are much smaller than the males."

The last is a doubtful point; as far as I have been able to gather evidence on the subject the female appears to be hornless, which allies *Pantholops* more to the antelopes and the gazelles. Major Kinloch may have taken some young males for females, the general colouring being much the same. In the 'Proceedings of the Zoological Society' for 1834, p. 80, there is an extract from a letter from Mr. Hodgson, which, with reference to previous correspondence, says: "The communications referred to left only the inguinal pores, the number of teats in the female, and the fact of her being cornute or otherwise, doubtful. These points are now cleared up. The female is hornless, and has two teats only; she has no marks on the face or limbs, and is rather smaller than the male. The male has a large pouch at each groin, as in *Ant. dorcas*; that of the female is considerably smaller." Mr. Hodgson further remarks that "the *chiru* antelope can only belong either to the gazelline or the antelopine group. Hornless females would place it among the latter; but lyrate horns, ovine nose, and want of sinus, would give it rather to Gazella, and its singular inguinal purses further ally it to *Ant. dorcas* of this group. But from Gazella it is distinguished by the accessory nostrils, of inter-maxillary pouch, the hornless females, the absence of tufts on the knees, and of bands on the flanks. The *chiru*, with his bluff bristly nose, his inter-maxillary pouches, and hollow-cored horns, stands in some respects alone."

Hodgson was apparently not well acquainted at the time with saiga, or he would have certainly alluded to the affinity. Kinloch has the following regarding its habits:—

"In Chang Chenmo, where I have met with it, the elevation can be nowhere less than 14,000 feet, and some of the feeding grounds cannot be less than 18,000. In the early part of summer the antelope appear to keep on the higher and more exposed plains and slopes when the snow does not lie; as the season becomes warmer, the snow, which has accumulated on the grassy banks of the streams in the sheltered valleys, begins to dissolve, and the antelope then come down to feed on the grass which grows abundantly in such places, and then is the time when they may easily be stalked and shot. They usually feed only in the mornings and evenings, and in the day-time seek more open and elevated situations, frequently excavating deep holes in the stony plains, in which they lie, with only their heads and horns visible above the surface of the ground. It is a curious fact that females are rarely found in Chang Chenmo; I have met with herds of sixty or seventy bucks, but have only seen one doe to my knowledge during the three times that I visited the valley."

GENUS ANTELOPE (*restricta*).

Horns in the male only; abnormal cases of horned females are on record, but they only prove the rule. No muffle; sub-orbital sinus moderate, somewhat linear; no canines; groin-pits large; feet-pits present. In the skull the sub-orbital fossa is large.

No. 461. ANTELOPE BEZOARTICA.

The Indian Antelope (*Jerdon's No.* 228).

NATIVE NAMES.—*Mrig* or *Mirga*, Sanscrit; *Harna, Hirun, Harin* (male) and *Hirni* (female), Hindi; also *Kalwit*, Hindi, according to Jerdon; *Goria* (female) and *Kala* (male), in Tirhoot; *Kalsar* (male) and *Baoti* (female), in Behar; *Bureta*, in Bhagulpore; *Barout* and *Sasin*, in Nepal; *Phandayet*, Mahrathi (*Jerdon*). *Hiru* and *Bamuni-hiru*, Mahrathi; *Chigri*, Canarese; *Irri* (male), *Sedi* (female), and *Jinka*, Telegu; *Alali* (male) and *Gandoli* (female), of Baoris.

HABITAT.—In open plain country throughout India except in Lower Bengal and Malabar. In the Punjab it does not cross the Indus. Dr. Jerdon says: "I have seen larger herds in the neighbourhood of Jalna in the Deccan than anywhere else—occasionally some thousands together, with black bucks in proportion. Now and then, Dr. Scott informs me, they have been observed in the Government cattle-farm at Hissar in herds calculated at 8000 to 10,000." I must say I have never seen anything like this, although in the North-west, between Aligarh and Delhi, I have noticed very large herds; in the Central provinces thirty to forty make a fair average herd, though smaller ones are more common. These small parties generally consist of does, and perhaps two or three young sandy bucks lorded over by one old black buck, who will not allow any other of his colour to approach without the ordeal of battle. I have lately heard of them in Assam, but forget the precise locality.

DESCRIPTION.—Form supple and elegant, with graceful curves; the neck held up proudly; the head adorned with long, spiral, and closely annulated horns, close at the base, but diverging at the tips in a V form. In very large specimens there are five flexures in the horn, but generally four. They are perfectly round, and taper gradually to the tips, which are smooth; the bony cores are also spiral, so that in the dry skull the horn screws on and off. The colour of the old males is is deep blackish-brown, the back and sides with an abrupt line of separation from the

Antelope bezoartica.

white of the belly; the dark colour also extends down the outer surface of the limbs; the back of the head, nape and neck are hoary yellowish; under parts and inside of limbs pure white; the face is black, with a white circle round the eyes and nose; the tail is short; the young males are fawn-coloured. The females are hornless, somewhat smaller, and pale yellowish-fawn above, white below, with a pale streak from the shoulder to the haunch.

SIZE.—Length, about 4 feet to root of tail; tail, 7 inches; height at shoulder, 32 inches. Horns, average length about 20 inches—fine ones 22, unusual 24, very rare 26. Sir Barrow Ellis has or had a pair 26½, with only three flexures; 28 has been recorded by "Triangle" in *The Asian*, and 30 spoken of elsewhere, but I have as yet seen no proof of the latter. The measurement should be taken straight from base to tip, and not following the curves of the spiral. I have shot some a little over 22, but never more. I believe, however, that the longest horns come from the North-west.

This antelope is so well known that it is hardly necessary to dilate at length on it; every shikari in India has had his own experiences, but I will take from Sir Walter Elliot's account and Dr. Jerdon's some paragraphs concerning the habits of the animal which cannot be improved upon, and add a short extract from my own journals regarding its love of locality:—

"When a herd is met with and alarmed, the does bound away for a short distance, and then turn round to take a look; the buck follows more leisurely, and generally brings up the rear. Before they are much frightened they always bound or spring, and a large herd going off in this way is one of the finest sights imaginable. But when at speed the gallop is like that of any other animal. Some of the herds are so large that one buck has from fifty to sixty does, and the young bucks driven from these large flocks are found wandering in separate herds, sometimes containing as many as thirty individuals of different ages.

"They show some ingenuity in avoiding danger. In pursuing a buck once into a field of *toor*, I suddenly lost sight of him, and found, after a long search, that he had dropped down among the grain, and lay concealed with his head close to the ground. Coming on another occasion upon a buck and doe with a young fawn, the whole party took to flight, but the fawn being very young, the old ones endeavoured to make it lie down. Finding, however, that it persisted in running after them, the buck turned round and repeatedly knocked it over in a cotton field until it lay still, when they ran off, endeavouring to attract my attention. Young fawns are frequently found concealed and left quite by themselves."—*Elliot.*

Jerdon adds: "When a herd goes away on the approach of danger, if any of the does are lingering behind, the buck comes up and drives them off after the others, acting as whipper-in, and never allowing one to drop behind. Bucks may often be seen fighting, and are then so intently engaged, their heads often locked together by the horns, that they may be approached very close before the common danger causes them to separate. Bucks with broken horns are often met with, caused by fights; and I have heard of bucks being sometimes caught in this way, some nooses being attached to the horns of a tame one. I have twice seen a wounded antelope pursued by greyhounds drop suddenly into a small ravine, and lie close to the ground, allowing the dogs to pass over it without noticing, and hurry forward." ('Mamm. of India,' p. 278.)

I have myself experienced some curious instances of the hiding propensities spoken of by Sir Walter Elliot and Dr. Jerdon. In my book on Seonee I have given a case of a wounded buck which I rode down to the brink of a river, when he suddenly disappeared. The country was open, and I was so close behind him that it seemed impossible for him to have got out of sight in so short a space of time; but I looked right and left without seeing a trace of him, and, hailing some fishermen on the opposite bank, found that they had not seen him cross. Finally my eye lighted on what seemed to be a couple of sticks projecting from a bed of rushes some four or five feet from the bank. Here was my friend submerged to the tip of his nose, with nothing but the tell-tale horns sticking out.

This antelope attaches itself to localities, and after being driven away for miles will return to its old place. The first buck I ever shot I recovered, after having driven him away for some distance and wounded him, in the very spot I first found him; and the following extract from my journals will show how tenaciously they cling sometimes to favourite places:—

"I was out on the boundary between Khapa and Belgaon, and came across a particularly fine old buck, with very wide-spreading horns; so peculiar were they that I could have sworn to the head amongst a thousand. He was too far for a safe shot when I first saw him, but I could not resist the chance of a snap at him, and tried it, but missed; and I left the place. My work led me again soon after to Belgaon itself, and whilst I was in camp there I found my friend again; but he was very wary; for three days I hunted him about, but could not get a shot. At last I got my chance; it was on the morning of the day I left Belgaon. I rode round by the boundary, when up jumped my friend from a bed of rushes, and took off across country. I followed him cautiously, and found him again with some does about two miles off. A man was ploughing in the field close by; so, hailing him, I got his bullocks and drove them carefully up past the does. We splashed through a nullah, and waded through a lot of rushes, and at last I found myself behind a clump of coarse grass, with a nullah between me and the antelope. They jumped up on my approach, and Blacky, seeing his enemy, made a speedy bolt of it; but I was within easy range of him, and a bullet brought him down on his head with a complete somersault. Now this buck, in spite of the previous shot at him, and being hunted about from day to day, never left his ground, and used to sleep every night in a field near my tent."

This antelope has been raised by the Hindoos amongst the constellations harnessed to the chariot of the moon. Brahmins can feed on its flesh under certain circumstances prescribed by the 'Institutes of Menu,' and it is sometimes tamed by Fakirs. It is easily domesticated, but the bucks are always dangerous when their horns are full grown, especially to children. The breeding season begins in the spring, but fawns of all ages may be seen at any time of the year. The flesh of this species is among the best of the wild ruminants.

The next group of antelopes are those with smooth horns, without knots; spiral in some African species, but short and straight, or but slightly curved in the Indian ones. Females hornless. There are but two genera in India, *Portax* and *Tetraceros.*

GENUS PORTAX—THE NYLGAO.

Horns on back edge of frontal bone behind the orbit, short, recurved, conical and smooth, angular at the base; bovine nose with large moist muffle; small eye-pits; hind legs shorter than the front; tail long and tufted; back short, sloping down from high withers; the neck deep and compressed like a horse, with a short upright mane; on the throat of the male under a white patch is a long tuft of black hair. In the skull the nasal opening is small, and the molars have, according to Dr. Gray, supplementary lobes. Dr. Jerdon says: "There is a small pit in front of the orbit, and anterior to this a small longitudinal fold, in the middle of which there is a pore through which exudes a yellow secretion from the gland beneath."

The female has sometimes in an abnormal condition been found with horns. Mr. J. Cockburn, in a letter to *The Asian* (11th of November, 1879, p. 40), describes such a one.

No. 462. PORTAX PICTUS *vel* TRAGOCAMELUS.

The Nylgao or Blue Bull (*Jerdon's No.* 226).

NATIVE NAMES.—*Nilgao*, *Nilgai*, or *Lilgao*, *Lilgai*, *Rojra* or *Rojh*, *Rooi* (female), Hindi; *Guraya*, Gondi; *Maravi*, Canarese; *Manupotu*, Telegu.

HABITAT.—India generally, from the Himalayas to the south. It is not common south of the Ganges, nor, according to Jerdon, is it found in the extreme south of India.

DESCRIPTION.—A horse-like animal at the first glance, owing to its lean head, long, flat, and deep neck, and high withers, but with cervine hind-quarters, lower than in front. The male is of an iron grey colour, intensified by age; the inside of the ears, lips, and chin are white; a large white patch on the throat, below which is the pendant tuft of black hair; the chest, stomach, and rings on the fetlocks, white; mane, throat-tuft and tip of tail, black. The female is a sandy or tawny colour, and is somewhat smaller than the male.

SIZE.—Length of male, 6½ to 7 feet; tail 18 to 22 inches; height at shoulder, from 13 to 14½ hands; horns, from 8 to 10 inches.

The nilgao inhabits open country with scrub or scanty tree jungle,

Portax pictus.

also, in the Central provinces, low hilly tracts with open glades and valleys. He feeds on beyr (*Zizyphus jujuba*) and other trees, and at times even devours such quantities of the intensely acrid berries of the *aonla* (*Phyllanthus emblica*) that his flesh becomes saturated with the bitter elements of the fruit. This is most noticeable in soup, less so in a steak, which is at times not bad. The tongue and marrow-bones, however, are generally as much as the sportsman claims, and, in the Central provinces at least, the natives are grateful for all the rest.

He rests during the day in shade, but is less of a nocturnal feeder than the sambar stag. I have found nilgao feeding at all times of the day. The droppings are usually found in one place. The nilgao drinks daily, the sambar only every third day, and many are shot over water. Although he is such an imposing animal, the blue bull is but poor shooting, unless when fairly run down in the open. With a sharp spurt he is easily blown, but if not pressed will gallop for ever. In some parts of India nilgai are speared in this way. I myself preferred shooting them either from a light double-barrelled carbine or large bore pistol when alongside; the jobbing at such a large cow-like animal with a spear was always repugnant to my feelings. They are very tenacious of life. I once knocked one over as I thought dead, and, putting my rifle against a tree, went to help my shikaree to *hallal* him, when he jumped up, kicked us over, and disappeared in the jungle; I never saw him again. A similar thing happened to a friend who was with me, only he sat upon his supposed dead bull, quietly smoking a cigar and waiting for his shikarees, when up sprang the animal, sending him flying, and vanished. On another occasion, whilst walking through the jungle, I came suddenly on a fine dark male standing chest on to me. I hardly noticed him at first; but, just as he was about to plunge away into the thicket, I rapidly fired, and with a bound he was out of sight. I hunted all over the place and could find no trace of him. At last, by circling round, I suddenly came upon him at about thirty yards off, standing broadside on. I gave him a shot and heard the bullet strike, but there was not the slightest motion. I could hardly believe that he was dead in such a posture. I went up close, and finally stopped in front of him; his neck was stretched out, his mouth open and eyes rolling, but he seemed paralysed. I stepped up close and put a ball through his ear, when he fell dead with a groan. I have never seen anything like it before or since, and can only suppose that the shot in the chest had in some way choked him. I have alluded to this incident in my book on Seonee; it was in that district that it occurred.

The nilgao is the only one of the deer and antelope of India that could be turned to any useful purpose. The sambar stag, though almost equal in size, will not bear the slightest burden, but the nilgao will carry a man. I had one in my collection of animals which I trained, not to saddle, for such a thing would not stay on his back, but to saddle-cloth. He was a little difficult to ride, rather jumpy at times, otherwise his pace was a shuffling trot. I used to take him out into camp with me, and made him earn his grain by carrying the servants' bundles. He was not very safe, for he was, when excited, apt to charge; and a charge from a blue bull with his short sharp horns is not to be despised. In some parts the Hindoos will not touch the flesh of this animal, which they believe to be allied to the cow. It has much more of a horsey look about it. McMaster says that in some parts of the Coimbatore district the natives described this creature to Colonel Douglas Hamilton as a wild horse, and called it by a name signifying such. He also notices the resemblance of the Gondi name *Guraya*, to the Hindi *Ghora*.

GENUS TETRACEROS.

Horns four, conical, smooth, slightly bent forward at tip, the anterior ones very short, sometimes rudimentary, which has led to the distinction of a separate species by some naturalists; slightly ringed at the base. The posterior ones situated far back on the frontal bone, the anterior ones above the orbits; eye-pits small, linear; muffle large; feet-pits in the hind feet; no groin-pits; four mammæ; canine teeth in the males; females hornless. The skull is characterized by the large sub-orbital fossæ which occupy nearly the whole cheek. The various species—*sub-quadricornutus* of Elliot, *iodes* and *paccerois* of Hodgson—are but varieties of the following only Indian species.

No. 463. TETRACEROS QUADRICORNIS.

The Four-horned Antelope (Jerdon's No. 227).

NATIVE NAMES.—*Chowsingha*, *Chowka*. Jerdon also gives *Bherki*, *Bekra*, and *Jangli-bakra*, but I have also heard these names given by natives to the rib-faced deer (*Cervulus aureus*); *Bhir-kura* (the male) and *Bhir* (female) Gondi; *Bhirul* of Bheels; *Kotri*, Bustar; *Kond-guri*, Canarese; *Konda-gori*, Telegu (*Jerdon*). Kinloch also gives *Doda*, Hindi.

Tetraceros quadricornis.

HABITAT.—Throughout India, but not in Ceylon or Burmah.

DESCRIPTION.—A small brownish-bay animal, slightly higher at the croup than at the shoulder, which gives it a poky look, lighter beneath and whitish inside the limbs and in the middle of the belly; fore-legs, muzzle, and edge of ears dark; fetlocks dark, sometimes ringed with lighter colour. The colouring varies a good deal. The horns are situated as I have before described; the anterior ones are subject to much variation; sometimes they are absent or represented merely by a black callous skin; others are merely little knobs; the largest seldom exceed an inch and a-half, and the posterior horns five inches.

SIZE.—Head and body, 40 to 42 inches; height at shoulder, 24 to 26 inches; at croup a little higher.

This little antelope, the smallest of Indian hollow-horned ruminants, is very shy and difficult to get, even in jungles where it abounds. It was plentiful in the Seonee district, yet I seldom came across it, and was long before I secured a pair of live ones for my collection. It frequents, according to my experience, bamboo jungle; but, according to Kinloch, Jerdon and other writers, it is found in jungly hills and open glades, in the forests, and in bushy ground near dense forests.

It is an awkward-looking creature in action, as it runs with its neck stuck out in a poky sort of way, making short leaps; in walking it trips along on the tips of its toes like the little mouse-deer (*Meminna*). The young are stated to be born in the cold season. General Hardwicke created great confusion for a time by applying the name *chikara*, which is that of the *Gazella Bennettii*, to this species. It is not good eating, but can be improved by being well larded with mutton fat when roasted. McMaster believes in the individuality of Elliot's antelope (*T. sub-quadricornutus*), but more evidence is required before it can be separated from *quadricornis*. The mere variation in size, or the presence or absence of the anterior horns and the lighter shade of colour, are not sufficient reasons for its separation as a species, for the *quadricornis* is subject to variation in like manner.*

BOVINÆ—CATTLE.

These comprise the oxen, and wind up the hollow-horned ruminants as far as India is concerned. There are in the New World some other very interesting animals of this group, such as the musk-ox (*Ovibos*), and the prong-horned antelope (*Antilocapra*), which last so far resembles the Cervidæ that the horns, which are bifurcate, are also annually shed. They come off the bony core, on which the new horn is already beginning to form.

The Bovines are animals of large size, horned in both sexes, a very large and broad moist muffle, massive bodies and stout legs. The horns, which are laterally wide spread, are supported on cores of cellular bone, and are cylindrical or depressed at the base. The nose broad, with the nostrils at the side. The skull has no sub-orbital pit or fissure, and the bony orbit is prominent; grinders with a well-developed supplementary lobe; cannon bone short. In India, the groups into which

* See notes in Appendix C, p. 529.

this sub-family may be divided, are oxen, the buffaloes, and the yaks. There are no true bison in our limits, the commonly so-called bison being properly a wild ox. The taurine or Ox group is divided into the *Zebus*, or humped domestic cattle; *Taurus*, humpless cattle with cylindrical horns; and *Gavæus*, humpless cattle with flattened horns.

According to Dr. Jerdon, in some parts of India small herds of zebus have run wild. He says:—

"Localities are recorded in Mysore, Oude, Rohilkund, Shahabad, &c., and I have lately seen and shot one in the Doab near Mozuffernugger. These, however, have only been wild for a few years. Near Nellore, in the Carnatic, on the sea-coast there is a herd of cattle that have been wild for many years. The country they frequent is much covered with jungle and intersected with salt-water creeks and back-waters, and the cattle are as wild and wary as the most feral species. Their horns were very long and upright, and they were of large size. I shot one there in 1843, but had great difficulty in stalking it, and had to follow it across one or two creeks."

GENUS GAVÆUS.

Massive head with large concave frontals, surmounted in *G. gaurus* by a ridge or crest of bone; horns flattened on the outer surface, corrugated at the base, and smooth for the rest of the two-thirds, or a little more; wide-spreading and recurved at the tips, forming a crescent; greenish grey for the basal half, darker towards the tips, which are black; muffle small; dewlap small or absent; the spinous processes of the dorsal vertebræ are greatly developed down to about half the length of the back; legs small under the knee, and white in colour; hoofs small and pointed, leaving a deer-like print in the soil, very different to the splay foot of the buffalo.

No. 464. GAVÆUS GAURUS.

The Gaur, popularly called Bison (*Jerdon's No.* 238).

NATIVES NAMES.—*Gaor* or *Gavri-gai*, *Bun-boda*, Hindi; *Boda* and *Bunparra* in the Seonee and Mandla districts; *Pera-mavo* of Southern Gonds; *Gaoiya*, Mahrathi; *Karkona*, Canarese; *Katuyeni*, Tamil; *Jangli-kulgha* in Southern India; *Pyoung* in Burmah; *Salandang* in the Malay countries. Horsfield gives the following names under his *Bibos asseel: As'l Gayal*, Hindi; *Seloi*, Kuki; *P'hanj* of the Mughs and Burmese, and some others which he considers doubtful.

HABITAT.—Regarding this, I quote at length from Jerdon, whose inquiries were carefully made. He says: "The gaur is an inhabitant of all the large forests of India, from near Cape Comorin to the foot of the Himalayas. On the west coast of India it is abundant all along the Syhadr range on Western Ghâts, both in the forests at the foot of the hills, but more especially in the upland forests and the wooded country beyond the crest of the Ghâts. The Animally hills, the Neilgherries, Wynaad, Coorg, the Bababooden hills, the Mahableshwar hills, are all favourite haunts of this fine animal. North of this, it occurs to my own knowledge in the jungles on the Taptee river and the neighbourhood, and north of the Nerbudda; a few on the deeper recesses of the Vindhian mountains. On the eastern side of the peninsula it is found in the Pulney and Dindigul hills, the Shandamungalum range, the Shervaroys, and some of the hill ranges near Vellore and the borders of Mysore. North of this, the

Gavæus gaurus.

forest being too scanty, it does not occur till the Kistna and Godavery rivers; and hence it is to be found in suitable spots all along the range of Eastern Ghâts to near Cuttack and Midnapore, extending west far into Central India, and northwards towards the edge of the great plateau which terminates south of the Gangetic valley. According to Hogdson it also occurs in the Himalayan Terai, probably however only towards the eastern portion, and here it is rare, for I have spoken to many sportsmen who have hunted in various parts of the Terai, from Sikhim to Rohilkund, and none have ever come across the gaur at the foot of the Himalayas."—'Mam. of Ind.,' p. 303. (See also Appendix C, p. 530.)

In the Central provinces the gaur is found in several parts of the bamboo-clad spurs of the Satpura range. My experience of the animal is limited to the Seonee district, where it is restricted to the now closely preserved forests of Sonawani in the south-east bend of the range, and a few are to be seen across occasionally, near the old fort of Amodagarh, on the Hirri river.

It is also more abundant on the Pachmari and Mahadeo hills. On the east of the Bay of Bengal it is found from Chittagong through Burmah to the Malayan peninsula. It was considered that the gaur of the eastern countries was a distinct species, and is so noted in Horsfield's Catalogue, and described at some length under the name of *Bibos assecl;* but it appears that all this distinction was founded on the single skull of a female gaur, and is an instance of the proneness of naturalists to create new species on insufficient data. He himself remarks that when the skin was removed it was evident that the animal was nearly related to *Gavæus gaurus*, or, as he calls it, *Bibos cavifrons*. Mr. G. P. Sanderson shot a fine old male of what he supposed to be the wild *gayal*, and he says: "I can state that there was not one single point of difference in appearance or size between it and the bison of Southern India, except that the horns were somewhat smaller than what would have been looked for in a bull of its age in Southern India;" and this point was doubtless an individual peculiarity, for Blyth, in his 'Catalogue of the Mammals of Burmah,' says: "Nowhere does this grand species attain a finer development than in Burmah, and the horns are mostly short and thick, and very massive as compared with those of the Indian gaurs, though the distinction is not constant on either side of the Bay of Bengal."

Jerdon supposes it to have existed in Ceylon till within the present century, but I do not know on what data he founds his assertion.

DESCRIPTION.—I cannot improve on Jerdon's description, taken as it is from the writings of Hodgson, Elliot, and Fisher, so I give it as it stands, adding a few observations of my own on points not alluded to by them:—

"The skull is massive; the frontals large, deeply concave, surmounted by a large semi-cylindric crest rising above the base of the horns. There are thirteen pairs of ribs.* The head is square, proportionately smaller than in the ox; the bony frontal ridge is five inches above the frontal plane; the muzzle is large and full, the eyes small, with a full pupil (? iris) of a pale blue colour. The whole of the head in front of the eyes is covered with a coat of close short hair, of a light greyish-brown colour, which below the eyes is darker, approaching almost to black; the muzzle is greyish and the hair is thick and short; the ears are broad and fan-shaped; the neck is sunk between the head and back, is short, thick,

* The true bison has fourteen pairs of ribs.—R. A. S.

and heavy. Behind the neck and immediately above the shoulder rises a gibbosity or hump of the same height as the dorsal ridge. This ridge rises gradually as it goes back, and terminates suddenly about the middle of the back; the chest is broad; the shoulder deep and muscular; the fore-legs short, with the joints very short and strong, and the arm exceedingly large and muscular; the hair on the neck and breast and beneath is longer than on the body, and the skin of the throat is somewhat loose, giving the appearance of a slight dewlap; the fore-legs have a rufous tint behind and laterally above the white. The hind-quarters are lighter and lower than the fore, falling suddenly from the termination of the dorsal ridge; the skin of the neck, shoulders, and thigh is very thick, being about two inches and more.

"The cow differs from the bull in having a slighter and more graceful head, a slender neck, no hump; and the points of the horns do not turn towards each other at the tip, but bend slightly backwards, and they are much smaller; the legs too are of a purer white. The very young bull has the forehead narrower than the cow, and the bony frontal ridge scarcely perceptible. The horns too turn more upwards. In old individuals the hair on the upper parts is often worn off. The skin of the under parts when uncovered is deep ochrey-yellow."—'Mammals of India,' p. 302.

The fineness of the leg below the knee is another noticeable feature, and also the well-formed pointed hoof, which leaves an imprint like that of a large deer. Mr. Sanderson states in his book that the bison, after a sharp hunt, gives out an oily sweat, and in this peculiarity he says it differs from domestic cattle, which never sweat under any exertion. This I have not noticed.

The period of gestation seems to be about the same as that of the domestic cow, and the greatest number of calves are born in the summer.

SIZE.—I cannot speak personally, for I regret now that I took no measurements in the days when I was acquainted with these magnificent animals, but the experiences of others I give as follows:—

Sir Walter Elliot gives—

	Ft.	In.
Nose to root of tail	9	6½
Height at shoulder (over 18 hands!)	6	1½
,, at rump	5	3
Tail	2	10½
Length of dorsal ridge	3	4
Height of ,,	0	4½
Head from muzzle to top of frontal ridge	2	1¾
Breadth of forehead	1	3½
Ear	0	10½
Circumference of horn at base	1	7½
Distance between the points of the horns	2	1

I give the measurements of two fine heads :—

	Ft.	In.	Ft.	In.
From tip to tip round the outer edge and across the forehead	6	2	6	11
Across the sweep	2	9	3	2½
Circumference at base	1	7	1	5
Between tips	1	7	1	10½

The following careful measurements are recorded by Mr. Blyth ('J. A. S. B.,' vol. xi., 1842, p. 588), and were furnished to him by Lieut. Tickell from the recently-killed animal, in order to assist in the setting up of the specimen in the Asiatic Museum :—

	Ft.	In.
A string passed along the back to root of tail	8	8½
From frontal ridge to tip of muzzle	2	0
Horns apart anteriorly at base	1	0½
Tip to tip of horns	2	3¼
From nose to centre of eye	1	0¾
Eye to root of horn	0	4¼
Eye to base of ears	0	6
Humerus, &c.	1	11¼
Radius	2	8
Metacarpus	0	9¾
Pastern, &c., and hoof	0	7¼
Pelvis	1	4½
Femur	1	7¼
Tibia and fibula	1	10
Metatarsus	1	4
Pastern to end of hoof	0	7½
Height perpendicularly, about	5	9
Length of dorsal ridge	2	5½
Tail, root to tip of hairs	3	1¾
Circumference of head behind horns	3	11
,, ,, neck behind ears	4	0½
,, ,, chest	8	8
,, ,, muzzle	1	9¼
,, ,, forearm close to axilla	1	11¼
,, ,, thigh close to body	3	0¾
,, ,, thigh close above hock	1	6

I feel tempted to let my pen run away with me into descriptions of the exciting scenes of the past in the chase of this splendid creature—the noblest quarry that the sportsman can have, and the one that calls forth all his cunning and endurance. As I lately remarked in another publication, I know of no other animal of which the quest calls forth the combined characteristics of the ibex, the stag and the tiger-hunter. Some of my own experiences I have described in 'Seonee;' but let those who wish to learn the poetry of the thing read the glowing, yet not less true pages of Colonel Walter Campbell's 'Old Forest Ranger;' and for clear practical information, combined also with graphic description, the works of Captain J. Forsyth and Mr. G. P. Sanderson ('The Highlands of Central India' and 'Thirteen years among the Wild Beasts').

The gaur prefers hilly ground, though it is sometimes found on low levels. It is extremely shy and retiring in its habits, and so quick of hearing that extreme care has to be taken in stalking to avoid treading on a dry leaf or stick. I know to my cost that the labour of hours may be thrown away by a moment of impatience. In spite of all the wondrous tales of its ferocity, it is as a rule a timid, inoffensive animal. Solitary bulls are sometimes dangerous if suddenly come upon. I once did so, and the bull turned and dashed up-hill before I could get a shot, whereas a friend of mine, to whom a similar thing occurred a few weeks before, was suddenly charged, and his gun-bearer was knocked over. The gaur seldom leaves its jungles, but I have known it do so on the borders of the Sonawani forest, in order to visit a small tank at Untra near Ashta, and the cultivation in the vicinity suffered accordingly.

Hitherto most attempts to rear this animal when young have failed. It is said not to live over the third year. Though I offered rewards for calves for my collection, I never succeeded in getting one. I have successfully reared most of the wild animals of the Central provinces, but had not a chance of trying the bison.

No. 465. GAVÆUS FRONTALIS.

The Mithun or Gayal.

NATIVE NAMES.—*Gayal*, *Gavi* or *Gabi*, *Gabi-bichal* (male), *Gabi-gai* (female); *Bunerca-goru* in Chittagong and Assam; *Mithun*.

HABITAT.—The hilly tracts east of the Brahmaputra, at the head of the Assam valley, the Mishmi hills, in hill Tipperah, Chittagong, and then southwards through Burmah to the hills bordering on the Koladyne river.

DESCRIPTION.—Very like the gaur at first sight, but more clumsy looking; similarly coloured, but with a small dewlap; the legs are white as in the last species. In the skull the forehead is not concave as in the gaur, but flat, and if anything rather convex. The back has a dorsal ridge similar to that of the gaur.

The *gayal* is of a much milder disposition than the *gaur*, and is extensively domesticated, and on the frontiers of Assam is considered a valuable property by the people. The milk is rich and the flesh good. There are purely domesticated *mithuns* bred in captivity, but according to many writers the herds are recruited from the wild animals, which are tempted either to interbreed, or are captured and tamed. In Dr. F. Buchanan Hamilton's MS. (*see* Horsfield's 'Cat. Mammalia,

E. I. C. Mus.') the following account is given: "These people (i.e. the inhabitants of the frontiers) have tame gayals, which occasionally breed, but the greater part of their stock is bred in the woods and caught; after which, being a mild animal, it is easily domesticated. The usual manner employed to catch the full-grown gayal is to surround a field of corn with a strong fence. One narrow entrance is left, in which is placed a rope with a running noose, which secures the gayal by the neck as he enters to eat the corn; of ten so caught perhaps three are hanged by the noose running too tight, and by the violence of their struggling. Young gayals are caught by leaving in the fence holes of a size sufficient to admit a calf, but which excludes the full-grown gayal; the calves enter by these holes, which are then shut by natives who are watching, and who secure the calves. The gayal usually goes in herds of from twenty to forty, and frequents dry valleys and the sides of hills covered with

Gavæus frontalis.

forest." Professor Garrod, in his *Ungulata* in Cassell's Natural History, quotes the following account from Mr. Macrae concerning the way in which the Kookies of the Chittagong hill regions catch the wild gayal: "On discovering a herd of wild gayals in the jungle they prepare a number of balls, the size of a man's head, composed of a particular kind of earth, salt and cotton. They then drive their tame gayals towards the wild ones, when the two herds soon meet and assimilate into one, the males of the one attaching themselves to the females of the other, and *vice versâ*. The Kookies now scatter their balls over such parts of the jungles as they think the herd most likely to pass, and watch its motions. The gayals, on meeting these balls as they pass along, are attracted by their appearance and smell, and begin to lick them with their tongues, and, relishing the taste of the salt and the particular earth composing them, they never quit the place till all the balls are consumed. The Kookies, having observed the gayals to have once tasted their balls, prepare a sufficient supply of them to answer the intended purpose, and as the gayals lick them up they throw down more; and it is to prevent their being so readily destroyed that the cotton is mixed with the earth and the salt. This process generally goes on for three changes of the moon or for a month and a-half, during which time the tame and the wild gayals are always together, licking the decoy balls, and the Kôokie, after the first day or two of their being so, makes his appearance at such a distance as not to alarm the wild ones. By degrees he approaches nearer and nearer, until at length the sight of him has become so familiar that he can advance to stroke his tame gayals on the back and neck without frightening the wild ones. He next extends his hand to them and caresses them also, at the same time giving them plenty of his decoy balls to lick. Thus, in the short space of time mentioned, he is able to drive them, along with the tame ones, to his *parrah* or village, without the least exertion of force; and so attached do the gayals become to the *parrah*, that when the Kookies migrate from one place to another, they always find it necessary to set fire to the huts they are about to abandon, lest the gayals should return to them from the new grounds."

NO. 466. GAVÆUS SONDAICUS.

The Burmese Wild Ox.

NATIVE NAME.—*Tsoing*, Burmese; *Banteng* of the Javanese.

HABITAT.—"Pegu, the Tenasserim provinces, and the Malayan peninsula, Sumatra, Borneo and Java; being domesticated in the island of Bali" (*Blyth*).

DESCRIPTION.—This animal resembles the gaur in many respects, and it is destitute of a dewlap, but the young and the females are bright chestnut. The bulls become black with age, excepting always the white stockings and a white patch on each buttock.

SIZE.—About the same as the last two species.

This animal has bred in captivity, and has also interbred with domestic cattle. Blyth says he saw in the Zoological Gardens of Amsterdam a bull, cow, and calf in fine condition. "The bull more especially has an indication of a hump, which, however, must be specially looked for to be noticed, and he has a broad and massive neck like the gaur, but no raised spinal ridge, nor has either of these species a deep dewlap like the gayal" ('Cat. Mamm. Burmah'). The banteng cow is much slighter in build, and has small horns that incline backwards, and she retains her bright chestnut colour permanently.

GENUS POEPHAGUS—THE YAK.

Somewhat smaller than the common ox, with large head; nose hairy, with a moderate sized bald muffle between nostrils; broad neck without dewlap; cylindrical horns; no hump or dorsal ridge, and long hair on certain parts of the body. Requires an intensely cold climate.

NO. 467. POEPHAGUS GRUNNIENS.

The Yak or Grunting Ox.

NATIVE NAMES.—*Yak, Bubul, Soora-goy, Dong*, in Thibet; *Bun-chowr*, Hindi; *Brong-dong*, Thibetan.

HABITAT.—The high regions of Thibet and Ladakh, the valley of the Chang Chenmo, and the slopes of the Kara Koram mountains (*Kinloch*).

DESCRIPTION.—"In size it is somewhat less than the common or domestic ox. The head is large, and the neck proportionally broad, without any mane or dewlap, having a downward tendency; the horns are far apart, placed in front of the occipital ridge, cylindrical at the base, from which they rise obliquely outward and forward two-thirds of their length, when they bend inward with a semi-circular curve, the points being directed to each other from the opposite sides; the muffle is small; the border of the nostrils callous; the ears short and hairy. At the withers there is a slight elevation, but no protuberance or hump, as in the Indian ox. The dorsal ridge not prominent; body of full dimensions; rump and hinder parts proportionally large; limbs rather small and slender; hoofs smooth, square, and well defined, not expanded as in the musk-ox; anterior false hoofs small, posterior large; tail short, not reaching beyond the houghs, naked for some inches at the root, very bushy, lax, and expanded in the middle; colour black throughout, but varying in tint according to the character of the hairy covering; this, on the anterior parts, the neck, shoulders, back, and sides, is short, soft, and of a jet-black colour, but long, shaggy, pendulous, and shining on the sides of the anterior extremities, and from the medial part of the abdomen over the thighs to the hinder parts" (*Horsfield*, 'Cat. Mam. Ind. Mus.').

GENUS BUBALUS—THE BUFFALOS.

Horns very large, depressed and sub-trigonal at the base, attached to the highest line of the frontals, inclining upwards and backwards, conical towards the tip and bending upwards; muffle large, square. No hump or dorsal ridge; thirteen pairs of ribs; hoofs large.

No. 468. BUBALUS ARNI.

The Wild Buffalo (Jerdon's No. 239).

NATIVE NAMES.—*Arna* (male), *Arni* (female), *Arna-bhàinsa*, *Jangli-bhains*, Hindi; *Mung*, Bhagulpore; *Gera-erumi*, Gondi; *Karbo* of the Malays; *Moonding* of the Sundanese.

HABITAT.—In the swampy terai at the foot of the hills from Oude to Bhotan, in the plains of Lower Bengal as far west as Tirhoot, in Assam and in Burmah, in Central India from Midnapore to Rajpore, and thence nearly to the Godavery; also in Ceylon.

DESCRIPTION.—This animal so closely resembles the common

Bubalus arni.

domesticated buffalo that it seems hardly necessary to attempt a description. The wild one may be a trifle larger, but every one in India is familiar with the huge, ungainly, stupid-looking creature, with its bulky frame, black and almost hairless body, back-sweeping horns, and long narrow head.

SIZE.—A large male will stand 19 hands at the shoulder and measure $10\frac{1}{4}$ feet from nose to root of tail, which is short, reaching only to the hocks. Horns vary greatly, but the following are measurements of large pairs: In the British Museum are a pair without the skull. These horns measure 6 feet 6 inches each, which would give, when on the head, an outer curve measurement of nearly 14 feet. Another pair in the British Museum measure on the skull 12 feet 2 inches from tip to tip and across the forehead, but these horns do not exactly correspond in length and shape.

The buffalo never ascends mountains like the bison, but keeps to low and swampy ground and open grass plains, living in large herds, which occasionally split up into smaller ones during the breeding season in autumn. The female produces one, or sometimes two in the summer, after a period of gestation of ten months.

Forsyth doubts their interbreeding with the domestic race, but I see no reason for this. The two are identically the same, and numerous instances have been known of the latter joining herds of their wild brethren; and I have known cases of the domestic animal absconding from a herd and running wild. Such a one was shot by a friend of mine in a jungle many miles from the haunts of men, but yet quite out of the range of the wild animal. Probably it had been driven from a herd. Domestic buffalo bulls are much used in the Central provinces for carrying purposes. I had them yearly whilst in camp, and noticed that one old bull lorded it over the others, who stood in great awe of him; at last one day there was a great uproar; three younger animals combined, and gave him such a thrashing that he never held up his head again. In a feral state he would doubtless have left the herd and become a solitary wanderer. Dr. Jerdon, in his 'Mammals of India,' says: "Mr. Blyth states it as his opinion that, except in the valley of the Ganges and Burrampooter, it has been introduced and become feral. With this view I cannot agree, and had Mr. Blyth seen the huge buffalos I saw on the Indrawutty river (in 1857), he would, I think, have changed his opinion. They have hitherto not been recorded south of Raepore, but where I saw them is nearly 200 miles south. I doubt if they cross the Godavery river.

"I have seen them repeatedly, and killed several in the Purneah district. Here they frequent the immense tracts of long grass abounding in dense, swampy thickets, bristling with canes and wild roses; and in these spots, or in the long elephant-grass on the bank of jheels, the buffalos lie during the heat of the day. They feed chiefly at night or early in the morning, often making sad havoc in the fields, and retire in general before the sun is high. They are by no means shy (unless they have been much hunted), and even on an elephant, without which they could not be successfully hunted, may often be approached within good shooting distance. A wounded one will occasionally charge the elephant, and, as I have heard from many sportsmen, will sometimes overthrow the elephant. I have been charged by a small herd, but a shot or two as they are advancing will usually scatter them."

The buffalo is, I should say, a courageous animal—at least it shows itself so in the domesticated state. A number of them together will not hesitate to charge a tiger, for which purpose they are often used to drive a wounded tiger out of cover. A herdsman was once seized by a man-eater one afternoon a few hundred yards from my tent. His cows fled, but his buffalos, hearing his cries, rushed up and saved him.

The attachment evinced by these uncouth creatures to their keepers was once strongly brought to my notice in the Mutiny. In beating up the broken forces of a rebel Thakoor, whom we had defeated the previous day, I, with a few troopers, ran some of them to bay in a rocky ravine. Amongst them was a Brahmin who had a buffalo cow. This creature followed her master, who was with us as a prisoner, for the whole day, keeping at a distance from the troops, but within call of her owner's voice. When we made a short halt in the afternoon, the man offered to give us some milk; she came to his call at once, and we had a grateful draught, the more welcome as we had had nothing to eat since the previous night. That buffalo saved her master's life, for when in the evening the prisoners were brought up to court martial and sentenced to be hanged, extenuating circumstances were urged for our friend with the buffalo, and he was allowed to go, as I could testify he had not been found with arms in his hands; and I had the greatest pleasure in telling him to be off, and have nothing more to do with rebel Thakoors. Jerdon says the milk of the buffalo is richer than that of the cow. I doubt this. I know that in rearing wild animals buffalos' milk is better than cows' milk, which is far too rich, and requires plentiful dilution with water.

There is a very curious little animal allied to the buffalo, of which we have, or have had, a specimen in the Zoological Gardens at Alipore—the *Anoa depressicornis*; it comes from the Island of Celebes, and seems to link the buffalo with the deer. It is black, with short wavy hair.

Before passing on to the true Cervidæ I must here place an animal commonly called a deer, and generally classed as such—the musk-deer according to some naturalists. There is no reason, save an insufficient one, that this creature should be so called and classed, there being much evidence in favour of its alliance to the antelopes. In the first place it has a gall bladder, which the Cervidæ have not, with the exception, according to Dr. Crisp, of the axis ('P. Z. S.'). On the other hand it has large canine tusks like the muntjacs, deerlets, and water-deer, and, as these are all aberrant forms of the true Cervidæ, there is no reason why

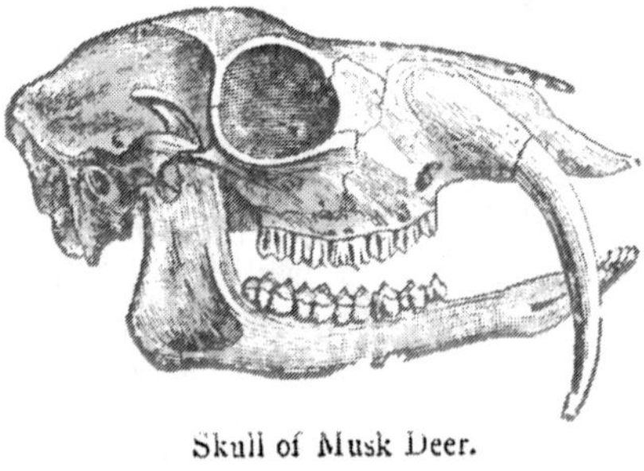

Skull of Musk Deer.

the same character should not be developed in the antelopes. Its hair is more of the goat than the deer, and the total absence of horns removes a decided proof in favour of one or the other. The feet are more like some of the Bovidæ than the generality of deer, with the exception, perhaps, of *Rangifer* (the reindeer), the toes being very much cloven and capable of grasping the rocky ground on which it is found. A very eminent authority, however, Professor Flower, is in favour of placing the musk-deer with the Cervidæ, and he instances the absence of horns as in favour of this opinion, for in none of the Bovidæ are the males hornless. There are many other points also, such as the fawns being spotted, some intestinal peculiarities, and the molar and pre-molar teeth being strictly cervine, which strengthen him in his opinion. (*See* article on the structure and affinities of the musk-deer, 'P. Z. S.' 1879, p. 159.)

GENUS MOSCHUS—THE MUSK DEER.

Canines in both sexes, very long and slender in the male; no horns; feet much cloven, with large false hoofs that touch the ground; the

Moschus moschiferus.

medium metacarpels fused into a solid cannon bone; in the skull the intermaxillaries join the nasals; hinder part of tarsus hairy; fur thick, elastic, and brittle; muffle large; no eye, feet, or groin-pits; a large gland or præputial bag under the stomach in the males, which contains the secretion known in commerce as "musk."

No. 469. MOSCHUS MOSCHIFERUS.

The Musk Deer.

NATIVE NAMES.—*Kastura*, Hindi; *Rous*, *Roos*, and *Kasturé*, in Kashmir; *La-lawa*, Thibetan; *Rib-jo*, Ladakhi; *Bena* in Kunawur (*Jerdon*); *Mussuck-naba'*, Pahari (*Kinloch*).

HABITAT.—Throughout the Himalayas at elevations above 8000 feet, extending also through Central and Northern Asia as far as Siberia.

DESCRIPTION.—It is difficult to describe the colour of this animal, for it so constantly changes; and, as I do not know the creature personally,

Moschus moschiferus.

I think it better to give the recorded opinions of three writers who have had personal experience. Markham describes it as a dark speckled brownish-grey, nearly black on the hind-quarters, edged down the inside with reddish-yellow; the throat, belly, and legs lighter grey. Leith Adams ('P. Z. S.' 1858, p. 528) says: "Some are very dark on the upper parts, with black splashes on the back and hips; under-parts white or a dirty white. Others are of a yellowish-white all over the upper parts, with the belly and inner sides of the thighs white. A brownish-black variety is common, with a few white spots arranged longitudinally on the back—the latter I found were young." Kinloch writes: "The prevailing colour is brownish-grey, varying in shade on the back, where it is darkest, so as to give the animal a mottled or brindled appearance."

SIZE.—Length, about 3 feet; height, 22 inches.

The musk-deer is a forest-loving animal, keeping much to one locality. It bounds with amazing agility over the steepest ground, and is wonderfully sure-footed over the most rocky hills. It ruts in winter, produces one or two young, which are driven off in about six weeks' time by the mother to shift for themselves. They begin to produce at an early age—within a year. The musk bag is an abdominal or præputial gland which secretes about an ounce of musk, worth from ten to fifteen rupees. It is most full in the rutting season; in the summer, according to Leith Adams, it hardly contains any. The musk does not seem to affect the flavour of the meat, which is considered excellent.

CERVIDÆ—THE DEER.

Of the horned ruminants these are the most interesting. In all parts of the world, Old and New, save the great continental island of Australia, one or other kind of stag is familiar to the people, and is the object of the chase. The oldest writings contain allusions to it, and it is frequently mentioned in the Scriptures.

"Like as the hart desireth the water brooks,"

sang David. It is bound up in history and romance, and the chase of it in England is to this day a royal pastime.

However, to come back from the poetry of the thing to dry scientific details, I must premise that the two main distinctions of the Cervidæ, as separating them from the Bovidæ, are horns which are not persistent, but annually shed, and the absence of a gall bladder, which is present in nearly all the Bovidæ. The deer also, with one exception (the reindeer, *Rangifer tarandus*) have horns only in the males.

Regarding the shedding of these horns, it is supposed that the operation is connected with the sexual functions. It is a curious fact that castration has a powerful effect on this operation; if done early no horns appear; if later in life, the horns become persistent and are not shed.

Captain James Forsyth (in his 'Highlands of Central India'), was of opinion that the Sambar does not shed its horns annually, and states that this also is the opinion of native shikaris in Central India. This, however, requires further investigation. I certainly never heard of such a theory amongst them, nor noticed the departure from the normal state.

There have been several classifications of the Cervidæ, but I think the most complete and desirable one is that of Sir Victor Brooke (*see* 'P. Z. S.' 1878, p. 883), which I shall endeavour to give in a condensed form. Dr. Gray's classification was based on three forms of antlers and the shape of the tail. But Sir Victor Brooke's is founded on more reliable osteological details. As I before stated in my introductory remarks on the Ruminantia, the first and fourth digits, there being no thumb, are but rudimentary, the metacarpal bones being reduced to mere splints; the digital phalanges are always in the same place, and bear the little false hoofs, which are situated behind and a little above the large centre ones, but the metacarpal splint is not always in the same place; it may either be annexed to the phalanges, or widely separated from them and placed directly under the carpus. The position of these splints is an important factor in the classification of the Cervidæ into two divisions, distinguished by Sir Victor Brooke as the *Plesiometacarpals*, in which the splint is near the carpus, and the *Telemetacarpals*, in which the splint is far from the carpus, and articulated with the digital phalanges. All the known species of deer can be classified under these two heads; and it is a significant fact that this pedal division is borne out by certain cranial peculiarities discovered by Professor Garrod, and also, to a certain extent, by an arrangement of hair-tufts on the tarsus and metatarsus. In the Old World deer, which are with few exceptions *Plesiometacarpi*, those which have these tufts have them above the middle of the metatarsus, and those of the New World, which are, with one exception, *Telemetacarpi*, have them, when present, below the middle of the metatarsus.

There is also another character in addition to the cranial one before alluded to, which was also noticed by Professor Garrod. The first cranial peculiarity is that in *Telemetacarpi*, as a rule, the vertical plate developed from the lower surface of the vomer is prolonged sufficiently downwards and backwards to become anchylosed to the horizontal plate of the palatals, forming a septum completely dividing the nasal cavity into two chambers. In the *Plesiometacarpi* this vertical plate is not sufficiently developed to reach the horizontal plate of the palatals. The second cranial peculiarity is that in the Old World deer (*Plesiometacarpi*), the ascending rami of the premaxillæ articulate with the nasals with one or two exceptions, whereas in the New World deer (*Telemetacarpi*), with one or two exceptions, the rami of the premaxillæ do not reach the nasals. It will thus be seen that the osteological characters of the head and feet agree in a singularly fortunate manner, and, when taken in connection with the external signs afforded by the metatarsal tufts, prove conclusively the value of the system. In India we have to deal exclusively with the *Plesiometacarpi*, our nearest members of the other division being the Chinese water-deer (*Hydropotes inermis*), and probably *Capreolus pygargus* from Yarkand, the horns of a roebuck in velvet attached to a strip of skin having been brought down by the Mission to that country in 1873–74.

Now comes the more difficult task of subdividing these sections into genera—a subject which has taxed the powers of many naturalists, and which is still in a far from perfect state. To all proposed arrangements some exception can be taken, and the following system is not free from objection, but it is on the whole the most reliable; and this system is founded on the form of the antler, which runs from a single spike, as in the South American *Coassus*, to the many branches of the red deer (*Cervus elaphas*); and all the various changes on which we found genera are in successive stages produced in the red deer, which we may accept as the highest development; for instance, the stag in its first year develops but a single straight "beam" antler, when it is called a "brocket," and it is the same as the South American brocket (*Coassus*). On this being shed the next spring produces a small branch from the base of this beam, called the brow antler, which is identical almost with the single bifurcated horn of the *Furcifer* from Chili. The stag is then technically known as a "spayad." In the third year an extra front branch is formed, known as the tres-tine. The antler then resembles the rusine type, of which our sambar stag is an example. In the fourth year the top of the main beam throws out several small tines called "sur-royals," and the brow antler receives an addition higher up called the "bez-tine." The animal is then a "staggard." In the fifth year the "sur-royals" become more numerous, and the whole antler heavier in the "stag," whose next promotion is to that of "great hart" of ten or more points. The finest heads are found in the German forests. Sir Victor Brooke alludes to some in the hunting Schloss of Moritzburg of the 15th to 17th century, of enormous size, bearing from 25 to 50 points—50 inches round the outside curve, 10 inches in circumference round the *smallest* part of the beam, and of one of which the spread between the coronal tines is 74 inches. Professor Garrod mentions one as having sixty-six points, and states that Lord Powerscourt has in his possession a pair with forty-five tines. The deer with which we have to deal range from the elaphine, or red deer type, to the simple bifurcated antler of the muntjac, which consists of a beam and brow antler only. We then come to the rusine type of three points only—brow, tres, and royal tines, and of this number are also the spotted and hog deer of India, but the arrangement of the tines is different; and following the rusine type comes the rucervine, in which the tres and royal tines break out into points—the tres-tine usually bifurcate, and the royal with two, three or more points. The arrangements of the main limbs of the horns is strictly rusine—that is to say, the external and anterior tine is equal to or shorter than the royal tine, whereas it is the reverse in the axis (spotted deer), and therefore this genus should come between the two. Even in the sambar and axis there is a tendency to throw out abnormal tines. There are many examples in the Indian Museum, and I possess a magnificent head which bears a large abnormal tine on one horn, and a faint inclination in the corresponding spot on the other horn to do likewise. I have no doubt, had the animal lived another year, the second extra tine would

Stag with Horns matured.

have been developed. Professor Garrod has three phases of the rucervine type, which he calls the normal, the intermediate, and the extreme. The first has both branches of the beam, tres and royal of equal size (*ex.* Schomburgk's deer); the second has the tres-tine larger than the royal (*ex.* our swamp deer); and the extreme type is that in which the royal is represented merely by a snag, the whole horn being bent forward (*ex.* the Burmese *Panolia Eldii*). The true cervine type of horn I have already described in its progress from youth to age. The Kashmir and Sikim stags are the representatives of this form in India. In Japan there is an intermediate form in *Cervus sika* which has no bez-tine.

Deer have large eye-pits, but no groin-pits; feet-pits in all four, or sometimes only in the hind feet. The female has four mammæ.

Stag with Horns in velvet.

At the time of reproduction of the antlers a strong determination of blood to the head takes place, enlarging the vessels, and a fibro-cartilaginous substance is formed, which grows rapidly, and takes the form of the antler of the species. The horns in their early stage are soft and full of blood-vessels on the surface, covered with a delicate skin, with fine close-set hairs commonly called the velvet.

"As the horns ossify the periosteal veins become enlarged, grooving the external surface; the arteries are enclosed by hard osseus tubercles at the base of the horns, which coalesce and render them impervious, and, the supply of nutriment being thus cut off, the envelopes shrivel up and fall off, and the animals perfect the desquamation by rubbing their horns against trees, technically called 'burnishing.'"—*Jerdon.*

We now begin with the simplest form of tine we have, viz. with one basal snag only.

GENUS CERVULUS—THE MUNTJACS OR RIB-FACED DEER.

Of small size, slightly higher at the croup than at the shoulders; short tail; large pits in hind feet; no groin-pits; no tuft on the metatarsus. This genus is specially characterised, according to Sir Victor Brooke, by the absence of the lateral digital phalanges on all four feet; the proximal ends of the metacarpals are however present; horns situated on high pedicles of bone, covered with hair, continued down the face in two longitudinal ridges, between which the skin is ridged or puckered; horns small, composed of a single beam with a basal snag; skull with a very large, deep sub-orbital pit; forehead concave; large canine tusks in the upper jaw; moderate, moist muffle.

NO. 470. CERVULUS MUNTJAC *vel* AUREUS.

The Muntjac or Rib-faced Deer (Jerdon's No. 223).

NATIVE NAMES.—*Kakur*, *Bherki*, *Jangli-bakra*, Hindi; *Maya* Bengali; *Ratwa*, in Nepal; *Karsiar*, Bhotia; *Siku* or *Suku*, Lepcha; *Gutra*, *Gutri*, Gondi; *Bekra* or *Baikur*, Mahrathi; *Kankuri*, Canarese; *Kuka-gori*, Telegu; *Gee*, Burmese; *Kidang*, Javanese; *Muntjac*, Sundanese; *Kijang*, Malayan of Sumatra; *Welly* or *Hoola-moolia*, Singhalese.

HABITAT.—India, Burmah, Ceylon, the Malay peninsula, Sumatra, Java, Hainan, Banka and Borneo.

DESCRIPTION.—Between the facial ridges the creases are dark brown, with a dark line running up the inside of each frontal pedestal; all the rest of the head and upper parts a bright rufous bay; chin, throat, inside of hind-legs, and beneath tail, white; some white spots in front of the fetlocks of all four legs; fore-legs from the shoulder downwards, the legs under the tarsal joints, and a line in front of hind-legs, dark blackish-brown. The doe is a little smaller, and has little black bristly knobs where the horns of the buck are.

SIZE.—Head and body, about 3½ feet; tail, 7 inches; height, 26 to 28 inches. Jerdon gives the size of the horn 8 to 10 inches, but in this he doubtless included the pedicle, which is about 5 inches, and the horns, from 2 to 5 inches. Of the only specimen I have at present in my collection the posterior measurement from cranium to tip of horn is $6\frac{1}{2}$ inches, of which the bony pedicle is 3 inches.

It is a question whether we should separate the Indian from the Malayan animal. The leading authority of the day on the Cervidæ, Sir Victor Brooke, was of opinion some time back (*see* 'P. Z. S.,' 1874,

Cervulus aureus.

p. 38), that the species were identical. He says: "In a large collection of the skins, skulls, and horns of this species, which I have received from all parts of India and Burmah, and in a considerable number of living specimens which I have examined, I have observed amongst adult animals so much difference in size and intensity of coloration that I have found it impossible to retain the muntjac of Java and Sumatra as a distinct species. The muntjacs from the south of India are, as a rule, smaller than those from the north, as is also the case with the axis and Indian antelope. But even this rule is subject to many exceptions. I have received from Northern India perfectly adult, and even slightly aged, specimens of both muntjac and axis inferior in size to the average as presented by these species in Southern India. These small races are always connected with particular areas, and are doubtless the result of conditions sufficiently unfavourable to prevent the species reaching the full luxuriance of growth and beauty of which it is capable, though not sufficiently rigorous to prevent its existence." In a later article on the Cervidæ, written four years afterwards, he seems, however, to qualify his opinion in the following words: "This species appears to attain a larger size in Java, Sumatra, and Borneo than it does on the mainland; and I think it not improbable that persistent race characters may eventually be found distinguishing the muntjac of these islands from that of British India."

The rib-face is a retiring little animal, and is generally found alone, or at times in pairs. Captain Baldwin mentions four having been seen together at one time, and General McMaster mentions three; but these are rare cases.

It is very subtle in its movements, carrying its head low, and creeping, as Hodgson remarks, like a weasel under tangled thickets and fallen timber. In captivity I have found it to be a coarse feeder, and would eat meat of all kinds greedily.

Its canine teeth are very long and sharp, and have a certain amount of play in the socket, but I am unable to state whether they are ever used for any purpose, whether of utility or defence. Its call is a hoarse, sharp bark, whence it takes its name of barking deer. What Jerdon says about the length of its tongue is true; it can certainly lick a good portion of its face with it.

For excellent detailed accounts of this little deer I must refer my readers to Kinloch's 'Large Game Shooting,' and a letter by "Hawkeye," quoted by McMaster's 'Notes on Jerdon.' My space here will not allow of my quoting largely or giving personal experience, but both the above articles, as well as Captain Baldwin's notice, nearly exhaust the literature on this subject in a popular way.

The next development of antler is the rusine type, in which the main beam divides at the top into two branches, making with the basal tine a horn of three points only.

GENUS RUSA—THE RUSINE DEER.

Antlers with a brow tine, the beam bifurcating into a tres and royal tine; muffle large; lachrymal fossa large and deep; ante-orbital vacuity very large; rudimentary canines in both sexes, except in the hog deer; tail of moderate length; no feet-pits. The males heavily maned.

NO. 471. RUSA ARISTOTELIS.

The Sambar (*Jerdon's No.* 220).

NATIVE NAMES.—*Sambar* or *Samhar*, Hindi; *Jerai* and *Jerao* in the Himalayas; *Maha* in the Terai; *Meru*, Mahrathi; *Ma-oo*, Gondi;

Rusa Aristotelis.

Kadavi or *Kadaba*, Canarese; *Kannadi*, Telegu; *Ghous* or *Gaoj*, Eastern Bengal, the female *Bholongi* (*Jerdon*); *Schap*, Burmese (*Blyth*); *Gona-rusa*, Singhalese (*Kellaart*).

HABITAT.—Throughout India from the Himalayas to Cape Comorin; through Assam round to the east of the Bay of Bengal, down through Burmah to the Malay peninsula; it is also found in Ceylon.

DESCRIPTION.—The sambar stag is a grand animal, with fine erect carriage, heavily maned neck, and with massive horns of the rusine type. In size it is considerably larger than the red deer, and, though its horns are not so elegant, it is in its *tout ensemble* quite as striking an animal. In colour it is dark brown, somewhat slaty in summer; the chin, inside of limbs and tail, and a patch on the buttocks yellowish or orange yellow. The head of the sambar is very fine; the eye large and full, with immense eye-pits, which can be almost reversed or greatly dilated during excitement. The ears are large and bell-shaped, and the throat surrounded by a shaggy mane—truly a noble creature. The female and young are lighter.

SIZE.—A large stag will stand 14 hands at the withers, the length of the body being from 6 to 7 feet; tail about a foot; ears 7 to 8 inches. The average size of horns is about 3 feet, but some are occasionally found over 40 inches. Jerdon says: "some are recorded 4 feet along the curvature; the basal antler 10 to 12 inches or more." A very fine pair, with skull, in my own collection, which I value much, show the following measurements: right horn, 45 inches; left horn, 43 inches; brow ant'er from burr to tip, 18¼ inches circumference; just above the burr, 9 inches; circumference half-way up the beam, 7¼ inches. On the right horn underneath the tres-tine is an abnormal snag 9 inches long. The left horn has an indication of a similar branch, there being a small point, which I have no doubt would have been more fully developed had the animal lived another year.

I have had no experience of deer-shooting in the regions inhabited by the Kashmir and Sikim stags, which are approximate to our English red deer; but no sportsman need wish for a nobler quarry than a fine male sambar.

As I write visions of the past rise before me—of dewy mornings ere the sun was up; the fresh breeze at daybreak, and the waking cry of the koel and peacock, or the call of the painted partridge; then, as we move cautiously through the jungle that skirts the foot of the rocky range of hills, how the heart bounds when, stepping behind a sheltering bush, we watch the noble stag coming leisurely up the slope! How grand he looks!—with his proud carriage and shaggy, massive neck, sauntering slowly up the rise, stopping now and then to cull a berry, or to scratch his sides with his wide, sweeping antlers, looming large and almost black through the morning mists, which have deepened his dark brown hide, reminding one of Landseer's picture of 'The Challenge.' Stalking sambar is by far the most enjoyable and sportsmanlike way of killing them, but more are shot in *battues*, or over water when they come down to drink. According to native shikaris the sambar drinks only every third day, whereas the nylgao drinks daily; and this tallies with my own experience—in places where sambar were scarce I have found a better chance of getting one over water when the footprints were about a couple of days old. An exciting way of hunting this animal is practised by the Bunjaras, or gipsies of Central India. They fairly run it to bay with dogs, and then spear it. I have given in 'Seonee' a description of the *modus operandi.*

When wounded or brought to bay the sambar is no ignoble foe; even a female has an awkward way of rearing up and striking out with her fore-feet. A large hind in my collection at Seonee once seriously hurt the keeper in this manner.

Those who have read 'The Old Forest Ranger,' by Colonel Campbell, have read in it one of the finest descriptions of the stalking of this noble animal. I almost feel tempted to give it a place here; but it must give way to an extract from a less widely known, though as graphic a writer, "Hawkeye," whose letters to the *South of India Observer* deserve a wider circulation. I cannot find space for more than a few paragraphs, but from them the reader may judge how interesting the whole article is:—

"The hill-side we now are on rapidly falls towards the river below, where it rushes over a precipice, forming a grand waterfall, beautiful to behold. The hill-side is covered with a short, scrubby rough-leafed plant, about a foot and a-half high. Bending low, we circle round the shoulder of the slope, beyond the wood. The quick eye of the stalker catches sight of a hind's ears, at the very spot he hoped for. The stag must be nigh.

"Down on all-fours we move carefully along, the stalker keenly watching the ears. A short distance gained, and the hind detects the movement of our heads. At the same moment the upper tines of the stag's antlers are in sight; he lies to the right of the hind, about 120 yards distant, hidden by an inequality of the ground. Be still, oh beating heart! Be quiet, oh throbbing pulse! Steady, oh shaky hand, or all your toil is vain! Onward, yet only a few paces! Be not alarmed, oh cautious hind! We care not for you. Crouching still lower, we gain ground; the head and neck of our noble quarry are in sight; the hind still gazes intensely. Presently she elongates her neck in a most marvellous manner. We still gain. On once more we move, when up starts the hind. We know that in another moment she will give the warning bell, and all will vanish. The time for action has arrived. We alter our position in a second, bring the deadly weapon to bear on the stag; quickly draw a steady bead, hugging the rifle with all our might, and fire! The hinds flash across our vision like the figures in a magic lantern, and the stag lies weltering in his couch."

GENUS AXIS.

Horns of the rusine type, but with the tres-tine longer than the royal or posterior tine; beam much bent; horns paler and smoother than in the sambar; large muffle and eye-pits; canines moderate; feet-pits in the hind-feet only; also groin-pits; tail of moderate length; skin spotted with white; said to possess a gall-bladder.

No. 472. AXIS MACULATUS.

The Spotted Deer (*Jerdon's No.* 221).

NATIVE NAMES.—*Chital, Chitra, Chritri-jhank* (the male), Hindi; *Chatidah* in Bhagulpore; *Boro-khotiya*, Bengali at Rungpore; *Buriya*, in Gorukpore; *Saraga*, Canarese; *Dupi*, Telegu; *Lupi*, Gondi (*Jerdon*); *Tic-mooha*, Singhalese (*Kellaart*); *Sarga, Jati, Mikka*, Canarese (*Sanderson*).

HABITAT.—Throughout India, with the exception of the Punjab; nor is it found, I believe, in the countries east of the Bay of Bengal. It is however obtained in Ceylon, where it has been classed by Kellaart as a distinct species, *A. oryzeus*.

DESCRIPTION.—General colour like that of the English fallow deer, yellowish or rufous fawn, spotted with white; the spots on the sides low down assuming an elongated shape, forming lines; a dark dorsal stripe from nape to tail; head brownish, unspotted; muzzle dark; ears dark externally, white within; chin, throat, and under-parts whitish, as also the inside of limbs and tail; the horns frequently throw out snags on the brow antler.

SIZE.—Length, 4½ to 5 feet. Height at shoulder, 36 to 38 inches. I regret I cannot give accurate measurements just now of horns, as I am writing on board ship, with all my specimens and most of my books boxed up, but I should say 30 inches an average good horn. Jerdon does not give any details.

This deer is generally found in forests bordering streams. I have never found it at any great distance from water; it is gregarious, and is found in herds of thirty and forty in favourable localities. Generally spotted deer and lovely scenery are found together, at all events in Central India. The very name *chital* recalls to me the loveliest bits of the rivers of the Central provinces, the Nerbudda, the Pench, the Bangunga, and the bright little Hirrie. Where the bamboo bends over the water, and the *kouha* and *saj* make sunless glades, there will be found the bonny dappled hides of the fairest of India's deer. There is no more beautiful sight in creation than a *chital* stag in a sun-flecked dell when—

> "Ere his fleet career he took
> The dewdrops from his flanks he shook;
> Like crested leader, proud and high,
> Toss'd his beam'd frontlet to the sky;
> A moment gazed adown the dale,
> A moment snuff'd the tainted gale,
> A moment listen'd to the cry
> That thicken'd as the chase drew nigh;
> Then, as the headmost foes appeared,
> With one brave bound the copse he clear'd."

Axis maculatus.

Here I may fitly quote again from "Hawkeye," whose descriptions are charming: "Imagine a forest glade, the graceful bamboo arching overhead, forming a lovely vista, with here and there bright spots and deep shadows—the effect of the sun's rays struggling to penetrate the leafy roof of nature's aisle. Deep in the solitude of the woods see now the dappled herd, and watch the handsome buck as he roams here and there in the midst of his harem, or, browsing amongst the bushes, exhibits his graceful antlers to the lurking foe, who by patient wood-craft has succeeded in approaching his unsuspecting victim; observe how proudly he holds himself, as some other buck of less pretensions dares to approach the ladies of the group; see how he advances, as on tiptoe, all the hair of his body standing on end, and with a thundering rush drives headlong away this bold intruder, and then comes swaggering back! But, hark—a twig has broken! Suddenly the buck wheels round, facing the quarter whence the sound proceeded. Look at him now, and say, is he not a quarry well worth the hunter's notice?

"With head erect, antlers thrown back, his white throat exposed, his tail raised, his whole body gathered together, prepared to bound away into the deep forest in the twinkling of an eye, he stands a splendid specimen of the cervine tribe. We will not kill him; we look and admire! A doe suddenly gives that imperceptible signal to which I have formerly alluded, and the next moment the whole herd has dashed through the bamboo alleys, vanishing from sight—a dappled hide now and again gleaming in the sunlight as its owner scampers away to more distant haunts."

Jerdon is a follower of Hodgson, who was of opinion that there are two species of spotted deer—a larger and smaller, the latter inhabiting Southern India; but there is no reason for adopting this theory; both Blyth, Gray, and others have ignored this, and the most that can be conceded is that the southern animal is a variety owing to climatic conditions. Multiplication of species is a thing to be avoided of all naturalists—I have, therefore, not separated them. McMaster too writes: "I cannot agree with Jerdon that there are two species of spotted deer." And he had experience in Southern India as well as in other parts. He states that the finest *chital* he ever came across were found in the forests in Goomsoor, where, he adds, "as in every other part of Orissa, both spotted deer and sambar are, I think, more than usually large."

No. 473. AXIS PORCINUS.

The Hog Deer (*Jerdon's No.* 222).

NATIVE NAMES.—*Para*, Hindi; Jerdon also gives *Khar-laguna*, Nepal Terai; *Sugoria* also in some parts. *Nuthurini-haran* in some parts of Bengal; *Weel-mooha*, Singhalese (*Kellaart.*)

HABITAT.—Throughout India, though scarce in the central parts; it is abundant in Assam and Burmah, and is also found in Ceylon, but is stated not to occur in Malabar.

DESCRIPTION.—"Light chestnut or olive-brown, with an eye-spot; the margin of the lips, the tail beneath, limbs within, and abdomen, white—in summer many assume a paler and more yellow tint, and get a few white spots, and the old buck assumes a dark slaty colour; the horns resemble those of a young spotted deer, with both the basal and upper tines very small, the former pointing directly upwards at a very acute angle, and the latter directed backwards and inwards, nearly at a

Axis porcinus.

right angle, occasionally pointing downwards" (*Jerdon*). McMaster says: "I can corroborate Jerdon's statement that the young of this deer are beautifully spotted; but, although I have seen many specimens, dead and alive, and still more of the skins while I was in Burmah, I do not remember having remarked the few white spots which he says many of them assume in summer." The fawns lose their spots at about six months.

SIZE.—Length, 42 to 44 inches; tail, 8 inches; height, 27 to 28. Average length of horns, 15 to 16 inches.

This animal is seldom found in forest land; it seems to prefer open grass jungle, lying sheltered during the day in thick patches, and lies close till almost run upon by beaters or elephants. Its gait is awkward, with some resemblance to that of a hog carrying its head low; it is not speedy, and can easily be run down by dogs in the open. McMaster writes: "Great numbers of these deer are each season killed by Burmans, being mobbed with dogs." The meat is fair. Hog deer are not gregarious like *chital;* they are usually solitary, though found occasionally in pairs.

The horns are shed about April, and the rutting season is September and October. This species and the spotted deer have interbred, and the hybrid progeny survived.

The next stage from the rusine to the cervine or elaphine type is the rucervine. In this the tres-tine, as well as the royal tine, throw out branches, and in the normal rucervine type the tres and royal are equal as in Schomburgk's deer, but in the extreme type, *Panolia* or *Rucervus Eldii* of Burmah, the tres-tine is greatly developed, whilst the royal is reduced to a mere snag. The Indian swamp-deer (*Rucervus Duvaucelli*) is intermediate, both tres and royal tines are developed, but the former is much larger than the royal. In none of the rucervine forms is the bez-tine produced.

GENUS RUCERVUS.

Horns as above; muzzle pointed. Canines in males only.

NO. 474. RUCERVUS DUVAUCELLI.

The Swamp-Deer (*Jerdon's No.* 219).

NATIVE NAMES.—*Bara-singha,* Hindi; *Baraya* and *Maha* in the Nepal Terai; *Jhinkar* in Kyarda Doon; *Potiyaharan* at Monghyr (*Jerdon*); *Goen* or *Goenjak* (male), *Gaoni* (female), in Central India.

HABITAT.—"In the forest lands at the foot of the Himalayas, from the Kyarda Doon to Bhotan. It is very abundant in Assam, inhabiting the islands and churs of the Berhampooter, extending down the river in suitable spots to the eastern Sunderbunds. It is also stated to occur near Monghyr, and thence extends sparingly through the great forest tract of Central India" (Jerdon's 'Mamm. Ind.'). I have found it in abundance in the Raigarh Bichia tracts of Mundla, at one time attached to the Seonee district, but now I think incorporated in the new district of Balaghat. In the open valleys, studded with sal forest, of the Thanwur, Halone, and Bunjar tributaries of the Nerbudda, may be found bits reminding one of English parks, with noble herds of this handsome deer. It seems to love water and open country. McMaster states that it is found in the Golcondah Zemindary near Daraconda.

DESCRIPTION.—Smaller and lighter than the sambar. Colour rich light yellow or chestnut in summer, yellowish-brown in winter, sometimes very light, paler below and inside the limbs, white under the tail. The females are lighter; the young spotted.

SIZE.—Height, about 44 to 46 inches; horns, about 36 inches. They have commonly from twelve to fourteen points, but Jerdon states he has seen them with seventeen.

Like the spotted deer this species is gregarious; one writer, speaking of them in Central India, says: "The plain stretched away in gentle undulations towards the river, distant about a mile, and on it were three large herds of bara singhas feeding at one time; the nearest was not more than five hundred yards away from where I stood. There must have been at least fifty of them—stags, hinds, and fawns, feeding together in a lump, and outside the herd grazed three most enormous stags" ('Indian Sporting Review,' quoted by Jerdon).

NO. 475. RUCERVUS *vel* PANOLIA ELDII.

The Brow Antlered or Eld's Deer.

NATIVE NAMES.—*Thamin*, in Burmah; *Sungrai* or *Sungnaie*, in Munipur, Eastern Himalayas, Terai, Munipur, Burmah, Siam, and the Malay peninsula.

DESCRIPTION.—In body similar to the last, but with much difference in the horns, the tres-tine being greatly developed at the expense of the royal, which gives the antlers a forward cast; the brow-tine is also very long. In summer it is a light rufous brown, with a few faint indications of white spots; the under-parts and insides of ears nearly white; the tail short and black above. It is said to become darker in winter instead of lighter as in the last species.

SIZE.—Height from 12 to 13 hands.

This deer, which is identical with *Cervus frontalis* and Hodgson's *Cervus dimorpha*, and which was discovered in 1838 by Captain Eld, has been well described by Lieutenant R. C. Beavan. The following extracts have been quoted by Professor Garrod; the full account will be found in the 'Journal of the Asiatic Society of Bengal.' The food of this species seems to consist of grass and wild paddy. "In habits they are very wary and difficult of approach, especially the males. They are also very timid and easily startled. The males, however, when wounded and brought to bay with dogs, get very savage, and charge vigorously. On being disturbed they invariably make for the open instead of resorting to the heavy jungle, like hog deer and sambar. In fact the thamyn is essentially a plain-loving species; and although it will frequent tolerably open tree-jungle for the sake of its shade, it will never venture into dense and matted underwood. When first started the pace of the thamyn is great. It commences by giving three or four large bounds, like the axis or spotted deer, and afterwards settles down into a long trot, which it will keep up for six or seven miles on end when frequently disturbed."

The next phase of development of which we have examples in India is the true cervine or elaphine type of horn in which the brow-tine is doubled by the addition of the bez; the royal is greatly enlarged at the expense of the tres-tine, and breaks out into the branches known as the sur-royals.

GENUS CERVUS.

Horns as above, muzzle pointed, muffle large and broad, with a hairy band above the lip; hair coarse, and usually deep brown, with a light and sometimes almost white disc or patch round the tail, which is very short; eye-pits moderate.

No. 476. CERVUS CASHMIRIANUS.

The Kashmir Stag.

Cervus Wallichii of Jerdon (No. 217).

NATIVE NAMES.—*Hangul* or *Honglu* in Kashmir; *Barasingha*, Hindi.

HABITAT.—Kashmir. Jerdon also gives out that it is found throughout great part of Western and Central Asia, as far as the eastern shores of the Euxine Sea, and that it is common in Persia, where it is called *maral*; but according to careful observations made by Sir Victor Brooke the *maral* is a distinct species, to which I will allude further on. In Kashmir it frequents the Sind valley and its offshoots; the country above also.

DESCRIPTION.—Brownish-ash, darker along the dorsal line; caudal disk white, with a dark border; sides and limbs paler; ears light coloured; lips and chin and a circle round eyes white. The male has very long and shaggy hair on the lower part of the neck. The colour of the coat varies but little; at times it is liver-coloured or liver-brown, sometimes "bright pale rufous chestnut," with reddish patches on the inner sides of the hips. Jerdon says: "The belly of the male is dark brown, contrasting with the pale ashy hue of the lower part of the flanks; the legs have a pale dusky median line. In females the whole lower parts are albescent."

SIZE.—Length, 7 to 7½ feet; height, 12 to 13 hands; tail, 5 inches. The horns are very large and massive, with from ten to fifteen, or even more, points. Jerdon states that even eighteen points have been counted, but such cases are rare. Dr. Leith Adams says the largest he ever measured were four feet round the curves. "A. E. W." in his

Cervus Cashmirianus.

interesting papers on Kashmir game, published in *The Asian*, gives the following measurements of two heads :—

Length of horns.	Girth above brow antler.	Divergency at tips.		Where obtained.
inches.	inches.	Greatest.	Least.	
47	$7\frac{3}{4}$	56 in.	29 in.	Sindh Valley
46	8	50 in.	32 in.	Ditto

I once saw a beautiful head at a railway-station, the property of an officer who had just come down from Kashmir, the horns of which appeared to me enormous. The owner afterwards travelled with me in the train, and gave me his card, which I regret I lost, and, having forgotten his name, I was never enabled to write to him, either on the subject of the horns or to send him some papers he wanted on Asiatic sheep.

Dr. Leith Adams writes: "They (the horns) are shed in March, and the new horn is not completely formed till the end of October, when the rutting season commences, and the loud bellowings of the stags are heard all over the mountains." Of this bellowing Sir Victor Brooke says it is just like the voice of the Wapiti stag, which this animal closely resembles, and is quite different from that of the red deer. "In the former it is a loud squeal, ending in a more gutteral tone; in the latter it is a distinct roar, resembling that of a panther." Sir Victor Brooke also points out another peculiarity in this deer: namely, that "the second brow antler (bez) in *Cervus Cashmirianus*, with very rare exceptions, exceeds the brow antler in length; a peculiarity by which the antlers of this species may be distinguished from those of its allies."

The female gives birth in April, and the young are spotted.

The points on which this stag differs from the *maral* are the longer and more pointed head of the latter.

No. 477. CERVUS AFFINIS *vel* WALLICHII.

The Sikhim Stag (*Jerdon's No.* 218).

NATIVE NAME.—*Shou*, Thibetan.

HABITAT.—Eastern Himalayas; Thibet in the Choombi valley, on the Sikhim side of Thibet.

DESCRIPTION.—Jerdon describes this stag as "of very large size; horns bifurcated at the tip in all specimens yet seen; horns pale, smooth, rounded, colour a fine clear grey in winter, with a moderately large disk; pale rufous in summer." Hodgson writes of the horns: "Pedicles elevate; burrs rather small; two basal antlers, nearly straight, so forward in direction as to overshadow the face to the end of the nasal; larger than the royal antlers; median or royal antlers directed forward and upwards; beam with a terminal fork, the prongs radiating laterally and equally, the inner one longest and thinnest." Jerdon adds: "Compared with the Kashmir stag this one has the beam still more bent at the origin of the median tine, and thus more removed from *C. elaphus*, and like *C. Wallichii* (*C. Cashmirianus*). The second basal tine or bez antler is generally present, even in the second pair of horns assumed. Moreover the simple bifurcation of the crown mentioned above is a still more characteristic point of difference both from the Kashmir *barasingha* and the stag of Europe.

Regarding the nomenclature of this species there seems to be some uncertainty. Jerdon himself was doubtful whether the *shou* was not *C. Wallichii*, and the Kashmir stag *C. Cashmirianus*. He says: "It is a point reserved for future travellers and sportsmen to ascertain the limits of *C. Wallichii* east and *C. affinis* west, for, as Dr. Sclater remarks, it would be contrary to all analogy to find two species of the same type inhabiting one district."

Sir Victor Brooke writes: "Should *Cervus Wallichii* (*Cuvier*) prove to be specifically identical with *Cervus affinis* (*Hodgson*), the former name, having priority, must stand.

SIZE.—Length, about 8 feet; height at shoulders, 4½ to 5 feet. Horns quoted by Jerdon 54 inches round curve, 47 inches in divergence between the two outer snags. Longest basal tine, 12 inches; the medians, 8 inches.

An allied stag, *Cervus maral*, is found in Circassia and Persia. Sir Victor Brooke mentions a pair kept for some years in one of his parks, which never interbred with the red deer, and kept apart from them. "The old stag *maral*, though considerably larger in size, lived in great fear of the red deer stag." Another very fine species, *Cervus Eustephanus*, was discovered by Mr. W. Blanford inhabiting the Thian Shan mountains. As yet it is only known from its antlers, which are of great size, and in their flattened crowns closely resemble Wapiti horns.

TRAGULIDÆ—THE CHEVROTIANS OR DEERLETS.

Animals of small size and delicate graceful form, which are separated from the deer and oxen by certain peculiarities which approximate them to the swine in their feet. They are, however, ruminants, having the complex stomach, composed of paunch, honeycomb-bag and reed, the manyplies being almost rudimentary; but in the true ruminants the two centre metacarpals are fused into a single bone, whilst the outer ones are rudimentary. In the pig all the metacarpal bones are distinct, and the African Tragulus closely resembles it. The Asiatic ones have the two centre bones fused, but the inner and outer ones are entire and distinct as in the swine. The legs are, however, remarkably delicate, and so slight as to be not much thicker than an ordinary lead pencil. The males have pendant tusks, like those of the musk and rib-faced deer.

GENUS TRAGULUS.

Has the hinder part of metatarsus bald and callous.

No. 478. Tragulus napu.

The Javan Deerlet.

Native Name.—*Napu.*

Habitat.—Tenasserim and the Malay countries.

Description.—Above rusty brown, with three whitish stripes ; under-parts white, tail tipped with white, muzzle black.

Tragulus napu.

Tragulus kanchil is another Malayan species yet smaller than the preceding ; it may be found in Tenasserim. It is darker in colour than the last, especially along the back, with a broad black band across the chest.

GENUS MEMINNA.

Hinder edge of metatarsus covered with hair.

No. 479. Meminna Indica.

Indian Mouse Deer.

Native Names.—*Pisuri*, *Pisora*, *Pisai*, Hindi and Mahratti ; *Mugi* in Central India ; *Turi-maoo*, Gondi ; *Jitri-haran*, Bengali ; *Gandwa*, Ooria ; *Yar* of the Koles ; *Wal-mooha*, Singhalese.

HABITAT.—In all the large forests of India; but is not known, according to Jerdon, in the countries eastward of the Bay of Bengal. It is common in the bamboo forests of the Central provinces, where I obtained it on several occasions.

DESCRIPTION.—"Above olivaceous, mixed with yellow grey; white below; sides of the body with yellowish-white lines formed of interrupted spots, the upper rows of which are joined to those of the opposite side by some transverse spots; ears reddish-brown" (*Jerdon*). The colour however varies; some are darker than others.

Mouse Deer.*

SIZE.—Length, 22 to 23 inches; tail, $1\frac{1}{2}$ inches; height, 10 to 12 inches. Weight, 5 to 6 lbs.

The above measurements and weight are taken from Jerdon. Professor Garrod (Cassell's Nat. His.) gives eighteen inches for length and eight inches for height, which is nearer the size of those I have kept in confinement; but mine were young animals. They are timid and delicate, but become very tame, and I have had them running loose about the house. They trip about most daintily on the tips of their toes, and look as if a puff of wind would blow them away.

They are said to rut in June and July, and bring forth two young about the end of the rainy season.

* (From Sir Emerson Tennant's 'Ceylon,' by permission of Messrs. Longmans.)

TRIBE TYLOPODA—THE CAMELS.

This name, which is derived from the Greek τύλος, a swelling, pad, or knot, and πούς, a foot, is applied to the camels and llamas, whose feet are composed of toes protected by cushion-like soles, and not by a horny covering like those of the Artiodactyli generally. The foot of the camel consists of two toes tipped by small nails, and protected by soft pads which spread out laterally when pressed on the ground. The two centre metacarpal bones are fused into one cannon bone, and the phalanges of the outer and inner digits which are more or less traceable in all the other families of the Artiodactyli are entirely absent.

The dentition of the camel too is somewhat different from the rest of the Ruminantia, for in the front of the upper jaw there are two teeth placed laterally, one on each side, whereas in all other ruminating animals there are no cutting teeth in the upper jaw—only a hard pad, on which the lower teeth are pressed in the act of tearing off herbage.

The stomach of the camel is the third peculiarity which distinguishes it. The psalterium or manyplies is wanting. The abomasum or "reed" is of great length, and the rumen or paunch is lined with cells, deep and narrow, like those of a honeycomb, closed by a membrane, the orifice of which is at the control of the animal. These cells are for the purpose of storing water, of which the stomach when fully distended will hold about six quarts. The second stomach or reticulum is also deeply grooved.

The hump of the camel may also be said to contain a store of food. It consists of fatty cells connected by bands of fibrous tissue, which are absorbed, like the fat of hibernating bears, into the system in times of deprivation. Hard work and bad feeding will soon bring down a camel's hump; and the Arab of the desert is said to pay particular attention to this part of his animal's body.

There are two species of true camel, *Camelus dromedarius*, with one hump only, most commonly seen in India, and *C. bactrianus*, the two-humped camel, a shorter, coarser-looking, and less speedy animal.

There never was a creature about whom more poetical nonsense has been written. He has been extolled to the skies as patient, long-suffering, the friend of man, and what not. In reality he is a grumbling, discontented, morose brute, working only under compulsion and continual protest, and all writers who know anything of him agree in the above estimate of his disposition. The camel is nowhere found in a wild state.

ORDER EDENTATA.

THESE are animals without teeth, according to the name of their order. They are however without teeth only in the front of the jaw in all, but with a few molars in some, the Indian forms however are truly edentate, having no teeth at all. In those genera where teeth are present there are molars without enamel or distinct roots, but with a hollow base growing from below and composed of three structures, vaso-dentine, hard dentine and cement, which, wearing away irregularly according to hardness, form the necessary inequality for grinding purposes.

The order is subdivided into two groups: *Tardigrada*, or sloths, and *Effodientia* or burrowers. With the former we have nothing to do, as they are peculiar to the American continent. The burrowers are divided into the following genera: *Manis*, the scaly ant-eaters; *Dasypus*, the armadillos; *Chlamydophorus*, the pichiciagos; *Orycteropus*, the ant-bears, and *Myrmecophaga*, the American ant-eaters.

Of these we have only one genus in India; *Manis*, the pangolin or scaly ant-eater, species of which are found in Africa as well as Asia.

GENUS MANIS.

Small animals from two to nearly five feet in length; elongated cylindrical bodies with long tails, covered from snout to tip of tail with large angular fish-like scales, from which in some parts of India they are called *bun-rohu*, or the jungle carp; also in Rungpore *Keyot-mach*, which Jerdon translates the fish of the *Keyots*, but which probably means *khet-mach* or field-fish—but in this I am open to correction. The scales overlap like tiles, the free part pointing backwards. These form its defensive armour, for, although the *manis* possesses powerful claws, it never uses them for offence, but when attacked rolls itself into a ball.

In walking it progresses slowly, arching its back and doubling its fore-feet so as to put the upper surface to the ground and not the palm. The hind-foot is planted normally—that is, with the sole on the earth.

The tongue is very long and worm-like, and covered with glutinous saliva; and, much of this moisture being required, the sub-maxillary glands are very large, reaching down under the skin of the neck on to the chest.

The external ear is very small, and internally it is somewhat complicated, there being a large space in the temporal bone which communicates with the internal ear, so that, according to Professor Martin-Duncan, one tympanum is in communication with the other.

These animals are essentially diggers. The construction of their fore-arms is such as to economise strength and the effectiveness of their excavating instruments. The very doubling up of their toes saves the points of their claws. The joints of the fore-fingers bend downwards, and are endowed with powerful ligaments; and in the wrist the scaphoid and semi-lunar bones are united by bone, which increases its strength. As Professor Martin-Duncan remarks: "Every structure in the creature's fore-limbs tends to the promotion of easy and powerful digging, and, as the motion of scratching the ground is directly downwards and backwards, the power of moving the wrist half-round and presenting the palm more or less upwards, as in the sloths and in man, does not exist. In order to prevent this pronation and supination the part of the fore-arm bone, the radius, next to the elbow, is not rounded, but forms part of a hinge joint." He also notices another interesting peculiarity in the chest of this animal, the breast-bone being very long; the cartilage at end large, with two long projections resembling those of the lizards. There is no collar-bone.

No. 480. MANIS PENTADACTYLA *or* BRACHYURA.

The Five-fingered or Short-tailed Pangolin (Jerdon's No. 241).

NATIVE NAMES.—*Bajar-kit*, *Bajra-kapta*, *Sillu*, *Sukun-khor*, *Sal-salu* Hindi; *Shalma* of the Bauris; *Armoi* of the Kols; *Kauli-mah*, *Kauli-*

Manis pentadactyla.

manjra, *Kassoli-manjur*, Mahratti; *Alawa*, Telegu; *Alangu*, Malabarese; *Bun-rohu* in the Deccan, Central provinces, &c.; *Keyot-mach*, in Rungpore; *Katpohu*, in parts of Bengal; *Caballaya*, Singhalese.

HABITAT.—Throughout India. Jerdon says most common in hilly districts, but nowhere abundant. I have found it myself in the Satpura range, where it is called *Bun-rohu*.

DESCRIPTION.—Tail shorter than the body, broad at the base, tapering gradually to a point. Eleven to thirteen longitudinal rows of sixteen scales on the trunk, and a mesial line of fourteen on the tail; middle nail of fore-foot much larger than the others. Scales thick, striated at base; yellowish-brown or light olive. Lower side of head, body, and feet, nude; nose fleshy; soles of hind-feet dark.

SIZE.—Head and body, 24 to 27 inches; tail, about 18. Jerdon gives the weight of a female measuring 40 inches as 21 pounds.

This species burrows in the ground to a depth of a dozen feet, more or less, where it makes a large chamber, sometimes six feet in circumference. It lives in pairs, and has from one to two young ones at a time in the spring months. Sir W. Elliot, who gives an interesting detailed account of it, says that it closes up the entrance to its burrow with earth when in it, so that it would be difficult to find it but for the peculiar track it leaves (*see* 'Madras Journal,' x. p. 218). There is also a good account of it by Tickell in the 'Journal As. Soc. of Bengal,' xi. p. 221, and some interesting details regarding one in captivity by the late Brigadier-General A. C. McMaster in his 'Notes on Jerdon.' I have had specimens brought to me by the Gonds, but found them very somnolent during the day, being, as most of the above authors state, nocturnal in its habits. The first one I got had been kept for some time without water, and drank most eagerly when it arrived, in the manner described by Sir Walter Elliot, "by rapidly darting out its long extensile tongue, which it repeated so quickly as to fill the water with froth."

The only noise it makes is a faint hiss. It sleeps rolled up, with the head between the fore-legs and the tail folded firmly over all.

The natives believe in the aphrodisine virtues of its flesh.

NO. 481. MANIS AURITA.

The Eared Pangolin (Jerdon's No. 242).

HABITAT.—Sikhim, and along the hill ranges of the Indo-Chinese frontier. Dr. Anderson says it is common in all the hilly country east of Bhamo.

DESCRIPTION.—Tail shorter and not so thick at the base as that of the last; the body less heavy; smaller and darker scales; muzzle acute; ears conspicuous; scales of head and neck not so small in proportion as in *M. pentadactyla.*

SIZE.—Head and body of one mentioned by Jerdon, 19 inches; tail, $15\frac{1}{4}$ inches.

No. 482. MANIS JAVANICA.

The Javan Ant-eater.

HABITAT.—Burmah and the Malayan peninsula; also Tipperah.

DESCRIPTION.—To be distinguished from the two preceding species by the greater number of longitudinal rows of scales, *M. pentadactyla* having from eleven to thirteen, *M. aurita* from fifteen to eighteen, and *M. Javanica* nineteen. Taking the number of scales in the longitudinal mesial line from the nose to the tip of the tail in *M. pentadactyla.* it is forty-two; in *aurita* forty-eight to fifty-six; in *avanica* as high as sixty-four; on the tail the scales are: *M. pentadactyla*, fourteen; *M. aurita* sixteen to twenty; *M. Javanica* thirty.

I am indebted to Dr. Anderson's 'Zoological and Anatomical Researches' for the following summary of characteristics:—

"*M. pentadactyla* by its less heavy body; by its tail, which is broad at the base, tapering gradually to a point, and equalling the length of the head and trunk; by its large light olive-brown scales, of which there are only from eleven to thirteen longitudinal rows on the trunk, and a mesial line of fourteen on the tail; and by its powerful fore-claws, the centre one of which is somewhat more than twice as long as the corresponding claw of the hinder extremity. *M. aurita* is distinguished from *M. pentadactyla* by its less heavy body; by its rather shorter tail, which has less basal breath than *M. pentadactyla*; by its smaller and darker brown, almost black scales in the adult, which are more numerous, there being from fifteen to eighteen longitudinal rows on the trunk, seventeen rows being the normal number, and sixteen to twenty caudal plates in the mesial line; and by its strong fore-claws, the middle one of which is not quite twice as long as the corresponding claw on the hind foot.

M. Javanica is recognised by its body being longer and more attenuated than in the two foregoing species; by its narrower and more tapered tail; by its longer and more foliaceous or darker olive-brown scales, of which there are nineteen longitudinal rows on the trunk, and as many as thirty along the mesial line of the tail; and by the claws of the fore-feet being not nearly so long as in *M. Jaurita*, and being but little in excess of the claws of the hind-feet.

APPENDIX A.

FAMILY MYOXIDÆ—THE DORMICE.

THESE small rodents approximate more to the squirrels than the true mice; but they differ from all others intestinally by the absence of a cæcum. They have four rooted molars in each upper and lower jaw, the first of each set being smaller than the other three, the crowns being composed of transverse ridges of enamel. In form they are somewhat squirrel-like, with short fore-limbs, and hairy, though not bushy, tails. The thumb is rudimentary, with a small, flat nail; hind-feet with five toes.

The common English dormouse is a most charming little animal, and a great pet with children. I have had several, and possess a pair now which are very tame. They are elegant little creatures, about three inches long, with tails two and a-half inches; soft deep fur of a pale reddish-tawny above, pale yellowish-fawn below, and white on the chest. The eyes are large, lustrous, and jet-black. The tails of some are slightly tufted at the end. They are quite free from the objectionable smell of mice. In their habits they are nocturnal, sleeping all day and becoming very lively at night. I feed mine on nuts, and give them a slice of apple every evening; no water to drink, unless succulent fruits are not to be had, and then sparingly. The dormouse in its wild state lives on fruits, seeds, nuts and buds. In cold countries it hibernates, previous to which it becomes very fat. It makes for itself a little globular nest of twigs, grass, and moss, pine-needles, and leaves, in which it passes the winter in a torpid state. "The dormouse lives in small societies in thickets and hedgerows, where it is as active in its way amongst the bushes and undergrowth as its cousin the squirrel upon the larger trees. Among the small twigs and branches of the shrubs and small trees the dormice climb with wonderful adroitness, often, indeed, hanging by their hind feet from a twig, in order to reach and operate on a fruit or a nut which is otherwise inaccessible, and running along the lower surface of a branch with the activity and certainty of a monkey" (*Dallas*).

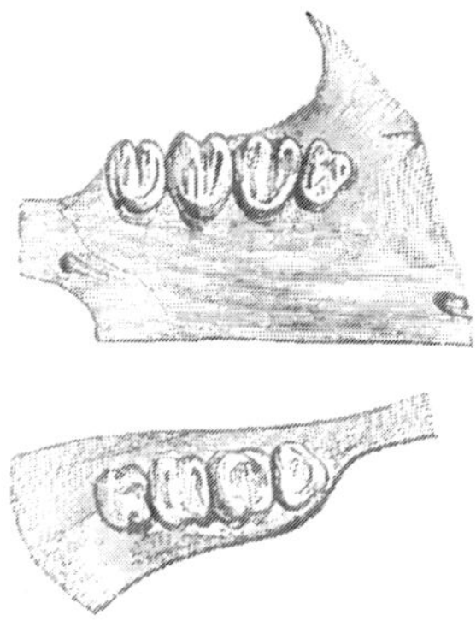

Dentition of Dormouse (magnified).

This little animal is supposed to breed twice in the year—in spring and autumn. It is doubtful whether we have any true *Myoxidæ* in India, unless *Mus gliroides* should turn out to be a *Myoxus*. The following is mentioned in Blanford's 'Eastern Persia': *Myoxus pictus*—new species,

Myoxus.

I think; I regret I have not the book by me at present—also *Myoxus dryas*, of which I find a pencil note in my papers. Mouse-red on the back, white belly with a rufous band between; white forehead; a black stripe from the nose to the ears, passing through the eye.

APPENDIX B.

Osteology of the Skull of Platanista Gangetica, page 251.

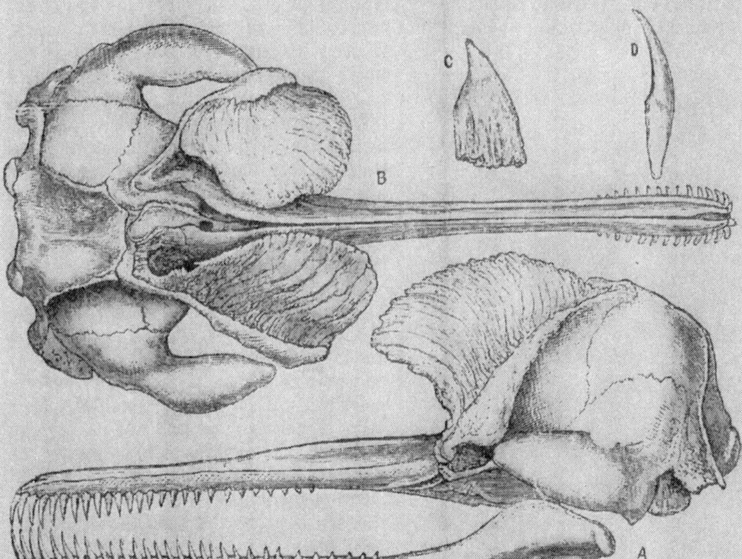

A. Side view. B. Upper view. C. Back tooth. D. Front tooth.

The above illustration was by accident omitted from the text.

APPENDIX C.

NOTES ON SOME OF THE FOREGOING SPECIES.

The Slow Loris, p. 31.—This creature sometimes assumes the erect posture, though in general it creeps. The following illustration shows an attitude observed and sketched by Captain Tickell, as the animal was about to sieze a cockroach. When it had approached within ten or twelve inches, it drew its hind feet gradually forward until almost under its chest; it then cautiously and slowly raised itself up into a standing position, balancing itself awkwardly with its uplifted arms; and then, to his astonishment, flung itself, not upon the insect, which was off "like an arrow from a Tartar's bow," but on the spot which it had, half a second before, tenanted.

Trade Statistics of Fur-skins, p. 139.—The Philadelphia *Times*, in an article on furs, says that the best sealskins come from the antarctic waters, principally from the Shetland Islands. New York receives the bulk of American skins, which are shipped to various ports. London is the great centre of the fur trade of the world. In the United States the sea-bear of the north has the most valuable skin. Since 1862 over 500,000 have been killed on Behring Island alone. In 1867 there were 27,500 sea-bears killed; in 1871 there was a very large decrease, only 3,614 being killed. There were 26,960 killed in 1876; and in 1880 the number killed was 48,504, a large increase. Sea-otter fur is about as expensive as any, and some 48,000 skins are used yearly. Over 100,000 marten or Russian sable skins are annually used. Only about 2,000 silver foxes are caught every year; and about 6,500 blue foxes. Other fox skins are used more or less. About 600 tiger skins are used yearly, over 11,000 wild cat skins, and a very large trade is being carried on in house cat skins. Aout 350,000 skunk and 42,000 monkey skins are utilised annually. The trade in ermine skins is falling off, as is also the trade in chinchilla. About 3,000,000 South American nutrias are killed every year, and a very large business is carried on in musk-rat skins. About 15,000 each of American bear and buffalo skins were used last year. There are also used each year about 3,000,000 lamb, 5,000,000 rabbit, 6,000,000 squirrel, and 620,000 filch skins; also 195,000 European hamster, and nearly 5,000,000 European and Asiatic hares.

Tigers, p. 168.—Since writing on the subject of the size of tigers I have received the following extract from a letter addressed to the editor of *The Asian*. Both the animals were measured on the ground before being skinned, and in the presence of all whose names are given :—

"Tiger shot on the 6th of July, 1882. Party present: C. A. Shillingford, Esq.; J. L. Shillingford, Esq.; F. A. Shillingford, Esq.; A. J. Shillingford, Esq. Length of head, 1 ft. 8½ in.; body, 5 ft. 6½ in.; tail, 3 ft. 6½ in.; total length, 10 ft. 9½ in. Height at shoulder, 3 ft. 7 in.

"Tiger shot on the 17th of March, 1883. Party present: The Earl of Yarborough; A. E. Fellowes, Esq.; Col. R. C. Money, B.S.C.; Capt. C. H. Mayne, A.D.C.; Lieut. R. Money; J. D. Shillingford, Esq. Length of head, 1 ft. 8 in.; body, 5 ft. 7 in.; tail, 3 ft. 5½ in.; total length, 10 ft. 8½ in. Height at shoulder, 3 ft. 8½ in.; girth of head round jaw, 3 ft. 1½ in.; girth of body round chest, 4 ft. 7 in.

"The latter animal, though not so long as the former, was the larger animal of the two, being more massively built, and by far the finer specimen of a tiger. He was shot by Mr. Fellowes while out shooting in the Maharajah of Darbhanga's hunt in the Morung Terai."

The following is an extract from a letter lately received by me from General Sir Charles Reid, K.C.B., with reference to an enormous tiger killed by him :—

"I had a tiger in the Exhibition of 1862, and which is now in the museum at Leeds, which was the largest tiger I ever killed or ever saw. As he lay on the ground he measured 12 feet 2 inches—his height I did not measure—from the tip of one ear to the tip of the other 19½ inches. I never took skull measurements, nor did I ever weigh a tiger. I had another in the International Exhibition, which measured 11½ feet fair measurement as he lay on the ground. The one at Leeds 12 feet 2 inches, as before mentioned, is not now more than 11 feet 6 inches. Mr. Ward was not satisfied with the Indian curing, and had it done over again, and it shrunk nearly a foot. The three tigers* mentioned are the largest I ever killed—all Dhoon tigers."

Elephants, p. 394.—The two Indian elephants now in the Zoological Society's Gardens, in Regent's Park, are interesting examples of the growth of these animals in captivity. I regret extremely that I have not been able to get accurate statistics regarding them before leaving England; I was obliged to put off several proposed visits to the Gardens in consequence of ill

* The third tiger is one which Sir Charles Reid has had set up, and is now in his house; it measured, as he lay on the ground, 10 ft. 6 in. He then goes on to say that his father-in-law had killed in the Dhoon four or five tigers over 11 feet, and that the late Sir Andrew Waugh told him he had killed one in the same place 13 feet. He says: "I believe the Dhoon tigers are the largest and finest beasts that are found in any part of India." Their coats are longer and thicker also.

health, and am now correcting the final proof-sheets of this work on board ship, preparatory to posting them at Suez, so I must trust to memory for what I heard concerning them.

The large male, *Jung Pershad*, must be close upon nine feet high, and the female, *Suffa Kulli*, at least seven feet; and I was astonished to find that they were the same that I had seen as little things in the Prince of Wales's collection in 1876. *Suffa Kulli's* age is not more than fifteen, yet she has been in a fair way of becoming a mother. There was no doubt as to the possibility, and she seemed to show some signs of it, but it ended in disappointment; however it is hoped that she will yet prove that these noble animals may be bred in captivity.

Osteology of the feet in Ruminantia, p. 414.—The following illustrations were inadvertently omitted from the text in the above page.

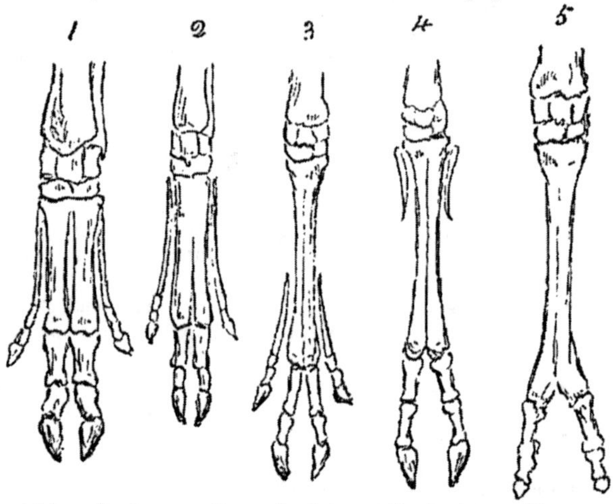

1. Pig, or African deerlet. 2. Javan deerlet. 3. Roebuck. 4. Sheep. 5. Camel.

Wild Boar, p. 417.—A few days before leaving England, I called to say good-bye to an old friend well known in Calcutta and Lower Bengal, Dr. Charles Palmer. He asked me whether I had ever heard of a boar killing a tiger, and, on my answering in the affirmative, he told me he had just heard from his son, who had witnessed a fight between these two animals, in which the boar came off victorious, leaving his antagonist dead on the field.

Ovis Polii, p. 427.—Mr. Carter in one of his letters to me says: "I see that you make the biggest horns of *Ovis Polii* 53 inches from tip to tip. In a photo of one brought down by the Yarkhand Expedition, which had a foot rule laid close, so as to scale it, the distance from tip to tip is nearly five feet."

I do not know which particular head is referred to, but two out of the three measurements given by me were of the finest heads brought down by the Expedition. There may have been a smaller pair with a wider spread, as the 73-inch horns I also mention, and which Sir Victor Brooke, to whom I sent a photograph, tells me is the finest head he has heard of, has only a spread of 48 inches.

Ovis cycloceros, p. 435.—I gave from 25 to 30 inches as an average size for the horns of this species, but Captain W. Cotton, F.Z.S., writes to me that he sent home a pair of ovrial horns from Cabul, 35½ inches, and that there is a pair in the R.A. mess at Attock 38½ inches, but very thin. They were looted in the Jowaki campaign. This sheep has bred freely in the Zoological Society's Gardens, and two hybrids have been born there from a male of this species and the Corsican mouflon, *Ovis musimon*.

I mentioned that there is in the Gardens a specimen of *Ovis Blanfordi.* I see by the Society's list that this was presented by Captain Cotton; the habitat given is Afghanistan.

The Wild Goat of Asia Minor, p. 447.—Mr. Carter writes to me: "In one of your letters you mention the Scind ibex, which is a wild goat. I have a photo of a head 31 inches round curve, but Mr. Inverarity, barrister, Bombay, says he has seen one 52½. The animal is not much bigger than the black buck." This last agrees with the estimate I formed from the specimens in the Indian Museum, Calcutta.

Tetraceros sub-quadricornutus, p. 480.—It is doubtful whether Elliot's antelope should stand as a separate species; Blyth was against it, and Jerdon followed him, and I incline to think that it is only a variety. Dr. Sclater, to whom I mentioned the subject, appeared to me to agree in this view, but I see he includes it in his list of the Society's mammals. Being adverse to the multiplication of species, I gave it the benefit of the doubt, and included it with *T. quadricornis;* but, as I have received one or two letters from writers whose opinions are entitled to consideration, I mention them here, merely stating that I still feel inclined to doubt the propriety of promoting *sub-quadricornutus* to the dignity of a species. Dr. Gray was certainly of opinion it was separate; but then, great naturalist as he was, his peculiar foible was minute sub-division.

The claims of Elliot's antelope to separate rank are: absence of the anterior horns, or with only a trace; smaller size; lighter colour; but even the larger, darker *quadricornis* is sometimes without the anterior horns; and, unless some other marked difference is found in the skull, it is hardly sufficient to warrant separation. However, I will give what others say on the subject.

"I can scarcely agree with you as to Elliot's antelope not being a good species, I have therefore taken the trouble of having a most accurate and full-size sketch of the skull of one made, and if you will compare it with those of the ordinary *quadricornis* I think you will see a well-marked difference. Dr. Gray wrote to me, and said that there was the recognised species of *sub-quadricornutus*."—Letter from Mr. H. R. P. Carter, "Smoothbore" of the *Field*.

The following is an extract from a letter signed "Bheel," addressed to the editor of *The Asian*, which appeared in that paper:—

"In the jungles of Rajputana, especially about the Arravelli Range, I have shot repeatedly very small, exceedingly shy deer, called by the Bheels and shikaries in this part 'bhutar.' They are very much smaller than the four-horned antelope, having very sharp thin horns about two inches in length, which are perfectly smooth, as if polished, and black. The colour of the skin is light brown, somewhat like a chinkara, white inside the limbs and under the belly. The hair on the skin is short, smooth and glossy. The feet are exceedingly small, about one-third in size smaller than that of the four-horned antelope. They are very retiring little creatures, and very difficult to bag. They run, or, more appropriately, bound with amazing swiftness when disturbed, and disappear like some passing shadow. These little deer live on the lower spurs of the hills, and are generally found in pairs. They are very plump, and appear to be always in good condition. The last one I shot was last year. The females are hornless.

"The four-horned antelope is described accurately by Mr. Sterndale, only that, in my humble opinion, I do not consider it to be the smallest of the ruminant species. The 'Bheel' name for this creature is 'fonkra.' It is found in the thick jungles at the foot of the hills. It selects some secluded spot, which it does not desert when disturbed, returning invariably to its hiding-place when the coast is clear. I noticed this very particularly. The hair of the 'fonkra' is comparatively much longer than the bhutar's, and the colour is a great deal darker. Could Mr. Sterndale kindly let me know the Latin name for the 'bhutar'? I am sure it can't be *Cervulus aureus* (kakur, or barking deer), because the colour given of this deer is a beautiful bright glossy red or chesnut, while, as I have mentioned above, the colour of the bhutar is light brown."

"Bheel's" "bhutar" is evidently Elliot's *sub-quadricornutus.*

The Gaur.

The Gaur, p. 482.—Jerdon doubted the existence of this animal in the Himalayan Terai, according to Hodgson's assertion ; but Hodgson was right, for I have a letter before me which I received some time back from Dr. W. Forsyth, stating that a few days previously a companion of his shot a large solitary bull (6 feet 1 inch at the shoulder) in the Terai, and he himself knocked one and lost another the day before he wrote. The local name is *gauri-gai*.

I also received a letter through the columns the *The Asian* from "Snap-shot," vouching for the existence of the *gaur* in the Darjeeling Terai.

Another correspondent of *The Asian* writes regarding the naming of this species :—

"In referring to Mr. Sterndale's descriptions of the gaur and gayal, in your issues of the 28th March and 11th April, I trust that that gentleman will not be offended by my making a few remarks on the subject, and that he will set me right if I am in the wrong. I see that he has perpetuated what appears to my unscientific self a mistake on the part of the old writers—Colebrooke, Buchanan, Trail, and others, who I fancy got confused, and mixed up the animals. The local name for the Central Indian ox is over a large tract of country the gayal, or gyll ; and this, being the animal with the peculiar frontal development, was most probably named bos, or *Gavæus frontalis*, whilst the mithun, or Eastern Bengal animal, was the gaur. It seems to me, therefore, that the names should be transposed. Will Mr. Sterndale consider this, if he has not already done so ; and, if I am wrong, tell me why the animal with peculiar frontal development, and called the gayal locally, should not have been named *frontalis*, whilst the animal called mithun, with nothing peculiar in his frontal development, is so called?

"Orissa, *April 15th*, 1882. "CHAMPSE.

"P.S.—Do any of the Eastern Bengal races call this mithun gayal?"

I think Hodgson's name *Bibos cavifrons* is a sufficient proof that *Gavæus gaurus* is applicable to the animal with the high frontal crest, which is the species inhabiting the Himalayan Terai, and is locally known as the *gaur*, or *gauri-gai*. It is known as *gayal* in some parts of India, but, where the people are familiar with the *mithun*, the *gaur* is called *asl'gayal*, from whence Horsfield's name *Bibos asseel*. Probably the *mithun* was called *frontalis*, under ignorance of a species with a still greater frontal development.

Gavæus frontalis interbreeds freely with domesticated cattle of all kinds. In the Society's Gardens are several hybrids between this and *Bos Indicus*, one of which hybrids again interbred with American bison (*Bison Americanus*), the progeny being one-half bison, and one-quarter each *frontalis* and *Indicus*.

APPENDIX D.

As many specimens are spoilt by either insufficient curing, or curing by wrong methods, I have asked Mr. Geo. F. Butt, F.Z.S., who was for many years manager to Edwin Ward, whom he has now succeeded, to give me a page or two of useful hints on the preservation of skins. The following notes are what he has kindly placed at my disposal. I know of no one I can more strongly recommend for good work than Mr. Butt. Some of his groups are works of art, with most lifelike finish. I have just seen a bear set up by him which seems almost to breathe.

Notes on Skinning the Mammalia and the Preservation of Skins. By Geo. F. Butt, F.Z.S., Naturalist to the Royal Family, 49, Wigmore Street, London, W.

The quadruped killed, the first and important step is to plug up the nostrils and throat with cotton-wool or tow, as also any wound from which blood may escape. Place the animal on its back, make a longitudinal incision with the knife at the lower part of the belly (the vent), and thence in as straight a line as possible extending to the chin bone, taking particular care that during the operation the hair is carefully divided and not cut. Vertical incisions may then be made extending down the inside of each leg to the claws. The skin can then be turned back in every direction as far as the extent of the incisions will admit of—the legs may now be freed from the skin. Next make a straight incision down the under part of the tail to the tip, turn the skin back until it is free. Having executed this, there remains only to remove the skin from the back and head; to do this place the carcase on its side, and with the scalpel carefully separate the skin by drawing it towards the head, in skinning which care being taken to cut the ears as close to the skull as possible, leaving the cartilage in the skin; the eyelids, also nose and lips, should be carefully skinned without injury. The skin is now free from the carcase. Turn the ears inside out, the nostrils, lips, and feet, removing all cartilage and flesh.

Place the skin open on the ground with the fur side down, and remove a the flesh and pieces of fat adhering; scrape the skin well, so as to get away all the loose particles of under-skin or pelt. When this has been thoroughly done, take powdered alum plentifully, and, with a *very* small quantity of common salt, rub well into the skin, especially into the ears, nostrils, lips, and feet, so that every portion of the skin is powerfully impregnated. Allow the skin to lie in this condition for an hour or so, then place it on a line or branch to dry. The operation should be carried on in the shade, if possible.

If the specimen is not for stuffing it may be pegged out to dry on the ground, but in no one instance should a skin be unduly strained out of shape, which is often done in order to make it appear larger than it really is, a mistake which is very common.

When this operation is completed, and the skin dry, it is ready for packing, and should be folded, with the fur or hair inside, and placed in a sound box or case well protected against the visits of ants, beetles, or moth.

Where it is intended that the animal should be ultimately stuffed whole, it is necessary to preserve the leg bones. These should be separated from the trunk at the os humeri or shoulder-joint, and at the os femoris or thigh bones; these bones cleanse from flesh.

The skull in every instance should be preserved: remove the flesh and brain; to do this place the skull in boiling water for five or ten minutes—in the case of small skulls for five minutes only, care being taken that the teeth are not lost. In packing skulls each one should be tied up in paper, marked with a corresponding number to the skin to which it belongs, and packed firmly, to prevent rolling about, the result of which is often broken teeth and disappointment.

Another excellent method for the preservation of skins of mammalia, where convenience will permit, and which can be followed with confidence, is as follows: After the skin has been treated according to the directions given —viz. thoroughly scraped and cleansed of all adherent particles of flesh, &c. —place it entirely in a tub or cask in which a solution or pickle has been previously prepared, as follows: to every gallon of cold water add 1 lb. powdered alum, ½-oz. saltpetre, 2 oz. common salt; well mix. Allow the skin to remain about a couple of days, after which hang it up to dry and for packing.

INDEX.

A.

B.

C.

D.

E.

F.

G.

H.

I.

K.

L.

M.

* By oversight this species has been twice described.